# THE SANTANDER REGIME

# IN GRAN COLOMBIA

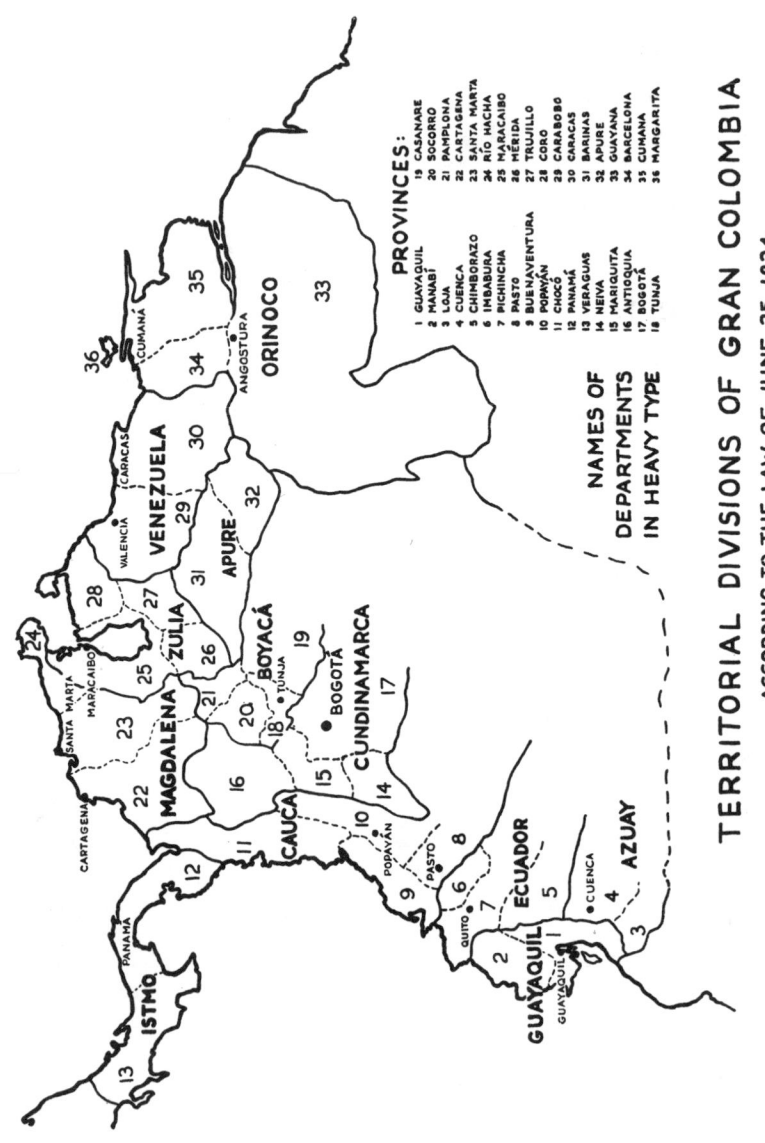

# THE SANTANDER REGIME
# IN GRAN COLOMBIA

BY

DAVID BUSHNELL

GREENWOOD PRESS, PUBLISHERS
WESTPORT, CONNECTICUT

*Copyright © 1954 by The University of Delaware*

Reprinted by permission
of University of Delaware Press

First Greenwood Reprinting 1970

SBN 8371-2981-8

PRINTED IN UNITED STATES OF AMERICA

# Foreword

THE present volume does not pretend to be a definitive treatment of an entire period in Colombian history or of the whole administration of Vice-President Santander. So great is the lack of research studies bearing on particular aspects of the period, and so great is the mass of still untouched documentary sources, that it is unlikely the present generation will ever see anything of the sort. Nevertheless, I hope that this volume, even with a more limited objective, will fulfill some useful purpose. Simply by presenting a fairly broad though detailed survey of the domestic scene of Gran Colombia—which has heretofore been neglected in favor of military and diplomatic events—it should suggest numerous topics for further investigation, and it should make investigation easier by serving as a general work of reference. Such a reference is especially needful since the political, economic, and religious issues of the period are so completely interwoven and are thus impossible to unravel except in constant relation to one another. Moreover, the study does introduce some new material, and it offers for consideration (even if sometimes in rather tentative form) a number of new interpretations.

Two points of organization require a brief word of explanation. First, the term "Santander regime" as used in the title is primarily a chronological device marking off that part of the history of Gran Colombia during which Francisco de Paula Santander and his chief associates, the liberals of New Granada, played the dominant role in domestic affairs. In a strict sense this period runs from the end of 1821, when Santander first became acting Chief Executive for the entire republic, until September, 1827, when he was permanently replaced by Bolívar. For most purposes, however, it is best to begin in August, 1819, when Santander was placed in charge of the provisional patriot administration in New Granada just after the battle of Boyacá. It is true that he had no legal authority then over Venezuela and Ecuador, but the patriot-held sections of Venezuela were dependent financially and to some extent militarily on the authorities at Bogotá, and Ecuador can be disregarded since it did not become an effective part of Gran Colombia until 1822. The period covered is therefore 1819-27; and the object of this study is to discuss all the major aspects of internal development during those years. Thus no attempt is made to review the war with Spain or Colombian foreign relations save in so far as they affect internal development. Neither will the treatment of the period be limited to a study of the specific policies of the Santander administration, even though its failures and achievements will naturally provide the principal unifying theme from one chapter to the next.

The second point that requires clarification is the application of chronology to each chapter in particular. When a historical study deals with so broad a subject a strictly chronological treatment from start to finish is obviously out of the question; hence the arrangement of material is for the most part topical. On the other hand, the political evolution of Gran Colombia up to the promulgation of the Constitution of Cúcuta and also the political crisis that began in 1826 and ultimately led to the fall of Santander both lend themselves to a purely narrative treatment, and they have been handled accordingly. A certain amount of overlapping inevitably results: there are provisions of the Colombian constitution and incidents of the crisis of 1826 that also serve to illustrate general developments discussed in the topical chapters. I can only hope that outright repetition has been kept to a minimum, since any alternative form of organization would seem to present even greater difficulties.

There remain only acknowledgments, which must as usual be wholly inadequate. First and foremost is the debt of gratitude which I owe to Professor C. H. Haring, under whose guidance this study had its inception as a doctoral dissertation at Harvard. It has passed through numerous stages since that time, but doubtless it retains—and proudly displays— the birthmarks of its origin. Indeed my debt to Professor Haring goes back to the day I first entered one of his classes as a sophomore. In every sense, therefore, this volume is a by-product of his teaching, and I sincerely hope that the efforts he spent on its author may not prove wasted!

Thanks are also due to Harvard University, to the Social Science Research Council, and to the University of Delaware for fellowships and other research assistance that have made it possible to gather data directly in the archives and libraries of Bogotá. I cannot mention all the individuals who have aided me, but I would like to single out Roberto Cortázar, Secretary until recently of the Academia Colombiana de Historia; Enrique Ortega Ricaurte, head of the Archivo Histórico Nacional; José Manuel Pérez Ayala, on whose friendship I imposed at the Biblioteca Nacional; and Julia Borda de Villar, who dominated the Archivo del Congreso at the time of my principal research efforts. Last but not least I wish to include my wife, Virginia Starkes Bushnell, who typed countless pages of illegible manuscript, worked on the map and charts, and twice endured the climate of Bogotá while her husband labored in the archives.

D. B.

# Abbreviations Used in Footnote Citations

A.C. . . . . . . . . . . Archivo del Congreso, Bogotá.
          Cámara-, Senado-, or Miscelánea- followed by a number will indicate a volume in one of the three major series of documents in the Archivo. Volumes in it are listed by both Arabic and Roman numerals, according to two different systems; the former is the more convenient and is used in citations unless otherwise indicated.

Actas . . . . . . . . . Printed minutes of the Congresses of Gran Colombia, edited by Roberto Cortázar and Luis Augusto Cuervo. Separate volumes are listed fully in the bibliography; in footnotes the volume is specified by an added symbol— e.g., Cúcuta, Cámara-1824.

Acuerdos . . . . . . Acuerdos del Consejo de Gobierno. 2 vols., Bogotá, 1940-1942.

A.H.N. . . . . . . . . Archivo Histórico Nacional, Bogotá.
          Corresp.-Cámara: Correspondencia del Poder Ejecutivo con la Cámara de Representantes (ministry of origin indicated in parentheses).
          Corresp.-Senado: Correspondencia del Poder Ejecutivo con el Senado (Secretaría del Interior exclusively).
          Interior y Relaciones: Secretaría de lo Interior y Relaciones Extranjeras.

Arch. Sant. . . . . . Archivo Santander. 24 vols., Bogotá, 1913-1932.

Blanco . . . . . . . . José Félix Blanco and Ramón Azpurúa, eds., Documentos para la historia de la vida pública del Libertador. 14 vols., Caracas, 1875-1878.

Codif. Nac. . . . . Codificación nacional de todas las leyes de Colombia desde el año de 1821. Bogotá, 1924—.

Corresp. . . . . . . . Bolívar y Santander. Correspondencia 1819-1820. Bogotá, 1940.

Groot . . . . . . . . . José Manuel Groot, Historia de la Gran Colombia. Caracas, 1941. (Vol. 3 of his Historia eclesiástica y civil de la Nueva Granada.)

Lecuna, C.L. . . . . Vicente Lecuna, ed., Cartas del Libertador. 10 vols., Caracas, 1929-1930. Vol. 11, New York, 1948.

Lecuna, C.S. . . . . Cartas de Santander. 3 vols., Caracas, 1942.

N.A. . . . . . . . . . . National Archives, Washington, D. C.

O'Leary . . . . . . . Simón B. O'Leary, ed., Memorias del General O'Leary. 32 vols., Caracas, 1879-1888.

Restrepo . . . . . . . José Manuel Restrepo, Historia de la Revolución de la República de Colombia. 3rd ed., 8 vols., Bogotá, 1942-1950.

# TABLE OF CONTENTS

| CHAPTER | PAGE |
|---|---|

1. Venezuela, New Granada, and Quito.................... 1
2. The Creation of Gran Colombia....................... 10
   From Boyacá to Cúcuta: the Provisional Government (10); The Congress of Cúcuta (14); The Completion of Independence (22).
3. The Santander Regime: Political Reform and Administrative Problems .......................................... 26
   The Progress of Innovation (26); The Use of Extraordinary Authorizations (31); Practical Difficulties of Administration (34); The Achievement of Santander (40).
4. The Judicial and Legislative Powers..................... 45
   The Courts, Crime, and Litigation (45); The Education of Congress (50).
5. Personal and Factional Conflicts 1821-1826.............. 58
   The Nariño-Santander Feud and the New Federalism (58); The Later History of the Nariño Faction (65); Friction Between Bolívar and Santander (69).
6. The Financial Crisis (I): The Revenue System............ 76
   The Reform of the National Tax System (77); Problems of Financial Management (83); The War, the Tobacco Monopoly, and the Mints (87).
7. The Financial Crisis (II): Debts, Deficits, and Recriminations 92
   The Mounting Deficit (94); The Growth of the Internal Debt (96); The Political Impact of the Financial Crisis (107).
8. The Foreign Debt as a Fiscal Expedient and Political Issue.... 112
   Negotiations in London 1820-1824 (112); Repercussions of the 1824 Loan (116); The Use of the 1824 Loan (118); The Later History of Colombian Foreign Credit (123).
9. Economic Reconstruction and Development.............. 127
   The Advance of Laissez Faire (129); Capital Investment and Public Improvements (134); Immigration and Land Settlement (143).
10. Policy and Practice in Foreign Trade.................... 151
    Import Duties and Regulations (151); Exports and Export Taxes (159); The Pattern of Foreign Trade (162).
11. The Liberals and the Masses: Slavery and the Indian Question 166
    The Decline of Slavery, and Related Questions (167); Liberalism and the Indian (174).

## TABLE OF CONTENTS

| CHAPTER | | PAGE |
|---|---|---|
| 12. | Education in the Santander Regime..................... | 183 |
| 13. | The Religious Question (I): Clericals and Anti-Clericals..... | 195 |
| | The Clergy in the War and Post-War Era (195); Anti-Clericalism, "Liberal Catholicism," and Freemasonry (205). | |
| 14. | The Religious Question (II): Anti-Clerical Reforms 1821-1826 .................................................. | 214 |
| | The First Major Reforms: the Progress of Toleration and Decline of the Monasteries (214); Limitations on Clerical Privilege and Income (219); Mortmain and *Censos* (223). | |
| 15. | The Religious Question (III): Church and State in Gran Colombia .................................................. | 229 |
| | The Struggle for the *Patronato* (229); The Church Policy of Santander (237); The Clerical Counterattack (244). | |
| 16. | The Colombian Army in War and Politics............... | 249 |
| | The Nature of the Army of Liberation (249); Army Reduction and Alternative Means of Defense (257); Reforming the Military System (266). | |
| 17. | Military Claims and Veterans' Unrest.................... | 275 |
| | The Handling of the Claims Backlog (275); The Veterans' Problem on the *Llanos* (279); The Infante Affair (282). | |
| 18. | The Venezuelan Problem............................... | 287 |
| | Liberalism and Federalism in Caracas (289); The Official Hierarchy (294); Páez, Peña, Guzmán: the Birth of an Unholy Alliance (298); The Other Venezuelan Departments (305). | |
| 19. | The Plight of Ecuador................................ | 310 |
| 20. | The Year of Crisis: 1826............................. | 318 |
| | The Reelection of Bolívar and Santander (318); The Revolt of Páez (323); The Reaction of Santander and Bolívar (329); The Subversion of Ecuador and the Pilgrimage of Guzmán (332). | |
| 21. | The Return of Simón Bolívar and the Fall of Santander...... | 338 |
| | From Guayaquil to New Granada (338); The Settlement of Venezuela and the Final Breach with Santander (343); The End of the Santander Regime (348). | |
| | Appendix: A Note on Colombian Financial Statistics........ | 360 |
| | Bibliography ......................................... | 362 |

Chapter I

## Venezuela, New Granada, and Quito

THE three colonies that made up the Viceroyalty of New Granada belonged definitely to the second rank of Spanish possessions in the New World, just as they have belonged to the second rank of Latin American republics for most of the years since they obtained their independence. The Captaincy-General of Venezuela, the "Kingdom" of New Granada, and the Presidency of Quito enjoyed in the year 1810 neither the aristocratic prestige of Peru nor the fabulous, though slightly exaggerated, mineral riches of Mexico. They had entered upon the world scene only occasionally, as when Admiral Vernon made his ill-fated descent upon Cartagena. Their own inhabitants were as little prepared as anyone else for the brief glory that was to be theirs when, under the leadership of Simón Bolívar, they combined to play the most decisive single role in the liberation of Spanish America.

This does not mean that they were altogether lacking in importance as parts of the Spanish Empire. Venezuela, to begin with, was in some respects the most successful non-mining colony that Spain possessed. Its exports were not as great either absolutely or in proportion to population as those of Cuba, but Venezuela had a more balanced economy, with grazing on the interior plains or *llanos* of the Orinoco basin and plantations of cacao, coffee, and indigo along the lower Andean ranges that faced the Caribbean coast. Venezuela was the world's leading producer of cacao, and also one of the colonies that produced a yearly cash surplus to ship home to the Spanish treasury.[1]

Venezuelan society was headed by a small creole aristocracy that owned the best land and produced the export crops; especially in the neighborhood of Caracas, this was done with the aid of Negro slaves. The great estate system had also begun to take root in the *llanos,* notably in the western province of Barinas, but in the *llanos* as a whole property divisions were often poorly defined, the cattle existed more or less wild, and the cowboy *llaneros* of mixed Spanish, Indian, and Negro descent were almost as uncivilized.[2] The *llaneros* resembled the Argentine *gauchos* in

[1] See Eduardo Arcila Farías, *Economía colonial de Venezuela* (México, 1946).

[2] Rafael Tovar Ariza, "Causas económicas, políticas, sociales, y culturales de la disolución de la Gran Colombia," *Revista de las Indias* (Bogotá), January, 1938, p. 86.

1

most essentials, and they were destined to serve as a skilled cavalry on both sides of the coming struggle. Another class that deserves separate mention is that of the merchants who handled the colony's steadily increasing trade. Although white like the great landowners, they tended to be Spanish rather than creole, or at least to maintain close connections with commercial interests in Spain. In either case they favored the Spanish mercantilistic system that prohibited direct legal trade with countries outside the Empire, and this fact, plus the merchants' normal incentive to buy cheap and sell dear, led them into conflict with the *hacendados*, whose obvious interest was to sell dear and buy cheap by opening the colonial commerce to as many competing firms as possible.[3] As it turned out, this could be fully achieved only by revolution, but substantial progress was made before 1810 by large-scale smuggling and by the intermittent relaxation of the Spanish navigation laws for the purpose of legalizing trade with foreign interlopers when war prevented Spain from even attempting to supply all her colonists' needs. This progress simply whetted the appetite of the creole landowners. Combined with the unpopularity of Spanish commercial interests and the broader intellectual contacts afforded by intensive trade and smuggling, it helped to make the Venezuelan aristocracy one of the groups that welcomed the idea of independence most enthusiastically when the time came.[4]

In name Venezuela was subject to the Viceroy of New Granada, who reigned at Santa Fe, the present Bogotá. In practice and in law, the Captain-General of Venezuela was to all intents and purposes an independent ruler under the Spanish Crown. To Venezuelans, therefore, the term New Granada meant not a great Viceroyalty to which they also belonged but a specific territory lying between them and the Presidency of Quito, and roughly equivalent to modern Colombia. Certainly New Granada was very different from Venezuela. It did have scattered tropical and semi-tropical plantations, and it had its share of the *llanos* in the eastern province of Casanare. It also had one substantial nucleus of great agricultural landholdings in the central region surrounding Bogotá. Here, however, the crops were temperate-zone products such as wheat, for in New Granada the Andes rose sharply above the Venezuelan average. Almost everywhere in New Granada there were also small urban industries, especially in the province of Socorro, a center of textile production; and in the West, along the Cauca Valley and the Pacific slopes of the

---

[3] Arcila Farías, *op. cit.*, 363-365.

[4] On the influence of foreign contacts upon sentiment for independence, see Alexander von Humboldt, *Personal Narrative of Travels to the Equinoctial Regions of the New Continent* (7 vols., London, 1822-1829) III, 196-197, 429, 472.

Andes, New Granada contained the chief gold-mining territory of the Spanish Empire.⁵

Gold was for New Granada, up to a point, what hides, cacao, and indigo were for Venezuela. Mining provided the bulk of the colony's exports and also, directly or indirectly, of the royal taxes. It was a source of great wealth for a few families such as the Arboledas and the Mosqueras of Popayán. However, mining employed relatively few people, among them the only significant concentration of Negro slaves in New Granada, and had somewhat less direct importance for society as a whole than did the export agriculture of Venezuela. The mining industry simply paid the bill for the rest of the colony's imports, because agriculture and manufacturing, with a few exceptions, were for local consumption or export to neighboring provinces only. In fact, Cartagena on the coast obtained its flour from abroad because bad and costly transportation made it impractical to bring flour from the central highlands.⁶

In the society of New Granada there were fewer slaves and proportionately fewer men with great private fortunes than existed in Venezuela. The division of wealth and property was relatively more equal, although less equal in Popayán and Bogotá than in Socorro. There was a slightly higher population density, more concentration of inhabitants in the larger towns, and more, though still not much, of what might be called a middle class.⁷ Unlike Venezuela, New Granada had most of its population far in the interior, and this fact in conjunction with the greater difficulties of internal communication and a less active foreign trade tended to keep New Granada more isolated from the cultural and technological movements of the outside world. The hold of traditional religion on the minds of the people, which was perceptibly weakening in Venezuela, was much firmer in New Granada. At the same time, methods of production were highly rudimentary. There was little of the advanced capitalistic farming of the Caracas plantations; in much of New Granada not even the plow was known, and in Bogotá the wheelbarrow had not yet come into general use.⁸

Yet in a few important respects New Granada enjoyed a higher intellectual development than Venezuela. There was greater activity in the

⁵ See Pedro Fermín de Vargas, *Pensamientos políticos y memoria sobre la población del Nuevo Reino de Granada* (Bogotá, 1944), and also Luis Eduardo Nieto Arteta, *Economía y cultura en la historia de Colombia* (Bogotá, 1941), 12-14.

In the present study the term New Granada will always be used in its more limited sense unless the Viceroyalty as a whole is specified.

⁶ Vargas, *op. cit.*, 38-40.

⁷ *Ibid.*, 100; Tovar Ariza, "Causas . . . de la disolución de la Gran Colombia," *loc. cit.*, 87.

⁸ Vargas, *op. cit.*, 8; Richard Bache, *Notes on Colombia* (Philadelphia, 1827), 242.

professions, thanks in part to the status of Santa Fe as a viceregal capital with the bureaucracy and everything else that went with it. The more even distribution of property allowed a wider diffusion of at least a little learning, and the "national character" of the *granadinos* gave special impetus to the legal profession. A competent Spanish general described them as generally timid, and thus explained the fact that in New Granada "one writes much, and the judges are overwhelmed with work," whereas in Caracas "disputes are ended by means of the sword." [9] However, New Granada produced more than lawyers. The Spanish scholar José Celestino Mutis, sent to New Granada on a scientific mission by Charles III, succeeded in starting a movement for investigation in the natural sciences which won praise and recognition even in Europe and was ably carried on after his death by a native *granadino,* Francisco José de Caldas.

The third element of the Viceroyalty was the Presidency of Quito, corresponding to modern Ecuador. As its ruler had lower rank than the Captain-General of Venezuela, he was more genuinely subject to the viceroy in Bogotá, but the connection between Quito and the territory of New Granada had been permanently sealed only in 1740, and even then did not entirely supersede the earlier dependence on Peru.[10] Socially, Quito still had far more in common with Peru, having a narrow creole aristocracy alongside a clear majority of pure Indians who lived their own lives as far as the former would let them. The economic importance of the Presidency was almost negligible. Only in Guayaquil did it have a major export crop, cacao, and it had no mines like those of New Granada. The bulk of the population lived in the temperate highlands, which could no more export their crops than the plain of Bogotá. Instead they produced food for local consumption, animals for meat and wool, and coarse textiles. The latter made Ecuador the chief manufacturing district of the viceroyalty, but Ecuadoran textiles had lost their hold on the Peruvian market when Charles III opened the Pacific coast to direct trade with Spain, and they retained only the far from prosperous domestic market and that of the mining camps of western New Granada. A good indication of the general state of Ecuador toward the end of the Eighteenth Century was the special royal decree reducing the yearly rate on mortgages (*censos*) owed to the Church from the normal 5% to 3%.[11] Ecuadoran property owners had convinced the court that they simply could not afford to pay more. Economic stagnation did not, of course, impair the strict division of society into two unequal classes; and it helped to produce an atmosphere of isolation more pronounced than that of New Granada.

[9] Report of Don Pablo Morillo, March 27, 1816, Blanco VII, 253.

[10] Tovar Ariza, "Causas . . . de la disolución de la Gran Colombia," *loc. cit.,* 81-82.

[11] Petition of the Quito municipality, September 21, 1823, A.C., Senado-4, 288-289; Nieto Arteta, *op. cit.,* 23.

The economic difficulties of Quito may help to explain why, despite its backwardness, it became the scene of the first major conflict of the War of Independence. In no part of the viceroyalty, however, did the struggle begin as an outburst of long-oppressed masses against the iniquities of the colonial system. Indeed the vast majority was everywhere either unconscious of those iniquities or relatively indifferent to them. The legal prohibition of trade outside the Empire was keenly felt and resented by the plantation interests of Venezuela, but certainly not by the Ecuadoran Indians, and it was readily evaded by contraband trade with the Antilles. The prohibition of industrial or other activities that competed with those of the mother country was occasionally denounced as oppressive, or perhaps as merely pointless,[12] but there is no evidence that any important line of production was thwarted by Spanish decrees alone, and much less that this was a burning popular issue. More important was the exclusion of creoles, by custom rather than by law, from most positions of distinction in Church and State, and the social snubs administered by European-born Spaniards that went with the exclusion policy. This two-fold discrimination heads the list of colonial grievances in José Manuel Restrepo's classic history of the Colombian Revolution.[13] On the other hand, it was something that affected mainly the creole elite of landowners and professional men; the average man could not aspire to become an archbishop or to sit on one of the high courts, and he would not be ruled out for reasons of nationality if he sought a clerkship in the postal service. In fact, the upper-class creoles were themselves too tepid in their resentments, too disunited, and too steeped in the tradition of respect for the Spanish king to strike forcefully against his government solely on their own initiative.

There were of course exceptions to all that has just been said, showing that a change was gradually preparing. One was the revolt of the *comuneros* in New Granada in 1781, although it was essentially a mass protest over an increase in taxes, and this was not entirely unprecedented under the colonial regime. More significant for the War of Independence proper were the propaganda and the plotting of Antonio Nariño in New Granada and Francisco Miranda in Venezuela, since both had become frankly convinced of the need for separation from Spain. The Spanish regime was not even remotely threatened, however, until events in Spain forced the hands of the creole leaders. The kidnapping of Ferdinand VII by Napoleon in 1808 and the establishment by Spanish patriots of a series of juntas to rule in his absence suggested to the creoles that they might organize juntas of their own for exactly the same purpose. The Spanish juntas received the loyalty of Spanish administrators on the spot, so that the first news of Ferdinand's difficulties brought no decisive action any-

[12] Cf. Vargas, *op. cit.*, 104-105.
[13] Restrepo I, xlvii.

where in the viceroyalty. Then, after the middle of 1809, a revolt finally did take place in Quito. The creoles were overwhelmingly in favor of establishing a regional junta, and with a patriot bishop from New Granada to help overcome the scruples of the more timid, a junta was formally set up. But Quito alone was too weak to stage a revolution. Neither Peru to the south nor New Granada to the north was yet ready to follow suit, and the movement was speedily crushed.

Educated *granadinos* had been quick to sympathize with Quito, but had done nothing when their viceroy joined the coalition that crushed the patriot revolt. Action came only when the reigning Spanish junta had been forced to retreat to the Isle of León in Cadiz harbor and dissolved itself, in February, 1810, in favor of an improvised regency. The next step was taken, moreover, in Caracas, where a Venezuelan junta was set up on April 19, and as this was the first successful junta formed anywhere in America it has convinced Venezuelans ever since that Caracas is truly "the cradle of liberty." The fact is, of course, that Caracas was the nearest colonial capital to Europe and therefore heard the news first. As it reached other colonial centers, similar juntas were created: at Cartagena on May 22, and at Bogotá, just a little late, on July 20. Caracas deserved slightly more credit for declaring full independence on July 5 of the following year, but again Cartagena was not far behind, coming through with a similar declaration in November. The bulk of New Granada waited two more years. Yet the formal declaration was really a minor detail. It would be unjust to dismiss the original juntas created to rule in Ferdinand's name as merely a hypocritical maneuvre to deceive the masses, but creole leaders everywhere were determined once they had begun to take command of the government that they would never again return to a purely colonial status. At the most Ferdinand could have been recognized as a constitutional monarch reigning over a congeries of Spanish American kingdoms, each with an administration staffed by ambitious creoles. Since neither the Spanish rump government in 1810 nor Ferdinand VII when he finally regained his throne would accept anything of the sort, the first juntas could be followed only by full independence or unconditional submission. And in the meantime, their *de facto* independence was nearly complete.

The course of events after the establishment of local juntas varied widely in different parts of the viceroyalty, but the period as a whole can be aptly described by a term originally used for New Granada: *La Patria Boba,* the Foolish Fatherland. During the six years from 1810 to 1816 the chief occupation of the *granadinos* appears to have been not preparation for a common defense against the Spanish enemy but rather the drafting of constitutions. It was widely assumed that federalism was the perfect form of government; hence each province, and often just one section of a province, had to be a sovereign state; and each sovereign state, not to mention each confederation of sovereign states, produced one or more constitutions. Most of these exhibited more lofty idealism than practical statesmanship. Mariquita adopted the Golden Rule as Article 7 of its constitution, and almost all of them were crammed with details that belonged in a penal code or municipal ordinances rather than in a frame of government.[14] The basic difficulty of the *granadinos,* however, was not the technical defects of their constitutions but their inability to agree upon a general organization for all of New Granada. Bogotá and Cundinamarca, led by Nariño until he fell prisoner to the Spaniards, sought a strong central leadership to ward off the vengeance of Spain. Cundinamarca would naturally assume the dominant role, and as a preliminary measure absorbed various of the surrounding "sovereign states," not always against their will. But the rest of New Granada formed a loose confederation of its own under the title of the United Provinces and was soon plunged into a state of intermittent civil war with Cundinamarca.

Venezuela had likewise been undergoing its *Patria Boba,* and formed itself into a single federation of sovereign states. There was no similar flurry of constitution-making, in part merely because the royalist reaction came too soon. The leadership of Caracas was resented by Maracaibo and Coro to the west, which remained staunchly royalist; the *llaneros* and others of mixed race resented the leadership of the generally patriot creole aristocracy,[15] and easily succumbed to Spanish urging that they rob and massacre the whites for the glory of God and the King. The result was a total collapse of the first Venezuelan Republic in 1812. However, a few leaders, including Simón Bolívar, escaped to New Granada, where they found a base from which to draw men and resources for a second liberation of Venezuela. This time the noble ideals of the first republic were sternly set aside in order to deal with an enemy whose principal methods were extortion and brutality. Bolívar himself proclaimed a "War to the Death," which meant the general massacre of Spaniards. He made little effort to conserve resources or to curb his own troops; the result, as a *granadino* patriot exclaimed with horror, was simply "robbery reduced to a system."[16] Unfortunately, the *llaneros* remained hostile and civilian bystanders could no longer find much difference between the two sides. Bolívar was victorious long enough to win his preferred title of *Libertador,* but Venezuela was soon reduced to submission once more, and was nearly ruined in the process. Again Bolívar turned to New Granada, where he repaid the United Provinces for their support of his last Venezuelan campaign by helping them finally to subdue Cundinamarca. But

[14] José María Samper, *Derecho público interno de Colombia* (2 vols., Bogotá, 1886), I, 77-84, 103, 109.
[15] Cf. Arcila Farías, *op. cit.,* 370-372.
[16] Eloy G. González, *La ración del boa* (Caracas, 1908), 44; cf. *ibid.,* 7-69.

in the meantime Ferdinand VII had regained his throne, set his house in order, and dispatched the first regular Spanish army of any size to reach America since 1810. It arrived in Caracas in May of 1815 under the leadership of Don Pablo Morillo, and it soon continued on to New Granada, where internal dissensions were already hastening the collapse of the Foolish Fatherland.

In Quito a second patriot coup had been staged in 1810 and had been suppressed in the same manner as the first, by troops sent from Lima. By the middle of 1816, consequently, all the principal cities of the viceroyalty were again in Spanish hands. Some of the lesser cities, however, were not. A group of *granadino* patriots headed by the former law-student Francisco de Paula Santander had made their escape to the *llanos* of Casanare; on the Venezuelan *llanos* the cowboy population was being won over at last to the patriot side by José Antonio Páez, who now succeeded in promising even more loot than the Spaniards. Finally, patriot guerrillas remained active in the East of Venezuela, and they were soon reinforced by the arrival of refugees from the Antilles—naturally including Simón Bolívar, who came to assume command. His past defeats and aristocratic background created some difficulties for him in his relations with the *llaneros,* and his forces were no match for the Spanish regulars guarding the Venezuelan Andes. But neither was the Spanish infantry a match for Páez' horsemen on the *llanos;* the patriot redoubt was held, the war went on, and the Venezuelan population continued its steady decline.

There was some further discord between the *llaneros* and Santander, but Bolívar recognized his true talents and put him to work organizing a stable patriot government in Casanare. And though Bolívar almost to the end was tempted to undertake the liberation of Caracas instead, the reports of Santander convinced him that he should try to invade New Granada from a base in Casanare. The advantages of the move were obvious. The main Spanish force was concentrated in Venezuela; New Granada had been ravaged to a far lesser extent by warfare, and so would be a superior base for future operations; and the population was strongly prepared to welcome the patriots.[17] The Spaniards had been proceeding on the assumption that the region would only be safe if all potential leaders were exterminated. Some of the younger and less prominent figures of the *Patria Boba* were able to save their lives by an abject though insincere submission, but there was little mercy for the rest. Not only this, but taxes were increased in order to pay the cost of conquest and repression; and as Santander bitterly remarked, the making of over 500 patriot martyrs

[17] Lecuna, *C.S.* I, 6-9, 24-30, 34-45; Pedro Julio Dousdebés, *Trayectoria militar de Santander* (2nd ed., Bogotá, 1940), 222; Vicente Lecuna, *Crónica razonada de las guerras de Bolívar* (3 vols., New York, 1950), II, 300-301.

caused less hostility to Spain than a rise in taxes.[18] As against these advantages of an assault upon New Granada there was the problem of crossing the Andes over one of their most difficult trails with an army habituated to the warm climate of the *llanos*. Many Venezuelan troops simply refused to come along. Yet the invasion was a success; and Bolívar's victory at Boyacá, on August 7, 1819, delivered over the heart of the viceroyalty at one stroke to the patriots. The war was far from ended, but the subsequent liberation of Caracas and Quito, and even the final independence of Peru and Bolivia, were part of a logical chain of events that had its beginning at Boyacá.

---

[18] Santander to Bolívar, October 1, 1819, Lecuna, *C.S.* I, 49.

Chapter II

## *The Creation of Gran Colombia*

THE remainder of the military struggle with Spain, from Boyacá to the expulsion of the last Spanish forces from the viceroyalty, does not directly concern the theme of this volume. But in the last analysis the military achievement of independence was only a first step. It removed Ferdinand VII and his agents from the political scene, but it could not in itself determine the institutions of the new republic. Indeed it would be hard even to find a name for the country in which the battle of Boyacá was fought: Only one of the provinces of New Granada had remained independent after 1816: this was Casanare, and there had been no serious attempt to set up a government-in-exile for all New Granada on the eastern *llanos*. Under the leadership of Santander, in fact, Casanare had accepted subordination to the provisional Venezuelan government which Bolívar established at Angostura in the province of Guayana. There were also numerous *granadinos* serving in that government, including the scholarly *antioqueño*, Francisco Antonio Zea, who held the rank of Vice-President of Venezuela. All this, needless to say, fitted in admirably with Bolívar's dream of ultimately uniting Venezuela and New Granada in a single republic. But on the field of Boyacá he was simply a conquering general from the Venezuelan *llanos*, and the precise status of New Granada remained obscure. Bolívar did not greatly clarify matters when he declared that the Congress he had improvised at Angostura was the depository of the sovereignty of both countries, and in the same breath that their union must be truly voluntary, subject to ratification by a *granadino* assembly.[1]

### *From Boyacá to Cúcuta: the Provisional Government*

In the short run minor inconsistencies could be safely forgotten, since the immediate problem was to carry on the war. With regard to political organization Bolívar simply ordered that in general no changes should be made in the Spanish administrative system, and before leaving Bogotá he placed that system under the direction of Santander with the title of Vice-President of New Granada. Santander and the Vice-President of Venezuela would handle the details of administering all patriot-held territory, while Bolívar would coordinate the common war effort. The

[1] *Arch. Sant.* II, 263.

Liberator also established a high court in place of the *Audiencia* of Santa Fe, providing for a right of appeal from its decisions to himself. And he decreed that each province should have both a civil and a military ruler, with the latter enjoying a clear superiority for reasons of war-time necessity.[2] The real basis of government, of course, was highly personal. Santander stated with slight exaggeration that he had "no other rule of procedure than the instructions and conduct" of Bolívar,[3] and other officials took their instructions in turn from one or the other of the two leaders. At times their orders were in conflict, as when Bolívar and Santander each named a different governor for the newly-liberated sections of the province of Cartagena,[4] but some confusion was unavoidable when the two men were not always on the same spot and the exact limits of their respective functions had not been carefully worked out. It is also true that they did not always see eye to eye on specific problems, with Santander generally urging greater tactfulness in squeezing supplies and recruits out of the *granadinos* and serving as a restraint upon some of the more grandiose projects of the Liberator. The latter, however, was ready to thank the Vice-President for his "impertinences,"[5] and there is no reason to doubt that by and large the two men formed an unusually happy combination.

Santander was assisted in his work by two ministers whom Bolívar appointed at his suggestion: Alejandro Osorio and Estanislao Vergara, veteran patriots of the *Patria Boba* who had managed by personal influence and bribery respectively to survive the era of Spanish "Pacification." Santander also found use for the two men who were later to become his most conspicuous political supporters. One of them, Francisco Soto, now went as governor to his native Pamplona; the other, Vicente Azuero, served in a judicial capacity at Bogotá. It was worth noting that both men, like Santander himself, were from the eastern provinces of New Granada, a region that enjoyed a slightly more progressive social organization than New Granada as a whole and was to become a liberal stronghold throughout the nineteenth century.[6] It was still too early, however, to think in terms of regional and factional differences. For the moment all responsible patriots were united to serve the common cause, and in the words of José Manuel Restrepo this was "the most glorious period in the public

---

[2] *La Gazeta de Santa Fe de Bogotá,* August 29 and October 31, 1819; January 16, 1820; Alejandro Osorio and Estanislao Vergara, *Memoria correspondiente al año de 1820* (Bogotá, 1821), 61-62.

[3] Santander to Bolívar, May 19, 1820, *Corresp.,* 181.

[4] Harold A. Bierck, Jr., *Vida pública de Don Pedro Gual* (Caracas, 1947), 172-190.

[5] Bolívar to Santander, April 18, 1820, *Corresp.,* 78.

[6] Eduardo Acevedo Latorre, *Colaboradores de Santander en la organización de la república* (Bogotá, 1944), 24, 35, 45-46, 229.

life of General Santander." [7] It was marred only by his cold-blooded decision to massacre the Spanish officers taken at Boyacá on vague charges of conspiracy. Even this move, which has been roundly condemned by many of the same persons who defend Bolívar's "War to the Death," at least served as a sufficient example to ward off any serious royalist plotting at Bogotá in the future and to strengthen the will of lukewarm patriots through fear of Spanish retaliation.[8] For the rest, not everything was done well, but the basic problems of consolidating the new regime and fighting the war at the same time were met with a remarkable degree of success.

Even while this was being done, a Republic of Colombia had been organized, at least on paper. Bolívar was called back to Angostura in December of 1819 to cope with a military revolt that stemmed from such factors as jealousy of his own preeminence and the ineffective leadership of Vice-President Zea. Whether because of the Liberator's personal magnetism, the news of Boyacá, or the prospect of sharing the treasure abandoned in Bogotá by the fleeing viceroy, the revolt was peacefully liquidated as soon as Bolívar arrived on the scene. Then, as a fitting culmination of his triumph, the Venezuelan Congress formally proclaimed in a brief Fundamental Law the union of Venezuela, New Granada, and Quito as the Republic of Colombia. No permanent organization was adopted, however. Acting now as supreme legislative body for all "Colombia," the Congress named Bolívar and Zea President and Vice-President of the Republic and created two additional Vice-Presidents, one with special responsibility for Venezuela and another for New Granada, or Cundinamarca as all of it was now to be called. Santander was of course given the latter position, which was essentially the same as he already held. It was provided that a third regional vice-presidency would be created later for Quito, as soon as it was wrested from the Spaniards. Other than this only the broadest details of government were sketched in, and a permanent constitution was left to be drafted by an assembly called to meet at Cúcuta, close to the border of New Granada and Venezuela, on January 1, 1821.[9]

The founding of Gran Colombia* is commonly dated back to the decision at Angostura, and the principle of unity was not seriously threatened until 1826. Actually, the acceptance of Bolívar's personal leadership

[7] Restrepo V, 245.
[8] Restrepo V, 172-174.
[9] Restrepo V, 177-180, 376-379.

---

* "Gran" Colombia is a term invented by later historians to distinguish Bolívar's creation, comprising the whole viceroyalty, from the modern Colombia, which is really just New Granada. At the time it was of course called merely Colombia, and in this study the terms will be used interchangeably.

by both sections of the old viceroyalty, the common patriotism which a joint war effort inspired, and the common sense of preserving a single front against Spain would probably have made the union almost inevitable in any case. Certainly the immediate practical effect of the Fundamental Law and most other enactments passed at Angostura was slight save in the immediate vicinity of the Congress. Even there Bolívar, assuming emergency war powers, was able to override its decisions at will. Bolívar sent orders to Bogotá that the law of union should be "solemnly proclaimed in the towns and in the armies, inscribed in all the municipalities, and executed in all the Department of Cundinamarca, as Congress orders."[10] Santander, however, did not act on the principle that everything done at Angostura was automatically binding on New Granada. He expressed sympathy with the idea of union, but before proclaiming it he obtained the approval of a junta of notables in Bogotá. With the consent of Bolívar, furthermore, he sometimes chose not to enforce the lesser enactments of the Angostura Congress in his own territory.[11] Indeed it appears that he was not always happy about the idea of recognizing its higher authority. This could well be seen in the air of persecution which he and the high court at Bogotá assumed in the face of a law passed at Angostura authorizing the Venezuelan *Alta Corte* to act both as a local appeal court and also as the supreme tribunal of the new republic. Santander and the judges of the Bogotá court, which was not mentioned in the law, chose to believe that the latter had been implicitly abolished; the court suspended its operations, and the Vice-President complained at great length of Venezuelan ingratitude. Bolívar then showed that the interpretation placed on the law in Bogotá had been quite unreasonable, and the court was reopened, but the incident had served to underscore once again the excessive vagueness of political relationships under the provisional regime.[12]

There was also some sniping between Venezuelans and *granadinos* with regard to the election of deputies for the coming Congress of Cúcuta. In the lack of reliable statistics it had been decided that each province should send exactly three deputies, and this gave rise to complaints in New Granada that the more sparsely inhabited provinces of Venezuela were unduly favored.[13] Venezuelans, in turn, were quick to point out that a good part of their homeland, including Caracas, was still under Spanish occupation at election time and thus could not participate in the voting at all. But fortunately the elections went smoothly by and large, and they were in some respects the most democratic ever held in Gran Colombia

[10] Lecuna, *C.L.* II, 126-128.
[11] Groot, 55-56; *Corresp.*, 178-179, 197.
[12] Blanco VII, 172; *Corresp.*, 181, 191-196; A.C., Senado-7, 1-4.
[13] Cf. Lecuna, *C.L.* II, 150.

since not only could anyone vote who owned $500* in real property or practiced a scientific, liberal, or mechanical profession but also all soldiers were made voters *ex officio*. The latter provision generously increased the size of the electorate, although apparently many soldiers did not take advantage of it. It extended the suffrage to foreigners, if they were volunteers in the Colombian army, and to a substantial number of illiterates, including many army officers. Nor is there any evidence of important irregularities.[14] The end result of the elections, in any case, was to assemble at Cúcuta a group of men of unusual character and ability. They included priests, lawyers, and *hacendados*, and there would have been numerous generals and colonels as well if most of those chosen had not been kept away by what was considered more urgent business. The group was generally young, thanks in large part to the high mortality of patriotic leaders in the Pacification; many of the *granadinos*, especially, had been conspicuously silent or even publicly royalist only a few years before, but this was mainly the result of Spanish terrorism and nothing else.[15]

## The Congress of Cúcuta

When the Congress finally met, several months late, only one voice was raised against making permanent the union of Venezuela and New Granada. This was the voice of the eccentric Dr. Manuel Baños, who wished to see his native New Granada organized as a "theocratic principality," whatever that might be, united only in some kind of loose military alliance with Venezuela.[16] It is surprising that there were not more voices raised to question the unilateral inclusion of Ecuador in the new republic, since the only part of the Presidency of Quito that had obtained its independence as yet was Guayaquil, and no part was represented at Cúcuta. However, only a few independent souls such as the "Colombian Cato," Dr. Félix Restrepo, had any serious qualms of conscience on this score. The rest frequently denied any thought of claiming to speak for the Ecuadorans, but that is precisely what they did.[17]

A more serious debate was in order when it came to deciding what type of union Colombia should be: whether a centralized union with a

[14] Detailed records of the voting in Venezuela can be found in A.H.N., Congresos XXIV, 36-403, and A.C., Senado-8, 3-61. The apparent lack of any undue pressure on the voters can be inferred from the fact in General Páez' own voting district in Achaguas, for instance, the *llanero* chieftain took only fifth place among men chosen for the electoral college that was to make the final choice of deputies.

[15] Joaquín Tamayo, *La Gran Colombia* (Bogotá, 1941), 78.

[16] *Actas:* Cúcuta, 124, 779.

[17] *Ibid.*, 44, 70, 800-801.

---

* In this volume $ refers always to Colombian pesos, whose value in the period under consideration was substantially the same as that of the United States dollar.

single executive and legislature or a federation of sovereign states. On either side the arguments were much the same as those employed from one end of Latin America to the other when the same issue came up. Centralists affirmed that Colombia had "neither the enlightenment nor the customs" requisite for a successful federation; there were hardly enough intelligent and public-spirited citizens to staff one set of executive, legislative, and judicial branches, much less a national set plus additional sets for all the sovereign states. It was assumed by this reasoning that neither local officials nor the people themselves could understand and abide by the complex rules marking off state and national functions under a federal system, and the disasters of the *Patria Boba* were cited as further and presumably unanswerable proof of the inadequacy of federalism. Then, too, it was observed that a strong central government would cause a good impression in Europe. The most pressing of all arguments, however, was the claim that centralization was far and away the most practical method of carrying on the war with Spain and hastening its successful conclusion. The federalist case was argued for the most part on a more theoretical plane. Its supporters stressed the universally admitted principle that federalism was more in line with the theory of pure republicanism, pointed to its success in the United States, and claimed of course that sovereign states would provide a barrier against executive tyranny. They added, among other things, that "federation is an ark of perfumes." The practical side of the federalist argument was shown in such considerations as the stated fear that a centralized government would unload the debts of other departments upon the back of Cundinamarca, and that it would turn New Granada into a Venezuelan colony.[18]

The last two statements reveal the main source of federalist sentiment. It was not Venezuela, which later helped to break up Colombia under the federalist banner; apparently those Venezuelans who came to Cúcuta felt the need of a central union to finish the job of liberating their homeland, and had at the same time been more thoroughly exposed to the vehement anti-federalism of Bolívar. Instead, the federalist stronghold was the interior of New Granada, the area farthest removed from Venezuela and the outside world, not to mention from the present theatre of war. Federalism was espoused above all by men who had taken an important part in the *Patria Boba* and had not, to the centralist way of thinking, learned their lesson. It reflected also a fear and distrust of

---

[18] *Ibid.*, 41-124, 779-780.
The supporters of federalism did not always make clear whether they wanted Venezuela, New Granada, and Quito organized as three great states in a federation, or whether they wanted the federal states to correspond roughly to the provincial divisions, as in the *Patria Boba*. But either way, the arguments pro and con were basically the same.

Venezuelan militarism as represented by the armies of Bolívar,[19] but it certainly cannot be dismissed as a badge of doctrinaire liberalism as it was destined to become in later years. Few Colombians, in fact, would have denied in 1821 that they were in some sense liberals. But as some distinctions must be made, it is best to reserve the term especially for those who construed liberalism to imply not only constitutional government but also an economic system based as far as possible on laissez faire, an attack on the privileges of the Roman Catholic Church, and a general reform of society in accord with whatever enlightened principles might be in vogue in western Europe. In this sense liberalism was most faithfully represented by the younger professional men who were already attaching themselves to the fortunes of Santander; and the most prominent members of this group, Francisco Soto and Vicente Azuero, were both firm supporters of centralism at Cúcuta. Santander himself, having abandoned the federalist views he held during the *Patria Boba,* was also in favor of the new system, and almost certainly the influence of Bolívar had much to do with the change. It is likewise probable that Santander and his supporters were influenced by the fact that he was already ruling New Granada itself along centralist lines and was likely to have an equally important role in any central union to be set up for all Colombia.

It has sometimes been argued that the Congress of Cúcuta did not really have a free choice at all, but was forced to accept centralism because Bolívar would have nothing else. One need not assume that he would have used force or the threat of force to prevent the establishment of a federalist system. In view of his known dread of federalism, which he held to be the root cause of earlier patriot failures, it was obvious enough that he would take direct offense at a federalist constitution; he might carry out one of his innumerable threats to resign, or at the very least cooperate poorly with the federal authorities, and few deputies cared to face either eventuality. It was not just Bolívar they were afraid of, for the army as a whole had shown wide discontent at the mere idea of replacing the existing government, which was essentially military in nature, with a constitutional regime,[20] and it is also true that known federalists voted in favor of centralism when the latter system was finally adopted by the overwhelming vote of 41 to 10. Yet there is no evidence that the result was due primarily to intimidation or fear of the military. A more important factor appears to have been the honest decision of many theoretical federalists that centralism was best fitted to the purpose of fighting the war with Spain, and that some measure of federalism could then be adopted later on when peace returned. This view obtained wide

[19] *Ibid.*, 83, 781-782; Santander to Bolívar, September 26, 1820, Lecuna, *C.S.* I, 124-125; Diego B. Urbaneja to Soublette, June 5, 1821, Blanco VII, 611.
[20] Restrepo V, 345, 387.

support when expressed at Cúcuta, notably by Alejandro Osorio, and might be termed the Great Compromise of the Colombian constituent convention. It was openly reflected in the provision that a new convention should be held at the end of ten years in order to consider the advisability of constitutional reform.[21]

It cannot be denied, moreover, that the degree of centralization adopted at Cúcuta went beyond what was likely to be found practicable in normal times. Latin American federalists have justly been accused of breaking up the unified territorial divisions of colonial times in order to create wholly artificial "sovereign" states. The Congress of Cúcuta went to the other extreme and placed three colonies that had been very loosely connected with each other under the immediate direction of a single central administration. It went much farther than the law of union adopted at Angostura, which had preserved Venezuela, New Granada, and potentially Quito as separate entities under the immediate command of regional vice-presidents. The three were now to be divided into a number of medium-sized departments, all equally subject to the central authorities and consisting of two or more of the colonial provinces. The new departments were supposed to be more convenient to govern, and, since they had no colonial traditions behind them, less likely to provide a focus for popular separatism. The "Department of Venezuela" thus bore little resemblance to the former Captaincy-General; it was nothing but a bloc of territory surrounding Caracas, theoretically on an equal plane with the Departments of Zulia on the west and Orinoco on the east. This arrangement was to prove in many places highly unpopular, and artificial as well. Both in Venezuela and in Ecuador it was found necessary at first to establish a *Jefe Superior* with some kind of general authority over all the territory previously ruled from Caracas or Quito: only when the republican regime had been more or less consolidated could this post be abolished. On the other hand, to have retained the three great colonial divisions permanently would have been to invite the growth of regional autonomy at the expense of the national authorities. To have abolished the three in favor of merely four, as Bolívar at one point suggested,[22] would have had the disadvantages of dismantling traditional units without the convenience of having smaller territories to administer.

Once the main question had been settled, the details of the constitution were filled in fairly easily. Municipal government preserved much the same outward form as under the colonial regime, with its *alcaldes* and *regidores,* and was made strictly subject to both departmental and national

[21] *Actas:* Cúcuta, 68-69, 77, 95-99, 111-112; William M. Gibson, *The Constitutions of Colombia* (Durham, 1948), 66.
[22] Letter of Pedro Briceño Méndez to Diego B. Urbaneja, May 24, 1821, A.C., Senado-5, 132.

authorities; the latter were represented at the local level by a special officer known as the *juez politico*. Next came the province, which was retained out of deference for tradition even though the provincial governors had no very clear function in the Colombian system: the intendants who were placed in charge of the various departments were the really basic cogs in the new mechanism of regional government. Both governors and intendants were to be appointed by the president with the consent of the Senate. At the center of government, power was apportioned among the Chief Executive, two houses of Congress, and an *Alta Corte* in roughly the same manner as in the United States: the presidential veto was the same, and members of the higher judiciary were to be selected by joint action of the other two powers. There was a definite movement among *granadino* deputies, especially the federalists, to limit the presidential power further, but they were overcome by a combination of strong-government Venezuelans such as Pedro Gual and future *santanderistas* such as Francisco Soto.[23] The theoretical supremacy, as in other republican regimes, rested with the law-making body, which was Congress; but in practice, thanks to his control over both central and provincial administration, the president was its equal if not in some cases its superior. His power was to be heightened in any emergency by the typical Latin American device of "extraordinary faculties," which was carefully enshrined in Article 128 of the new constitution. And, finally, the rights of Colombian citizens to the enjoyment of life, liberty, and property were safeguarded by conventional but specific guarantees.[24]

Individual rights definitely were not taken to include a democratic system of elections. The word democracy was itself looked on with disfavor at Cúcuta, and not solely to quiet European suspicions. Suggestions for an elective Supreme Court found very little favor among the deputies,[25] and all positions that actually were made elective were to be filled by a complex system of electoral colleges rather than by direct vote. The right to vote was limited to the same groups that had qualified to elect deputies to the Constituent Congress, except that this time suffrage was given to anyone who owned $100 instead of $500 in real property and was not specifically extended to the military without regard to their other qualifications. A few weak voices were raised in favor of allowing any "honorable poor" to vote, but the demand was never an important one. It was observed in the course of the debate that property qualifications had been in use "since the most remote antiquity," and the Legislative Commission firmly stated that "a rigorously democratic election does not suit us, will not suit us for many years . . . and perhaps will never be

[23] *Actas:* Cúcuta, 108, 248-252, 298, 462, 467-468, 803-804; Gibson, *op. cit.,* 61.
[24] Gibson, *op. cit.,* 58, 61-64.
[25] *Actas:* Cúcuta, 263-265.

preferable to the one that is proposed." [26] A clear indication of where the sympathies of the "honorable poor" chiefly lay can be seen in the fact that a broader suffrage found more support with clerical-minded conservatives than with orthodox liberals. Progressivly higher property qualifications were then imposed for the right of holding elective office, although they were not so high in this case as to exclude most liberal intellectuals.[27]

When the deputies had finished with the constitution they turned to function as an ordinary legislative assembly. They had of course "legislated" even before this, as in their momentous decision to abolish slavery through gradual emancipation,[28] but it was only after the constitutional problems were cleared away that the assembly really set to work to pass those specific laws and decrees which could not be postponed until the meeting of the first regularly-elected Congress. In the field of taxation, and in some other aspects of social and economic policy, the deputies at Cúcuta produced far-reaching measures of reform; these will all be considered in due course. On political and administrative questions, however, they continued to be guided by a mood of caution. The one noteworthy reform was the abolition of press censorship and the institution of a jury procedure for the trial of press offenses. The demand of a perfectionist minority to establish trial by jury for all criminal offenses as one of the Natural Rights of Man had been sensibly rejected, but the Congress of Cúcuta chose to follow the example of the Spanish liberals in making its press law an opening wedge for the jury system, which would ultimately, it was hoped, be applied far more widely.[29]

Aside from this there was little innovation. The constitution itself had already provided for the retention of the entire body of Spanish law, subject only to the reservation that any law or decree contrary to the principles of republicanism was automatically void.[30] Rather more important, since it was less inevitable, was the subsequent adoption of the Ordinance of Intendants of New Spain, the administrative code of Spanish Enlightened Despotism overseas, as a temporary basis of departmental and provincial government. This decision was subject to the usual condition stating ". . . in all that is not contrary to the present system of government," [31] but according to the terms of the very same law this did not mean that the republican separation of powers, formally enshrined in the trinity of Executive, Congress, and *Alta Corte,* would have to be

[26] *La Gazeta de la Ciudad de Bogotá,* November 25, 1821, Cf. *Actas:* Cúcuta, 239-240, 286, 297, 437-440.
[27] Gibson, *op. cit.,* 53-55.
[28] See below, p. 168.
[29] *Codif. Nac.* I, 39-47; *Actas:* Cúcuta, 325, 491-493.
[30] Gibson, *op. cit.,* 65.
[31] *Codif. Nac.* I, 99.

applied at all the lower levels of government as well. On the contrary, both intendants and provincial governors would have some judicial functions, and only a last-minute alteration prevented the *juez político,* at the municipal level, from sharing in the regular legal jurisdiction of the *alcaldes.* Similarly, civil and military functions, though technically separate, could still be united in the same person. This provision was a natural result of war-time conditions, but it left one more conflict with republican principles to be removed by later legislation. There was, moreover, at least one case in which a major republican principle was disregarded without any apparent excuse: for it was provided that once the membership of the existing municipal councils had been renewed by the provincial electoral colleges all future elections were to be made by the outgoing members themselves.[32]

An exceptional procedure was also followed in the first election for president and vice-president, who were chosen by the Congress of Cúcuta itself so that the new constitution might take immediate effect. For the office of president, Bolívar was the obvious choice: there were only nine votes cast against him. It was known in advance, however, that Bolívar had no intention of abandoning his military command in order to direct the dull work of civil administration. He was therefore granted special permission to lead the army in person, with "extraordinary faculties" in those areas "where he personally makes war," while the immediate control of government in the greater part of the republic was to be entrusted to the vice-president.[33] The latter position accordingly took on unusual importance in the new regime, and it was far more bitterly contested. On the first ballot no less than seven candidates shared the total vote, even though two of them were very definitely out in front: Antonio Nariño, who had only recently returned from a long period of captivity in Spain, and Santander. Of the two men, Nariño had perhaps the more obvious qualifications. He was a *granadino,* which was essential as long as the president was Venezuelan; he had a long and distinguished patriot record; he had gained ample experience at practical politics both at home and abroad. Santander, though a talented administrator and also a *granadino,* had been almost unknown until after Boyacá and he was not yet even thirty years of age.

The candidacy of Santander was strengthened, on the other hand, by Nariño's personal unpopularity with a large body of the deputies. There was, to begin with, a hard core of violently anti-Nariño sentiment in New Granada derived from unburied grudges of the *Patria Boba;* it was strongest among the close admirers of Santander, who had personally been on bad terms with Nariño ever since he deserted the "Precursor" in

[32] *Ibid.,* I, 97-104, 155; *Actas:* Cúcuta, 624-626.
[33] *Actas:* Cúcuta, 458, 558; *Codif. Nac.* I, 109-110.

order to join the federalist side in the civil wars of 1812. It was a firm ally of Santander who aired the sensational and not very accurate charges that Nariño had needlessly surrendered to the Spaniards at Pasto, and that he was a willfully insolvent debtor to boot. The latter charge was particularly unjust since the fact was that Nariño had long ago borrowed money, quite legally, from the funds he was handling as treasurer of tithes for the Bogotá archdiocese, and had then defaulted only because he was suddenly arrested for his patriot activities and ordered to repay what he had borrowed ahead of schedule. It is thus doubtful that such charges as these were enough to prevent the election of Nariño. Far more important was the erratic behaviour of Nariño in recent months. He had become provisional Vice-President of Colombia in the spring of 1821, and as such he had formally opened the Congress of Cúcuta. He had then proceeded to show rather little respect for Congress. He was discourteous at the very least toward the widow of an English officer who came to Cúcuta seeking the payment of money owed to her late husband; he arrested another foreign officer who protested too strongly over the incident, and he took great offense when the Congress asked him to account for his actions. Nariño was subjected to such a barrage of criticism on the floor of Congress that he was finally compelled to resign his office. All in all, it is perhaps surprising that he fared as well as he did in the election for a permanent vice-president under the new constitution; only on the eighth ballot did Santander finally obtain the requisite two-thirds majority.[34]

The flare-up of partisan sentiment caused by the vice-presidential election was paralleled by additional wrangling on the question of choosing a capital city. Ultimately a city named in honor of Bolívar was to be founded for this express purpose, but in the meantime the government needed a temporary resting-place. The choice of Bogotá was bound to impose itself, since it was located near the center of the republic and possessed all the facilities to accommodate a host of Congressmen and civil servants. The discomforts of Cúcuta were a strong argument in its favor. Even so, it was necessary first to overcome the opposition of some Venezuelans who disliked a capital so far from home, not to mention the fear of Francisco Soto that mob violence in Bogotá as in revolutionary Paris would exert an unwholesome pressure upon the republic's leaders.[35]

When Bogotá finally won out, the only major task still remaining for the Congress to perform was to choose the members of the first Colombian Senate. Senators were to serve eight-year terms, and unlike the members of the Chamber of Representatives they were to be chosen only in part at

[34] Antonio Nariño, *Defensa del General Nariño* (Bogotá, 1823), 4-11, 48-49; Restrepo V, 338-339; Urbaneja to Soublette, June 5, 1821, Blanco VII, 611; *Actas:* Cúcuta, 141, 145, 182, 558, 749-750, 796-799.
[35] *Codif. Nac.* I, 118-119; *Actas:* Cúcuta, 561-564.

each election. Hence in order to have a full membership for the Senate's first meeting the deputies at Cúcuta saw fit to vote this time for the entire body themselves. Their selections, by and large, were shrewdly made, with the result that the Senate was definitely superior in ability to the lower house, which was filled from the outset by indirect popular election. Despite the inclusion of the staunchly conservative Bishop of Mérida, Rafael Lasso de la Vega—who had only recently embraced the cause of independence—the Senate was also a more liberal body, and it was therefore destined to cooperate far more closely with the administration of Santander.[36]

Bolívar, on his part, filled out that administration by formally naming the first cabinet secretaries before he relinquished executive control to Santander. Fittingly enough, he chose two *granadinos* and two Venezuelans. The *antioqueño* José Manuel Restrepo became Secretary of Interior, a position in which he was to earn the reputation of a devoted public servant and a convinced liberal who nevertheless knew how to temper his principles with common sense. José María Castillo y Rada of Cartagena, who became Secretary of Finance, was more doctrinaire in his opinions and less effective as an administrator. Yet both men remained at their posts during the entire administration of Santander, an their collaboration with the Vice-President was on the whole eminently successful. Venezuela was represented in the cabinet by the respected patriot Dr. Pedro Gual as Secretary of Foreign Relations and by General Pedro Briceño Méndez, a close friend of Bolívar, as Secretary of War. Both were destined to leave the administration while Bolívar was still absent at the front of his armies, but they were replaced by Santander himself with two of their compatriots, Dr. José Rafael Revenga and General Carlos Soublette. And with the partial exception of Revenga—who disagreed openly yet sincerely with Santander over the English loan of 1824—the four Venezuelans were fully equal to their associates both in zeal for the public welfare and in their loyal cooperation with Santander.[37]

## *The Completion of Independence*

By the time the Congress of Cúcuta closed its sessions in October, 1821, Colombian armies had confined the Spanish forces in Venezuela and New Granada to little more than the fortress of Puerto Cabello, the Isthmus of Panama, and the ultra-royalist province of Pasto. In Ecuador, Quito remained in Spanish hands, but Guayaquil already enjoyed an independent government. The war of liberation, therefore, was drawing

[36] *Actas:* Cúcuta, 744-755.
[37] Eduardo Acevedo Latorre, *Colaboradores de Santander en la organización de la república* (Bogotá, 1944), 68-152.

to its close. The task ahead was complicated, however, by the fact that the territories still under Spanish occupation had been formally included in the Colombian Republic without the consent of their chosen representatives. They were in a worse position than Caracas, which had been liberated too late to elect deputies of its own but had been represented indirectly at Cúcuta by the numerous *caraqueños* who were chosen for other provinces. This was hardly a serious injustice in the case of Pasto and Puerto Cabello, which were integral parts of New Granada and Venezuela respectively, but the Presidency of Quito was a different matter. Even Panama, although it had legally been under the direct control of the viceroy at Santa Fe, had not forgotten the semi-independent status it once enjoyed under its own *Audiencia* and had fairly little sense of unity with the rest of New Granada.

Fortunately the Panamanians were not diehard royalists like the people of Pasto, and were quite willing to accept a reasonable transaction. In November of 1821, while Bolívar was preparing an armed descent upon the Isthmus, they deposed the Spanish authorities in a bloodless revolution and offered to join Colombia at once if certain conditions were granted. The most important of these were the preservation of all military and civil officers in their current positions and the recognition of debts that had been assumed by the patriot junta established on the Isthmus as a result of the coup. As the debts included some that had been contracted in Panama by the Spanish authorities, their recognition was contrary to Colombian policy. In effect, the Panamanian junta proposed a treaty between sovereign states rather than the simple incorporation of a territory so implicitly regarded as Colombian by the deputies at Cúcuta that they had none of the qualms of conscience on including it that were evinced with regard to Quito. However, there was no time to waste in haggling; the Panamanian terms were accepted in full.[38]

The situation at Guayaquil was superficially the same as had existed in Panama. The province was regarded as naturally belonging to Colombia, but it had won independence through its own efforts in October, 1820, and had since existed under the exclusive control of a local patriot junta. There was a substantial party that favored formal annexation to Colombia and accepting the work of Cúcuta. But there was also a decided faction that favored union with Peru under the guidance of San Martín; and there was a third group, strongly represented on the governing junta, that believed Guayaquil could exist profitably as an independent commercial state after the model of the Hanseatic towns. It is quite impossible to assess the exact strength of any one party. In the last analysis, however, a completely free choice was out of the question. The Congress

[38] Blanco VIII, 221-222. The question of Panamanian debts is discussed below, p. 103.

of Cúcuta had laid claim to the entire Presidency of Quito, including Guayaquil; and even though the deputies apparently assumed this claim would be freely ratified by the peoples concerned, Bolívar was frankly prepared as a last resort to annex the region by force.[39]

The first step was to liberate Andean Ecuador, which was done chiefly by a Colombian army under Sucre that landed at Guayaquil under the protection of the independent junta and proceeded inland to win the decisive battle of Pichincha in May of 1822. This victory marked the end of Spanish rule in Ecuador, and indirectly it compelled the royalists in Pasto to surrender as well. A further result was the final annexation of Quito to Colombia by a form of popular acclamation. Pichincha did not automatically deliver Guayaquil to Colombia, but possession of the Ecuadoran highlands merely strengthened the Liberator's resolve to obtain it, since Guayaquil was their only convenient outlet to the sea. As soon as possible he marched to the port city, and by a show of force and determination easily won a vote for union with Colombia. The form of a free choice was maintained, and after Pichincha it probably represented a genuine majority decision. Whether it really did or not must remain a matter for speculation.[40]

With the acquisition of Guayaquil the republic had won its desired frontiers; the main interest in the War of Independence—and Bolívar personally—now moved on to Peru. The only regular Spanish army still on Colombian soil was that based on Puerto Cabello in northern Venezuela, and its defeat, which finally came late in 1823, was only a matter of time. The granting of diplomatic recognition by the United States in 1822 and by Great Britain three years later attested before all the world that Colombia was a success. To be sure, even after a territory had been won, it was sometimes necessary to cope with continuing disorders fomented by Spanish agents or by domestic royalists. The province of Pasto soon regretted its submission and became the scene of endemic royalist revolt. There were occasional royalist guerrillas elsewhere too; and all such activities combined to create a truly critical situation toward the end of 1822 and beginning of 1823. Land communication between Ecuador and New Granada was cut off by the *pastusos;* domestic royalists briefly seized the city of Santa Marta; there were miscellaneous disorders and alarms in other parts of the republic. To make matters worse, the Spanish forces still at Puerto Cabello staged a surprise descent on Maracaibo and were threatening an invasion deep into the interior.

Rising to meet this challenge, Santander fulminated new decrees against "internal conspirators," and Colombian army officers initiated a

[39] Cf. Lecuna, *C.L.* III, 4-7.

[40] On this general subject see William H. Gray, "Bolívar's Conquest of Guayaquil," *Hispanic American Historical Review* XXVII (1947), 603-622.

virtual scorched-earth policy in Pasto. The first regular Congress in 1823 did its part by authorizing the immediate deportation of all suspected royalists and *desafectos* anywhere in Colombia.[41] And yet within a few months the scare had passed. Indeed it is apparent that the danger from internal enemies was never so great as was believed by Colombian leaders at the time. The most active supporters of Ferdinand VII had usually retreated with the Spanish armies before the first advance of the patriots. Others were formally expelled by the action of patriot commanders, and those who remained came more and more to accept Colombian independence as at least a *fait accompli*. Some of the most rabid of royalists were transformed into perfectly sincere patriots as they recoiled in horror before the progress of liberalism in the mother country following the Spanish revolution of 1820.[42] Even the hardy mountaineers of Pasto— whose royalism was more a product of extreme localism and ignorance than a conscious political theory—began to see the light when Col. José María Obando was sent out as governor by Santander and proceeded to practice conciliation in place of the previous wanton repression.[43] By 1825, if not sooner, royalism in Colombian politics had become little more than an epithet to be flung at those who were not "disaffected" toward independence as such but merely toward the particular program of political, social, and economic reform upon which the republican regime now boldly embarked.

---

[41] *Codif. Nac.* I, 199-200. The expulsion law gave rise to long and bitter debate, in which conservative elements—apparently fearing that the term *desafecto* could be stretched to include anyone of reactionary social or political views, even if not technically a royalist—sought to limit the wide discretionary power that was granted to the Executive. In actual practice, however, the law was very little used in most parts of Colombia. See A.C., Senado-23, 90-93; Actas del Senado (secret sessions) June 11 and 12, July 1, 1823; *Actas:* Congreso-1823, 185, 190-191, 482.

[42] The official and semi-official press never tired of reminding the clergy, especially, of the sad plight they would be in if they had fallen into the hands of heretical Spanish liberals. Cf. *El Patriota* (Bogotá), February 5, 1823.

[43] For Obando's own account—which obviously exaggerates his own merits and the iniquities of his predecessors—see his *Apuntamientos para la historia* (Lima, 1842), 27-45.

Chapter III

## The Santander Regime: Political Reform and Administrative Problems

EVEN before the problems of national security—both external and internal—were finally disposed of, the Colombian Congress and administration were attempting to bring the political institutions adopted at Cúcuta more nearly into line with liberal thinking. There was no serious question as yet of changing the constitution, although such a move was suggested by some opposition leaders. There was much wider agreement on the need to alter the detailed division of governmental functions and the territorial organization that had been worked out once the constitution was signed. In these matters the Constituent Congress had done its work hastily, and many of its decisions were admittedly provisional in nature. No one felt that perfection had already been attained. The main dispute concerned merely the precise degree of ideal republicanism and bureaucratic symmetry that was practicable for the moment, and a measure of caution was advocated not only by old-fashioned conservatives but also, from time to time, by Santander himself. The Vice-President was a good liberal, but he was also a practical politician, and he knew from experience the concrete difficulties that stood in the way.

### The Progress of Innovation

The most glaring violation of liberal principles in the entire administrative system had been the combination of theoretically incompatible functions in the hands of the governors and intendants. Under the Ordinance of Intendants of New Spain, provisionally adopted for Colombia at Cúcuta, they had been given both executive and judicial powers; and as the separation of powers was deemed the very cornerstone of republican government this arrangement found few defenders. According to the Secretary of Interior, José Manuel Restrepo, it was not only unwise but really unconstitutional. Still another objection to the practice was the fact that many army officers disliked serving as governor or intendant so long as those positions required the performance of judicial functions. Judicial business in itself was apparently distasteful to them, and the routine subordination to the higher courts that it entailed was even more distasteful. Since Santander nevertheless desired to employ the services of military men, he at one point refused to submit any nominations for either of the two posts unless Congress agreed to revise their functions.[1]

The feelings of the military did not carry as much weight with Congress as with Santander, since the appointment of professional soldiers to any kind of civil office was conventionally believed to involve a threat of military despotism. Santander, though a general himself, could sympathize with this view up to a point. However, he did not always have enough capable civilians to choose from, and by combining the position of governor or intendant in the same hands with the provincial or departmental military command he could both save money and eliminate possible conflicts between civil and military authority. In all regions threatened with Spanish invasion this practice was also advisable for strategic reasons.[2] Though never universal, it had existed ever since the liberation of New Granada and had been approved by the deputies at Cúcuta. A clear majority of the first intendants and governors named by Santander under the new constitution had thus been military *comandantes* as well, and even when civil and military functions were not united, the civil heads might still be army officers.[3]

Yet it was only a matter of time before Congress got around to making a definitive reform of departmental government, and the legislation that resulted, in 1825, was designed both to ensure the formal separation of judicial and executive powers and to end the union of civil and military commands. The first objective was accomplished mainly by transferring the judicial business of intendants and governors to new magistrates especially created for the occasion, the *jueces letrados de hacienda,* of whom there was to be one for every province. A curious sidelight is the fact that the judicial functions of governors and intendants were legally abolished almost two months before the new magistracies were created. The second part of the program was also achieved, over Santander's vigorous protest, by prohibiting the combination of civil and military commands in the same person save on a temporary basis and in cases of extreme necessity.[4] Even this provision did not rule out the appointment of individual army officers to civil posts, but here the necessity of obtaining senatorial confirmation

---

[1] José Manuel Restrepo, *Exposición . . . del Despacho del Interior* (Bogotá, 1824), 6; A.H.N., Corresp.-Senado (Interior), June 14, 1823; A.C., Senado-20, 71-74.

[2] A.H.N., Corresp.-Cámara (Interior), January, 1825 (first message) and March 21, 1825.

[3] *Codif. Nac.* I, 100; *Acuerdos* I, 11-12; *La Gazeta de la Ciudad de Bogotá,* December 23, 1821; A.C., Senado-2, 54-55.

[4] *Codif. Nac.* II, 17-35, 121-150; A.C., Senado-28, 385.
 As the term implies, the *juez letrado de hacienda* was concerned above all with cases in which the treasury was involved, but he had certain other jurisdiction as well.

was bound to act as a restraint if the Vice-President ever attempted to name too many.

The most significant change made in government at the municipal level was the creation in 1825 of still another new judicial office, the *juez letrado de primera instancia*. This measure was not quite enough to introduce a complete separation of powers in local government, since the municipal *alcaldes* still retained cognizance of the less important cases.[5] It was designed to bring about greater efficiency, however, and it helped to provide a much-desired symmetry—on the French model—in the hierarchy of officials. For the *juez letrado* existed alongside the *juez político* (now rechristened *jefe político*), who was the local agent of the national executive, and also the *comandante de plaza* if the town had a military garrison. This set of officials thus corresponded exactly to the *juez letrado de hacienda*, governor, and *comandante de armas* theoretically existing in every provincial capital, and the *Corte Superior*,[6] intendant, and *comandante general* assigned to every department.

In order to have bureaucratic arrangements equally symmetrical in a geographic sense, Congress held to the ideal of making all departments, all provinces, and all "cantons" or municipalities roughly equivalent in size and importance. This had originally been proclaimed as a guiding principle at Cúcuta, but it had not always been followed in practice. Subsequent Congresses thus sought to obtain a greater perfection by continually creating new territorial units and readjusting the boundaries of the old ones. The region most affected by these changes was the Venezuelan *llanos*, most of which had belonged at first to the Department of Venezuela, whose capital was Caracas. The result had been to create a department which was much greater in size and population than the national average, while at the same time the difficulty of maintaining order among the unruly *llaneros* made it advisable to have a higher authority on the spot. Hence after some preliminary reshuffling of provincial lines a brand new Department of Apure was erected on the *llanos* themselves. The latter step created a unit of standard size, and brought an intendant and *comandante general* to the city of Barinas. On the other hand, Apure was still far below average in population and resources, so that two years later it had to be combined with the province of Guayana, hitherto subject to the Intendant of Orinoco at Cumaná, in still another new department.[7]

[5] *Codif. Nac.* II, 138-141, 147.

[6] The creation of *Cortes Superiores*, which in a great many departments was never actually carried out, is discussed in detail in the following chapter.

[7] *Codif. Nac.* I, 225, 305, II, 300. A confusing detail is the fact that the combination of Apure and Guayana was now to be called the Department of Orinoco; the department that formerly bore this name thus had to be given the new title of Maturín. In this study, however, the Department of Orinoco will always mean the original department whose capital was Cumaná.

In other parts of Colombia there was somewhat less tampering with provincial and departmental boundaries, but everywhere the readjustment of municipal divisions was a favorite game of Colombian politicians. Especially in New Granada, municipal organization had been particularly unstable during the *Patria Boba,* when the vogue of federalism encouraged a great number of dependent outlying settlements to declare their own municipal autonomy. The Pacification had generally brought a return to the status quo, which continued through the Congress of Cúcuta, but when later Congresses went to work the trend to smaller city units was resumed. Not only was it assumed that cantons should all be of about the same size, but Congress also sought to create as many of them as possible so that the benefits of a republican administration might be felt at first hand by more people. The reform was carried out in part by legislative fiat, in part by authorizing the Executive to create new cantons as it saw fit. The result was the creation, at least on paper, of several dozen new municipalities.[8]

It was obvious that for the moment Colombia lacked the resources to carry out every detail of the administrative network decreed by Congress. Hence the Executive was given fairly wide discretion both in setting up the new municipalities and in filling all the offices that formed the ideal bureaucratic pyramid; and as long as it was given this leeway, the Santander administration was quite as enthusiastic as anyone else about the new political order. It is worth noting, however, that the reforms adopted were designed almost solely to further bureaucratic symmetry, the separation of powers, and the mutual independence of civil and military authorities. There was certainly no move toward political decentralization, even though federalist sentiment was still very much alive and served as a constant source of harassments for the administration.[9] Indeed, the only compromise ever made with federalist ideas was the creation, in 1825, of *juntas provinciales*—rump assemblies, drawn from the membership of the provincial electoral colleges, which were to meet once a year to "propose" needed legislation, to "inform" the authorities about conditions in the province, and to do nothing at all.[10] Furthermore, any move towards a greater democratization of the Colombian regime was likely to be dismissed as mere "Jacobinism" in the official and semi-official press.[11]

[8] A.C., Senado-2, 262-263, 269-276, Senado-27, 93-99; *Codif. Nac.* I, 305-309, II, 65.

[9] Federalism as a political issue was associated mainly with the following of Nariño at Bogotá and the more extreme opposition groups of Venezuela. It is treated more fully below, pp. 58-64, 290-291.

[10] *Codif. Nac.* II, 31-32.

[11] Cf. *La Indicación* (Bogotá), August 10, 17, and 24, 1822. *La Indicación* was published by Dr. Vicente Azuero, who generally reflected the administration viewpoint and was really a member of Santander's "brain trust." Azuero stressed the fact that the popular will was limited by "public utility," the chief aim of government; and for the people to overrule public utility would be unjust

It was clearly recognized that liberalism would be incompatible with any true democracy so long as the masses remained ignorant, impoverished, and more susceptible to the influence of the Church than to that of liberal merchants and professional men; hence no extension of the suffrage was even taken under consideration. A more serious proposal was the demand to give some sort of popular assemblies a right to suggest candidates for governor and intendant. Even some of Santander's closest supporters tended to favor a reform of this nature; yet it was always rejected by the Vice-President himself, not only because he opposed any diminution of his own prerogatives but also because the proposal seemed incompatible with a centralist constitution. When such a measure was finally approved by Congress in 1827, it was firmly vetoed by Santander.[12]

Particularly revealing is the suspicious treatment regularly meted out to the municipalities, which had been the one more or less popular element in the colonial regime. It is true that in one respect Congress did advance the cause of municipal democracy, for it ultimately put an end to the method of having new members of the town councils selected by the outgoing officers of the previous year. Even here, however, the attempt of Congress to substitute direct popular election was blocked by Santander. In his veto message the Vice-President warned that "frequent meetings of the people" for such purposes as the election of public officials were against the teaching of "very famous *políticos*," and that it would be "absurd" to give local governments a more popular origin than Congress itself. "A day can come," he argued, "when perverse men placed in the municipalities might allege their purity of origin and plunge the republic into chaos." [13] As a result, Congress agreed to have municipal officers indirectly chosen by a miniature electoral college.[14] The functions of municipal government, moreover, were always severely limited by the republican regime: hemmed in between a *jefe político* and a *juez letrado,* town officers were actually more restricted in some ways than they would have been under a Spanish *corregidor.* Similarly, by a special law of municipal finance Congress denied local governments the right to deviate in the slightest from a uniform system of revenue and expenditure without obtaining its prior consent. Thanks to this measure one village in Antioquia had to petition Congress even for the right to build public pens for storing pigs at a *real* a head, and the proud city of Bogotá had to pass up a better offer for the rental of its common lands simply because the law required leases to be made for a term of exactly two years.[15]

[12] *La Gaceta de Colombia,* July 22, 1827. Cf. *La Indicación,* September 28, 1822 and January 18, 1823 for a view different from Santander's.
[13] *La Gaceta de Colombia,* September 3, 1826; A.H.N., Corresp.-Cámara (Interior), January, 1825 (first message).
[14] *Codif. Nac.* II, 27.
[15] *Codif. Nac.* II, 72-85; A.C., Cámara-15, 430-431, Cámara-16, 169-170.

All this is perhaps surprising in view of the part played by the *cabildos* in launching the independence movement, but past services in this case made little impression on Santander, who spoke of the *cabildos* as "so indifferent to the public good, and so little capable of promoting it." [16] The limitation of municipal functions was also one way of reconciling the ideal of numerous magistrates in direct contact with the people with the unfortunate fact that at the lower levels these magistrates were not too well educated and were inclined to be more conservative than either the national administration or Congress. In any case, town magistrates were seldom very happy under the new regime. If they were not actually complaining about their election to municipal office, which was no longer a favorite outlet for creole ambitions, they were likely to be assailing the encroachment of new-fangled national officials on their own prerogatives.[17]

## *The Use of Extraordinary Authorizations*

One other seeming inconsistency in Colombian political practice was the willingness of a Congress so obviously committed to republican principles to grant the administration special authority from time to time to take measures that normally lay outside its legal functions. The grant might take the form of "extraordinary faculties" in the strict sense, which were semi-dictatorial powers to deal with a military or other emergency, or it might be a delegation of congressional authority to make the final decisions —in effect, to legislate—on some specific problem. In either case the procedure was accepted only as a necessary evil, which presumably would disappear as soon as the republic was set upon a really firm footing. But in the meantime grants of one sort or another were made so frequently as to become one of the major features in the politics of Gran Colombia.

The basic provision on the subject of "extraordinary faculties" was Article 128 of the Constitution of Cúcuta, which permitted the Executive to take emergency measures under a state of virtual martial law in any region threatened by foreign invasion or internal rebellion. If Congress was in session at the time, it was supposed to give its consent; if Congress was not in session the Chief Executive could proceed on his own initiative, reporting his actions to Congress as soon as it met again. Under the terms of this article the Congress of Cúcuta issued its law of October 9, 1821, that made an indefinite grant of "extraordinary faculties" in all regions serving as a theatre of the war with Spain and in all "recently

[16] Santander to Diego B. Urbaneja, August 23, 1821, A.H.N., Congresos XXIV, 639. The fact that a small town in Guayana dared to suggest an improved system of tithe collections brought forth an angry reply from Bogotá in which the town council was told to treat in future only "the matters that are entrusted to it, without attempting to form *reglamentos* or perform other acts which are peculiar to the legislative body." (A.C., Senado-20, 522.)

[17] Cf. A.H.N., Congresos XXV, 885, 861, 863, 867, 869-870.

liberated" territories as well. It was thought necessary to define these faculties by listing them one by one, but the definitions were so vague that they did little if anything to limit the Executive: one article flatly granted the power "to organize the country that is being liberated in any way that the President or Chief Executive sees fit. . . ." [18]

The effect of this measure was to give the Executive almost absolute powers to use if needed in such areas as northern Venezuela, where the Spaniards retained Puerto Cabello until late in 1823, and Ecuador, which was a theatre of war until the battle of Pichincha in May of 1822 and remained a "recently liberated" area even after that. Hence customs-houses in Venezuela were able to raise export duties above the legal rates on the plea that more money was needed to prosecute the war. At the same time, and for similar reasons, Bolívar was suspending virtually all the fiscal reforms of the Congress of Cúcuta in Ecuador.[19] Only in 1824 did Congress get around to withdrawing the grant of "extraordinary faculties" made at Cúcuta, and even then it merely replaced the former law with another of its own. The new measure was designed to restrict the powers conferred by defining them still more carefully, but in reality its definitions were almost as vague and meaningless as those of 1821. Thus newly-liberated provinces were deleted from the list of areas where "extraordinary faculties" might be used, but Congress still permitted declaration of a state of siege in provinces that were merely contiguous to one threatened by invasion or revolution. This clause could be and was construed to cover the whole of Ecuador due to its proximity to the war in Peru.[20] In fact the main significance of the law was simply that it also prohibited Bolívar from exercising emergency powers as President of Colombia while remaining in charge of military operations outside the country. This did not affect the nature of the powers themselves, even though it set off a dispute between Bolívar and Santander that must be discussed in another connection.[21]

Nevertheless, "extraordinary faculties" were always the subject of widespread criticism, some reasonable and some not so reasonable. Even the awkward attempts of Congress to define them more fully reflect a clear uneasiness over their possible abuse; and as the war tapered off and Colombia began to enter upon the road to normalcy they did in fact become less necessary. In 1825 Congress made a new grant of emergency powers to cover the special case of rumored disorders in central Venezuela, but as it happened the grant was never used, and in the same year the wartime state of siege was finally ended by administrative decree even

[18] William Marion Gibson, *The Constitutions of Colombia* (Durham, 1948), 58; *Codif. Nac.* I, 109-110.

[19] See below, pp. 156, 311.

[20] *Codif. Nac.* I, 388-390.

[21] See below, pp. 72-75.

in Ecuador. Not satisfied with this, the Chamber of Representatives decided the following year to repeal every measure without exception having to do with "extraordinary faculties," including all decrees issued by the Executive by virtue of the faculties in question. This would have left the administration nothing but the bare words of Article 128 to permit their use in the future. The Senate was in substantial agreement, but the details were never quite worked out, and in the end Congress did not carry through its threat.[22]

Although "extraordinary faculties" attracted by far the most attention, they were related in principle to the roughly similar technique of delegating to the Executive discretionary powers for such commonplace activities as drawing municipal boundaries and approving army uniforms. These were all legally the concern of Congress, but Congress chose not to exercise its power directly. The Congress of Cúcuta, in particular, had no time to lay all the foundations for the new republic, and it therefore authorized Santander to adjust territorial divisions, set up government offices, and above all to regulate the size of the armed forces and raise internal loans at his own discretion.[23] After 1823, when normal legislative processes began, many of the more sweeping grants of power finally lapsed, but discretionary control over the armed forces was provisionally continued by the Congress of 1823, and countless miscellaneous tasks were subsequently thrust upon the Executive, from the determination of a bureaucratic salary scale to the establishment of a temporary educational curriculum.[24] Such practices led *El Constitucional,* which was the chief independent liberal organ of Bogotá, to complain that Congress showed "an implicit confidence in the Executive, much greater, without dispute, than that which is compatible with the interests" of the Colombian people.[25] The same editorial made clear, on the other hand, that it condemned the Congress as negligent rather than the Executive as desirous of arbitrary power.

Sometimes, it is true, Santander specifically asked for greater discretionary powers. He vetoed a bill that retained final decision on the design of military uniforms in the hands of Congress, since he could neither wait for Congress to give advance approval to any contract with suppliers nor risk a later invalidation of contracts already made. He therefore obtained from Congress the power to settle designs himself.[26] On other occasions discretionary powers were clearly thrust on Santander

[22] A.C., Cámara-6, 91-104. The Venezuelan emergency decree of 1825 is discussed in detail below, pp. 300-301.
[23] Cf. *Codif. Nac.* I, 98, 106, 120.
[24] *Codif. Nac.* I, 198, 252-253, II, 241.
[25] *El Constitucional,* April 14, 1825.
[26] A.C., Actas del Senado, January 9, 1826; *Codif. Nac.,* II, 193-194.

against his will: such was the case when Congress commanded the Vice-President to decide what ports should be open to foreign trade, and thus to face the storm of criticism that was sure to come from ports that were passed over.[27] Whether such powers were sought after or not, however, the effect was to give Santander a very real share in the legislative function, and so even more influence on the development of Gran Colombia than his position as Chief Executive alone would indicate.

## Practical Difficulties of Administration

Unfortunately, no amount of extraordinary powers could solve all the problems facing the Colombian administration: they might provide helpful short-cuts, but they could never conjure up material or other resources that did not exist. The mere setting up of untried republican organs of government was in fact a task of the utmost difficulty. Superficially, it would seem that many of the republican magistrates had only to fulfill the same functions as the officials of the colonial regime under a slightly different set of titles, but even when offices were basically identical—which was not always the case—the more important colonial office-holders were likely to be gone, and capable replacements were hard to find. The prolongation of the war first in the extremes of the republic and then beyond its borders in Peru created an endless demand for men, money, and supplies that would have strained the administrative system even if the experienced civil servants of the viceroyalty had remained at their desks. In many areas, both public order and official routine had to be re-established from the ground up.

Not only this, but the high degree of political centralization adopted at Cúcuta was sufficient in itself to make the task of the Colombian Chief Executive even harder than that of the former viceroys. It is true that the viceroy's judicial and legislative functions had been transferred to the *Alta Corte* and Congress, but this did not always make the work of administration easier, and Congress promptly transferred at least some of its functions right back to the Executive. Moreover, any alleviation of duties in this respect was more than offset by the need to assume direct responsibility for Venezuela and Ecuador, over which the viceroy had exercised little more than nominal authority. Not only were there obstacles of distance and terrain that had to be overcome—it was a hard journey of many weeks' duration to such points as Guayaquil and Cumaná—but the Venezuelans and to a lesser extent the Ecuadorans tended to feel a loss of dignity in the new arrangement and became as a result rather hard to deal with. This aspect of the problem, however, is one that can best be treated apart, for the complexity of conditions in Venezuela and Ecuador was such that either section would have been hard to govern under

---

[27] *Actas:* Cámara-1824, 325; *Codif. Nac.* I, 423.

any conceivable political organization. Suffice it to say for the present that even with "extraordinary faculties" it was never, easy to make central authority effective in the outlying regions of the republic, and that the weakness of central control did not necessarily mean that a firm local authority then fulfilled the same functions. Instead, local officials might well evade their responsibility altogether, relying on the inadequacy of communications with Bogotá and on the lack of any deep popular sentiment in favor of strict obedience to the central authorities.

When centralist institutions were combined with the colonial tradition of shifting responsibility from the lower to ever higher levels of government, the result was often to bog down the national authorities in a mass of inconsequential detail. Among the matters taken up at plenary cabinet sessions were such trivia as the appointment of an interim doorman at the Bogotá mint or an official archivist for the Intendancy of Venezuela; it can only be hoped that Santander and his ministers did not thrash out the merits of each candidate as they went down the list. A more vital matter, but still rather out of place in a Council of State, was settlement of a dispute between the Intendant of Cundinamarca and the city of Bogotá over the best place to hold markets.[28] In their own departments, fortunately without reference to the cabinet as a whole, the ministers had to decide such questions as whether the *oficial mayor* of the *contaduría de tabacos* at Socorro might take leave to go fetch the wife he had left in Barinas ten years ago, or how to feed prisoners in the Pasto jail. In the former case Finance Secretary Castillo y Rada graciously offered his consent, but in the latter he felt compelled to scold the intendant who had raised the problem for wasting precious time with it.[29] Indeed it was obvious that many small problems of this nature did not actually have to be submitted to Bogotá even under the Constitution of Cúcuta. But here the very unfamiliarity of the new system directly added to the burdens of those who administered it: until detailed procedures had been worked out in practice many subordinate officials invariably sought to remain on the safe side by avoiding decisions of their own.

Administration was further complicated—and slowed down—by the exaggerated sense of etiquette inherited from Spanish officialdom. Among the trivial questions referred to the entire cabinet was whether the *Corte Superior del Centro* might communicate with the intendants merely through its secretary, or whether the president of the court had to sign all messages himself.[30] Santander on his part gave great offense to the *Alta Corte Marcial* by failing to place his signature on official letters addressed to it; the court tried to retaliate by sending its correspondence to

[28] *Acuerdos* I, 271, II, 207, passim.
[29] A.H.N., Departamento de Boyacá II, 383; A.C., Cámara-6, 294.
[30] *Acuerdos* I, 58-59.

the war ministry signed only by a secretary rather than by the presiding judge, but the correspondence was then returned unanswered.[31] An even greater amount of time was wasted by the *Corte Superior del Centro* and the *Contaduría General* at Bogotá in drawing up protests, counter-protests, and *expedientes* designed to prove either that the court might "demand" information from the *Contaduría* or that it had merely the right to "request" it.[32] It is no doubt significant that so many of the more striking disputes of this nature can be found in the relations between administrative officers and the judiciary, which had so recently been raised to the status of a separate and equal power, but they were parallelel within the various levels of the bureaucracy itself.

It would appear also that newly-created officials seldom enjoyed the traditional respect that had surrounded colonial civil servants. The prestige of the *jueces letrados de primera instancia*, in particular, was further undermined by the not entirely disinterested attacks of municipal *alcaldes*. Neither did the citizenry always take very kindly to the tampering with time-honored territorial divisions. Municipalities that were carved up in order to create new cantons from their outlying districts were seldom happy about it, and in some cases the new cantons themselves were not much happier. The citizens of Moniquirá sought and obtained revocation of their municipal status on the interesting grounds that they were too ignorant to fulfill the functions of a town government and too poor to pay for one.[33] When it came to creating whole new provinces still more problems arose: the Ecuadoran city of Ambato felt deeply insulted to be included in the new province of Chimborazo simply because the shift entailed subordination to lowly Ríobamba rather than to metropolitan Quito as in the past.[34]

This leaves one more purely administrative problem to be considered, and almost certainly it is the most serious of them all: the lack of qualified public servants. The Chamber of Representatives truthfully complained in 1824 that "the Republic lacks illustrated men, both because of the disasters of the war and because of the . . . colonial and oppressive system with which the Spanish government ruled these peoples."[35] Additional reasons of a social and economic nature could easily be listed, but the fact itself was inescapable. It is no doubt true that little formal education or experience was needed for the bulk of administrative posts, and also that the lower levels of the bureaucracy would very often retain their

[31] A.C., Senado-7, 252-254.

[32] A.C., Senado-7, 57-71. This question had to be referred to Congress for a final decision.

[33] A.H.N., Interior y Relaciones CIX, 788, 864-882. For a similar case (Funza) see A.C., Senado-53, 111.

[34] A.C., Senado-42, 40-41.

[35] *Actas:* Cámara-1824, 333.

pre-independence public servants. On the other hand, in many areas there was a shortage even of men with an average facility at reading and writing. In all but a few there was an even greater shortage of men with specialized training. It is hard to imagine any country in Latin America today without a positive surplus of certified lawyers, but it was asserted on the floors of the Colombian Congress in 1823 that there were somewhat over 200 in a population of nearly 3,000,000, and the figure seems roughly confirmed by partial statistics on legal talent gathered by the administration. At one point only seven lawyers could be counted in the city of Popayán.[36] This was a serious matter, for not only were there judicial posts to fill, but legal training was useful in many executive offices. Moreover, the lawyer shortage was a sure symptom of the general lack of "illustrated men," if only because higher education in Spanish America had traditionally been either juridical or theological.

There was of course no real lack of lawyers and other "illustrated men" in Bogotá itself, for that is where many of those from outlying provinces had found their way. But even at the center of government, salaries were seldom alluring, and because of military expenditures they could seldom be paid in full.[37] Low pay, as one might expect, made it difficult to maintain high standards of either efficiency or honesty in public service. Nor was the supply of candidates for office in Bogotá ever large enough to compel the less fortunate to take positions in Trujillo or Río Hacha or Panama. Hence such a reform as the institution of *jueces letrados* could not have been fully carried out everywhere even if the necessary funds had been available, which they were not. It is likewise significant that the first three men named lieutenant governor (*teniente asesor*) of Casanare, which was hardly a promising spot for a *letrado*, resigned the position as soon as they were appointed.[38] As for the *jefes políticos*, the financial bond which they were supposed to post had to be overlooked repeatedly in practice thanks to the dearth of acceptable candidates. In fact any candidates at all were sometimes welcome. In suggesting three names for the position of *jefe político* of Cúcuta, the governor of Pamplona province frankly remarked that "none of these . . . individuals has the intelligence necessary to perform said office; but they are wealthy men, and if they wish to do a service for the Republic they can pay the clerks they need from their own pockets. . . . "[39]

[36] *Actas:* Congresos-1823, 167; A.H.N., Interior y Relaciones CXXI, 285-286, 355-356, 544-557.

[37] The practice of withholding regular sums from government salaries in order to make up the treasury's operating deficit is discussed more fully below, p. 100.

[38] *Acuerdos* I, 15, 21, 23.

[39] A.C., Senado-19, 71-72, 83, 88-95. When the Intendant of Boyacá finally offered the job to one of the gentlemen in question, he nevertheless replied that he was too poor to accept it.

The common practice of having one man fill two positions was another sign of the lack of qualified officials and at the same time one of the major techniques for getting around it. Presumably government efficiency often suffered, but that could not be helped. The tendency to unite civil and military commands is one obvious example of the practice, although in that case the personnel shortage was only one of the reasons for it. An even clearer example is afforded by the use of Congressmen in both administrative and judicial posts. Some of the men elected to Congress already held positions in the other branches of government; still more obtained executive and judicial appointments after their election, and generally the only constitutional requirement was that they suspend their other duties while Congress was in session.[40] Thus, according to one count, 69 out of the 103 members of the Congress of 1826 held positions of some sort to which they had originally been nominated by Santander.[41] The chief spokesman of the administration in Congress, Senator Francisco Soto, was also public attorney and prosecutor (*fiscal*) before the *Corte Superior del Centro* and later the *Alta Corte* itself. For that matter, several leaders of the conservative opposition bloc were judges of the same *Corte Superior,* and in either case the practice of combining executive and judicial office with membership in Congress was widely criticized as contrary to the theoretical separation of powers. A campaign to end it was spearheaded on the floors of Congress itself by the Caracas priest José Antonio Pérez, a systematic oppositionist who would have refused Congressmen the right to accept any position whatever the Executive had power to give; after leaving Congress, he added, they still should not be eligible for appointment until the Executive Power itself changed hands. Even some pro-administration liberals sympathized with Father Pérez' general objective.[42] Indeed Santander himself did not entirely oppose that objective, personally recommending that the judges of a *Corte Superior* be declared ineligible for Congress. When Congress passed a somewhat

[40] *Actas:* Cámara-1824, 171-172; A.H.N., Corresp.-Cámara (Hacienda), May 13, 1823. There were a few offices, such as governor and intendant, which were legally incompatible with membership in Congress, but even this could often be evaded by giving Congressmen "provisional" appointments, in which case the rule did not apply.

[41] *La Gaceta de Cartagena,* June 11, 1826. The figures come from a source which was hostile to the administration and was attempting to prove that Congress had been suborned by Santander. They are impossible to check with accuracy because the number of members and the number of those holding other official posts varied constantly. And they include clergymen who had obtained their posts in the hierarchy through aid of the *patronato.* There is no doubt, however, that they substantially reflect the true situation.

[42] A.C., Senado-33, 19-20; *La Gaceta de Cartagena,* December 31, 1825 and January 7, 1826; *La Miscelánea* (Bogotá), November 27, 1825; *Actas:* Senado-1824, 830-831.

watered-down version of Pérez' project he vetoed it simply because he felt it was technically unconstitutional, and because he wished that it had not gone quite so far.[43]

The combination of more than one position in the same hands was not always to the liking of the incumbent, since he could not simultaneously draw two full salaries. All too frequently, however, he had no choice in the matter. In the case of Congressmen, it was decided soon after the first regular Congress had opened for business that no member could resign his seat save for a good excuse and with the consent of his respective chamber. If a member was also judge or bureaucrat he would just have to take a vacation until the session was over, unless for some very special reason he obtained permission from Congress to return to his job.[44] He might conceivably resign his other position, but he was unlikely to do so since Congress did not offer year-round employment. Indeed the administration would surely do its best to dissuade him from such a step in view of the difficulty of replacement. In many cases it curtailed the right of resignation just as vigorously as Congress, for compulsory public service was regularly exacted in all branches of government. Sometimes the law itself stated that one could not resign without due cause; this was true of such posts as collector of direct taxes and also of municipal offices. The Intendant of Magdalena once commanded the leading citizens of Lorica to attend the election of municipal officers in person so that if they were chosen they could be forced to accept on the spot, before they had a chance to think up excuses.[45] In the case of some other positions—*jefe político,* for instance[46]—the same policy of compulsion was occasionally adopted without apparent legislative sanction. No proof is available that this was done by virtue of specific orders from the central administration, but the latter could hardly plead ignorance of the abuse. The custom was especially unjust when salaries were so hard to pay on time, and it is thus surprising that there was so little protest outside the ranks of the victims: one of the few statesmen who seem to have expressed doubts in public regarding the practice was Antonio Nariño.[47] But as a practical matter it was not always easy to compel a man to serve unwillingly. Dr. José Ignacio Márquez, as Intendant of Boyacá, fined one obstinate citizen $25 for refusing to become tobacco administrator at Pamplona; but the appointee still refused to take office.[48]

[43] A.H.N., Corresp.-Cámara (Interior), April 26, 1823; A.C., Senado-34, 270-273, 409-410; A.C., Actas del Senado, January 28, 1826.
[44] *Actas:* Congreso-1823, 415; A.C., Senado-15, 186, 306; A.C., Actas del Senado, April 1, 1826.
[45] *Codif. Nac.* I, 81, II, 28; *La Gaceta de Cartagena,* February 14, 1825.
[46] Cf. A.C., Cámara-13, 318-320.
[47] *Actas:* Congreso-1823, 167.
[48] A.H.N., Departamento de Boyacá III, 861-865.

## The Achievement of Santander

Under such conditions the mere fact that a functioning administration was set up, that it proved capable of supplying the armed forces, and that it maintained internal tranquillity in all but a few limited areas has never ceased to arouse admiration for the executive talents of Vice-President Santander. The praise has come not only from his confessed admirers but also from such hostile writers as José Manuel Groot, although the latter always reserve their greatest praise for the earliest years of his government, when fewer controversial issues were raised.[49] Especially after the lapse of so many years, however, it is not easy to find concrete evidence for an abstract quality such as administrative talent. The mere survival of Colombia, despite the implications of the Vice-President's flatterers, is not sufficient proof. For the most part one must form a rough impression from the way in which he met each problem in turn, always with the aid of his ministers; and the best confirmation of the general praise is the fact that by and large he pursued his course with relative moderation and common sense, even when common sense conflicted with the orthodox liberalism that was dear to him in theory. There are exceptions, but it is unlikely that Bolívar himself would have made fewer serious mistakes. When he finally assumed the presidency in person, Bolívar simply made different kinds of mistakes, and he made them just as consistently.

Moreover, there can be no doubt that Santander at least attempted to be a very conscientious ruler. One can dismiss first of all the various allegations that he made illicit profits from his office. Despite all the time and effort that have been expended for the purpose of proving such charges, only one has ever been truly supported by concrete evidence, and that one is distinctly a borderline case. Santander did not come to office a rich man, his salary was irregularly paid, and even though his stingy entertaining ultimately won him the ill-will of the diplomatic set[50] the expenses of his position were heavy. He therefore accepted the offer of Bolívar to grant him a legal military bonus by means of an illegal short-cut which consisted of a decree falsely dated back to the period when the Liberator had authority to make the award solely on his own initiative. The bonus was paid in the form of an estate near Chiquinquirá and a house in Bogotá, both of which were probably assessed at much less than their real value, but the latter detail was a normal occurrence in military bonuses.[51]

---

[49] Cf. Groot, 57, and Daniel F. O'Leary, *Bolívar y la emancipación de Sur-América* (Rufino Blanco-Fombona, ed., 2 vols., Madrid, n.d.), II, 125.

[50] Cf. Hildegarde Angell, *Simón Bolívar* (New York, 1930), 240.

[51] Lecuna, *C.L.* II, 187, 217; Juan Francisco Ortiz, *Reminiscencias* (2nd ed., Bogotá, 1914), 94.

We also know that the Vice-President worked late hours at his desk for the public good. "I work like a pen-clerk," he wrote of himself in August, 1821; "I am, besides, a general and corporal, I am the *alcalde* to hear law-suits, and believe me that I do not have time to eat."[52] In later years Santander obtained more secretarial help, but he also obtained more work. He was methodical in his habits, setting aside regular hours each week for conferences with the secretaries of state and the Intendant of Cundinamarca, and he encouraged the same orderliness in others. The Vice-President decreed, among other things, that all petitions and reports must be submitted to the government with their pages numbered.[53] A still better example of Santander's attention to detail is his veto message of January, 1825, on the *Ley orgánica de tribunales*. Not only did he lecture the Senate on when the conjunction "or" should be written *u* instead of *o*, but he reported not less than three minor grammatical errors in the law and found time to observe that *expresarán siempre* would be "more elegant" than *siempre expresarán*. He also suggested some much-needed substantive changes.[54] Presumably many of the defects in the law were discovered originally by José Manuel Restrepo, the cabinet secretary within whose sphere it came, but Restrepo must have been inspired at least in part by the Vice-President's own thoroughness. It may be argued that to correct legislative grammar is a waste of time. But in a state where authority was highly centralized and the most unimportant matters were constantly being referred to the national executive, it is an indication that Santander was temperamentally well fitted for his job.

The one quality, however, for which Santander is most admired by Colombian Liberals today is his uncompromising devotion to constitutional legality. There is no doubt an element of fiction as well as of fact in the hallowed tradition of Santander, *"El Hombre de las Leyes,"* for he was quite capable of stretching a point of law when it suited his purposes. No ruler of an infant republic totally lacking in precedents for constitutional government could help but do just that. On other occasions he merely hid behind a legal technicality in order to escape criticism for failure to meet some urgent problem in full and on time; one of his favorite excuses was always to allege that a particular measure could only be taken with the specific consent of Congress. Santander's reputation as "Man of Laws" is nevertheless deserved by and large, and nowhere can this be seen more clearly than in his general respect for civil liberties, which constitute, after all, the most important single aspect of constitutional legality. During Santander's entire administration as Vice-President of Colombia probably the most famous instance of alleged tampering with

[52] Lecuna *C.S.* I, 159.
[53] *La Gaceta de Colombia*, January 13 and February 24, 1822.
[54] Message of January 3, 1825, A.C., Senado-22, 56, 58, 66, 68-69.

the rights of the opposition on his part was the official order for Col. Francis Hall to leave Caracas after becoming the sponsor of a strongly anti-government newspaper, *El Anglo-Colombiano;* but as Hall had been commissioned to do a scientific survey for the Colombian government, not to engage in oppositionist propaganda, the move was clearly justified.[55]

Santander's respect for the rights of the opposition is particularly striking in view of the fact that he was personally highly irritable when subject to political attack. He tended to look upon criticism of his administration as a personal affront, and he repeatedly bothered Congress with demands that it clear his name by investigating even the pettiest charges of his enemies.[56] He also requested Congress to pass a law curbing unbridled criticism of the government in representations placed before the courts.[57] However, it is significant that he sought to obtain this objective by due process of law. It was another arbitrary impulse that led the Vice-President to regard the manifesto in which the Caracas city council swore allegiance to the Constitution with some rather meaningless qualifications as a serious case of seditious propaganda which should be punished as such. But what Santander did, quite typically, was to instruct the Intendant of Venezuela to prefer charges in normal fashion before the local press jury, and when it returned a unanimous verdict of not guilty he promptly let the matter drop.[58]

Santander did perhaps have one unfair advantage in building up his reputation for scrupulous and often doctrinaire legality: the various special authorizations that allowed him to wield more power than he would normally enjoy as Chief Executive and still remain technically within the letter of the law. But it must be said that he showed considerable restraint even in the use of "extraordinary faculties," which were the powers most easily subject to abuse. Unlike Bolívar, who would cite "extraordinary faculties" as an excuse for issuing decrees on practically any subject that came to mind, Santander used them primarily for their literal objective, which was to deal with internal conspiracy, war preparations, and the like; and he appears to have been quite faithful in later reporting his emergency decrees to Congress for its approval.[59] He recognized the possi-

[55] A.C., Actas del Senado (secret sessions), February 3, 1825. For a good collection of arbitrary acts charged against Santander see *Cartas al Señor Ex-Jeneral Francisco de Paula Santander* (Bogotá, 1837-38). Some of these appear to have a foundation in fact, especially those relating to the period of provisional military government before the Constitution of Cúcuta; but in no case has a really serious offense been proven.

[56] See, e.g., A.H.N., Corresp.-Cámara (Interior), February 13, 1826, for a request that Congress investigate a story that Santander had made an excursion into the country with an "apostle of the monarchic system."

[57] *La Gaceta de Colombia,* September 5, 1824.

[58] *El Anglo-Colombiano* (Caracas), May 11, 1822.

[59] Cf. A.H.N., Corresp.-Senado (Interior), May 9, 1823.

bility that such powers could be abused by the subordinates to whom they had to be delegated in practice, and he sought to forestall such abuses by laying down precise conditions under which the powers might be used.[60] Indeed he recognized implicitly that he might abuse them himself. Even without a special law from Congress, he was always entitled by the Constitution of Cúcuta to assume "extraordinary faculties" when needed to ward off a threatened invasion. But Santander was afflicted with doubts as to whether he could legally act in such a case simply on the basis of *datos fundados* that such an invasion was imminent or whether he would have to wait until the invasion materialized. He referred the matter to Congress for its opinion, and was told that he did not need to wait. Then, to be doubly sure of his position, he proceeded to ask Congress to define by law just what sort of *datos* might legitimately be considered *fundados*.[61]

It obviously took more than hard work and good intentions on the part of the Vice-President to make a success of the government as a whole. It took similar qualities in subordinate officials, and it has already been seen that these were hard to find. The most that can be said is that Santander did not, as is sometimes charged, consistently aggravate the shortage of administrative talent by limiting his favor to his own unconditional supporters. The men whose names he submitted to Congress as candidates for major executive and judicial posts included both uncompromising independents and, on one occasion, the bitterest of all his congressional critics, the *cartagenero* Juan de Francisco Martín.[62] In the latter case Santander may have meant simply to challenge De Francisco to see if he could do any better in managing the affairs of state, and as it turned out Congress finally selected an alternative candidate; but at least there is no reason to assume that all the Vice-President's non-partisan appointments represent a base effort to buy political support.

To be sure, no listing of the virtues of Santander can obscure the fact that the Colombian administration left very much to be desired. In its lower reaches the existence of widespread corruption was everywhere taken for granted, and the reports of foreign observers are studded with stock phrases regarding "the disposition of the local authorities to exercise arbitrary powers." [63] Neither was the government of Colombia outstanding for efficiency in the performance of its day-to-day functions. This is a quality for which the colonial regime had not been famous, and Colombia

---

[60] Cf. instructions to the *Comandante General* of Cauca Department, *Acuerdos* II, 54-55.

[61] *Codif. Nac.* I, 293; A.H.N., Corresp.-Cámara (Interior), January 25, 1825.

[62] *La Gaceta de Colombia,* June 11, 1826.

[63] Dispatch from Todd to Secretary of State, February 28, 1823, N.A., Colombia Dispatches II.

faced even greater obstacles than the Viceroyalty of New Granada. Hence not only did much of the excellent legislation issued by Congress remain largely unenforced in practice, but even the protection of life and property against common criminals was notoriously ineffective. And yet the situation could easily have been worse. The critics of Santander would have it that all bad laws were carried out while the good ones remained a dead letter, but this is unlikely *a priori*. It is contradicted, in fact, by the painfully slow but yet real progress made in such fields as education, all of which must be taken up in more detail over the following chapters. Not only this, but the worst corruption was always to be found in the revenue service, where temptations were peculiarly great, and in the armed forces, which were not always amenable to control by the Vice-President. Military and financial organization, in any case, had complexities all their own, and they, too, must be considered apart.

Finally, it is well to note that most of the complaints about a "disposition . . . to exercise arbitrary powers" refer either to the Colombian army or to the lower levels of the civil government, both municipal and provincial. In other sectors of the administration concrete and authenticated charges of misgovernment are surprisingly few. It was by no means difficult to win a hearing for one's complaints against major Colombian officials in Congress and the press, and actual impeachment proceedings were begun against roughly a half dozen of them. The Chamber of Representatives maintained a "Committee on Infraction of the Constitution and Laws" for just this purpose. For the most part, however, the charges submitted to Congress—to "the brilliant justification and most distinguished goodness of that peerless Congress," [64] as one petitioner had it—were either irrelevant, or unfounded, or just impossible to prove. Two of the most sensational of all impeachment trials dealt merely with the "abuse" of a *comandante de armas* in breaking up a smuggling ring and that of an official of the government tobacco monopoly in financing the state's business by a highly irregular procedure—out of his own pocket.[65] As long as the Constitution of Cúcuta was really in force, only one of the provincial and departmental heads was undoubtedly guilty of major abuses against the rights of citizens. This was Colonel Vicente Castro, Governor of Loja, who was accused of various arbitrary arrests and related irregularities. He was saved at the last minute from a formal impeachment trial only through the fact that Santander and the *Corte Superior del Sur* both beat Congress to him.[66]

---

[64] A.C., Cámara-12, 134.

[65] On these two cases see below, pp. 65-66 and 89.

[66] *Actas:* Cámara-1825, 355; *El Colombiano del Ecuador*, (Quito), April 17, 1825.

Chapter IV

## *The Judicial and Legislative Powers*

IN WRITING the history of the Latin American republics it is customary to pay no attention to the national judiciary, and very little to the internal workings of the legislative branch. Up to a point this neglect is justified, for Latin American political development has been characterized from the outset by the concentration of power in the hands of the Chief Executive; the same can be said of dictatorships and of ostensibly constitutional regimes. But it is easy to carry neglect too far. Certainly the political life of Gran Colombia—where the courts and Congress had by no means lost all independence—cannot be accurately studied without giving due consideration to both the law-making process and the administration of justice. Both have been touched on already, but they must now be appraised in their own right. For not only did they provide ample subject-matter for some of the chief partisan controversies of the day, but their problems in themselves throw additional light on the general obstacles to be overcome in setting up the republican regime.

### *The Courts, Crime, and Litigation*

There is more than a superficial resemblance between the colonial *Audiencias* of Bogotá, Caracas, and Quito and the *Cortes Superiores de Justicia* that replaced them after the attainment of independence. Yet the changes brought about by the new regime were at bottom quite as important as the remaining similarities. The *Audiencia* had been a very special form of court: its main business was judicial, but it was an administrative council as well. Thanks to the republican separation of powers, the Colombian appeal courts had been stripped of all non-judicial functions. At the same time they had been granted cognizance of many judicial and quasi-judicial appeals formerly settled by administrative officials. Unlike an *Audiencia*, a Colombian *Corte Superior* was regularly entitled to hear appeals from ordinary courts-martial and to review all legal controversies relating to fiscal administration.[1] The establishment of a supreme court on Colombian soil was a further innovation. Appeals from the three colonial *Audiencias* had gone to Spain if they had been

[1] Report of *Corte Superior de Justicia del Centro,* December 12, 1825, in A.C., Senado-42, 2-4; *La Gaceta de Colombia,* September 30, 1827. To hear military cases the court would be formally converted into a court-martial through the addition of certain army officers to the panel of judges.

permitted at all; from the regional *Cortes Superiores* they might go to the *Alta Corte de Justicia* in Bogotá, and they were allowed far more frequently. In the view of Colombian judges themselves, however, the most important difference was that members of the *Audiencias* had "answered only to God for their operations,"[2] whereas republican magistrates were bound also to respect the laws and the rights of citizens. This was theoretically true not only as a general proposition but also in terms of the detailed political and judicial guarantees written into the Colombian constitution; and if legal provisions were not enough, there was a conscientious body of legislators and an untrammelled press to keep the judges responsible to more than God alone.

Unfortunately, Colombian judges also had far more cases to settle. The *Corte Superior del Centro* at Bogotá affirmed that it was called upon to handle twice as many civil and three times as many criminal cases as the *Audiencia* of Santa Fe, and overwork of this sort was a major reason for the decision of Congress that ultimately an equivalent *Corte Superior* should be created in every department.[3] But even when such courts were set up in Cartagena and Popayán the situation apparently grew no better. One explanation for this phenomenon was of course the transfer to the regular courts of cases which had been decided elsewhere in days before the separation of powers. It would appear, too, that the breath of liberty had made men more willing to go to court in defense of their natural rights. Another reason, however, was the fact that the attainment of independence had been followed by an increase in crime. It is difficult to estimate how serious this was, since accurate statistics are lacking. It is also difficult to reconcile reports of a crime wave with the amazement of foreign travelers over the security with which great sums of money were carried almost unguarded through the mails.[4] The testimony for some increase in crime is nevertheless too great to be disregarded, especially as concerns thefts of merchandise along the Magdalena River, animal rustling on the *llanos,* and the dangers to life and property in the very capital of Colombia.[5]

[2] Report of *Corte Superior del Centro, loc. cit.,* 4-5.

[3] *Ibid.; La Gaceta de Colombia,* December 18, 1825; A.C., Senado-2, 324. Until 1826 the *Corte Superior del Centro* served a somewhat wider territory than the *Audiencia*—in particular, the Cauca, which had previously belonged to the judicial district of Quito—but this would not suffice to account for so great a difference.

[4] Charles Stuart Cochrane, *Journal of a Residence and Travels in Colombia* (2 vols., London, 1825) II, 47, 373-374; Carl August Gosselman, *Reise in Columbien* (2 vol., Straslund, 1829) I, 191-192.

[5] See e.g., Hamilton to Planta, March 8, 1825, in C. K. Webster, ed., *Britain and the Independence of Latin America* (2 vols., London, 1938) I, 386; *El Constitucional* (Bogotá), October 13 and 20, November 24, 1825. Murder was apparently rare in Colombia, but all varieties of crime were common enough as compared with the colonial era (cf. Restrepo I, xliii).

The precise reasons for all this were a matter of controversy, but the general increase in judicial business which it helped to bring about had results that were obvious to all. For one thing, the proverbial slowness of Spanish justice was carried over into the republic. It was admitted in 1826 that the case of one criminal had been under review for twelve years, which was longer than the maximum sentence applicable to his offense.[6] During the same year the *Alta Corte* managed to deliver a final decision in only 36 cases,[7] although this was not so much a reflection on its own judges as on the lower courts, which all too frequently failed to perform their own job satisfactorily. The *Alta Corte* thus gave repeated scoldings to the *Corte Superior del Centro* for its assorted errors and delays, and the latter court in turn scolded the ignorant and sometimes illiterate rural *alcaldes* who started cases off wrong in the first place. The *Corte Superior* was so sensitive to criticism of itself on this score that it once fined each member of the Bogotá city council $50 for presuming to complain about the slowness of judicial processes.[8]

Colombian judges were further harassed by the need to interpret a mass of new and unfamiliar legislation, and by the exceedingly complex problem of deciding which decrees of the Spanish kings were incompatible with republican principles and thus no longer valid. It is little wonder that their decisions showed occasional inconsistencies: the *Alta Corte* decided within the space of half a year, first that retired army officers could no longer enjoy the military *fuero* and then that they still did enjoy it.[9] The scarcity of qualified personnel naturally affected the judiciary as well as the Executive Power, and so did the irregular payment of government salaries. The latter circumstance may help to explain why two judges of the *Corte Superior del Centro* were found guilty by the *Alta Corte* of illegally pocketing certain gambling fines.[10] Nevertheless, it would be rash to assume that the quality of justice was in any way worse than it had been under the Spanish regime: the fact was simply that independence had not ushered in the hoped-for utopia in the administration of justice any more than in other fields of national life.

In some respects, indeed, the judiciary was the most nobly republican of Colombian institutions. The *Corte Superior del Centro* in Bogotá had

[6] *El registro judicial de la República de Colombia* (Bogotá), September 6, 1826.

[7] *El Conductor* (Bogotá), February 2, 1827.

[8] *El Huerfanito Bogotano,* May 5, 1826. The technical offense, presumably, was contempt of court.

[9] *La Miscelánea* (Bogotá), May 21, 1826; A.C., Senado-36, 122-128. The immediate cause of this reversal was the change of one judge in the composition of the tribunal, but it still indicates the difficulty of laying down a consistent judicial course through the maze of new republican institutions.

[10] *El Correo de Bogotá,* April 9, 1824.

some regrettable eccentricities, but its counterpart in Caracas was at least a mildly stabilizing influence in the most turbulent section of Colombia.[11] The *Alta Corte* itself contained some of the best minds of the republic. The shrewd but unscrupulous Venezuelan, Dr. Miguel Peña, was a questionable asset, but in Vicente Azuero it possessed one of the outstanding figures of Santanderean liberalism, and Dr. Félix Restrepo, who enjoyed the widest prestige of all the judges on the court, was the very personification of republican virtue. One of Restrepo's favorite maxims, we are told, was that it would be better to let the universe be destroyed than to commit a single act of injustice.[12] Such sentiments were immoderate, but their practical effect was all to the good: the enlightened spirit of the *Alta Corte* is well illustrated by its request that the lower courts delete all references to the race of a defendant in submitting cases for review.[13] It was equally on the alert against the mistreatment of citizens by either civil or military officials. When a court-martial failed to impose a prison sentence upon the army officer who assaulted Bogotá's leading yellow journalist, Dr. José Félix Merizalde, it was the supreme court in its military capacity as *Alta Corte Marcial* that intervened to decree punishment.[14]

According to some, the attempt to be scrupulously fair in all things was an excessive leniency that merely encouraged crime. Conservative elements were thus inclined to blame the recent increase in crime on the mildness of the courts and administration in handling criminals, and on the unwise liberality of Colombian laws. "The transition to an absolutely liberal government," the town fathers of Bogotá solemnly proclaimed, "is deadly."[15] No doubt the city of Bogotá was attempting to shift its own share of the blame onto someone else's shoulders, but such charges cannot be dismissed entirely. The *Alta Corte* itself observed that the section of the constitution which required the drawing up of an *información sumaria* of a crime before proceeding to the arrest of the criminal generally played into the hands of the latter. Secretary of Interior José Manuel Restrepo, who was a nephew of the supreme court judge, tried to center the blame for the prevalence of crime upon the inadequacy of Colombian jails and the laxity of minor officials, but he gave as a contributing factor the law of 1824 which sought to define when and how a magistrate could force his way into private dwellings. When the law was originally passed it had been attacked for giving too little protection to

[11] See below, pp. 296-297.

[12] Guillermo Hernández de Alba, *Vida y escritos del doctor José Félix de Restrepo* (Bogotá, 1935), 30-31.

[13] *El Constitucional*, December 22, 1825.

[14] *Sucinta exposición de la causa del teniente-coronel José M. Barrionuevo* (Bogotá, 1825).

[15] Municipalidad de Bogotá, *HH. RR. de la provincia de Bogotá* (Bogotá, 1826).

individual rights; three years later Restrepo was by no means the only one to make exactly the opposite complaint.[16]

The truth of the matter seems to be that the crime problem arose chiefly as an outgrowth of the War of Independence itself. While the war lasted on Colombian soil it had disrupted the usual mechanism of public order; even when it was finished it left behind a troublesome legacy of wandering deserters and disgruntled veterans. An added factor at Bogotá was the growing pains of an isolated colonial town transformed overnight into a great capital with its hordes of new officials, foreign diplomats, and assorted adventurers. But whatever the reason may have been, the situation had to be dealt with. The convinced liberal was interested above all in creating *Cortes Superiores* for every department and placing a *juez letrado* (*de hacienda* or *de primera instancia*) in every province and canton; the judicial backlog could thus be dealt with, and quick, impartial justice for all would go far towards ridding the nation of crime. On the other hand, if liberalism itself was to blame for crime the obvious solution was to temper justice with summary hearings and heavier penalties. In the end Congress tried to please both schools of thought. It created all the new judicial posts that were demanded—not that all of them were ever filled in practice[17]—but it also enacted a special law in 1826 for the purpose of shortening legal procedure in the punishment of thieves.

There were some protests in Congress against the articles of this law that permitted arrest on little more than the verbal denunciation of one "honest citizen" and excluded the presentation of new evidence in the court of second instance, but the measure as a whole met with little opposition. It provided the death penalty for all robberies that involved injury to persons or buildings, and incorporated a number of clauses for the strict repression of vagabonds, including "those who under pretext of studies live without subjection to their respective superiors, without fulfilling their scholastic obligations, and delivered over to idleness." [18] Despite all this the new law did not put an end to robberies. It doubled the number of cases that were carried before the *Corte Superior del Centro*, and for this very reason they could not be handled as quickly as directed. Secretary Restrepo himself saw fit to complain about the lack of executions

[16] *El Constitucional*, March 30, 1826, and July 12, 1827. Cf. complaint by the Intendant of Cundinamarca in A.C., Senado-53, 171.

[17] For lack of both funds and lawyers the government did not even try to set up the legally-authorized *Cortes Superiores* in three of the twelve departments, and not all of the others were actually opened. *Codif. Nac.* VII, 294; *El Constitucional*, January 26, 1826.

[18] *Codif. Nac.* II, 356-363; A.C., Actas del Senado, April 22, 1826; A.C., Miscelánea 1824-1829 *bis*, 61-62.

resulting from the law.[19] However, it apparently did invigorate the prosecution of thieves, and it was at least one of the factors that helped to bring the post-war crime wave under control at last.

## The Education of Congress

If conservatives were unhappy about the administration of justice, almost everyone was dissatisfied in one way or another with the Colombian Congress. Its members were accused of wasting time in talk while accomplishing nothing constructive, of collecting their own salaries instead of solving the financial crisis, and so on *ad infinitum*. When the Congress of 1823 prorogued its sessions beyond the legal minimum, it was promptly charged that the one object had been to obtain extra pay.[20] The Senate was spared some of the criticism because its smaller size was an aid to efficiency, and because its top-heavy liberal majority won it the consistent favor of at least one political sector; but the Chamber of Representatives was so evenly divided that it had no friends at all.

It is thus surprising that more than one traveler from the Anglo-Saxon world had high praise for the Colombian Congress.[21] It may well be, however, that Anglo-Saxons took a more realistic view of what to expect from a legislative body, especially in a country with no legislative traditions. This is, in fact, the one field where the thesis that Latin America lacked all previous experience in the arts of self-government may be accepted without qualification. Santander perhaps went too far in implying that excess talk was distinctive with new deputies,[22] but inexperience was very definitely a reason why long sessions had to be spent simply in working out minor rules of procedure before the first regular Congress could get underway. It was necessary, for instance, to argue out whether the preliminary draft of a law should always begin with the set formula *"El Senado y la Cámara de Representantes, etc."* or whether it was not presuming too much to use the complete phrase when a bill had not yet even left the chamber of its origin.[23]

Some other debates on internal rules and regulations were no doubt entirely superfluous, such as the heated controversy in the lower house over the proper costume for Congressmen to wear. The Senate disposed of this point with a vague "decent but moderate," but the Representatives had to determine specifically whether the clergymen among them could decently wear priestly garments on the floor.[24] It is also true that Con-

[19] *La Gaceta de Colombia*, March 11, 1827; *El Conductor*, February 6, 1827.
[20] *Actas:* Senado-1824, 604-606.
[21] Cf. William Duane, *A Visit to Colombia* (Philadelphia, 1826), 514; *Letters Written from Colombia* (London, 1824), 167-175.
[22] Lecuna, *C.S.* I, 229.
[23] *Actas:* Congreso-1823, 44.
[24] *Ibid.*, 55; *El Noticiosito* (Bogotá), May 23, 1824.

gressmen occasionally used their position for improper financial advantage, placing a dependent on the payroll or perhaps collecting undue travel allowances.[25] Nevertheless, the modern historian may express surprise that petty abuses such as these were no more frequent, while the more serious charges of financial corruption that were made at the time are seldom at all conclusive. No doubt many Congressmen did make handsome profits when a part of the English loan of 1824 was used to pay off the internal debt; but this was not necessarily illegal, many who were not in Congress profited just as much, and it scarcely follows in any case that the expectation of personal gain is what originally moved Congress to vote the loan.[26] Neither can one accept the notion that countless Congressmen sold themselves to Santander for judgeships, sinecures, and clerical benefices. Many did receive appointments, and probably some Congressmen allowed their political views to be swayed by the hope or the realization of such favors. On the other hand, it has already been seen that the shortage of qualified officials positively required one branch of government to raid the personnel of another, and one need not automatically impugn the motives of either Santander or his appointees.

One can even pardon a certain measure of venality among those Congressmen who came to Bogotá when so many of their fellows flatly refused to make the journey. Congress was not a year-round job, and salaries were paid only during sessions. Travel money was provided for legislators from distant provinces, but no allowance was made for unusual expenses, and the sums offered were not always enough to offset the discomfort of traveling hundreds of miles on muleback over mountain trails or ascending the Magdalena in an open boat. At one point Ecuadoran Congressmen found the land route to Bogotá cut off by the *pastusos* and the sea by privateers; and frequently travel allowances could not be paid at all because of the financial embarrassment of departmental treasuries.[27] The disadvantages of serving in Congress were naturally felt the more keenly the farther away from Bogotá a Congressman lived. Venezuelans and Ecuadorans regularly charged that the distance to Bogotá had been underestimated in calculating travel allowances; but even when the Intendant of Venezuela improperly accepted a higher estimate and improperly offered to pay in advance the cost of a round-trip plus congressional salaries for a full session he was unable to obtain more than scattered representation for his department at the opening of Congress in

[25] *El Correo de Bogotá,* April 30, 1824.
[26] Cf. attack in *El Chasqui Bogotano,* No. 3 (1826), and below, pp. 120-122.
[27] A.C., Cámara-1, 308-311, Senado-37, 80-86, Senado-16, 24, 39-43, Senado-54, 62.

1823.[28] Indeed several of the Venezuelans who were elected to Congress during the decade of Gran Colombia, including none other than General Páez, complained that the frigid climate of the capital city was more than their constitutions could possibly endure.[29]

This widespread unwillingness to serve naturally explains the decision of Congress that no one could refuse his election without establishing due cause. As a result, numerous volumes of the Congressional Archives are given over to the medical histories of statesmen who alleged that they were too sick to accept the honor and the complaints of dire poverty put forth by those who claimed to lack the legal property qualifications.[30] Congressmen who could not get their excuses accepted were then fined for the support of those who arrived on time and had to be fed and housed in Bogotá while waiting for a sufficient quorum to open for business. Brushing aside some rather dubious medical certificates, Congress forced the distinguished Venezuelan patriot Martín Tovar to pay not quite $722 under this ruling. His fellow Venezuelan, Colonel Francisco Carabaño, was fined no less than $3000 for his own repeated offenses, although—unlike Tovar—he never got around to paying it; he was also formally expelled from Congress, but this was no great hardship since he had never taken his seat.[31] After the first year Congress tried to reduce absenteeism by offering a special allowance for members from the provinces who chose to remain in Bogotá between sessions,[32] and that is one reason why Congress in 1825 finally managed to begin its labors on the day prescribed by the constitution. Even so, Congress was never without a substantial list of vacancies, and the fact that the absent members were primarily from Ecuador and Venezuela gave undue weight to New Granada in legislative deliberations. Immediately after the first Congress opened in 1823 the proportion of Representatives present to absentees was 36 to 7 for New Granada, 10 to 16 for Venezuela, and 2 to 17 for Ecuador.[33] The balance righted itself somewhat in later years, but never completely. The unfortunate result was to weaken the prestige of Congress in the outlying departments, and to encourage the notion that it was a tool of selfish *granadino* interests surrounding Vice-President Santander.

Still another source of trouble was the division of Congress into two increasingly hostile factions, the conservative and pro-clerical *Montaña*

---

[28] A.C., Senado-19, 18, 21, 24, Senado-37, 53, Senado-53, 93, Cámara-12, 71-73; A.H.N., Congresos IX, 73-76, Corresp.-Cámara (Hacienda), January 25 and February 11, 1825.

[29] A.C., Senado-37, 125; A.H.N., Congresos IX, 43.

[30] *Actas:* Congreso-1823, 7-8, 60; A.C., Senado-8, 225.

[31] *El Colombiano* (Caracas), January 18, 1826; *La Gaceta de Colombia,* May 28, 1826.

[32] *Codif. Nac.* I, 276-277, 348-349.

[33] A.H.N., Congresos IX, 98-99.

and the liberal *Valle*. By this terminology borrowed from the French Revolution, the nickname of the Jacobins sitting on the highest tiers of the National Convention was most inappropriately given to their exact opposites in Colombia, the men who had accepted republican and constitutional government but did not care to see it joined with any major changes in the social and religious status quo. This division was supplemented by strictly personal quarrels, of which the most important was the feud between the supporters of Santander and the friends and relatives of Nariño. Both the ideological and the personal issues at stake will be dealt with in subsequent chapters. However, the intensity of partisan feeling had a direct bearing on the institutional history of the Colombian Congress in that it distinctly tended to reduce legislative efficiency. This did not greatly affect the Senate, which had been chosen originally by the Congress of Cúcuta and was overwhelmingly liberal in sympathy. The Chamber of Representatives, on the other hand, had been elected by the provincial electoral assemblies. It was therefore more closely in touch with popular opinion, and it contained a strong conservative faction alongside the contingent of the *Valle*.

A foretaste of the wrangling that was to follow was afforded soon after the opening of Congress in 1823 when the extremists of the *Valle* began to challenge the election of several conservative members of the lower house on the grounds that they lacked the necessary qualifications for office. In some cases the charges were patently false, in others they may have had some technical justification; but none were really argued on their merits, so it is just as well that finally everyone was allowed to take his seat. Then, in 1824, a climax was reached with the deposition of Dr. Ignacio Herrera as President of the Chamber of Representatives. Herrera was a conservative statesman of the *Patria Boba* and a relative of Nariño; on most issues he was to be found among the adherents of the *Montaña*, and he was one of those whose credentials had been challenged the year before. Having failed in that attempt, the liberals now baited him consistently until he at length committed a "most grave offense against the social order," which was the technical way of describing an undignified scene of name-calling and general disorder on the floor of the house. This lost him the presidency and virtually compelled him to resign his seat in Congress.[34] Apart from such major crises as the deposition of Herrera, there were minor incidents with disconcerting regularity, and the *Valle* made full use of *El Correo de Bogotá* and other organs of opinion to hurl insults at the members of the *Montaña* before a still wider audience. The conservatives were at a disadvantage in the latter phase of the struggle since the Bogotá press was predominantly liberal. They did

[34] A.C., Senado-15, 148, 170-171, 203-210, Senado-23, 487-494; *Actas:* Cámara-1824, 246, 254-255.

seek to have Congress take some kind of disciplinary action against the *Correo,* but the *Valle* had little trouble in warding off the move.[35]

Not only did factional squabbling of this sort cause a considerable loss of time and energy, but it left a residue of bitterness that made constructive cooperation harder to obtain when needed. Moreover, the division was so close in the lower house that it took only a few absences or the shift of a few votes one way or the other for the Representatives to change their mind, or to take a diametrically opposite stand on two different issues. More often than not the liberals still had their way in the end, and it is probably just as well that there was an effective opposition to act as a restraint when moderation was needed. But there was always a certain unpredictability to the behaviour of the lower house, and this in turn served to complicate its relations with the consistently liberal Senate.

In the light of so many adverse factors, the total achievement of the Congress of Gran Colombia is definitely impressive. Congress was not always efficient, but its members were ready to work hard if necessary, with night meetings a regular occurrence during the latter part of every session. The total output of legislation was satisfactory: an average of roughly one measure every other day was issued during the sessions from 1823 to 1826 inclusive. Many of these were minor decrees on honors and the like, but others were comprehensive pieces of legislation arising from the need to give to all phases of national life—customs duties, courts, education, and so forth—a formal, legal organization in keeping with the principles of the new regime. The quality of legislation, to be sure, was not always on a par with its quantity. In the *Ley orgánica de tribunales* as originally passed Santander found not only grammatical errors but also the absurdity of speaking in one place of *jueces letrados de primera instancia* as already existing, and in another of the time "when they shall be established," and without anywhere prescribing the manner of their appointment or defining their powers.[36] The general import duty law of 1826 contained minor inconsistencies that were not detected until it had been printed in the *Gaceta*.[37] And yet this was no worse than could have been expected in view of the inexperience of Colombian legislators and the fact that so much of their work had to be done in haste in order to meet new situations that were not provided for in pre-existing Spanish law codes. In any case, there was always Santander to catch the worst mistakes; his veto messages would be full proof of his political acumen even if no other monument of his work survived. Citing the authority of

[35] *El Correo de Bogotá,* April 30, May 7 and 14, 1824; A.C., Senado-25, 5-8.
[36] Santander to Congress, January 3, 1825, A.C., Senado-22, 56-68.
[37] A.C., Actas del Senado, April 4, 1826.

Jeremy Bentham, Santander explained that "the words of laws should be weighed like diamonds," [38] and he really practiced what he preached. One example is his detailed message concerning the *Ley orgánica de tribunales,* which has been cited more than once already. Even more interesting, perhaps, is his careful disquisition on how Congress should rephrase a law ending discrimination against illegitimates so that it would not suggest to foreigners that they constituted a major problem in Colombia.[39]

The care with which Congress usually studied Santander's veto messages is an indication of the generally good relations obtaining between the Legislative and Executive Powers, without which the work of Congress would almost certainly have been far less effective. This achievement is a tribute to the good sense of both sides, and it is really a minor miracle in view of the exalted opinion which each had of its own rights and dignity. Neither the Congressmen who described each other's speeches in the minutes as "luminous observations" [40] nor the Vice-President who imagined that one day without a Chief Executive could plunge the nation into chaos[41] were necessarily easy to get along with. Yet the Vice-President also took as generous a view as possible when it came to defining the exact scope of legislative functions. His stated objective was to have "laws for all imaginable cases," [42] including the most improbable case of what to do if *a*) the Chief Executive's term should expire before either the newly-elected President or the new Vice-President turned up to take office, *b*) the President of the Senate then took over following the constitutional procedure, and *c*) the latter died in office with Congress out of session and so unable to replace him.[43] Santander's desire to have Congress define as exactly as possible the conditions under which he might assume "extraordinary faculties" is another good illustration. He further humored the Congressmen by giving them first priority in paying salaries from his chronically depleted treasury, even to the point of allowing some payments of slightly dubious legality.[44] This was in line with his general policy to

[38] *La Gaceta de Colombia,* April 11, 1824.
[39] *Acuerdos* II, 34; A.H.N., Corresp.-Cámara (Interior), March 29, 1825.
[40] Cf. *Actas:* Congreso-1823, 608.
[41] A.H.N., Corresp.-Senado (Interior), July 12, 1824.
[42] A.H.N., Corresp.-Senado (Interior), May 18, 1824.
[43] A.H.N., Corresp.-Senado (Interior), July 12, 1824. And presumably with the Vice-President of the Senate also dead or otherwise unavailable. Curiously enough, Santander neglected to pose the problem of what to do if the Vice-President elect (though not the President) was on hand but Congress had not yet assembled to receive his oath of office. When this really happened in 1827, Santander took the easy way out and since he was both the new and the old Vice-President merely stayed in office himself.
[44] A.H.N., Corresp.-Cámara (Hacienda), June 6, 1823, April 14, 1824, and March 7, 1825.

interfere as little as possible in the management of Congress' domestic affairs: he scolded the lower house for appointing two secretaries instead of only one as legally provided,[45] but he apparently did nothing about it.

Needless to say, a certain amount of friction was unavoidable in working out relations between the two powers when there were no colonial precedents to point the way. When Santander offered to supply Congress with a guard of honor there were some legislators who construed his suggestion as a threat to their independence, and others who deemed it merely superfluous; a long debate followed before the guard was finally declined with thanks.[46] When he asked Congress to decide where he and his ministers might sit when their official duties took them to its halls he unwittingly set off still another complex argument. José Antonio Marcos, a clerical deputy from Guayaquil, feared republicanism would certainly be doomed if the Chief Executive delivered a message to Congress while seated in an *asiento preferente;* Manuel Baños, the same who had proposed a "theocratic principality" at Cúcuta, felt the liberty of Congress required the Chief Executive to keep away altogether. Since Congress could not agree on the details of seating and precedence, Baños had his way, and Santander's formal messages were all delivered in writing. The treatment of the Secretaries of State fortunately did not pose quite as many difficulties. There was general agreement that they might report on their activities in person, taking their seats at random. The real question was whether they could stay to witness congressional debate on the information they had offered, and despite the request of Santander that they should be allowed to do so, the decision was that they should not. The *Montaña,* in particular, felt that this would be a threat to legislative freedom, and enough independent liberals sided with them to form a majority.[47]

A similar dispute arose when the first Congress prorogued its sessions by a mere joint resolution, which did not require executive sanction. Santander nevertheless chose to regard this decision as a legislative act and pointedly affixed his own signature without being invited. He refused to budge from his interpretation even after Congress passed a special law establishing its own authority in the matter; he merely vetoed the measure, and Congress had to pass it again over his veto.[48] Santander fared somewhat better in a major controversy that arose over the dating of Colombian laws. Congress decreed that laws should always be cited by the date on which they were finally passed by both houses, rather than by the date of

[45] A.H.N., Corresp.-Cámara (Interior), April 6, 1824.

[46] *Actas:* Congreso-1823, 20; A.C., Senado-15, 98-100, 106, 159.

[47] *Actas:* Congreso-1823, 27-28; *Codif. Nac.* I, 211; A.C., Senado-7, 138-139, Senado-15, 275-277, 283, 291-294, 476.

[48] A.C., Senado-20, 13; A.H.N., Corresp.-Senado (Interior), June 22, 1824; *Actas:* Senado-1824, 230; *Codif. Nac.* I, 313-314.

the Chief Executive's signature; Santander formally disagreed, he vetoed Congress' decree, and in this case, thanks to the Senate's relative lack of interest, the veto stood firm.[49] The one drawback was that Congress continued to cite laws in its way and Santander in his. This practice created a good bit of confusion; among historians, in fact, the confusion has continued ever since.

Fortunately most questions of mere procedure were fought out on a high plane of principle—a good bit higher, indeed, than the intrinsic importance of the issues usually required. On other questions both Vice-President and Congress sometimes lost their tempers. Santander argued repeatedly with the lower house over who was to blame for the nation's financial difficulties, and he showed considerable annoyance when complaining that the Representatives prefaced all tax bills with the statement that they were issued at the suggestion of the Executive while regularly omitting such a preamble from more popular measures.[50] He also permitted criticism of the Chamber of Representatives in the official *Gaceta*, much to the annoyance of both the *Montaña* and independent liberals.[51] These incidents, however, were not enough to offset the generally successful collaboration that existed between Congress and administration, and they concern almost solely Santander's relations with the lower house. With the Senate there were seldom any hard feelings at all, which was especially fortunate since it was principally the Senate that had to confirm the Vice-President's nominations of the more important civil, military, and ecclesiastical officials. Only very rarely was a nomination rejected. The one really important official to be denied confirmation was José Rafael Revenga, whose appointment as Minister to Great Britain was defeated ostensibly because he was little esteemed in Europe, but probably also because his honesty and tactlessness had won him personal enemies at home, and conceivably because Antonio Nariño wanted the job for himself.[52]

---

[49] A.H.N., Corresp.-Cámara (Interior), April 1, 1826; A.C., Actas del Senado, April 3, 1826.

[50] A.H.N., Corresp.-Cámara (Interior), March 12, 1825.

[51] Cf. *Actas:* Cámara-1825, 127.

[52] A.C., Actas del Senado (secret sessions), June 26, 1823; Senado-22, 3, 7, 23-24. Santander was especially annoyed because Revenga had already left for his post; he himself supplied the theory that Nariño was to blame. (Lecuna, *C.S.,* I, 223).

Chapter V

## Personal and Factional Conflicts 1821-1826

IF THE political history of Gran Colombia cannot be studied without some discussion of the courts and Congress, neither can it be portrayed solely in terms of institutional development. In all history there are personal factors, irrational perhaps, that play their part in guiding events, and this is particularly true of Latin America in the nineteenth century, when the cast of characters on the political scene was narrowly confined by a retarded economic and educational development. Even on the most abstract issues a man's position may have been determined primarily by personal loyalties and antagonisms; in other cases the issue itself was at bottom little more than a clash of personalities. It may be easy to dismiss the issues of this sort as lacking in long-range significance, but they are often the ones that aroused the most interest and excitement at the time, and it is not too much to say that larger trends were in some measure influenced by their outcome.

### The Nariño-Santander Feud and the New Federalism

The personal conflict between Nariño and Santander was in fact the first real test faced by Santander after becoming Vice-President of Colombia. It was essentially a legacy of the *Patria Boba,* and the detailed story of its origin is obviously beyond the scope of this study: suffice it to say that in 1812 Santander was one of the younger officers who abandoned the centralist armies of Nariño in order to support the federalist United Provinces in the first civil war of New Granada, and that to the older man and his associates Santander's course had every appearance of treason. By 1821, when the Constitution of Cúcuta was drawn up, the issue that had divided them was ostensibly a thing of the past. Santander was now wholly committed to centralism, and Nariño was not yet ready to abandon his previous ideas.[1] However, this momentary agreement was offset by the fact that the two men were pitted against each other as opposing candidates for the vice-presidency, and it certainly did not serve to wipe out the antagonism existing between them. Santander addressed kind words to the Precursor while he was at Cúcuta, returned the house seized from him by the Spaniards in 1794, and gave him some of the property of the former Jesuits in payment of back salaries; yet in writing to Bolívar

[1] Blanco VII, 604-606. Nariño actually submitted his own private draft of a centralist constitution to the deputies at Cúcuta.

he privately warned the Liberator to be on guard against Nariño as a dangerous rival and prophesied only trouble from his return to political life.[2]

Santander took what he considered a further conciliatory step by appointing Nariño in October, 1822, as *Comandante General* of the Department of Cundinamarca. Whether the Precursor could have been permanently satisfied with a position as subordinate to his youthful rival is highly doubtful; and the fact that Santander did not attempt a genuine private reconciliation, or even seek out the advice of Nariño as that of a respected elder statesman, can hardly have improved the relations between them. Certainly the appointment of Nariño to the *comandancia* did nothing to prevent a public revival of his struggle with Santander. The dispute found a theoretical basis now as in 1812 in the conflict between federalism and centralism, but this was a slightly artificial issue to be raised only a year after the Congress of Cúcuta had decided in favor of the latter, and the two men, furthermore, had now changed sides. Santander remained true to the centralist cause he had so recently adopted; but Nariño now fought openly for federalism. The debate is difficult to follow, for Nariño did not make clear just what kind of federalism he wanted, or precisely when he wanted it. He had declared at Cúcuta that federalism was an ultimate ideal to be adopted some time after independence was definitely established, but he did not claim frankly in 1822 that this time had already come. The Congress of Cúcuta had made it almost impossible to introduce any fundamental change in the constitution before the year 1831; and though the partisans of Nariño decried this provision as contrary to popular sovereignty, they denied any intention of carrying out a reform illegally. The vagueness of the demand, however, did not prevent it from proving highly embarrassing to the Santander administration. Nor is there any reason to doubt that this is precisely what Nariño intended it to be.[3]

The extent of the embarrassment actually caused, and also something of the nature of the conflict, can be seen by first considering the elements that made up Nariño's immediate following. Nariño's followers are virtually as important as he was, for it is difficult to judge exactly how far he personally provided the leadership of the new-style federalist movement. Obviously those *granadinos* who had fought to the end for federalism at Cúcuta needed little encouragement to return to the fray; and it is wholly probable that in some cases disaffected elements merely

[2] Blanco VIII, 434; Santander to Bolívar, September 9, 1821, Lecuna, *C.S.* I, 160.

[3] See Antonio Nariño, *Los Toros de Fucha* and *Segunda Corrida al Patriota* (Bogotá, 1823); *El Insurgente* (Bogotá), November 1, 8, and 22, 1822. *El Insurgente*, if not actually written by Nariño, was at least under his immediate influence (cf. Groot, 210).

exploited the Precursor's name for purposes of their own. But certainly the chief sponsors of the current federalist agitation were Nariño's personal friends and relatives, who were numerous indeed in the Bogotá area, and his former collaborators from the *Patria Boba,* who were likely to be his friends and relatives as well. The conflict thus became, among other things, a clash of generations. It reflected the belief of Nariño and other surviving leaders of the *Patria Boba* that their accumulated wisdom and experience were needed to place Colombia on a firm foundation, and it reflected the even stronger belief of the Santanderean liberals that their predecessors had met with nothing but failure and should consequently make way for new leadership. *El Insurgente,* which spoke for the Nariño faction, frankly scoffed at the fact "that youths who have been able to obtain no more knowledge than what the reading of two books or two constitutions can give them should wish to take an ascendancy over everyone." [4] In its extreme form the reply of the bookish upstarts was to cast doubt upon the patriotism of the leaders who failed to prevent the Spanish reconquest in 1816. This technique was used above all against men like Dr. Ignacio Herrera and Dr. José Ignacio de San Miguel, both of whom had participated in the formal surrender of Bogotá to Morillo. But similar charges were leveled even against Nariño; and for that matter Herrera was one of Nariño's relatives.[5].

Regional antagonisms were also involved in the conflict. Nariño was a stalwart *bogotano;* Santander was a provincial from Cúcuta come to rule over the metropolis of New Granada. The resentment in Bogotá can only have been increased by the fact that so many of the Vice-President's close associates were also men from the provinces, like the Azueros of Socorro and Francisco Soto of Pamplona. Indeed the federalists' appeal to Bogotá regionalism was both clear and direct. As Dr. San Miguel eloquently expressed it in a typical broadside, "Cundinamarca is the one that has worked and cooperated most for independence with arms, with monies, with men . . .; and would it be right for her to lose the fruits of her efforts, of her sacrifices, subjecting her violently to a government that does not suit her?" [6] It can hardly be that centralism as such is what did not suit Cundinamarca and its capital Bogotá, for their central location should have made them supporters of a highly unified government. It was simply a central government with Santander and his friends rather than the *bogotanos* themselves in the places of command. There was likewise a distinct resentment against the predominance of Venezuelans in the military affairs—not to mention the presidency—of the new republic, although this was seldom expressed directly for obvious reasons of tact and ex-

[4] *El Insurgente,* October 25, 1822.
[5] Cf. Juan Nepomuceno Azuero, *Respuesta a un papel que . . . han publicado los doctores Ignacio Herrera y José Ignacio de San Miguel* (Bogotá,1823), 2-15.
[6] José Ignacio de San Miguel, *S.A.B.* (Bogotá, 1822).

pediency. However, Dr. San Miguel must have had the pronounced anticlericalism of Caracas in mind when he spread the alarm that other sections might seek to attack the religion of Cundinamarca. This remark was coupled, interestingly enough, with a rather indiscreet compliment to the religious fervor of royalist Pasto.[7]

The whole campaign of the Bogotá federalists, in fact, had obvious conservative tendencies. The Precursor himself cannot be fitted into any neat ideological brackets, least of all can he be dismissed as a pro-clerical reactionary. Nevertheless, such friends and allies as Herrera and San Miguel were frank supporters of the religious status quo. The sentiment of Bogotá, which was so ardently courted by the Nariño faction, was relatively conservative on matters of religious and economic reform; and the oppositionist stand of the local federalists inevitably attracted malcontents of all varieties. In any case, the theoretical issue of federalism was often quite forgotten in the midst of miscellaneous attacks on the liberal administration. Nariño never had as much newspaper space at his disposal as did the Vice-President, but he had on his side some of the best satirists and pamphleteers present in the capital. Among these were the respected and independent-minded Alejandro Osorio, who had been a minister of Santander up to the Congress of Cúcuta, and Dr. José Félix Merizalde, the foremost scandal-monger of Gran Colombia. Nariño's own skill as a pamphleteer was far from negligible: his *Toros de Fucha* and the *Corridas* that came as sequels to it were far superior in style to any equivalent compositions of Santander. Coming to a peak in the first half of 1823, these productions represent the one brief flowering of opposition journalism in Bogotá during the years of the Santander regime.[8]

Last but not least, the agitation in Bogotá coincided with federalist movements in other parts of Colombia, notably Venezuela and Ecuador. These were generally unrelated to it, and must be dealt with separately in later chapters. But at least federalist sentiment had nowhere been stilled entirely by the verdict of the Constituent Congress, and federalists of all varieties found common ground in their criticism of the central administration. Quite a few were elected to Congress, from Caracas and Quito as well as from Bogotá. The Caracas federalists were particularly violent, claiming not only that the national government was too powerful but that the constitution itself had not been legitimately adopted. They held this to be the case because some provinces, including their own, had not been represented at Cúcuta, and because the constitution had not been confirmed by a popular referendum.[9] The obvious implication was that

[7] *Ibid.* For a contemporary reference to the anti-Venezuelan leanings of the Bogotá federalists see J.N. Azuero, *Respuesta,* 17-18.

[8] David Bushnell, "The Development of the Press in Great Colombia," *Hispanic American Historical Review* XXX, 438-439 (November, 1950).

[9] *El Anglo-Colombiano* (Caracas), *passim.* See also below, p. 291.

no one was really bound to respect it, and such a conclusion could only lend weight to the stand taken by the Nariño faction.

The administration could hardly let insinuations of this sort go unchallenged, no matter where they originated. Except for its personal attacks on certain *caraqueño* federalists, the official *Gaceta de Colombia* specialized in rather general arguments along the order of in-union-there-is-strength.[10] However, the case against federalism was stated in somewhat more detail by Vicente Azuero's *La Indicación*, whose arguments were specifically aimed in the direction of Caracas but obviously took in Nariño as well. Azuero cited legal principles to prove the binding character of the constitution, and added that it should certainly be given a fair trial before proposing reforms. He revived the argument used at Cúcuta to the effect that Venezuela, New Granada, and Ecuador were much too large to become states in a real federation, while smaller units would necessarily degenerate into petty local oligarchies (i.e., Nariño and all his relations?) for lack of sufficient able men to staff their separate governments.[11] By and large *La Indicación* stated its case ably, and in a dignified manner. Dignity was unfortunately must less evident in the concurrent rantings of *El Correo de la Ciudad de Bogotá*, in which Azuero also had a hand; its own preference in anti-federalist arguments was apparently the old and slightly irrelevant thesis that Herrera and San Miguel had betrayed New Granada to Morillo.[12]

The administration forces as a whole sought to place the federalists in the worst possible light by implying that they were all seeking constitutional reform at once, by illegal means. Some of them, especially in Venezuela, were demanding just that; but not even in Caracas was a federalist coup imminent, and Santander himself had to admit that Nariño's behaviour in Bogotá was outwardly quite harmless.[13] It is noteworthy that misrepresentation or at least exaggeration of the federalist objectives was a particular stock-in-trade of *El Patriota*, which was founded by Santander as an outlet for his personal views early in 1823, ostensibly to rally popular morale after the sudden recapture of Maracaibo by the Spaniards. Being designed for the average reader, *El Patriota* made a point of oversimplifying issues; and Santander could not resist the temptation to use it as a means of airing his feud with Nariño. The Vice-President's self-delusion with regard to the federalist peril may have been wholly sincere, but it is still obvious that both his common sense and his

---

[10] Cf. *La Gaceta de Colombia*, November 24 and December 1, 1822.

[11] *La Indicación* (Bogotá), August 3 to December 14, 1822.

[12] Cf. *El Correo de la Ciudad de Bogotá*, March 23 and April 10, 1823. This title is not simply a full version of *El Correo de Bogotá*, which is so frequently cited in the text; they were published by virtually the same staff, but at different periods.

[13] Letter to Bolívar, February 6, 1823, *C.S.*, I, 200-201.

official dignity had momentarily left him. He accused the Precursor of jealousy toward himself, which was no doubt correct, and of insufficient patriotism, which certainly was not. If Nariño's supporters held positions under the centralist regime they were urged to be true to their principles and resign; if they did not enjoy a government salary, they were accused of being dissatisfied merely because they had been overlooked in making appointments.[14]

If one can believe the charges of his enemies, Santander went beyond mere words in his struggle with Nariño. A certain army officer was vaguely alleged to have been persecuted by the Secretary of War because of pro-Nariño sentiments, and *El Insurgente* announced that it finally had to suspend publication because of the unfavorable official reaction to its propaganda.[15] Unless this statement means simply that the editors disliked having the Vice-President dislike them there is no evidence whatever to support its implications of foul play. Nariño himself publicly admitted that Bogotá enjoyed a free press.[16] On the other hand, Santander did finally ease Nariño out of the *Comandancia General* of Cundinamarca, remarking to Bolívar at the time on his mortal hatred for "this man."[17] And he did nothing whatever to discourage Francisco Soto and Diego Fernando Gómez from reviving the same personal attacks that had been used to block Nariño's election to the vice-presidency in 1821 in an all-out effort to prevent his being seated as Senator in 1823. This maneuvre coincided with an attempt to exclude several of Nariño's partisans, especially Herrera and San Miguel, from their seats in the lower house. Perhaps the greatest emphasis was placed this time on the notion that Nariño lacked the legal residence requirement for his position; but if he had been away from home until shortly before his election it was because he had been taken to Spain as a prisoner of the king.[18]

Not to be outdone by his adversaries, Nariño showed in his defense that he was quite as skilled at personal defamation as they were. The terms he used were even less elegant, and so the solution was for the Senate to grant him his seat while at the same time expurgating a portion of his remarks from the record.[19] *El Patriota* then announced that the Senate's decision would usher in an era of general reconciliation. Yet Santander hardly acted in a conciliatory spirit when he joined this pious hope with a word of praise for Senator Soto and his lone vote against the

[14] *El Patriota,* January 26 to April 13, 1823.
[15] *El Noticioso* (Bogotá), No. 2 (1823); *El Insurgente,* November 22, 1822.
[16] Antonio Nariño, *Segunda Corrida al Patriota* (Bogotá, 1823).
[17] Letter to Bolívar, February 20, 1823, Lecuna, *C.S.* I, 204.
[18] Antonio Nariño, *Defensa del General Nariño* (Bogotá, 1823).
[19] *Actas:* Congreso-1823, 60, 124-125; see also ms. biography of Diego F. Gómez by his wife, Biblioteca Nacional (Bogotá), Sala No. 1, Vol. 12,100, f. 211.

seating of Nariño.²⁰ Not even with Nariño's death, in December, 1823, did the quarrel end. It is difficult to believe the whole statement of Canon Francisco Xavier Guerra to the effect that he had to call off his funeral oration in eulogy of Nariño because of evidence that it would bring *gravísimos perjuicios* down upon him, but it is still entirely probable that Santander expressed disapproval of his plans. Indeed the *Correo de Bogotá* heatedly affirmed that if Guerra was really planning to laud the *Patria Boba* at the expense of the present constitutional system, as rumored, then the government would have been entirely justified in forbidding the speech as seditious.²¹

The federalist question itself, however, had by that time begun to fade into the background. Probably the activities of Santander had less to do with this result than the resolute opposition of Bolívar. From the start he had expressed solidarity with the Vice-President, assailing Nariño vaguely for his "crimes" and depicting San Miguel as a former royalist who was even now a supporter of absolutism. At one point Bolívar expressed determination to return to Bogotá from Ecuador in order to combat factious federalists and uphold the constitution, and he specifically asked Santander to congratulate Azuero on his journalistic campaigns. The Liberator's official message to the first regular Congress pointedly warned that no law passed in defiance of the constitution would be obeyed by him; he would uphold Colombian institutions by the sword if necessary.²² Bolívar ultimately cautioned the Vice-President to end his public feuding with Nariño, but his vehement opposition to federalism, which was duly publicized by Santander, naturally carried much weight with Colombian opinion. It was a major reason why federalism was firmly opposed both by Venezuelan military leaders and by the aristocracy of Popayán, whose chief spokesman in Bogotá, Senator Jerónimo Torres, helped write the anti-federalist articles of the *Gaceta*.²³ There was talk in Congress of rebuking Bolívar for the outspoken tone of his recent message, but the motion failed in the end, with the Santanderean liberal bloc vigorously supporting the Liberator.²⁴ After that federalism was gradually forgotten, at least in Bogotá, until it was revived during the constitutional crisis of 1826-27.

[20] *El Patriota,* June 1, 1823.

[21] Francisco Xavier Guerra, *Al Público,* printed broadside in Biblioteca Nacional (Bogotá), Sala No. 1, Vol. 6257; *El Correo de Bogotá,* February 20, 1824.

[22] Bolívar to Santander, September 29 and October 27, 1822, January 14, 1823, Lecuna, *C.L.* III, 100, 107, 135; Blanco VIII, 584-586.

[23] Santander to Bolívar, February 6, 1823, Lecuna, *C.S.* I, 200-201.

[24] *Actas:* Congreso-1823, 30-31; A.C., Senado-15, 228-230.

## The Later History of the Nariño Faction

The Nariño faction survived both the decline of the federalist issue and the death of Nariño. It continued to exploit the provincialism of Bogotá and Cundinamarca and to take a generally conservative stand on the issues of the day. The followers of Nariño increasingly lost their separate identity within the opposition as a whole; but what still distinguished them from other oppositionists was the particular set of real or imagined personal grievances which they possessed over and above any ideological differences with the administration. Thanks to such personal antagonisms, the general struggle between *Valle* and *Montaña* often centered around a series of *causes célèbres* that involved the friends and relatives of Nariño. These petty crises provided much of the human interest element in national affairs for a few more years, and several of them are highly revealing for the study of behaviour and personalities in Colombian politics.

The most striking of them all was the *affaire* Márquez, in which the Nariño faction itself took the offensive only to see its victim triumphantly vindicated at last. The origins of the struggle go back to 1822, so it is also an example of the type of agitation engaged in by the Precursor's following during his lifetime. It began when Colonel Remigio Márquez was sent as military *comandante* to Mompós, a way-station on the Magdalena between interior New Granada and the coast, and given a special commission to combat smuggling. In the course of fulfilling his duties, Márquez was accused of committing innumerable arbitrary acts against peaceful merchants, not to mention uttering praise of military rule and insulting the constitution. All the charges were then relayed to Congress, where a movement was launched to impeach him in punishment for his misdeeds and at the same time to prevent him from taking the seat to which he had been elected in the Colombian Senate.[25] It is not impossible that there was an element of racial prejudice in this campaign, for Márquez was part Negro, and he was accused among other things of seeking to provoke race warfare by appealing to the *pardo* or mulatto class of the Magdalena valley. However, the main factor behind the charges was the natural indignation of merchants whose comfortable techniques of violating the customs laws had suddenly been interrupted. The guilty parties received chief support precisely from the Nariño faction, not only because the affair seemingly offered a chance to annoy the administration but also because several of them were related by ties of blood or friendship to Nariño and his followers. The best-known offender, indeed, was Antonio Nariño y Ortega, son of the Precursor, who

[25] A.H.N., Congresos XXV, 551-552, 561-562; *El Insurgente,* October 25, 1822; Antonio Nariño y Ortega, *Al Público* (Bogotá, 1822); various manifestos in Biblioteca Nacional, Sala No. 1, Vol. 7, 483, ff. 493-499.

had been caught in the act of tampering with customs documents and arrested on the spot.²⁶

As the merchants and their accomplices were not without influence either in Cartagena or in Bogotá, their effort to present Márquez as the real villain in the piece came very close to success. They promptly appealed to the *Corte Superior del Centro,* where a majority of the judges —who included none other than Dr. Ignacio Herrera—happened to be personal friends or relatives of Nariño. Instead of excusing themselves from taking cognizance in the case, as required presumably by decorum if by nothing else, the judges in question gave orders for the contraband seized by Márquez to be brought to Bogotá and delivered provisionally to one of the apparent smugglers. At Mompós and at Cartagena additional forces set to work to undermine Márquez' anti-smuggling campaign. An attempt was made to depose him as *comandante* by means of a *cabildo abierto,* using the pretext that he was incompetent to defend the region against royalist bands in the neighboring province of Santa Marta; and even though this strategem failed, the Intendant of Magdalena later compelled him to leave his sick bed and depart from Mompós on 24 hours' notice.²⁷ The Santander administration, however, came finally to Márquez' defense and decreed the suspension and trial of all the officials who had plotted against him at Mompós. Furthermore, the proceedings against him in Congress, which finally came to a head in the sessions of 1824, had the same outcome as the earlier attempt to unseat Nariño: once the accused had delivered his full defense, the movement against him collapsed. There was not even any need to go through with the scheduled trial of Márquez before the Senate, for the official prosecutor who had been appointed by the lower house took the unusual step of withdrawing all his charges.²⁸ There is no indication whether any of the enemies of Márquez were ever punished,²⁹ but morally, at least, they had suffered a notable defeat.

The *affaire* Márquez coincided with various lesser controversies that also involved the Nariño faction and, in particular, the judges of the *Corte Superior del Centro.* The behaviour of this court was in fact a constant source of difficulties for the administration, despite the fact that

²⁶ A.C., Senado-27, 21, 25.

²⁷ A.C., Senado-27, 14-33; A.H.N., Congresos XXV, 558; Remigio Márquez, *Preservativo contra los ataques de una facción* (Cartagena, 1823).

²⁸ *Acuerdos* I, 169; A.H.N., Congresos XXV, 702-704; *Actas:* Senado-1824, 9-10; A.C., Senado-10, 100-101.

²⁹ Cf. *Vindicación de la inocencia de algunos vecinos de la Ciudad de Mompóx* (Cartagena, 1824), 17, 22. This refers to the subsequent acquittal of those who tried to depose Márquez at Mompós. Apparently no specific laws had been broken in this part of the affair, which had gone no farther than the stage of agitation. The author has not had opportunity to trace the final outcome of the smuggling case.

its judges owed their appointment in large part to Santander himself.[30] Presumably the Vice-President had intended a show of broadmindedness when he originally sponsored such men as Ignacio Herrera for the judiciary, but the result was to give the Nariño faction a special foothold in the higher courts. The quality of justice also suffered, through the repeated injection of partisan controversy, but for this both sides were really to blame. There is, moreover, at least one other factional dispute involving the *Corte Superior del Centro* and the adherents of Nariño that deserves more than passing consideration. This might be termed the *affaire* López Ruiz, although the original figure was soon almost forgotten in the dense ramifications of the case.

What originally happened was that Sebastián López Ruiz went to court to obtain the goods of a certain deceased friar and that the *Corte Superior del Centro* awarded them instead to an arm of the Church. It was never clearly shown which side had the better legal claim to the property, and no truly impartial verdict was ever delivered on the case. There is considerably less doubt regarding the technical point that the appeal court had no business handing down a final decision when it did, but should first have returned the case to a lower level for the correction of procedural defects. However, a more important fact is that the judges split strictly along the lines of their political and religious sympathies, with such pro-Santander liberals as Diego Fernando Gómez supporting the lay claimant López Ruiz and the rest of the court upholding the rights of the Church. Ignacio Herrera was not present to vote on the question, but the court was still controlled by his allies, of whom the most prominent was José Joaquín Ortiz, an experienced lawyer, veteran patriot, and another relative of Nariño.[31]

It was now the turn of the Vice-President's supporters to take the offensive, charging the judges responsible for the decision against López Ruiz with an arbitrary act of the most serious nature. The preliminary round occurred in the Congress of 1823. The legislators asked to see certain documents relating to the case; the court refused. It went on to ask whether Colombia had "snatched despotism and arbitrariness from the hands of one man to deposit them in the midst of a Senate;" and in retaliation for such disrespectful language, the Senate despotically fined each of the judges concerned $200—a fine which they actually paid.[32] Then, in the Congress of 1824, it was proposed to impeach the judges

[30] *El Correo de la Ciudad de Bogotá*, April 24 and May 1, 1823, would have it that Santander had to overcome the opposition of both Bolívar and the *Alta Corte* in order to launch Herrera upon his career in the Colombian judiciary.

[31] A.C., Senado-27, 282-283; Senado-29, 235-239. At the moment Herrera was under automatic suspension from his post in view of the fact that there was a case pending against him personally in the courts.

[32] A.C., Senado-20, 167-184; *Actas:* Senado-1824, 144.

for the López Ruiz decision itself. This move had much to do with the deposition of Ignacio Herrera as President of the Chamber of Representatives, since a decision to refer the matter to a committee hostile to the whole Nariño clan is what occasioned the outburst that cost Herrera his post.[33] Herrera's conduct, needless to say, did his party more harm than good, and in the end the Representatives formally voted to accuse the guilty judges before the Senate. However, the close balance of forces in the lower house, not to mention its general unpredictability, was clearly shown in the decision not to include Ortiz in the charges. The exception was based originally on the dissenting vote which he had left on the record of the court; but he was still excepted even when it was demonstrated that he had really supported the court's decision and had entered his written protest only after the event, just in time to escape prosecution.[34]

In view of such apparent favoritism, the pro-administration bloc that controlled the Senate refused to act on the Chamber's accusation, and instead the Senate placed charges of its own against Ortiz before the *Alta Corte*. From this point on, López Ruiz was nearly forgotten. The issue now revolved about bringing Ortiz to justice for fraud and, as a first step, evicting him from the seat which he also held in the lower house of Congress. The quarrel dragged on through the sessions of 1825 and was noisily argued in the press, all with no result save much harsh talk and ill-will. In November of the same year, when the *Alta Corte* finally opened proceedings against Ortiz and suspended him from the *Corte Superior,* the Chamber of Representatives legally had no choice but to suspend him likewise. However, the Chamber preferred to believe that Ortiz had not consciously sought to falsify the record but had merely changed his mind, and it therefore allowed him to retain his seat. Only when the members of the *Alta Corte* depicted the vote in favor of Ortiz as an act that "threatened . . . the destruction of the social order" and offered to resign in protest did the lower house finally reverse itself.[35]

Slightly over a year later the *Alta Corte* actually acquitted Ortiz. Presumably the technical basis for this decision is explained somewhere in the records of the court, but it attracted no public discussion at the time, and in the end about the only thing definitely proven by the *affaire* López Ruiz-Ortiz was that Colombian politics were capable of sinking to a rather unedifying level of personal bickering in between the great debates of

[33] A.C., Cámara-7, 143.
[34] A.C., Senado-27, 282-283; Senado-29, 235-239, 246; *El Correo de Bogotá,* April 30, 1824; Juan Nepomuceno Azuero, *El Dr. Merizalde y el Notiziozote* (Bogotá, 1825), 16-18.
[35] Alta Corte de Justicia, *Colección de documentos . . . oponiéndose a que la Cámara de Representantes diese asiento en su seno al Dr. Joaquín Ortiz* (Bogotá, 1826), 7-11, 25; *Actas:* Cámara-1825, 143, 155, 199; A.C., Senado-27, 286, Cámara-14, 57-59.

principle.³⁶ The real climax had already come and gone with the suspension of Ortiz from Congress early in 1826; and it had been followed by a gradual decline in the importance of the Nariño faction as a political force and public issue. Starting with the Venezuelan revolt of April, 1826, there were more important things to worry about, and the resentment of Nariño's followers toward the Santander administration and everything connected with it was offset at least in part by their equally pronounced distrust of Venezuela.

## Friction Between Bolívar and Santander

There is one more essentially personal question that requires separate and extended treatment. This is the complex subject of relations between Bolívar and Santander, who were not always on the best of terms even before 1826. The difficulties between them centered in large part around constitutional issues, and they involve a number of simple misunderstandings. But underlying them there was always a clash of personalities, with the impatient genius of Bolívar pitted against the methodical and legal-minded cautiousness of Santander. These early differences seem to have aroused fairly little open comment at the time, but they were fully thrashed out in public as part of the later political duel between the two men, and they are still being argued over today. Moreover, they foreshadow to a great extent the issues that were destined to divide the two men permanently a few years later.

It has already been noted that there were a few minor disagreements between Bolívar and Santander even in the months following Boyacá. Santander annoyed the Liberator above all, perhaps, by constant talk of their joint "responsibility" to future generations,³⁷ which was an oblique way of emphasizing the need for scrupulous legality (in so far as conditions allowed) and for the careful avoidance of all arbitrary acts. Some years later Santander appears to have annoyed Bolívar all over again with his fretting about Nariño and his endless references to the trouble he would face in enforcing strict respect for the constitution upon Congress. But Bolívar still preferred Santander to the federalists,³⁸ and he too played the part of the legalist in his resistance to federalist agitation, and also in obtaining Congressional permission for his project to go to Peru and accept personal command of all the forces still fighting against Spain. The latter is especially notable in view of the fact that even San-

---

³⁶ *El registro judicial de la República de Colombia* (Bogotá), June 22, 1827. The most likely supposition would seem to be the absence of any positive proof of harmful intent. Unfortunately, the author cannot say either what finally happened to López Ruiz.

³⁷ Cf. Bolívar to Santander, May 20, 1820, Lecuna, *C.L.* II, 170.

³⁸ Cf. Bolívar to Santander, September 23, October 27, and December 6, 1822, Lecuna, *C.L.* III, 94, 107, 121.

tander felt legislative sanction was not absolutely necessary.[39] On the other hand, it was a wise move politically, for there was a strong body of opinion that opposed allowing Bolívar to go on the grounds that he was needed at home to mop up the remaining pockets of Spanish resistance, to ward off new invasions, and to help organize the country—presumably in the place of Santander. Whatever may have been the precise motives on either side, the Santanderean liberals successfully supported Bolívar's petition, and a bloc of mixed conservatives and independents provided the opposition.[40]

It was only when Bolívar had reached Peru that real trouble between the two leaders arose. First there were petty disagreements over the diplomatic mission which Bolívar entrusted to Bernardo Monteagudo simply to get him out of Peru, and over a few other cases in which the Liberator appeared to have exceeded his faculties or infringed on those of Santander. Bolívar promptly confessed his faults, giving the reasons for his course of action, and succeeded in reassuring his Vice-President.[41] The latter's slowness in sending military reinforcements then gave rise to more serious disputing. Bolívar had shipped a good-sized army to Peru in advance of his own departure in August of 1823, but this did not prevent him from sending repeated requests to Santander for still more men and supplies. By the end of 1823 he was demanding no less than 12,000 troops, including 1,000 *llaneros;* by the following February the number was ranging from 12,000 to 16,000, and it was to include, of all things, a group of naval officers, of whom Colombia had scarcely any more than Peru. Naturally all were to come fully equipped. As Bolívar candidly expressed to Sucre, he had asked for 12,000 men simply in the hope of getting 6,000, but when the 6,000 did not come either he began complaining that Santander and the Colombian administration had fallen down on the job. Soon he was predicting dire ruin on every side and offering to resign; finally he suspended his correspondence with Santander altogether.[42]

It was of course true that there were persons in Colombia who took no interest in aid to Peru, feeling that Colombia need trouble herself only with the expulsion of Spaniards from her own borders. Such sentiments were expressed above all in Bolívar's homeland, Venezuela, and by enemies of Santander; they were vigorously assailed in the official press.[43] Nor is there evidence that at any time Santander questioned the

[39] Message to Congress, May 10, 1823, A.C., Senado-22, 12-15.
[40] *Codif. Nac.* I, 184-185; *Actas:* Congreso-1823, 111, 128-129, 131; A.C., Senado-25, 245-250; A.C., Actas del Senado (secret sessions) May 13 and 15, 1823.
[41] Cf. Lecuna, *C.S.,* I, 245-246; *C.L.* III, 311.
[42] O'Leary XX, 171, 219, 414, 432, 445-446, 449-450, 477; Blanco IX, 216-217; Lecuna, *C.L.* III, 255, 260, 309-310, 322, IV, 7, 14, 149, 200.
[43] Cf. *El Cometa* (Caracas), March 17, 1825; *La Gaceta de Colombia,* July 25, 1824; Lecuna, *C.S.,* I, 298-299.

importance to Colombia of bringing the Peruvian war to an end. He was indeed a little slow in delivering the aid which Bolívar now requested, but at least he had an impressive list of excuses. First and foremost stood probably the weakest of them all, the claim that he had no legal authorization to order more Colombian troops and supplies outside the country. Santander began to harp on this point even before Bolívar's annoyance was strongly evident, insisting that he had been given discretionary authority to raise troops for the defense of Colombia, but not for the defense of anyone else, and that none of his other powers could be stretched to cover the point either. According to this argument, the aid could be sent only under a specific grant of power from Congress, and Congress remained out of session until April, 1824. The Vice-President's stand was summed up in one of his most famous political pronouncements: "Si en la obediencia de la Constitución se encuentra el mal, el mal será."[44]

Whether this was quibbling or devotion to duty depends in large measure on one's personal estimate of Santander, and actually there is something to be said on either side. Santander had upheld the legality of aid sent to Peru by Bolívar himself in the months immediately following Pichincha, even though the Liberator's action was not specifically provided for in the "extraordinary faculties" which he then exercised in Ecuador.[45] It is also difficult to see why a ruler whose country was at war needed special legislative permission to pursue the enemy over the frontier and give direct military assistance to a friendly state with which his own government had signed a formal defense pact. On the other hand, Santander's respect for the letter of the law was too persistent a trait for his sincerity to be entirely questioned in this instance. He clearly felt that Bolívar's latest requests represented something over and above what Colombia could normally be expected to provide on the basis of either self-defense or treaty obligations. Having just emerged from his first bout with the Nariño faction in Congress, and fearing to make any false step as he felt his way in the management of new republican institutions, Santander was presumably more anxious than ever to forestall the charge of infringement on legislative functions.

Nor were these the only considerations. Troops and supplies on the scale demanded were hard to provide, for military service was deeply unpopular and the treasury usually empty. The security of the homeland still came first: with Spanish forces in Puerto Cabello until November of 1823, and after that in the Antilles, northern Colombia could not be denuded of troops. Nevertheless, even while waiting for Congress to act, Santander had not been wholly inactive. He was already devising ways and means of dispatching whatever forces Congress might decree; and

[44] Lecuna, *C.S.* I, 265-268; Santander to Chamber of Representatives, April 23, 1824, A.C., Cámara-5, 57.
[45] Message to Congress, May 10, 1823, A.C., Senado-22, 12-15.

he had issued his orders for the first contingents to gather at Guayaquil pending the time when they would be allowed to proceed farther.[46]

When at length Congress met, Santander explained his own conduct, obtained congressional approval, and put the legislators to work at framing the needed special authorizations. These were held up by some rather idle discussions, including a secret senatorial debate over the need to delete any statement implying that aid to Peru was in Colombia's own interest lest this be taken as an excuse for Peru not to pay for assistance rendered. However, in a little over a month, on May 6, 1824, the job was finished.[47] The Vice-President now completed the necessary arrangements for Bolívar to receive some 12,000 men, although it is perhaps doubtful that anyone really expected them all to arrive. In fact throughout the entire troop-raising episode Santander's orders were often impossible to carry out on a local level; in some places the recruits mutinied, in others the enlistments had to be abandoned altogether. In no case was there time for troops that left the northern departments in May or later to reach Peru in time for the decisive battle of Ayacucho, although several thousand were then en route.[48]

By that time still another issue had arisen to strain the relations between Bolívar and Santander, and it is perhaps the one that has been most frequently misrepresented. On May 17 Santander had sent Congress a message asking: 1) whether Bolívar, now that he was in Peru, legally retained any of the "extraordinary faculties" granted to him by the Congress of Cúcuta; 2) whether those faculties might still be exercised in Ecuador by General Bartolomé Salom, to whom Bolívar had expressly delegated them before his departure; 3) whether Bolívar, from Peru, could issue commands binding on officials in Colombia, particularly in Ecuador; and 4) whether promotions he issued solely on his own initiative for Colombian troops in Peru would remain valid when the men returned home.[49] Obviously Santander would not have felt compelled to ask for a ruling on these points had he not questioned some of the powers that Bolívar was currently exercising, and it is quite true that these powers were in need of clarification. This was really a problem that should have been thought of before he left. Hence Santander's message need not be taken as an underhanded rebuke to Bolívar, and

[46] Certain other troops actually reached Peru, but these either had been requested by Bolívar before his own departure from Guayaquil or were sent by virtue of orders issued from Lima to Ecuador, without directly approaching the Vice-President. See O'Leary XX, 541; *La Gaceta de Colombia,* August 29, 1824; Lecuna, *C.S.* I, 290-291; Vicente Lecuna, *La entrevista de Guayaquil* (Caracas, 1948), 299, note 54.

[47] A.C., Senado-10, 106; Actas del Senado (secret sessions) April 29 and 30, May 4, 1824; *Codif. Nac.* I, 289-290.

[48] Lecuna, *C.S.* I, 293-294, 302, 304, 310; A.C., Senado-20, 442-444.

[49] *Actas:* Senado-1824, 302; *La Gaceta de Colombia,* June 13, 1824.

much less as an effort to reduce him to impotence. Even without the powers specified by the Vice-President, Bolívar had all the authority he needed for most purposes simply as a Colombian commanding general and as legal Dictator of Peru by invitation of the Peruvian authorities. Santander might have handled the matter more tactfully, but there is no reason to question his statement that his main motive was to place everything on a sound legal footing and so forestall any charge that he had been a party to the improper use of "extraordinary faculties." [50]

Congress, as it turned out, went farther than the Vice-President specifically requested. Indeed the legislators took this occasion to carry out a general reform of "extraordinary faculties," replacing the existing law on the subject, which had been passed by the Congress of Cúcuta, with another of its own. As pointed out already in a different connection, the new measure did not greatly alter the nature of those faculties themselves. But it made clear that Bolívar could not exercise them in his present position, or wield any power at all over Colombia so long as he remained in Peru. It thus annulled Bolívar's power completely on the first three points covered in Santander's message. As for promotions, the law allowed the Colombian Executive to grant them at will to troops serving outside the republic, and permitted delegation of this authority to anyone at all, which would naturally include Simón Bolívar. Finally, the law reaffirmed the Liberator's right to lead the nation's armies in person whenever he returned to Colombian soil.[51]

The last article gave rise to some misunderstandings because it did not expressly state that Bolívar could also lead Colombian armies in Peru, but otherwise the law was eminently logical. If it deprived Bolívar of all authority as President of Colombia, this was primarily the result of his own decisions: first of all, his insistence that he would accept the presidency only on condition that the Vice-President take full administrative responsibility save in those regions where he was personally directing the war; and in the second place, his resolve to go to Peru. Nevertheless, the law was not passed without some opposition. The decision to end outright the Liberator's "extraordinary faculties" was sponsored essentially by the Santanderean liberal bloc in Congress, although there is no real proof that it was originally suggested by Santander himself. It was opposed both by independents with a special fondness for Bolívar, such as Senators Jerónimo Torres and Joaquín Mosquera of Popayán, and by the conservative oppositionists of the lower house. These groups sought to grant Bolívar at least some authority over Ecuador even while he was in Peru, and in view of the proximity of Ecuador to the war theatre this was not wholly unreasonable. The demand that he automatically be

---

[50] Letter to Bolívar, May 21, 1824, Lecuna, *C.S.* I, 295.
[51] *Codif. Nac.* I, 388-390; cf. above, p. 32.

endowed with full "extraordinary faculties" whenever he again set foot on Colombian soil was less reasonable, for by that time there might be no excuse for anyone to exercise them; but both provisions were defeated in the end.[52]

Santander attenuated the effect of the law somewhat by decreeing on his own authority that Ecuador must remain under a regime of "extraordinary faculties" simply on the grounds of its closeness to the Peruvian war, by delegating those faculties on the spot precisely to General Salom, and by instructing Salom to grant Bolívar any aid he might request. Santander's decree further provided that Bolívar might exercise "extraordinary faculties" in Ecuador—by delegation from himself—if he should return there before the war emergency ended.[53] It is not clear that Bolívar ever studied the contents of this decree, but at least Santander personally assured him that in Ecuador things would continue as before. No doubt realizing the Liberator's great fondness for "extraordinary faculties," he also sought to place full responsibility for the law in its final shape upon Congress, ascribing it chiefly to uneasiness over the military promotions granted by virtue of emergency powers either by Bolívar or by himself. This explanation was actually rather improbable, since the law turned out to be especially generous on the subject of promotions, and since the two Venezuelan deputies whom Santander named as the chief critics of his own promotion decrees—Cayetano Arvelo and Juan José Osío—had been firm supporters of "extraordinary faculties" for Bolívar in the Congressional debate.[54]

Bolívar, in any case, was prompt to take offense at the law. He chose to take the most extreme interpretation of the limits imposed on him, resigning his personal leadership of Colombian troops to Sucre. He retained only the authority he held as head of all civil and military government in Peru. Bolívar felt essentially that he was being stripped of his power by Congress without so much as a word of thanks, and instead with a tactless statement in the preamble of the law about the *inconvenientes* of "extraordinary faculties." All this, moreover, by instigation of the Vice-President. Bolívar's offense was shared by Sucre and the Colombian army in Peru, which proceeded to draw up a lengthy protest against the "atrocious" conduct of Santander, especially in having questioned the legitimacy of their promotions. The army was so annoyed, Bolívar said, that Sucre had to grant still more promotions to quiet their

[52] *Actas:* Cámara-1824, 253, 304; *Actas:* Senado-1824, 334, 378, 767; A.C., Senado-26, 307-308, 402-409.

[53] *Codif. Nac.* VII, 208-209.

[54] Santander to Bolívar, May 21 and August 6, 1824, Lecuna, *C.S.* I, 295, 305-306.

despair.[55] Though Bolívar was assured by José Manuel Restrepo that Santander was still a loyal friend and had meant no harm by his original message to Congress, he himself wrote that he felt the Vice-President had been "generous at my expense." Bolívar added that he had quickly recovered from this as from all other angers,[56] and certainly the law did not hinder the progress of the war in the slightest. Unfortunately, Bolívar had not so much forgiven as temporarily forgotten. His relations with Santander resumed their previous cordiality, but there was nothing to prevent the late grievances from being dragged out again by Bolívar and his adherents in any future controversy.

[55] Bolívar to Santander, November 10 and December 20, 1825, Lecuna, *C.L.* IV, 203, 226-227; Daniel F. O'Leary, *Bolívar y la emancipación de Sur-América* (Rufino Blanco Fombona, ed., 2 vols., Madrid n.d.) II, 336-339.

For a discussion of the actual effect of the law on Bolívar's position see Vicente Lecuna, "El Ejército Libertador y la Ley del 28 de julio," *Boletín de la Academia Nacional de Historia de Venezuela* XXVIII (1945), 3-23, and sources cited therein. In reality, Congress appears to have taken for granted Bolívar's personal right to lead Colombian troops in Peru, being concerned essentially with "extraordinary faculties" in the strict sense, and especially with their use in Colombia. It did *not* repeal its authorization for Bolívar to assume full direction of the war in Peru, much less cancel his general's commission.

[56] Restrepo to Bolívar, February 6, 1825, O'Leary VII, 253-254; Bolívar to Restrepo, March 7, 1825, Lecuna, *C.L.* IV, 277-278.

Chapter VI

## The Financial Crisis (I): The Revenue System

WHEN all was said and done, no mere political crisis could rival the disastrous state of Colombian finances. If the task of administering a new government was difficult, the task of paying its expenses was harder still. The situation was particularly serious because Colombia had undertaken a greater share in the winning of Spanish American Independence than would have corresponded to her on the basis of national resources alone. The result was a condition of latent bankruptcy which contributed more than any other one factor to the collapse first of Santanderean liberalism and ultimately of the Bolivarian dictatorship as well, and which adversely affected nearly every project for internal reform.

The financial crisis was complicated by the fact that so many reform projects concerned the field of government finance itself. Administration leaders felt that a sound policy of public finance was the first requirement for national economic health, and as good nineteenth-century liberals they firmly believed that taxation was a necessary evil which should be carefully adjusted so as to interfere as little as possible with "natural" economic laws. Finance Secretary José María Castillo y Rada asserted in his *Memoria* for 1826, which is the definitive statement of Colombian revenue policy, that "the fiscal laws of every country should be judged principally according to their influence on the good or bad fortune of agriculture." [1] He further assumed that a vigorous and unhampered economy would naturally yield more taxes for the state, while moderate assessments would always produce more than oppressive taxation simply by reducing the incentives for evasion and creating a greater demand for the goods and services taxed. This general principle Dr. Castillo applied with equal force to customs duties and to the stamp tax. At the same time he believed that taxation should be simplified for the benefit of both government and tax-payers, and nuisance taxes either abolished or consolidated. Castillo y Rada rounded out his exposition with an element of social science reminiscent of the *Federalist Papers:* "The major part of the expenses which a government makes in its internal administration have as their object to defend the rich against the poor, because if both were abandoned to their respective forces the first would very soon be despoiled." [2] From this he concluded that the rich should pay more taxes

[1] *El Constitucional* (Bogotá), February 9, 1826.
[2] *El Constitucional*, March 2, 1826.

in return for their protection, and that nothing could be fairer than direct taxes based on the wealth of the tax-payer. If all these principles were carried into practice, he thought, Colombia would take her true place among civilized nations. And the first step was to renovate the entire mechanism of colonial taxation—monopolies, *alcabala*, and the like—which was deemed to have been created not so much to raise revenue as to keep Colombians in bondage.[3]

## The Reform of the National Tax System

It was obviously impossible to reform everything at once, particularly in the midst of a struggle for existence. Reform would disturb the habits of taxpayers, and the new system would need to be firmly implanted before it could yield as much as the old. Immediately after Boyacá, therefore, Bolívar had ordered that the whole traditional framework of government finance be continued. Certain minor changes were made in fiscal administration, but the colonial taxes themselves were all retained, however repugnant to liberal principles. When Dr. Pedro Gual as provincial governor of Cartagena saw fit to abolish the Indian tribute and the state monopolies of tobacco and *aguardiente* he was vigorously rebuked by Santander. For the sake of uniformity, the *aguardiente* monopoly was even restored in parts of New Granada where it had lately been abolished by the Spaniards.[4]

A real opportunity for reform came only with the Congress of Cúcuta. By the time it met, New Granada was secure from Spanish threats; by the time it could pay serious attention to financial problems, Caracas too had been liberated. The central mission of the Congress was to create the basic conditions for liberal development, and fiscal reform could no longer be postponed entirely. The first of all tax reforms, fittingly enough, was directed against two of the most annoying colonial imposts: the internal customs duties and the special sales-tax on foodstuffs which was known as the *sisa*. Neither produced revenue in proportion to its effect in obstructing business, and both were abolished outright. Next came the general sales-tax or *alcabala*, whose normal rate had been 5%. It was more important as a source of revenue but it was also the most objectionable of all taxes in economic theory. It was therefore abolished for most purposes, to be levied henceforth only on sales of real estate and imported merchandise, and at the reduced rate of 2½%.[5]

Two other major items of the colonial revenue system were abolished at Cúcuta: the Indian tribute and the *aguardiente* monopoly. The former had been a convenient method of collecting the Indians' taxes in a single

[3] *El Constitucional*, February 9 through March 2, 1826.

[4] *La Gazeta de Santa Fe de Bogotá*, September 19, 1819, January 16 to 30, 1820; Santander to Bolívar, September 9, 1820, Lecuna, *C.S.* I, 115.

[5] *Codif. Nac.* I, 55, 89-90.

lump payment, in return for which they were exempted from most regular taxation, but it had overtones of oppression that could not be tolerated in a free republic. The Indians were now declared equal citizens, and consequently they were to pay exactly the same taxes as other Colombians.[6] The law abolishing the *aguardiente* monopoly was no less liberal in its intentions. Its eloquent *considerandos* stated:

"1. That in Venezuela the monopoly of *aguardientes* did not exist even under the Spanish yoke;

2. That this barbarous monopoly has produced nothing but misery . . . , chaining the industry of the farmer and obliging him not to undertake lucrative enterprises;

3. Finally, that when such restrictions are broken *aguardiente* can still be a source of public and private wealth." [7]

Accordingly, the distilling industry was now thrown open everywhere to all who desired to enter it. To make up for the resulting loss of revenue a series of new taxes was imposed on the private manufacture and sale of *aguardiente,* and the manner of collecting them was carefully prescribed in some 24 articles. Despite all hopes to the contrary, however, the new taxes yielded only a fraction of the revenue produced by the former monopoly.[8]

No other really important tax was ended by the Constituent Congress or by later Congresses, but numerous minor revenues were abolished at one time or another in accordance with liberal theory. The playing card monopoly was retained only long enough to sell off the decks inherited from the Spanish administration.[9] The sale of offices was ended as incompatible with republican government, although current holders of *oficios vendibles* were not necessarily dismissed.[10] On another occasion Congress abolished the state monopoly of chewing tobacco, which had been kept separate from the tobacco monopoly proper: this rather insignificant revenue had been found "highly grievous to the peoples who consume these articles," while the attempt to earn the government a 75% profit had simply played into the hands of contraband salesmen.[11]

[6] *Codif. Nac.* I, 116. This measure was suspended for a time in Ecuador; for a general discussion of the tribute, see below, pp. 175-176.

[7] *Codif. Nac.* I, 94.

[8] *Codif. Nac.* I, 94-97, 396-400. One worthy cause that suffered from this reform was the care of lepers, who had been supported in large part from the *aguardiente* monopoly. (A.C., Cámara-12, 317, 320, 338, 388, 407-408, 419).

[9] *El Constitucional,* July 26, 1827.

[10] *El Constitucional,* March 2, 1826; A.C., Actas del Senado, May 13, 1826.

[11] *Codif. Nac.* I, 380-381. This law declared free the manufacture of *chimó* and *mohó,* which were chewing compounds prepared with a special mineral soda known as *urao* that was extracted from a lake near Mérida. The *urao* itself continued under government control. See message of Santander to Congress, April 23, 1824, A.C., Senado-13, 136.

The various levies on foreign trade were not abolished, but the tariff structure was subjected to a general overhauling just the same. In the late colonial regime the duties collected at ports of the viceroyalty had been quite modest, but they were over and above those already paid by the same goods on export from Spain or from another colony; and if goods came from outside the Spanish Empire to begin with, the normal procedure was to have them landed first at a Spanish port, paying $36\frac{1}{2}\%$ import duty plus an additional 7% on being reexported. Moreover, the actual duty was calculated not from intrinsic value, but from a fixed tariff or *arancel*, of which there was one version for Venezuela and another for New Granada.[12] After Boyacá the confusion was increased for a time by the contradictory orders of Admiral Brión, Dr. Gual, Bolívar, and Santander. Bolívar usually had the last word, and for New Granada, at least, he used his advantage to impose a standard tax of 33% on all imports from French wines to medical supplies.[13] The Congress of Cúcuta finally attempted to establish a moderate and unified system for the entire republic. The regular Spanish import duties—*almojarifazgo, almirantazgo* and the rest—were consolidated into a single tax that was to be levied everywhere by the *arancel* of New Granada; and the standard rate to be charged was to vary from 15% to 35% depending on the nature of the article involved. Export duties were unified at the same time, and in general were to be considerably lower than they had been during the colonial regime.[14]

Actually the Congress of Cúcuta did not quite attain its twin objectives of simplicity and moderation. Separate tonnage and anchorage duties were retained, not to mention a confusing assortment of nuisance taxes and miscellaneous port duties, both national and municipal, which bore on foreign trade. For a time there was also the special *alcabala* on imported goods. In 1824 this and some of the nuisance taxes were consolidated into a 3% *derecho de consumo,* while other minor charges were abolished or carefully regulated by the Congress of 1826.[15] Such reforms as these, however, did not answer the widespread charges of both doctrinaire liberals and foreign traders that the basic import duty schedule—the rate from 15% to 35% levied according to a static *arancel*—was itself unreasonably high. In actual fact, the rate was definitely lower than the

[12] Cf. *Actas:* Cúcuta, 391; *Reglamento, tarifa, y arancel aprobados y mandados observar por el exmo. señor virey* (Cartagena, 1817).

[13] *Corresp.* 93; H.L.V. Ducoudray-Holstein, *Memoirs of Simón Bolívar* (Boston, 1829), 267.

[14] *Codif. Nac.* I, 56-58, 64-65, 68.

[15] *Codif. Nac.* I, 69, 128-129, 350-352, II, 344-346; *El Constitucional,* February 23, 1826; A.C., Cámara-1, 346-348.

combined colonial and Spanish duties on non-Spanish goods under the colonial mercantile system. Even so, foreign trade had to support a heavy burden of taxation, and some reduction was achieved by the Congress of 1823. More relief was afforded to Colombian importers by Congress in 1826 when it substituted *ad valorem* duties for the *arancel*. Prices in the *arancel*, though seldom exhorbitant, had been frequently out-dated. The use of commercial invoices to determine values incidentally increased the possibilities for fraud, thus tending to reduce still further the amounts actually paid. This reform was accompanied by a slight increase in the general level of rates, but its frank intent was one of eliminating unreasonable charges, and it was followed by another law abolishing outright the *derecho de consumo,* which meant in practice a flat reduction of 3% in all import levies.[16]

If the new regime did not slash customs duties even farther with a view to encouraging trade—and thus, in the long run, increasing the government's revenue also—it was primarily because of the immediate need for funds in the national treasury. For the same reason good liberals like Vicente Azuero helped to defeat a proposal in the Congress of Cúcuta for the abolition of the tobacco monopoly, which had been a highly lucrative source of revenue during the late colonial regime even though its yield had suffered a disastrous decline since the start of the war. The salt monopoly was retained, and was extended to salt-works which had been privately operated during the Spanish regime. Even the gunpowder monopoly was specifically upheld by act of Congress, although the state factories were in such bad condition that the main effect of the measure was simply to make the government sole importer.[17] Nor was anything done about the tithes, which Castillo y Rada termed a "monstrous tribute." [18] One reason for retaining the tithe system was, of course, the fear of clerical opposition, but equally important was the fact that the government could neither forego its own traditional share in the proceeds of the tithes nor undertake to support the clergy instead from its general revenues. Few taxes were more objectionable on principle than the stamp tax; as Nariño's *Insurgente* pointed out, it imposed a fee even for exercising the inalienable right of petition. Yet not only was the use of stamped paper continued under the republic, for a time it actually became more expensive. The charges were later reduced again only because sales

[16] *El Constitucional,* July 15, 1824, January 27, 1825, and February 9, 1826; Robert A. Humphreys, *British Consular Reports on the Trade and Politics of Latin America* (London, 1940), 266 note 2, 281; *Codif. Nac.* II, 207, 247-248. For a more detailed discussion of customs policy, see Chapter 10.

[17] *Actas:* Cúcuta, 669-671; A.C., Senado-13, 136; *Codif. Nac.* I, 209-210; *El Constitucional,* March 2, 1826.

[18] *El Constitucional,* February 9, 1826.

had fallen off.[19] Finally, the new regime carefully preserved the Royal Fifth (*quinto*) on precious metals, and countless insignificant revenues such as the impost on cockfighting, which produced exactly 16 pesos and 6 *reales* in the Department of Cundinamarca for the fiscal year 1825-6.[20]

At the same time Colombia sought to develop a few new sources of revenue that had been overlooked or else inadequately exploited by the colonial authorities. The relaxation of Spanish restrictions on the entry of foreigners somewhat increased the government's income from its national domain, because it was now in a position to lease almost anything that came to mind to British speculators.[21] But the most notable innovation was in the field of direct taxation, which was universally held to be the variety most in accord with republican principles and was also a favorite of other Latin American reformers such as Rivadavia in Buenos Aires. Santander had toyed with the idea of a direct property tax in the months following Boyacá, only to decide that it would be too difficult to enforce,[22] but the Constituent Congress was bolder. It also had to make up in some way for the loss of the *alcabala;* and its solution was the *contribución directa*.

The new tax was a levy of 10% a year on the income produced by land and capital (12½% if the property was held in entail or mortmain), and either 2% or 3% on such personal income as government salaries, depending on their amount. Each taxpayer was required to make a public declaration of property, subject to review by a board of respected citizens; but as it was deemed impossible to determine the exact income derived from any property, it was arbitrarily assumed that mining and manufacturing capital would produce 5% a year, commercial capital 6%, and landed property 5%. When 10% of the latter figure was taken, the tax really amounted to an annual capital levy of ½%. Once a final assessment was arrived at, collection of the tax was entrusted to agents named for every parish by the *juez político*. A collector could not refuse the appointment under any circumstances, and to prevent laxity both *juez*

[19] *El Insurgente* (Bogotá), September 25, 1822; *Arch. Sant.* VII, 317-318; A.C., Senado-17, 579; *Codif. Nac.* I, 106-109, 283-285. See table in next chapter for stamped paper revenues. There appears to be no complete and reasonable explanation for the decline.

[20] A.C., Senado-38, 105. The tax was not quite so contemptible in Azuay, where it produced $322, and in Orinoco where it gave $408.

[21] Col. James Hamilton actually rented eight Indian missions from the provisional government at Angostura, and allegedly made a handsome profit. It would seem that Vice-President Zea allowed the rental to be counted against interest payments due to Hamilton from the treasury; and in any case, Bolívar strongly disapproved of the whole transaction. See Lecuna, *C.L.* II, 181, 202; Karl Richard, *Briefe aus Columbien* (Leipzig, 1822), 54.

[22] *Corresp.*, 178.

*político* and collector were to receive 2½% of the money that passed through their hands.[23]

The *contribución directa* was a very rough approximation to the ideal form of taxation, so it is well that the great majority of Colombians who earned under $150 a year and either owned no property or owned less than the minimum requirement of $100 were excused from paying it. Supporters of the new tax denied the charge that it was just another tithe, pointing out that it was theoretically based on income rather than gross production, but in practice tithes were automatically reduced in quantity in a bad crop year, while the *contribución directa* assumed that a given property would always produce the same income. The methods of assessment and collection were cumbersome to say the least. Hence constant changes had to be made in the administrative procedure, and Santander felt compelled to obtain special power from Congress to diminish assessments when a given property clearly produced less than the assumed return. In due course, the Vice-President hoped, the government would have sufficiently trustworthy economic data for Congress to estimate the nation's fiscal needs each year and then fix an annual rate for direct taxation in much the same way as property taxes were assessed in the United States. Castillo y Rada even assumed that if the proper reforms were carried out the *contribución directa* would yield not less than $3,100,000 a year. But meanwhile, in fiscal 1825-6, the yield was $195,000, or a good bit less than the *alcabala*.[24]

A fiscal expedient closely related to the *contribución directa* was the series of "extraordinary contributions" imposed by Congress from time to time and variously called *subsidio*, *auxilio patriótico*, or simply *contribución extraordinaria*. These levies were really a compound of forced loan, *contribución directa*, and head-tax. Like the former, they were emergency measures, either to support the war effort or, as in the case of the 1826 *auxilio patriótico*, to pay interest on the foreign debt. There was usually not even a pretense of promising repayment, but forced loans were not always repaid either, and at least the *auxilio patriótico* was supposedly to be credited against future payments due under the *contribución directa*. The "extraordinary contributions" also resembled the *contribución directa* in that they were levied on income and property. On the other hand, they charged different rates, and like a head-tax they sacrificed ideals of fiscal

[23] *Codif. Nac.* I, 79-85.

[24] A.C., Senado-13, 138; A.H.N., Corresp.-Cámara (Hacienda), March 17, 1825; *Codif. Nac.* II, 118-119; *El Constitucional*, February 16 and March 2, 1826. In an effort to put the *contribución directa* on a more scientific footing, the Congress of 1826 transformed the part paid by the business and professional classes into a *derecho de patentes*, which was really a system of license fees (*Codif. Nac.* II, 363-370). But this was in some ways even less scientific than the original tax, and it was never given a real trial because of the political disturbances that began the same year.

justice to the need for prompt and simplified collection. Thus the *subsidio* of 1823 placed a uniform assessment on all the members of certain professions and taxed property by a scale that began at 1% and levelled off to about one-third of 1% on the highest valuations, presumably because it was easier to collect taxes from the poor than from the rich. Santander asked that this strange practice be reversed for the *contribución extraordinaria* in 1824, but instead Congress decided to take exactly ½ of 1% on all taxable property and income. Only in 1826 was a progressively graded tax applied, for the *auxilio patriótico,* and then only on civil and ecclesiastical salaries: these could not well be concealed and so the tax ranged as high as one-sixth in the upper brackets.[25]

The assorted inequalities that studded the "extraordinary contributions" were mitigated to some extent by the fact that like the *contribución directa* they carried an exemption to protect the poorest classes. Probably the special levy of 1824, with exemptions as low as $50, is the only one that came even within striking distance of the average man. Yet it should be noted that the "extraordinary" property tax in 1823 and 1826 contained not only a minimum but also a maximum assessment. This feature was supported even by Santander, who once predicted that hardly anyone would be so honest as to declare property worth over $20,000.[26] No doubt he thought that time, trouble, and perjury could be saved by not asking wealthy citizens to do so in the first place.

## Problems of Financial Management

The disappointing yield of direct taxation is illustrative of the fact that mere legislation on fiscal matters was only a first step. The money still had to be gathered in, and in practice financial officers were hampered to an unusually high degree by the same variety of obstacles that made all government difficult in the first years of the new republic. Thus the general lack of experienced public officials was especially serious in the field of finance since it was in many ways the most technical of all government functions. As Vice-President of Cundinamarca, Santander was forced to attend in person to countless small details of fiscal routine, while over in Caracas Bolívar had to entrust the regional *Dirección de Rentas* provisionally to a certain Spanish merchant who allegedly was bankrupt.[27] Up to a point it might almost be said that the choice of Castillo y Rada as Secretary of Finance was a further illustration of the personnel problem. He was a fine theorist, and there is no proof whatever for the occasional

[25] *Codif. Nac.* I, 182-184, 301-303, II, 399-402; *Actas:* Cámara-1824, 160 · *Actas:* Senado-1824, 501.
[26] Message to Congress, June 2, 1824, A.C., Senado-6, 58. Actually, the maximum assessment in 1826 was based on a valuation of $200,000.
[27] O'Leary XVIII, 379, 396.

implications of personal dishonesty. Yet he was not an outstanding administrator, and he acquired a special reputation for arriving late to work.[28]

The situation was perhaps worst of all when it came to collecting a tax such as the *contribución directa,* which was heartily unpopular with the chief contributors. In the last analysis, the assessment of direct taxes admittedly had to be based on either "general rumor" or "a minute and inquisitorial examination of books and correspondence," and neither method was really satisfactory. By its very novelty the tax was constantly raising intricate technical problems. For these reasons practically nobody ever wanted the job of collecting it, and despite the government's legal right to compel anyone to take the position, in practice the tax was never collected in full. The collection might be omitted in an entire canton, and even in Bogotá, where it was always in arrears, it once went uncollected for an entire semester. All this was not only because collectors were hard to find but also because it was inexpedient to demand too much energy from those who finally took on the job lest they find some way to abandon it.[29]

As in other branches of administration, the extreme political centralization stemming from the Constitution of Cúcuta did not really help matters. At the center of government, Castillo y Rada had probably more trivial matters referred to him for a decision from other parts of the republic than anyone else in the administration. But at the same time, really effective central control was so hard to maintain in outlying provinces that often it broke down entirely. Conditions were especially bad in the richest and most independent-minded department of all, Venezuela, where financial officers were frequently years behind schedule in preparing their balance sheets and even farther behind in having them approved by their superiors. At the other end of the republic, in Guayaquil, and also in some of the ports of New Granada, taxes were levied whose nature was quite unknown to the central authorities at Bogotá. Equally significant are the numerous circular letters in which Castillo y Rada desperately pleaded with local officials to look through their archives and see if there were any fiscal laws or decrees that perchance were not currently being enforced.[30]

Then there was the nearly invincible popular habit of cheating the government which was generally blamed on "our ancient oppressors" but

[28] Hamilton to Planta, March 8, 1825, in C. K. Webster, ed., *Britain and the Independence of Latin America* (2 vols., London 1938) I, 385; Watts to Clay, November 14, 1826, N.A., Colombia Dispatches IV; *El Noticiosote* (Bogotá), March 8, 1825; Groot, 492.

[29] *La Gaceta de Colombia,* October 5, 1823, July 17, December 11 and 18, 1825; A.C., Senado-33, 291; A.H.N., Corresp.-Cámara (Hacienda), March 17, 1825.

[30] *El Constitucional,* February 23, 1826; *La Gaceta de Colombia,* June 11, 1826.

had certainly found new outlets in the confusion of the war and post-war periods. Even the most enlightened measures might be seized upon in order to defraud the treasury: the law allowing printed matter to pass through the mails free of charge for the sake of encouraging learning led straight to the practice of wrapping up one's personal letters in a post-free newspaper.[31] Another problem was the illegal extraction of precious metals bound for Jamaica or elsewhere without payment of either *quinto* or export duties; this was a practice that tended to increase after the ancient oppressors left, so that other factors clearly were involved as well. Most serious of all was the matter of goods illegally imported, which Castillo y Rada once estimated as providing up to 60% of the nation's total import trade. The main solution suggested by Dr. Castillo was naturally to cut down import duties, thus rendering contraband less attractive; a similar measure, he believed, would reduce the illegal extraction of precious metals. The fact was, however, that duties were already lower than they had been under the colonial regime—and that smuggling was even more widespread.[32]

It was obvious that the evasion of import duties and other taxes on such a grand scale would not have been possible without considerable laxity, to say the least, in matters of fiscal administration. One reason for this was naturally the lack of adequate personnel, but it was not the only reason: habits created by ancient oppressors, war-time disruption of administrative routine, and the difficulties of centralized control were all aggravating conditions. So too was the fact that military requirements seldom left funds enough to pay the civil service its legal salaries in full. In any case, the existence of widespread corruption was everywhere taken for granted: almost every mail, said Dr. Castillo, brought anonymous revelations about his subordinates.[33] Corruption was worst precisely where most was at stake, in the customs service. Nothing but a long record of toleration could explain the storm of indignation that arose when Col. Remigio Márquez suddenly cracked down on smuggling at Mompós. Four years later, in 1826, José Rafael Revenga wrote that all but one of the customs administrators on the Atlantic Coast should be dismissed at once.[34] Nor was mere non-collection of taxes the only problem of this sort. There was wholesale waste and pilfering of confiscated property and other government assets, and abuses in military contracts were so constant that they cannot have been due solely to inexperience. It is true that contracts for naval supplies, which constituted a largely un-

[31] *La Gaceta de Colombia,* May 25, 1823.
[32] *La Gaceta de Colombia,* March 18, 1827; *El Constitucional,* February 23 and March 2, 1826.
[33] *La Gaceta de Colombia,* July 17, 1825.
[34] Revenga to Bolívar, May 21, 1826, O'Leary VI, 514.

familiar field, were generally the most onerous, but it hardly seems probable that ignorance alone led Colombian officials to buy tar worth $3.50 a barrel from a United States citizen for $25.[35]

All efforts of the administration to deal with this situation merely emphasize how difficult it was to overcome. As early as October, 1819, Santander decreed that any financial employee found guilty of fraud should be put to death *sumariamente*. If the offender were merely guilty of "little zeal" he would be conscripted into the army or put to forced labor in Guayana. This rule was suspended only in June, 1822, and then not because the problem had ceased but rather for the sake of "economizing" the use of "extraordinary faculties."[36] However, it was also true that severity alone could never end corruption. Hence the administration began to stress the need to increase its employees' pay if they were to remain honest; and then when Congress finally authorized a general pay increase Santander vetoed the bill on the plausible grounds that he lacked the funds to carry it out.[37] The Vice-President's next move was to ask Congress for the right to dismiss finance officers merely on the basis of a reasonable suspicion of corrupt practices. Under existing laws he could only suspend suspects who then had to be restored to their jobs unless charges could be conclusively proven in the courts, and it turned out that fraud was as hard to prove as to prevent—for much the same reasons. The Congress of 1826 therefore granted this request, although it seems that few officials were actually removed as a result.[38] Indeed shortly afterwards a good part of the republic was in a state of rebellion, and many officials were thus placed wholly beyond the reach of Santander.

It would of course be easy to exaggerate the amount of inexperience, insubordination, and outright corruption that plagued the Colombian fiscal administration, for presumably many tax-collectors were honest and highly capable. Others, however, were not; and no amount of zeal at the higher bureaucratic levels could have solved the problem completely. As a result, it was frequently proposed that the government should by-pass its own employees by farming out sources of revenue to private entrepreneurs. The latter would presumably introduce good business methods so as to increase both honesty and efficiency, while private enterprise in all forms was dear to liberal theorists. As tax-farming was a good colonial

[35] MacPherson to Secretary of State, May 6, 1826, N.A., Cartagena I. The problems involved in management of confiscated property are discussed below, pp. 276-278.

[36] A.C., Senado-2, 10; *El Correo de la Ciudad de Bogotá,* June 20, 1822.

[37] A.H.N., Corresp.-Cámara (Hacienda) April 11, 1825; Santander to Congress, January 3, 1826, A.C., Cámara-5, 168.

[38] *La Gaceta de Colombia,* August 21, 1825; *El Constitucional,* February 9, 1826; *Codif. Nac.* II, 200; O'Leary VI, 519.

tradition, and was still one method employed in the collection of tithes, conservative elements could hardly object to it. The government itself, finally, would naturally strive to make sure that any future contracts would be free from the abuses formerly associated with the practice.

The first practical suggestion to this effect was apparently the request of Santander, in July of 1823, for a legislative decree authorizing him to rent the saltworks of Zipaquirá to a group of English investors. As they had offered to pay three years' rental in advance, Congress was quite willing to give its consent, and the contract was signed. Unfortunately, the promoters had been counting on obtaining settlement of debts owed to them by the Colombian government before they made their advance payment; the government refused to pay, and the whole negotiation fell through.[39] Even so, the salt monopoly was always the revenue held most suitable for private management, and ultimately Congress decreed that all saltworks without exception should be farmed out. This decision was heartily endorsed by Castillo y Rada, who proceeded to auction off the Zipaquirá works all over again, this time to native investors.[40] There was, moreover, an intermittent demand for farming out other sources of revenue as well. But except for the rental of certain government mining properties nothing else was done. In fact it is obvious that there was a limit to the amount of revenue that could be administered by private businessmen without meeting many of the same obstacles as the government itself.

## The War, the Tobacco Monopoly, and the Mints

The greatest obstacle of all is one that has only been touched on so far, and has nothing directly to do with the quality of financial officials. This is the War of Independence as such, and when the immediate effects of the war are combined with all other adverse factors it is sometimes surprising that any money was collected at all. For the war created general confusion and disrupted communications, thus facilitating the non-payment of taxes and encouraging officials to evade responsibility. It also destroyed many of the very sources of government revenues. This was especially true of a levy on production such as the tithes, which provided income for the state as well as for the church. Not only was a tax of this sort unusually hard to collect under war-time conditions, but production itself had decreased in some regions as a result of the struggle, and a great many *hacendados* claimed to be ruined whether they really were or not. Hence the corps of functionaries engaged in the collection of tithes went farther and farther into arrears, and the government had little choice but to allow fairly

[39] *Codif. Nac.* I, 258; *Acuerdos* II, 55; *La Gaceta de Colombia,* November 14, 1824; A.C., Senado-15, 111; A.C., Cámara-14, 284-288.
[40] *Codif. Nac.* II, 315-318; *El Constitucional,* March 2, 1826; *La Gaceta de Colombia,* September 2, 1827.

liberal terms. The fact that the tithe-collectors included such worthy citizens as Dr. Vicente Azuero and General Domingo Caicedo was no doubt an added reason for leniency, and by April, 1825, over half a million pesos was overdue in the archdiocese of Bogotá alone.[41]

The war was an even worse calamity for the tobacco monopoly, which was hurt above all by the diversion of its operating capital to military expenses. The state tobacco factories thus could not pay the growers in full or on time for their tobacco, and the latter then cut down production, went on strike against growing any tobacco whatsoever, or sold their crops to bootleggers who could pay them handsomely in cash and still undercut the state monopoly.[42] Castillo y Rada once asked Congress whether he might compel the growers to give their tobacco to the government on credit, but the nation's credit standing was so low that this would scarcely have been a real solution. In addition, there were the usual problems of dishonest officials and the like, and the unsettled conditions of wartime had allowed widespread evasion of the laws prohibiting the introduction of foreign tobacco. By the latter process, many Colombians had unfortunately acquired a taste for the Virginia or Havana products, and the Congress of Cúcuta had thus seen fit to make tobacco imports legal at a high rate of duty; the measure was a provisional one, and the duty was specifically designed to protect the interests of state factories, but in practice any form of competition was harmful to the monopoly. Then, too, the very principle of state monopoly was repulsive to liberal economic thinking, so that many good Colombians felt fewer inhibitions about cheating the government when it came to tobacco than they did in the payment of regular taxes.[43] Finally, there was a bitter dispute with the growers over the amount that should be deducted from their payments for loss of weight through drying; this was another indirect result of the war, since it stemmed mainly from an attempt to reestablish stricter colonial regulations after a temporary war-time relaxation.[44]

When all these factors were taken together the result was that no other major revenue made such a poor showing as compared with the colonial period. The exact extent of the decline is hard to judge, since the

[41] A.C., Senado-26, 79-81. On the situation in Popayán see A.H.N., Congresos XXVII, 124-142. Naturally not all defaulting was due to war conditions, since collectors were permitted to use the money they received for private speculation pending the time when it was due to be finally handed in.

[42] *Observaciones sobre el comercio de la Nueva Granada* (Bogotá, 1831), 11; A.C., Cámara-1, 290-292; *El Venezolano* (Caracas), January 3, 1824.

[43] *La Gaceta de Colombia*, August 22, 1824, August 21 and 28, 1825.

[44] A.C., Cámara-6, 260-292 contains an *expediente* on this topic. The administrator of the monopoly at Honda stated in June, 1826, that this was the sole cause of the decline in production, which was no doubt an exaggeration. However, it is true that by that time some of the other causes, such as lack of capital, had become less severe.

figures available are not always reliable and do not always distinguish between gross sales and net profits. Yet in colonial Venezuela alone in some years the sales had reached nearly a million pesos. In 1825-6, in all Colombia the sales were roughly $800,000 and the profit $288,000. As late as 1827 profits in Venezuela were scarcely a quarter of what they had been, and at Panama tobacco sales fell at times to $3 daily.[45] Needless to say, any hope of exporting great amounts of government tobacco to Europe, which had been one reason for retaining the monopoly,[46] simply failed to materialize.

It was equally natural that the government should receive as much of the blame for the situation as did the real culprit, which was the War of Independence, and it never tired of seeking expedients to save both its reputation and its revenue. One of the first measures had been to grant draft-exemption to tobacco growers. Later the administration sought and obtained a renewed prohibition of foreign tobacco, although smuggling went on and the monopoly itself occasionally imported United States tobacco to sell at a handsome profit when for some reason its own factories could not meet the demand.[47] Apparently on his own initiative, at least one tobacco official attempted to rescue the monopoly by virtually merging it with his private business. Thus the *factor* at Piedecuesta, Facundo Mutis, received tobacco at the state factory in return for tickets which he later exchanged for merchandise in his own private business. The growers did not get full value for their crops by this scheme, but what they got was better than nothing; the treasury itself fared better than it could have otherwise, and the only loser was Mutis, who had actually financed the monopoly with his own capital, and had not been reimbursed for all his advances. Yet the plan was admittedly illegal, and the Intendant of Boyacá was subjected to a noisy impeachment trial for tolerating Mutis' procedure. Even though the intendant was finally acquitted, Congress failed to grant full exoneration to the *factor,* so that others were presumably discouraged from following his example.[48]

Still another method by which it was hoped to reinvigorate the tobacco monopoly was the appropriation of $540,000 from the funds of the English loan of 1824 for use by the factories. There is no indication how much of this sum was actually spent as planned, or whether it was spent correctly; in any case, the measure led to no great or immediate increase in revenue. A final attempt was the law of 1826 which authorized the

[45] Eduardo Arcila Farías, *Economía colonial de Venezuela* (México, 1946), 332; Blanco XI, 544; A.C., Senado-13, 16, Senado-38, 102.
[46] Cf. *Codif. Nac.* I, 72.
[47] O'Leary XVIII, 401-402; *Codif. Nac.* I, 208-209; *Documentos que el Poder Ejecutivo presenta . . . en asuntos conexionados con el empréstito de 1824* (Bogotá, 1826), 17.
[48] *Actas:* Senado-1824, 477-493; A.C., Senado-4, 401-418.

government to raise the prices paid by the monopoly to the growers and reduced those charged to consumers, but this was a virtual admission that the whole system of monopoly profits was unsound.[49] Indeed there were some timid suggestions that the one real solution was to abolish the monopoly altogether. The proposal came chiefly from a few areas such as the provinces of Socorro and Caracas, where a direct interest in tobacco production was combined with a relatively wide diffusion of theoretical liberalism, but at no time did it receive the attention it deserved at Bogotá.[50]

The peculiar problems that afflicted the tobacco monopoly did not affect the government's salt business to any great extent, in part because it did not require such large operating capital. Conditions in the tobacco monopoly were roughly paralleled, however, by the state of the mints— which were basically a monopoly of coinage—and of all the related taxes on precious metals. Revenue from these sources had fallen off badly, and again the main reason was the war. Mining slaves had been conscripted for military service and properties damaged; at Popayán the mint itself was hurt. Money that should have been used to pay miners for the precious metals coined by the state mints was used for other purposes, and especially for prosecuting the war. As in the tobacco industry, the result was either a slackening of production or an added inducement for illicit sales to private individuals. In the latter case the metal was usually smuggled out to the West Indies, where prices were definitely higher than in Colombia; and not only did the mints lose their profit, but the treasury was further defrauded of the *quinto* that was levied on all precious metals without exception.[51]

All in all the Bogotá mint—which suffered less than that of Popayán —received one-fourth less gold and silver in 1820-1827 than it received in 1800-1807, and the *quinto* came to yield only half of what it had produced for Spain. The customs revenues were also affected, for until 1826 there was a moderate export duty on coined gold, the only form of precious metal that could legally be taken from the country, and obviously this was not paid when the metal was smuggled out in bulk. A comprehensive reform and reduction of all imposts on mining was therefore presented by Castillo y Rada as one solution to the general problem; he

---

[49] *Codif. Nac.* II, 342-343, VII, 207-208, 373-376; *Documentos que el Poder Ejecutivo presenta*, 15-16.

[50] For suggestions to end the monopoly, see A.H.N., Congresos XXV, 865; A.C., Cámara-8, 132-136; *El Cometa* (Caracas), November 17, 1824; *La Revista Semanal* (Caracas), April 15, 1826. Socorro had abolished the monopoly on its own initiative in 1812 (Luis Eduardo Nieto Arteta, *Economía y cultura en la historia de Colombia*, Bogotá, 1941, 50).

[51] José María Castillo y Rada, *Memoria de Hacienda* (Bogotá, 1823), 10, and also his *Memoria* for 1826 in *El Constitucional*, February 9 to March 2, 1826.

also suggested the founding of new mints at Panamá and Cartagena so that gold from the Isthmus and the Chocó would not need to make the difficult trip to Popayán or Bogotá. However, neither of his suggestions was adopted by Congress. Just as in the case of the tobacco monopoly, part of the English loan was used for supplying new capital to the mints, and this may help to account for a rise in the amount of gold entering the Bogotá mint after its lowest point had been reached in 1824-5. Even so, neither the operations of the mints nor the income from other mining taxes ever returned fully to colonial levels.[52]

The low profit of the Colombian mints was at least a sign that the government had generally resisted the temptation to solve its fiscal problems by currency depreciation. It did issue a certain amount of depreciated silver, at times with legal authorization and at times without it. And it even resorted to false-dating the coins in order to conceal what it was doing. But there was no experimentation at all with paper money—despite the existence of legislation specifically providing for it—and gold remained always the basic currency standard. Indeed not enough silver of any sort was minted to have an appreciable effect either on the general price level or on the plight of the Colombian treasury, which operated steadily at a loss.[53]

---

[52] See table to Chapter 7 and also Aníbal Galindo, *Historia económica y estadística de la hacienda nacional* (Bogotá, 1874), Table 14; *El Constitucional*, February 23 and March 2, 1826; *Documentos que el Poder Ejecutivo presenta*, 15.

[53] Guillermo Torres García, *Historia de la moneda en Colombia* (Bogotá, 1945), 31-32; *Codif. Nac.* I, 12-13.

Chapter VII

## *The Financial Crisis (II): Debts, Deficits, and Recriminations*

WHEN a balance was struck between the abolition of old taxes and the creation of new ones, the growing importance of some and the decline of others, it turned out that the Colombian government was actually better supplied with revenue than its colonial predecessor. One would hardly expect this, to judge from the laments of Colombian officials, but it still appears to have been the case in the two fiscal years 1824-5 and 1825-6, which were the nearest approach to normal ever attained in Gran Colombia and also the years for which the most complete—though not always the most accurate—statistics are available. (See Table.[1]) The most serious losses on the books of the Colombian treasury were shown by the tobacco monopoly, which never wholly recovered from the effects of the war, and by the different revenues from *aguardiente,* for the new liquor taxes never brought in as much money as the former monopoly. The virtual extinction of the *alcabala,* on the other hand, was offset by the *derecho de consumo,* which replaced it for a time on foreign merchandise, and by the new *contribución directa,* for even though the latter never lived up to expectations it did produce more than its critics would usually admit. The abolition of the Indian tribute was also less serious than might appear because the Indians were henceforth supposed to pay all regular taxes instead, and even more because it was delayed until 1825 in the one area where the tax was most important, Ecuador. The profit from the mints of Bogotá and Popayán fell off sharply at first but did not lag too far behind the colonial figures once the mints had returned to a peace-time footing, and the salt monopoly more than held its own. The customs, finally, showed a striking improvement thanks to the collection of all duties at American ports, the inauguration of a fairly liberal commercial policy, and an influx of foreign capital that stimulated trade. They became much the most important source of government income, and if one could believe Dr. Castillo's exact figures for 1825-6—which one decidedly cannot—they alone amounted to more than the grand total of colonial revenues.

[1] See Appendix for a discussion of the sources from which the table was compiled, and for extended qualifying remarks on the customs, *alcabala,* and tribute totals, as well as on the grand total that appears for 1825-6. Suffice it to say here that the latter is particularly misleading.

## FINANCIAL CRISIS (II): DEBTS, DEFICITS, AND RECRIMINATIONS

### REVENUES OF THE VICEROYALTY OF NEW GRANADA BEFORE AND AFTER INDEPENDENCE

| Class of Revenue | Average for Last Years Before 1810 | Fiscal Year 1824-5 | Fiscal Year 1825-6 |
|---|---|---|---|
| Tobacco monopoly (gross receipts) | $1,170,000 | $859,067 | $800,519 |
| Aguardientes | 345,048 | 60,564 | 29,429 |
| Customs: | | | |
|   Import duties | | 1,888,007 | 3,178,198 |
|   Export duties | | 467,849 | 582,100 |
|   Derecho de consumo | | 148,011 | 424,854 |
| Total (including miscellaneous) | 658,000 | 2,651,118 | 5,688,019 |
| Alcabala | 627,880 | 119,902 | 78,598 |
| Stamped paper | 113,000 | 55,866 | 62,294 |
| Tribute | 290,089 | 172,051 | 138,068 |
| Salt monopoly | 79,000 | 187,905 | 215,333 |
| Tithes and vacantes | 319,000 | 254,837 | 248,719 |
| Mints | 150,000 | 101,993 | 142,152 |
| Quinto | 78,240 | 32,748 | 34,738 |
| Cockfighting | 2,200 | | 860 |
| Contribución directa | | 194,559 | 144,169 |
| "Extraordinary contributions" | | 122,322 | 35,001 |
| Internal loans | | 516,189 | 254,217 |
| Foreign loans | | | 2,437,195 |
| Total of the above and all other categories | $5,326,088 | $6,196,725 | $12,156,375 |

## The Mounting Deficit

Unfortunately, the expenses of the new republic had increased even more spectacularly than its revenues. The vicregal treasury, to begin with, had not needed to support a Congress, yet no republic was complete without one, and if every department had ever sent its full quota of legislators to Bogotá the cost would have run to nearly $1000 a day for sessions that lasted at least four months each year. This alone would have taken roughly half of the meagre profits still being made by the tobacco monopoly, so from a fiscal standpoint the problem of Congressional absenteeism might almost be called a blessing in disguise.[2] Neither had the Viceroy of New Granada any need for diplomatic agents in foreign lands, whereas the Colombian foreign service cost slightly under $85,000 in the fiscal year 1825-6—or more than the combined product of *quinto* and *aguardientes*—and would have cost far more if all the posts existing on paper had been filled.[3] The expansion of the Judicial and Executive Powers which was necessary in order to give the people all the benefits of a liberal administration was likewise a heavy fiscal burden, but Dr. Castillo warned that the cost of government could not be wantonly slashed in a new nation where everything still remained to be done.[4] Part of the added expense was due to the effort to create a symmetrical arrangement of departments and provinces, each with its own superior officials in military affairs, civil administration, finance, and so forth: this was often more logical than the colonial system had been, but it usually created new positions to fill. At the higher levels, at least, the salaries to be paid were also fairly generous, although here symmetry was abandoned to the extent of allowing the Intendant of Venezuela $4000 a year, while the Intendant of Cundinamarca, where living expenses were low, was to have only $2500. Even allowing for such regional variations and for the fact that public officials did not always receive their full salaries, the cost of bureaucracy was high. The civil payroll in 1825-6 was only $7185 for the Department of Cauca, but rose to five times that much in Guayaquil, and to well over $300,000 in Cundinamarca, although in the latter figure most Congressional salaries are also included.[5]

[2] *Codif. Nac.* I, 111, 252-254, II, 86-87; *Actas:* Cámara-1824, 209.

[3] A.C., Senado-38, 105. The Secretaría de Relaciones Extranjeras was awarded nearly $300,000 in the budget for 1826-7; however, this included such purely theoretical items as $18,632 for a legation in Denmark that was never set up. (*Ibid.*, 91-92).

[4] *El Constitucional*, February 9, 1826.

[5] A.C., Senado-38, 105. For data on salary scales see *Codif. Nac.* I, 75, 112-113, 252-254, and *La Gaceta Oficial del Departamento del Istmo* (Panamá), October 5, 1823. The latter gives the final scale as decreed by Santander, and is considerably less generous than the original decree of the Congress of Cúcuta, which assigned every intendant $6000 and every governor $4000.

Most serious of all was the problem of military expenditures. The viceroyalty had existed down to 1810 with only the most rudimentary defenses. Colombia, on the other hand, had to fight a War of Independence that could not be safely ended until the whole continent was free; and it left the nation with a swollen military establishment headed by Generals-in-Chief with a monthly salary of $300 and the right to a war bonus of not less than $25,000. Naturally the military did not receive their full salaries any more than the civil bureaucracy, for the entire yield of Colombian taxation was not enough to pay the sum technically appropriated for national defense. Even so, military salaries, war supplies, and related expenses were always much the greatest drain on the treasury. In the fiscal year 1825-6, for which the fullest records are available, roughly three-fourths of the government's regular operating expenses were military; or to look at it another way, the army and navy together cost well over $5,000,000, which is about as much as total government revenue had been under the colonial regime.[6] In earlier years the proportion of military expenses had almost certainly been higher still, although there are few real statistics to prove it. But even when the fighting moved on to Peru and finally ended altogether there was no great decline in military expenses. There was always a possibility of new Spanish incursions and civil strife, there were old bills yet to be paid, and a large army was hard to get rid of without offending influential generals and colonels. Even the relatively sheltered Department of Boyacá spent more on its garrison than on anything else, while only a few remote spots such as Casanare ever possessed a civil salary budget that outweighed its military payroll.[7]

Chiefly because of the armed forces, therefore, Colombian accounts remained in a state of chronic unbalance. It was significant that the Chamber of Representatives adopted the custom during the war of discussing major financial issues in secret session rather than frighten the nation's friends and give encouragement to the foe by revealing too many unpleasant truths. Congress itself did not know what the true state of national finances was, because adequate statistical records were never available. Nevertheless, taking official budgetary pronouncements as correct only to the nearest million pesos—which is a more than adequate precaution—it is still obvious that normal revenues were never equal to the government's fiscal requirements. In 1823 the government's income seems to have been approximately $5,000,000, but for the same year its

[6] The complete official financial statement for 1825-6 can be found in A.C., Senado-38, and its military figures are more complete than some other items. If anything, the estimate of three-fourths may be too low. The proportion cited does not, however, take into consideration the gross expenditures of the tobacco monopoly, which form a rather special case, or expenditures made directly in England and the United States with funds of the English loan of 1824.

[7] A.H.N., Departamento de Boyacá II, 869, 896-897, 926, 947-950, III, 30, 38, 191-195, 260.

financial needs were calculated at $14,000,000 or more.⁸ In the spring of 1824 a budget of $13,000,000 was submitted to Congress, but in the fiscal year 1824-5 only half that amount was collected, and this included a half million pesos from internal loans.⁹ In the course of fiscal 1825-6 the government actually claimed a paper surplus of better than $3,000,000 over and above expenses of approximately $9,000,000; but in this case both income and expense columns were inflated by Colombian bookkeeping methods, and part of a foreign loan is included in revenue. José Manuel Restrepo, who was in a position to know, doubted that at any time the ordinary revenues alone had exceeded seven millions.¹⁰ At the very most the record of 1825-6 suggested that if all went well there was hope for a balanced budget in the not too distant future.

## *The Growth of the Internal Debt*

Budget figures are not quite so alarming as they first appear, because no one seriously expected to find and spend all the money that was theoretically needed. Yet the results of fiscal insolvency were clear enough, and the most obvious of these results—as well as the chief means of dealing with the budgetary deficit itself—was a rapid expansion of the Colombian national debt, both foreign and domestic. Foreign credit became a significant factor after 1824, when a substantial Colombian loan was raised in London; it then served to check the rise of internal indebtedness, at least temporarily. But borrowing abroad did not offer a complete solution by any means for Colombia's financial crisis. It was in some respects a cure worse than the disease, and it must be considered separately in the following chapter. Even internal borrowing might in the long run create still further difficulties all its own, especially when the government of Gran Colombia was already burdened from the start with debts inherited from its predecessors. Nevertheless, it was clearly unavoidable, and it took almost every form, voluntary or otherwise, that Colombian ingenuity could think up.

The administration was usually least successful whenever it attempted to float a general internal loan on a nationwide basis. A fine illustration is the fate of the $500,000 domestic loan decreed by Congress in 1823, which was also by far the most ambitious venture of its kind.¹¹ In seeking

⁸ A.H.N., Corresp.-Cámara (Hacienda) April 19, 1823; A.C., Senado-26, 227.

⁹ *El Constitucional,* February 16, 1826.

¹⁰ A.C., Senado-38, 101-105; Restrepo VII, 299.

¹¹ Under authorization from the Congress of Cúcuta, the administration had previously attempted to raise loans for $80,000 early in 1822, and $300,000 later in the same year to recoup the loss of Maracaibo. Neither one produced much more than half of what was sought. See *Actas:* Congreso-1823, 113; *La Gaceta de Colombia,* October 27, 1822; Restrepo VI, 117. The first citation mentions a loan of $30,000 sought late in 1822 under the decree of Cúcuta, but this probably is a mistaken reference to the $300,000 loan.

FINANCIAL CRISIS (II): DEBTS, DEFICITS, AND RECRIMINATIONS 97

to carry out the decree of Congress, Santander offered lenders a discount of 10% and interest of 6%, and he promised to approach only those who could pay with comfort; he also promised to use the proceeds of an expected English loan in order to pay back the $500,000. Yet when the merchants of Bogotá were asked for $40,000 as their share in the loan they gave less than $3000, and in the nation's capital the loan was saved from disaster only when the single firm of Arrubla and Montoya, whose members were personal friends of Santander, agreed to advance $50,000; their own generosity, moreover, was influenced by the fact that two of the partners were going to London to negotiate the projected foreign loan and thus would be in a position to obtain immediate repayment.[12] Elsewhere there was no one to save the day. Cartagena, where the intendant was still trying to collect an earlier loan, gave nothing at all; the Intendants of Venezuela and Cauca—assigned $50,000 and $20,000 respectively —obtained nothing either since they were in the process of collecting local loans on their own authority. As the time for realizing the English loan drew near, Santander tried once more to make the internal loan effective, issuing $220,000 in debt certificates which were to be exchanged for money or supplies at any discount the intendants could obtain. This time Cartagena gave $4000, although her merchants were known to have far more available, and Panama a gratifying $30,000, but in general the effort was no more successful than the last.[13]

One reason for such disheartening results was the very size of the deficit that made loans necessary: the chances of repayment were uncertain, and even if interest should be paid it could not match the usurious rates obtained in commercial lending. The other reason was that investors had already been exploited by a never-ending series of informal and generally involuntary loans imposed locally by the decree of either civil or military officials. Sometimes these were frankly termed "donatives," the chief difference being that in the latter case there was not even a pretense of promising repayment. In either case the procedure was arbitrary by its very nature, but it was not necessarily illegal. Emergency powers of almost any sort could be stretched to cover the raising of forced loans, and the Congress of Cúcuta had specifically confirmed the right of the Executive to raise money to support the war effort virtually as it saw fit.[14]

[12] *Codif. Nac.* I, 255, VII, 152-153; *La Gaceta de Colombia,* September 7, 1823; A.H.N., Corresp.-Cámara (Hacienda), April 6, 1824; A.C., Senado-2, 209-210. Castillo y Rada in his *Cuentas del empréstito del año de 1824* (Bogotá, 1826), B, indicates that Francisco Montoya lent still more on his own, although this was not mentioned in the *Gaceta* at the time.
[13] A.H.N., Corresp.-Cámara (Hacienda), April 6, 1824; A.C., Senado-2, 207, 213-214, 218, Senado-13, 48, 52, 79-81, Senado-26, 228.
[14] *Codif. Nac.* I, 120. For that matter, there was usually some compulsion used even in raising more conventional loans, such as that described above.

Improvised forced loans had been especially common in the period immediately after Boyacá. Santander expressed sorrow for the poor merchants of New Granada who had "neither the means nor the occasion to acquire and replace what we take away from them," [15] but he did not swerve from his harsh duty. He was particularly well pleased with the province of Antioquia, from which nearly $400,000 was extracted in the first year of liberation both by draining provincial treasuries of all the funds they contained and by the exaction of loans from private citizens, religious foundations, and the *tesorería de diezmos;* all this, he added, had been obtained without complaint! If the latter observation is strictly true, however, it does not reflect a normal reaction. Santander himself felt compelled to remind Bolívar that there was a point beyond which funds could be obtained for his army only at the risk of serious political unrest.[16]

As additional territory was liberated, new subscribers were found for the government's forced loans. If the loyalty of a newly-acquired province was not entirely certain it was sometimes decided to proceed cautiously at first, as happened in the case of Maracaibo; but in general pro-Spanish elements were always required to make the heaviest contributions.[17] Nor did the extension of patriot rule put an end to demands on Bogotá and New Granada. Even after the fall of Caracas, Bolívar continued to write Santander from time to time with urgent requests for $50,000 or so in cash to be dispatched at once, ordering him to seize any funds on hand in the Bogotá treasury and then obtain the rest locally from private citizens.[18] In fact everywhere when the authorities were hampered by lack of funds, which was most of the time, the normal solution was to call in some wealthy merchants and draw up quotas for a new forced loan. The methods employed were the same whether the amount involved was $350 for the military hospital in Mérida or $90,000 for the siege of Puerto Cabello and support of Páez' soldiers. The resistance of the lenders was also similar. Bolívar could scarcely contain his indignation when the people of Mérida did not want to give $350 to cure wounded veterans, and the Intendant of Venezuela was far from successful in collecting the $90,000 needed by Páez. This departmental loan served as a good excuse for Caracas merchants not to participate in the nationwide loan of $500,000 decreed by the Congress of 1823, but they still did not pay their quotas, and when at length the intendant needed to clear the way for

[15] Santander to Bolívar, May 21, 1820, *Corresp.,* 184.
[16] Santander to Bolívar, September 26, 1820, Lecuna, *C.S.* I, 123; May 19 and 21, September 22, 1820, *Corresp.,* 182-184, 232.
[17] O'Leary XVIII, 126, 184, 358, 388, 405-406, XX, 32, 182; *Corresp.,* 9.
[18] Cf. O'Leary XVIII, 450-451.

FINANCIAL CRISIS (II): DEBTS, DEFICITS, AND RECRIMINATIONS   99

launching still another loan he simply took it in his own hands to issue drafts on the tardy lenders.[19]
The problem of raising forced loans was not really so simple as that. It was politically inexpedient to place leading citizens in jail for not paying an unpopular exaction. Colonel José Ucrós, as Intendant of Magdalena, further pointed out that nothing could be gained by confiscating property in payment of either loans or taxes since the government would then find no one to buy it. For that matter, the merchants' excuses were sometimes valid. Ucrós agreed that the war—and no doubt war loans—really had ruined many fortunes, and he noted that one normally wealthy merchant had been forced to beg $400 in order to meet a particular loan assessment.[20] Whether justified or not, however, the resistance of private lenders was reason enough to prefer other sources of credit when available. One technique was to borrow a part of the tithes, either from the individual collectors or from the semi-official tithe treasuries. It was also possible to "borrow" from special revenues technically reserved for debt service or some other object, or an official might simply intercept money en route to one of his colleagues.[21] But such methods as these were not enough, so that private citizens were always asked for more. It is thus fortunate that the need for internal loans diminished gradually as war emergencies became less frequent and the domestic revenue system more firmly established. When the English loan of 1824 finally materialized, forced loans were largely abandoned—for the time being.[22]

In practice it was often difficult to distinguish between forced loans and the standing debt for military supplies which had not been paid for at the time of acquisition. The latter debt was due, in part, to the regular purchase of supplies on credit; but when supplies had been commandeered by the military authorities, as so frequently happened, the debt really represented a forced loan in goods. This was another perfectly normal procedure: the government decreed in 1822 that since it did not "for the moment have sufficient means to supply the different corps of operations" a commanding officer might just take what he needed, issuing a formal receipt that was to serve as a legal government obligation.[23] All too often

[19] O'Leary XVIII, 256; A.C., Senado-8, 218, Senado-13, 34, 48, 62, 64.
[20] A.C., Senado-2, 214, Cámara-5, 67.
[21] Cf. Alejandro Osorio and Estanislao Vergara, *Memoria correspondiente al año de 1820* (Bogotá, 1821), 34; A.H.N., Depto. de Boyacá III, 27. The Governor of Santa Marta once retained for local use $2000 from an urgent remittance being sent from Cartagena to the forces operating against Maracaibo (A.C., Cámara-5, 68).
[22] The balance sheet of the regional treasury office in Bogotá, which recorded loans and revenues received in central New Granada, featured $123,663 in internal loans for 1821, $159,096 in 1822, $66,973 in fiscal 1823-4, and $7 in 1825-6 (*La Gaceta de la Ciudad de Bogotá*, January 13, 1822; *La Gaceta de Colombia*, March 23, 1823 and December 19, 1824; *El Constitucional*, November 16, 1826).
[23] *Codif. Nac.* VII, 115.

receipts and promises of repayment were omitted, but even when the formalities were carefully complied with such practices were bound to have an adverse effect on popular morale.

The greatest single item in the internal debt, however, was incurred not by borrowing money or taking supplies on credit but by simply failing to pay civil and military employees what was legally owed them for their services. When wages could not be paid in full or on time the remainder automatically became a national debt to be satisfied at some future date. The system bore some resemblance to a modern payroll savings plan, but with the difference that the savings were compulsory, and that they varied in amount from month to month depending on financial contingencies. Neither could the obligations which the government gave in lieu of wages be cashed on demand at the nearest bank, and some debts of this nature were actually repudiated in the end.[24]

Sometimes an executive or legislative decree directed that soldiers and civil servants should be paid only a third or a half of their salaries in cash. On other occasions it was merely provided that they should be paid as much as possible: "however small" that sum might be, as the Guayana Congress once expressed it.[25] In practice if not in theory, the latter system was almost always followed. Santander himself, whose very generous salary was legally exempt from any kind of deduction, was actually paid $34,000 in the period from January, 1822, to March, 1824, and became a government creditor for the $6,500 remaining. Each of his ministers received about as much as he was owed, and a national debt of approximately $2000 apiece was declared in their favor. It need hardly be added that other officials saw as much or more of their legal salaries go merely to swell the national debt. There were months when the statement of the Tunja treasury showed no outgo for government salaries whatever, and soldiers could be required to subsist for a whole year without pay, kept alive by a daily ration which was itself often incomplete.[26] The debt owed for personal services was further increased by the fact that it included lavish sums owed to veterans of the Venezuelan

[24] For a case in which certain wage debts owed to the military were partially repudiated, on the basis that it was impossible to determine exactly how much was really owed, see *Codif. Nac.* II, 354-355.

[25] *Codif. Nac.* VII, 11. The deputies did not foresee any discount in the allotment made to their own standing committee or *Diputación Permanente,* but Bolívar reduced its pay just the same (A.C., Senado-5, 18-28).

The final decision on this matter, made by the Congress of 1823, was to abolish all formal discounts and leave the government to pay whatever it could (*Codif. Nac.* I, 252-254).

[26] A.C., Cámara-1, 207; A.H.N., Departamento de Boyacá II, 869, III, 30. For the honor of Santander it should be added that in earlier years he had given up far more of his legal salaries (*La Gaceta de Colombia,* April 13, 1823). The problem of military salaries is discussed more fully below, pp. 252, 275-279.

FINANCIAL CRISIS (II): DEBTS, DEFICITS, AND RECRIMINATIONS 101

campaigns of 1816-19 under the bonus legislation of Angostura and Cúcuta.[27]

Then, too, there were debts in all categories that had been simply invented by self-styled government creditors. This was particularly easy to do at a time when even legal obligations had been accumulated faster than anyone could really keep track of them. Commanding officers sometimes failed to leave receipts for the cattle they took, and the receipts could be lost. The records of monetary loans and salary debts were often kept almost as informally, and as all this was not necessarily the fault of the creditors, public faith required that witnesses be accepted if need be in lieu of documentary proof. Hence one of the most fertile fields for fraud in all Colombia was the business of manufacturing false claims against the treasury. The central *Comisión de Liquidación* complained of an "enormous covetousness" that led citizens first to prove how many cattle they owned before the war, then acquire witnesses to swear that all had been eaten up by Colombian troops, and finally have the debt approved by a lax or corrupt official.[28] It was also possible to find a general who would certify for bonus purposes that one's nephew had died a colonel rather than a mere captain; this was done by General Mariño for Bolívar's sister, much to the Liberator's annoyance.[29]

One more aggravating factor—and a highly controversial issue in its own right—was the responsibility of the Colombian government for obligations incurred even before the battle of Boyacá and the subsequent act of union passed at Angostura. It was generally accepted that the creditors of the *Patria Boba* and of the provisional governments established on the *llanos* during the Spanish "Pacification" should receive at least something in return for their sacrifices. Yet it was not quite so generally agreed that Caracas should help to pay the debts of Quito and vice versa. Furthermore, the *Patria Boba* and the withdrawal to the *llanos* had been precisely the times when confusion was greatest, and the passage of time and destruction of records now made it all the harder to detect false claims. Much was at stake in the issue, for a single individual might claim that the earlier patriot government of Quito had owed him $80,000.[30] As equity was clearly on the side of the lenders, and Colombia was to be a unitary state, the Congress of Cúcuta declared after some hesitation that in general all "credits contracted by the glorious cause of independence" were to be considered a "sacred obligation" of the national

[27] *Codif. Nac.* I, 74-78, II, 389.
[28] *Codif. Nac.* II, 318-323; A.C., Senado-2, 280-281.
[29] The fraud had been discovered and annulled by the Secretary of War, General Briceño Méndez (Lecuna, *C.L.*, III, 312).
[30] A.C., Cámara-15, 218-219.

treasury.³¹ Even so, this could refer only to debts legitimately contracted, and thus there was still wide disagreement in applying the rule to individual claims. What, for instance, should be done about the experimental paper money issued at Cartagena in 1813? The money had apparently been subject to widespread counterfeiting and speculation, and it was not clear that the issues had been duly guaranteed by the Congress of New Granada. Neither was it entirely clear that such a guarantee was necessary. A religious issue was injected by the fact that the money had been used mainly to pay off ecclesiastical mortgages or *censos*. Thus the clergy had the most to gain if the currency was recognized as a "sacred obligation." The administration wisely referred the whole matter to Congress, which finally decided in favor of recognition.³² However, the obligations of the *Patria Boba* did not in general receive high priority under the new regime, and this particular item was likely to rank among the lowest as far as Santander himself was concerned.

A roughly similar problem was raised in connection with debts left by the former Spanish authorities. There was little thought of redeeming all the debts of the ancient oppressors save conceivably as part of a negotiated peace, and least of all of paying debts for money used in Spain or in fighting against independence. There were other obligations, however, which had been contracted by the Spanish regime for the sake of useful local improvements or the legitimate defense of the colony against foreign enemies. Most of this debt was now owed to persons and corporations of unquestioned patriotism, and other creditors had simply held mortgages on property which was later transferred to the Spanish state for reasons which did not concern them at all. The case for recognition was further strengthened by the fact that Colombia almost invariably sought to collect debts which were owed to rather than by the Spanish crown.³³

The situation was complicated by the fact that so much of the colonial debt took the form of clerical *censos* imposed either on a specific piece of state property or on the general income of a particular treasury. Once again, the sums involved were considerable. Some of the smaller provincial treasuries were burdened with no *censos* whatsoever, and that of Caracas, where clerical holdings were less important than in New Granada, recognized surprisingly little. That of Popayán, on the other hand, owed a principal of $331,796; with interest unpaid since early in the *Patria Boba*, the debt totalled well over half a million by the end of 1825. The

---

³¹ *Codif. Nac.* I, 139.

³² *Actas:* Cámara-1824, 64; *La Gaceta de Colombia,* June 26, 1825; A.C., Senado-38, 114; *Codif. Nac.* II, 389. The decision of Congress was to recognize all *censos* that had been assumed by the state "in the different epochs of the revolution;" and the latter in effect is what had happened at Cartagena.

³³ See in particular *Actas:* Cámara-1824, 196; Jerónimo Torres, *Observaciones sobre la obligación . . . de reconocer los capitales reconocidos a censo en este país por el gobierno antiguo* (Bogotá, 1826); A.H.N., Depto. de Boyacá III, 913-918.

total for the whole republic was at least $1,400,000 and probably more.[34] Much of the principal of this debt had actually been sent to Spain, so that presumably there was no serious question of recognizing the entire sum. Yet the first Colombian authorities were careful not to assume a hard and fast responsibility for any *censos* whatever, even though some of the payments due were actually made. The Congress of Cúcuta made no decision one way or the other, and in the following years payment on a given obligation at a given moment depended primarily upon the current financial situation. At least so the Vice-President informed Congress; in practice, there is some reason to suspect that the character of the individual clergymen with claims upon the colonial *censos* was also taken into account.[35]

There were likewise a few cases in which very substantial Spanish debts were solemnly recognized *in toto* for reasons of political expediency. One aspect of the bloodless revolution effected in Panama was the agreement of the patriot leaders to recognize $656,847 owed by Spain to inhabitants of the Isthmus for back salaries, pensions, loans, and similar items; at least indirectly, and despite all claims to the contrary, much of this debt had helped finance the war against Colombia. It was nevertheless accepted in its entirety as a condition of Panama's incorporation into the republic, and a later attempt in Congress to question its recognition as a dangerously expensive precedent was explicitly rejected.[36] There was still better reason not to recognize the sum of over $100,000 owed to the business community of Guayaquil as the result of a war loan raised by the Spanish regime in 1819; yet all that was owed to patriotic Americans, or roughly half of it, was formally accepted by Bolívar, presumably in an effort to overcome local indifference toward joining Colombia.[37] In due course there appeared a strong campaign to recognize all pre-revolutionary debts provided that *a*) they were owed to Colombian citizens, and *b*) they had not been used solely for the benefit of Spain. This demand was sponsored primarily by the more conservative elements, in part because the interest of the clergy was involved, and no doubt in part because many creole aristocrats, notably in Ecuador, had substantial claims of their own to press. One argument put forward in Congress was that failure to recognize colonial *censos* would be unjust to all the souls in purgatory who had been receiving *sufragios* paid for out of the income

[34] A.H.N., Depto. de Boyacá III, 913-918; A.C., Senado-43, 504, 514-520, 523, 575.

[35] A.H.N., Corresp.-Cámara (Hacienda), January 15, 1825. Cf. payments to Senator Manuel B. Rebollo and Dr. J. N. Azuero, as also to various notables in Venezuela, A.C., Senado-43, 499, 519-523.

[36] *Debates de la Cámara del Senado . . . sobre el reconocimiento del acta de la independencia de Panamá* (Cartagena, 1826); *Codif. Nac.* II, 390; A.C., Actas del Senado, April 12, 1826; A.C., Senado-38, 111.

[37] A.C., Senado-43, 557, 562-570.

they produced. Probably a zeal for abstract justice moved Dr. Félix Restrepo to join in the demand; for reasons that are not entirely clear Castillo y Rada and José Manuel Restrepo joined too. Thus the measure passed the lower house as early as 1824, and it was adopted with suitable qualifications by the Senate two years later. It was vetoed by Santander. He did not flatly oppose the measure, but in view of the nation's financial difficulties he wisely suggested the need for further study, and in the end the payment of interest continued to depend essentially upon the whim of Colombian officials.[38]

However difficult it might be to decide which debts to pay, it was harder still to pay them. Exactly how hard would depend on the net amount involved, but the government itself had only the vaguest notions as to the size of its domestic obligations: Castillo y Rada could not even supply Congress with a comprehensive table of the sums owed to government employees for unpaid back salaries.[39] Moreover, if money were at hand to pay either interest or principal the amount of the debt could always be expected to increase overnight, not only through outright falsification of claims but also because many creditors never took the trouble to press their claims until there was some hope of obtaining payment. There is no doubt, however, that the accumulated debt was a large one. Its highest level was presumably reached at some point in 1824, since the English loan raised in that year actually permitted some net reduction in the internal debt. But even in 1825 the most conservative estimate of that debt seems to have been the figure of $10,000,000 cited by Joaquín Mosquera in the course of a Senate debate on fiscal policy, and this total must be taken as an absolute minimum. In the same year, and again in 1826, Colombian speculators were seriously proposing that the government should raise a new loan in Europe for as much as $20,000,000, primarily for the purpose of retiring the whole remainder of the internal debt. Not all of this amount would have been available for the main objective, but the proposal reflects a definite belief on the part of some that a good bit more than $10,000,000 might be still outstanding. And in 1826, with the English loan largely spent, the domestic debt resumed its former progress upward.[40]

[38] *Acuerdos* II, 148; *Actas:* Senado-1825, 99-101, 134-136; A.C., Actas del Senado, January 3, April 14, 1826; A.C., Senado-6, 96, Senado-13, 168-171, Senado-35, 412, Senado-43, 469-470, 507, 539-547.

[39] A.H.N., Corresp.-Cámara (Hacienda), April 21, 1825; A.C., Senado-38, 112.

[40] *Actas:* Senado-1825, 765. The loan of 1824 and the proposed loan of 1825 are discussed in detail in the following chapter. Although from three to four million pesos of the 1824 loan funds seem to have been used to pay off domestic obligations, it is impossible to say how much of this represents a net reduction; probably most of it, but some additional internal borrowing was still going on as occasion demanded. Neither can one be sure how much of the decline is accounted for in the estimate of $10,000,000.

In order to bolster public confidence in the ultimate payment of this debt, Colombian legislators from the outset had reserved certain classes of national property and revenue specifically for the satisfaction of government creditors. The Congress of Cúcuta decreed that property confiscated from enemies of the republic should be used precisely for the payment of bonuses to the Colombian armed forces. If royalist estates were not enough, vacant lands and other forms of national property could be used for the same purpose.[41] The Congress of 1824 further destined certain minor funds such as the income from government-owned mines to the payment of debts in general. Two years later, in a definitive treatment of the subject, Congress greatly extended the list of revenues and properties reserved for domestic creditors. The tenth part of municipal revenues, the entire proceeds from the sale of stamped paper, and various other classes of income were set aside for the payment of interest exclusively; the principal of all debts, meanwhile, was to be amortized gradually from the mass of national lands and from certain other state properties.[42] As might have been expected, however, this system never worked very well. The revenues earmarked for debt service were not generally the most productive, and there was a strong tendency for hard-pressed officials to make use of them to meet any momentary deficit instead of setting them aside as legally required. Some interest was actually paid from the funds reserved for that purpose by the Congress of 1826, but in the first year, roughly speaking, it was less than a third of the amount legally due. Likewise the military were always slow in receiving payment of their salary and bonus claims, despite the fact that they possessed a theoretical lien on state property; for one thing, they had been granted land-warrants worth more than the available confiscated estates, and they showed little interest in accepting unoccupied public domain instead.[43]

In the last analysis, of course, the national debt was guaranteed by the entire wealth and income of the Colombian state. Thus not only did some creditors receive satisfaction from the proceeds of the English loan,

[41] *Codif. Nac.* I, 74-78. It should be added in this connection that, in certain cases, royalists deported only on suspicion of hostile activities were allowed to retain title to their land in Colombia; but usually royalist exiles, whether voluntary or involuntary, lost all or most of what they owned.

[42] *Codif. Nac.* I, 385-386, II, 391-392. At the same time Congress fixed the interest on debts for military supplies, internal loans, etc. which had been registered with the *Comisión de Liquidación* at 5%; in general they had been receiving this in theory already (cf. *Codif. Nac.* VII, 63-65). The interest on salary debts, which had been drawing no interest at all, on the Panamanian independence debt, and on the debt from redemption of *censos* in the *Patria Boba* was fixed at 3%. It is worth noting that the normal interest on *censos* was 5%.

[43] *La Gaceta de Colombia,* May 13, August 12 and 19, 1827; O'Leary XXVI, 9-11.

but some other debts were actually paid in cash from general treasury funds. In still other cases government obligations were accepted in lieu of taxes or in payment of debts to the state monopolies. The chief example of the latter method was the conversion of miscellaneous debt claims into special drafts or *vales* to be used in payment of duties at the customhouses. But even when *vales* of this sort had been formally issued they would not always be accepted on demand. The customs were the greatest single source of government revenue, so that usually only a fourth of the duties on any shipment could be paid in *vales*. Indeed the intendants still complained that the payment of *vales* ate up all their revenues, and whenever the financial situation was particularly bad payment was suspended altogether; suspensions could not be decreed more frequently simply for fear that merchants would retaliate by stopping the flow of credit. As a result, there were always more customhouse *vales* in existence than could be amortized within a reasonable time, and this naturally meant that they were subject to much speculative depreciation.[44]

The same speculation extended to the land-warrants given to soldiers and veterans and to many other types of obligations. Because of the different classes of certificates involved and the inevitable fluctuations in the government's ability to pay them, their market price varied widely even during the brief period of relative financial ease afforded by the English loan of 1824. Customhouse drafts that were selling for 85% might drop to 30% or less if payment were suddenly interrupted, and there were soldiers who complained that they sold their right to back wages and bonuses for a mere 5% of face value. Speculation was of course a profitable business for some. The merchants engaged in foreign commerce were almost the only ones who could actually use *vales* in payment of import duties, and they extracted every possible advantage from their privileged position when acquiring the *vales* of others. A number of prominent army officers reaped substantial profits both by speculation in the general market and by buying up their own soldiers' land-warrants.[45] But the average creditor was less fortunate. Nor could the government itself find much comfort in the debased market value of its obligations, which all too clearly reflected its own basic insolvency and the lack of public confidence in the promises it made.

[44] *Codif. Nac.* VII, 251-252; A.C., Senado-13, 16, 48, Senado-20, 76-77, 117; A.H.N., Corresp.-Cámara (Hacienda), April 6, 1824; *La Gaceta de Colombia,* March 11, 1827; O'Leary VII, 523. In 1826 Congress destined an eighth of the customs revenues to pay the foreign debt, with the result that Santander reduced the normal amount payable in domestic debt certificates to an eighth also (*Codif. Nac.* II, 390; *La Gaceta de Colombia,* February 4, 1827).

[45] Cf. *El Patriota de Guayaquil,* December 10, 1825; *El Registro* (Bogotá), May 24, 1827; A.C., Senado-17, 170-171.

## The Political Impact of the Financial Crisis

Needless to say, the unbalanced budget made its influence felt far beyond the realm of national credit and other purely fiscal operations. It has already been pointed out that financial difficulties are one reason why the ideal judiciary and bureaucracy which had been created on paper could never be fully established, and that they made it hard to recruit capable civil servants even for the posts that were really filled. They likewise caused the army to feel neglected by the civil authorities, since even its legitimate needs could not always be attended to, and thus helped it to acquire the dangerous habit of looking out for its own interests. For lack of funds the execution of measures for popular education, the manumission of slaves, and many other liberal objectives was always strictly limited. Nor was merit alone sufficient reason to obtain a pension from the Colombian government. Some pensions, both civil and military, were actually paid, but countless other claims were put off on the pretext that no general law on the subject had yet been passed; and no serious effort was made to pass one because it was obvious that there would be no money to pay the pensions in any case. Hence even the most deserving war widows usually remained pensionless unless supported by a private grant from the salaries of Bolívar or Santander.[46]

Scarcely less unfortunate was the fact that fiscal policy and administration became, as a result of the deficit, a burning political issue. For the average citizen was inclined to forget that wars and basic republican institutions were necessarily expensive. During the colonial period the Spanish authorities had collected their taxes, met a full payroll, and generally paid their operating expenses in cash. The situation was now radically altered; and the more conservative Colombians, together with many liberals who were personally disaffected toward the administration, came easily to the conclusion that the regime itself was somehow to blame.

The liberals' tax reforms were probably subject to the most vigorous attack of all. It was widely alleged that colonial taxation had been both more productive and less oppressive than that of the republic. As a general proposition this was quite untrue, but it was widely believed just the same. As Bolívar himself put it, "the old taxes had the advantage of being habitual and therefore were considered mild." [47] They were especially mild when levied on someone else, so that the fiscal panacea proposed by the white aristocracy of Ecuador was naturally the restoration of the Indian tribute. Even Nariño's faction at Bogotá proposed restoration of the tribute, arguing that the Indians should be glad to pay for the special benefits they allegedly derived from independence—and over-

[46] O'Leary XVIII, 279; *La Gaceta de Colombia*, April 13, 1823; A.C., Cámara-3, 199, 242-248, 265-268, 330.
[47] *La Gaceta de Colombia*, December 17, 1826.

looking the fact that abolition of the tribute had been offset, at least in some small part, by the imposition of regular taxes on the Indians.[48] Another favorite target was the new system of *aguardiente* taxes. The pro-Nariño *Insurgente* correctly pointed out that the extinct monopoly had produced far more revenue, and that the new taxes had frequently bogged down in hateful regulations and red-tape. Similar charges were aired in Congress and in the *juntas provinciales,* while it was conveniently forgotten that other revenues such as the customs had more than made up for the net loss from *aguardiente.* However, there was no universal demand to restore the monopoly. Too many independent businessmen had entered the field for full state control to be restored without trampling on important private interests; thus many critics proposed only a modification of the new system.[49]

Traditionalists reserved their chief energies for what was in many ways the worst of their various causes. The *alcabala* had not been "mild," and it was less productive than its supporters claimed, but its restoration was at the heart of the conservative financial program. This was coupled with a demand to abolish its official substitute, the *contribución directa,* which was portrayed with some exaggeration as a financial inquisition, an obstacle to sound business, and a total failure as a source of revenue. It was even claimed that direct taxes were a particular hardship on the poor, although the only reasons given for this statement were that the poor could not cheat as easily as the rich, that merchants would just pass the tax on to consumers, and that the *contribución directa* failed to make exceptions in favor of property that earned less than the average return.[50] The last argument alone was entirely relevant, but it was ultimately taken care of by Congress, and the poor usually had no taxable property in the first place. The fact of the matter was, of course, that the *contribución directa* had been a bold attempt to tax those who were best able to pay, while the *alcabala,* like any sales-tax, always bore hardest on the poor. Hence government spokesmen were not far from the truth when they charged that opposition to the *contribución directa* came essentially from wealthy landowners, clergy, and similar groups that had been relatively little harmed by the *alcabala* but were now ordered to pay a fixed percentage of their capital and/or income into the national treasury. Even

[48] *La Gaceta de Colombia,* December 18, 1825; *El Insurgente* (Bogotá), November 15, 1822.

[49] *El Insurgente,* October 5 and 15, 1822; *La Gaceta de Colombia,* January 22, 1826; *El Observador Caraqueño,* February 26, 1824; A.C., Senado-13, 103, Cámara-3, 233; A.H.N., Congresos XXVII, 469-471.

[50] *El Insurgente,* November 8, 1822; *El Observador Caraqueño,* April 15, 1824; *El Patriota de Guayaquil,* Semestre 11, Nos. 4 and 11; *El Noticiosote* (Bogotá), March 25, 1825; *El Chasqui Bogotano,* November 12, 1826; *El Censor* (Bogotá), November 23, 1826.

General Juan José Flores, who was no liberal zealot, asserted that only selfish property-owners wanted the tax abolished outright.[51]

Selfish or not, the opposition was strong enough for Santander to toy repeatedly with the idea of suspending the new tax. He once suggested that it should at least be given a new name—with the part paid by the clergy entitled a *don gratuito* or something of the sort—and he obligingly decreed that it might be paid in depreciated government obligations or even in the form of army rations.[52] In three successive years there was a strong movement in Congress, centering in the *Montaña* of the lower house, to abolish the *contribución directa* entirely and restore the *alcabala* in its place. Each time, however, the move was defeated, because the much-berated direct taxation had its defenders as well. Doctrinaire liberals were consistently fond of it, and it was supported also by some of the richest and most active merchants of New Granada, including Cartagena's Juan de Francisco Martín, who was a leading opponent of the Santander administration. Nor was this wholly surprising, for an enlightened businessman could hardly fail to see that in the long run the *alcabala* would be even worse.[53] Above all, the government remained formally committed to the principle of direct taxation, despite its occasional relaxation of the measure in practice. Castillo y Rada felt that the abolition of the *contribución directa* in order to make way for a revived *alcabala* would be "an offense to the lights of our time, a false step, a detour from the sea which the republic had so majestically entered upon, a shameful retrogression. . . ."[54] This same statement he applied to all the other conservative demands for revision of the tax structure, and as long as Santander remained in command no "shameful retrogression" was made.

Criticism was directed not only against new forms of taxation but also against the swollen republican bureaucracy, which was repeatedly contrasted with the alleged austerity of the colonial regime. According to a manifesto from the town fathers of Barichara it was sprawling and inefficient bureaucracy and not the war that caused the government's financial plight. Everywhere new officials such as the *jueces letrados* were assailed as useless parasites who drew heavy salaries and yet oppressed the citizenry by exacting fees. Such arguments were not wholly objective when they

---

[51] *La Gaceta de Colombia,* April 3, 1825; A.C., Miscelánea 1824-9 bis, 47-48; *El Constitucional de Boyacá* (Tunja), December 2, 1825 (reprinted in *La Gaceta del Istmo de Panamá,* January 22, 1826); Flores to Bolívar, October 29, 1826, O'Leary IV, 12-13.

[52] *Actas:* Cámara-1824, 297, 302; *Acuerdos* II, 141; A.C., Senado-13, 138; *La Gaceta de Colombia,* November 21, 1824 and February 25, 1827. The tax actually was suspended by Congress in 1823 for the duration of the *subsidio* of that year.

[53] *Actas:* Congreso-1823, 526-528; *Actas:* Cámara-1825, 150, 187, 191-192, 216, 237, 255, 264; A.C., Senado-33, 264-266.

[54] *El Constitucional,* March 2, 1826.

came, as they frequently did, from municipal dignitaries who had lost some of their functions to newly-created national officials, and they overlooked the fact that the bureaucracy never sprawled as far in practice as it did on paper. But they were echoed by many conservatives, in due course by Bolívar himself.[55] And they did contain at least a grain of truth.

The brunt of the attack fell upon all those who had anything to do with the collection and administration of revenue, from the lowliest tax-collector to the Secretary of Finance and the Vice-President himself. Many of these officials were assumed to be superfluous, and the others obviously were not doing a very good job: there was the deficit, once again, to prove it. The political effectiveness of such attacks can be clearly seen from the eagerness with which Castillo y Rada and Santander attempted to make Congress take its full share of the blame. In fact finances were beyond a doubt the one subject that most often strained the generally cooperative relationship between the administration and Congress. Santander correctly pointed out in this connection as in so many others that with the republican separation of powers the executive branch could no longer be expected to do everything by itself; hence one of his self-righteous retorts to criticism was that the laws Congress passed were inadequate to create and administer the required amount of revenue. Even when Congress did act, complained the *Gaceta,* it often did nothing but grant the Executive discretionary power to raise funds or to reform fiscal agencies, without making a single practical suggestion and without agreeing to share the responsibility for success or failure.[56]

It is no doubt true that the general inexperience of Colombian Congressmen, like the scarcity of capable civil servants, was an especially serious handicap whenever the task at hand concerned financial statistics, credit manipulations, and all the technical details of revenue and expenditures. The regularity with which "definitive" enactments on one financial problem after another were found wanting and had to be replaced in whole or in part is proof that Colombia's fiscal legislation was far from perfect. Congress, however, sought to shift responsibility back onto the Executive by charging that the administration never supplied it with all the detailed information which it requested and which was necessary as a basis for drawing up more successful revenue laws. This charge, too, was perfectly accurate—and Castillo y Rada was among the first to admit it. But he hastened to explain that he could do no better because he himself worked "without known data, in isolation, and as circumstances de-

[55] Cf. A.H.N., Congresos XXV, 686, 863-873 and XXVII, 111-117; *El Noticiosote,* April 24, 1825. Bolívar's opinion is given in *La Gaceta de Colombia,* December 17, 1826.

[56] *La Gaceta de Colombia,* July 17, 1825. Cf. O'Leary XX, 220-222.

manded;" [57] and this in turn was mainly because subordinate officials in the provinces could never be relied upon to submit full and punctual accounts to Bogotá as legally provided.

The Chamber of Representatives was always much more insistent on the question of responsibility than was the Senate, since it was in the former that money bills had to originate, and the Senate was in any case more friendly to Santander. Indeed the Senate always was careful to fasten Congress' share of the blame for whatever ailed Colombian finances on the lower house primarily. But in reality, of course, all attempts to foist the blame on any one group or person served only to obscure the fundamental causes of the financial crisis. And the fact that everyone joined so eagerly in the quest for a scapegoat shows merely how the underlying condition of insolvency had frayed tempers on every side.

[57] *La Gaceta de Colombia,* May 22, 1825.

## Chapter VIII

# The Foreign Debt As a Fiscal Expedient and Political Issue

THE operating deficit, the depreciation of *vales*, and all related ingredients of the financial crisis quite naturally suggested to Colombian statesmen the possibility of foreign credit as a solution to their difficulties. In its origin, to be sure, the foreign debt was as haphazardly incurred as the domestic. Indeed at times the two tended to overlap, since the leading suppliers of arms and ammunition whose claims were included in the "internal" debt had always been foreigners by nationality.[1] Yet even when his account was listed with the domestic debt a foreigner was accorded special treatment so as to uphold the patriots' reputation abroad. Furthermore, ever since the start of the Revolution the provisional authorities of Venezuela and New Granada had been sending agents to Europe to obtain military supplies and enlist foreign legionnaires. Other patriots residing abroad sometimes assumed the same role with or without legal authority, and either way the result was a mass of debts which were often contracted without due formalities and irregularly spent. Nor was it long before English investors learned from bitter experience that they had little chance of being paid whether their claims were legitimate or not.

### Negotiations in London 1820-1824

In order to remedy this situation and so to clear the way for obtaining still further assistance Bolívar gave plenary powers as financial and diplomatic agent in Europe late in 1819 to Francisco Antonio Zea, the first Vice-President of Colombia. Zea emphasized the prestige of his office by living on a lavish scale in London, and his work was made easier by military successes at home. Even so, he found that the first step toward a restoration of Colombian credit would have to be a formal agreement with the disgruntled creditors of earlier patriot agents, and rather than waste his time in haggling he indiscriminately accepted their claims to the amount of over £500,000. This represented both miscellaneous debts incurred in Great Britain and a certain amount of war supplies delivered

---

[1] The Law of Public Credit of May 22, 1826, defined the "foreign debt," strictly speaking, as consisting of formal loans contracted abroad (*Codif. Nac.* II, 389-390). If an individual merchant or contractor with bills to collect happened to be a foreigner he was listed as such by the *Comisión de Liquidación*, but his claims were included in the "domestic" debt.

but not paid for in cash in Guayana. Zea accepted terms that were undignified to say the least: three members of an official debt commission in Bogotá were to be appointed by the foreign creditors and interest was to be 10% a year, or 12% if paid in Colombia. However, Zea was then able to obtain a new loan for £140,000 from the relatively small firm of Herring, Graham, and Powles, who were the principal creditors from his first transaction, and with this sum he actually began to make interest payments. And he floated still another loan at two-thirds discount in order to have £20,000 for his expenses on an unsuccessful peace mission to Spain.[2]

In the spring of 1822, finally, Zea raised Colombia's first major foreign loan for the sum of £2,000,000, again from Herring, Graham, and Powles. The loan was made at a discount of only 20%, which was not really excessive, but much of it was paid in the obligations which Zea had issued earlier, and which had frequently been bought up at a fraction of their face value by the lending firm. There were also sums retained in London for future interest, commissions, and so forth, so that only a third of the loan was to be paid in cash; and not all of that was actually delivered.[3] Nor did Zea's operations put an end to those of other self-styled Colombian agents. In particular Don Luis López Méndez, whose credentials from the former Venezuelan Republic had expired, sought both to undermine Zea's transactions and to carry out others on his own initiative. Unlike Zea, he was personally far from extravagant, but he created countless difficulties for Colombian financiers by freely granting contracts and issuing debentures on the most onerous terms, both for military supplies and for the recruiting of unwanted and over-ambitious expeditionary legions.[4]

All these happenings aroused great displeasure in Colombia, especially since the first news of Zea's operations usually reached Bogotá by means of the press rather than through his own dispatches. Almost as soon as the home government heard of his first arrangements with English creditors it began to think of recalling him; in the end even his original spon-

[2] Pedro A. Zubieta, *Apuntaciones sobre las primeras misiones diplomáticas de Colombia* (Bogotá, 1924), 276, 285-287, 314-317; Harold A. Bierck, *Vida pública de Don Pedro Gual* (Caracas, 1947), 236; Pedro Ignacio Cadena, *Anales diplomáticos de Colombia* (Bogotá, 1878), 82-84, 453-456.

[3] Zubieta, *op. cit.,* 328, 375-379.

[4] O'Leary XVIII, 203-204; Zubieta, *op. cit.,* 284-285, 299-302; Cadena, *op. cit.,* 63-78, 87; Raimundo Rivas, *Escritos de don Pedro Fernández Madrid* (Bogotá, 1932), 332-333. Cadena, who seemingly accepts Méndez' sincerity, describes him as a radical democrat; it is worth taking note that in 1827 he was a leader in the invasion of Ecuador undertaken by mutinous Colombian troops in opposition to the rule of Bolívar.

sor, Bolívar, was calling him "Colombia's greatest calamity."[5] For reasons hard to explain—perhaps because his own reports were so slow in arriving—he was not definitely notified that his financial powers had lapsed until October of 1821. By that time the Constitution of Cúcuta had reserved to Congress the final authority to make foreign loans, and the new central administration headed by Santander chose to retain Zea as its political representative only. Yet the change was not published in Europe, so that he was free to continue his money-raising operations in the apparent belief that his government did not really mean what it said. Only after Zea had obtained his last and greatest loan for £2,000,000 was his reduced status made clear to all, and it was still later—on the very eve of his death—that he was actually recalled from Europe. On the other hand, as Zea had personally exceeded his faculties, the government refused to assume responsibility for the £2,000,000; and it was even less willing to recognize the latest debts incurred by López Méndez, who had been ordered home as early as November, 1820.[6]

It could not be denied, however, that foreign credit was still badly needed: the methods of Zea and López Méndez, not their basic objectives, had earned the condemnation of Bogotá. Once a conservative economy bloc had been overruled, therefore, Congress solemnly promised to make payment for all money and materials which had actually been received under the terms of Zea's various transactions. It was assumed that Colombia would probably be forced to recognize a somewhat larger indebtedness than justice required, but this was deemed a necessary sacrifice if the republic hoped to obtain more loans in the future. Ultimately a similar policy was adopted in favor of the creditors of López Méndez.[7] It is perhaps significant, moreover, that General Carlos Soublette as *Jefe Superior* of Venezuela issued drafts against the repudiated Zea loan without being rebuked from Bogotá.[8]

In fact even while Zea was carrying on in Europe, the authorities in Colombia had become engaged in negotiations of their own for foreign credit. Dr. Justus Erich Bollman, "an adventurer par excellence" in the opinion of Bierck, had come to Colombia originally during the Congress of Cúcuta in order to inspect platinum mines for the London investment firm of Baring Brothers, but while he was there he also agreed on the terms of a loan for $2,000,000 in cash and war materials to be guaranteed by the salt works of Zipaquirá. As it turned out, Bollman died before

[5] Bolívar to Santander, January 14, 1823, Lecuna, *C.L.* III, 135; see also O'Leary XVIII, 203-204, 482, and Bierck, *op. cit.*, 237.

[6] Zubieta, *op. cit.*, 330-331; *Codif. Nac.* I, 203-205, 259-260; Blanco VIII, 562; *Acuerdos* I, 71, 92-93.

[7] *Acuerdos* II, 55; O'Leary VIII, 377, XVIII, 203-204; *Codif. Nac.* I, 203-205; A.C., Senado-15, 497; Senado-25, 192; Senado-53, 100.

[8] A.C., Senado-26, 15-16; Zubieta, *op. cit.*, 397.

returning to London to have the agreement ratified by his employers,[9] and the loan consequently failed to materialize. Numerous other projects for foreign loans were suggested to the government at Bogotá from time to time; at one point a group of merchants almost succeeded in raising a loan for Colombia in the United States, only to meet with failure because of the doubtful treatment accorded the 1822 loan. Ultimately Santander decided, in spite of his experience with Zea, that it would be best to send a new financial mission to negotiate directly in London. For this purpose he obtained from the Congress of 1823 a special authorization to borrow as much as $30,000,000 in Europe. If this remarkable sum could be obtained, it was thought, pre-existing foreign debts could be consolidated, the internal deficit overcome, and economic development speeded through the injection of foreign capital.[10]

Santander reasoned that it would be well to keep the raising of new funds technically separate from the final settlement of old business, which meant principally reaching an agreement with Zea's creditors. He therefore commissioned his two good friends, Manuel Antonio Arrubla and Francisco Montoya, who wanted to go to London anyway on their own business, to obtain the former; the settlement of Zea's affairs was reserved for Colombia's first fully-accredited Minister to London, Manuel José Hurtado. In the end Hurtado was able to fulfill his part of the project only by accepting virtually all the transactions Zea had made from the time he reached England; the one real concession he obtained was the promise of Herring, Graham and Powles to deliver the funds they still owed from the loan of 1822. This agreement used up one-third of the $30,000,000 that Santander had been authorized to borrow, but at least it restored Colombia's reputation in London financial circles. Coming at the same time as favorable news from the war fronts, it enabled Arrubla and Montoya to obtain £4,750,000 ($20,000,000) in April, 1824, from the highly respectable firm of Goldschmidt and Company. The loan was made at the unprecedented discount of only 15%, the interest was 6%, and in general its terms were far less objectionable than those usually obtained by Zea.[11]

[9] Bierck, *op. cit.*, 239-240; Zubieta, *op. cit.*, 381. This proposal has usually been stated in pounds rather than in pesos, but A.H.N., Corresp.-Cámara (Hacienda), April 19, 1823, makes it clear that the transaction was made under the decree of the Constituent Congress (*Codif. Nac.* I, 124) which provided for foreign borrowing up to a maximum of 3,000,000 pesos. It is worth adding that Bollman's mission was originally suggested by Zea.

[10] A.H.N., Corresp.-Cámara (Hacienda), April 19, 1823, January 15, 1825; *Codif. Nac.* I, 206-207; Francisco de Paula Santander, *El Vicepresidente de Colombia da cuenta a la república de su conducta* (Bogotá, 1828), 17.

[11] Santander, *op. cit.*, 17; *Exposición del Poder Ejecutivo al Congreso de 1825 sobre la negociación del empréstito* (Bogotá, 1825); Manuel José Hurtado, *Manifestación sobre su manejo en el empréstito de 1824* (Panamá, 1828), doc. P; A.C., Senado-43, 465-466.

### Repercussions of the 1824 Loan

The loan nevertheless aroused wide opposition in Colombia, both from those who sincerely disapproved of its terms and from oppositionists who found it expedient to lay charges of any sort against the Santander administration. There was no question of denying ratification to the loan itself when it was submitted to Congress, but several of its terms were severely criticized, and the legislators flatly refused to accept the supplementary articles making Goldschmidt the republic's commercial agent in Great Britain and guaranteeing the firm a right of preference whenever a new English loan might be contracted. A qualified approval, replied Santander, would ruin the nation's foreign credit, and he promptly announced that he had been mistaken in asking Congress to ratify the loan agreement in the first place: the original authorization for raising a loan he now construed as broad enough to cover whatever arrangements were entered into. To make this thesis more palatable, Santander pointed out that the commercial agency clause could be interpreted as referring only to government purchases and not to consular business, and that the requirement to prefer Goldschmidt as agent for a new loan could be evaded by allowing them to raise a loan of £100 and then contracting a real loan with someone else, or by simply signing any loan contract in Calais. But such arguments did not satisfy Congress, where clerical conservatives, Venezuelan separatists, and even many administration supporters joined forces to pass the decree of qualified ratification over an executive veto.[12]

Goldschmidt promptly charged that Colombia had not kept faith with her agreements and threatened to declare the entire transaction null and void. This was no empty threat, as the lending firm still possessed a part of the loan funds at the time; hence in 1826 Congress meekly instructed the Executive to "conciliate the interests" of both parties by further discussion.[13] But unfortunately it was also revealed in the course of the debate that at least one other firm whose qualifications were beyond dispute had offered to contract the loan at a slightly more favorable discount than Goldschmidt. According to the testimony of the Venezuelan statesman José Rafael Revenga, who had been in London at the time and was now serving as Foreign Secretary in Santander's cabinet, the offer had been entirely feasible. It was perhaps odd that in spite of this Revenga had submitted a generally favorable report on the loan when first contracted.[14]

[12] *Codif. Nac.* II, 116-117; *Exposición que . . . hace la Comisión de Hacienda sobre el empréstito colombiano de 1824* (Bogotá, 1825); A.H.N., Corresp-Cámara (Hacienda) April 2 and 22, 1825; *Actas:* Cámara-1825, 231, 240, 301, 318-319; *El Noticiosote* (Bogotá), April 21 through 28, 1825.
[13] A.C., Senado-48, 150-151; *Codif. Nac.* II, 346-347.
[14] A.H.N., Corresp.-Cámara (Hacienda), February 10, 1825. Revenga later wrote to Bolívar that the negotiators had done the best they knew, but that the loan should still have been obtained on slightly better terms (Letter of May 5, 1825, O'Leary VI, 494).

However, the real question was simply whether the Colombian agents had received news of the second offer in unequivocal form before the deadline they had set for reaching a settlement, and whether or not it was accompanied by other conditions that either were unacceptable in themselves or served to offset the more favorable discount.[15] Neither of these points could really be cleared up, since Revenga's charges were based not on documentary proof but solely on his personal interpretation of what the rival investment firm had meant by its offer.

In all probability both Arrubla and Montoya in 1824 and Revenga in 1826 were acting in good faith. In the end, Congress rejected the latter's charges and the administration as a whole firmly identified itself with the negotiators in opposition to Revenga.[16] But in practice the fine points of the dispute made no difference, since most parties to the debate understood little or nothing of international high finance. The main thing was that a respected member of Santander's cabinet had seemingly accused his administration of betraying the nation's interests, and had thus confirmed by implication all that the opposition in Congress and the press had been saying from the start. The agency clauses and the discount rate, moreover, did not exhaust the opposition charges. The government was accused of incompetence at the very least in allowing interest to run from a conventional date which was actually earlier than the date the contract was signed, and in allowing interest on the entire loan before the last installments had been delivered. It was accused of much worse in granting 1% commissions both to Hurtado and to Arrubla and Montoya, although neither the commissions nor the interest arrangements lacked precedents in the dealings of other countries. Much was said and more was suggested, finally, concerning the rapidity with which the $30,000,000 decreed by Congress was used up by the administration.

Such charges as these became the principal stock in trade of *La Gaceta de Cartagena*, which was then under the direction of Juan Bautista Calcaño, a Venezuelan agitator who was also a friend of the *Comandante General* of Magdalena, Mariano Montilla. Calcaño hinted that he possessed secret sources of information about the loan, and the ill-tempered replies of the official *Gaceta de Colombia* simply gave his paper a notoriety which it otherwise could not have attained.[17] Calcaño's viewpoint was

[15] Francisco Montoya and Manuel Antonio Arrubla, *Nuevos documentos relativos a la conducta de los comisionados por el gobierno para negociar en Londres el Empréstito de 1824* (Bogotá, 1826), 101-147; A.H.N., Congresos VII, 813.
[16] Montoya and Arrubla, *Nuevos documentos*, 150; A.H.N., Congresos VII, 813.
[17] Some of the replies were composed by Santander himself; cf. Blanco IX, 722. Probably Representative Juan de Francisco Martín had a hand in writing *La Gaceta de Cartagena*'s disquisitions on the loan, but the viewpoint of the paper is most conveniently summarized in Calcaño's own *Análisis de la negociación del empréstito de 1824* (Cartagena, 1825).

ably expressed in Congress by Juan de Francisco Martín, a wealthy Cartagena merchant who earlier had supported most administration projects. (De Francisco now found charges of misappropriating confiscated property suddenly and vigorously pressed against him both in the courts and in *La Gaceta de Colombia*.[18]) All attacks on the loan were eagerly repeated by the dissident factions of Venezuela, while the Caracas priest José Antonio Pérez seconded the tirades of Señor de Francisco in the Chamber of Representatives. In Cundinamarca most good liberals rallied to the administration's support, but the strongly liberal and ultra-respectable *Constitucional,* which itself reflected British interests, agreed that the negotiations had been mismanaged. Enough had been said, in any case, to arouse a strong undercurrent of popular skepticism regarding the government's financial practices. The loan issue did not prevent Santander's ultimate reelection, although it certainly reduced his margin of victory; and it weakened faith in the administration at precisely the time when other aspects of its program were coming under increasing attack and revolution was preparing in Venezuela.[19]

## *The Use of the 1824 Loan*

There is one aspect of the loan debate that deserves closer study not only because of its political significance but because of its importance for the Colombian economy. This is the use of the loan funds: or, as the opposition put it, the "disappearance" of $30,000,000, presumably into the hands of administration leaders. As even the British Minister accepted charges of Santander's personal mishandling of the loan,[20] the matter clearly bears investigation. And the first thing to note is the fact, constantly emphasized in the *Gaceta,* that the 1824 loan was really for $20,000,000 and not $30,000,000, since one third of the latter sum had been applied to the refunding of Zea's obligations. Then there were the sums subtracted for rate of discount, two years' advance payment of interest, commissions, and so forth, which further reduced the amount actually received by Colombia until it was only about half of what Con-

[18] *La Gaceta de Colombia,* July 2, 1826.

[19] For samples of the loan discussion see *El Constitucional* (Bogotá), March 17 and August 4, 1825, May 4, 1826; *La Gaceta de Cartagena,* May 7 and 14, 1826; *El Noticiosote* (Bogotá), April 21 through 28, 1825; *El Chasqui Bogotano,* Nos. 3 and 9 (1826). The last two papers were both issued by Dr. J. F. Merizalde, Bogotá's first yellow journalist, and a man usually close to popular feeling. His strictures on the loan are significant even though in line with his own prejudices he sought to lay most of the blame on Congress.

[20] Hildegarde Angell, *Simón Bolívar* (New York, 1930), 240. Angell, though inclined to agree, points out that the diplomatic colony was generally prejudiced against Santander because of his stingy entertaining.

gress had decreed.²¹ Of the part that Colombia did not actually receive, all went to English brokers and investors except for the commissions paid to Hurtado, Arrubla, and Montoya. Hurtado's, to be sure, was certainly too high, since it was based not only on his own settlement of the 1822 Zea loan but on the loan acquired by Arrubla and Montoya; yet it was arranged without the prior consent of the administration, and it drew an official protest from Bogotá. Arrubla and Montoya were not so extravagantly paid even though they, unlike Hurtado, were close friends of Santander. Together they received only 1% of the loan they personally obtained for Colombia, and this commission had to cover all of their far from negligible expenses from the day they left Bogotá.²²

As for the money that was duly received by the Colombian government, Congress had decreed that it be used, in a rough order of preference, for the payment of "domestic" debts owed to individuals of foreign nationality; for the payment of interest on the foreign debt; for the development of such national revenues as the tobacco monopoly and the mints; for the costs of the war with Spain—including payment of internal loans and supply debts already incurred for the same purpose; for diplomatic salaries abroad; for the payment of certain salary debts to government employees; and for the payment of interest on the registered domestic debt. As an afterthought it was decided later to use up to $1,000,000 of the loan funds in order to revive Colombian agriculture through a program of loans to deserving farmers.²³ Unfortunately, it is seldom easy to determine exactly how much was spent for any of these purposes. Castillo y Rada loyally published the *Cuentas del empréstito* in 1826, but some of his broader classifications, such as £893,508 remitted in money and materials by Colombia's agent in London, and £162,765 changed into pesos by a Jamaica merchant, do not explain precisely what the money was used for. Probably Castillo himself did not always know, since local officials never sent him their full accounts, and there is no reason to assume that he was willfully suppressing information. He frankly admitted that some funds had been "borrowed" for purposes not authorized by Congress, including, among other things, the salaries of its members. He also revealed that $715,000 had been forwarded to the tobacco monopoly and the mints as capital in order to "foment the

---

²¹ The supplies, cash, and credits listed by Castillo y Rada as actually received after deducting the cost of the loan itself totalled £3,622,745 out of £6,750,000 face value. The former figure apparently includes the liquid settlement of the previously unpaid portion of the 1822 loan. See Castillo y Rada, *Cuentas del empréstito del año de 1824* (Bogotá, 1826).

²² Santander, *op. cit.*, 36; Castillo y Rada, *op. cit.*, A; A.H.N., Corresp.-Cámara (Hacienda), January 15, 1825. To be exact, Arrubla and Montoya received £20,137 apiece, which Santander termed "a miserable sum," and Hurtado somewhat over £53,000.

²³ *Codif. Nac.* I, 206-207, 294, 296-297, 391; II, 100-101.

national revenues." As for fomenting agriculture, $320,000 was actually set aside for farm loans; and it is worth noting that virtually all of this sum and most of the tobacco fund as well was sent to Venezuela, whose inhabitants nevertheless complained that they did not receive all they deserved from the loan.[24]

A much greater part of the loan was used for current military expenses. Even before news of its signing reached Bogotá, Santander had been pledging the loan funds in payment of naval contracts, and Congress had hopefully authorized the Executive to issue advance drafts against them in order to pay for sending reinforcements to Bolívar in Peru. Nearly £200,000 was subsequently used to pay these drafts, and on another occasion the Department of Venezuela was specially authorized to draw £62,500 more for defense costs. Additional funds were used to buy war materials directly in Great Britain, and to pay for acquisitions by the Colombian purchasing agent in the United States.[25] In all likelihood much of the money thus used for military expenses was actually misspent. However, there is no proof that illegal profits reached administration leaders in Bogotá, and probably most of any illicit gains that were made went to high-priced foreign suppliers.

It was only when it came to paying off back debts of the Colombian government that any Colombian with business initiative had a chance to derive personal advantage from the loan, and a great many of them actually did. Castillo y Rada included in the *Cuentas del empréstito* a list of foreign and domestic creditors who as a result of the loan had been given sterling drafts in payment of claims amounting to nearly £600,000. This did not include £21,700 taken personally by Arrubla and Montoya in London in return for advances they had made the government in 1823. Subsequently *La Gaceta de Colombia* published lists indicating that about $750,000 in miscellaneous internal debts had been paid from the loan funds at the treasuries of Bogotá, Maracaibo, and Cartagena, apparently using sums not accounted for in detail in the *Cuentas del empréstito*.[26]

[24] Castillo y Rada, *op. cit.*, C, D.; *Documentos que el Poder Ejecutivo de Colombia presenta . . . en negocios conexionados con el empréstito de 1824* (Bogotá, 1826), 15-17. For a typical Venezuelan complaint see *El Argos*, No. 11, cited in *El Constitucional*, September 22, 1825. It would of course be hazardous to assume that all the money forwarded to the provinces for a certain purpose was actually spent as directed. See, e.g., report of General Bermúdez, December 1, 1825, in Biblioteca Nacional (Bogotá), Sala 1, Vol. 12,104, No. 31.

[25] Castillo y Rada, *op. cit.*; A.C., Senado-26, 5, 11, 13; *Codif. Nac.* I, 294, VII, 202-203.

[26] Castillo y Rada, *op. cit.*; *La Gaceta de Colombia*, February 11 through May 13, 1827, passim; Hurtado, *Manifestación*, Doc. P.

The tables in the *Gaceta* included all payments made in pesos from the loan funds at the treasuries in question, and it is not always clear whether a particular listing represents the payment of back debts, current military expenditures or something else again; hence the figure given cannot be regarded as anything but a very rough approximation. It is, however, a distinctly conservative estimate.

Nor do the published lists exclude the possibility—better still, the likelihood—that still other debts were paid one way or another with money ultimately derived from the English loan. In any case, there was much talk of speculative profits and outright fraud in connection with the payments made to Colombian creditors, and there is little reason to doubt that the charges had some basis in fact.

Even so, it does not follow that Santander and his ministers were personally robbing the treasury. It was well known that many government obligations had originally been issued far in excess of the goods and services actually received, and it would be surprising indeed if none of the debts that were paid with the proceeds of the English loan fell into this category; but such obligations may still have been issued in good faith on the part of the responsible official, and even if they had not been, it was far from easy to detect the fraud when final payments were authorized in Bogotá. It was likewise true that many valid obligations had been bought up by speculators for a fraction of their value, but as this was not usually illegal the government cannot automatically be blamed for making payment. Then, too, it is wholly conceivable that favoritism was sometimes shown in deciding which debts to pay and which not to pay, but this would be hard to prove objectively, and need not have been strictly illegal so long as the debts belonged to the general categories approved for payment by Congress.[27] Certainly there was no systematic discrimination, for all varieties of Colombians received some benefit.

Satisfied creditors ranged all the way from the "Colombian Cato," Dr. Félix Restrepo, to the arch-critic of the loan, Juan de Francisco Martín. De Francisco also made full use—to the extent of at least $120,000—of the arrangement whereby anyone could convert pesos into pounds for commercial transactions by purchasing sterling drafts against the loan funds; and neither De Francisco nor the house of Arrubla had to pay the full amount in pesos on first obtaining such drafts in Colombia. Other prominent figures, notably the President of the Senate Luis Andrés Baralt, acted as brokers for friends and neighbors at home in obtaining settlement of their claims at Bogotá. Once again it must be noted that Venezuela was not forgotten: individual *caraqueños* do not figure prominently in the public tables of satisfied creditors, but the businessmen of Maracaibo are there in force, and the *caraqueños* finally obtained payment of Soublette's drafts on the Zea loan of 1822.[28] The class of army

[27] The basic legal requirement was to prefer debts which had been a) incurred for war purposes and b) certified by the *Comisión de liquidación* — particularly if such debts were owed to foreigners — over debts for back salaries incurred under the regular discount system adopted at Cúcuta. Other salary claims, including military bonuses, apparently were not to be paid from the loan (*Codif. Nac.* I, 296-297).

[28] Castillo y Rada, *op. cit.,* B, D, F; A.H.N., Departamento de Venezuela VI, 720-721.

officers was not neglected either. General Urdaneta, for instance, was reimbursed for certificates which had originally been issued for supplies taken by his own armies and had now been endorsed in his favor.[29] The chief spokesmen of Santander's own party, on the other hand, were less prominently favored. The published lists included only $3000 for Vicente Azuero, and nothing for Francisco Soto. Neither did the Vice-President's name appear, and the only member of his cabinet to be listed was the *antioqueño* businessman José Manuel Restrepo, who cashed an unspecified "document of credit" worth £350 and obtained $9000 for a house that he sold to the state.[30]

To be sure, nothing of what has just been said excludes the possibility of secret "kick-backs" from interested creditors, improper payments received under the name of third parties, or any similar corrupt practices on the part of members of the administration. But it is at least significant that no concrete evidence of such irregularities has ever been produced. Very seldom have charges of corruption even gone so far as to mention specific names, and the one figure who is cited most often as having been party to some irregular transaction with Santander is José Antonio Marcos, a conservative congressman from Guayaquil who was scarcely close to the Vice-President.[31] It is of course possible that the administration was seeking to buy Marcos' support through improper payments from the loan funds, but it is also possible that officials in Bogotá were unwittingly deceived by him, or even that Marcos was entirely innocent. Certainly there is no compelling proof one way or the other. In fact the critics of the administration would have been on firmer ground if instead of implying the existence of flagrant corruption among the Vice-President's inner circle they had simply pointed out that the government was frankly neglecting some of the other objectives of the loan in favor of retiring as much as possible of the internal debt. In practice it never spent all the money legally appropriated for such purposes as "fomenting" agriculture and the national revenues, and in the end it preferred paying domestic creditors even to meeting its foreign obligations, which ranked much higher under the appropriation decree of Congress.[32]

[29] Cf. *La Gaceta de Colombia,* February 11, 1827, and other lists cited above.

[30] Payment of the last item would have been illegal if regarded as payment of a debt, since it did not fit into one of the debt categories that might legally be paid from the loan, but it might have been justified under the heading of "fomento de las rentas públicas," since it saved the treasury the expense of future building rentals.

[31] Cf. *Cartas al Señor Ex-Jeneral Francisco de Paula Santander* (Bogotá, 1837-38), 48. Marcos was actually listed in the *Gaceta* (March 11, 1827) as having received $500 on account of Manuel Antonio Marcos, who had lent that sum to the government at Guayaquil.

[32] See below, p. 125.

## The Later History of Colombian Foreign Credit

Not satisfied with the windfall of the 1824 loan, Colombian speculators immediately set to work on plans for raising still another. This time the objective was solely to pay interest on the existing foreign debt and retire the remainder of the internal debt, of which the greater part was still outstanding despite all the progress that had been made. The amount envisaged for the new loan ranged as high as $20,000,000. It was formally proposed in 1825 and again in 1826 by the German-Colombian entrepreneur Juan B. Elbers, who offered to undertake the technical assignment of converting domestic into foreign obligations; it was warmly supported in Congress by his friend Juan de Francisco Martín; and it was endorsed with equal vigor by Castillo y Rada. The argument was that the nation's total indebtedness would not be increased, and that the injection of so large an amount of foreign capital would invigorate the Colombian economy; at the same time the plan would permanently end the depreciation of government *vales*, thus benefiting any poor soldiers who had not yet sold their land-warrants to the speculators. If anything was left over after buying up the last *vale*, it could be paid directly into the national treasury.[33]

It was overlooked that only in the latter case was there much chance that the money would even stay in Colombia long enough to invigorate the economy. As merchants were the chief holders of the internal debt, it was probable that most of the funds they received would go to flood Colombia with a mass of English consumer goods that she could not otherwise have afforded, and this result would have done more harm than good to the national economy. To a certain extent exactly the same thing had already happened with the loan of 1824. No one was a good enough economist, however, to attack the project clearly along these lines. Instead the opposition simply pointed out that until Colombia proved she could really pay for the last loan it would be difficult to obtain another on anything like acceptable terms; if the loan project ended in spectacular failure then Colombia's foreign credit really would be ruined for a long time to come. The case for common sense was strongly stated by Senator Joaquín Mosquera, who added his own fears that the plan would enslave Colombia to British capitalists and suggested that the internal debt be repaid instead by a combination of the *alcabala* and a head-tax. Nor was popular opinion slow to grasp the fact that the whole project had been thought up essentially by and for speculators in government obligations.[34]

[33] *El Noticiosote*, April 28, 1825; *El Constitucional*, February 23, 1826; A.C., Senado-34, 127-129; Senado-44, 194-209.

[34] Joaquín Mosquera, *Observaciones sobre el empréstito decretado por la Hon. Cam. de RR.* (Bogotá, 1825); Mosquera to Bolívar, April 21, 1826, O'Leary IX, 32-33; *El Noticiosote*, April 28, 1825.

The opposition case found confirmation in the fact that mere discussion of the new loan plan tended to undermine Colombian bond prices on the London market. The appearance of a European financial crisis early in 1826, moreover, soon rendered the whole scheme hopelessly impractical. This development was admittedly the most important though not the only factor in causing Santander himself to throw his full weight against the plan, although he hesitated until its supporters had already suffered a virtual defeat in Congress.[35] The year 1826, in any case, marked the final collapse of Colombian foreign credit. This collapse can be ascribed in part to political difficulties—especially the revolt of Páez in Venezuela— which permanently undermined the stability of the central government. Yet there were other reasons of a purely financial order. To begin with, the British money crisis forced the house of Goldschmidt into bankruptcy, carrying with it a sizeable remnant of the 1824 loan which had been left in its hands for safekeeping by Hurtado rather than being deposited in a bank. This in itself was a serious loss, and an embarrassing one since not less than £49,531 in drafts against the funds were still outstanding.[36] Hurtado was already unpopular because of his commissions and because of his choice of a pro-Spanish merchant as money-changing agent in Jamaica. He was now called a latter-day patriot who had speculated on the bond market in cooperation with Goldschmidt and Co., and a strong party in Congress believed that he should personally repay the loss suffered by the republic.[37] The entire episode, needless to say, was highly damaging to the prestige of the administration. Santander did his best to cast the whole blame on his Minister to London, but Arrubla and Montoya had shared the responsibility for Hurtado's decision with regard to disposition of the loan funds, and the Vice-President himself had expressed approval when informed of it.[38]

The collapse of Goldschmidt was promptly followed by Colombia's defaulting on the loan of 1824. The amount withheld in advance for

[35] Santander to Chamber of Representatives, April 21, 1826, A.C., Cámara-5, 181; A.C., Senado-44, 193, and Actas de la Cámara de Representantes (secret sessions), April 12, 1826. For political reasons some years later Santander greatly exaggerated his opposition to the project (*El vicepresidente da cuenta*, 16-17).

[36] Hurtado, *op. cit.*, docs. N and S; A.C., Senado-53, 100.

[37] *Actas:* Senado-1824, 806; *El Chasqui Bogotano*, No. 14 (1826); A.H.N., Congresos XXVII, 109-110. Canning himself had looked with disfavor on Hurtado's connections with the mercantile class in London, but stated in January, 1825, that he knew of nothing that would reflect on his integrity (C.K. Webster, *Britain and the Independence of Latin America*, 2 vols., London, 1938, I, 382).

[38] *Exposición del Poder Ejecutivo al Congreso de 1825*, 24; *Documentos que el Poder Ejecutivo de Colombia presenta*, 10-12; Hurtado, *op. cit.*, doc. K. Hurtado was finally cleared of all charges in connection with the loan of 1824 under the Bolivarian dictatorship, after the disgrace and exile of Santander. (O'Leary IX, 576).

interest and amortization had now been used up, so that even before this Santander was looking desperately for special funds with which to make the interest payments that fell due starting in July of 1826. He asked the intendants to part with a quarter of their customs revenues for this very purpose, although only the Intendant of Guayaquil was willing and able to do so. He had carefully arranged for Peru to use part of an expected English loan for the payment of war debts owed to Colombia, but because of the financial depression in England the Peruvian loan never materialized. Santander had also instructed Hurtado to seek an emergency loan in London on any terms he could obtain, but this plan did not work either, particularly since it had been assumed that Goldschmidt was the firm most likely to oblige.[39] On the contrary, the collapse of Goldschmidt entailed the loss of Colombian funds that might otherwise have been applied toward the July interest.

When Santander learned that the Goldschmidt firm had gone into bankruptcy his first reaction was to redouble his efforts to gather money at home. He even thought of shipping off some $300,000 in cash still left over from the loan funds in Colombia, although for some reason the plan was never carried out. Instead the money was used at least in part to make new payments on the domestic debt.[40] Then, at the last minute, help was received from a wholly unexpected quarter. The Ecuadoran patriot Vicente Rocafuerte, who was then serving as Mexico's envoy to Great Britain, granted Hurtado a friendly loan of £73,000 from Mexican government funds in London.[41] This was not enough to pay everything that was owed, but it delayed the total collapse of Colombian credit for a few months longer.

In its own effort to solve the immediate crisis, meanwhile, the Colombian Congress had done nothing but approve in advance whatever measures the Executive might choose to take. It had also decreed an *auxilio patriótico* in the hope of meeting payments of interest and amortization due in November and January. As a supposedly permanent solution, finally, the Law of National Credit signed on May 22 had expressly reserved an eighth of all customs duties, the total profit of the tobacco monopoly, and various other revenues for the payment of the foreign debt.[42] It was hoped that this law also would start to take effect before the end of the year. In practice, however, these particular revenues were mainly derived not from peaceful Cundinamarca but from the very depart-

---

[39] Santander to Chamber of Representatives, April 21, 1826, A.C., Cámara-5, 183; *Documentos que el Poder Ejecutivo de Colombia presenta*, 15; *La Gaceta de Colombia*, June 18, 1826.

[40] Santander, *El vicepresidente da cuenta; La Gaceta de Colombia*, March 11 through April 8, 1827.

[41] Zubieta, *op. cit.*, 468.

[42] *Codif. Nac.* II, 390, 399-403; A.C., Actas del Senado, May 22 and 23, 1826.

ments that were most constantly in turmoil after the middle of 1826, and the funds were thus appropriated illegally for other purposes.[43] The interest was not paid for a long time after July of 1826. Yet even in normal times payments could not long have been maintained, since the total annually due for both interest and amortization was $2,100,000. As this was roughly a third of the revenue that might be expected in an average year, the remarkable thing is that English investors had been willing to part with the $30,000,000 (minus discount . . .) in the first place.[44] The loan was, in short, a temporary relief at best for Colombia's financial ills; and it left behind quite as many problems for succeeding generations as it seemingly had solved for the administration of Santander.

---

[43] O'Leary XXVI, 9-11.

[44] Indeed the gradual decline in Colombian bond prices, which could be traced to a growing realization of Colombia's basic insolvency, was a contributing factor to the failure of Goldschmidt, and thus, indirectly, to the English banking crisis. See *El Constitucional,* September 15, 1825, and July 20, 1826.

Chapter IX

## Economic Reconstruction and Development

NO MATTER what fiscal expedients were adopted in the short run, Colombia could never enjoy true financial stability until the general level of economic life was radically altered. Despite the presence of a few flourishing industries, the mass of the population struggled along not far from the subsistence level, and was wholly unable to pay all the taxes that were needed. For budgetary as well as humanitarian reasons, therefore, Colombian leaders hoped that independence might soon usher in an era of plenty. The relative prosperity of the United States was held up as an example of what Colombia might attain through a wise combination of republican government and liberal economics; and by the same token all existing economic ills were blamed on the same tattered scapegoat of "Spanish oppression." Indeed one of the blackest crimes of the colonial regime was held to have been a willful suppression of information regarding the new science of Political Economy. Had they known true economic principles, recited a well-coached pupil of Dr. Francisco Soto, Colombians would have been free even before 1810.[1]

Naturally there was some disagreement as to just what constituted true economic principles. The younger patriots led by Santander were more prepared for sweeping liberal reforms than was the circle of Nariño; merchants and intellectuals were more receptive to new ideas than were the landowners. Nor did all true principles suit the local interests of every province, with the result that any program for economic reform was likely to arouse strong opposition in some quarter. Yet the supporters of orthodox liberalism, which in economics meant the closest possible approximation to laissez faire, had some very clear advantages: they controlled the central administration and the leading newspapers, and they were united behind a consistent economic policy. They could not always have their own way, but at least they possessed an influence out of proportion to their numbers.

Before the economy could be transformed along liberal lines, however, it was necessary first to overcome those obstacles which arose not from colonial restrictions but from the material impact of the War of Independence itself. Military science was not yet sufficiently developed to do much damage to land or buildings, and there was little machinery to be destroyed. Much of the labor force, on the other hand, had died in

---

[1] *El Constitucional*, (Bogotá), August 11, 1825.

military service or had been diverted from productive enterprise to war purposes. The same had happened to the beasts of burden without which an agricultural economy could scarcely function, while cattle had been eaten up without much thought being given to replacement. The dispersal of whole villages in flight from passing armies had caused commercial agriculture to lose ground to purely subsistence farming in some areas.[2] The business community had seen a substantial part of its operating capital drained off in war loans, and repayment was slow in coming if it came at all. In general, conditions were most serious in Venezuela, as that is where the fighting had raged longest and with the greatest bitterness. Statements that the population of Venezuela had fallen off by one-half were obviously exaggerated, but even a decline of merely a fifth, which is as good an estimate as any,[3] could not help but have far-reaching effects on the regional economy. As for animals, the war created such a shortage on the *llanos* that if available at all they sold for many times their previous amount, and it was some time before conditions could even begin to return to normal.[4]

In terms of abstract justice it was widely thought that not only should all war loans be repaid but an indemnity should be granted for damages suffered in the course of the struggle. There was, of course, no chance of doing any such thing in practice.[5] The most that could possibly be done was to grant special assistance to areas that had suffered more than the usual amount of destruction, and in fact both Congress and administration were deluged with pleas from one province after another for the remission of taxes on the grounds that this was essential to economic recovery. The plight of Casanare won particular sympathy from its former ruler Santander, who suggested that its tobacco crop be exempted from the tithes;[6] but only one region succeeded in having a special relief measure passed through Congress. This was the province of Río Hacha, which had not only been ravaged by war but had seen its capital and only

[2] Gaspar Theodore Mollien, *Viaje por la República de Colombia en 1823* (Bogotá, 1944), 252.

[3] For a higher estimate cf. Francis Hall, *Colombia: Its Present State* (2nd ed., London, 1827), 10. A resume of pre-revolutionary estimates of Venezuelan population can be found in Josiah Conder, *Colombia* (Boston and Philadelphia, 1830), 4-5; they in general differ only slightly from Restrepo's figure of 900,000 (Restrepo I, xx), which may be compared with the total (probably too low) of roughly 660,000 given by the census of 1825 (Restrepo VII, 300).

Naturally not all of the decline was due to casualties in battle. The expulsion of royalists and the impact of war hardships on the civilian population also played a part, but in addition Latin America's War of Independence (unlike World War II) seems to have had a definitely adverse effect on the birth rate.

[4] Cf. Karl Richard, *Briefe aus Columbien* (Leipzig, 1822), 95; *El Constitucional*, July 12, 1827.

[5] Cf. report of a Senate committee on this topic, A.C., Cámara-3, 330.

[6] A.H.N., Corresp.-Cámara (Interior), July 7, 1823.

port burned to the ground by mutinous Irish legionnaires. It was thus granted a one-year exemption from most customs duties by the Congress of Cúcuta, and when the recapture of Maracaibo by the Spaniards late in 1822 made it a center of military operations once more, Congress allowed the importation of foodstuffs duty-free for a period of ten years. As an added favor, Congress later appropriated $10,000 to rebuild the local church.[7]

The decision to appropriate $1,000,000 of the English loan funds for an agricultural lending program also granted some relief to the most important single economic class. The generosity of Congress was partially offset, however, by the caution of the administration. Only $320,000 was actually set aside by Santander, and only for the Department of Venezuela, which received the lion's share, is there definite proof available that the funds were used as intended.[8] The grants to individual estate-owners were reasonable enough, exceeding $3000 in a few cases; on the other hand, those who needed the money most were probably excluded by the strict conditions set up, including the requirement of a mortgage equal to double the amount that was advanced.[9] At least there seems to have been little if any political favoritism in making the distribution. Two sisters of the Intendant of Venezuela received some $3000, but the application of Secretary of War General Carlos Soublette was turned down, while several pronounced critics of the administration succeeded in obtaining loans as requested.[10]

## The Advance of Laissez Faire

There were no other significant measures giving direct relief to either geographic regions or economic classes. For the rest, recovery was left primarily to the operation of natural economic forces. Indeed even though the agricultural loan project had been originally proposed by Santander,[11] his basic conviction was that private enterprise should always be preferred as the force to solve the nation's economic problems. In answer to one call for help he bluntly replied that as ruler he could not "directly promote either agriculture or mining, whose prosperity results from indi-

[7] *Codif. Nac.* I, 59, 272-273, II, 243-244.

[8] *La Gaceta de Colombia*, February 5, 1826; *El Colombiano* (Caracas) December 7, 1825. This does not mean that Orinoco and Ecuador, which were also assigned funds, did not actually use the money in whole or in part, but simply that the author has found no mention of the distribution. It should be borne in mind that Congress had frankly authorized Santander to spend less than a million pesos if he deemed it advisable (*Codif. Nac.* II, 100-101).

[9] This was perhaps to offset the interest rate of 6%, which was too low to please Santander (*La Gaceta de Colombia*, June 12, 1825). For a criticism of the terms, see *El Indicador del Orinoco* (Cumaná), October 22, 1825.

[10] *El Colombiano*, December 7, 1825.

[11] A.C., Senado-34, 203.

vidual effort and resources."¹² In the opinion of Santander and his supporters the proper sphere for official action was to be found mainly in removing any barriers to private initiative that had been left over from the colonial regime. If these could not yet be abolished outright, then they should at least be manipulated in such a way that private enterprise could function to its best advantage.

The first major steps toward abolishing out-dated restrictions had been taken as early as the Congress of Cúcuta. Such fiscal reforms as the abolition of internal customs barriers and the *alcabala* were designed to give greater freedom to commerce even at the expense of government revenue. And it is interesting to note that when the *derecho de consumo* was finally abolished in 1826 the official motive was not so much to reduce taxation on foreign trade as to increase the freedom of commercial movement by eliminating the additional inspections and general inconvenience which its collection entailed.¹³ Equally significant was the abandonment of the colonial guild system as contrary to the principles of free competition. The guilds were never formally legislated out of existence, and the basic features of the system were reaffirmed in a local ordinance of the Intendant of Cundinamarca in 1822 and later in the Congressional draft of a general law on provincial administration. Most good liberals, however, held that the guilds were obviously contrary to constitutional provisions against private monopoly, and the intendant promptly withdrew his ordinance when this reasoning was explained to him by Vicente Azuero's *Indicación*. The Senate likewise deleted the objectionable provisions from the law on provincial administration before it was finally passed. As a result, the guild system as such simply died out under official disfavor.¹⁴

The attack on the guilds could not help but involve also the *consulados* of Caracas and Cartagena, although here it was not quite as successful. The *consulados* were, essentially, merchant guilds, but they combined this role with miscellaneous public service, not to mention the functions of a court of commercial law. Hence there were many protests when the Congress of Cúcuta resolved that they were neither "republican" nor useful and decreed their formal extinction. The same law abolished the special commercial tribunals that had existed in certain other centers, which shared many of the characteristics of the *consulados* even though they did not enjoy quite the same exalted privileges. Opposition to this measure was especially strong in Venezuela, where commerce had been

[12] *La Gaceta de Colombia,* February 11, 1827. This was in answer to the *Junta Provincial* of Mompós. Cf. *El Patriota* (Bogotá), May 20, 1823 and *La Gaceta de Colombia,* April 15, 1827.

[13] *Codif. Nac.* II, 247-248.

[14] *La Indicación* (Bogotá), August 17 through 31, 1822; A.C., Senado-28, 419, 426.

most highly developed and the people had least confidence in the new republican officials to take over the work of the institutions that had just been abolished. But except for the more doctrinaire liberals within its ranks the merchant class elsewhere in Colombia was also generally hostile to the reform. Accordingly, Bolívar used his "extraordinary faculties" to reestablish the commercial tribunal of Guayaquil, and soon afterward he permitted Cuenca to have one too where none had existed before. Even many original supporters of the reform appear to have regretted it before long, and in 1824 Congress set up a new system of commercial tribunals for the whole republic, by which it sought to give merchants an expeditious means for settling their own disputes while at the same time avoiding any trace of monopolistic practices.[15]

Of somewhat wider significance was the liberals' attempt to abolish or curtail forms of land tenure that were held to obstruct the free transfer of real property and the development of private initiative along the lines of laissez faire. In this connection clerical mortmain was considered the worst offender, but in practice the question of church lands was more a religious than an economic issue, and it must be treated as such in a later chapter. The opposition to entailed estates, on the other hand, was based solely on economic theory, and they were legislated out of existence with fairly little difficulty.[16] Moreover, at least a little progress was made toward abolition of the various forms of collective landownership, which was equally repulsive to liberal thinking. The ultimate objective was clearly shown when the Congress of Cúcuta decreed that the Indians' communal lands should all be divided up into private holdings. This measure had little practical effect in the short run—it was virtually impossible to enforce—but at least it established a principle that was to guide the nation's Indian policy down to the present day.[17]

When it came to dealing with the common lands or *ejidos* of non-Indian municipalities the liberal objective was exactly the same, although in this case no progress at all was made save the gradual education of public sentiment through agitation in Congress and the press. There was at first little question of abolishing the *ejidos* all at once, but with the support of most good liberals Santander proposed to Congress that they should at least be made subject to voluntary alienation without arbitrary restrictions. Even this mild suggestion was defeated by the conservative bloc in the Chamber of Representatives when the liberals tried to insert it into the comprehensive law of 1825 dealing with municipal finance.

[15] *Codif. Nac.* I, 152, 335-339, VII, 109, 112; *Actas:* Cúcuta, 769; *Actas:* Senado-1824, 538; *La Gaceta de Colombia,* November 10, 1822; A.C., Cámara-4, 242-244, 296-297.

[16] *Actas:* Senado-1824, 81-82, 121-122, 239-241; *Codif. Nac.* I, 332-333.

[17] Cf. Juan Friede, *El indio en lucha por la tierra* (Bogotá, 1944) and Chapter 11, below.

However, the supporters of the reform refused to admit defeat, one reason for their obstinacy being the fact that Santander's good friend Juan Manuel Arrubla wanted to give his handsome but money-losing theatre, the *Coliseo,* to the city of Bogotá in exchange for some of its town lands. This more than anything else is really what had moved the Vice-President to broach the subject in the first place.[18] A year later he went so far as to urge that municipalities, colleges, and assorted religious institutions be not only permitted but required to divest themselves of their landholdings for the sake of stimulating the economy and increasing the sphere of private initiative. The Vice-President's suggestion was daring to say the least, and Congress now seemed generally disposed to accept the liberal argument. But there was no time to act upon the problem during the sessions of 1826.[19]

The following Congress was more conservative in sympathy and had too many political crises on its mind to bother with the *ejidos,* so that land reform ceased to be a legislative issue without anything more having been accomplished. It is fairly clear, moreover, that liberal notions on the evils of communal ownership still had not penetrated very far into the popular mind. In 1824 the town authorities of Barinas argued that the *ejido* principle should actually be extended as a means of repairing the physical destruction caused by war and earthquake. Their thesis was that house lots were really city property, which had merely been lent to private families on condition of being properly used; consequently, if the ostensible owners did not now repair the buildings placed upon them the lots should revert to the municipality.[20]

The same survival of traditional economic thinking could be seen in the defeat of liberal efforts to remove colonial restrictions upon rates of interest. The legal status of money-lending was slightly obscure to begin with; the *Corte Superior del Sur* once felt required to ask Congress whether it was legal to receive any interest at all. In general, however, Spanish legislation had limited interest rates to 5%.[21] This did not prevent rates of 36% from being asked in practice, but doctrinaire liberals demanded a law openly establishing the freedom of interest rates on the ground that all limitations were a relic of "scholastic theology." The absence of such

[18] A.H.N., Corresp.-Cámara (Interior), March 9, 1825; *El Noticiosote* (Bogotá) March 20, 1825; A.C., Cámara-12, 100-105, Senado-33, 136. The city government, which derived one third of its income from its *ejidos* (A.C., Cámara-16, 162), was not enthusiastic about Arrubla's proposal, but it was presumably hoped that if a law made the transfer possible then a later, more drama-conscious city administration might prove amenable.

[19] A.C., Senado-6, 91-95; below, p. 226.

[20] A.C., Senado-27, 242-263. The outcome is not indicated.

[21] Guillermo Torres García, *Historia de la moneda en Colombia* (Bogotá, 1945), 135; A.H.N., Interior y Relaciones, CXIV, 654-657.

limitations in the United States was stressed as one major reason for Anglo-American prosperity. The reform was strongly opposed, needless to say, by most of the clergy, including the Senator-Bishop Rafael Lasso de la Vega of Mérida who insisted that it was the special prerogative of the Church to fix rates of interest. The Bishop could not convince his fellow Senators, but the *Montaña* in the lower house twice defeated the reform by a narrow majority,[22] and Colombian liberals were thus reduced to defending the interests of money-lenders in other ways. From their position in the judiciary they upheld the practice of committing willfully insolvent debtors to prison, vigorously opposing the claim that it was incompatible with Colombian institutions. Indeed Dr. Vicente Azuero insisted that malice in a debtor should be assumed until it was proven otherwise.[23] At the Congress of Cúcuta Santander himself was given a stinging rebuke for daring to grant a debt moratorium to the widow of a patriot martyr. She would not have been reduced to penury even if she had paid her debts; thus the action was construed simply as an arbitrary violation of property rights, and the liberal majority in Congress was sincerely horrified.[24] This was frankly an unusual slip for Santander, who later reminded Congress that "the respect which [theorists] recommend for property is superior to any other, to the extent that there is a writer of reputation who states that the violation of personal security would be more tolerable than that of property." [25]

It was somewhat harder to make sure that provincial and local officials would always grant security and freedom to private enterprise. Internal commerce continued to be hampered by frequently arbitrary municipal regulations which were ostensibly for the purpose of safeguarding public health, assuring a stable food supply, collecting taxes, or advancing some other worthy object, but were equally effective at interfering with business in general and sheltering the growth of local monopolies. As a matter of fact, new regulations were sometimes deemed necessary in coping with special war-time and post-war conditions: in order to curb an epidemic of cattle-rustling, the governor of Apure province set up a complex system of transport restrictions, certificates, and the like for all dealings whatsoever in hides, much to the annoyance of licit as well as illicit traders. With much less justification a governor of Barcelona in 1822 was requiring official permits for all commercial movement of cattle and food-

---

[22] *La Gaceta de Colombia*, February 26, 1826; *La Miscelánea* (Bogotá), September 25, 1824 and September 28, 1825; *Actas:* Cámara-1825, 317; A.C., Cámara-13, 159-160; A.C., Actas del Senado, January 10, February 10 and 15, 1826.

[23] A.C., Senado-7, 123-126; Senado-36, 146-154; *La Gaceta de Cartagena*, January 3, 1824.

[24] *Actas:* Cúcuta, 571-573; A.C., Senado-12, 106, 111, 116-117.

[25] *Actas:* Congreso-1823, 199.

stuffs over to Guayana.[26] There was, however, a growing opposition to restrictive practices of all kinds, and there was no feeling of respect for local autonomy to dissuade either Congress or administration from making sporadic attempts to deal with the problem. A case in point is the municipal finance law of 1825, which sought among other things to prevent abuses in the levying of municipal imposts and to standardize them as far as possible throughout Colombia.[27] Unfortunately, this law by its very inflexibility tended to create new problems in place of the ones it solved.

## Capital Investment and Public Improvements

One aspect of the general lessening of restrictive practices that deserves special attention is the changed attitude toward foreign capital investment that was immediately ushered in by the coming of independence. It was obvious that a successful program of economic development required the cooperation of both foreign money and foreign technical skills; hence not only were colonial restrictions largely abandoned in this respect but positive encouragement was offered as well in so far as it was thought compatible with the concept of private initiative. A Congressional committee reporting on the possibility of an interoceanic canal actually asserted that foreign investors should be granted preference over any native entrepreneurs in building one because in this fashion not only would a useful project be carried out but new capital would come to circulate inside Colombia.[28] The same welcome for things foreign was expressed in more general terms by José Manuel Restrepo when he observed that "in this century of philosophy the nations of Europe hasten to receive America into the community of nations: they offer the new states their discoveries in all fields, and the enlightenment of their advanced civilization, with no more interest than to benefit humanity, to dissipate ignorance, and to establish a commerce which offers mutual advantages to Europeans and to Americans."[29] When this doctrine was applied to tariff policy or immigration not all Colombians found the advantages as mutual as did Restrepo; foreign capital, however, aroused less opposition than foreign wheat and foreign heretics. For that matter, there was so much that needed to be done that native businessmen were eager to launch still other useful projects entirely on their own. The one drawback was that both native and foreign entrepreneurs suffered from an overly optimistic view of Colombia's short-run possibilities.

[26] *El Venezolano* (Caracas), April 23, 1824; A.H.N., Congresos IX, 814-816.
[27] *Codif. Nac.* II, 72-85.
[28] A.C., Senado-27, 100.
[29] *El Constitucional* (Bogotá), July 12, 1827.

The most promising field for capital investment—or at least so it appeared—was mining, traditionally the major industry of western New Granada. Production had suffered from the effects of the war, although the mining industry had not been systematically ruined in New Granada as in New Spain. For one thing, placer workings were predominant, so that there were fewer expensive installations to destroy. On the other hand, there were still mining properties in need of rehabilitation for one reason or another, there were marginal deposits that might be made to yield a profit under more modern methods, and there were mines directly operated by the state that might benefit from being rented out to private management. It was also hoped that new deposits could be found and worked; and mining development of any variety fitted in well with liberal notions of Colombia's place in the world economy. *El Correo de la Ciudad de Bogotá,* which tended to reflect official thinking, was entirely willing to let the more efficient British factories replace Colombian production of coarse textiles, suggesting that Colombians should be content to emphasize mining as an alternative source of wealth.[30] Europeans on their part were no less willing to emphasize mining, for the inexhaustible nature of Latin America's mineral riches was everywhere taken for granted.

One of the first problems to absorb the attention of Congress and Santander was accordingly that of working out a liberal system of mining concessions. When Congress sought to impose too many restrictions borrowed from the Mining Ordinances of New Spain, the Vice-President insisted that foreign investors must not be scared away by an excessive control over their operations, and in the end he obtained a broad authorization to lease government-owned mines more or less as he saw fit, while following traditional Spanish legislation in the case of "mines that have not yet been discovered." [31] The latter clause, however, was presumably to be interpreted in the light of republican principles and institutions. The government then granted concessions to a number of mining associations formed especially for the occasion, with a highly illustrious list of sponsors on both sides of the Atlantic. Santander alleged that he himself was offered £60,000 merely to lend his name to one British mining company,[32] and there was a distressing amount of speculation with spurious mining claims. However, the more important concerns seem to have been reputable enough, even if the results seldom corresponded to the full hopes of Colombian and English promoters.

The renowned emerald mines of Muzo, which had reverted to direct government control after being abandoned by the previous management,

[30] *El Correo de la Ciudad de Bogotá,* April 18, 1822.
[31] Message to Congress, June 4, 1823, A.C., Senado-17, 520-521; *Actas:* Congreso-1823, 366; *Codif. Nac.* I, 265.
[32] *La Voz de la Verdad* (Bogotá, 1825), 12.

were farmed out to the Bogotá patrician José Ignacio París, the Peruvian metallurgist Mariano Rivero, and the English adventurer-entrepreneur Charles Stuart Cochrane. Rental was 10% of production, and the venture appears to have been reasonably successful. Certain silver mines in the vicinity of Mariquita, which had been worked sporadically in the past but were also unused at the moment, were leased to the Colombian Mining Association, whose capital was supplied in large part by Goldschmidt and Company and whose titular president was Manuel José Hurtado, the Colombian Minister to Great Britain. It was hoped that the silver mines could be made profitable by bringing in English equipment, and the company actually sent over a hundred English miners to help out; but conditions at Mariquita were less favorable than was stated in the prospectus, and the progress made was very slow. Then there was the Cartagena and Anglo-Colombian Mining Association, which obtained a grant of all government mines, including those not yet discovered, in the province of Cartagena. Its nominal capitalization was £1,500,000, but it accomplished even less than Goldschmidt and Hurtado.[33]

The government was not directly involved in the rental of the copper mines of Aroa in Venezuela, which belonged to the family of Bolívar. As they had not been worked for some time, Charles Stuart Cochrane was able to rent them for only $10,000 a year; he brought over a few English miners and then sold his rights to the Bolívar Mining Association for $150,000, presumably in stock. Cochrane remained in charge of the project as agent for the Association, and ultimately died from the unhealthy climate of Aroa. His successor was Robert Lowry, the United States Consul at La Guaira, who also died on the job, but the obstacles were finally overcome, and the mine began to give investors a return on their capital. In fact the Association was well enough pleased to offer to buy the mines outright for £38,000.[34] There was also one rather unconventional mining venture involving the same Charles Stuart Cochrane that should be mentioned if only for its romantic interest. This was the lake-draining enterprise in central New Granada in which he became associated with José Ignacio París. The objective was both to reclaim land for colonization and to uncover some of the Chibcha treasures that the legend of *El Dorado* and the like seemed to locate somewhere beneath the surface of the water.[35]

[33] *La Gaceta de Colombia,* January 2, 1825; Carl August Gosselman, *Reise in Columbien* (2 vols., Straslund, 1829), I, 198-199, II, 289-290; *El Constitucional,* March 10, 1825; *The Present State of Colombia* (London, 1827), 319-320; Mollien, *op. cit.,* 385.

[34] Correspondence of Bolívar's representatives relating to the Aroa mines may be found in O'Leary II, 367; VIII, 381, 388-389, 392, 393; IX, 316, 333-336.

[35] Charles Stuart Cochrane, *Journal of a Residence and Travels in Colombia* (2 vols., London, 1825), II, 201-205, 246; A.H.N., Miscelánea de la República XXI, 241.

Probably the most ambitious and at the same time least workable of all mining projects were those that concerned the exploitation of platinum. In theory, the sale and export of platinum was a fiscal monopoly of the Colombian treasury, which had been set up by the Congress of Cúcuta for the same reasons that led Colombia to preserve the colonial monopolies of salt and tobacco: the short-run need for added revenue. It was felt that platinum was ideally suited to this purpose since it was also a natural monopoly of Colombia. But little was produced for sale, and though platinum enjoyed a high price in Europe as a curiosity the foreign demand was easily met by smuggling the metal out to Jamaica. A domestic market would have been created if the laws passed by successive Congresses for issuing a platinum currency had ever been carried out, but this could not be done chiefly because of the difficulty of refining the metal in Colombia. Francisco Antonio Zea's plan for the Bank of England to issue platinum coins in Great Britain had equally little effect. Colombians were slow to lose their enthusiasm, however, and the Congress of 1826 gave careful consideration to the proposal of an English promoter to establish a platinum refinery in Colombia and earn literally millions of pesos for the government both by coining the metal in Colombia and by selling it abroad in bars. A law to authorize the program was duly passed, requiring the concessionaires to raise the operating capital themselves and also to train young Colombians in the process of platinum refining, presumably so that foreign assistance could be dispensed with when the agreement expired. The following February a formal contract was signed with English interests, but apparently nothing else was accomplished.[36]

One reason for the difficulties faced by mining companies and all other groups interested in internal development was the inadequacy of transportation within Colombia, and considerable effort was spent in trying to meet this problem as well. The government recognized that it had neither the technical resources nor the funds to do the job; and even though Colombian leaders were committed to the doctrine of free competition, they realized that no ordinary private company could undertake it either. Hence the principal method used was the granting of exclusive privileges, and at least in the field of steam navigation there was no lack of applicants for the concessions. The greatest prize of all was naturally the right to introduce steam navigation on the Magdalena, a project that was destined sooner or later to affect every aspect of the *granadino* economy. This privilege ultimately went to Juan Bernardo Elbers, a German adventurer who had been a leading supplier of the patriot armies in the

---

[36] A.C., Senado-48, 44, 47-48; *Codif. Nac.* I, 87-88, II, 378-381; *La Gaceta de Colombia,* February 18, 1827. The Spanish authorities had also tried to maintain platinum as a state monopoly, but with so little success that it really had to be established anew by Colombia.

War of Independence and had subsequently made Colombia his adopted country.[37]

The contract granted to Elbers in July of 1823 provided that for twenty years he would have sole right to operate steamboats on the Magdalena, gave his employees exemption from military service, and allowed him the use of all lands necessary for his project. In return he was to carry the Colombian mails free of charge, observe certain maximum freight charges which were actually quite generous, build connecting canals from the Magdalena to Cartagena and Santa Marta, and construct a road from the terminus of steam navigation up to Bogotá. The agreement seemed at first glance highly favorable to both parties. In practice, Elbers had agreed to do far more than he was able. He began service in January, 1824, only by hiring a small ship that was then promptly withdrawn; when his own vessels arrived, it was found that they were ill-adapted to the river and thus gave rather irregular service. Elbers' attempt to reopen the colonial *Canal del Dique* linking Cartagena with the Magdalena drew him into a petty squabble with the local authorities, and only a part of the road to Bogotá was ever finished. His organization of a broad company with prominent Colombian businessmen as directors and Bolívar as "Patron" was of no avail; indeed his privilege was ultimately revoked by Bolívar himself on the technically justifiable grounds that he had not fulfilled the entire contract. Nevertheless, his steamers really had been carrying passengers and freight on the Magdalena, even if sporadically; and many passengers preferred to run the risk of being stuck on a sandbar rather than face the known discomforts of making the entire trip in an open *bongo*.[38]

After the achievement of Elbers on the Magdalena, the opening of steam navigation on the Orinoco had to come as something of an anticlimax. Yet the region to be served was far from negligible, and there was even talk of linking the Orinoco system with the Amazon by steamboat over the Río Casiquiare.[39] There was less competition for the privilege in this case principally because the two leading contestants agreed to go into business together. One of them, the Venezuelan Congressman Miguel Palacio, had mainly his local knowledge and connections to offer; the other, James Hamilton, was a Scotch entrepreneur whose career in Colombia had closely paralleled that of Elbers. The two obtained a con-

[37] Robert Louis Gilmore and John Parker Harrison, "Juan Bernardo Elbers and the Introduction of Steam Navigation on the Magdalena River," *Hispanic American Historical Review* XXVIII (1948), 338, note 8.

[38] For a full survey of the problem see Gilmore and Harrison, "Juan Bernardo Elbers," *loc. sit*. See also Gosselman, *op. cit.*, II, 291, 297-299; A.H.N., Correspondencia del Libertador Presidente, 173, 186-187; *El Constitucional*, November 8, 1827.

[39] A.C., Cámara-4, 276.

cession in terms very similar to the Magdalena contract, although fortunately no roads or canals were involved this time. When the first steamer did not arrive before the legal deadline, Congress graciously extended the time limit by special decree. The trouble was that ships had to be built to order in England, and when one delay followed another Santander at last felt compelled to rescind the contract, ordering Hamilton to pay a fine of $20,000 for non-fulfillment under the terms of his privilege. Palacio, as a mere associate, apparently was not involved in the fine, and there is no evidence that Hamilton ever paid it—although it may have been applied against the substantial debts owed to him by the Colombian treasury. In due course Hamilton finally did place a steamboat on the Orinoco; but this was too late to regain his monopoly.[40]

The one steamboat concession which was carried into effect without delay was the exclusive privilege for steam navigation on Lake Maracaibo and the adjoining Río Zulia. It was granted to the German-American Christian Louis Mannhardt, who was acting in the name of one George Suckley. Mannhardt had already brought a ship to Colombia in the expectation of using it on the Magdalena; and when Elbers got the Magdalena concession instead, Mannhardt simply transferred his vessel to Lake Maracaibo. However, the local trade offered by the area was of less importance than the commerce of the Magdalena, and the contract was soon voided for failure to maintain service.[41] Various other exclusive concessions were requested from time to time for steamship operation along the coast from the Magdalena to the Orinoco and up the small western rivers to the gold mines of the Chocó and the province of Buenaventura,[42] but nothing came of any of the proposals.

Equally unsuccessful were the projects to build canal, cart railway, or through highway to link the Atlantic and Pacific Oceans. Bolívar himself imagined that with a half year's preparation he could have a canal cut across the Atrato River route in the province of Chocó. He gave instructions accordingly, and nothing happened.[43] Foreign and domestic promoters besieged the Congress of Cúcuta and all later Congresses with similar schemes designed for either the Atrato or the Isthmus of Panama: the list of persons interested in one way or another in these projects affords a virtual political and economic Who's Who of Gran Colombia. By and large, the Panama route was preferred for the canal or whatever else it might be; and in Congress, at least, there was a noticeable preference for

[40] *Codif. Nac.* I, 266-268, 328-329; *El Constitucional,* November 17, 1825 and June 28, 1827; A.H.N., Corresp.-Cámara (Interior), January 25, 1826; *Acuerdos* II, 262-263; *Present State of Colombia,* 188.

[41] *Codif. Nac.* II, 53-55, VII, 498; *Present State of Colombia,* 192; A.C., Senado-27, 40-41.

[42] Cf. *El Colombiano* (Caracas), November 10, 1824; A.C., Senado-29, 1-2.

[43] O'Leary XIX, 170.

Hislop and Company of Jamaica as the firm to do the job. The administration, on the other hand, rather unrealistically preferred to keep the management of such a strategic enterprise in Colombian hands. It apparently favored a group of prominent businessmen and politicians headed by Senator Jerónimo Torres of Popayán. However, no contestant ever obtained more than a permit to survey the land. Not only were the material obstacles almost insurmountable, but there were political considerations that had yet to be worked out; it was even urged that a canal would dangerously facilitate future Spanish invasions.[44]

In part, at least, to prepare for the day when a canal really would be built, Colombian leaders were also interested in developing new ports along the Pacific coast. Bolívar had scarcely reached Ecuador in the course of his campaigns when he began to consider ways and means of opening a more direct route than that of Guayaquil to link Quito with the sea. A suitable port existed at Esmeraldas, but it was not of much use since there was not a passable trail to connect it with the highlands. Hence as a first step Bolívar offered generous tax exemptions to anyone who would settle along the route from Quito to Esmeraldas and ordered customs duties at the port drastically reduced so as to encourage its use by merchants sending goods to Quito. The Liberator even sought to settle fugitive slaves along the new route, and his various tax exemptions and privileges were specifically confirmed by Congress; but unfortunately the colonists were hard to find, and the road itself was much too difficult to build.[45]

Representatives of the Cauca Valley were no less interested in the development of Buenaventura, where an excellent harbor existed and had been used intermittently, but where facilities for handling trade on a large scale were non-existent since the area roundabout was virtually uninhabited. With the full support of the administration, therefore, a law was passed giving settlers at Buenaventura free public lands and even wider tax privileges than those granted for Esmeraldas. As Buenaventura naturally lacked good road connections with the interior, an earlier law had already authorized the Executive to contract for a new highway from the Cauca Valley down to the port. The contractors were to have the exclusive right to introduce and use improved mining machinery in certain nearby rivers, but in over two years only one specific proposal for building

[44] Blanco VIII, 71-73; *La Gaceta Oficial del Departamento del Istmo,* June 20, 1824; A.H.N., Miscelánea de la República XXI, 268, Congresos XII, 18-19, 537, Corresp.-Cámara (Interior), February 11 and March 4, 1826; A.C., Senado-27, 290-291, Senado-29, 3-5.

[45] O'Leary XX, 161-162, 561-562; *La Gaceta de Colombia,* September 8, 1822; *Codif. Nac.* II, 225; Robert A. Humphreys, *British Consular Reports on the Trade and Politics of Latin America* (London, 1940), 250-251.

## ECONOMIC RECONSTRUCTION AND DEVELOPMENT 141

the road had been made, and it was not found satisfactory.[46] It is thus doubtful that the free land and tax privileges attracted many settlers. As a matter of fact, there was always a good supply of legislative provisions granting lands, toll privileges, tax reductions, and so forth not only to Colombian road-builders generally but also to persons who would merely open inns along existing trails and highways.[47] But in general there was not sufficient capital available for extensive road-building in Colombia, nor sufficient traffic and security for investment to warrant bringing the capital from abroad. Hence the only major items of road construction that even reached the advanced planning stages were Elbers' promised but undelivered road from Bogotá to the Magdalena and one rather dubious highway from Caracas to La Guaira.

The latter provides another good example of the excess haste which marred so many early projects for internal development. In April, 1825, a detailed plan for a cart railway from La Guaira to Caracas was presented by an English firm with wide business interests in Venezuela; the promoters had already surveyed the land, offered what seemed to be quite liberal terms, and promised to charge less than the animal convoys on the existing road, which would remain open for anyone who chose to use it. Then, a few weeks later, a newly-formed *Sociedad Emprendedora de Caracas* offered a plan of its own to build an improved highway down to the coast provided it might charge tolls and carry all freight shipments along the road exclusively on its own vehicles. The scheme was advertised as offering the advantages of native management, and the proposed rates were carefully adjusted with a view to undercutting the English company's offer. When the latter responded by slashing its own proposed rates, the Caracas society just as promptly revised its scheme so as to beat the English again. The members of the *Sociedad Emprendedora* included virtually all the leaders of business and high society in Caracas— among them the business competitors of the English company, and in particular the chief representatives of United States interests. The Intendant Juan de Escalona was included, though his rival, General Páez, was not. The society promised to raise $1,500,000 in order to do the job. However, members needed to pay for only 1% of their pledges to begin with, and it was probably hoped that the bulk of the necessary capital would come from 10,000 shares which were to be sold in Great Britain. The plan was thus wholly improvised both in its technical planning and in its claims to financial support; yet it was endorsed by the cities of La Guaira and Caracas, many of whose officials were found among its sponsors. As soon as Congress convened in the following year, Santander added his own personal endorsement. Congress, in turn, granted the

[46] A.C., Actas del Senado, June 7, 1827; *Codif. Nac.* II, 103-104, III, 286-288; *El Constitucional,* June 28, 1827.
[47] *Codif. Nac.* I, 245, II, 96-98.

desired concession, with the customary privilege of draft exemption for the company's employees. Then came the revolt of Páez, in April of 1826, and the project was laid aside.[48]

Similar concessions were granted for other theoretically useful but often ill-conceived projects. One of these was a system of mechanized pearl-fishing for which certain English interests represented by the omnipresent Charles Stuart Cochrane obtained an exclusive privilege from the Congress of 1823. It had been observed that dangerous fish and other adverse factors had led to a decline in Colombian pearl-fishing, and supposedly all the obstacles would now be overcome by the use of a specially designed diving-bell. As a necessary inducement the promoters were given a monopoly of the use of their diving-bell in Colombian waters; in return, they were to satisfy the *quinto* on all the pearls they found and yield up their equipment to the state on expiration of the privilege. Special provisions were drawn up in case the company should find a pearl *"tan extraordinaria que su valor venga a ser imaginario."* In practice, it was found that the new machinery was no more capable of finding valuable pearls in quantity than were individual divers.[49] Equally unrealistic was Cochrane's plan to set up a series of copper rolling-mills along the Venezuelan coast, particularly in the neighborhood of the Aroa mines. Fuel and transportation problems and the lack of an adequate internal market did not deter Congress in 1823 from granting him the exclusive right to establish such mills, with the requirement that he train six young Colombians as apprentices in each one of them. Cochrane and his sponsors were to begin work within two years. Yet according to his own statement, by that time he had simply begun construction of the necessary machines; Congress thus refused to grant him an extension, and he was fined $8000 for non-fulfillment of his contract, a fine from which he was probably saved by his untimely death.[50]

This does not quite exhaust the list of concessions granting full or partial monopoly rights for the establishment of some useful enterprise. However, it should not be thought that every project of this sort was uncritically accepted. As Santander put it, "exclusive privileges can be conceded only for those things difficult to introduce without a substantial capital, or without very special knowledge." [51] He thus decried as "ruinous" a plan for a paper monopoly, and it was never accepted. Neither

[48] *El Colombiano,* May 11, June 8 and 22, 1825; A.C., Senado-34, 501-505, 508, 511, 518, 521, 525-527; A.H.N., Corresp.-Cámara (Interior), January 9, 1826; *Codif. Nac.* II, 214-218.

[49] *Codif. Nac.* I, 280-282, VII, 166-168; *El Constitucional,* April 7, 1825; *Present State of Colombia,* 322.

[50] *Codif. Nac.* I, 238-239; A.C., Senado-34, 51; A.H.N., Miscelánea de la República XXI, 236.

[51] A.H.N., Congresos XII, 414.

did the proponents of exclusive concessions to make beer and vinegar find favor with either Executive or Congress.[52] And in the realm of agriculture, which was Colombia's basic industry, the principle of exclusive privileges could scarcely be applied at all. The closest approach to it was the decision of Congress in 1824 to give temporary exemption from the tithes to anyone who established new plantations of coffee, indigo, and cacao. The law was vigorously assailed by the more orthodox clerical spokesmen on the basis that tithes were instituted by divine right and no civil authority could legitimately tamper with them, but such arguments found little support even among conservative laymen. Instead there were numerous demands to extend the same system to other crops, and even to grant exemptions to anyone who introduced the use of ploughs in a community where ploughing had not formerly been practiced. Congress did not do this, but on second thought it did agree to extend the duration of the coffee, indigo, and cacao exemptions in such a way that new plantings of cacao, for instance, would pay no tithes at all until the year 1840.[53] For the rest, it was hoped that the progress of agriculture would be furthered by innovations in the tax structure and by the program of foreign immigration that went hand in hand with the encouragement of foreign capital investment.

## *Immigration and Land Settlement*

The immigration policy of Gran Colombia was officially based on the assumption that Colombia possessed a wealth of resources not yet exploited, that one reason for this neglect was the sparsity of population, and that underpopulation was in large part due to Spain's fanatical hostility toward the entrance of foreigners in her dominions. The Congress of Cúcuta therefore issued what was thought to be an extremely generous law on the subject of naturalization, inviting foreigners to come and "form one family with native Colombians," who had been "deprived up to now of their fraternity and of the industry, the arts, and the useful knowledge, and all the blessings" which a flow of immigrants would have offered. Spanish Americans, under the terms of the law, could be naturalized simply on request; others could obtain citizenship after not more than three years of residence, although it would be granted sooner to anyone who acquired either a Colombian wife or a specified amount of rural property.[54]

[52] *Acuerdos* II, 120; *Actas de las sesiones de la Cámara de Representantes* (Bogotá, 1826), January 27. The only monopoly project involving light consumer goods to be adopted was one for the establishment of a playing card factory. It seems to have been accepted with some misgivings, and the original article forbidding all importation of competing decks was vetoed by Santander as an "odious" restriction (*Acuerdos* II, 253; *Codif. Nac.* III, 320).

[53] *Codif. Nac.* I, 295, II, 312-313; *Actas:* Senado-1824, 30, 46, 73-74.

[54] *Codif. Nac.* I, 49-50.

In the first 20 months of this law only 27 persons were naturalized, and these few included men such as James Hamilton, the future pioneer of steam navigation on the Orinoco, who had been established in business in Colombia for some years already.[55] This result was hardly surprising, since the law had not had time to take full effect and the War of Independence was not yet over, but it was nevertheless something of a disappointment. Moreover, recent events in Venezuela had served to strengthen the conviction of Colombian statesmen that immigration was necessary. Race tension had contributed to several outbreaks of violence in the Venezuelan *llanos*, and fear was widely expressed that Spanish and "Haitian" agents would create a general state of race warfare if some effective measures were not promptly taken. The administration itself was caught up in the general feeling of alarm, and among the measures it proposed was to strengthen the white minority by giving still more encouragement to immigration. The idea immediately found a favorable reception in Congress, although it was thought best to discuss the problem in secret session. The result, in any case, was a new and comprehensive attack on the problem of immigration by the Congress of 1823.[56]

One of the steps taken was to liberalize even further the general requirements for naturalization adopted at Cúcuta.[57] In addition, Congress now attempted to provide land on easy terms for the new immigrants to settle on. This detail was rather neglected by the Congress of Cúcuta, which had merely passed a law for the registration and clarification of all private land titles and for the sale of unclaimed public lands to anyone who wanted them at $2 per *fanegada*\* in the coastal provinces, $1 in the interior, and at auction prices wherever special conditions made them unusually desirable. Squatters already established on the national domain were promised that they would have preference in such sales, but if their occupation was at all recent they would still have to pay the legal price or run the risk of losing what they had.[58] This law was not repealed by the Congress of 1823, but it was supplemented by a new measure authorizing the distribution of up to 3,000,000 *fanegadas* of the national domain for the express purpose of encouraging immigration; in carrying out this project the Executive could dispense with the formalities of land sales prescribed at Cúcuta, could draw up rules for the social and political

[55] *La Gaceta de Colombia,* September 22, 1822, January 19 and June 15, 1823.

[56] A.C., Senado-17, 230-232, Senado-25, 113-114, 156; A.C., Actas del Senado (secret sessions), May 5, 1823. Fear of racial tension was no doubt a motive for the law of Cúcuta as well, but there is no evidence that it was given as much weight then as in 1823.

[57] *Codif. Nac.* I, 201-203.

[58] *Codif. Nac.* I, 125-128.

\* A *fanegada* was a measure 100 *varas* or Spanish yards square (*Codif. Nac.* I, 123).

organization of immigrant blocs, and was limited only in that no more than 200 *fanegadas* could be given to a single immigrant family. In the case of group colonization under the terms of this measure, citizenship might be granted from the very day of arrival.[59]

The colonization law of 1823 at least resulted in the granting of numerous contracts to specially-formed immigration companies. The administration ceded lands without payment in quantities ranging from 20,000 to 200,000 *fanegadas*. It gave options to take additional tracts at cut-rate prices, and these could apparently be paid for in government *vales*. The contractors, on their part, assumed full responsibility to find immigrants and bring them to Colombia, but it was arranged that once colonies were set up they would enjoy substantial tax-exemptions, and they were frequently promised special privileges of local self-government as well. Santander offered even a qualified freedom of worship, which is more than was legally enjoyed by native-born Colombians: the colonists could not publicly hold non-Roman Catholic rites, but by implication private worship would not be interfered with.[60] A large proportion of these grants were made in the coastal provinces, which were not generally as well suited to conventional white immigration as were the highlands. However, the coastal lowlands were less densely populated, they had the greatest concentrations of Negroes and mulattoes to be overcome, and they offered fewer obstacles to the development of transportation.

Practically everyone with an eye for business opportunities sought to participate in the colonization game. Liberal politicians like Diego Fernando Gómez and Vicente Azuero, conservatives like Senator Jerónimo Torres, wealthy merchants like Juan de Francisco Martín and Juan Manuel Arrubla, military leaders like Mariano Montilla, not to mention a wide assortment of foreigners—all were among the sponsors and directors of societies receiving land grants for colonization. Many were government officials; indeed the administration was frank in admitting that any persons established in or near Bogotá had an unfair advantage in obtaining contracts, and so in December, 1825, it rather tardily announced that the last 684,000 *fanegadas* would be saved for distribution to purely provincial companies.[61] However, no matter who obtained the contracts, it was usually taken for granted that capital would have to be raised in London for bringing the prospective colonists over and getting them well started. Some native speculators appear to have obtained contracts simply in order to transfer their rights for a proper consideration to English investors and then forget the whole business. There was also a tendency

[59] *Codif. Nac.* I, 187-188.

[60] Cf. contracts in *La Gaceta de Colombia,* April 10 and September 25, 1825. A complete series can be found in A.H.N., Libro Primero de Contratos.

[61] *La Gaceta de Colombia,* December 25, 1825.

for the concessionaires to combine their holdings into mammoth land corporations for greater financial or at least speculative strength. A National Colonization Company was organized by a group of Bogotá merchants with title to 500,000 *fanegadas*. In London the Colombian Association for Agriculture and Other Purposes was conceived and set up jointly by Goldschmidt and Company, certain other interested firms, and even a few Members of Parliament. Its nominal president was Manuel José Hurtado, and it possessed a stated claim to over one million acres.[62]

It was of course much easier to form colonization companies than to find colonists willing to go to Colombia. The Vice-President saw fit to blame the resulting delays on unsettled political conditions in Colombia, including principally the Páez revolt of 1826, and it can easily be imagined that such developments did make immigration far less attractive. But political conditions were only one of the many perfectly obvious reasons why potential European settlers preferred the United States. As a result, only the Colombian Association for Agriculture ever began the settlement program for which it had contracted, and all or virtually all the contracts made finally had to be cancelled because they were not being carried out.[63] Even the Association for Agriculture was far from successful in its first endeavours. It managed to bring nearly 200 Europeans to La Guaira for settlement in the province of Caracas, but on their arrival they found that the public lands to which they had legal option had not yet been marked out, and local agents of the corporation had to provide others instead. There is little indication of what happened to the immigrants themselves, but at least one seems to have been killed by a peon in his employ, and probably many of the others left Colombia in disappointment as soon as possible.[64]

The hoped-for tide of immigrants thus failed to materialize. Colombia continued to receive only driblets, and generally speaking agriculture was precisely the industry that benefited least. In the province of Cumaná, for instance, out of the grand total of thirteen foreigners who were naturalized by December, 1825, eleven were merchants, presumably living in the chief towns, and only two were engaged in agriculture.[65] Moreover, a great many of the foreigners who did take up residence in Colombia

[62] *El Constitucional,* June 2 and 23, 1825; A.H.N., Miscelánea de la República XXI, 231; *La Voz de la Verdad* (Bogotá, 1825), 12.

[63] *La Gaceta de Colombia,* January 14 and May 13, 1827; Angel and Rufino J. Cuervo, *Vida de Rufino Cuervo* (2 vols., Paris, 1892), I, 40, note; *El Constitucional,* June 28, 1827.

[64] *El Colombiano,* December 14, 1825, and September 27, 1826; *La Gaceta de Colombia,* January 22, 1826; A.C., Senado-48, 115-116. The murder victim is not positively identified as one of the Association's recruits, but that appears to be the sense of the report.

[65] *El Indicador del Orinoco* (Cumaná), January 14, 1826.

showed no interest in becoming Colombian citizens even when naturalization was offered on the most liberal terms. In the case of businessmen, who formed much the most important group, this fact in itself was enough to create a number of ticklish problems for both domestic politics and international relations.

From the first years of the independence movement British subjects and North Americans especially had begun to play an important role in import and export trade within Colombia, and their superior connections abroad, not to mention the ultimate protection of their home governments, had given them in many cases a distinct competitive advantage over native businessmen. The national authorities had felt it expedient to offer foreigners a general exemption from internal forced loans, even though local officials often violated this rule in practice and sometimes tried to place heavier financial burdens on foreigners than on anyone else.[66] As a result, a good bit of jealousy and resentment was built up, and early in 1822 Santander took what then seemed the easiest way out by ordering a more or less literal enforcement of Spanish restrictive legislation that had not been expressly repealed. In particular, he issued a decree in February of that year requiring foreigners to employ Colombian consignment agents for the distribution of imported goods throughout the country. They might still practice any mechanical craft and even set up retail shops if they wished, provided only that they paid the same taxes as Colombians, but the right to engage directly in wholesale trade was denied them.[67]

The Vice-President's decree pleased Colombian importers, and it does appear to have encouraged some foreign merchants to take out citizenship papers. It was vigorously assailed, needless to say, by the foreigners themselves; those Colombian newspapers that reflected English influence described it as illiberal in theory, and also as an arbitrary infringement of privileges tacitly granted years before when the Spanish regulations were not being enforced.[68] As a matter of fact, the decree was considerably mitigated in practice. Foreign consuls, who were commonly importers themselves, were not covered by its terms, and the United States consul at La Guaira claimed immunity not only for himself but for his business agent in Caracas. Since the Colombian constitution granted a vaguely privileged status to foreigners who had performed outstanding service on behalf of the Republic, the Intendant of Venezuela further exempted a few deserving private merchants from the general prohibition of wholesale trade.[69] Nevertheless, Santander soon decided that his decree should be

[66] A.H.N., Interior y Relaciones CXVII, 749-753.
[67] *Codif. Nac.* VII, 73-74.
[68] *El Anglo-Colombiano* (Caracas), May 11, 1822; *El Constitucional*, June 10, 1824.
[69] A.H.N., Interior y Relaciones CXVII, 882, 888-891; N.A., Colombia Dispatches II, July 29, 1823.

revoked. He felt that it had served to keep away "the foreign capitalists whom we need so much to give life to our agriculture;" that the scarcity of able and trustworthy Colombian merchants tended to create a harmful commercial monopoly; and that foreigners, having fewer connections in the country, were less able to corrupt the customs officials and so should be actively encouraged to engage in commerce. Congress came around to the same opinion, and despite all predictions that foreign merchants would ruin native industries or drain off the country's gold, a new law passed in July, 1824, granted complete commercial equality to anyone who voluntarily subjected himself to the nation's tax laws.[70]

The rivalry between Colombian and foreign importers was really one special phase of a fairly widespread hostility toward the influx of foreigners in general, whether naturalized or not. Another side to this hostility was the fear of some clerical elements that foreigners would introduce heretical notions of religion, a love for senseless luxuries, and the relaxation of morals: it was on grounds such as these that the chief opposition was offered to all plans for the encouragement of immigration.[71] However, such views found more favor with the masses than with the leaders of Colombian society, who felt on the contrary that contact with foreigners would help to eradicate the "corruption of customs" which already existed, and which was ascribed, of course, to "three centuries of Spanish oppression." Even Colombian importers objected much less to foreigners as such than to business competition. The English, who came in force both to fight in Colombian armies and to develop the economy, were particularly admired; they were copied even in such minor details as hand-shaking and shouting "hip, hip, hip, huzza" for Simón Bolívar.[72] Equally significant was the wide support enjoyed by two very typically English institutions, the Colombian Bible Society and the Bogotá Racing Club. The former, which must be considered at length in a different connection, had actually a higher degree of Colombian participation, but the Racing Club is just as good an example of cultural influence. Its stated objectives were to introduce Bogotá to the "delights" of horseracing, and naturally to "improve the breed of that excellent animal the horse."[73] With few exceptions all Bogotá race horses were owned by members of the British colony, yet the Racing Club as well as the Bible Society had Santander as its official patron, several leading merchants joined the board of directors, and two cabinet members agreed to serve as Stewards. Since gambling was also a popular Colombian vice, it was

[70] A.H.N., Corresp.-Cámara (Interior), July 14, 1824; *Codif. Nac.* I, 394-395; *Actas:* Senado-1824, 793-796; A.C., Senado-29, 277-280.
[71] See below, p. 245.
[72] *El Preguntón* (Bogotá), No. 7, 1823; Cochrane, *op. cit.*, II, 166.
[73] *El Constitucional,* June 2, 1825.

ECONOMIC RECONSTRUCTION AND DEVELOPMENT 149

hardly surprising that prominent Colombians turned out en masse to view the races.[74]

Neither the establishment of foreign merchants nor the introduction of horse-racing, however, served to correct the state of underpopulation which had been the chief official motive for encouraging immigration in the first place, and it occurred to few Colombians that vacant lands might be used instead by their landless fellow citizens. For most purposes other than foreign colonization, the last word on land distribution had been said by the public land law of Cúcuta, and that law was not really very liberal in its terms. If it had been strictly enforced, which it fortunately was not, the law might have caused the eviction of countless squatters on public lands, and would probably have evicted many small landowners from their own farms simply because they could not establish the validity of their titles. The minimum price of $1 per *fanegada* which it set for the sale of the national domain was not exactly reasonable either: critics pointed out that at this price a square league of the Venezuelan *llanos* would cost $3600, whereas such land previously had never been worth more than $500, and had sold at times for as little as $40.[75] As a result, dealings in land under this legislation appear to have been limited mainly to a relatively small number of large-scale and essentially speculative purchases, paid for not in cash but in debt certificates.[76] A Congressman from the *llanos* proposed a new law which would have granted full ownership of public lands to anyone who had made use of them for a space of ten years, but this proposal was never finally adopted. The administration bloc led by Senator Francisco Soto strongly opposed too great a reduction in land prices, and Santander himself vetoed one land law precisely

[74] *El Constitucional,* June 2, 16, and 23, July 7, and August 18, 1825.

[75] *Codif. Nac.* I, 125-128; *El Constitucional,* July 22, 1824; *El Observador Caraqueño,* April 22, 1824. The Congress of Cúcuta did offer a clear title, free of charge, to anyone whose occupation of public lands dated from *tiempo inmemorial,* or who held them by "a just prescription;" but certain legal formalities were still required, and it is doubtful that many squatters ever complied with them.

[76] One public land transaction which aroused great controversy at the time was the acquisition of an extensive tract between Río Hacha and Maracaibo by Col. Mauricio Encinoso, who hoped to invite the Goajira Indians to live on or near his land and thus become "civilized." It is doubtful that many accepted his invitation, and Encinoso was soon involved in a long and bitter dispute with the *Junta Provincial* of Maracaibo, which suspected that his real objective was to acquire a monopoly of the brazil wood trade. See A.C., Senado-47, 10, 14-15, and on the general problem of public lands, *El Constitucional,* March 2, 1826, which reproduces the relevant portions of Castillo y Rada's memoir for 1826. For the highly interesting speculations of Juan de Dios Aranzazu, see Luis Augusto Cuervo, ed., *Epistolario de Rufino Cuervo* (3 vols., Bogotá 1916-22) I, 7, 10-11, 15, and *passim.*

because it would have allowed provincial officials to sell too much land too cheaply.⁷⁷

In fairness it must be added that the Santander administration was seeking mainly to prevent an uncontrolled speculation in public lands which would have permanently alienated all the best of the national domain before there was any sizeable number of bona fide settlers to use it. There were at least a few persons, moreover, who clearly recognized the social and economic weaknesses of the predominant great estate system and agitated for a wider distribution of land among individual small landowners. This thesis was particularly well expressed by *El Huerfanito Bogotano*, which seems to have been a mouthpiece for Catholic humanitarianism. The English-dominated *Colombiano* of Caracas attacked the *latifundios* also, on the grounds that their owners so seldom made full use of the land, and there were always particular types of large landholdings that were very generally condemned. It has already been mentioned that entailed estates were abolished in 1824, and Colombian liberals managed to whittle away slowly but surely at mortmain holdings as well.⁷⁸

It does not follow that such measures had any far-reaching effect upon the average size of landed estates or the patterns of rural settlement: at most they may have increased the turnover of landed property within the ranks of the well-to-do minority. On the other hand, there is certainly no evidence that the rural masses were as yet generally dissatisfied with the economic order. There was social unrest in much of Venezuela, but the system of landholding was only one of the reasons for it. Only in Antioquia was there a vigorous and expanding rural population seeking to increase the number of small homesteads. What the *antioqueños* wanted primarily was a share of vacant national lands, and their need moved Santander rather belatedly to request permission to distribute the public domain for settlement by native Colombians on as liberal terms as those offered to foreign immigrants.⁷⁹ Congress did nothing about this, but at least there is no indication that those *antioqueños* who helped themselves to the national domain just the same were seriously hampered by the authorities.

---

⁷⁷ *Actas:* Congreso-1823, 509; *Actas:* Senado-1824, 123; *Acuerdos* I, 236-237. Interior Secretary Restrepo, on the other hand, felt that the present price of public lands was definitely too high. See *El Constitucional*, July 22, 1824.

⁷⁸ *El Huerfanito Bogotano*, May 19, 1826; *El Colombiano*, April 12, 1826. On clerical mortmain see below, pp. 223-228.

⁷⁹ A.C., Cámara-10, 166-172; Santander to Congress, January 17, 1825, Senado-36, 4.

Chapter X

## *Policy and Practice in Foreign Trade*

DESPITE the attention lavished on problems of internal development, the most important single aspect of Colombian economic policy was clearly the regulation of foreign trade. In so far as Colombia possessed more than a subsistence economy, her economic life was largely geared to the exchange of precious metals and agricultural produce for foreign manufactures. Foreign trade, passing through the customs houses, was far and away the primary source of government revenue. Moreover, it provided a perfect field both for a test of conflicting economic theories and for the expression of antagonistic regional interests. If foreign trade did not become as explosive an issue as in the United States and Argentina during the same period it was mainly because the agricultural interests of the northern provinces were so strong that the laissez faire dogma of the liberals had to be modified to suit their requirements, while those groups that felt themselves seriously injured by foreign trade policy were usually weak enough to be disregarded. But it need hardly be added that no economic group could ever be treated to its entire satisfaction, and that in the end trade and tariff issues became at least one underlying factor in the creation of political discontent.

### *Import Duties and Regulations*

In practice, of course, no one seriously desired to accept the full logic of economic liberalism and introduce a policy of complete free trade. Even the most doctrinaire liberals regarded this merely as an ideal to be attained at some future point, and for the present they had to be content with only a gradual reduction in the scale of duties. As pointed out before in dealing with fiscal policy, this process culminated in the tariff legislation of 1826, which provided for *ad valorem* duties ranging from 7½% to 35% on most Colombian imports.[1] The stated objective of the Colombian government was to seek further reductions whenever possible, and in general the tariff was conceived of as a revenue measure primarily.

Nevertheless, it was inevitable that the tariff should also be used to some extent as an instrument of general economic policy. The first tariff law passed by the Congress of Cúcuta carefully provided for duty-free introduction of most tools, paintings, antiquities, and other articles deemed particularly necessary for material and spiritual progress. Care was like-

[1] *Codif. Nac.* II, 204-212.

wise taken to impose higher rates on such luxuries as silks and furniture than on unfinished metals and ordinary textiles,[2] and these arrangements set a pattern that was generally followed in subsequent legislation. A few articles were either excluded altogether or subjected to prohibitory duties for reasons that were frankly protective. The list of prohibited articles actually increased from year to year until the trend was at last reversed by the Congress of 1826. Even then the more important prohibitions were left in force, in part because the liberals, despite their theoretical fondness for free trade, were convinced that some protection was necessary, and in part because it was inexpedient to reject the claims of powerful economic interests.

Perhaps the most powerful vested interest of them all was the national treasury, which consistently sought to protect the state monopolies against foreign competition. Foreign tobacco, for instance, was excluded by Congress altogether after a brief experiment with a 50% import duty. The duty in this case had left a substantial revenue for the state, since United States tobacco could still be sold at a profit in Colombia thanks to the artificially high prices charged by the *estanco;* but the monopoly itself had suffered, and Venezuelan tobacco-growers were equally unhappy. Indeed the protests of officials in Venezuela led Santander to suspend tobacco imports even before they were finally forbidden by law. The Congress of 1824 likewise prohibited the introduction of salt, which was another government monopoly, and even though the gunpowder monopoly was too decrepit to fill Colombian needs, Congress at least made the importation of powder illegal for private citizens.[3]

Even when no state monopoly was involved, the agriculturalists of Venezuela and northern New Granada were usually strong enough to gain special favors in customs legislation. Considered as a whole, they were the largest single economic interest group, and they had been obviously hard hit by the war. The Congress of Cúcuta thus began by forbidding outright the importation of coffee, cacao, indigo, and sugar.[4] The inclusion of coffee and cacao in the list was superfluous since they were imported nowhere; they were Colombia's two leading export crops. Indigo, on the other hand, although it ranked third, was produced mainly in Venezuela. It was regularly imported from Guatemala into Ecuador for the coloring of local textiles, and the absence of Ecuadoran representatives at Cúcuta provided the opportunity for what appears to have been among other things a frank effort of Venezuelan producers to win the southern market for themselves. The prohibition was particularly unjust since transportation costs from the north coast plantations to Ecuador

[2] *Codif. Nac.* I, 57, 60-61.

[3] *Codif. Nac.* I, 59-60, 208-210, 334; *Acuerdos* I, 40; *La Gaceta de Cartagena,* April 16, 1823; A.C., Senado-20, 136.

[4] *Codif. Nac.* I, 62-63.

were infinitely higher than the costs of doing business with Guatemala. As for sugar, Ecuador was again the region that suffered: there were some producers in Guayaquil and elsewhere who were delighted to receive protection, but Ecuador as a whole was accustomed to obtaining much of its sugar supply from Peru, and that would now become impossible. The producers of Venezuela and Cartagena may well have hoped that ultimately they could replace Peru as a supplier, but this was extremely unlikely since their own sugar industry was badly run down as a result of the war and a shortage of slave labor; indeed some kind of protection was really needed just to keep foreign sugar out of the local market in the northern departments. It is thus fortunate for the Ecuadorans that Congress finally agreed to make a special and temporary exception in their favor. A common interest in the importation of sugar won them the support of Panama, and in 1826 the opposition of Congressmen from Venezuela and Magdalena had to give way. Hence the Congress of that year reluctantly permitted the introduction for three years of either sugar or indigo at Guayaquil, and of sugar on the Isthmus, subject only to some rather high specific duties.[5]

An unusually complicated problem was posed by the introduction of Jamaica rum and other liquors, which was consistently opposed by both sugar and distilling interests. The Congress of Cúcuta had placed a high duty on such imports, but this proved to be an ineffective deterrent. A wide taste for Jamaica rum had developed when it was first brought in on a large scale during the War of Independence; the Jamaica product was cheaper than any Colombian equivalent; and the duty was not too hard to mitigate in practice by suborning the necessary officials or by concealing a part of the shipment. Therefore the Congress of 1823 flatly prohibited the importation of all liquors derived from cane sugar, and further increased the duties on all other varieties of strong drink. The measure was taken, interestingly enough, at the urging of Dr. Castillo y Rada, whose liberal principles were overcome in part by his concern over the decline in Colombian distilling taxes, and no doubt also because his native Cartagena was one of the regions most affected.[6] Even this did not satisfy the producers themselves, who marshalled an interminable list of arguments to show that protection of native *aguardiente* required the prohibi-

[5] *El Patriota de Guayaquil,* February 11 and 25, 1826; *El Constitucional* (Bogotá), January 26, 1826; *The Present State of Colombia* (London, 1827), 280-282; A.C., Senado-35, 374, Actas del Senado, February 28 and March 2, 1826; *Codif. Nac.* II, 329.

[6] Eduardo Rodríguez Piñeres, ed., *La vida de Castillo y Rada* (Bogotá, 1949), 129; A.C., Senado-4, 354; *Codif. Nac.* I, 260-261. From a purely fiscal viewpoint whatever might be gained in distilling taxes would be offset by the loss in import duties; but the low state of the former was a very sensitive matter since it reflected on a major liberal reform, the abolition of the *aguardiente* monopoly.

tion of all liquor imports whatsoever. It was pointed out that rum was being brought in labelled *ginebrón,* with the result that on one occasion the visiting French educator Pierre Comettant had to be drafted as official gin-taster for the port of Maracaibo. It was feared that Colombians might acquire a permanent taste for French brandy, and even the general evils of drink were played upon in this campaign to exclude foreign in favor of native liquors.[7] However, despite the support of the Santander administration, the exclusion of all foreign distilled liquors did not pass. In fact there remained a strong school of thought opposed to the absolute prohibition of any article whatsoever as contrary to liberal principles and ineffective in practice, and in the tariff law of 1826 legal entry was permitted once again for cane liquors, subject to a high specific duty. The same treatment was extended simultaneously to salt, gunpowder, and even snuff, though not to tobacco generally; but all other prohibitions remained technically in force.[8]

Other interest groups did not win even a short-lived victory. The agriculturalists of interior New Granada waged an intermittent campaign for the exclusion of United States flour, which was extensively used in the coastal provinces, and they were strongly supported both by the City of Bogotá and by the more conservative representatives of the central provinces in Congress. *El Noticiosote,* which usually gave a fair reflection of popular prejudices, expressed the fear that at the present rate Colombia would soon be importing not only wheat flour but even *chicha.* Yet the liberal professional men who spoke for Cundinamarca and Boyacá in official circles could generally see no compelling reason to abandon free-trade principles in this respect. The wheat-growing area, therefore, did not present a strong united front. Then, too, transportation costs from the plain of Bogotá to the Caribbean coast would have made the inferior native product unreasonably expensive. As a result, flour was merely subjected to the high specific duty befitting an article of luxury, and this was not enough to stop the flow of imports.[9]

Much the same was in store for Colombia's primitive manufacturing

[7] *La Gaceta de Cartagena,* March 19, 1825; A.C., Senado-10, 1-2, Senado-27, 347-350, Senado-30, 198-201, Cámara-8, 127-131; A.C., Correspondencia del Senado 1823-1825, 127.

[8] *Actas:* Senado-1824, 769; A.C., Senado-20, 137, Senado-43, 30, Correspondencia del Senado 1823-1825, 127; *Codif. Nac.* II, 211-212.

[9] *Actas:* Congreso-1823, 448, 484; José Ignacio de San Miguel, *Señor Pedro Palotes* (Bogotá, 1822), 14; *El Noticiosote* (Bogotá), March 27, 1825; A.C., Senado-23, 75. Admittedly some administration liberals supported the exclusion measure: Francisco Montoya, who was close enough to Santander to be chosen as one of the loan negotiators in London, sponsored a bill for this purpose in Congress. However, the main support always came from conservative elements.

industries, which suffered chiefly though not exclusively from the "inexplicable mania" for English textiles. Even in Boyacá, the manufacturing heart of New Granada, English cloths competed successfully with the native product. The textile industry of highland Ecuador was restricted to an ever smaller share of the market it had formerly enjoyed for cheap cloths in the mining region of western New Granada, and was challenged by European textiles even in Quito and Cuenca. No doubt the situation was not quite so bad as domestic producers sought to imply, and foreign travelers may sometimes have exaggerated the trend out of pride in Europe's industrial superiority. Nevertheless, there was bound to arise a strong demand in some quarters for protection, and the town fathers of Bogotá asked support for miscellaneous native industries just as they asked for the exclusion of foreign wheat. So did the more old-fashioned *granadinos* in Congress. In highland Ecuador, which had no major exports and was thus far more dependent on the fate of domestic manufacturing, the same demand was both more vehement and more widespread.[10]

However, New Granada manufacturers and artisans suffered from the same lack of united support as the wheat-growers. Venezuela was scarcely interested in the problem at all. As for Ecuador, it had been unrepresented at Cúcuta and was distinctly under-represented in later Congresses because of the difficulty of communications. The administration itself cited the rights of consumers as against those of producers, and pointed out that a moderate tariff produced more revenue, thanks to the greater volume of trade, than did a high one. Or as José Manuel Restrepo observed, the damage to Ecuadoran industry was regrettable, but the benefits of cheap foreign goods to the nation as a whole were even greater. The army, which was the greatest single consumer of textiles, frequently preferred British products.[11] In the end, therefore, no concerted effort was ever made to protect manufacturers, and least of all to give them the exaggerated support afforded to the agricultural interests of Venezuela. Boot-makers, cabinet-makers, and the like received more consideration in the tariff schedule than weavers, in part simply because the goods they made were not usually intended for popular consumption.[12]

[10] *El Correo de la Ciudad de Bogotá,* April 18, 1822; *El Chasqui Bogotano,* November 12, 1826; *La Gaceta de Colombia,* December 4, 1825, October 1, 1826; Gaspar Theodore Mollien, *Viaje por la República de Colombia en 1823* (Bogotá, 1944), 92; A.C., Cámara-16, 27-28.

[11] *El Constitucional,* January 26, 1826, July 12, 1827; *La Gaceta de Colombia,* March 5, 1826.

[12] Under the legislation of 1821 boots and shoes paid maximum duties of 30% and ordinary textiles no more than 22½%; for 1826 the figures were 35% and 22½% respectively. No simple comparison is possible between the two years, as the first figures are levied according to a static *arancel,* and the latter are *ad valorem.* Because of this (and other complications) it is unfortunately impossible to express the trend of import duties in a chart such as that given below for export duties.

It should not be imagined, of course, that tariff measures were always uniformly applied in practice. Smuggling was used both to evade payment of duties and to circumvent prohibitory legislation, while "extraordinary faculties" or other emergency powers could be used for all kinds of tampering with the scale of duties. The Intendants of Venezuela and Magdalena occasionally suspended all regular import duties on needed foodstuffs in periods of scarcity, prohibiting their export at the same time.[13] For purely financial reasons in 1822 Bolívar used his special faculties in Ecuador to retain the customs system originally adopted by the independent government of Guayaquil; this levied a basic rate of 30% on foreign goods, which was definitely higher than the Colombian average, but the extra revenue was badly needed so that Guayaquil might serve as an arsenal for military operations in Peru.[14] As a concession to local sentiment and local conditions, furthermore, Bolívar decided not to enforce the prohibition of sugar and indigo at Ecuadoran ports. In the latter case his decision was immediately countermanded by a special decree of Congress,[15] and the national tariff rates were also extended to Ecuador as soon as financial conditions allowed. In practice, however, it is doubtful that the exclusion of sugar and indigo was ever complete in Ecuador, and in 1826, as observed already, Congress itself had to meet the Ecuadorans part-way.

An important side-issue to the debate over what products should be allowed to enter the republic was the question of the ports through which they should be allowed to come. The question was chiefly important for the Caribbean coast of New Granada, where Cartagena and Santa Marta fought to retain their colonial monopoly of foreign trade. As both ports were situated at a distance from the main route to the interior, the Magdalena River, they were not always able to handle cargo most effectively. In particular their monopoly was challenged by the small port of Sabanilla, which lay only a short distance overland from the present terminus of river navigation at Barranquilla. The port of Sabanilla had officially been opened for foreign trade while Cartagena was still occupied by the Spanish. When Cartagena was taken by the patriots, its superior harbor and port facilities made it certain that it would receive the bulk of the trade that had previously gone to Sabanilla, but the latter quite naturally sought

[13] *La Gaceta de Cartagena,* February 23, 1824, April 30, 1825; *El Colombiano* (Caracas) April 26, 1826.

[14] Cf. *Reglamento provisorio para el comercio nacional y extranjero* (Guayaquil, 1821); O'Leary XX, 91, 110; A.C., Cámara-1, 215-216. If goods passed through Panama en route to Ecuador, the Guayaquil customhouse would collect the difference between 30% and the duties already paid on the Isthmus.

[15] *Codif. Nac.* I, 243-244; *Actas:* Congreso-1823, 260-261.

to remain open for any trade it could legally get. It was nevertheless closed to all foreign commerce by the Congress of Cúcuta, and a later campaign against the Cartagena "monopolists" in the Congress of 1824 failed to reopen the smaller port. Congress insisted that Santander take responsibility for any final decision regarding the opening or closing of ports, and when he reluctantly undertook to draw up a definitive list of ports for foreign trade he reaffirmed the decision of Cúcuta.[16] From the start exceptions had occasionally been made, permitting the Cartagena "monopolists," among others, to make use of Sabanilla in special cases, but this was for export purposes only.[17] With the aid of the *cartagenero* Secretary of Finance, Dr. Castillo y Rada, the Cartagena merchants further saw to it that the Atrato River, which had also been opened to foreign trade as a war measure, was closed as effectively as Sabanilla when the war was over. It stayed closed despite strong protests from the Chocó, which could be safely disregarded, and from the commercial interests of the Cauca valley, who were really less contemptible and were strongly backed by their intendant.[18]

There were also certain cases in which preferential duties were imposed on the basis of either the nationality of the ships engaged in import trade or the ports from which they sailed. Following accepted mercantilistic practice, and apparently without opposition, the Congress of Cúcuta established special discounts on customs and tonnage duties if goods were imported in Colombian ships.[19] Since the Colombian merchant marine was small indeed, this provision did not seriously hurt foreign shipowners. Somewhat more important was the preference granted at Cúcuta in the case of goods brought directly to Colombia from European ports, whether carried in native or in foreign vessels. Under this provision the duties were at least 5% less than they would be otherwise. The purpose was simply to end Colombian dependence on the middlemen of Jamaica, St. Thomas, and other West Indian islands who had come to dominate trade between northern Europe and the Spanish Main during the late colonial period thanks to their favorable location for smuggling, and had consolidated their position by being the first to take advantage of the legal opening of patriot-held ports to non-Spanish trade during the War of Independence. During the war they had performed a useful

[16] Blanco VIII, 218-219; *Codif. Nac.* I, 138, VII, 213; *La Gaceta de Cartagena* No. 174; A.H.N., Congresos XXV, 654, 668.

[17] Cf. *La Gaceta de Cartagena,* October 8 and 28, 1825, regarding the exception made in favor of Juan de Francisco Martín.

[18] A.C., Senado-47, 75-88, Actas del Senado, July 5, 1827 (A.M.).

[19] *Codif. Nac.* I, 58, 69. A similar discount was later applied to various lesser port duties (*Codif. Nac.* II, 345).

function in supplying the new nation; but now they were considered parasitic "monopolists" who increased the cost of imported goods through extra handling and insurance charges.[20]

The same discount did not at first apply in trade between Colombia and the United States. One reason was no doubt the fact that such trade was not dependent to the same extent on West Indian merchant houses: hence no special inducement was needed. The omission was nevertheless discriminatory, and it was ascribed by United States diplomats both to Colombian resentment over the Florida treaty with Spain and to a desire to hasten diplomatic recognition by economic pressure.[21] Whatever its precise origin, such discrimination was soon recognized as illiberal by the Colombian authorities, and in 1823, in response to diplomatic protests, the reduced rate was extended to direct trade with the United States.[22] The preference for goods carried by Colombian shipping did not last long either. Not only was equality granted to the ships of Peru, Chile, and Central America out of Spanish American solidarity but it was demanded by Great Britain as a condition for signing a commercial treaty in 1825. And once equal treatment was accorded Great Britain it had to be given to the United States under the most favored nation principle, for the United States had already signed a commercial treaty.[23] It was naturally withheld, on the other hand, from all nations which did not formally recognize Colombian independence and sign a commercial pact. The Anglo-Saxon powers thus obtained from the outset a juridically favored position in Colombian trade. Swedish overtures for a treaty in 1823[24]

[20] *Codif. Nac.* I, 58; *Actas:* Cúcuta, 390; A.C., Senado-10, 42.

[21] Todd to Adams, May 20, 1823, N.A., Colombia Dispatches II, and May 29, 1823, in William R. Manning, ed., *Diplomatic Correspondence of the United States Concerning the Independence of the Latin American Nations* (3 vols., New York, 1925), II, 1254; Lowry to Adams, March 20, 1822, N.A., La Guaira I. The Florida treaty was the explanation given by Todd, who apparently received his information from Dr. Miguel Peña, judge of the *Alta Corte* and a former deputy at Cúcuta.

[22] *Codif. Nac.* I, 190-191. The direct trade rebate was also extended to other Latin American countries on products originating within their borders, and to Asiatic trade (*Codif. Nac.* I, 264).

[23] *Codif. Nac.* I, 213, 221, II, 90, 194-196. In some respects Britain had received more than equal treatment, since she forced Colombia to agree that at the end of a seven-year period reciprocal privileges in British ports would be given to Colombian-owned ships only if they had been built in Colombia and were predominantly manned by Colombian citizens. This would obviously exclude almost any Colombian vessel capable of crossing the Atlantic, but Colombia felt compelled to yield lest Mexico and Buenos Aires get ahead in the competition for British trade and investment. (Cf. *Acuerdos* II, 44-45.)

[24] Todd to Adams, May 29, 1823, N.A., Colombia Dispatches II; Blanco VIII, 636-637.

came to nothing, and the French government, despite the protests of French merchants, was not even willing to begin negotiations.[25]

## Exports and Export Taxes

The levying of export taxes provided still another battleground for conflicting interests. Everyone agreed that such duties were an evil both in theory and in practice: they were condemned by liberal economists, and they impaired the nation's capacity for earning foreign exchange. No one seriously challenged Castillo y Rada's thesis that they should ultimately be done away with. However, neither could it be denied that in the short run the treasury needed the revenue they provided.[26] Good liberal though he was, Santander repeatedly used his veto power to restrain Congress from whittling away at export duties too rapidly.[27] The chief problem was simply to find a rate for any given export that would yield the greatest possible revenue without seriously hampering the flow of trade or excessively burdening Colombian producers.

The first step, which was taken at the Congress of Cúcuta, was to abolish the export levies of the Spanish regime and replace them with a standard *ad valorem* tax of 5%, which was generally a good bit less than had formerly been paid. The figure was reduced again to 4% in 1824. This rate did not apply, however, to the bulk of the nation's export volume, since everything important and much that was unimportant received special treatment at all times. (See Table.) Thus cacao, which was by far the chief export of Guayaquil, shared leadership in Venezuela with coffee, and was important also in New Granada, was originally subject to a duty of 10%. The basic rate was exceeded in this instance on the grounds that cacao was a virtual monopoly of Colombia and could well bear the extra charge. Moreover, under the separate tax system provisionally retained in Ecuador by order of Bolívar, cacao paid a specific duty amounting to roughly 30% *ad valorem;* indeed the prospect of seeing this particular revenue cut by two-thirds was one of the chief

---

[25] The Bogotá administration promptly disavowed, however, the extravagant threat made by Zea to cut off all trade with any nation that did not recognize Colombian Independence. Cf. Pedro A. Zubieta, *Apuntaciones sobre las primeras misiones diplomáticas de Colombia*, (Bogotá, 1924), 325-328.

[26] See Castillo's memoir for 1826 in *El Constitucional*, February 23, 1826, and also criticism of export taxes from two widely different viewpoints in *La Miscelánea* (Bogotá), September 25, 1824, and *El Colombiano del Ecuador* (Quito), November 2, 1825.

[27] Santander to Congress, April 23, 1823, A.C., Senado-13, 137; June 2, 1824, A.C., Senado-64; *Actas*, Cámara-1824, 232-233.

## COMPARATIVE EXPORT DUTIES

|  | Law of<br>29 September 1821 | Law of<br>10 July 1824 | Law of<br>13 March 1826 |
|---|---|---|---|
| Basic rate | 5% | 4% | 4% |
| Coffee | free | 6% | free |
| Sugar | free | 4% | 4% |
| *Aguardiente* | free | 4% | 4% |
| Hides | 10% | 10% | 10% |
| Cacao | 10% | 15% | 10% |
| Indigo | 10% | 5% | 5% |
| Mules | $15* | $20* | $20* |
| Horses | $15* | $16* | $16* |
| Cattle | $12½ | $12½ | $12½ |
| Minted gold | 3% | 3% | free |
| Minted silver | forbidden | forbidden** | free |
| Cotton | free | free | free |
| Rice | 5% | free | free |
| Corn | 5% | free | free |
| Quinine | 5% | 4% | free |
| Manufactures | 5% | 4% | free |

\* Could be prohibited at discretion of the Executive.

\*\* Save at Panamanian ports and Guayaquil, where export was permitted on payment of 3% duty.

Sources: *Codif. Nac.* I, 64-65, 329-331; II, 212-214.

reasons for Bolívar's refusal to enforce the customs legislation of Cúcuta in the South. When the national customs system was finally extended to Ecuador, the general rate on cacao was increased from 10% to 15% so as to recoup some of the expected loss in revenue. Yet this was done over strong protests, for it was claimed that the Colombian export tax had already caused an increase in cacao exports from Guatemala, and the rate was again reduced to 10% in 1826.[28]

Coffee presented just as many difficulties when it came to finding the ideal level of duties. Originally, it was exempted from all export duties whatsoever. This was done not only because the planting economy had been hurt by the war—which was even truer in the case of cacao, since it required more careful attention—but also because coffee very definitely was subject to foreign competition. On the other hand, coffee was still a crop that commanded an ample foreign market, and it recovered quickly

---

[28] *Actas:* Senado-1824, 530-531; A.C., Actas del Senado, February 23, 1826; *Reglamento provisorio* (Guayaquil); A.C., Senado-26, 488-489, 504; *El Constitucional,* September 15, 1825.

when peace was restored. Thus no real crisis ensued when the Intendant of Venezuela used his "extraordinary faculties" to impose a temporary regional levy of 10% on coffee exports in 1822.[29] Two years later a general export duty of 6% was imposed by Congress, only to be removed in 1826 when Castillo y Rada announced an increase in foreign competition.[30]

The third great agricultural export of Venezuela, indigo, was subjected to a 10% duty at Cúcuta, but the rate was cut to 5% in 1824 since the product was neither unique with Colombia nor of very high quality. Producers of cotton were in an even less favorable position for foreign trade. Cotton had once been a major export of both Venezuela and Cartagena, but it was still produced as inefficiently as ever and was cleaned by hand, while United States production had risen sharply in both quantity and quality with the use of the cotton gin; the world price of Colombian cotton had fallen by as much as two-thirds since 1810. Hence cotton was exempted from export duties by the Congress of Cúcuta, and in this case all subsequent legislation allowed the exemption to stand. Sugar was likewise exempted at Cúcuta, since production methods were inefficient and the crop was threatened indirectly by the influx of Jamaica rum. Later a moderate duty was imposed, but its place on the free list was more than filled by a number of other products that for one reason or another were thought to need special encouragement: quinine, which had once been a major export of New Granada but had lost its market through unethical tampering with the quality; corn and rice, which were of major interest to a few areas and faced heavy competition abroad; and, finally, Colombian manufactures.[31]

A peculiarly difficult problem was presented by the grazing industry of the Venezuelan *llanos*. It had been hard hit by the war, yet horses and mules were in steady demand in the Lesser Antilles, which, it was thought, could obtain them economically from no other source. The production of hides, similarly, had greatly declined, but there was a steady market overseas. To complicate matters further, draft animals were urgently needed at home for agricultural recovery; for this reason there was a persistent demand, especially in Venezuela where the needs of agriculture were greatest, to restrict or simply to forbid the extraction of horses and

[29] *Actas:* Cúcuta, 393; *El Iris de Venezuela* (Caracas), September 30, 1822; *El Anglo-Colombiano* (Caracas), July 13, 1822; José María Castillo y Rada, *Memoria de Hacienda* (Bogotá, 1823), 7; A.C., Senado-6, 54. The latter measure (which was applied to certain other articles as well) was highly unpopular and was frowned on by Castillo y Rada, but the administration at least granted formal approval.

[30] *El Constitucional,* February 23, 1826.

[31] A.C., Senado-26, 489, Correspondencia del Senado 1823-1825, 340; *The Present State of Colombia,* 270-276.

mules.³² Hence a compromise was clearly in order: the export of live animals was subjected to fairly high specific duties, while the Executive was granted special authority to forbid their export altogether whenever it seemed advisable. This authorization was actually used in different areas more than once.³³ As for the hides, they were consistently taxed at the special rate of 10%.

The duties on agricultural and pastoral exports were mainly a concern of Venezuela and Guayaquil. Highland Ecuador virtually had no exports. New Granada was concerned above all with precious metals, and at first only minted gold could legally be sent out of the country, subject to a tax of 3%.³⁴ This was a substantial reduction from the 6% charged by the colonial tariff, but silver could not be exported at all because it was needed for coinage, and gold exports in any other form were forbidden so that the traffic might be controlled more easily and all taxes, including the profit of the mint, carefully collected. The same rate of 3% was followed in the highly controversial *derecho de extracción presunta*, which was imposed on all imports that were not directly taken in exchange for Colombian exports; the assumption was that gold was smuggled out in payment, so a tax was charged just as if it had passed through the customs house. This provision was especially unpopular in Venezuela, which had no gold of its own to export and also bore the brunt of the regular export taxes on agricultural produce. Both in response to such criticism and in the hope of encouraging trade in general, the *derecho de extracción presunta* was abandoned in 1824. Moreover, by the first months of 1826 the shortage of silver had become less acute, and general economic conditions were sufficiently stabilized to permit a more liberal policy with regard to precious metals. As a result, the Congress of 1826 decreed that both gold and silver in minted form could be exported without limitation, and free of duty.³⁵

## *The Pattern of Foreign Trade*

The precise effect of Colombian tariff policy on the course of foreign trade is difficult to judge, especially since no reliable trade figures are available. Both Colombian and foreign statistics are inadequate, and the

---

[32] A.C., Senado-20, 137, Actas del Senado, March 3, 1826; *Actas:* Cúcuta, 404.

[33] Cf. *La Gaceta de Cartagena,* November 13, 1824. This policy, together with the high duties, apparently caused an increase in breeding in the British West Indies (*Present State of Colombia,* 290).

[34] Certain exceptions had to be granted for local conditions in Panama and Ecuador. See *Acuerdos* I, 29, and Table of Export Duties.

[35] *Actas:* Cúcuta, 635-636; *El Constitucional,* September 15, 1825, February 23, 1826; A.C., Actas del Senado, February 25, 1826; *Codif. Nac.* II, 213. Even certain other forms of gold and silver (though not all forms) could now be exported, subject to varying specific duties.

POLICY AND PRACTICE IN FOREIGN TRADE          163

Colombian figures, above all, fail to account for the very substantial portion of foreign trade that did not pass through customs. Yet it is clear that there were important changes in the nature of Colombian foreign commerce in the period immediately after independence, and that official trade policy was at least one of the various reasons for those changes. This is particularly evident in the case of import trade, where the ending of the Spanish monopoly, combined with a mildly liberal tax policy, made it definitely easier to acquire foreign manufactures than it had been under the colonial regime. Then too, with the English loan of 1824 merchants were enabled to carry on an unprecedented importing spree. Thus Colombian imports rose steadily from 1821 through 1825, when they far surpassed colonial figures. In fact at that time in legal trade imports were at least half again as much as exports, the result being a heavily unfavorable trade balance.[36]

Obviously Colombia was not receiving any great amount of goods free of charge, so presumably the difference was made up, chiefly by borrowed sterling and by the illegal (and thus unrecorded) extraction of precious metals. Nevertheless, the figures that exist do reflect a basic difficulty: Colombian demand for foreign manufactures, especially after years of war-time privation, was indefinitely expansible, whereas the foreign demand for coffee and cacao was not, and neither was the Colombian production of gold and silver. Some readjustment in trade was obviously necessary, but the crisis was delayed as long as the English loan lasted. Unfortunately, the loan was soon spent in its entirety. Starting with the year 1826 there was consequently a marked decline in imports,[37] for which

[36] Until much more research is done it would be folly for a historian to commit himself in print concerning the total of either imports or exports in any given year. Some usable figures do exist listing articles of trade by individual ports, but such tables are hard to use in making estimates for the nation as a whole: they are not always calculated on the same basis, and what may be a good year for statistics in Cartagena may be a bad one in La Guaira. The easiest way to reach a rough approximation of import totals is simply to take the import duties collected and multiply by four or five, since the average duty charged was rather constant in the neighborhood of 20-25%. With import duties officially listed as over $3,000,000 in 1825-6, and even making all conceivable allowances, the resulting total will still exceed any estimates available for the colonial period by several millions.

There is no easy way to estimate total exports, but the trade deficit is beyond dispute. Customhouse figures for La Guaira and Puerto Cabello in 1824-5, for instance, show over $3,000,000 imports and under $2,000,000 exports (*Present State of Colombia*, 162); a similar relationship existed at Guayaquil (cf. R. A. Humphreys, *British Consular Reports on the Trade and Politics of Latin America*, London, 1940, p. 240) and at Cartagena (cf. A.H.N., Aduanas de la República I, 161, 420, 468).

[37] Colombian figures for 1826-7 are especially inadequate, but figures for imports through La Guaira, as well as United States and British figures for exports to Colombia, leave no doubt as to the decline. See N. A., consular dispatch February 9, 1828, La Guaira II; United States Bureau of Statistics (Treasury Department), *American Commerce* (Washington, 1899), 3304; Humphreys, *op. cit.*, 344-351.

political disturbances in Colombia and the European financial depression can be only partly to blame. Imports were simply finding the natural level set by Colombia's ability to pay, and customs revenues fell with them.

Not only did exports fail to keep pace with imports, but also there were a few noticeable changes in their composition. Only in the last years of the colonial regime had coffee been able to compete with indigo for second place among agricultural exports, but at least in Venezuela it was now a rival of cacao for first place. By 1825 Venezuelan coffee exports had approximately regained the level of the last years before independence, even though the total value was slightly less as a result of a steady fall in prices.[38] Cacao was still feeling the effects of the war, and was also affected adversely by the decline of slavery since it was more typically the product of a slave economy. Hence despite Colombia's supposedly firm grip on world cacao markets its relative importance was declining; production had been falling slightly even before the war, and the recorded exports from Venezuela in 1824-5 were less than half the pre-war total. This was offset in part by a slight increase in prices, while in Guayaquil production was not seriously diminished.[39] Even so, in the nation as a whole coffee was gaining at the expense of cacao; and it is entirely reasonable to assume that the heavier export tax on cacao was one of the factors responsible for this trend. No tax privileges, on the other hand, were enough to help the declining cotton industry, so that cotton virtually disappeared from the list of Colombian exports. Neither did such minor exports as rice, corn, and quinine acquire much practical importance, at least for the nation as a whole, despite the preferred treatment accorded them. New Granada, therefore, had to rely as usual on its mineral exports. In the colonial period it had exported more gold than everything else combined, and the chief export from republican Cartagena was again simply money.[40]

There was also a change in the direction of Colombian foreign trade after independence. Spain not only lost her previous trade monopoly but since peace had not been signed was excluded altogether. Great Britain now enjoyed unchallenged leadership as a source of Colombian imports.

[38] *Present State of Colombia*, 162. The average price in the last years before 1810 was around $12 per quintal (cf. Mollien, *op. cit.*, 449); it rose to a wartime high occasionally in excess of $20 in 1819-22 and then fell to a figure well below colonial levels (cf. "price currents" in *La Gaceta de Caracas, El Venezolano*, and *El Colombiano*).

[39] Alexander von Humboldt, *Personal Narrative of Travels in the Equinoctial Regions of the New Continent* (7 vols., London, 1822-1829) IV, 67, 230, 241, 245-248; *Present State of Colombia*, 163, 264-267. See periodicals cited above for "price currents."

[40] Carl August Gosselman, *Reise in Columbien* (2 vols., Straslund, 1829) I, 92; Humphreys, *op. cit.*, 260.

The British share in Colombian export trade was considerably less, and that of the United States proportionately greater.[41] However, Colombian trade with the United States was of a different variety from that with Great Britain. The United States did not seriously compete with Great Britain in manufactured goods, sending instead "provisions"—flour, salt meats, lard, and the like—which were consumed in quantity in the Caracas area and along the coastal lowlands, where it was more profitable to grow plantation crops, and where "provisions" could be obtained more economically from overseas than overland from the interior of Colombia. Trade with the United States was also noteworthy in that Colombia did not show an unfavorable official balance.[42] The only other countries that figured at all prominently in Colombian foreign trade were France and Germany, but neither one could really compete with either British manufactures or United States "provisions," and they were further hampered by the lack of diplomatic relations with Colombia; hence both lagged well behind the two leaders.

Regardless of the countries of origin, a regrettably high proportion of Colombian imports still arrived by way of West Indian middlemen. It had been assumed that the tariff preference for "direct" imports would induce Europeans to send their goods to the Spanish Main without stopping in the Antilles, but unfortunately the West Indians had contacts with Colombian distributors and with corruptible customs officials that newcomers could not match. Likewise native importers, who had grown used to sending small ships out to Kingston or St. Thomas, lacked the means for trading personally with London. Goods were still being brought to Guayaquil after being grounded at both Kingston and Panama instead of traveling more economically by way of Cape Horn. In the latter case, however, Jamaica merchants were often taking a loss simply to keep their hand in the market; elsewhere, too, there were signs that the West Indian "monopolists" were losing their grip, and it was obvious that sooner or later the tariff discrimination would have to take its effect.[43]

[41] One of the few usable breakdowns of Colombian trade by countries is a table for La Guaira in the year 1827 prepared by the United States consulate. It reveals that the United States took roughly a third of La Guaira's exports, France one fifth, and Great Britain and Germany a sixth each. Imports came one-third from Great Britain, one-fourth each from Germany and the United States, and one-ninth from France (Dispatch of February 9, 1828, N.A., La Guaira II). These figures give a rough indication of the position of the leading countries, but it would be hazardous to take the exact figures as typical of any other year or of a different port. No similar figures are available for Cartagena, but as the chief export of New Granada was bullion it is likely that a considerably higher share went to Great Britain, directly or by way of Jamaica. In any case there is no doubt at all that Great Britain sold far more than she bought.

[42] *American Commerce*, 3304. If reexports are included, the balance is shifted.

[43] Mollien, *op. cit.*, 423-424; Humphreys, *op. cit.*, 240-243, 257-258; *Letters Written from Colombia* (London, 1824), 152, 205.

## Chapter XI

## *The Liberals and the Masses: Slavery and the Indian Question*

AS LONG as the Colombian government felt that in economic affairs its basic role was simply to create the conditions in which private enterprise could work to best advantage, the common man was for the most part expected to shift for himself. It was now fashionable to attack almsgiving as a boon to laziness, and what might be termed labor legislation was devoted mainly to keeping the poorer classes from becoming a public nuisance. Congress was particularly interested in reforming the *bogas* who so constantly abused the passengers they conveyed in their primitive craft up and down the Magdalena, and it passed a law for just this purpose, subjecting them to a stringent and rather complicated mechanism of government controls. In due course Congress also made vagrancy a national offense and decreed that "vagrants" should be put to work on such useful projects as sailing the Colombian Navy.[1] For that matter, even non-vagrants were liable to conscription for unpaid road work.[2]

By and large, however, the lot of the lower classes was not so miserable as might be assumed. Wages were low, averaging one or two *reales* a day in the interior of New Granada; they might go as high as four in port towns, but there prices were also higher. Health conditions, especially in the coastal lowlands, were usually deplorable. Yet the climate seldom required elaborate clothing and shelter, and certainly no one was in danger of actual starvation. One of the things that struck the attention of travelers from Europe is the fact that even meat was cheap enough to be a regular item of popular consumption. Indeed the *Corte Superior* of Guayaquil ascribed the multitude of vagrants among the local populace —a "horde of savages," to use its own graphic term—precisely to the fact that anyone could earn enough in two days to subsist for a whole week.[3] There were two special groups, moreover, that were not left solely to shift for themselves in the social and economic reforms of the period: the slaves and the Indians. Both groups had been accorded a particular legal status under the colonial regime that set them apart from the rest of the population, and there was consequently a mass of illiberal

[1] *Codif. Nac.* II, 25, 330-332, 361-362.
[2] *Codif. Nac.* II, 76-77.
[3] A.C., Senado-36, 179-182.

166

custom and legislation that had to be done away with first before they could take their proper place as citizens.

## The Decline of Slavery, and Related Questions

Slavery had not been a general phenomenon in the Viceroyalty of New Granada. It was estimated that in 1810 the slaves numbered only 138,000 out of a total population of nearly 3,000,000.[4] These slaves were concentrated principally along the coasts, in the minefields of the western provinces, and in the plantation districts of central Venezuela, and as these regions included precisely the ones that provided the bulk of Colombian exports, it followed that slavery was a force to be reckoned with. However, it was less to be reckoned with politically than economically. The mining and coastal regions were on the whole sparsely settled, and were therefore weakly represented in government. The Caracas area was of course a different matter, but its political power was still outweighed by that of central and eastern New Granada, which by no means rested on a slave economy. All opponents of slavery, furthermore, had a powerful ally in the political and economic philosophy of the Enlightenment, which was distinctly hostile to it and now strongly colored both official and private thinking in the new republic. Scarcely anyone dared to assert that slavery was morally justified, and the slaveowners of Gran Colombia were destined to fight at most a delaying action against the process of emancipation.

Perhaps the chief foe of slavery was the war itself. By 1825 slightly over 100,000 slaves could be counted in the republic,[5] and only part of the decline could be accounted for by natural causes and voluntary manumission. Many slaves had simply run away from their masters under cover of war-time disorders and confusion. Others had been invited to leave, and not always willingly, so that they might serve in the ranks of one or the other of the contending armies. The best known example of this practice, although by no means the only one, is Bolívar's order of February, 1820, for the recruiting of 5000 slaves in western New Granada; they were to serve in the patriot armies for two years and then would obtain full personal liberty. For fear of its effects on the mining industry, Santander at first protested against the order, but he carried it out as best he could despite the injured cries of Cauca slaveowners.[6] Moreover, since the slaves who obtained freedom in return for military service were

[4] Restrepo I, xx.
[5] Restrepo VII, 300.
[6] *Corresp.* 51-52, 75-76, 139, 167, 180. Bolívar did not, of course, obtain as many slaves as he asked for. For a full treatment of this question (and of slavery in general) see Harold A. Bierck, "The Struggle for Abolition in Gran Colombia," *Hispanic American Historical Review* XXXIII, 365-386 (August, 1953).

necessarily drawn from the active male population, the effect of such measures on the institution itself was greater than numbers alone would indicate.

Many Colombians—including the Liberator—were not content with such haphazard methods of emancipation. Bolívar's decision to draft slaves into the army was due in part to the obvious need for manpower, and also to the fear he expressed again and again that free citizens would be killed off in war while slaves stayed safely home, thus upsetting permanently the balance between white and dark races. But he also really believed in emancipation. He frankly deplored the hypocrisy of fighting for independence while denying freedom to thousands of individual Colombians; he freed his own slaves early in the struggle, and under his influence the Angostura Congress declared openly for the general abolition of slavery.[7] It was left for the Congress of Cúcuta to devise practical steps toward this end, and one of the first measures placed before it when it opened in May of 1821 was Dr. Félix Restrepo's bill to give personal freedom to every child born henceforth in Colombia.

Restrepo had sponsored a similar law in the province of Antioquia during the *Patria Boba,* and he supported the plan at Cúcuta with all his oratorical talents and with a wide array of citations from the Bible and from political scientists. He pointed out that a slave's master exercised executive, legislative, and judicial powers at the same time, which was highly irregular, and also that free labor had shown its economic superiority both in ancient Rome and in New Granada. Despite this, for the present Restrepo asked only a law of free birth, together with certain improvements in the treatment of the slave population and the establishment of a special tax on inheritances with which to buy the freedom of slaves who had been born too soon to be liberated automatically by his law. The second great *antioqueño* in Congress, José Manuel Restrepo, joined a group of Venezuelan deputies in asking additional safeguards for the "property rights" of existing slaveowners, but no one seriously opposed the measure as such. Two clerical deputies demanded immediate universal emancipation, while others declared the freedom of their own slaves amid tears and applause on the very floor of the house. By July 21 Restrepo's proposal in all its essentials had become law, and Colombians can well be proud that it is the first piece of general legislation in the *Codificación Nacional.*[8]

In the short run this law was not very effective as a means of abolishing slavery. It did not free a single slave outright, and Congress expressly declared that it had not meant even to imply that slaves then owned by

---

[7] Bierck, "Struggle for Abolition," *loc. cit.,* 368; Bolívar to Santander, April 18, 1820, *Corresp.,* 75-76, and April 20, 1820, Lecuna, *C.L.* II, 152.

[8] *Actas:* Cúcuta, 205-207, 213-216, 225-226, 232-233, 243-244, 253-257, 283, 287-288, 293; *Codif. Nac.* I, 14-16.

the state should be set at liberty, although their freedom was subsequently decided as a matter of general policy by the Bogotá administration.[9] Nor did the machinery set up for the manumission of slaves ever work well. The special inheritance taxes were not collected very faithfully: the manumission board at Caracas stated that up to June of 1827 about one fourth of the amount legally due had been collected, and even of that a great part had been misspent. At Cumaná no one at all was freed for four years, and in the nation as a whole only 471 were recorded as having been set free under the terms of the law by the start of 1827.[10] Fortunately cases of voluntary manumission continued, and they were encouraged by favorable publicity in the *Gaceta,* but this was hardly a basic solution. Moreover, demands for broadening the law passed at Cúcuta were few, and they were uniformly unsuccessful.

The Santander administration, on its part, recognized the inadequacy of the existing law, and would certainly have liked to see slavery liquidated more rapidly,[11] but for the present it was willing simply to preserve the gains already made against the counterattack of the slaveholders. *El Observador Caraqueño* was virtually alone in its insistence that "slavery ... is absolutely necessary for the preservation of our people," and in its assertion that Colombian slaves were really better off than free laborers in Europe.[12] Yet in Caracas even the rabidly liberal *Cometa* assailed the manumission law as being "generous with the property of others," [13] and everywhere in slaveholding regions groups of *hacendados,* provincial juntas, and town fathers drew up protests against specific features of the law. One complaint was that it made no provision for the reduction of *censos* or mortgages upon slave-property that was to be gradually abolished under the free-birth principle; this is perhaps the one complaint that was fully justified, and legislation to meet it was proposed several times in Congress.[14] Even so, the Church vigorously opposed any reduction in its own income from the *censos,* and nothing was done. Still more frequent objections were made to the provision requiring slaveowners to care for their slaves' free offspring during infancy in return for receiving their services without pay up to the age of eighteen. Difficult calculations

[9] A.C., Senado-49, 249; *La Gaceta Oficial del Departamento del Istmo* (Panamá), March 14, 1824.

[10] *El Indicador del Orinoco* (Cumaná), October 29, 1825; *El Constitucional* (Bogotá), July 12, 1827; Bierck, "Struggle for Abolition," *loc. cit.,* 373-377, 379-380.

[11] For evidence of feeling in the administration camp on the topic of slavery cf. *La Indicación* (Bogotá), December 28, 1822, and *La Miscelánea* (Bogotá), January 29, 1826.

[12] *El Observador Caraqueño,* January 15, 1824.

[13] *El Cometa,* September 22, 1824.

[14] A.C., Senado-27, 347-348, Cámara-14, 158-160; *Actas:* Senado-1824, 802.

were made to prove that the food and clothing of slave children cost far more than such services would be worth, and it was thus proposed repeatedly that either the owners should be granted a special indemnity for their expenses or else the children should be made to serve until they were considerably older than eighteen. Forty or fifty was the age suggested by a group of wealthy *cartageneros,* including Juan de Francisco Martín, who lauded the intent of the manumission law but asserted that the freedom of the few must not be placed higher than the general welfare.[15]

It was not only the technical aspects of the manumission law that aroused complaint, for the anti-slavery atmosphere which it reflected had encouraged slave labor to become more inefficient than ever. Some slaves took the law as a sign that slavery was now to be abolished altogether and promptly sought to desert their masters, thus giving rise to serious disorder in the mining districts of western New Granada.[16] A larger number, seeing that slavery was officially condemned and was being slowly liquidated, became merely less responsive to their owners' commands and eagerly carried all complaints of mistreatment to public officials. The Intendant of Ecuador, in view of this fact, proposed allowing them wide freedom in changing masters simply as a means of allaying their unrest. This proposal was put forward mainly on the basis of expediency, but it is also true that the slaves' complaints very often found a favorable reception. The *Alta Corte* in Bogotá was prepared for purely humanitarian reasons to intervene in their behalf, and the floors of Congress became a forum for the discussion of wrongs done to individual slaves.[17] This sympathy, needless to say, was all to the good, yet slaveowners retorted that it merely augmented the problem of maintaining discipline. According to the city council of Barbacoas, only "the harshness of a miner with lash in hand" could make the slaves "fulfill their duty." [18]

A further complication was the fact that in many of the areas where slavery had played a basic role in the economy there was no adequate supply of free labor to make up for the decline in both numbers and

[15] The complaints of José Rafael and Joaquín Mosquera, both of them important slaveholders as well as leaders in Congress, and of the Popayán provincial assembly can be found in A.C., Senado-26, 90; *El Constitucional,* January 26, 1826; *El Correo de la Ciudad de Bogotá,* February 13, 1823; and *La Indicación,* December 14 and 28, 1822. See also A.C., Cámara-3, 24-31.

[16] Gaspar Theodore Mollien, *Viaje por la República de Colombia en 1823* (Bogotá, 1944), 265; A.C., Senado-29, 299. The declaration of the Angostura Congress had led to similar results (Blanco VII, 169-171; Alejandro Osorio and Estanislao Vergara, *Memoria correspondiente al año de 1820,* Bogotá, 1821, pp. 41-42).

[17] A.H.N., Congresos XXVI, 712; A.C., Senado-10, 125-131, Cámara-12, 218-232.

[18] A.C., Senado-29, 299.

efficiency of the slave population. This was especially true in the mining industry, where war recruitment had made its greatest inroads on the slave supply, and where the work itself was least attractive: the mine slave who gained freedom did not usually want his old job back even for wages, and other free labor could be obtained only at a price which employers were grieved to pay. Hence the city of Barbacoas also asserted that five youths of good family had been forced to go work the mines in person, thereby forfeiting "the brilliant role which their forefathers had played in the civil world." [19] This was no doubt regrettable, but a still more serious result of the labor situation was its impact on production. Mineral output was necessarily hurt, and outside the mining regions so was the production of sugar and certain other staple crops.[20] To be sure, the complete disaster so freely predicted by the slaveowners never did quite materialize; but still, all things considered, their present lot was not an entirely happy one.

Slaveowners were in fact so discouraged by their endless grievances that one of their principal spokesmen, Senator Jerónimo Torres, frankly advised them that it was no use continuing the struggle any longer. The Senator observed first the horrors of slavery and then the injustice of the manumission law; he pointed out that many schools and churches derived their income from slave labor and he finally suggested that all slaves be freed at once, put to work at compulsory "free" labor, and required to make a yearly contribution toward indemnifying their former owners.[21] Torres' proposal was not a really practical solution, even though normally he was one of the most clear-headed men in Bogotá. It merely illustrates the gravity of the situation, and certainly it was never taken very seriously. Neither did the Colombian administration show any real inclination to make concessions to the slaveowners. Within the ranks of the clergy, similarly, a humanitarian sympathy for the slaves was combined with firm resistance to any tampering with *censos*. Thus all attempts to limit or amend the manumission law continued to be overruled in Congress by Santanderean liberals, pro-clerical conservatives, or both together, and the complaints even of such eminent slaveowners as the Mosqueras and Arboledas of Popayán were met with scorn in the Bogotá press.[22] Venezuelan protests had equally little effect, despite the Venezuelans' well-known sensitivity regarding any neglect of their interests at Bogotá.

The question of emancipation could not be separated entirely from

[19] A.C., Senado-29, 301.
[20] *The Present State of Colombia* (London, 1827), 268-269, 280-282, 291-292, 299-300; Carl August Gosselman, *Reise in Columbien* (2 vols., Straslund, 1829) II, 102; A.H.N., Interior y Relaciones CXIV, 593-595.
[21] Jerónimo Torres, *Observaciones de G.T. sobre la ley de manumisión* (Bogotá, 1822).
[22] Cf. *La Miscelánea*, January 29, 1826.

certain other issues involving the relationship between white and colored races. The repercussions of the manumission law are enough to show that the decline of slavery as an institution had not put an end to all racial tension, but the latter involved freemen as well as slaves, the mulatto as well as the full Negro. This could be seen most clearly of all in the frequent alarms over the imminence of race warfare that were heard from Guayaquil to Cumaná. Especially in Venezuela and the Cauca there was· a widespread fear that royalist agents would seek to stir up and exploit the resentment of the slaves and free colored population against the dominant creoles, just as they had done earlier in the *Patria Boba*, and to a certain extent these fears were actually justified. The royalist guerrillas of Pasto and Patía quite naturally did recruit some runaway slaves, although never so many as was feared by the Popayán aristocracy. Likewise Spanish agents were apparently responsible in part for at least one small uprising on racial lines among the mulattoes and Indians of eastern Venezuela.[23]

But Spanish machinations were not always to blame for racial unrest. Negroes did not need to be told by anyone that their race was still denied complete freedom and social equality, and many of them were obviously unhappy with their lot. In fact the present tension dated back at least to the closing years of the colonial period, when free men of color had made their first real advance toward a higher social status, and had thereby come in conflict with the prejudiced resistance of the creoles. Moreover, it was seriously affirmed by assorted Congressmen and administration spokesmen that Haiti, like Spain, was attempting to foment race conflict and had even stationed some 300 secret agents in Venezuela for that very purpose; this was one reason why Bolívar's republic refused even to establish relations with the homeland of his benefactor Pétion.[24] Supposedly, Haiti was trying to exert pressure on the Colombian authorities lest they accept the bid of the white inhabitants of Santo Domingo to join Colombia. There is certainly no concrete evidence to support all the charges of Haitian intrigue, but such charges still helped to maintain the general fear of racial strife. There was consequently much thought given to the need for preventive measures, and it is significant that no responsible Colombian leader held out systematic repression as the course to follow. Fairly wide agreement existed on the need to keep the colored

[23] John P. Hamilton, *Travels Through the Interior Provinces of Colombia* (2 vols., London, 1827) II, 58; T.C. Mosquera to Bolívar, September 21, 1824, O'Leary IX, 73; A.C., Cámara-5, 29-30; O'Leary XX, 136-137, 177.

[24] On the general subject of Haitian spies see A.C., Cámara-14, 327; Senado-17, 230; Actas del Senado (secret sessions) May 5, 1823 and April 17, 1824. It was later suggested that Colombia might recognize Haiti but see to it that she send no consuls to coastal cities with a large colored population (J. Fernández Madrid to Bolívar, April 18, 1829, O'Leary IX, 342).

race numerically inferior, whether by drafting slaves for the battlefronts or by encouraging white immigration from Europe. Equally important, however, in the eyes of both Bolívar and Santander, was the need to continue without interruption on the road to general emancipation: by this means the colored race would come to see that its objectives were attainable by peaceful means, and would give up any thought of seeking long overdue justice by force of arms. Thus fear, in the last analysis, is precisely one of the reasons why Colombia stood firm in defense of the manumission law.

Jerónimo Torres, on his part, was convinced that the only way to secure internal tranquillity was to abolish the Negro race altogether, but to do so by love alone. Once the slaves had been freed and set to compulsory free labor under his own ingenious scheme, he felt that the authorities should round up vagabonds and prostitutes from the main cities and send them off to live with the former slaves; a steady process of miscegenation would then finish the Negro problem for all time.[25] The notion was obviously absurd, but it forcibly illustrates the fact that racial problems were not seriously complicated by irrational demands for *apartheid*. Despite the slaveowners' lobby and the Haitian spy scare, the condition of Colombian Negroes was steadily improving, and not only through the progress of emancipation. On the contrary, the nation's present rulers were aware that emancipation was not enough by itself, and that it would lose much of its true meaning if slaves were technically set free only to remain thwarted in their legitimate hopes for advancement by a wall of official and unofficial discrimination. Admittedly, many Negroes just released from slavery would not be prepared for all the responsibilities of citizenship, but as long as emancipation was gradual this danger could be tolerated, and an important safeguard existed in the property requirements for voting and holding office. Hence the principle of full racial equality became an official dogma of the new regime, even among many who found it hard to accept all the practical implications: it was energetically affirmed in public pronouncements and official school texts,[26] not only as a major legal conquest of the Revolution but also as the only lasting solution to racial tensions. The Santander administration fought against such traditional practices as the exclusion of mulattoes from institutes of higher learning, on the grounds that they were incompatible with republican principles; the *Alta Corte,* which typified all the nobler ideals of Colombian liberalism, rebuked lower courts for even mentioning a man's race in judicial documents.[27]

[25] Torres, *op. cit.,* 37-38.

[26] Cf. Pedro Acevedo, *Noticia sobre la jeografía política de Colombia* (New York, 1827), 28.

[27] *Acuerdos* I, 163; *El Constitucional,* December 22, 1825; *El registro judiciario de la República de Colombia* (Bogotá), February 1, 1826, June 22, 1827.

New careers, moreover, were opening up for the colored population. The most obvious of these was perhaps the army, where Negroes and mulattoes, especially from among the *llaneros*, had found an important place in the corps of officers. By virtue of their rank they had earned themselves the right to dance with white ladies of high society.[28] At the other extreme, the *junta provincial* of Guayaquil formally petitioned the government not to send mulatto officers to serve in the local garrison,[29] and this is only one of many signs that prejudice was far from dead; but at least it was declining. In Congress there were also men of mixed white and Negro descent; they were very few but this was in part merely because so few could meet the constitutional requirements.

## *Liberalism and the Indian*

The needs of Colombia's Indian population were ostensibly handled along much the same lines, with complete legal equality as the goal in sight, but the similarity between the Indian and Negro problems is mainly confined to their theoretical aspects. Although they constituted a substantial minority in New Granada and a majority in Ecuador, the Indians[30] were neither feared nor subjected to discrimination. There was simply no occasion for the one or the other, since they preferred to live by themselves and seldom attempted to play a part in the life of the nation as a whole. Indeed the Indian was rather widely idealized—from a safe, romantic distance—and was occasionally seen as the natural ally of the white man in any conflict with the Negro and mulatto.[31] The Chamber of Representatives hoped to gain not only better race relations but also "many useful discoveries" through the inclusion of Indian languages in the official school curriculum.[32] Last but not least, it was officially assumed that the War of Independence had been fought in large part for

---

[28] Cf. Mollien, *op. cit.*, 317.

[29] A.H.N., Miscelánea de la República XXI, 248.

[30] In case there is any room for doubt on the matter, it should be made clear that the term "Indian" is used not in a racial but in a social sense—i.e., referring to those Indians who had preserved as much as possible of their distinctive Indian culture and who lived on the margin of (or wholly outside) creole-mestizo society. It thus includes some who actually had non-Indian "blood," but excludes other Indians who had already been more or less "integrated" in the general culture of country.

[31] Cf. A.C., Actas de la Cámara de Representantes (secret sessions), April 8, 1825, referring to the *llanos* of Casanare; Mollien, *op. cit.*, 265, referring to Popayán.

[32] *Codif. Nac.* II, 232. There is no evidence that these languages were actually taught as required, and for some reason their inclusion in the curriculum was made over the opposition of the Senate (A.C., Actas del Senado, February 23 and March 2 and 3, 1826).

the Indians' sake: Bolívar and his generals were tiresomely extolled as the final "avengers" of the fallen Incan Empire. There was considerably less talk of avenging the fallen Chibchas, perhaps because they were less known abroad. Certainly the Chibchas showed little desire to do the avenging themselves, for the Indians in general took no interest in the great struggle. There were exceptions, of course, and Bolívar tried earnestly to make more. He once urged the use of Indians to garrison the Spanish Main, stating that the wilder they were the better, since the wild ones would be missed the least and were less likely to have suffered already by the ravages of contending armies.[33] It is perhaps doubtful that very much, if anything, ever came of this idea, and probably nothing did; indeed the royalists would seem to have been generally more successful in overcoming the Indians' natural apathy than were the patriots. If they did serve the Colombian cause, with either their persons or their property, it was usually the result of open or implied coercion.[34] The new regime nevertheless refused to penalize the Indian for his backwardness, ascribing it as might be expected to the long centuries of "Spanish oppression." The Congress of Cúcuta therefore set out with all good intentions to redeem "this considerable part of the population of Colombia which was so vexed and oppressed by the Spanish government."[35] It sought first of all to give the Indian civil equality by relieving him both of the obligation to pay the "tax known by the degrading name of tribute" and of the illiberal system of holding his lands in common, unlike the rest of Colombians who shared the advantages of full private ownership.

Even before the Congress met, different groups of Indians had been petitioning Colombian officials for an end to the tribute—"prostrated at the feet of Your Excellency," as they more than once addressed Santander.[36] They founded their request not so much on theories of equality as on the supplies and transportation they had furnished the patriot armies, and in a few exceptional cases the request was granted. However, both true equality and financial necessity required that the Indians share the burdens of state, so that the patriots refused to abolish the tribute outright until new legislation should require the Indian to contribute in some other manner.[37] This legislation is what the Congress of Cúcuta provided, abolishing the tribute at last and subjecting the Indians instead to the same forms of taxation as all other citizens. The measure was

[33] O'Leary XVIII, 607.
[34] Juan Friede, *El indio en lucha por la tierra* (Bogotá, 1944), 100-101.
[35] *Codif. Nac.* I, 116.
[36] A.H.N., Indios, 16, 112-113. Naturally the Indians' zeal was dampened when they learned that other taxes would be imposed on them to make up the loss.
[37] Osorio and Vergara, *Memoria*, 29-30; *La Gaceta de Santa Fe de Bogotá*, January 30, 1820; A.H.N., Indios, 16, 77, 86-90, 107-121, 129-139.

accepted at first almost without question, for the tribute had not been a major source of revenue in Venezuela or New Granada. The local situation in Ecuador was different, but Ecuador was still under Spanish rule, and the objections of its non-Indian inhabitants were not felt until Sucre arrived on the scene with his Army of Liberation and proceeded to enforce the law of Cúcuta. Bolívar then reversed the action of his lieutenant. He did not cherish the tribute on principle, as did many Quito aristocrats, but he feared that it would be some time before the Indians could pay as much in regular taxes as they had paid in tribute. As he badly needed money for the war in Peru, he therefore used his "extraordinary faculties" to suspend the effects of the law in the southern departments. Even at Bogotá this action was considered reasonable, and when Bolívar's "extraordinary faculties" were repealed in July, 1824, a decree of Santander expressly continued the tribute in Ecuador for the duration of the struggle. But as it turned out this was not for very long, and subsequent demands for restoration of the tax were sternly ignored by Santander and his colleagues.[38]

The decision to liquidate the Indians' *resguardos* or communal lands, unlike the abolition of the tribute, was entirely unsolicited. Yet both measures were accomplished by the same law of Cúcuta. The Congress decreed that as soon as possible the communal lands should be divided up among the Indians themselves, taking account of the needs of individual families, but that the division should take place within five years at the latest. Meanwhile the Indians were to continue using their lands in the traditional fashion, with the special provision that any surplus should be rented out, the proceeds going to the support of a primary school and of the local priest. As a final concession to the Indians after their centuries of "degradation," all the *resguardos* were to remain tax-exempt pending the final distribution.[39]

It will surprise no one to learn that this legislation was never fully carried out. The division of the *resguardos* in Ecuador was suspended at the same time as Bolívar decreed the continuation of the tribute. Elsewhere in Colombia it was delayed by the technical difficulties of surveying and distributing different types of land, by lack of funds to pay for the operation, and by the opposition of the Indians themselves, who drew up numerous petitions against the measure. The administration confessed that it would be "almost impossible to make the division to the satisfaction of the Indians," who clung with great obstinacy to "what they call their

[38] *El Constitucional,* January 26, 1826; *La Gaceta de Colombia,* December 18, 1825. In 1823-4, the tribute furnished one-third the income of the Quito treasury (*La Gaceta de Colombia,* January 2, 1825).

[39] *Codif. Nac.* I, 116-117.

privileges"—in other words, to their tradition of communal ownership.⁴⁰ In practice, therefore, little land was distributed, but this did not end the Indians' complaints. Even when the division was not carried out within the stated period, the basic requirement remained on the statute books as a threat to the Indians' "privileges." Furthermore, there were a great many conflicts arising from the provision about renting of surplus lands, the so-called *sobrante de resguardos*. It seems that the rental terms were often imposed on the Indians without consulting their real interest, and that they did not always receive the full amount: one group of Indians complained that their "imbecility and misery" made it impossible for them to collect what was owed. On other occasions land was rented that was not really surplus at all, and the Indians had to defend themselves against attempts to use the proceeds to support schools not for Indian children but for the creoles and *mestizos*, which was certainly against the spirit if not always the letter of the law.⁴¹

Not content with asserting the equality of the Indian in taxation and land tenure, the Congress of Cúcuta further declared him capable of performing all public offices and repealed colonial restrictions on the residence of non-Indians in his villages. It sought to abolish even the term *indio* in favor of *indígena*, which supposedly did not have the same connotation of racial discrimination. Moreover, since the Indians were to be equal to everyone else, the Congress felt that they should defend their interests in the same way as other citizens: thus the colonial position of *protector de indios*, whose duty had been to help the Indians in all kinds of legal disputes, was now limited in function essentially to cases involving still undivided communal lands. This measure was inspired both by liberal doctrines of equality and by the fact that colonial protectors had frequently abused their charges. Actually, its effect went somewhat farther than might appear, because Congress did not specify how the office should be filled under the republican regime, and this omission often served as an excuse to put off filling it at all.⁴²

Fortunately the stern doctrines of civil equality and laissez faire were tempered in practice by a certain amount of humanitarian concern for the *indígena* as a particularly helpless member of the Colombian nation. Higher judicial and administrative officials at times showed laudable eagerness to preserve the *resguardos* against the more arbitrary encroachments, and Santander himself agreed to commute the death sentence of one army deserter because, among other things, he was an *"indígena muy*

⁴⁰ *El Constitucional,* January 26, 1826. See also A.H.N., Indios, 86-90, Corresp.-Senado February 4, 1825; A.C., Cámara-10, 159-164.

⁴¹ A.H.N., Indios 4, 131; Interior y Relaciones, CXIV, 623, A.C., Cámara-4, 235-237, Senado-48, 415.

⁴² *Codif. Nac.* I, 116-117; *Actas:* Senado-1824, 112-113; *El Fósforo* (Popayán), June 19, 1823; A.C., Senado-36, 199-205; Senado-48, 422-424.

*rústico.*" [43] Nor was the education of the Indians to be restricted solely to the schools subsidized from their own lands—which, of course, were not always set up. At one point twelve Indian youths came in to attend the Lancasterian public school established at Popayán, although they found confinement so hard to endure that they ultimately went home. Similarly, the government offered scholarships to provide a secondary education for Indians who could "read and write correctly," and it urged all rectors to treat "students of this unhappy class" with a special paternal interest.[44]

Anti-clericalism served to reinforce humanitarian sentiments when it came to limiting the tribute of goods and services paid by the Indian to the Church. The Congress of Cúcuta strictly prohibited the arbitrary exaction of unpaid Indian labor "by any class of persons," by which must be understood primarily municipal officers and parish priests. The Congress likewise exempted Indians from the payment of parish fees to their priests for a period of five years, which was later extended by Santander.[45] Unfortunately, labor might still be exacted illegally, and neither was the abolition of parish fees everywhere observed. The Intendant of Cundinamarca thus felt compelled to issue a vigorous protest and a decree to match against both the unpaid labor required of Indian servant girls in the houses of priests and the "scandalous usage" of closing Indians in a church building until they paid fees wrongly demanded of them.[46] The latter abuse, however, was probably less common than the intendant implied, while the various personal services rendered by the Indians to the clergy were not always performed against their will.

The measures which have been considered so far had to do primarily with the mass of Indians who lived a settled existence, in regions where there was at least a pretense of enforcing Colombian legislation. A more complex problem was presented by the wilder Indians who either had not been fully subdued by Spain or had taken advantage of the anarchy of the war years to reassert their tribal independence. There was real doubt whether Congress had a right to redeem or do anything else to these tribes: one overscrupulous deputy at Cúcuta challenged the article of the Constitution dealing with national boundaries on the ground that it paid no heed to the rights of "independent Indian nations." [47] Even when the

[43] *Acuerdos* II, 117-118.

[44] Hamilton, *op. cit.*, II, 75; *La Gaceta de Colombia,* May 5, 1822.

[45] *Codif. Nac.* I, 116; A.H.N., Indios 38.

On these two points (and on much else of its Indian legislation) the work of the Congress of Cúcuta was clearly foreshadowed by Bolívar's decree of May 20, 1820 (*Codif. Nac.* VII, 16-17).

[46] *El Correo de Bogotá,* March 26, 1824. Cf. Friede, *op. cit.,* 19; *El Constitucional de Boyacá* (Tunja), June 16, 1826; A.C., Senado-12, 363.

[47] *Actas:* Cúcuta, 121. The deputy was Manuel María Quijano, who was not an orthodox liberal and was perhaps inspired by a clericalism of the Las Casas variety.

## The Liberals and the Masses

Congress did assert jurisdiction over everything within the theoretical limits of the old viceroyalty, the Santander administration interpreted its decision in such a way as to grant "uncivilized" Indians at least a quasi-independent status. The sections where they lived were Colombian territory, and any land they did not actually need could be sold by the national government as part of its public domain, but they themselves, it was announced, were in some way not really subject to Colombian laws.[48]

It was officially estimated that over 200,000 "uncivilized" Indians existed, of whom 144,143 were said to be so wild that not even the names of their tribes were known.[49] The government still hoped that as many as possible of the Indians in question might be induced to share the benefits of Colombia's liberal institutions, and in seeking to win their friendship it set out to be as generous as its finances permitted. Santander accordingly asked Congress for a special appropriation with which to "civilize" wild Indians, and Congress responded in 1824 with a law authorizing the grant of lands, tools, and so forth to any tribe that wished to settle down to a civilized existence. Under the terms of this law Santander provided that up to 200 *fanegadas* of public land could be given free to any one family, which was exactly the same quota allowed to European immigrants under the colonization law of 1823. Subsequently the Indians of Casanare were offered full exemption from military service as an added inducement to become civilized. However, not much happened. The Governor of Casanare reported that with some aid from private enterprise two new Indian towns had been established in his jurisdiction, and that many more Indians had become interested in civilizing themselves as a result of free handouts of tools and provisions. On the other hand, their interest could be maintained by gifts alone: the *Jefe Político* of Eastern Casanare once feared he would actually be eaten up if he visited certain groups of Indians without bearing gifts. And as there was never enough money to give what was needed, progress was necessarily slow. A second law passed in 1826 had little more effect. It expressly appropriated $100,000 per year for wild Indians, but for obvious reasons this amount was never available.[50]

The Executive was no more successful in reviving missionary activity by the religious orders, whose efforts had been seriously disrupted since 1810. Especially in Guayana and Casanare, where the missions had enjoyed a high degree of success in the late colonial period, they had suffered a sharp decline as a result of damage inflicted by passing armies,

---

[48] *Acuerdos* I, 187, 262-264.

[49] José Manuel Restrepo, *Memoria . . . del Despacho del Interior* (Bogotá, 1827).

[50] *Codif. Nac.* I, 403, II, 334; *La Gaceta de Colombia,* October 31, 1824, July 16, 1826; A.H.N., Indios, 221-229, 237, 247-248, 252, 256, 262, 265-266; A.C., Senado-28, 108, 119-120, 123.

the great amount of commissary provisions extracted from them in the course of the war, and the preoccupation of their political and religious wardens with the affairs of independence.[51] If the missions could now be put back on a sound footing, they might play an important part in the general civilizing program, and every scheme for this purpose received enthusiastic support from such zealous churchmen as the Bishop of Mérida, Lasso de la Vega. Yet the friars themselves showed little cooperation. The government repeatedly demanded missionary friars for service on the *llanos* and elsewhere, but their superiors were not always very helpful in supplying the numbers requested, and at times the missionaries sought to desert en route before they reached their destination. Missionary work was in fact so unpopular that one entire convent in Bogotá drew up a formal protest when just four of its members were ordered to the *llanos*.[52]

The inadequacy of both civil and ecclesiastical efforts to attract the wilder Indians was particularly regrettable since the entire Spanish system of frontier defense was breaking down. One reason for this was precisely the decline of once-flourishing mission outposts. Another was the interruption of subsidies paid by the Spaniards to select Indian tribes simply in return for their good behaviour, since in Colombia as in the United States such payments were often suspended after independence. The administration claimed that it lacked legal authorization, not to mention funds, for making the payments; and there was also some disagreement in official ranks as to whether they were desirable.[53] Furthermore, the war had interfered not merely with subsidies but also with all other traditional contacts between government officers and tribal chiefs; and Spanish agents naturally used any opportunity they could find to turn the Indians' latent resentment toward whites and *mestizos* in general into a struggle of royalist guerrillas against the patriots. All in all, the situation was a serious one. Indian tribes staged intermittent raids on Colombian

[51] Baltasar de Lodares, *Los franciscanos capuchinos en Venezuela* (3 vols., Caracas, 1929-31) II, 299, 318-333; Marcelino Ganuza, *Monografía de las misiones vivas de Agustinos Recoletos (Candelarios) en Colombia* (2 vols., Bogotá, 1921) II, 55, 207-250.

[52] A.H.N., Correspondencia del Libertador Presidente, 180, 196, 221-223, Miscelánea de la República XXI, 269-271, 275, 292, 317, 331. An attenuating circumstance is the fact that numerous royalist clergymen had been sent to frontier outposts as a security measure during the war; hence one friar demanded an official statement that he was not being punished for disloyalty before he would depart to minister to the Indians around Lake Maracaibo. However, the readiness of the friars to see an aspersion on their honor and patriotism in assignments to mission duty is scarcely compatible with either Christian humility or a zeal to extend the faith wherever they might be called.

[53] Mollien, *op. cit.*, 349; *La Gaceta de Colombia*, February 13, 1825.

settlements in Casanare; in Guayana, Indians who had deserted the missions took to assaulting those who did not desert; in the Goajira peninsula they not only harassed surrounding settlements but attacked military convoys passing through the territory.[54]

When the government could turn its attention from frontier raids it had to consider the related problems posed by the influence of even friendly foreign powers among remote Indian tribes. Fear of British intrigue among the Indians of Guayana and other outlying provinces was one reason for the entire "civilizing" program:[55] it was also a factor in the decision to exclude potential immigrant colonies from the sections which Colombia claimed of the Mosquito Coast. The most serious difficulty of all involved the trade carried on directly between Jamaica merchants and Indians of the Goajira peninsula. Such trade had been forbidden under the colonial regime with varying success, but at first it was more or less tolerated by the republican authorities. This leniency was due both to the difficulty of enforcing the law and to the fear of antagonizing Great Britain at a time when British recognition was a major objective of Colombian foreign policy. Not until March, 1822, did the authorities at Bogotá formally order the seizure of a ship illegally engaged in the Goajira trade. This step was accompanied by a partial tightening of restrictions, but it was frankly taken mainly just to see how the British would react. The reaction was unfavorable; and Dr. Félix Restrepo declared that Colombia had no business interfering with the trade of an "independent" Indian nation anyway. There followed a period of conflicting Colombian orders, thinly veiled British threats to "protect" the trade, much diplomatic correspondence, and some philosophic discussion on the status of "independent" Indians. The final decision was not entirely pleasing to Santander, but it was dictated by obvious common sense. This was the issue that brought the definitive statement that wild Indians were not really subject to Colombian laws, and the corollary for the present situation was exemption of the Goajira tribe from most of the country's commercial legislation. They might trade directly with the British, chiefly bartering cattle for rum, provided the foreign ships first stopped at the nearest licensed port for the necessary redtape, an inspection designed to keep illicit arms from being taken to the Indians, and the payment of little more than token duties. The system still was not easy to enforce, but at least there was to be no attempt to impose either the full customs tariff or the legal prohibition of importing rum. At the

[54] A.H.N., Indios, 103-104, 307, Departamento de Boyacá III, 441; A.C., Senado-25, 116, Cámara-16, 56-58; O'Leary XVIII, 309-310.
[55] A.H.N., Congresos IX, 135; *La Gaceta de Colombia,* September 12, 1824.

same time it was decided that merchants trading with the Mosquito Indians, who presented a similar problem, had only to pay the reduced charges to a Colombian commercial agent abroad and then sail directly for the Indian coast.[56]

The decision to allow the wilder Indians to trade outside the Colombian customs system is perhaps a special case, but it still illustrates the difficulties inherent in treating the Indian population on a basis of absolute civil equality. In Goajira the Indians did not care to be full-fledged citizens with the right to vote and hold office, provided they met all the legal requirements, and yet without the right to buy Jamaica rum at bargain prices from English interlopers. Seldom were the Indians in any region pleased with the requirement to own their lands on the same terms as other citizens; and it does not appear that the substitution of regular taxation for the colonial tribute was invariably popular. Neither, for that matter, did the Colombian authorities always practice what they preached as concerns equal treatment of the Indian minority. They did not quite abandon the term *indio,* even in official decrees,[57] and despite the best of intentions they even found it hard to eschew the word *salvaje.*[58] Local officials in the provinces often mistreated the Indians by deed as well as by word. The fact remains, however, that a sincere attempt had been made to do what was right, as dictated by both Christian brotherhood and Natural Law: there is little evidence that as yet the exponents of Indian equality were chiefly moved by base designs on Indian lands, although such designs certainly existed. Equality in practice was not always a benefit, but the republic's policies toward both Indians and Negro slaves were surely among the noblest of its intentions.

---

[56] A.C., Senado-2, 395, Senado-29, 126-152; A.H.N., Corresp.-Cámara (Hacienda), July 28, 1824, Miscelánea de la República XVI, 787, Congresos XII, 180-183, 190-191; *Acuerdos* I, 31-32; *La Gaceta del Istmo de Panamá,* December 12, 1824. This trade was definitely frowned upon by the *junta provincial* of Río Hacha as discouraging the civilization of the Indians (*La Gaceta de Colombia,* January 8, 1826). Santander himself observed that the trade in rum did the Indians no good, and that general smuggling was encouraged, but there was little he could do about it.

[57] Cf. decree of March 11, 1822, in *La Gaceta de Colombia,* May 5, 1822.

[58] See A.C., Actas del Senado, February 6, 1826, for reference to a law in which the derogatory term was not finally eliminated until third reading.

Chapter XII

## Education in the Santander Regime

THE preceding chapter has attempted to show that moral as well as material objectives were involved in the attitude of the Colombian regime toward the Negro and Indian minorities. The same can be said in a much more obvious sense of the educational program of the Santander administration, which was certainly as dear to the Vice-President's heart or dearer than any other project for the improvement of Colombia. On the one hand, it was necessary to expand the number and size of educational institutions as rapidly as possible so as to spread the rudiments of knowledge without which a nation cannot operate at full efficiency. On the other, it was sought to bring the spirit of Colombian education into line with the advances of early nineteenth century liberalism. "It is painful," wrote José Manuel Restrepo in his *Memoria* for 1826, "to have to forget the major part of what we learned in colonial education . . . and to study anew; but it is necessary in order to place us on a par with the enlightenment of the century." [1]

Hence education was always one of the first concerns of Colombian rulers. Bolívar had been in Bogotá scarcely a month after the victory of Boyacá when he ordered the convent abandoned by the royalist Capuchins, together with all its revenues, to be set aside for a free school to train orphans, the poor, and the sons of patriot martyrs. As it turned out, this particular school was never opened, but it set a pattern for future efforts to expand educational facilities, and in particular to expand them at the expense of the Church. Slightly later, while still serving as Vice-President of Cundinamarca, Santander issued orders for every village and every convent or monastery to set up a school of its own.[2] In 1821, finally, the Congress of Cúcuta set out to organize the educational system on a more or less permanent footing. First it announced that without knowing how to read "Citizens cannot basically know the sacred obligations which religion and Christian morality impose upon them, or the rights and duties of man in society;" then it decreed the establishment of a primary school for boys in every town of 100 or more families, made attendance compulsory from six to twelve years of age except when a legitimate excuse was offered, and provided for support of the school system by assessments against all who could afford to pay, the children of the poor

[1] *El Constitucional* (Bogotá), January 26, 1826.
[2] *La Gazeta de Santa Fe de Bogotá,* October 10, 1819, and October 22, 1820; Groot, 18.

being educated free of charge. The curriculum was to consist of the "three R's" plus religion, morality, and "the rights and duties of man in society." The same subjects, plus sewing and embroidery, were to be taught to young girls, save that there was no pretense of founding schools for all of them. With regard to higher education, the Founding Fathers called for a *colegio* (or *casa de educación*) in each province, teaching not less than grammar, rhetoric, philosophy, and "the branches of mathematics which are most important to the residents of the province"—and teaching as much more as the province could afford. Assorted revenues were assigned for the secondary schools, including general tax funds as a last resort; but their chief source of income was to be the capital holdings of the smaller Colombian convents, which were suppressed forthwith.[3]

The work of the Cúcuta Congress remained a model for all educational planning during the years of the Santander regime. Its main principles were reaffirmed by subsequent legislation and were given more concrete application in the Plan of Studies which was issued by Santander in 1826 as a detailed guide for Colombian educators to follow. As far as organization is concerned, the only important changes were made by the Congress of 1826 and were designed simply to round out the existing structure, remedying any major omissions, and applying to education the ideal symmetry already in use, at least on paper, for political, judicial, and military organization. There was now to be a primary school in each ward or parish, apparently whether it had 100 families or not, and also in each army corps; a rudimentary grammar school at the center of each canton; a *colegio* in each province; and, as a fitting climax to it all, a university for every department. With undue optimism Santander's Plan of Studies added that each parish school should be open by Christmas, 1827, and that its main room should be 36 feet wide "at the least and wherever possible." [4]

Needless to say, the legal provisions on width of floors were not the only parts of the official scheme of education that remained in practice a dead letter. And yet within a short time a surprisingly good start had been made. In primary education the most spectacular progress was to be found in the rapid extension of schools using the Lancasterian method of "mutual teaching," which was currently the rage in Europe and was specifically approved for use in Colombia by the Congress of Cúcuta. The method had already been introduced in Colombia by Fray Sebastián Mora of the Franciscan order, who learned it when deported to Spain in punishment for his patriot activities. On his return in 1820 Mora promptly established a small school in the miserable town of Capacho

[3] *Codif. Nac.* I, 21-30.
[4] *Codif. Nac.* VII, 402.

in western Venezuela. However, he was rescued from obscurity when he was brought to Bogotá by Santander the following year in order to found the first Lancasterian school in New Granada and thereby prepare the way for the general expansion of primary education under the dictates of the Constituent Congress. Mora's school in Bogotá was thus to serve as the first of three central "normal schools" of the Lancasterian method which Santander ordered set up in Bogotá, Caracas, and Quito; each of these was supposed to receive at least one student from every surrounding province, who would learn the new technique and then carry it to the people at home when the course was over. The Vice-President hoped that in this way it would soon be known throughout Colombia.[5]

Probably even more important for the spread of the Lancasterian method was the work done by a variety of traveling educational missions, of which the most successful was one entrusted to Mora himself. Once Mora had his Bogotá school running smoothly, he moved on to Popayán and ultimately to Ecuador, founding schools and training teachers as he went. His mission consumed several years, and was not complete until he had personally established the Lancasterian method in Loja and Cuenca, the southernmost provinces of the republic.[6] Mora's work was paralleled in the North by the mission of a French educator, Pierre Comettant, whose services were especially contracted in Europe by the Colombian agent José Rafael Revenga. Comettant's first assignment was to relieve Fray Sebastián at Bogotá; afterwards he moved to Caracas and then traveled along the Caribbean coast organizing Lancasterian schools as he went and engaging prominently in Masonic activities on the side. Comettant had constant difficulties in obtaining funds for his work, and not all his achievements were permanent; but meanwhile the *Gaceta del Istmo de Panamá* seriously affirmed that in his schools one could learn in a year what normally took five or six.[7] A still more famous traveling educator was Joseph Lancaster himself, the originator of the new system, who came from England to Caracas at the express invitation of Bolívar. Unfortunately, Lancaster accomplished less than either Mora or Comettant. He took over the management of the Lancasterian school already established in the Venezuelan capital, but he was soon embroiled in a dispute over finances with the Caracas municipality. As he himself loudly complained, he was "obliged *to borrow money to buy bread.*"[8] Since Bolívar's

[5] *Codif. Nac.* I, 29; *La Gaceta de Colombia,* April 21, May 5, and September 15, 1822.

[6] *La Gaceta de Colombia,* January 15, 1826; A.H.N., Congresos XXV, 440-443.

[7] *La Gaceta del Istmo de Panamá,* March 6, 1825. On Comettant see also *La Gaceta de Colombia,* September 15, 1822 and June 5, 1825; *La Gaceta de Cartagena,* April 30, 1825; *El Constitucional,* July 1, 1824; A.H.N., Congresos XII, 312.

[8] Lancaster to Santander, August 25, 1825, A.H.N., Interior y Relaciones CIX, 18. Italics Lancaster's.

personal offer of funds could not be very promptly turned into cash, he finally went home in disgust.[9]

Despite the unhappy fate of Mr. Lancaster personally, his teaching method had won remarkable acceptance. The openings and public exercises of Lancasterian schools were everywhere a major attraction, commemorated by masses and bullfights and attended by such dignitaries as the intendants in the provinces and the Vice-President in Bogotá. Their numbers increased rapidly, and so did the number of non-Lancasterian schools, which benefited somewhat less directly from the same primary-education craze. In 1823 the province of Bogotá alone boasted fifteen Lancasterian primary schools; by 1827 the Secretary of Interior reported that the country as a whole had 52 Lancasterian and 434 old-style primary schools for boys, with a total enrollment of about 20,000.[10] In a population of between two and three millions the latter figure is not high, but it was better than nothing.

Statistics, however, are not very instructive, for none are wholly reliable and there are few colonial totals to compare them with. Where comparative figures do exist, they are highly favorable to the republic: thus the province of Pamplona had one public primary school in 1810, 30 in 1822.[11] The main thing is that a real effort was being made to found new schools, and some of them were distinctly praised even by foreign observers.[12] Not only the government but also the clergy and private citizens had their hand in the good work, and the numerous cases of failure serve merely to emphasize the obstacles that were being gradually overcome. Thus even with the Lancasterian "normal schools" there was an obvious shortage of teachers, especially in such isolated spots as Río Hacha, which had to plead for a schoolmaster in the Cartagena press.[13] Equally or more serious was the lack of money, for the assessment system enacted by the Congress of Cúcuta was quite inadequate, and even a town the size of Maracaibo had trouble paying for any primary education at all. It was also necessary to contend with the laxity and indifference of many provincial officials who did not share the zeal of the national government; at Cúcuta no school was set up despite the fact that both teacher and funds were available.[14] These obstacles were

[9] Bolívar to Lancaster, March 16, 1825, Lecuna, *C.L.* IV, 295; *El Constitucional*, January 26, 1826.

[10] *La Gaceta de Colombia*, August 3, 1823; *El Constitucional*, June 24, 1824 and July 19, 1827.

[11] *La Indicación* (Bogotá), October 5, 1822. Cf. *La Gaceta de Colombia*, February 1, 1824.

[12] Cf. Col. John P. Hamilton, *Travels Through the Interior Provinces of Colombia* (2 vols., London, 1827) I, 254; William Duane, *A Visit to Colombia* (Philadelphia, 1826), 449-450.

[13] *La Gaceta de Cartagena*, January 7, 1826.

[14] A.H.N., Congresos XII, 312; *El Constitucional*, July 15, 1824.

doubly severe when it came to founding schools for girls: even the nuns, who were ordered by law to open schools for them, alleged lack of funds to do the job.[15] All things considered, one can only marvel that the number of children who received an education of some sort was no smaller.

The very same obstacles hampered the growth of secondary education. The supply of funds and teachers was insufficient, and such teachers as there were preferred the delights of Caracas and Bogotá to the quiet of Cumaná and Angostura. There were also special difficulties to overcome, such as the rivalry of Socorro and San Gil to be the seat of the same provincial *colegio*. This dispute was solved first by placing the *colegio* proper in San Gil while allowing Socorro to possess its own separate chair of philosophy, and finally by establishing a true *colegio* in each city; but this is not the only case in which the planned symmetry and centralization collided with the demand for at least a little secondary education in several different towns of a province.[16] Nevertheless, the five *colegios* existing in 1821 had grown to 21 *colegios* and one *casa de educación*—which was almost the same thing—by the start of 1827. Seven of the new institutions were schools that had existed before the War of Independence and were now simply revived, generally in expanded form, but there were ten that had been organized where nothing existed before, and in such places as Ibagué and the city of Antioquia this was no mean accomplishment.[17]

The increase in the number of universities was much less striking. The colonial regime had founded universities only in Bogotá, Caracas, and Quito, so that there were nine more to be created before every department could have its own as provided in the legislation of 1826. For the present, however, Santander decreed the establishment of new universities only at Tunja and Popayán, and as these were due to be organized just when the country was floundering in the political crisis set off by the Venezuelan revolt of 1826, only the University of the Cauca in Popayán became a functioning institution. A rector was named for the one at Tunja in the Department of Boyacá, but apparently that is as far as it got. This suited the people of Socorro and San Gil very nicely, for the departmental university was meant to absorb the more advanced courses of instruction given in their local *colegios,* and they had therefore been campaigning vigorously against the project for its creation.[18]

[15] *El Constitucional,* July 19, 1827.

[16] Juan de Dios Arias, "El Colegio de San José de Guanentá," *Conferencias dictadas en el Centro de Historia de Santander* (Bucaramanga, 1944?), 71-97, 102.

[17] *La Gaceta de Colombia,* October 19, 1823, April 10, 1825; *El Constitucional,* July 19, 1827. The number of students in 1827 was given as 2075.

[18] *La Gaceta de Colombia,* February 11, May 13, and June 10, 1827; A.C., Cámara-16, 226-229, and Senado-49, 1-12.

In any case, the most important institutional change at the university level was simply the reorganization of the three colonial universities so that they might take their place in the new educational system. In Bogotá, accordingly, the Dominican fathers' *Universidad de Santo Tomás* was now replaced by the official *Universidad Central de Bogotá*. The former had been little more than a central clearing-house for the granting of degrees, while the real work of teaching was done in the two *colegios* of San Bartolomé and Rosario. In 1826, by decree of Santander, all the courses given in the two *colegios* save Castilian and Latin grammar were transferred to the *Universidad Central*, and the Dominican university was superseded altogether. The result was a formal protest by the Rector of the *Colegio del Rosario* and a considerable struggle with the Dominican fathers, who denied that their university was legally suppressed and resisted the demand to surrender its archives to the *Universidad Central*. The Rector and the Dominicans were unsuccessful in all their pretensions, however; and though Santander was inclined to be lenient on the archives question, Bolívar turned out to be adamant. At most the Dominicans had some revenge by giving out degrees hand over fist in the last days of their university's existence, thus creating, as the saying went, *doctores al vapor*.[19]

The authorities also sought to encourage institutions of learning and culture outside the regular school and university system. First of all there had to be a national library, which was formed out of the public library of colonial Bogotá plus a few significant additions such as the collection of the *sabio* José Celestino Mutis. The library originally contained an estimated 10,000 to 12,000 books, which was not many, but it grew steadily: when jailed in the library building after the attempt on Bolívar's life in September, 1828, Santander personally counted 14,847.[20] Similarly, an *Academia Literaria Nacional* was organized in 1826 under a law which directed Santander himself to select the 21 original members. The choice was obviously difficult to make, since only *bogotanos* or public servants working in the capital could ever hope to participate directly in its activities, while at the same time political expediency if nothing else made it impossible to exclude provincials. The solution was to name thirteen *granadinos,* most of them regularly employed in Bogotá, seven native Venezuelans, of whom three could normally be found in the capital, and one Ecuadoran—the poet Olmedo. Several *académicos,* including Olmedo and the Venezuelan Andrés Bello, were not even in the country. However, this was not very serious as it turned out because the Academy met only a few times: it was little more than a way of honoring

[19] This phrase is from Groot, 419. See also *Acuerdos* II, 223, 227; A.H.N., *Miscelánea de la República* XXI, 338 and Congresos XXV, 248.

[20] *Codif. Nac.* VII, 77-78; *La Gaceta de Colombia,* January 4, 1824; Enrique Naranjo Martínez, *Puntadas de historia* (Bogotá, 1940), 168.

prominent citizens and of satisfying Colombians that they had an institution which was theoretically just like the academies of Western Europe.[21] Actually, many of the functions of the Academy were performed after a fashion, on a local scale, by private and semi-private *Sociedades Filantrópicas*, of which one existed—and held banquets—even in the remote and forbidding Chocó.[22]

Finally, there were certain state institutions designed to give instruction of a specialized nature. Bogotá in 1820 had possessed a short-lived military academy.[23] Three years later, under a contract made by Francisco Antonio Zea with a group of foreign scholars in Paris, the Colombian capital acquired a *Museo Nacional* with a mining school attached to it. According to the decree of Congress which approved the contract, the mining school was to receive at least one youth from each department, and the museum staff was to give instruction in sciences ranging from entomology to astronomy. This ambitious program was not fully carried out. Yet a few of the less exotic courses were actually given, and the mining school did formally open even though it never accomplished much. The Director of the *Museo,* the Peruvian Mariano Rivero, was so enthusiastic about his new tasks that he voluntarily ceded a quarter of his salary. He may well have had to cede even more in practice, for Zea had promised him the extraordinary sum of $4000 a year, almost twice the salary of a judge on the *Alta Corte.* Rivero and his colleagues did not do much teaching, but they carried on some excellent and useful researches on such topics as the milk of the "cow-tree" and the iron masses of the Cordillera Oriental.[24]

The museum and mining school were really part of a general reform movement which affected the quality and content as well as the quantity of Colombian education, and of which one aspect was a post-war revival of the scientific movement fostered by Mutis and Caldas in the late colonial regime. Thus the teaching of minerology had been ordered at the provincial *colegios* of Cali and Medellín even before a special school for mining was set up in Bogotá.[25] Some progress was also made in the field of medical education, where in truth progress was badly needed. There were whole provinces without a doctor: as one investigating committee lamented, "the people of Colombia absolutely lack surgeons and even

[21] *Acuerdos* II, 208; Restrepo VI, 435.
[22] *El Constitucional,* August 10, 1826.
[23] Alejandro Osorio and Estanislao Vergara, *Memoria correspondiente al año de 1820* (Bogotá, 1821), 22.
[24] *Codif. Nac.* I, 235-238, and VII, 171; *La Gaceta de Colombia,* September 7 and November 30, 1823, December 5, 1824; *Actas:* Senado-1825, 657-658; *El Constitucional,* April 27, 1826; Charles Stuart Cochrane, *Journal of a Residence and Travels in Colombia* (2 vols., London, 1825) II, 16.
[25] *Codif. Nac.* VII, 120, 145.

mere blood-letters, with notable prejudice to health."[26] Even in the latter part of 1822 the University of Caracas had exactly one medical student, and the situation in Bogotá was only slightly better. There medical instruction had been an unremunerated public service before the Revolution, and so it continued for a time under the republic. In due course, however, volunteer teaching was supplemented by that of two French doctors who gave formal classes in anatomy and physiology in return for a government stipend, and a part of this program was incorporated in the *Universidad Central* when it was set up, for the new university boasted a regular medical curriculum.[27] In provincial centers as well, medical instruction was encouraged by the administration; at one point there were actually more medical students in the provincial *colegio* of Tunja than in Caracas.[28] Not only this, but Santander's Plan of Studies for the first time required a doctor's degree for the practice of medicine in Colombia. This measure was not made retroactive to cover all current practitioners, and there is ample evidence of official laxity in enforcing medical standards even at Bogotá, but at least the ruling illustrates a growing awareness of the importance of formal training.[29]

A more important change in the nature of Colombian education was the steady decline of clerical influence. During the colonial regime most schools had been managed directly by the Church, and clerical influence was by no means eliminated under the republic. However, even though Colombian leaders were at first hesitant about asserting official control over the Church as a whole by means of the *patronato*, they never wavered in their claim that education of all varieties must be under the immediate guidance of the state. One of the measures taken by Santander as Vice-President of Cundinamarca was to bring the *colegio* of San Bartolomé back under public control after twenty years of episcopal management; and Bolívar not only gave prompt endorsement to this move but ordered that the same control should be exercised over all *colegios* whatsoever. Even ecclesiastical seminaries were placed under direct government regulation. When exceptions were made to the general rule, as in permitting the Bishop of Mérida himself to name the rector of a *colegio* which he

[26] A.H.N., Congresos XXV, 251.

[27] *La Gaceta de Colombia*, October 20, 1822 and August 14, 1825; A.H.N., Congresos XXV, 250. The Bogotá physician, José Félix Merizalde, one of the volunteer professors, cast serious doubt on the value of the newcomers' instruction, but there is no real way of determining the truth of his charges. They are presented in *El estudiante* and *El desengaño anatómico* (Bogotá, 1824).

[28] Cf. *El Constitucional de Boyacá* (Tunja), December 23, 1825; *La Gaceta de Colombia*, February 5, 1826.

[29] *Codif. Nac.* VII, 446; *La Gaceta de Colombia*, November 25, 1827. On the practicing of the mysterious Dr. Arganil see Alberto Miramón, *Los septembrinos* (Bogotá, 1939), 103-111.

founded and supported at Pamplona, it was only through a special delegation of authority on the part of Santander.[30] The mere tightening of state control did not, of course, prevent the liberal use of individual clergymen as teachers. The decrees of Santander often required that particular teaching posts be filled by members of the clergy, and the archbishop-designate of Bogotá, Dr. Fernando Caicedo, was named first rector of the *Universidad Central*.[31] Likewise, Church funds were extensively used for educational purposes, whether they consisted of the capital holdings confiscated from suppressed convents, the income from special clerical endowments traditionally assigned for use in education, or the voluntary contributions of individual clergymen. Gifts for education were made with particular lavishness by the ex-royalist Bishop of Popayán, Salvador Jiménez de Enciso, but they were also made by humble curates, and in every case the money was eagerly welcomed.[32] Nor was there any attempt to exclude religious education from the official school system. Church attendance on stated occasions was made compulsory for school children, although in 1826 the children of non-Roman Catholics were implicitly exempted.[33] The principal change was simply a shift of emphasis: with the decline of ecclesiastical control religion was to become a subordinate rather than the central element in Colombian education.

The new emphasis, needless to say, was to be placed on whatever doctrines were being expounded at the moment by the most popular liberal writers of western Europe. The respect shown for scientific studies is really one aspect of this development, but even more significant was the reform of the curriculum in such fields as political science, law, and liberal arts. For one thing, there were particular aspects of the social sciences that had been taught very little if at all during the colonial regime, and which had to be firmly established in Colombian schools before the nation could consider itself really up-to-date. Francisco Soto thus began a new course in political economy at San Bartolomé, using the text of the French liberal economist Jean Baptiste Say, and this moved the official *Gaceta* to remark gleefully that "from the conquest until now the words political economy, values, productive and unproductive capitals . . . had not resounded in our colleges.[34] For the moment political economy as a separate course was apparently taught nowhere else, but the

[30] Santander to Bolívar, May 26, 1820, *Corresp.* 187-189; *Codif. Nac.* II, 234, VII, 14-15, 146.
[31] Cf. *La Gaceta de Colombia,* November 19, 1826; *Codif. Nac.* VII, 134-135.
[32] Cf. *La Gaceta de Colombia,* May 8, 1825; *El Constitucional de Boyacá,* March 3, 1826.
[33] *Codif. Nac.* VII, 404.
[34] *La Gaceta de Colombia,* July 24, 1825. See also issue of November 21, 1824, and *Codif. Nac.* VII, 229.

government hoped that ultimately it might become a standard element in the Colombian curriculum. San Bartolomé also led the way in the formal teaching of French and English, although both subjects were to be offered at other institutions as soon as possible. Santander's Plan of Studies in 1826 required that they be taught at every *colegio* and university in Colombia. Neither language in itself had any ideological significance, but they were included in the curriculum not only for their commercial and diplomatic usefulness but also as a way of helping Colombians to familiarize themselves with the writings of the best modern authorities on the social and natural sciences. The encouragement of French and English thus went hand in hand with a campaign to limit the use of Latin, which was by contrast the language of the traditional and orthodox authorities. Latin also was too closely associated with "the syllogistic form of teaching used by the peripatetics," which was now formally banished from Colombian schools. The decline of Latin was profoundly lamented by such clerical conservatives as the Bishop of Mérida, Lasso de la Vega, but the trend could not be halted: the Congress of 1826 decreed that only certain legal studies, theology, and Scripture might be taught from Latin texts, while at the same time everything possible was done to eliminate the oral use of Latin in Colombian classrooms.[35]

The most controversial innovation of all, however, was the introduction of new textbooks of doubtful religious orthodoxy. This concerned both new courses like political economy and old ones like jurisprudence, and heading the list of controversial authors was the English philosopher Jeremy Bentham, undoubtedly the favorite writer of Santander and his liberal circle. From the outset Bentham had been cited with the most laudatory epithets by *La Gaceta de Colombia,* and his writings were placed on the curriculum at San Bartolomé and possibly elsewhere at an early date. Finally, in November, 1825, a decree of Santander made Bentham's text on principles of legislation compulsory for law students throughout the republic. This step unleashed a storm of criticism, for Bentham was a confessed materialist whose works were full of statements directly contrary to Roman Catholic orthodoxy. The clergy was almost unanimously indignant, and so were the more conservative laymen. Santander thus referred the problem for further study to the national *Dirección de Estudios* established by decree of Congress in 1826 in order to supervise all branches of Colombian education. One of the three Directors, Dr. Félix Restrepo, was opposed to Bentham altogether; the other two, Vicente Azuero and Estanislao Vergara, conceived the idea that as long as no entirely satisfactory alternative was available teachers might simply point

[35] *Codif. Nac.* II, 233, and VII, 238, 407, 431-433; *La Gaceta de Colombia,* February 1, 1824, March 13 and December 4, 1825; Pedro Leturia, S.J., *La emancipación hispanoamericana en los informes episcopales a Pío VII* (Buenos Aires, 1935), 130.

out the "mistaken" passages in Bentham as they went along, thus warning their students not to be misled. This suggestion was incorporated in the definitive Plan of Studies issued in October of 1826, but it still did not quiet the opposition. It would not suffice to delete a few passages from Bentham when his central doctrine of utilitarianism and everything that stemmed from it was basically in conflict with the Roman Catholic religion. In the end Santander had to authorize the *Dirección de Estudios* to import a different text if it saw fit, but there was no time to act on this suggestion before the end of the Santander regime.[36]

Bentham was only the most prominent of the authors who were under attack. Santander's decree of November, 1825, was also criticized for including the Protestant Wattel as a prescribed authority on international law, and the Plan of Studies a year later greatly extended the list of heretical or at least mildly unorthodox writers whose works were placed on the school curriculum. The Plan ordered children in primary school to learn good behaviour from the "moral catechism" of an author who was not a Roman Catholic in good standing. Even the required texts on canon law left a good bit to be desired from the orthodox viewpoint. It is thus easy to believe the charge of Groot that Congress entrusted the Executive with the job of issuing the full Plan of Studies rather than enacting it by legislative process precisely because the liberal majority feared to allow a full public discussion of the curriculum it had in mind. Indeed very few texts of any importance were wholly acceptable to conservatives.[37]

Although it was not always expressly stated at the time, Groot leaves no room for doubt that conservative elements often objected quite as strongly to the teachers as to the textbooks they used. Many instructors, it was felt, were leading the young to think of religion as a stupid waste of time and in general were undermining sound moral principles.[38] Nor could this charge be denied entirely, at least from the viewpoint of orthodox Roman Catholicism. Thus the teaching of legislation according to the textbook of Bentham was entrusted at Bogotá to Dr. Vicente Azuero, a freethinker who was quite frankly sympathetic toward the basic doctrines of the English philosopher. Whether Azuero's private character was good or bad, he could hardly be expected to point out as erroneous all the passages that were deemed contrary to good religion and morals by the fully or even moderately orthodox. Similar objections could be made against many other eminent liberals who assumed teaching assignments as a part-time occupation. Francisco Soto is one more obvious example,

[36] *Codif. Nac.* VII, 299, 450, 481-482; *La Gaceta de Colombia,* July 17, 1825, and September 9, 1827; Groot, 366, 466-467.
[37] Groot, 417-422; *Codif. Nac.* II, 241, and VII, 405.
[38] Groot, 291.

although in his special field of economics he was not so directly concerned with religious dogma. Even the clergymen who were named to high places in the field of education were usually chosen from the radical wing of the Colombian priesthood.

At the lower levels of instruction, and especially in the provinces, the atmosphere was not quite so liberal. José Manuel Restrepo complained that there were far too many teachers who still found it "painful to confess that very little that is useful can be learned from our ancestors" and who believed "that nothing should be taught but in Latin, condemning the contrary opinion as endangering the religion of Jesus Christ." [39] As a matter of fact, there were not enough qualified doctrinaire liberals to fill all the teaching positions in the country even if the government wanted them to, which it probably did not. Quite apart from all ideological considerations, moreover, there is no doubt that the teaching profession had come to include a high number of unusually gifted citizens. Among the liberals there were not only Soto and Azuero but also the brilliant young Rufino Cuervo and the future President José Ignacio de Márquez, who took time out from his duties as Intendant of Boyacá in order to teach at the provincial *colegio* in Tunja. The moderates were represented above all by Dr. Félix Restrepo, who taught philosophy at Bogotá.[40] The men chosen for the principal supervisory posts in the educational system both in Bogotá and in the departments were equally capable for the most part, including a good selection of clergymen and the conservative aristocrat Joaquín Mosquera as well as the inevitable Dr. Vicente Azuero.[41] The great difficulty in Colombian education was simply that the capable men at the top were always hindered both by the scarcity of human and material resources at their command and by the partisan controversies that so much of their work necessarily entailed.

---

[39] *El Constitucional,* July 22, 1824.

[40] *El Constitucional,* December 23, 1825; *La Gaceta de Colombia,* August 8, 1824; Guillermo Hernández de Alba, *Vida y escritos del doctor José Félix de Restrepo* (Bogotá, 1935), 28-29.

[41] *Acuerdos* II, 159, 234; *La Gaceta de Colombia,* February 11, 1827.

Chapter XIII

# The Religious Question (I): Clericals and Anti-clericals

NOT only in education but in its general campaign for reform and innovation, the success of Colombian liberalism was dependent to a great extent upon the attitude of the Roman Catholic Church. There was little difficulty with regard to harmless projects such as the founding of primary schools: despite later talk of clerical hostility to the spread of learning as such, these obtained effective Church support from the start. When it came to the liberals' notions of property reform, religious liberty, and methods of higher education, the situation was different. These questions and others like them involved fundamental interests of the Church, and often affected them adversely. On such issues, despite a long habit of obedience to the state, the Church was bound to fight for its own views. The clergy often fought with greater moderation, at first, than did its opponents, but its growing disaffection played a major role in the series of political crises that brought about the collapse of Gran Colombia.

## The Clergy in the War and Post-War Era

The "Religious Question" derived its importance principally from the far-reaching influence which the clergy still exercised in the life of the nation. Anti-clericals might lament this influence as a sign of degrading fanaticism, but it could not be disregarded. Foreign visitors agreed that parish priests enjoyed a nearly absolute moral authority over the mass of the population,[1] and Colombia made the most of this authority by repeatedly assigning the clergy as *ex officio* members of manumission juntas, primary education boards, and similar committees for the advancement of worthwhile causes. Or to cite the testimony of a conservative army officer, it was only for "fanaticism" that the people of the Cauca would willingly take arms and fight,[2] and the Cauca was not one of the most "fanatical" regions of Colombia. Even without recourse to arms the latent hostility of the religious masses served as an effective brake upon many favorite projects of the dominant liberal group. Santander himself announced more than once that he would have to oppose a measure not because he considered it wrong but simply because the people would deem it an attack on religion.

[1] Cf. Gaspar Theodore Mollien, *Viaje por la República de Colombia* (Bogotá, 1944), 354.
[2] Tomás C. Mosquera to Bolívar, November 21, 1827, O'Leary IX, 90.

The influence of the clergy was not lessened by the coming of independence as such. In some respects it was increased, for the clergy as a whole had lent effective support to the patriot cause. The *Gaceta* never tired of lauding "this clergy upon whose patriotism has been erected the throne of liberty," [3] and the picture of rampant clerical royalism invented by later liberal authors[4] is simply untrue. Don Pablo Morillo, who was in a position to know, stated of New Granada in 1816 (with some slight exaggeration) that "the *curas* are particularly disaffected; not one appears addicted to the cause of the king." [5] There were, of course, some royalist priests everywhere, and in certain regions they composed a distinct majority of the clergy, but there is no evidence that anywhere the clergy was significantly influenced either for or against Spanish rule by reason of its ministry alone: in the diocese of Mérida priests as well as laymen were divided between royalist Maracaibo and patriot Mérida,[6] and if in Pasto the priests were rabid royalists so too was everyone else. The essential patriotism of the Colombian clergy becomes all the more evident if one excludes from consideration its Spanish-born elements. The colonial authorities had reserved the chief positions in the Church as well as in civil administration for European Spaniards, and their influence, for obvious reasons, was usually exerted on behalf of the royalist cause. Of the three Spanish-born bishops who held office at the time independence was attained only Salvador Jiménez de Enciso of Popayán was ever truly reconciled to the new regime; and among the three native-born bishops—an exceptionally high proportion for the colonial regime—Bishop Lasso of Mérida had originally been selected precisely because he was then known as ultra-royalist in sympathy. The two creole bishops of Panamá and Santa Marta, on the other hand, gave valuable support to independence from the time their dioceses were liberated.[7]

The patriotism of the clergy was further increased by measures taken to discipline the more obvious royalist sympathizers. Voluntary exile was chosen by the Bishop of Cartagena and numerous others who fled before the advance of patriot armies, but if exile was not accepted voluntarily the patriots were perfectly willing to require it whenever they saw fit. This was done to the Bishop of Quito when it was decided that his conversion to the cause of independence had been insincere. It was seldom

[3] *La Gaceta de Colombia*, February 9, 1823.
[4] Cf. Julio Hoenigsberg, *Santander, el clero, y Bentham* (Bogotá, 1940), 13-21.
[5] Groot, 639.
[6] Mary Watters, *A History of the Church in Venezuela* (Chapel Hill, 1933), 54-55.
[7] On the Bishop of Panamá, a Peruvian, see *La Gaceta de Colombia*, March 17, 1822; on the Bishop of Santa Marta, a *bogotano*, see Groot, 92. The high proportion of creole bishops was an accidental result of the unusual number of vacancies then existing, and did not reflect any intentional shift in Spanish policy.

## The Religious Question (I): Clericals and Anti-clericals 197

necessary, however, to go so far, and most if not all of those actually deported were Spaniards. Others were confined to a different part of Colombia, as when Santander rounded up suspicious clergymen after Boyacá for shipment to Guayana, a fate which in some respects at least was worse than expulsion from the country. It was even thought advisable, for security reasons, to transfer a number of royalist nuns away from Pasto. A milder form of punishment was simply to remove a royalist priest from his office. This could mean either a brief suspension until such time as he convinced the authorities of his future good intentions or, in certain cases, a permanent demotion. The acting heads of the two vacant sees of Caracas and Bogotá were both replaced by their cathedral chapters under pressure from the government, although in neither case had they given any specific grounds for complaint. Their past record as royalists was in itself enough to disqualify them.[8]

But even some who had appeared the most hardened royalists performed valuable service for the new state once they had undergone a process of political conversion. The conversion of Bishop Lasso of Mérida derives special importance from the fact that it was the first break in the ranks of the royalist episcopate. It was due in part, admittedly, to his fear of Spanish liberalism following the Spanish revolution in 1820; he once wrote that precisely when Ferdinand VII swore allegiance to the Spanish liberal constitution the peoples of America had regained their fundamental sovereignty. But he also felt it his clear duty to stay loyally by his flock, and he was exposed to the personal magnetic charms of Simón Bolívar. In any case, Lasso not only changed sides but proclaimed his newly-acquired faith in "republican virtue," popular sovereignty, and social contracts in the pastoral letters which he gladly issued at the request of republican officials. With the same willingness he took up Bolívar's idea that he should personally write to Rome on behalf of Latin American freedom. He was the first bishop anywhere to do so, and the correspondence was genuinely effective.[9] Lasso took a seat in the Congress of Cúcuta, and he subsequently became a hard-working, fair-minded—and ultraconservative—member of the Colombian Senate.

Still more striking, perhaps, was the service rendered by Bishop Jiménez of Popayán. Jiménez had retreated to the royalist stronghold of Pasto, showering excommunications in his path, when the greater part of

---

[8] Julio Tobar Donoso, *La iglesia ecuatoriana en el siglo XIX* (Quito, 1934), 150-162, 171; Groot, 16, 38-39, 217; Nicolás E. Navarro, *Anales eclesiásticos venezolanos* (Caracas, 1929), 169-172.

[9] Rafael Lasso de la Vega, *Conducta del Obispo de Mérida* (Bogotá, 1823); Pedro Leturia, *Bolívar y León XII* (Caracas, 1931), 17-23; and especially Antonio Ramón Silva, *Patriotismo del clero de la diócesis de Mérida* (Mérida, 1911), 123-133.

his diocese was first occupied by Colombian forces; but he saw the light in time to lend a hand in the negotiations that brought the surrender of Pasto to Bolívar in May of 1822. He ultimately became as good a patriot as Lasso de la Vega, frankly proclaiming Bolívar to be the "tutelar angel of the republic." [10] Indeed Jiménez was the only Spanish-born bishop anywhere in America to remain permanently at his post after the defeat of Spain; he was also the only Spanish bishop to follow Lasso's example in placing the patriot case before the Vatican in his correspondence.[11] He was never elected to Congress and composed fewer pamphlets than the Bishop of Mérida, but in his quiet way he materially helped to cement the new regime, and it is probable that on more than one occasion the liberals of Bogotá wished that Lasso had been content to remain as inconspicuous.

Other members of the clergy had been doing their part for the national cause even before the much-publicized conversions of Lasso and Jiménez. Priests were repeatedly directed to explain in sermons that "the cause of Liberty has an intimate connection with the Doctrine of Jesus Christ," [12] but in many cases this reminder was hardly necessary. A typical example of the clergy's propaganda function was the solemn exercise held by the Franciscans of Bogotá in the spring following the Battle of Boyacá. Fourteen vehemently patriotic "propositions" were defended in turn for the edification of the capital, and their general tenor can be gathered from the conclusion that "to think the bull of Pope Alexander VI gives Spain a right to property over the countries of America argues either a mad temerity or a shameful ignorance." [13] Both willingly and unwillingly, the clergy also gave heavily to the war assessments which were euphemistically described as "loans" and "gifts." These were especially onerous in the case of royalist priests, who sometimes paid a virtual bribe to escape more drastic measures. Bishop Jiménez of Popayán issued a blanket authorization to arrest and confiscate the property of any priest who refused to pay his share in such contributions, and the Bishop of Panama made a special loan of cattle and other items worth $60,000 almost as soon as the Isthmus was liberated. This step was carried out in disregard of the laws of the Church, but the Bishop gladly offered

[10] Salvador Jiménez de Enciso y Cobos Padilla, *El Atalaya* (Bogotá, 1824), 203-204. On his part in the surrender of Pasto see Blanco VIII, 421.
[11] Pedro Leturia, S.J., *La emancipación hispanoamericana en los informes episcopales a Pío VII* (Buenos Aires, 1935), 169-185.
[12] *La Gaceta de la Ciudad de Bogotá*, March 12, 1820.
[13] *La Gaceta de la Ciudad de Bogotá*, April 23, 1820. This need not be taken in an anti-clerical sense, although it is true that anti-clericals usually made the most of Alexander's bull, and that good Churchmen usually preferred not to mention it.

to do it again for the support of the war in Peru, which was his own homeland.[14]

A final variety of assistance to the national cause was personal service by members of the clergy. A surprising number of priests and friars actually took up arms, and some filled posts of major responsibility under the new regime. The priest-Colonel José Félix Blanco, for instance, received a special commission to quiet unrest behind the front in the province of Santa Marta.[15] The most typical form of personal service, however, was participation in all manner of juntas, congresses, and assemblies, not only because this was deemed to be more in keeping with the clerical vocation, but also because such positions were often filled by popular election. The electoral college of Maracaibo in 1825 contained equal numbers of priests and laymen. The Colombian Senate was almost exclusively composed of laymen, but the Chamber of Representatives, which more accurately reflected popular sentiment, began its functions in 1823 with a membership that was one-third clerical. The clerical element would have been greater still if the provinces of Pasto and Bogotá had not been overruled by Congress itself when they insisted on electing two very popular friars among their Representatives; friars were considered legally ineligible in view of their vows of unquestioning obedience to their orders and their lack of the necessary property and residence requirements in civil society.[16]

As the prominence of clergymen in elective office will serve to indicate, independence had in some ways actually increased the opportunities for the Church to exert an influence upon national life. But if the Church was to maintain its position, it could well use whatever additional authority and prestige it had gained through its services to the republic. Even though the clergy could not truthfully be identified with the fallen regime, it had been indirectly weakened in several major respects since the start of the struggle for independence. For one thing, it was no longer as numerous as before. According to the census of 1825 the nation possessed 1694 secular priests, 1377 friars, and 789 nuns; there was consequently one priest or friar for slightly over 700 inhabitants, which is considerably better than the Latin American average today. Even so, the clergy had apparently fallen off by about one-seventh from pre-war levels. The population in general had also declined, and in somewhat the same proportion, but the general decline had not occurred for the same reasons.[17] Certainly war casualties and privations were a minor

[14] Groot, 154, 189-190; A.C., Senado-6, 54.
[15] *Acuerdos* I, 106-107.
[16] *El Aficionado* (Bogotá), No. 1 (1823); A.C., Senado-8, 165-166. 186. Senado-15, 167.
[17] Restrepo I, xx, xxxviii, and VII, 300-302.

factor in the case of the clergy; emigration and exile, which affected principally the Spanish-born clergy, were somewhat more important. The most alarming development, however, was a decline in the number of new recruits. There is evidence that this decline had begun under the impact of the Enlightenment in the late colonial period, but it was accelerated when independence opened up new careers in the army, government, and business, all of which made the alternative of a clerical vocation appear less attractive. No doubt the inroads made upon the wealth of the clergy by war damages, forced loans, and at least some of the reform measures of the new government also made the Church less desirable as a career. As a result, the old *colegio seminario* of Cartagena had to suspend the teaching of canon law and theology altogether for lack of students, and similar conditions could be found in other parts of Colombia. It was even observed that young girls were growing too independent-minded to become nuns.[18]

The problem of maintaining an adequate clergy was further complicated by its uneven distribution throughout the republic. In Ecuador the situation would not become serious for a long time; indeed the number of monks and friars in Quito was so excessive that the convents could not hold them all and discipline had to be sacrificed by allowing them to live on the outside, managing their own resources. In the less desirable provinces, however, the situation was serious already. Guayana, which was supposed to be the seat of a bishopric, contained only one secular priest and four friars in the census year 1825.[19] By that time, apparently, the royalist clergymen sent to Guayana by Santander had either perished or won parole.

In the first years of Gran Colombia there was also a vertical maldistribution. Exile and death had depleted both the cathedral chapters and the episcopate, and so many complex interests were at stake in deciding how to fill vacancies above the parish level under the new regime that no action was taken either at Rome or in Bogotá as long as the war still raged on Colombian soil. Of the eighteen posts in the metropolitan chapter of Bogotá, only five were still occupied at the start of 1823; Cartagena was likewise reduced to only three full canons.[20] As for the episcopate, the sees of Bogotá, Guayana, and Cuenca were vacant when Gran Colombia was founded; the bishops of Santa Marta and Panama died soon after their dioceses were freed; and the royalist bishops of Quito and Cartagena went into exile. This left only Lasso and Jiménez, for the archbishop of

[18] *La Gaceta de Cartagena,* October 29, 1826; William Duane, *A Visit to Colombia* (Philadelphia, 1826), 483.

[19] Tobar Donoso, *op. cit.,* 71-72, 243-244; José Manuel Restrepo, *Exposición . . . del Despacho del Interior* (Bogotá, 1827).

[20] Leturia, *Emancipación,* 157, 162.

Caracas was in Spain, where he had been sent by order of Morillo, and he also died late in 1822. By and large most episcopal functions could be carried on by a *Provisor,* Capitular Vicar, or interim head of the diocese under some other title, and the Pope was generally willing to grant special authorizations when needed. Yet the lack of bishops could not help but deprive the Church of firm leadership in a time of readjustment, and it was especially serious in Quito, where one *Provisor* was left by the exiled bishop and another named by the cathedral chapter. The result was a general uncertainty regarding the efficacy of the sacraments until the rift was healed and the Vatican retroactively validated the acts of both.[21]

In due course chapters and bishoprics were filled, by the law of *patronato* passed in 1824 and by the establishment of informal relations with Rome; both developments must be considered in a later chapter. However, the lack of bishops and canons was only one of the problems that arose in matters of church organization. Another difficulty was the mere fact of separation from Church authorities in Spain. In the case of the secular clergy little more was involved than the status of military chaplains, who had previously been dependent directly upon the Patriarch of the Indies. This problem was easily settled by placing them under the control of the respective dioceses.[22] The issue was somewhat more serious for the regular clergy, who had always left certain cases in canon law for a final decision by the heads of their orders in Spain. This was now impossible; and even if appeal to an enemy nation had not been out of the question, the Spanish liberals had left Discalced Augustinians no Spanish province to appeal to.[23] Once again, the natural solution was to expand the powers of the bishops or their substitutes. One *Provisor* at Quito claimed to exercise the same functions as the heads of the orders in Spain simply as a matter of course. Bishop Lasso, on the other hand, had the forethought to ask the Pope, and he succeeded in obtaining a bull that gave him the right to exercise a limited jurisdiction over the religious orders, at the same time as he won new privileges for the Provincials of the orders within his diocese. All of this was entirely reasonable, as even the dean of Senate anti-clericals, Dr. Francisco Soto, was ready to agree. Unfortunately, the bull had to be referred to Congress for its sanction under the law of *patronato,* and as it happened the Diplomatic Commission of the lower house saw a copy in which *episcoporum* was mistakenly written in place of *episcopo cum.* In its context this term suggested that the Pope intended to set up an extra-legal tribunal of

[21] Tobar Donoso, *op. cit.,* 157-166, 190-191.
[22] *Acuerdos* I, 188.
[23] Marcelino Ganuza, *Monografía de las misiones vivas de Agustinos Recoletos (Candelarios) en Colombia* (2 vols., Bogotá 1921) II, lii.

bishops in Colombia, and so the Chamber as a whole flatly refused its consent to the new arrangements. This confusion was ultimately cleared up, but Congress still had some doubts about other provisions of the same bull, and in the end Congress never did get around to permitting its execution.[24] The issue at stake thus remained without any clear solution.

The religious orders had deeper worries, however, than their relations with superiors in Spain. They had become a residence of "immorality and ignorance" in the words of Foreign Minister José R. Revenga; Lasso himself confirmed the friars' practice of wandering about from one place to another like vagabonds.[25] The religious orders were also hurt more than the secular clergy by the decline in clerical vocations: the anti-clerical *Cometa* of Caracas observed with undisguised pleasure that "no one becomes a friar any more."[26] What was perhaps worse, the existing friars evinced a strong desire to escape monastic life. To some extent they themselves appear to have become infected by anti-clerical agitation against the monastic ideals, and they no doubt observed also that their orders were the chief losers by the first anti-clerical reforms of the new regime. Still another factor was the war with Spain, and the wide disruption of missions and monasteries which it entailed, for it was hard to settle down to old routines once the excitement was over. The Dominican Ignacio Mariño rose to the rank of Colonel with the patriot forces in Casanare, returned to Bogotá after the liberation of New Granada, and proceeded to compose a tract in which he decried the injustice of forcing missionary friars to create new parishes in the wilderness only to have secular priests come out and enjoy the fruits of their labor once the hard work was done.[27] Similar complaints were heard from the regular clergy throughout the republic. Even a group of nuns in a Loja convent were caught by the yearning to escape, although they later issued a shamefaced retraction of their plea for secularization.[28]

In the case of the Loja nuns secularization could only have meant a return to civil life, and this was also demanded by a small minority of friars. Such extremists found little support for their pretensions, since religious vows could still be enforced under Colombian law,[29] but the more conventional demand for mere enjoyment of secular benefices was a

[24] Tobar Donoso, *op. cit.*, 173; Leturia, *Emancipación*, 149-150, 203-209; A.C., Actas del Senado, March 31, 1826; Senado-35, 84-103.

[25] Revenga to Ignacio Tejada, March 9, 1826, Blanco X, 216; Leturia, *Emancipación*, 149-150.

[26] *El Cometa* (Caracas), March 2, 1826.

[27] Ignacio Mariño, O.P., *Defensa del clero regular* (Bogotá, 1821).

[28] A.C., Senado-41, 141.

[29] For an extreme case cf. J.J. Joaquín Vela, *Guerra a la preocupación y defensa de los regulares* (Bogotá, 1826?); A.H.N., Miscelánea de la República XXI, 114-129.

slightly different matter. The administration was openly sympathetic; it interceded both with the Vatican and with Congress on the friars' behalf. The government would not, however, declare them generally eligible for secular benefices on its own initiative; and despite the presence of wide support in Congress, Bishop Lasso in his capacity as Senator of the republic was successful in heading off legislative action. Yet even without a special legislative order, the archdiocese of Bogotá displeased some of the secular clergy by its willingness to find special cases in which friars might act as curates. And despite a hard struggle with secular priests and city authorities the Dominicans retained undisputed possession of the greatest shrine in New Granada, the temple of Our Lady of Chiquinquirá, which yielded a "spiritual mine" in alms every year.[30] The fact that the temple of Chiquinquirá was happily tended by friars who lived in a monastery clearly suggests that material advancement and public recognition rather than mere release from convent walls were the real objectives of most discontented friars. Indeed the friars in mission outposts enjoyed even more personal freedom than many secular priests, but in spite of the abundance of regular clergy in Quito and Bogotá all Indian missions remained in a state of deplorable neglect.[31]

Disciplinary problems were not limited to the religious orders. The *Provisor* of Bogotá agreed that there was "a sufficient number of delinquent ecclesiastics" among the secular clergy as well. The practice of holding more than one position in the Church even when it was uncanonical to do so was admittedly common, and the government itself complained of the great number of priests who failed to live in their benefices.[32] Clergymen who had embarked upon a political career would very often be offenders in the latter respect; indeed one of the priests in Congress declared that he had not felt qualified to perform his priestly functions since the day he signed a royalist's death warrant as magistrate of the *Patria Boba*.[33] Even the education of the clergy was observed to be on the decline, since the war had disturbed clerical as well as lay instruction and post-war jurisdictional disputes over management of sem-

---

[30] A.H.N., Corresp.-Senado, March 3, 1826; A.C., Senado-12, 329-334, Senado-15, 473-474, Senado-40, 11-12, Cámara-7, 116-226, Actas del Senado, March 29, 1826.
The Dominicans themselves claimed that $10,000 to $20,000 in alms at Chiquinquirá meant a good year (Andrés Mesanza, *Apuntes y documentos sobre la orden dominicana en Colombia,* Caracas, 1936, p. 160); but others placed the figure a good bit higher. It was sarcastically alleged that the militant patriotism of the Dominican order was due to the fact that they could not take the Virgin of Chiquinquirá into exile with them (Duane, *op. cit.,* 439).

[31] See above, pp. 179-180.

[32] *La Gaceta de Colombia,* October 21, 1827.

[33] Gustavo Otero Muñoz, *Semblanzas colombianas* (2 vols., Bogotá 1938) I, 258. The reference is to Sen. Manuel Benito Rebollo.

inaries and colleges often made it hard to restore normal conditions of clerical training. Certainly the education of priests was not a major concern of the liberal government. The situation was especially serious in a vacant see like Quito, where candidates for the priesthood made the long trip to Popayán in order to receive their final ordination from a bishop who was in a poor position to discriminate between worthy and unworthy. To judge from the complaint of Manuel José Mosquera, however, Bishop Jiménez was also reduced to ordaining "some very idiotic and corrupt" individuals for his own diocese.[34]

Probably the most common complaint against the secular clergy was the charge that it lived in luxury through the exaction of improper fees and services. Few curates, said the French visitor Mollien, lacked an income of $1000 a year, and many enjoyed over $2000; the Bishop of Popayán was said to have a revenue of some $40,000 and was accordingly noted as a connoisseur of fine foods and beverages.[35] When such ample incomes were contrasted with the subsistence level of the mass of the population, it appeared outrageous to the clergy's critics that it should charge as much as $8 for a burial and $11 or $12 for the sacrament of marriage.[36] In the clerical stronghold of Ecuador the intendant joined the *junta provincial* in protesting against the "unlimited covetousness" of the clergy in the matter of parish fees, noting that it was aggravated by irregular demands for free personal service. Even Dr. Buenaventura Arias, right-hand man of Bishop Lasso, was accused of charging excessive fees by a Congressional committee otherwise favorable to the clergy.[37]

It is probable, however, that there is a measure of exaggeration in many accounts of clerical wealth and luxury. Clerical income from the tithes and mortgage holdings inevitably declined in many areas where agriculture was disrupted by war or where the regional economy was weakened by post-war readjustments. This is no doubt why Bishop Lasso of Mérida could complain in 1823 that his episcopal revenues, which should have amounted to $10,000, were actually less than $4000.[38] Even Mollien, who frequently complained of clerical wealth, was willing to admit that with the exception of its bishop the clergy of Popayán was not rich, and another foreign visitor asserted that the Dominicans of

[34] Tobar Donoso, *op. cit.*, 44-45, 199, 211-214.

[35] Mollien, *op. cit.*, 162, 266; Col. J. P. Hamilton, *Travels Through the Interior Provinces of Colombia* (2 vols., London 1827) II, 40-42, 72-73.

[36] See Charles Stuart Cochrane, *Journal of a Residence and Travels in Colombia* (2 vols., London 1825) II, 513 for a table of fees from Bogotá, and also the complaint of the town of Charalá in A.C. Senado-16, 174-175. On another occasion Charalá asked the right to name its own priest so as to avoid clerical "excesses and scandals." (Senado-55, 161-162).

[37] A.C., Cámara-16, 184; A.H.N., Congresos V, 538.

[38] A.C., Cámara-4, 185.

Chiquinquirá actually led a humble life regardless of their fabulous income.[39] In spite of all its shortcomings, in fact, foreign tourists generally formed a favorable view of the secular if not of the regular clergy. Richard Bache testified that he "invariably found them courteous, hospitable, and many, well informed," and that they showed a "benignity of manners to all who approached them, high or low."[40]

### Anti-clericalism, "Liberal" Catholicism, and Freemasonry

The Colombian Church was nevertheless faced with one problem which was far more serious than clerical luxury, lax discipline, or empty cathedral chapters. This was the first real weakening of its great moral influence over the population. The influence of the clergy was still infinitely more than that of any private institution, and at least in its powers of mass persuasion it was no doubt stronger than the government itself. Clerical prestige was not remotely threatened among the common people of Ecuador and New Granada. It was also great in Venezuela; but in central and eastern Venezuela there was an evident weakening of religious feeling even among the masses. This was particularly true in the case of the shifting population of the *llanos,* where the present generation had known little but war since infancy; it was suggested in Congress that the *llaneros* themselves would make a good mission field for Colombian friars.[41]

Among educated persons, furthermore, and above all among convinced liberals, the opinions of the Church obviously carried less weight than formerly. Once again the process was most apparent in Venezuela, in part because Venezuelans maintained the closest economic and intellectual relations with the outside world, but exactly the same tendency was evident to some extent almost everywhere. The aristocratic families of Popayán were generally conservative in their politics and economics, and in religion they were not basically anti-clerical. On the other hand, they were not greatly interested in defending the Church unless for reasons of political expediency; they, too, could speak loosely about the evils of "fanaticism," and they prided themselves on the relative lack of it in the Cauca Valley.[42] The officer class of the Colombian army held much the same sentiments. Military men often had little use for doctrinaire liberals who pointlessly antagonized the clergy, but they themselves were scrupulous neither in their morals nor in their religious observances; on both counts they scandalized

---

[39] Mollien, *op. cit.,* 266; Cochrane, *op. cit.,* II, 231-232.
[40] Richard Bache, *Notes on Colombia* (Philadelphia, 1827), 157.
[41] A.C., Senado-25, 119.
[42] Cf., e.g., J.R. Arboleda to Bolívar, January 22 and May 6, 1828, O'Leary IX, 216-218.

the more pious inhabitants of liberated Ecuador.[43] As for the professional classes, many of the older men were genuinely devout Roman Catholics, including some of the most prominent jurists of Ecuador and New Granada, but many others were very far from orthodox. This was especially true of the younger generation. The typical young lawyer, merchant, or bureaucrat was a liberal who believed in Montesquieu, Adam Smith, and most likely Bentham; he was an anti-clerical almost by definition. Indeed if we may trust the British observer John Hamilton, virtually all the younger men of better society in Bogotá were not only anti-clerical but shockingly irreligious. He consequently felt that a good dose of Bible-reading was in order.[44]

It would not be too much to say that an anti-clericalism of sorts had taken root even in some sectors of the clergy, for there were a few priests and friars who had progressed from the mere acceptance of political independence to a militant liberalism that frequently entailed either conscious or unconscious heresy. Typical of this group was Fray Antonio María Gutiérrez, who was transformed from an arch-royalist official of the Holy Inquisition into a zealous patriot and leading Bogotá Mason. Gutiérrez' prominence in educational circles provided him with an excellent opportunity to air his views, and he set off one of the chief intellectual wrangles of the decade by holding public exercises in the old *Universidad Tomística* in order to deny the validity of papal censures against Freemasonry.[45] A similar role in the secular clergy was played by Dr. Juan Nepomuceno Azuero, brother of Vicente, who was able to attract even wider attention thanks to his position as member of Congress. There was never a project directed against the general views of his Church which Dr. Azuero did not vigorously support; even the standard clerical dress appeared to him "a discredit in the eyes of enlightened men." [46] To be sure, not many clergymen went so far as Gutiérrez and Azuero, but a substantial minority was at least mildly sympathetic with their stand. Gutiérrez' exercises on papal censures were endorsed not only by a future bishop of Antioquia but also by the entire faculty of his university, which was directed by the Dominican order. A very similar spirit was shown by the special sermon in favor of religious toleration which was preached in Bogotá cathedral in 1825 in order to commemorate the anniversary of the Spanish conquest.[47]

[43] Cf. Pedro Fermín Ceballos, *Resumen de la historia del Ecuador* (5 vols., Guayaquil, 1886), IV, 22.

[44] Hamilton, *op. cit.,* I, 139-140.

[45] Groot, 224-225; *El Constitucional,* April 21 and May 12, 1825; *El Correo de Bogotá,* March 12, 1824.

[46] *El Constitucional,* July 1, 1824.

[47] *La Gaceta de Cartagena,* September 3, 1825.

Even so, the great majority of the clergy was sincerely orthodox, and orthodoxy was incompatible not only with religious toleration but also with education by Bentham and many other liberal notions of the proudly-announced "century of light." The clergy was also firmly opposed to any serious limitations on its property and income; and though the Church did not reject compromise altogether there was a rather narrow limit beyond which it would not voluntarily go. Certainly it would never go far enough to please the average liberal, or the anti-clerical whether liberal or not, and because of this a "Religious Question" had to arise sooner or later. There were undoubtedly some extremists who would have been happy to sever all connections with organized Christianity or else to espouse some form of Protestantism if it had been expedient to do so. It was much more common, however, for critics of the Colombian Church to insist that they were as good Roman Catholics as anyone else and then to rationalize their opposition to particular doctrines or practices by interpreting Roman Catholic theology and canon law to suit themselves. In some cases this approach could probably be labelled a frank attempt to deceive. More often it represented a measure of wishful thinking added to a sincere desire to liberalize the Church without completely severing the ties that bound it to Rome or unduly alarming the "fanatical" masses. But in either case the brand of "liberal" Catholicism that resulted was very far from agreeing with the official beliefs of the Roman Church.

One of the most basic heresies of Colombian liberals was their essentially Protestant attitude toward the Bible and the Early Church. "The solid foundation of the Christian faith," declared one Caracas liberal newspaper, "is the Gospel: the canons and theology form the political science of the Roman court." [48] Moreover, the Bible was to be interpreted by any believer. Another Caracas newspaper added that Colombians were "not bound to adopt anything which cannot be found in the Holy Books, on a fair and rational construction of the text." The same article added just one important qualification: namely, that the New Testament was to be followed more literally than the Old, which contained too many passages that might be construed in support of ecclesiastical claims to worldly power and material sanctions.[49]

From these beliefs it followed that one should mainly read the Bible in order to be a true Christian, and this is one aspect of "liberal" Catholicism that appealed to many of the unquestionably orthodox as well. It is thus easy to understand why Mr. James Thomson, an agent of the British and Foreign Bible Society, was greeted with such wide enthusiasm

[48] *El Cometa,* October 31, 1825, cited at length in *La Gaceta de Cartagena,* December 24, 1825.

[49] *El Colombiano,* March 22, 1826. The fact that *El Colombiano* was founded by British interests does not make its views less typical of Colombian liberalism in this respect.

when he entered Colombia by way of Guayaquil late in 1824. He later claimed to have disposed of some 600 Testaments in one day in that freethinking commercial center. He met some opposition in the more conservative Ecuadoran highlands, and was distinctly rebuffed by Bishop Jiménez at Popayán, but soon afterwards in Bogotá he scored his most striking triumph. Here Thomson proposed to establish a national society for the distribution of the Scriptures, and by playing down the fact that he himself and his home Society were Protestant he managed to find considerable support for his plans even within the clergy. Fray Antonio María Gutiérrez and his friends in the Dominican order were among the leading backers of the scheme; so were the rectors of San Bartolomé and the *Colegio del Rosario,* both of them leading clergymen; and so was the *Provisor* of the archdiocese, Dr. Fernando Caicedo, who was not an active liberal but usually went along with any scheme that had the support of the administration. For Santander had naturally given his blessing also. Two members of his cabinet—Dr. Pedro Gual and Castillo y Rada— became officers of Thomson's Colombian Bible Society when it was finally established.[50]

From the outset the Society sought to disarm criticism by promising to distribute only an edition of the Bible which was approved by the Roman Catholic Church. The Church, however, was to be represented by Dr. Caicedo, who declined to be an officer in the Society merely in order to fulfill this function with an outward appearance of impartiality. It was highly disingenuous, moreover, to claim that the British and Foreign Bible Society published a translation that met the requirements of the Council of Trent, when one of the principal aims of the movement was to distribute a popular edition that was not weighted down with the prescribed explanatory notes. A few months later the Society grew bolder in its propaganda, affirming that Colombia was indeed a Christian nation but that it possessed only mistaken notions of religion obtained from "small catechisms and arbitrary interpretations." [51] By this time the more conservative members of the clergy had launched a counter-attack against the Bible Society, and no doubt some of the priests who had been favorably disposed at first had changed their minds. Nevertheless, the Society continued to obtain loyal support from some members of the Bogotá clergy. The Rector of San Bartolomé sponsored public exercises in which one of his students defended "the utility of reading the Scriptures in vulgar tongue." [52] All in all not less than 2000 Bibles were received from London by the start of 1827. It is impossible to say

[50] *El Constitucional,* March 17 through April 7, and October 20, 1825; Tobar Donoso, *op. cit.,* 182-184.
[51] *El Constitucional,* June 23, 1825.
[52] *La Gaceta de Colombia,* July 24, 1825.

whether the Society carried out its plans to distribute the Bible free of charge in the schools and to the poor—who presumably could not read—and to set up a system of branches in the country; but the movement was definitely extended to Caracas, where the local clergy failed in its effort to gain a court injunction against the distribution of a noteless and heretical Bible.[53]

If the Bible ranked highest in the estimation of Colombian liberals, the practice of the Early Church did not lag far behind. And the Earlier the better, since the chief aim was to prove that Christianity was a purely spiritual force without the corruption of wealth and power. The leading reference was of course the New Testament, and the college students of Bogotá presented more public exercises in order to show that Christ had given no material powers to His Church; all non-spiritual prerogatives were the gifts of princes and peoples, who might take them back at will.[54] This was usually taken to mean that all matters of "external discipline"—which included almost everything but pure theology—should ultimately be regulated by the state rather than by the Church if they were to be regulated at all. The job of a priest was simply to "interpret the Bible and resolve moral problems."[55] He was expected to be kind, humble, and submissive, and, as Bishop Lasso complained, there was a tendency to judge the clergy by its positive virtues or the lack of them rather than by its exalted station as such. Indeed Lasso asserted that the extremes of humility required of the clergy by liberal theorists would make impossible the fulfillment of its mission, and led logically to a belief in the ministry of every Christian man.[56]

The history of the Early Church was used to prove everything from the justice of exempting new plantations from payment of tithes to the propriety of making the religious orders directly dependent on the episcopate. It was particularly hard on the "despotism of Rome," which Dr. Juan N. Azuero claimed to be at variance with the "doctrine of the most accredited Catholic canonists."[57] A Tunja clergyman more conservative than Azuero insisted that it is "a scandalous sin to pretend that the popes can extend their domination beyond advising, instructing, pleading . . .,"[58] while the Ecuadoran liberal Vicente Rocafuerte went to the logical extreme of asking Bolívar to sever all ties with Rome whatsoever.[59] The govern-

[53] *El Constitucional,* June 23, 1825 and January 25, 1827; *Acuerdos* II, 67.

[54] *La Indicación* (Bogotá), July 24, 1822.

[55] *La Gaceta de Colombia,* March 4, 1827.

[56] Rafael Lasso de la Vega, *Protesta del Obispo de Mérida* (Bogotá, 1824), 30-34.

[57] Juan N. Azuero, *El Dr. Merizalde y el Noticiozote* (Bogotá, 1826), 14-15.

[58] *El Constitucional de Boyacá* (Tunja), November 25, 1825. The quotation is from Dr. Bernardo de la Motta.

[59] Rocafuerte to Bolívar, January 8, 1824, O'Leary IV, 395-396.

ment itself claimed (in private) that it could recognize the position of the papacy only as an historical *fait accompli*, and for reasons of expediency.[60] The arguments against the powers of the papacy naturally received added weight from the Vatican's long record of supporting Spanish rule in America, which was duly traced back to the world-dividing bull of Alexander VI. Hence, the sending of a papal emissary to Chile was passed off in some quarters as one more royalist intrigue, despite the fact that his mission was really the first clear sign of Rome's willingness to accept the fact of Latin American Independence.[61]

Hostility to Rome went hand in hand with an indulgent and at times openly sympathetic attitude toward Protestant religions. Groot shrewdly observed this tendency even in the liberals' ridicule of the ritual use of Latin,[62] while English religion in particular won special praise for its alleged spirit of toleration. The need for toleration was in fact one of the principal conclusions drawn from study of the Early Church. Its benefits were emphasized by constant harping upon the horrors of the Spanish Inquisition, which once took up seven of the eight columns of the official *Gaceta de la Ciudad de Bogotá*.[63] The strange thing about the campaign for toleration was simply that there were almost no non-Roman Catholics in Colombia to require it. Groot therefore affirmed that the real objective was to win toleration for Masonry,[64] but Masons were receiving it as a matter of course already. Groot is certainly correct, however, in pointing out that the agitation involved much more than a demand for freedom of worship, since it was ultimately directed against all clerical obstruction of new ideas in religion, in education, or in any field of intellectual activity whatsoever. Such obstruction was the very essence of the much-decried clerical "fanaticism," which became one of the most hackneyed expressions in all the literature of the period. "All the horrors of fifteen centuries"—Inquisition, pogroms, Crusades, and the Spanish Conquest as interpreted by Las Casas—were carefully ascribed to this one cause. The students of Bogotá did their part too, as usual, presenting Voltaire's drama *Mahomet, ou le fanatisme* as part of the *fiestas nacionales* of December, 1823.[65]

It was not only on essentially religious grounds that the position of the

[60] Blanco X, 214-215, 224-225; Raimundo Rivas, *Escritos de don Pedro Fernández Madrid* (Bogotá, 1932), 383-388.

[61] *El Patriota de Guayaquil*, August 21, 1824, reprinted in *El Observador Caraqueño*, December 30, 1824; Pedro Leturia, S.J., *Bolívar y León XII* (Caracas, 1931), 39-52.

[62] Groot, 157.

[63] *La Gaceta de la Ciudad de Bogotá*, April 6, 1820.

[64] Groot, 293.

[65] *El Correo de Bogotá*, January 9, 1824.

Church was subject to attack. The accumulation of property in Church hands was criticized because it lacked Apostolic precedents and also because it interfered with the free play of economic forces. It is impossible to say to what extent the actual desire to transfer Church wealth into the hands of the anti-clericals had a part in such agitation, but the congressional campaign against clerical *censos,* which must be discussed at length in the following chapter, suggests that it was not an entirely negligible ingredient. Economic considerations were also cited in favor of religious tolerance, which was considered a prerequisite for any constructive program of foreign immigration; it was thought especially needful to permit foreign Protestant settlers to take Colombian Catholic wives.[66]

Anti-clerical agitation could not, of course, strike deep roots in popular opinion at so early a stage. The most effective force in moulding opinion remained the clergy itself. For the educated classes, however, the liberals really possessed better means of propaganda than did the Church. One of these, and perhaps the most important in the long run, was the system of state-controlled education which was used to bring Bentham and other heretical authors to the attention of Colombian youth. Almost equally important was the anti-clericals' domination of the press, which resulted directly from the popularity of liberal ideas among enterprising young intellectuals. All principal newspapers during the Santander regime were anti-clerical in tone, regardless of their stand on the English loan, the manumission law, or the personality of the Vice-President. The most outspoken of all—at least among the major organs—was *El Correo de Bogotá,* run by Santander's good friends Soto and Azuero. It stooped to virtual obscenity in accusing Bishop Lasso of mismanaging his *colegio* at Pamplona, while it cast aspersions on his admitted patriotism merely because he had replaced a symbol of Liberty with the image of a saint in the *sala rectoral.* One of the few entirely reasonable criticisms made by the *Correo* was its suggestion that the surplus clergy of Bogotá should take up missionary work in Casanare.[67]

Still another factor in the spread of anti-clerical sentiment was the sudden growth of Freemasonry. There is good evidence of functioning lodges—in which Spanish elements played a leading role—even before 1810, but the full development of Masonry had to wait for the attainment of independence. In 1820 lodges were founded both at Angostura and in Bogotá, the former by the English entrepreneur James Hamilton, and the latter by a Colombian merchant, Francisco Urquinaona. Further lodges

[66] Cf. *El Cometa* (Caracas), October 31, 1825, quoted in *La Gaceta de Cartagena,* December 24, 1825.
[67] *El Correo de Bogotá,* January 2 and 23, 1824.

were then founded at Caracas, Quito, and other urban centers.[68] Everywhere Freemasonry had a special appeal among army men as a sort of continent-wide officers' club. Bolívar himself merely dabbled in lodges during his youth and voiced strong opposition to their activities in Gran Colombia. Santander, on the other hand, was made a Venerable at Bogotá.[69] Masonry was so popular in military circles at Maracaibo that a bold attempt was made to display Masonic symbols even in church during funeral services for General Manuel Manrique, although in the end the local clergy saw to it that they were displayed only on leaving the building.[70] Bishop Lasso further complained that the vogue of Masonry was causing officers to neglect the spiritual guidance of their troops;[71] and it certainly was evidence of their personal indifference to the censures of the Papacy.

The anti-clerical implications of Freemasonry had least importance among the military, most of whom were no doubt more interested in its social than in its ideological functions. Masonry clearly had a wider significance among civilians; almost without exception the leading liberals and anti-clericals took membership in the early lodges while genuine conservatives usually stayed away. The entire Santander cabinet became Masons, and so did some of the more radical priests and friars. Fray Ignacio Mariño donated $2000 to the lodge *Fraternidad Bogotana*. Many prominent merchants also joined, especially those from Antioquia and the coastal cities. All of this, as Groot remarked, made the lodges highly attractive to curiosity-seekers and social-climbers, since they were the one place where anyone could freely mix with the notables of the day.[72] But even if many persons entered only for the reasons that Groot suggests, they were at once subjected to a strongly anti-clerical atmosphere. The

[68] Roscio to Bolívar, September 27, 1820, O'Leary VIII, 504-505; Nicolás E. Navarro, *La masonería y la independencia* (Caracas, 1928), 19; Mary Watters, *A History of the Church in Venezuela* (Chapel Hill, 1933), 107, note 118; Groot, 58-59, 221; Leturia, *Emancipación*, 161, 166-167.

Julio Hoenigsberg, *Influencia revolucionaria de la masonería en Europa y América* (Bogotá, 1944), treats the whole subject in a violently anti-clerical—and distinctly fanciful—vein.

[69] Navarro, *La masonería y la independencia*, and *Tópicos bolivarianos* (Caracas, 1933), 17-34; Groot, 221.

[70] *El Constitucional*, July 1, 1824; José Luis Azuola y Lozano, *El Doctor Azuola a Colombia* (Bogotá, 1824), June 12, 1824. The clergy, incidentally, was backed up by Santander, who feared to disrupt "good harmony among citizens." (*Acuerdos* I, 180). For a similar issue in Cartagena see Leturia, *Emancipación*, 166-167.

[71] A.H.N., Congresos XXVII, 715.

[72] Groot, 100, 105, 223, 628-633; Gustavo Otero Muñoz, *Semblanzas colombianas* (2 vols., Bogotá, 1938) I, 258. Groot is an invaluable though biased source, since he was a nephew of Francisco Urquinaona and in his youth was himself a Mason.

leading civilian Masons fully understood the meaning of their defiance of papal censures, and they were ready to make their membership a rallying-point for opposition to "fanaticism" of every sort. Masonry is one of the issues on which Santander, who was really more of a civilian intellectual than an army officer, was drawn into the most open and vehement disagreement with Colombian clericals. His private mouthpiece *El Patriota* tactlessly indulged in general ridicule of papal authority as a means of undermining the popes' condemnation of the Masonic order.[73]

Even before *El Patriota* had finished its campaign in favor of Masonry, Vice-President Santander himself had begun gradually to withdraw his support from the lodges, thus influencing many other prominent Masons to do likewise. Certainly in large part this shift resulted from Santander's fear of popular criticism, but it is also probable that the appeal of novelty was starting to wear off. In the following years two of the most outspokenly anti-clerical newspapers—*El Cometa* of Caracas and *La Miscelánea* of Bogotá—both publicly declared their opposition to Freemasonry. From the clerical viewpoint, on the other hand, the damage had already been done. Estrangement from the organized lodges did not necessarily produce an immediate change in anyone's viewpoint with regard to matters ecclesiastical. For that matter, Masonry itself had come to stay, and it continued to be a convenient symbol of heresy for Catholic pamphleteers.[74]

---

[73] *El Patriota*, August 17 and 24, 1823.

[74] Groot, 221-223, 228; *El Cometa*, February 7, 1826; *La Miscelánea*, April 2, 1826. The article in *La Miscelánea* was written by Alejandro Vélez, himself a renegade Mason (Otero, *Semblanzas*, II, 18-19).

Chapter XIV

# The Religious Question (II): Anti-clerical Reforms 1821-1826

WHEN it came to carrying their ideas into practice, Colombian anticlericals were in a more favorable position than their mere numbers would indicate. It has been seen in the previous chapter that they possessed excellent means of influencing the opinion of the educated classes; what is more, their influence was equally great in the Colombian Congress, which alone could basically alter the legal structure of power and privilege that the Church had enjoyed under the colonial regime. In this respect above all, the limitations on suffrage adopted at Cúcuta were favorable to the liberal cause. The Senate, which had been least democratic in the manner of its election, gave its approval to most anti-clerical measures by an overwhelming majority. The Chamber of Representatives contained a strong ultra-Catholic bloc and many of its members were themselves clergymen. But several of the priests in Congress had definite liberal tendencies, and in general the *Valle* maintained a slight majority of votes even in the lower house. Hence the anti-clerical program was more often checked by the prudence of its own supporters or by tactful use of the executive veto than by purely legislative opposition. Some of the most important reforms, moreover, were put through by the Congress of Cúcuta itself, before the religious question had become a heated political issue.

## *The First Major Reforms: The Progress of Toleration and Decline of the Monasteries*

Perhaps the one genuinely popular religious reform was the abolition of the Inquisition; in fact there would probably have been little protest even from the clergy if it had been formally abolished by decree in the first weeks after Boyacá, and scarcely anyone thought of continuing it in the traditional form. The Colombian authorities nevertheless saw fit to move cautiously at first. In his capacity as Vice-President of Cundinamarca Santander allowed the *comisaría* of the Holy Office in Bogotá to continue at least nominally in existence, and quite frankly as a concession to "fanaticism" he also drew up a set of regulations for a special court of dogma under episcopal authority. His provisions did not entirely please the clergy, but Santander did retain the traditional fines for willful failure to denounce heretics, and his administration sent out a circular officially

THE RELIGIOUS QUESTION (II): ANTI-CLERICAL REFORMS    215

instructing the clergy of New Granada to remit suspects whenever they were asked to do so.¹ In any case, the action of Santander afforded an obvious model for the definitive handling of the same problem at Cúcuta. By a law of August 22, 1821, which was adopted in its main outlines almost without opposition, the Constituent Congress permanently abolished the Inquisition, confiscating all its property in favor of the state. However, as the time was still not ripe for declaring full religious toleration, this step was taken ostensibly for the purpose of "preserving the Catholic religion in all its purity," and the ancient Inquisitorial function of trying heretics and imposing penalties in matters of faith was expressly transferred to the ordinary diocesan courts.²

In order to cope with this task the *Provisor* of the Bogotá archdiocese requested and obtained a grant of public funds with which to pay a *delegado del dogma,* but there was certainly no thought at any time of setting up an episcopal Inquisition. On the contrary, the *Provisor* solemnly promised to exercise jurisdiction in matters of faith "with a sweetness capable of correcting and not exasperating the criminal." ³ Indeed he had little choice but to correct sweetly, for the law had said nothing about temporal penalties. Thus the new arrangement appears to have had slight practical importance save perhaps for the maintenance of clerical discipline, and even in the latter case the government ordered the *delegado del dogma* always to observe the basic principles of republican fair play in procedural matters, whether or not such principles were agreeable to the canons of the Church. Foreigners, moreover, were left outside the scope of all legislation against heresy. They were not permitted to hold non-Roman Catholic services in public, and only British subjects obtained by treaty a guarantee of their right to perform Protestant ceremonies in the home; but a foreigner's freedom of conscience was expressly retained even if he became naturalized as a Colombian citizen, and it could be passed on to his descendants. Even the prohibition of mixed marriages was tacitly revoked later on by the Congress of 1826, although it prudently sidetracked a bill for outright repeal.⁴

A similarly indirect assault was made upon religious censorship. The matter had been left hanging by Santander's provisional regulations for a tribunal of faith; the Vice-President declared that "persons of illustra-

¹ Santander to Bolívar, October 7, 1820, *Corresp.,* 235; Guillermo and Alfonso Hernández de Alba, *Estudios históricos* (Bogotá, 1926), 175-182; A.C., Senado-10, 86-87. Presumably the *comisaría* or local agency of the Inquisition had nothing to do now that the prosecution of heretics was left to the ordinary church authorities.

² *Codif. Nac.* I, 47-48; *Actas:* Cúcuta, 478.

³ A.C., Senado-12, 319-320. See also *Acuerdos* I, 20-21.

⁴ *Acuerdos* I, 47; *Codif. Nac.* I, 48, II, 185, 272-275; A.C., Actas del Senado, January 6, 1826.

tion" might read any books they wanted, but he did not define his term or take a clear stand on censorship in general. The law of Cúcuta abolishing the Inquisition made it clear that the civil authorities retained all their prerogatives in the prohibition of books and related matters of "external discipline," and Dr. Castillo y Rada, who was serving as provisional Vice-President of Colombia at the time, declared that this precluded any inspection of books by the clergy. The issue was finally settled, however, only when the Constituent Congress passed its law dealing with press offenses. A few liberal extremists sought to delete all mention of religion from the law, while a conservative faction, consisting mainly of priests, sought not only to prohibit writings contrary to the Roman Catholic faith but also to give the clergy a decisive voice in determining what publications were at fault. In the end a middle course was chosen: writings "contrary to the Catholic religion" were declared "subversive" and penalized as such, but all cases were to be decided by the civil press juries. Supposedly the Church could add its own "spiritual" penalties to those meted out by the juries, but only the Bible was subject to prior censorship. Thus the clerical party was appeased, and at the same time a wide degree of freedom was assured. In practice this meant virtually as wide a degree as the writer himself thought expedient. Not even the agent of the British Bible Society attacked Roman Catholicism as such, but it was perfectly feasible to oppose accepted dogmas in print, and almost fashionable to attack the institutions of the Church. Even the Protestant Reformation could be praised, yet there seems to be no case of a publication that was officially condemned as "subversive" of the Roman Catholic faith. Nor did the press law apply to books imported from abroad, which would naturally include those most harmful to religious orthodoxy. The government did recognize a certain responsibility as protector of the Faith to forbid circulation of the more notoriously obscene and irreligious works, but the status of foreign books in general was always left conveniently obscure.[5]

Just as important as the progress made toward religious freedom was the assault begun on the religious orders, which had become symbols of all clerical wickedness. The monastic life itself was decried as obsolete and parasitic; those who embraced it were accused of hopeless ignorance and depravity. Hence the Congress of Cúcuta decided against compelling the friars to establish schools in their convents for fear that they would reduce education to a state of "shameful degradation," although precisely the same service was rather inconsistently required of the nuns. But this was really just a side-issue. As a comprehensive solution to the monastic problem, Miguel de Santamaría proposed that the orders of

[5] Groot, 143; *Actas:* Cúcuta, 326-328, 335-339, 345, 453-455, 460; *Codif. Nac.* I, 39-47; *Acuerdos* II, 67.

monks and friars should be abolished outright; Domingo Briceño asked to have all the men placed in one big convent, leaving the rest of their property to the state; and Alejandro Osorio suggested that they be sent off to the Indian missions. The venerable Félix Restrepo, despite his rather tolerant attitude toward the friars, seems to have opposed a sweeping confiscation of monastic property mainly out of respect for the private rights of the original donors. In the absence of any serious opposition in Congress the chief deterrent to hasty action was simply the friars' obvious popularity with the masses; and this was enough to cause still another compromise in religious policy. Basing its decision on both Spanish precedents and the canons of the Church, the Congress decided by a vote of 32 to 10 to close down all convents not having eight members on the day the law was signed, and the properties of the suppressed *conventos menores* were then applied to the cause of secondary education.[6]

The Congress fondly hoped that the conversion of convents into colleges would disarm much of the potential opposition to the law, for education was probably quite as popular as friars. The *junta provincial* of Ibarra actually submitted a plea to hasten the suppression of four local convents for the sake of advancing learning.[7] This petition, however, is almost unique; indeed the people of Ibarra, as distinct from the *junta provincial*, staged a mass protest against the closing of the very same convents. Provincial towns with one small monastery were naturally loathe to lose this distinction, and Dr. Juan Fernández de Sotomayor, who was himself one of the more liberal Colombian priests, complained that clergymen of undoubted patriotism had been turned against the new regime by the suppression of convents. He added that only his personal influence had permitted enforcement of the law in Mompós.[8] The religious orders themselves, needless to say, were still less happy about the measure. The Discalced Augustinians had enough members for a half dozen good-sized convents, but they were so unevenly distributed about the country that the order lost five of its six congregations and so had to crowd all its members into a single establishment at Bogotá. There was even some dispute as to whether this one was a genuine convent or technically a *colegio*. Whatever its correct title might be, the local prior insisted that one congregation was not enough to justify the existence of a whole

[6] *Actas:* Cúcuta, 313-316, 328-331, 339-340, 347-348, 354-355, 370, 375-382; *Codif. Nac.* I, 21-24.
 It should perhaps be emphasized that this law referred only to male congregations—not to nuns.

[7] A.C., Cámara-13, 79-80.

[8] Julio Tobar Donoso, *La iglesia ecuatoriana en el siglo XIX* (Quito, 1934), 193; A.C., Senado-25, 121.

Augustinian province; he therefore denied allegiance to his Provincial, and the order was further weakened by the long and undignified quarrel that resulted.[9] It is thus hardly surprising that each successive Congress was deluged with petitions for repeal or revision of the law of Cúcuta. The town fathers of liberal Panamá frankly stressed the expediency of yielding on this point to "the religious fanaticism which dominates the greater part of the ignorant populace,"[10] while the city of Tunja observed that convents were good for local business. The most common line of attack, however, was to cite the *tristes gemidos* of the faithful and darkly hint that the extinction of all religion was at hand if the law remained in force.[11] Popular sympathy with the friars was so pronounced that Bolívar advised a general suspension of the law almost as soon as it was passed, and Santander thought seriously of following this suggestion. He abandoned the idea when he failed to win the support of his cabinet, but he still adopted a policy of temporizing in particular cases when popular feeling seemed to demand it. This he did in part by interpreting the law in favor of the friars, as in the ruling that the minimum complement of eight friars per convent might include those who were out at the time holding secular benefices; in part by suspending the law in a particular area, as appeared essential for the preservation of order in the final pacification of Pasto; and in part, finally, by allowing the friars to continue using certain "suppressed" convents either as hospices or as temporary places of refuge until new homes could be found for them.[12] Exceptions to the law were made more numerous still by the maneuvres of the friars themselves, such as packing a *convento menor* at the last minute so as to give it eight members before the legal deadline and transferring the property of suppressible convents to those that were out of danger.[13]

The Colombian Congress, on its part, firmly refused to cooperate in the task of watering down the law. Indeed it wished to make the law even stricter, and it found an opportunity to do so when a dispute arose as to the status of Ecuadoran convents that had been still under Spanish rule on the day the measure was signed in August of 1821. It was not

[9] See Fray José María de los Dolores Pineda, *Ciencia demostrada sobre que hay provincia y provincial* (Bogotá, 1827); *Refutación del dictamen de cuatro jurisconsultos de Bogotá* (Bogotá, 1827); A.C., Cámara-16, 80-139. The Provincial ultimately won.

[10] A.C., Senado-41, 179-187.

[11] Cf. petition of Ecuadoran friars in A.C., Cámara-6, 127-135. For the Tunja petition see A.C., Senado-47, 55-58.

[12] A.C., Senado-3, 78, Senado-47, 21-28, Cámara-16, 188; *Acuerdos* I, 9; A.H.N., Miscelánea de la República XXI, 268.

[13] Cf. *El Constitucional* (Bogotá), June 15, 1826, and *El Observador Caraqueño,* January 29, 1824.

clear whether convents in such areas should be suppressed if they had lacked eight members in August, 1821, or only if they did not have them at the time they came under Colombian jurisdiction, or whether they might actually be closed on either count. The final decision was referred to Congress, which decided to close all convents in subsequently-liberated areas that had lacked the eight members at the time of "publication" of the law. Congress did not specify exactly how this term was to be understood, although at least the period of grace was extended somewhat. But it then tacked on another article that required the closing of any convent that should fall below the legal quota in the future or merely lacked sufficient income to support its friars decently.[14]

A final blow was struck against the religious orders by a law of March, 1826, which required novitiates to be at least 25 years of age before they could be admitted to a convent or monastery. Although this law was introduced to the public by a long article in the *Gaceta* that extolled its reasonableness and listed its many precedents, it was much more clearly aimed at destroying the religious orders than were the laws on *conventos menores*. Unlike the latter, it did not even make an exception in favor of the hospital order of San Juan de Dios; neither was it concerned in any way with the advancement of education. The proponents of the law frankly desired to put off the enslavement of unsuspecting youths until an age when they might know better, and this intent was by no means lost on the heads of the orders, who protested against the measure with even greater unanimity than they had shown against the suppression of *conventos menores*. Santander himself suggested that it be modified so as to allow the admission of *devotos* wearing the habits but not formally taking the vows of novitiates until they reached the required age, but Congress failed to act upon his suggestion.[15]

## Limitations on Clerical Privilege and Income

Although the most spectacular progress was made in the fight against religious intolerance and the monastic orders, scarcely any aspect of religious doctrine or organization was entirely exempt from attack. Some reform proposals, it is true, were too extreme to deserve serious consideration. The demand to permit clerical marriage[16] is obviously one of these, and Santander's suggestion to legalize abortion and divorce in certain limited cases[17] is really in the same category, despite the fact that he seldom proposed a reform he did not sincerely believe to be practicable.

[14] A.C., Actas del Senado, April 4, 1826; *Codif. Nac.* II, 276-278.
[15] *Codif. Nac.* II, 201-202; *La Gaceta de Colombia,* March 19, 1826; A.H.N., Congresos XXV, 766-774; *Acuerdos* II, 236.
[16] Cf. *El Cometa* (Caracas), March 2, 1826.
[17] A.H.N., Corresp.-Senado, March 28, 1827.

The proposal to exclude priests from Congress was not quite so unrealistic, since a bill to that effect actually passed the Senate and found wide support in the lower house, where it was notably backed by Dr. Mariano Talavera, himself a clergyman and a future bishop of Guayana.[18] However, the reform was never finally passed. A similar fate befell the movement to eliminate unnecessary religious holidays, which was really one of the most sensible suggestions of all. It was pointed out that 74 full days and 18 half days were lost through holidays in the archdiocese of Bogotá, that more time and money were wasted in preparing the celebrations, and that most crimes were committed either on holidays or on Sundays. Castillo y Rada officially asked Congress to enact a reform, and the Pope was urged to do the same. No figure of importance seriously opposed the idea; but unfortunately nothing was done save discuss the matter in detail and require government offices to remain open on the half-holidays.[19]

Efforts to limit the clergy's *fuero* or right of private jurisdiction and to increase its taxes were somewhat more successful. Both objectives reflected the belief that the clergy was essentially a profession like law or medicine, and that its members should be treated as far as possible in the same way as the mass of citizens. The *fuero*, in particular, was loudly denounced as an antiquated privilege unbecoming a new republic. Hence in the drafting of a new penal code Congress decided that no one should enjoy its benefits save in the case of faults committed *por razón de su estado*, and that every Colombian should suffer the same penalties for the same offenses regardless of his estate.[20] As it turned out, the penal code was not issued, since it was still undergoing revision when Bolívar's dictatorship did away with Congress; but it is still significant as revealing the ultimate objective of Colombian liberals. In several minor respects, moreover, the *fuero* had already been curtailed by other Colombian legislation. It was implicitly overruled in the handling of press offenses by the press law of the Constituent Congress, and expressly revoked in all cases of conspiracy, banditry, and fraud against the state. In a similar vein the Congress of 1825 eliminated the role of the prelates in authorizing clergymen to testify in civil courts.[21] It is true that these measures were no more than legislative dents in the *fuero*, but they were further signs of a widespread hostility towards the institution as such. The same

[18] *Actas:* Senado-1824, 835, and Cámara-1824, 277.

[19] *El Constitucional,* January 26, 1826; *El Constitucional de Boyacá* (Tunja), January 13, 1826; Juan N. Azuero, *El Dr. Merizalde y el Notiziozote* (Bogotá, 1825), 22-23; Raimundo Rivas, *Escritos de don Pedro Fernández Madrid* (Bogotá, 1932), 383-388; *Codif. Nac.* II, 149.

[20] A.C., Senado-34, 292, Miscelánea-2, 76.

[21] *Codif. Nac.* I, 39-47, 140; II, 151-181, 361; *La Gaceta de Colombia,* July 10, 1825; *Actas:* Senado-1824, 714-715.

hostility tended to favor a stricter judicial interpretation of existing laws and precedents relating to the *fuero*. The *Alta Corte* once fined the judges of the *Corte Superior del Centro* $100 apiece merely for having neglected "the strict duty which the laws impose to sustain and defend civil jurisdiction against the abuses of ecclesiastics." [22]

The financial policy of the new regime was likewise guided as far as possible by the principle that clergymen were no better than anyone else. For one thing, the clergy was required to contribute on much the same terms as other citizens to war loans and to the new systems of direct taxation. It was only a slight comfort that the *subsidio* of 1823 gave the ecclesiastical authorities a special role in collecting the clergy's assessments and graciously permitted the Colombian bishops to give "what their patriotism may persuade them," [23] for the very principle of equal direct taxation was repugnant to the clergy. When Congress was discussing the *subsidio* Bishop Lasso felt compelled to remind his fellow Senators of the "just punishment" that had been meted out to Henry IV, and other members of the clerical party made their own predictions of disaster in the lower house. The extension of the use of stamped paper to ecclesiastical courts was almost equally objectionable in the eyes of Lasso. The assumption that clergymen should contribute on equal terms with other citizens led in due course to the repeal of the *medias anatas* and other special taxes paid by the clergy alone, but the unwelcome premise upon which this relief was based perhaps explains the clergy's failure to show any great appreciation.[24]

While on the one hand the republican regime increased the clergy's taxes, on the other it sought to diminish the clergy's revenues. The tithes were assailed as a ruinous burden on the Colombian economy, and their enforcement by means of legal sanctions was looked upon by the entire liberal press as one more instance of out-dated clerical privilege that should now be done away with. The same proposal was offered by Castillo y Rada in his *Memoria* for 1826, and the Bogotá cathedral chapter was so

[22] *La Gaceta de Colombia,* May 23, 1824. This particular sentence was handed down in the sensational case of Dr. Manuel Fernández Saavedra, "The Apostle of Facatativá," who had sought protection of the *fuero* when brought to trial for having drawn up an edict that required outsiders to register with the town authorities and to establish, among other things, that they were good Christians. Actually there seems to be some truth in the clerical charge that the "Apostle" was being persecuted for becoming a renegade Mason; but at least the *Alta Corte* was leaving no stone unturned to keep his case fully in the hands of the civil authorities. There is a good summary of the affair in Groot, 240-243.

[23] *Codif. Nac.* I, 183. The *subsidio* and other forms of direct taxation are treated more fully above, pp. 81-87.

[24] A.C., Senado-27, 227; *Actas:* Congreso-1823, 350-351; *Codif. Nac.* I, 284, II, 50-51.

worried that it issued a circular calling on the clergy everywhere to rally to the defense of the tithe system before Congress. This was not really necessary, for not many Congressmen would have dared as yet to make the payment of tithes a purely voluntary matter; indeed it appears that Santander himself did nothing to back up the proposal of his Secretary of Finance. On the other hand, there were always special blocs of producers who demanded merely the abolition or reduction of tithes on their own crops, and temporary exemptions actually were granted for new plantations of cacao and certain other export staples. The clergy suffered no direct loss from this practice, but it did not fail to enter a vigorous protest against the precedent of tampering with its principal source of income.[25] And if no more serious attempt was made to abolish tithe-collections altogether, one major reason was simply that the state had traditionally shared in their proceeds and had every intention of continuing to do so. Rejecting the thesis of Bishop Lasso that the government's right was nothing but a papal concession to the kings of Spain and had therefore lapsed with the overthrow of Spanish authority, Colombia continued to receive both the *novenos reales* and the substantial income which the civil authorities had always obtained from vacant benefices as well. In fact Congress took it upon itself in 1826 to decree that all cathedral vacancies beyond a limited number should be left unfilled precisely to increase the government's income from *vacantes*.[26]

Priests who ministered wholly or mainly to the Indians were especially hard-hit financially by the legislation of Gran Colombia. Not only had the Congress of Cúcuta exempted Indians from the payment of parish fees, but at the same time the public treasury ceased to be responsible for the stipends which such priests had received under the colonial regime. The priests of Indian congregations were legally reduced henceforth to sporadic alms, plus whatever income they might receive from the rental of the *sobrante de resguardos,* from the tithes collected in the Indian parishes themselves, and, as a last resort, from a complex system of direct assessments upon the Indians. Unfortunately, the schoolmaster (if any) had a prior claim upon the *sobrante de resguardos,* the tithes of Indian parishes were seldom lucrative, and as the assessments were to be made only in a parish so poor that no other source of income existed they naturally could not yield much either. The inadequacy of these arrangements was one reason why Indian missions fared so badly, and almost everywhere the Indians' curates found some room for complaint. San-

[25] *El Constitucional,* February 9, 1826; *La Miscelánea* (Bogotá), April 2, 1826; *Actas:* Senado-1824, 73-74.

[26] *La Gaceta de Colombia,* April 7, 1822; *Codif. Nac.* I, 160, II, 325-326; A.C., Senado-14, 2-7. Lasso proposed that the *novenos reales* be used instead to send Colombian emissaries to Rome.

tander therefore requested Congress to reform the law, but Congress took no action at all save insofar as its laws on "civilization" of wild Indians could be construed as an authorization to pay missionary friars.[27]

Ecclesiastical fees were not deemed an evil only when paid by the Indians. Bolívar observed that they should be reduced generally so that people could have more money to pay in taxes,[28] and few subjects received greater attention from the Congress of 1823 than the relatively minor matter of the fees charged for *dispensas de impedimentos matrimoniales*. It was pointed out that most people did not want to marry their relatives in the first place, but even the priests in Congress agreed that the cost of dispensations was excessive. The fees in question were therefore abolished; yet they had become so important as a source of ecclesiastical revenue that the Church promptly threatened to close down the *curia* of Bogotá, and the government had to grant a special subsidy to take their place. Certain other charges were abolished a year later when Congress included the ecclesiastical courts in its general tariff of legal fees, although in the last analysis these measures did not have great importance for the mass of practicing Christians who were chiefly concerned with the cost of baptism, burial, and simple marriage without *impedimentos*.[29] However, the work of Congress was supplemented by that of regional officials, who often engaged in a running battle with churchmen deemed guilty of unreasonable exactions.

## Mortmain and Censos

Even if the Church had lost all its revenue from tithes and fees it would still have been left with a vast amount of wealth in the form of real estate and *censos*. Unlike the tithes, which were essentially a tax levied for the primary benefit of the Church, and unlike the various fees, which were payments for services rendered, this wealth was a private possession of the Church which logically should have partaken of the sacredness accorded to all property by liberal theory. The Church felt that it was even more sacred, since it was nominally owned by Jesus Christ. Colombian liberals, however, felt that property held by the Church was a distinctly inferior variety of private property, and they demanded the abolition or limitation of mortmain with much the same arguments that had been successfully used against entails. The reform was thought necessary both to encourage the free circulation of wealth and to increase the productivity of the property in question by applying methods of com-

[27] Tobar Donoso, *op. cit.*, 199; *Codif. Nac.* I, 116-117; A.H.N., Indios, 103-104, Corresp.-Cámara (Interior), January 23, 1826; A.C., Senado-48, 420.

[28] *Acuerdos* II, 215.

[29] *Actas:* Congreso-1823, 183, 439-440, 536; *Codif. Nac.* I, 189-190, 367; A.C., Cámara-4, 184, 188, 214.

petitive private enterprise. It was of course supported by Castillo y Rada in his *Memoria* for 1826. *El Venezolano*, representing the extreme anticlerical view, went on to assert that the Church had no right to hold property at all.[30] On the other hand, it was clearly advisable to proceed with great caution. Thus what might seem the first and greatest step towards abolition of mortmain—the suppression of *conventos menores*—was enacted as an educational measure, or at most as a measure to reform the religious orders. It was provided that the property of suppressed convents should not be placed on sale but should be administered as before, with the one difference that schools instead of friars should receive the proceeds; only five years later did the government obtain the legal right to sell anything that was not applicable to the use of the *colegios*, although it appears that some property had already been disposed of illegally.[31] As a result, the suppression of convents weakened the Church but did not have the same consequences economically as a true abolition of mortmain; the bulk of the convent property could logically remain in trust until the clerical party became strong enough to restore it to the orders, which was done at least in part under the Bolivarian dictatorship.

The opposition aroused by the closing of convents boded ill for efforts to deal with the problem of mortmain more directly. Liberals and anticlericals still made the attempt, but their one clear-cut success was scored when the Congress of 1824 wrote a prohibition of all future transfers of property to mortmain into the law abolishing entails. Religious foundations such as *capellanías* might still be set up if their property was specifically made alienable, but all forms of real estate given to the clergy to be held in mortmain as such would have to be sold at auction and their value paid to the national treasury. The state, in turn, would pay yearly interest on whatever the sale might bring; but the difficulty of obtaining the full value of the property in a sale of this sort, along with the much greater difficulty of collecting interest from the Colombian treasury, would be a strong deterrent to anyone considering a bequest to the Church.[32]

The only other real progress was made in the matter of clerical *censos*, which were in practice closely akin to ordinary mortgage holdings whether the principal of the debt was incurred by borrowing from the Church or was voluntarily assumed in a burst of piety. In connection with the growth of the national debt it has been pointed out that the burden of *censos* that had come to rest in one way or another upon the viceregal treasury was effectively reduced under the new administration. There was no hard and fast rule, but payments were made rather irregularly.[33] The main

---

[30] *El Constitucional*, February 9, 1826; *El Venezolano* (Caracas), November 12, 1822.

[31] *Codif. Nac.* II, 277. Cf. *El Patriota*, April 20, 1823.

[32] *Codif. Nac.* I, 332-333.

[33] Above, pp. 102-103.

## The Religious Question (II): Anti-clerical Reforms

argument, however, concerned *censos* for which private citizens were responsible, and the clamor against these was so general that a reduction in *censos* could be proposed even by members of the pro-clerical faction. This agitation affected every region of the republic, and it usually took one of three forms: a demand for the payment of interest in kind, for a reduction in the rate of interest, or for a reduction in the principal itself.

The first proposal came especially from Ecuador, and it carried somewhat less weight since Ecuador and Panama had long enjoyed the special privilege of paying only 3% instead of the usual 5% a year on their *censos*. Moreover, the distress cited by Ecuadoran *censuatarios* consisted primarily of rather general and intangible economic factors such as the shortage of specie and the stagnation of the regional economy that resulted from shifting patterns of trade. Elsewhere, and particularly in war-ravaged Venezuela, it was argued mainly that the value of property in land, cattle, and buildings upon which *censos* had been imposed was greatly reduced as a result of military destruction and other concrete calamities and that it was only fair to make a corresponding reduction in the interest or the principal of the *censos* themselves. The total volume of complaint in Venezuela and New Granada was possibly less than in Ecuador; but as their political influence was far greater, the relief measures which Congress finally passed were especially designed to suit their needs. Not only were patriot landowners relieved of any necessity to pay back interest on property that had been under seizure by the Spaniards, but machinery was set up for adjusting the principal of *censos* on property which had deteriorated as a result of war, earthquake, and other extraordinary causes. This relief was sometimes even more effective than appeared on paper, since it was not difficult to exaggerate one's losses, and since the civil authorities were likely to show a more tolerant attitude toward the landowners than toward the clergy. Furthermore, the *censos* could legally be scaled down as a result of war damages even when the real value of the property under lien was still greater than the original principal of the debt.[34]

Although no other measures to reduce the wealth of the clergy actually took effect, the Church was kept steadily on the defensive by a whole series of attacks on its worldly possessions. The Congress of 1824, in addition to curbing future gifts of property to mortmain, made a bold attempt to require all pious foundations and brotherhoods—*capellanías, obras pías, cofradías* and the like—to transfer their holdings to the state by means of a forced loan to support the war effort. The project was so controversial that the lower house felt compelled to discuss it in secret session; in the end it passed Congress only to be vetoed by Santander,

[34] A.C., Cámara-4, 255-257, Cámara-10, 36-40, 45-60; *Codif. Nac.* I, 431-434. On the operation of this law cf. complaint of Ramón Ignacio Méndez in A.H.N., Interior y Relaciones CXIV, 635.

who had several objections to the law but chiefly emphasized the danger of antagonizing public opinion.³⁵ The issue of Church wealth and property was then revived on a much grander scale during the sessions of 1826, which constituted the high-water mark of congressional anticlericalism. One of the first measures proposed that year was a law for the return of nuns' dowries to their families after death, as suggested by José Manuel Restrepo in his yearly *Memoria*. This would have effectively limited further additions to the wealth of nunneries. But the bill was soon shelved,³⁶ and the attention of Congress was taken up instead by a movement to permit and regulate the voluntary alienation of several different types of Church property. As *capellanías, obras pías,* and convents were all involved, the legislative proposals became somewhat complicated, but the intention was clearly to encourage the process of alienation. It was therefore proposed that if religious institutions did not want to sell their lands they should still be compelled to do so in certain cases on the grounds of maladministration or neglect. A measure containing this and many similar features was passed by both houses, but again it was only to meet with an executive veto. This time Santander actually declared that the law did not go far enough. If alienation was a good thing, he affirmed, it should be made frankly compulsory; and it should be applied also to municipal *ejidos* and to the property of *colegios,* which would presumably have included that already confiscated from the *conventos menores.* It is of course conceivable that Santander really wanted to sidetrack the measure and merely chose the most liberal pretext to do so. In any case, his new proposal won an immediately favorable response in Congress, but no further action was taken before adjournment, and the Congress of 1827 failed to take up where that of 1826 left off.³⁷

The Congress of 1826 came closer to success in a new attack on the problem of *censos*. First of all, there was a strong effort to reduce the interest on *censos* to a uniform 3% throughout the country.³⁸ This measure was hardly consistent with the liberals' general opposition to any restrictions on interest, and it is quite fitting that it did not pass. Later in the session, however, the liberals did manage to enact that *vales* of the registered internal debt should be accepted at face value for the purpose

³⁵ Message of May 20, 1824, A.C., Senado-6, 54.

³⁶ *El Constitucional,* January 26, 1826; A.C., Actas del Senado, January 30, February 8 and 17, 1826. This is one of those anti-clerical measures that were widely supported by provincial city governments as well as by liberal journalists of Bogotá. Cf. plea of Medellín (A.C., Cámara-8, 138-139) and Socorro (A.H.N., Congresos XXV, 865).

³⁷ A.C., Actas del Senado, January 26, February 16 and 17, 1826; A.C., Cámara-13, 242-248, Senado-6, 91-95, 100 ff. Cf. above, p. 132.

³⁸ A.C., Cámara-13, 60-61.

of retiring the burden of *censos* on any property at the option of the debtor. In effect this was a move to transfer the debt for *censos* from private individuals to the national treasury: landowners would find relief, and theoretically the clergy would receive the same interest from the *vales* as it had from *censos*. In practice, of course, the provision meant that debt certificates worth a fraction of their nominal value could be used in full for the redemption of *censos*, while it was very doubtful that the government could ever pay all the interest legally due. The liberals were delighted with their ingenuity, and the most respectable businessmen of Bogotá, who were also large holders of debt certificates, were enlisted firmly in their support. The clergy, on the other hand, was as bitterly opposed to this measure as to any reform that had issued from the Colombian Congress. Thus even before it became law a special bill had been adopted by the lower house for the purpose of repealing it, and in the end, despite administration protests, it was decided that the measure should take effect only on January 1, 1828. The Church won an additional reprieve from the Congress of 1827, and after assuming the dictatorship Bolívar suspended the provision indefinitely.[39]

It would nevertheless be easy to exaggerate the success of the Colombian Church in defending its wealth against the anti-clericals. It is true that the more extreme proposals to limit its property and income were finally defeated, although this result was primarily due to fear of public opinion rather than respect for the Church in Congress. However, if all the unsuccessful bills against mortmain, *censos,* and the dowries of nuns represented nothing but anti-clerical defeats there would be no reason to list them in such detail. Their real effect could be seen in the creation of a general atmosphere of insecurity for the material interests of the Church; and this insecurity not only embittered all aspects of the Church Question but led the clergy to dispose of a part of its holdings voluntarily while it could still do so on its own terms. It is impossible even to guess at the total value of Church property that was freely sold and of *censos* that were cancelled out by direct negotiation with the clergy, for such transactions were generally made surreptitiously, but there is no doubt at all that the sums involved were considerable. This was confirmed by the *Alta Corte,* which sought to annul clandestine sales where possible,[40] and by the Intendant of Ecuador, José F. Valdivieso, who proposed to extend government control over the administration of convent property lest it become so depleted by illegal alienations that the people would have to

[39] *Codif. Nac.* II, 394-395. See also A.C., Senado-43, 476; Actas del Senado, May 15, 16, and 23, 1826. A businessmen's protest against the suspending clause can be found in Cámara-16, 230-231, and press comments for and against in *La Miscelánea,* June 4, 1826, and *El Chasqui Bogotano,* No. 13. The latter is no doubt correct in its implication that many Congressmen stood to profit heavily by the redemption clause as originally adopted.

[40] *El Constitucional,* November 1, 1827.

support the friars with their own money.[41] Nor is this the only way in which mere agitation, even without positive laws, had worked against the material interests of the Church. It was also alleged that the campaign against *censos* had encouraged individual landowners to neglect their interest payments here and now, and there is little reason to doubt that the charge was substantially true.[42]

[41] A.C., Senado-34, 418-419.
[42] A.C., Cámara-13, 55-60.

Chapter XV

## *The Religious Question (III): Church and State in Gran Colombia*

ALTHOUGH the most significant anti-clerical reforms were accomplished by legislation, the ultimate victory of the liberals' religious program was also dependent in large measure upon the role of the administration. It has already been seen that the real effect of a reform was often determined by the attitude of the enforcing authorities, who mitigated in practice both the suppression of *conventos menores* and the continuing legal restrictions on religious freedom. All good liberals were convinced, moreover, that the administration could not play its role effectively unless it preserved the complex body of civil prerogatives in religious affairs which had constituted the royal *patronato*. In so far as the *patronato* meant a right to legislate on all manner of religious problems, it had been asserted from the outset by Colombian Congressmen, but the *patronato* also entailed the day-to-day exercise of government control over the Church, particularly in such matters as appointments and promotions, and administrative action of this sort could not be taken for granted quite so easily. It was nevertheless essential from the liberal point of view. If the Colombian Republic could maintain the same control over the clergy as that exercised by the Spanish kings there was a possibility of reforming the Church from within as well as from without, and the vast influence of priests and friars could be more firmly enlisted in support of the liberal regime. These objectives were fully shared by Vice-President Santander, who made the *patronato* the principal foundation of his religious policy even while seeking to make it more palatable to the clergy by granting concessions in other respects.

### *The Struggle for the Patronato*

The *patronato* was not just another anti-clerical reform. It had the full force of tradition behind it, and the political leaders of Gran Colombia supported it almost without exception, regardless of their general political beliefs and their attitude toward other aspects of the Church problem. This was one of the few issues on which the Azueros found room for agreement with Dr. Ignacio Herrera.[1] The clergy itself took no clear stand either one way or the other. Liberal churchmen naturally supported the *patronato*, while the militantly conservative elements usually maintained that it had been a special privilege granted by the papacy to the Spanish crown and that it had consequently lapsed with the overthrow of Spanish authority. However, there were numerous shadings in between. There were also exceptions, and in the last analysis the mass of clergymen were prepared to submit to the civil authorities regardless of their own theoretical beliefs, simply out of long habit acquired during the Spanish regime.

On the basis of mere logic there was still much to be said for the opposition case. The attempt to justify the *patronato* simultaneously by natural right and by the republic's inheritance of all the prerogatives of the tyrannical Spanish regime was an obvious inconsistency, and foes of the *patronato* made the most of it. Liberals argued that "Colombia is not of worse condition than the King of Spain," [2] but according to this thesis Colombia should also have retained intact all the other powers of hated Bourbon absolutism. Much was said on both sides about the precedents of the Early Church, yet the one historical fact which everyone could readily agree on was the specific papal grant of the *patronato de Indias* to the Spanish crown. The rights of lay patronage supposedly inherited from the colonial founders who had planned and built Colombian churches were equally indefinite; and, finally, the general admission that any system of patronage should ultimately obtain the sanction of a papal concordat led quite naturally to the suggestion that it would be wise to negotiate with Rome first and only afterwards adopt a permanent solution.[3]

Since Colombian liberals wanted the *patronato* for reasons that had little to do with Spanish law and Church History they were not to be dissuaded by mere logic, but there were also practical reasons to proceed slowly. The hesitation of many of the patriot authorities on this issue during the *Patria Boba* encouraged the foes of the *patronato* and inspired caution in its supporters, and as long as Spanish armies remained on Colombian soil it was unwise to antagonize the dissenting faction too

[1] Bolívar definitely was not an opponent of the *patronato,* despite certain inconsistencies in his position, and despite the efforts of some clerical admirers to prove the contrary; indeed he himself suggested one specific scheme for establishing the *patronato* to the cathedral chapter of Bogotá (Raimundo Rivas, *Escritos de don Pedro Fernández Madrid,* Bogotá, 1932, 361-364).

[2] *Actas:* Senado-1824, 574.

[3] For the best statements of the contending points of view see Capítulo Metropolitano de Bogotá, *Venganza de la justicia por la manifestación de la verdad en orden al patronato* (Bogotá, 1824); Rafael Lasso de la Vega, *Trabajos del Obispo de Mérida* (Bogotá, 1824), 8-16; Juan Nepomuceno Azuero, *Informe sobre los derechos del gobierno en la provisión de beneficios eclesiásticos* (Bogotá, 1824); Republic of Colombia, *Sobre el patronato* (Bogotá, 1823).

severely. The really active opposition was small, but it included such prominent figures as the Bishop of Mérida and, save for momentary lapses, the strategically important cathedral chapter of Bogotá.[4] Nor was it known exactly how Rome would react to a unilateral assertion of the *patronato,* and papal recognition was one of the major objectives of Colombian diplomacy. Hence at first Colombian legislators and administrative officials carefully avoided any categorical declaration. They did not hesitate to exercise particular functions of the *patronato* when it suited their purposes; but they did not apply the *patronato* consistently, and least of all in the matter of clerical appointments, which was the most important single aspect of the problem and for that very reason the most controversial. According to an interim arrangement adopted by the Congress of Angostura in January, 1820, parish priests were to be chosen directly by the ecclesiastical authorities, subject only to the formal approval of the Executive. Appointments at the higher levels simply were not made for lack of any agreement on the procedure to follow. Even at the parish level the law of Angostura was not uniformly observed, and almost anything could happen in practice: at one point Bolívar demanded that the *Provisor* of Bogotá give comfortable curacies to a list of worthy friars, reproved him for not obeying at once, and then declared that the government would not interfere at all in appointments to clerical benefices.[5]

The confusion was not remedied by the Congress of Cúcuta, even though a majority of the deputies clearly favored the *patronato.* This could be seen in the rejection of Lasso's thesis of full Church control over the tithes and in the reservation of civil prerogatives that was written into the law granting jurisdiction over heresy to the episcopal courts. On the other hand, the Congress still hesitated to declare Colombia formally in possession of the *patronato;* indeed it omitted all mention of religion whatsoever from the Colombian constitution. According to the thesis of Leturia this omission reflected the existence of widespread hostility to the *patronato* in Congress itself, and it is apparently true that Bishop Lasso went along with the other deputies on this point largely for fear that inclusion of an article on religion would entail the acceptance of civil patronage. As far as the majority of the Congress was concerned, it is just as likely that the omission was due to fear that a religious article would expressly or implicitly make Roman Catholicism the exclusive religion of the nation and thus set up a permanent obstacle to the advance

[4] Rivas, *op. cit.,* 358-361.
[5] *Actas:* Angostura, 268; O'Leary XVIII, 21, 24-25.

of toleration.⁶ In either case, however, the deputies obviously did not want to deal with the issue directly, and they provided that the basic question of clerical appointments should be submitted for further study to a special conference between the Executive Power and representatives of the various dioceses. Dr. Castillo y Rada affirmed that the calling of this assembly was mainly a gesture to "calm scruples," and was not to be understood as implying the renunciation of a single prerogative formerly exercised by the Spanish crown; but the decision still reflected a sensible mood of caution.⁷

As the Congress of Cúcuta took no decisive action, for the present much depended on the attitude of Santander, who had already demonstrated his conviction that basically the *patronato* was still in force. As Vice-President of Cundinamarca he had declared the vacancy of the Popayán see on his own authority when the bishop took flight before the advance of patriot armies. He had likewise upheld civil patronage in such minor matters as the naming of *mayordomos de fábrica* to handle the financial affairs of individual churches.⁸ After becoming Chief Executive of a united Colombia he continued to act in the same manner, and his position was conveniently symbolized in his own decree of December, 1821, prescribing exactly how he should be treated when he attended church on state occasions. "At the door of the church," he demanded, "six canons will go out to receive and give holy water to the head of the Republic: to wit, two dignitaries, two canons, one rationary, and another half-rationary, with all the choir chaplains, dressed in cape and *malla*." Once inside he would then take his place "on the Gospel side" and seated upon a throne, while to all lesser functionaries in his official retinue he similarly assigned stations according to their rank.⁹ Moreover, Santander was aided in asserting his control by the relatively complacent attitude of a majority of the clergy. The Bogotá cathedral canons, who were generally hostile to the *patronato* on theoretical grounds, had earlier dismissed Dr. Guerra y Mier as their *Provisor* simply on request of the civil authorities; they replaced him with Dr. Nicolás Cuervo, who meekly promised to excommunicate no heretic without express approval of the Santander administration; and Cuervo was ultimately succeeded by Dr. Fernando Caicedo, who formally apologized for his "excess zeal" in

⁶ Pedro Leturia, *Bolívar y León XII* (Caracas, 1931), 119-120; *Actas:* Cúcuta, 219, 222, 415-417; Groot, 128; Rafael Lasso de la Vega, *Conducta del Obispo de Mérida* (Bogotá, 1823), 19-24. Hence religion was relegated to the manifesto introducing the constitution to the people; by this means Roman Catholicism could be referred to as the religion of the people without seeming to give the words binding legal force.

⁷ *Codif. Nac.* VII, 36; Groot, 133.

⁸ A.C., Senado-4, 25-41; *La Gaceta Oficial del Departamento del Istmo* (Panamá), December 14, 1823 (referring to an earlier decree).

⁹ *La Gaceta de Cartagena,* July 2, 1825.

# The Religious Question (III): Church and State

daring to issue an edict against bad books on his own initiative.[10] The clergy showed a similar acceptance of the *patronato,* in practice if not always in theory, by appealing to the civil authorities to settle its own internecine disputes. Such had been the custom under the colonial regime, and because of the war-time disruption of the Church hierarchy there was no lack of jurisdictional quarrels to settle.[11]

The one element of the *patronato* which no one felt courageous enough to establish as yet was the full civil control of appointments as exercised by the Spanish colonial authorities. As a purely temporary solution, therefore, Santander fell back upon the compromise principle adopted at Angostura—appointment by the Church, with confirmation by the state—and sought to make it effective throughout the republic by his own decree of January 4, 1822. According to this measure the local prelates everywhere would select the lower clergy, subject to approval by the intendants, but the civil authority was entitled to reject a candidate only on grounds of suspected disloyalty. The decree still did not affect the cathedral chapters, where vacancies remained unfilled pending a final settlement, and much less did it deal with bishoprics. On the other hand, when the Bogotá chapter claimed early in 1823 that its work was threatened by a lack of able-bodied canons Santander promptly came to the rescue. He permitted the surviving members to select new candidates who would then be "presented" for their positions by the government itself; by the same process the canons were enabled to give one another some deserved promotions. This was of course an emergency measure, and it was not extended to other cathedral chapters. But it was reasonable enough, and it closely resembled the method used to fill parochial vacancies.[12]

The methods used in filling the Bogotá chapter nevertheless became the subject of heated controversy. Santander was criticized for sacrificing civil prerogatives simply because he had allowed the canons themselves to take the initiative.[13] At the same time he was attacked by foes of the *patronato* on the grounds that he had not waited for a concordat or even for the joint conference on Church appointments that had been called for by the Constituent Congress. This was only one aspect, moreover, of a nation-wide increase in agitation for and against the *patronato.* The inadequacy of half-measures had thus been clearly demonstrated; and it

[10] Groot, 217-218; A.H.N., Congresos XXVII, 305; *La Gaceta de Colombia,* May 26, 1822.

[11] Cf. O'Leary XX, 164-166; A.C., Senado-27, 270-273.

[12] *Codif. Nac.* VII, 41-43; *La Gaceta de Colombia,* February 9 and March 23, 1823.

[13] Santander replied to criticism of this sort in a message to Congress, July 23, 1824, A.H.N., Corresp.-Cámara (Interior).

is fortunate that the much-delayed ecclesiastical conference finally did meet at Bogotá in July of 1823. It was in many ways an unusual gathering, since a majority of the dioceses were represented by Congressmen or Church dignitaries who simply happened to be in Bogotá, regardless of whether they originally came from the diocese for which they spoke. That of Cartagena was represented by Dr. Castillo y Rada, who was a real *cartagenero* but was also a liberal layman, a Mason, and an ardent advocate of the *patronato*. Even so, the assembly reflected a growing clerical sentiment against state control. As a result the administration could obtain nothing but an agreement to uphold the decree of January, 1822, on appointment of the lower clergy and the proposal of a specific but still tentative procedure for filling the cathedral chapters. The latter would have allowed the government more choice than it had at the parish level —or than it had exercised in the case of the Bogotá canons—but all the suggestions of the conference were designed to last only until a concordat was signed with Rome, and Santander expressly reserved his own right to claim more extensive prerogatives in the future.[14] The real significance of the conference is simply that it marks the first comprehensive effort to deal with the problem of appointments. By the same token it was the first step toward a permanent settlement of the whole *patronato* controversy, even though that settlement finally turned out to be a very different one from what the conference itself envisaged.

The next step was for Congress to ratify or reject the agreements. The lower house readily accepted the provision that a definitive arrangement must await the sanction of a concordat with the Vatican. The Representatives began, however, with a frank declaration that the right of patronage belonged to the Colombian state, and they arranged for the more important cathedral dignitaries to be named directly by the Chief Executive subject to the approval of Congress, just as if they were high civil officials. Vacant bishoprics—with which the conference had not seen fit to deal—were to be filled in roughly the same manner, although it was assumed that all candidates for the episcopate would then be further approved by the Pope. But this was still not enough to satisfy the Senate, which felt the time was at last ripe to regulate the entire subject of Church-state relations and thus postponed the question until the following year in order to give time for drawing up a more ambitious measure. Thus in the end what Congress produced was a complete law of patronage, containing specific provisions for the calling of Church

[14] A.H.N., Congresos XXVII, 4-13, Corresp.-Cámara (Interior), July 11, 1823. About the only person who seemed really pleased with this outcome was Bishop Lasso; see his *Congratulaciones del obispo de Mérida a las iglesias de Colombia* (Bogotá, 1823).

councils by act of Congress, for the creation of new parishes by the intendants, and for careful government supervision of every function performed by the clergy. A concordat was still mentioned as desirable, but it seems to have been wanted mainly for the purpose of confirming a *fait accompli,* and naturally all papal bulls would have to be ratified by one or another of the branches of government before they could be considered valid in Colombia. The government might now veto nominations of parish priests on any grounds whatsoever. As in the original proposal of the lower house, higher Church officials were to be chosen henceforth by the Executive and Congress together, with the Pope also enjoying a voice in the case of bishops. Despite indignant protests from the clergy it was even provided that vacant bishoprics should be publicly advertised in the *Gaceta* so that all aspiring churchmen could submit their applications to the civil authorities.[15]

Rather surprisingly, perhaps, the final law of *patronato* passed through Congress almost without opposition. Bishop Lasso and the two fellow Senators who supported him were forced to take refuge in proposals for delay and in constant but futile sniping at specific details of the law. The opposition in the lower house was almost as powerless, since even the most conservative laymen frequently supported the *patronato,* or at least were fairly indifferent to its enactment. Once Congress forced the issue, moreover, the great majority of the clergy also fell into line. Lasso de la Vega himself appears to have gracefully admitted defeat.[16] The last bulwark of the opposition, interestingly enough, was to be found in Caracas, the most liberal of major Colombian cities. The cathedral canons of the Venezuelan capital announced that their consciences would not permit them to obey the law, and they threatened that ecclesiastical anarchy would result if their corporation should be dissolved for its refusal to cooperate. They admitted that many provisions of the law were acceptable in themselves, but they insisted that nothing should be done without papal confirmation; the chapter consequently proposed that all clerical appointments be made on a provisional basis until the signing of a concordat. Expediency, however, finally induced the Caracas churchmen to compromise. They accepted the law with some reservations, and in order to maintain their principles unblemished they simply pretended to act as though all government appointees to Church office had been selected on

[15] *Codif. Nac.* I, 354-366; A.C., Senado-17, 600-601, Senado-53, 218-219; *Actas:* Senado-1824, 594.

[16] Groot, 281; Rivas, *op. cit.,* 423-426; *La Gaceta de Colombia,* December 5, 1824, February 27, 1825.

the authority of the Church itself.[17] The Pope gave his consent to this fiction, and it appears to have become a general though unpublicized device throughout the Colombian Church.[18]

With the surrender of the national clergy there remained only one major problem outstanding: the filling of vacancies in the corps of bishops and archbishops, which were much the most important. It would have been revolutionary indeed to fill the highest places in the hierarchy without previously obtaining the express consent of the Vatican, and even the law of *patronato* had assumed that this consent must be obtained. It was requested, in fact, even before the law was issued, and before anything at all was done about filling the cathedral chapters. But unfortunately the task of establishing working relations with the Papacy was not easy. An understanding had been sought as far back as the *Patria Boba*, all to no avail. Then, after the founding of Gran Colombia, the attempt was made with renewed vigor. Bishops Lasso and Jiménez, Vice-President Santander, and the cathedral chapter of Bogotá all sent messages to Pius VII in which they ardently defended the patriot cause and pleaded for the establishment of relations between Colombia and the Holy See. Santander used this occasion to submit forthwith, on his own authority, a series of nominations for the vacant bishoprics. Taken as a whole, this flurry of correspondence created a profound impression in Rome; and the mere fact that Lasso received a cordial answer from the Pope was such a favorable omen that Santander ostentatiously kissed the papal signature.[19]

Yet no Colombian representative actually reached Rome to take advantage of the Pope's favorable disposition until the arrival of Ignacio Sánchez de Tejada in 1824. This was just when absolutism had been restored in Spain following the short-lived liberal regime and Pius VII had been succeeded as Pope by Leo XII. The new Pope was hard-pressed by the Holy Alliance and accordingly reluctant to make any clear commitment in favor of the Spanish American republics; in September, 1824, he issued a frankly pro-Spanish encyclical.[20] For a time he even yielded to outside pressure to the extent of expelling Tejada from papal territory. He had no intention whatever of granting a concordat, and much less of

---

[17] Cabildo metropolitano de Caracas, *Indicación de la súplica y observaciones que ha dispuesto hacer a la próxima legislatura* (Caracas, 1824); A.C., Senado-30, 147-170; Nicolás E. Navarro, *Disquisición sobre el patronato eclesiástico en Venezuela* (Caracas, 1931), 58-60, 65-66, 69. The Caracas protest was echoed in the dependent diocese of Guayana, where presumably the same solution was adopted. It is interesting to note that in Venezuela the *patronato* law of 1824 remained in force until the present century.

[18] Cf. Groot, 452; O'Leary IX, 192.

[19] Pedro Leturia, *La acción diplomática de Bolívar ante Pío VII* (Madrid, 1925), 127, 143, 263, 303-308. See also Leturia's *La emancipación hispanoamericana en los informes episcopales a Pío VII* (Buenos Aires, 1935), 134-137, 184-194.

[20] Leturia, *Emancipación*, 194-197.

recognizing the *patronato,* despite his *de facto* toleration of government-appointed canons. His personal feelings toward Colombia were not necessarily hostile, for as early as March of 1825 the Vatican privately resolved to supply the bishops requested by Santander, but the bishops still were not named.

Early in 1826, therefore, the Colombian government saw fit to intimidate the Pope with a threat to organize the Church independently of Rome. The Vice-President, it was decided, had every right to compel the existing bishops to install new ones, and otherwise to assume full power over the Church without reference to Rome.[21] It is not clear exactly what was said to the Vatican itself, but as Leturia has pointed out this was no idle threat. An autonomous Spanish American Church was a prominent scheme of the Abbé de Pradt, the favorite European propagandist of the independence movement, and there was at least a possibility that some such arrangement might be proposed at the Congress of Panama with the backing of Bolívar. Hence Leo met the challenge with a definite promise to name the bishops. His promise was then fulfilled at a meeting of the Consistory in May, 1827, when Lasso was given an auxiliary bishop for Mérida and other bishops were assigned to the vacant Colombian sees, including both Caracas and Bogotá. The Pope naturally drew up all the appointments in such a way that his action could not be construed as recognizing any inherent right of presentation on the part of the Colombian government. Nevertheless, the new bishops were all men who had been specifically approved by the Vice-President; together with one bishop for Bolivia, they were the first to be named for any of the former Spanish colonies; and, in practice if not in theory, the Pope's action was tantamount to an informal recognition of Colombian independence. The bulls of investiture did not meet the ideal requirements of the law of *patronato,* but the administration saw to it that the new bishops themselves took a formal oath to respect the prerogatives of the civil government. When they then proceeded to swear allegiance on their own to the even higher prerogatives of the Holy See, Santander was clearly displeased; he wisely refrained from making a public issue of it.[22]

## *The Church Policy of Santander*

Santander could well afford to overlook such minor inconsistencies as

[21] José Rafael Revenga to Texada, March 9, 1825, and Revenga to Restrepo, March 16, 1826, Blanco X, 213-217, 223-226.
[22] Leturia, *Bolívar y León XII,* 77-96; *Acuerdos* II, 241-243; Rivas, *op. cit.,* 460; A.C., Senado-54, 252; A.H.N., Corresp.-Senado, August 20, 1827. An auxiliary bishop for Mérida had not been specifically requested by Santander, but rather by Lasso de la Vega; but the candidate chosen was Dr. Buenaventura Arias, who had earlier been suggested by the Vice-President as a candidate for a different post in the episcopate.

the new bishops' double oath when the law of *patronato* had meanwhile given the government as much practical control over the Church as it possibly could want. He was thereby placed in an excellent position to carry out his own religious policy, which has inevitably been touched upon already more than once but deserves to be considered now in its own right. It was, in the last analysis, that of the majority of liberal intellectuals. Santander considered himself a loyal Roman Catholic, and he clearly thought that Christianity had a significant role to play in the life of the nation. But he just as clearly thought that the Church could play its role better if reformed in both doctrine and organization. His adherence to Freemasonry showed that he was not concerned over papal censures, while the prominent support that he gave to the Colombian Bible Society marked him as one of those who thought that Roman Catholicism had something to learn from the Protestant Reformation. As a ruler he braved the displeasure of the Church by lending the official press to anticlerical propagandists. *La Gaceta de Colombia* seldom ventured beyond vague denunciations of "fanaticism," [23] but its predecessor under the provisional government of New Granada, the *Gaceta de Bogotá*, had been less tactful, and Santander continued to lend it his moral support even after it ceased to be an official organ of his administration.[24]

The *patronato* itself served the cause of a liberalized Colombian Church most directly in its appointment provisions. It would now be possible to place reliable men in all the highest positions, and perhaps even to lead a few recalcitrant churchmen over to the cause of Enlightenment. The Vice-President publicly observed that "ecclesiastics like other men are led by hope and by rewards," [25] and the number of rewards available was further increased by the custom of naming clergymen to the chief positions in schools, colleges, and universities. In any event there was a clear tendency to use political criteria in making clerical appointments, while at the same time the requirements established by the Council of Trent were simply disregarded when it appeared convenient to do so.[26]

One almost inevitable requirement for Church office under the new system was Colombian patriotism. A majority of the first batch of candidates for the cathedral chapters whose names Santander submitted for approval under the law of patronage were not only good patriots but

[23] There were exceptions, however, one technique being to reproduce more outspoken articles from other papers as items of general interest. Cf. *La Gaceta de Colombia*, August 28, 1825.

[24] See Groot, 156-159, 163-164, and also David Bushnell, "The Development of the Press in Great Colombia," *Hispanic American Historical Review* XXX, 436 (November, 1950).

[25] A.H.N., Corresp.-Cámara (Interior), July 23, 1823.

[26] *Acuerdos* II, 26.

men who had suffered some form of persecution or hardship for their services to independence. The first appointment of all under the new law was fittingly offered to José Cortés Madariaga, the Chilean hero of the first Venezuelan Republic.[27] But patriotism was only a minimum requirement. Christian humility was also desired, and its meaning was clarified by *La Gaceta de Colombia* in writing the eulogy of the deceased bishop of Panama, Fray Higinio Durán. The bishop was especially praiseworthy, the *Gaceta* said, because he had lived "consecrated to his ministry of peace, preaching, and mildness," and this was proven precisely by the fact that he had never objected to a single act of the Colombian government.[28] It was qualities such as these that made Dr. Fernando Caicedo such an excellent candidate to propose for Archbishop of Bogotá; as *Provisor* and archbishop-designate he graciously yielded to all the demands of Santanderean liberalism, and after he had assumed his new office he proved equally helpful to Bolívar in consolidating a conservative dictatorship. The very highest degree of eligibility, however, was represented by Dr. Juan Fernández de Sotomayor, who was an able patriot, a liberal, a supporter of the *patronato,* and a Member of Congress to boot: although an immigrant from Cartagena he was rewarded with both the rectorate of the *Colegio del Rosario* and the *canongía doctoral* of Bogotá cathedral.[29]

Actually several of the priests in Congress obtained promotions even without possessing such obvious qualifications as Dr. Sotomayor, thus giving rise to the same charges of corruption and intrigue that were made with regard to the appointment of Congressmen to executive and judicial office. A good example is Dr. Andrés Beltrán de los Ríos, who was sent to Congress from Cuenca chiefly because he was a safe foe of impiety and because his opponent was a Mason. For a time the liberals would not even allow Beltrán to take his seat; but he soon distinguished himself on the floor delivering praises of Santander, and shortly thereafter he was named to the Cuenca cathedral chapter. *La Gaceta de Cartagena* assumed from this that clerical appointments were being frankly sold in return for political support, and the charge may well be at least partially justified —certainly Dr. Beltrán's speech cannot have prejudiced his chances.[30]

[27] A.C., Senado-20, 447-464, 485, 495-500, 526; Senado-35, 22-25, 51-52, 222-223, 292-293, 381-386; Miscelánea-2, 51. Madariaga did not accept the position offered.

[28] *La Gaceta de Colombia,* November 23, 1823. Actually, the bishop had protested very strongly against the expropriation of *capellanías de jure devoluto* by the Congress of Cúcuta (A.C., Cámara-4, 171-180).

[29] *La Gaceta de Colombia,* April 10, 1825.

[30] *Actas:* Cámara-1825, 69, 72; A.C., Senado-8, 262-279; *La Gaceta de Cartagena,* March 28, 1826.

On the other hand, there are also some cases in which the government either overlooked or grievously misjudged political considerations. Father José Antonio Pérez not only was named to the Caracas cathedral chapter but was firmly supported from Bogotá when the chapter itself sought to relegate him to a lower rank than the one for which he had been nominated; yet he was still dissatisfied, and he became one of the most vitriolic opponents of the Santander regime in Congress.[31] It should also be noted that many clergymen ultimately turned conservative after attaining distinction in large part on the basis of their liberal records. However, the tendency to grow conservative with age was not limited to the clergy.

The distribution of rewards was only one aspect of government control over the clergy. Another was the broad supervision of clerical discipline and clerical activities in general that was entrusted to the state not only by the *patronato* but by other laws as well; and the admitted relaxation of clerical life and customs certainly demanded vigorous official action. Unfortunately, very little was done about this problem in the midst of never-ending military, financial, and political crises. The government did try to compel the friars to fulfill their duty of carrying the Gospel to the Indians, but the friars, as observed already, refused to cooperate. What was needed was a basic reform of monastic life, which no one attempted to carry out. In fact the only disciplinary question that the administration was deeply interested in was that posed by the numerous clergymen who refused to show due respect for the government and its laws and who were therefore classified indiscriminately as "seditious preachers." A few of these, presumably, were royalist at heart, but most of the pro-Spanish element had already been dealt with. The main difficulty concerned priests who might be ardent patriots and endowed with all the other qualities of sainthood but who nevertheless insisted on delivering sermons about Masons and "impious philosophers" and strongly implied that the leaders of the government belonged to the same irreligious class. In dealing with this problem Santander did not have to wait for the law of *patronato* to be issued, since the case was covered both by his general police powers and by miscellaneous Spanish legal precedents. He saw to it that the archdiocese of Bogotá issued strict orders against "seditious preaching," and the *Provisor* withdrew preaching licenses from some of the offenders. As a matter of fact, even after the law of *patronato* was passed Santander continued to ask Congress for a special enactment on "seditious preachers," and if the proposed draft of a penal code had ever become law double fines would have been imposed

---

[31] A.H.N., Miscelánea de la República XXI, 263; *La Gaceta de Colombia*, July 17, 1825.

THE RELIGIOUS QUESTION (III): CHURCH AND STATE     241

on any clergyman guilty of causing popular tumult, with death for abetting revolution by sermons or pastoral letters.[32] Santander was not above taking direct action when particularly annoyed, as he demonstrated when he personally ordered one preacher out of the pulpit in the middle of his sermon.[33] The government was also quick to reprove the Bogotá cathedral chapter for so slight an offense as using the colonial *"Santa Fe de Bogotá"* in its correspondence: the term had been officially discarded soon after Boyacá and was therefore highly disrespectful if not downright subversive.[34] However, the classic example of disrespect for the authorities was the preaching of Dr. Francisco Margallo, a Bogotá clergyman renowned alike for his learning, his humility, and his patriotism. Dr. Margallo was by no means literally "seditious," but he liked to view with alarm, expressing both his fear that Masons would turn Bogotá cathedral into a lodge and his feeling that he would rather see the college of San Bartolomé burned to the ground than have heretical doctrines taught in its classrooms. When such remarks were repeated with proper exaggeration by his enemies, Margallo found himself in trouble more than once with the courts, Congress, and administration. Legal proceedings against him were always dropped before a sentence was imposed, but the *Provisor*, Dr. Fernando Caicedo, did act to discipline Dr. Margallo after one particularly noisy dispute with Vicente Azuero over the teaching of Bentham. He briefly suspended Margallo from priestly functions, confined him in a monastery, and sternly warned him in future to "measure his expressions" and stick to preaching the Bible and correcting vices. Adding insult to injury, Caicedo went on to praise the obviously heretical Dr. Azuero for his "religiosity." Even though Margallo emerged from the ordeal without showing the least sign of repentance, the prestige of the civil government had been strikingly upheld as a lesson to clergymen everywhere.[35]

[32] A.C., Senado-2, 62-63; Senado-34, 305, 308; A.H.N., Corresp.-Senado, May 19, 1824; *La Gaceta de Colombia,* March 13, 1825. A proclamation of 19 October 1823 in which Dr. Fernando Caicedo instructs preachers not to "alarm" the simple, etc., can be found in Biblioteca Nacional, Bogotá, Sala I, No. 11,212. Congress did discuss a special law on this subject, but it was never issued. Cf. A.C., Actas del Senado, January 4 and 5, 1826.

[33] Groot, 116, gives what seems to be the best account of the incident. The priest in question had been expelled from Popayán earlier as a royalist, but Groot insists that the sermon was by no means unpatriotic and supports his version with the authority of a patriot clergyman who participated in the scene.

[34] Rivas, *op. cit.,* 423-424.

[35] On the character of Margallo see Mario Germán Romero, "Apuntes biográficos del doctor Francisco Margallo y Duquesne," *Boletín de historia y antigüedades* XXXVIII, 1-116 (January, 1951). See also: Vicente Azuero, *Representación dirigida al Supremo Poder Ejecutivo contra el Presbítero Doctor Francisco Margallo* (Bogotá, 1826); *Actas:* Senado-1824, 246-247; A.H.N., Corresp.-Senado, May 11, 1824.

Especially in Venezuela, the civil authorities scarcely needed the example of Santander to show them what course to follow. In Caracas another priest well known for virtue and patriotism was actually sent to the public jail for reprinting a tract written by Dr. Margallo in opposition to the demand for religious toleration: it was deemed contrary to the laws and constitution of Colombia and was therefore condemned as seditious by the local press jury, although it had originally been published with impunity in Bogotá.[36] But certainly the clergy could not always be expected to take such rebuffs in its stride, and neither could it derive much satisfaction from the anti-clerical reforms so steadily issued by the Colombian Congress. Santander himself, moreover, was something of a moderate in religion as well as in politics. He shared the conventional liberal objectives, but he desired to attain them as far as possible by agreement with the clergy and without needlessly antagonizing public opinion. As a result, his religious policy often seems to present a clear contradiction between anti-clericalism on the one hand and appeasement of the clergy and the Catholic masses on the other. In *El Patriota* he warned his fellow liberals against going too far and too fast in religious reform, noting the disastrous consequences which such excesses had brought upon the liberals of Spain.[37] He encouraged full use of the press as a means of preparing public opinion for necessary changes in the future; but meanwhile, in order to lessen the clergy's annoyance, he took pains to lavish praise upon its head in his official pronouncements.

Santander likewise deplored the time wasted on religious polemics in Congress,[38] and his veto messages present an interesting record of his efforts to moderate the tone of anti-clerical legislation. He warned the Congress of 1824 not to embark upon rash measures for expropriating Church property, and he accordingly refused to sign the law it passed which would have exacted a forced loan from *obras pías* and *cofradías*. He explained on this occasion that "for laws to be well received by the people and easy to execute, they must temporize with the character of the people." [39] He was not true to his principle of moderation when he asked Congress two years later to compel the alienation of all estates belonging to religious bodies, but he may have thought that the public had by then been educated to accept the measure, or there may be other reasons behind his message.[40] He certainly had not abandoned caution altogether, for in the same year he decided to veto a law forbidding

[36] *La Revista Semanal* (Caracas), May 11, 1826; R. Lepervanche Parparcen, *Núñez de Cáceres y Bolívar* (Caracas, 1939), 104-105.
[37] *El Patriota* (Bogotá), February 5 and March 16, 1823.
[38] Message to Congress, April 21, 1826, A.C., Cámara-5, 182.
[39] Message of May 20, 1824, A.C., Senado-6, 54.
[40] Above, pp. 132, 226.

THE RELIGIOUS QUESTION (III): CHURCH AND STATE    243

burials within church buildings lest it arouse popular displeasure. Many clergymen had already voiced opposition to this practice, and almost simultaneously the government authorized the Intendant of Boyacá to enforce Spanish regulations against it, but Santander insisted that Congress had passed enough controversial laws for one year. He thus contented himself with a long article in the *Gaceta* praising the reform he had just rejected.[41] Another interesting veto was reserved for a rather technical measure concerning the salaries of those priests who had been elected to Congress. There were technical defects in the law which Santander quite properly pointed out, but he took special pains to object to the law's use of the term "national revenues" as applied to the tithes. Santander had never ceased to assert full civil control over the tithes, and the administration itself had previously referred to them frankly as "national revenue." Yet he now insisted that they were really something slightly different. Congress passed the phrase over his veto, but in the meantime Santander had successfully posed as the clergy's defender, and Congress would have to bear the brunt of any protests.[42]

It is still true that Santander welcomed more reforms than he vetoed, and apart from his marked willingness to compromise in the suppression of convents he generally showed little hesitation in enforcing them to the best of his ability. But his favors to the clergy were not limited to use of the veto power. Just as the clergy was expected to show decent respect for the republican regime, officers of government were expected to maintain the prestige of the Church by at least an outward observance of its rites. Officials in the provinces were specifically instructed to go to mass on the principal holidays. Santander himself set the example by taking part in all major festivals: during the early years he attended church so frequently that Groot imagined he was aiming to spy on the preachers.[43] Santander was even willing to go part way in assisting the clerical campaign against heretics and "impious philosophers." A decree of May 13, 1822, prohibited the circulation of works "such as" the writings of Arretino, "The Private Lives of the Twelve Caesars," and "The Pleasures of Julia." The following year Santander extended his measure to include, among other works, "The Philosophy of Venus,"

[41] See *Acuerdos* II, 146-147; *La Gaceta de Colombia*, May 28, 1826; *El Constitucional de Boyacá* (Tunja), April 7, 1826; A.C., Senado-6, 107-108. The *Sermón predicado por un cura del arzobispado de Santa Fé* was a tract against church burials published in Bogotá with the endorsement of the archdiocese. Actually, local officials had occasionally imposed similar reforms purely on their own initiative; see *El Constitucional de Boyacá*, December 16, 1825, and also A.C., Cámara-6, 121, for an order of Sucre with regard to Quito.

[42] *La Gaceta de Colombia*, March 5 and 19, 1826; A.C., Actas del Senado, February 14, 1826.

[43] Groot, 227; A.H.N., Miscelánea de la República XXI, 219.

"The Portable Theology," "Christianity Unmasked," and Dupuis' *Origine des cultes*. The last-named item and probably the rest as well were forbidden at the express desire of Dr. Caicedo.[44] It will be noted, however, that the Vice-President's index included only obscene literature and the more extravagantly irreligious writings. Such respectable heretics as Bentham and Voltaire were absent from the list, so that Santander's action in this case might be placed in the same category as his decision to veto the law against inside burials while signing measures infinitely more harmful to the clergy.

Even so, the various concessions granted by Santander to the clergy earned him frequent censures in liberal circles. He was accused of everything from encouragement of the "seditious preaching" he sought to prevent to the use of inquisitorial tactics in forbidding obscene and irreligious books.[45] To a certain extent he sought to forestall such criticism by his frequent explanations about the need to sacrifice ideals to expediency. It is probable, nevertheless, that the censures of anti-clericals were of real value in smoothing Church-state relations. The chief difficulty was simply that the complaints of the clerical party became even louder, for no temporary appeasement could offset the ultimate commitment of the Santander regime to a policy of religious reform.

## *The Clerical Counterattack*

The clergy's response to the assault of its critics—and at the same time its general attitude toward the liberal regime—can be studied best of all in the field of pamphleteering, for published tracts, unlike the sermons of alleged "seditious preachers," have been preserved in their original form down to the present day. And it would seem that at first the clergy showed considerable restraint while the *Gaceta de Bogotá* was ridiculing its practices and dogma and Freemasonry was expanding its influence under the sponsorship of high Colombian officials. The first tracts against heresy and "corruption of customs" were in general quite harmless, and the clergy's specific campaign against Masonry apparently was not carried over into print at all until a defense of the Masons had appeared with the Vice-President's blessing in *El Patriota*. Then Dr. Margallo began his career as a pamphleteer with an anti-Masonic treatise that bore the arresting title *El Gallo de San Pedro* and the formal endorsement of the archdiocese. *El Patriota* admitted that Margallo had stated his case reasonably and with moderation. It therefore invited further discussions in a similar vein, and its request was more than answered. Margallo himself led the field by turning out *El Perro de Santo Domingo* against "the pestilential

[44] A.H.N., Congresos XXV, 457-460.

[45] Cf. *La Miscelánea* (Bogotá), April 30, 1826, and *El Anglo-Colombiano* (Caracas), August 10, 1822.

air" of forbidden books, *El Serpiente de Moisés* against "the horrendous monster" of religious tolerance, and numerous other pamphlets, all ably written and sent forth with zoological titles.[46] Other churchmen did not lag far behind. Lasso de la Vega was a prolific writer of tracts against all manner of anti-clerical reforms, although his style was too obscure to attract the general reader. The Bishop of Popayán was stylistically more successful: his *Atalaya* was an excellent statement of the case for Roman Catholic orthodoxy, even if less outspoken than the works of the Bishop of Mérida. Timid souls such as Dr. Caicedo naturally remained on the sidelines of the debate, and "liberal" priests such as Juan N. Azuero penned an occasional reply. Yet there is every indication that the two bishops, Margallo, and others of like mind came closer to interpreting the sentiments of the clergy at large and of the Catholic masses. If anything, clerical opinion grew more critical each year as the intentions of the liberal regime became fully apparent.

The one theme that gave unity to the whole barrage of clerical propaganda was the peril of foreign Protestantism and freethinking. There can be no doubt that from the standpoint of public relations it was expedient to place more stress on this than on mere defense of the clergy's economic interests; but neither can one deny the sincere fervor with which such fears were expressed. Laws permitting immigration of non-Roman Catholics were not necessarily challenged directly, but it was made clear that the heresies foreigners professed were highly undesirable. Patriotic impulses were played upon in order to discredit the liberals who asserted that everything worth while came from abroad: from the viewpoint of clerical conservatives the chief items brought to Colombia from other lands were impiety and "corruption of customs," which included anything from useless luxuries to contraceptives.[47] Bishop Lasso suggested further that "the weak in faith" be prevented from making excursions to lands where toleration was practiced.[48] In the meantime, however, it was necessary to combat the exotic errors that had already taken root in Colombia. Freemasonry was always the one that suffered most abuse, being depicted both as a den of Bacchanalian rites and as the foreign heretics' fifth column. The Bible Society was likewise placed in the latter category by many clerical writers, despite the formal adherence of Dr. Caicedo and other chuchmen; the popular version it distributed was a tempting harlot,

---

[46] Bushnell, "Development of the Press," *loc. cit.,* 435-436, 441, and sources cited therein.

[47] Cf. José Ignacio de San Miguel, *Señor Pedro Palotes* (Bogotá, 1822), 15; *El Huerfanito Bogotano,* March 30, 1826; see also the serial *Tardes masónicas de la aldea* (Bogotá, 1823), 53-55. The feeling against heretical immigration can be gauged from Páez' proposal that the entry of needed immigrants be made as inconspicuous as possible (A.C., Senado-20, 546).

[48] Rafael Lasso de la Vega, *Mis sentimientos* (Bogotá, 1826), 25.

a tool of Luther, and an offense to the "holy obscurities" of the Scriptures.[49] Even a Protestant Bible could not quite be included in the "pestilential air" of bad books, but the works of countless foreign authors were, and in particular any that had won a place on the official Plan of Studies. Clerical pamphleteers were somewhat more tactful in their references to individual Colombian personalities. This restraint may have been based on principle, or it may represent only a fear that libel regulations would be enforced more strictly against themselves than against their liberal opponents. At the same time, the clergy failed even to bring charges against numerous anti-clerical writings that were contrary to Roman Catholic doctrine and thus "subversive" under any strict interpretation of the press law, presumably realizing that the gesture would be a mere waste of time and effort. But the clergy had sympathizers who were prepared to take more direct action against heresy. Even in Caracas it might be imprudent for a foreigner to refuse some public act of deference when confronted with the Host; in a small provincial town the consequences were serious indeed.[50] In Cuenca, and conceivably elsewhere, Freemasons were the target of popular rioting.[51] Moreover, such incidents were clearly abetted, consciously or otherwise, both by the writings of Catholic pamphleteers and by the sermons of the "seditious preachers" that Colombian liberals talked so much about. As the example of Margallo suggests, the same persons might often engage in both varieties of propaganda; and either way the net result was to maintain a lively atmosphere of ill-will toward all forms of religious unorthodoxy.

There was also one place where "seditious preachers" and the merely orthodox—not to mention their lay associates—could scarcely be curbed at all, and this was Congress. In the Senate there was no great problem. Lasso de la Vega was always outspoken, but his threats and pleadings appear to have been uttered in generally good spirits, with offense to none.[52] His fellow clergyman Ramón Ignacio Méndez, a former chaplain to Bolívar and soon to become Archbishop of Caracas, was actually expelled from the Senate for coming to blows with Diego F. Gómez over the law setting a minimum age for monastic vows.[53] However, in the

[49] *Tardes masónicas de la aldea,* 78-83; Francisco Margallo, *La Ballena* (Bogotá, 1825); José Manuel Fernández Saavedra, *A sus feligreses* (Bogotá, 1825).

[50] William Duane, *A Visit to Colombia* (Philadelphia, 1826), 92-93; *El Constitucional,* September 7, 1826; Carl August Gosselman, *Reise in Columbien* (2 vols., Straslund, 1829) II, 301-302.

[51] Julio Tobar Donoso, *La iglesia ecuatoriana en el siglo XIX* (Quito, 1934), 226.

[52] See tribute in *Letters from Colombia* (London, 1824), 168.

[53] A.C., Actas del Senado, January 12 to 14, 1826; Ramón Ignacio Méndez, *Manifiesta la injusticia con que el Senado de la República le ha expulsado de su seno* (Bogotá, 1826).

upper chamber the pro-clerical party was too small to matter: its true forum was the Chamber of Representatives. Even there the defenders of the clergy could usually be outvoted in the end, but they had many opportunities to obstruct and delay, and they invariably made the most of them. This was clearly reflected in the extreme violence of debates that characterized the lower house, reaching a climax in 1824 in the brawl that cost Dr. Ignacio Herrera his position as President of the Chamber.[54]

More than just the religious issue was involved in the fall of Dr. Herrera, but, significantly, he himself insisted that the liberals' animus against him was due primarily to his sponsorship of a measure declaring the Roman Catholic religion to be the foundation of the Colombian state.[55] Ostensibly this was a move to remedy the omission of any reference to religion from the Constitution of 1821, and it is by no means clear what practical effect it would have had if it had ever become law. Even so, it is a good illustration of the activities of the pro-clerical *Montaña* in the lower house. Naturally the Masons received their due share of attention, for a bill was introduced—in secret session, fittingly enough —for the precise objective of declaring their society illegal.[56] Indeed every desire of the clergy, and every grievance of the clergy against the civil authorities, was sure to find an ample hearing in the Chamber of Representatives; and the forces of *Montaña* and *Valle* were always divided evenly enough for the Chamber to deliver major rebukes on occasion to favorite schemes of the Colombian liberals. The successful fight to delay the use of government *vales* for the redemption of *censos* is a case in point.

Yet the *Montaña* was never strong enough to please either the mass of the clergy or the nation as a whole, which was still pro-clerical in its sympathies. Groot is basically correct in stating that "it was the government itself that formed an opposition party which did not exist; and this by protecting Masonry and philosophism."[57] The "government" in this case must certainly include a large part of Congress, and "philosophism" must be taken to cover the whole array of anti-clerical proposals. To be sure, there was little danger of overt rebellion solely on religious issues, for the clergy was too well trained in obedience to the state, and strategic positions in the hierarchy had been entrusted as far as possible to men favorably disposed toward the administration. The religious masses threatened at times to riot for the Faith but not to overthrow the government entirely. Nevertheless, religious discontent was a constant factor in the history of Gran Colombia. It played a part even in essentially political

[54] Above, p. 53.
[55] Ignacio Herrera, *Causa célebre de la separación del presidente de la Cámara de Representantes* (Bogotá, 1824).
[56] A.C., Senado-15, 101; *El Noticiosote* (Bogotá), June 27, 1824.
[57] Groot, 155, note.

controversies such as the federalist agitation of 1822-3, and despite the relative caution displayed by Santander himself in church affairs it was directed, in the last analysis, against the whole of the liberal regime. The crux of the matter is that the Santander administration lost much of its original popularity by its dabbling in anti-clericalism, and when it was finally challenged from another source the mass of the clergy and its admirers showed little interest in coming to the rescue.

Chapter XVI

## *The Colombian Army in War and Politics*

THE position of the Church in the life of the new nation finds many striking parallels in that of the Colombian army. The Church and the army were the only truly national institutions outside the civil administration itself; both, by their very existence, created problems that called for solution; and both were disaffected. The army did not have the same means as the clergy for swaying public opinion, but the weapons it did possess were just as effective in their own way. Hence of all the concrete weaknesses of the Santander regime none was more fatal in the long run than the fact that it lost the confidence of a great part of the armed forces. The real and imagined grievances of the military were not peculiar to any one class, rank, or region; and they stemmed from the very nature of the Colombian army as well as from political movements outside it. They were all the harder to cope with since the army on its part was wholly trusted by very few Colombian civilians, no matter what their political and religious leanings.

### *The Nature of the Army of Liberation*

In the first place, the army that created Gran Colombia, helped liberate Peru and Bolivia, and finally abolished its own homeland was a very large and expensive affair. Estimates of its size at one time or another ranged as high as 36,000 men, but as no one ever knew how many troops had deserted since the last count was made or how many existed only in official documents no statistics can really be trusted. Suffice it to say that what seem to be the most reliable estimates hover in the neighborhood of 25,000 to 30,000 men during the years up to and including 1825, when the war on the South American continent was finally ended.[1] This would be roughly 1% of the Colombian population, and that is a quite respectable figure. It is lower than comparable figures for the War of Independence in the English colonies, but Colombia was even less prepared to stand the effort and expense. It has been seen in an earlier chapter that the

[1] The figure of 36,000 was given by the U. S. agent Todd to Secretary of State in dispatch of November 2, 1820, N.A., Colombia Dispatches I. For other estimates see Pedro Briceño Méndez, *Memoria del Secretario . . . de Guerra* (Bogotá, 1823), 5; Briceño Méndez to Congress, May 24, 1823, A.C., Senado-25, 167; *The Present State of Colombia* (London, 1827), 206; official table in A.C., Senado-29, 117. The latter gives the most detailed figures of all, with a total of 24,895 officers and men as of October, 1825, including those away in Peru.

military expenditures of the Colombian government were roughly three-fourths of its total, and that they were the chief underlying cause of fiscal insolvency. But the army still did not have enough for its needs.

Caution is also necessary in discussing the internal composition of the army. It is fairly clear, however, that it was one of the more democratic, socially speaking, of the nation's institutions. The creole aristocracy naturally held the greatest share of the commanding positions, but the army had grown too fast and too unevenly for any one social class to fill them all. Thus men of humble origins such as José Antonio Páez had reached the very highest ranks, and illiteracy was no bar to becoming a colonel. Certainly much the best way for a man of mixed race to obtain a high place in the administration, social esteem, or a seat in Congress was to rise up through the armed forces.[2]

Another generalization that may safely be made is that a disproportionate number of army officers came from Venezuela.[3] This was especially true of the highest ranks, and it can easily be explained by the fact that in Venezuela the war had lasted longest and with least interruption. The proportion of Venezuelans was somewhat lower among the troops, for common soldiers were more likely to die or desert, and those units that moved on to fight in New Granada and Ecuador regularly obtained replacements on the spot. In addition, a good number of both officers and men were foreign volunteers who had come out for money, adventure, or a chance to serve mankind. The main trouble with the foreign legionnaires was that they demanded preference when it came to pay, food, and general treatment, and were often of little use unless they received it; Englishmen, as Páez learned, were not much good without shoes. Many of them had been irregularly enlisted abroad at excessive ranks, which gave rise to constant wrangling when they got to Colombia. Hence Bolívar at a rather early date closed the door to new recruits, and the legionnaires thus remained a small minority in the army as a whole. Nevertheless, since so many of them had received superior training in Europe, and since the numbers involved on both sides of the struggle were relatively

[2] Cf. Rafael María Baralt and Ramón Díaz, *Resumen de la Historia de Venezuela desde el año de 1797 hasta el de 1830* (2 vols., Bruges 1939), II, 215; Macpherson dispatch, March 30, 1827, N.A., Cartagena I.

[3] This is evident from numerous sources. In a list of Colombian generals and colonels appearing in *El Conductor* (Bogotá), February 6 and 20, 1827, 74 are definitely from Venezuela, 29 from New Granada, 18 from foreign countries, 4 from Ecuador. The writer cannot postively identify 28 remaining, but even if not one was from Venezuela, the latter would still have more than New Granada and Ecuador combined. The list in question is apparently intended to be complete, which it is not; but it must be nearly so, and it definitely includes all officers holding major commands. Let us hope that some future investigator will attempt a more complete breakdown in the Bogotá archives—the results should be highly revealing.

so small, the foreign volunteers were sometimes just enough to provide the margin of victory.[4] The foreigners can in any case be overlooked in examining recruitment and social characteristics of the Colombian rank-and-file. Theoretically, all able-bodied males were liable to military conscription, but as a last resort the upper classes could always buy their way out by hiring a substitute, and in due course Congress gave young men "in the career of letters" the same deferred status enjoyed by "only sons of widows."[5] Nor does it follow that men who did not escape service were methodically processed by a selective service board. As often as not the draft took the form of arbitrary impressment, including even the time-honored recruiting technique of ambushing able-bodied worshippers on their way to and from church.[6] There was always a tendency, moreover, to use conscription as a means of getting undesirables out of one's own province, especially when no concrete charge could legally be proven against them. When ordered to send recruits to Bolívar's army in Peru the *Comandante General* of Zulia announced that he would give preference to *"los desafectos, sospechosos, y licenciados que casualmente hubieran quedado . . . del ejército enemigo."* [7] Military service was likewise a normal punishment for royalist prisoners of war, and it was especially recommended for vagrants by more than one act of Congress. The courts sometimes condemned common thieves to army service, preferably in Peru, although in this case the *Alta Corte* ultimately declared the practice illegal.[8]

The extensive use of such irregular recruiting methods was due not only to the traditionally low respect accorded the soldier's vocation but also to the low efficiency of both civil and military administration. Above all, it was due to the violent unpopularity of military service with the Colombian people, which made normal functioning of any conscription mechanism virtually impossible. Nor is it hard to find reasons for the general dislike of being drafted. It may have been caused in part, as the government claimed, by the same inherited "spirit of servility" that was

[4] See Alfred Hasbrouck, *Foreign Legionaries in the Liberation of Spanish South America* (New York, 1926), *passim,* and *Archivo del General José Antonio Páez* (Bogotá, 1939), 283.

[5] *Codif. Nac.* II, 292-295. Some attempts to limit the right to hire a substitute were made; however, it is doubtful that many wealthy youths ever had to serve in the ranks against their will. Indeed some Congressmen were frankly aghast at the notion of drafting the rich, since they could serve just as well by giving money, and the poor were poor simply out of laziness (A.C., Cámara-4, 139-140).

[6] J. C. Mejía Mejía, "Nueva contribución al clero de Pasto," *Boletín de Estudios Históricos* (Pasto), V, 93.

[7] Report of Manuel Manrique, November 21, 1823, A.C. Senado-XIII, 43.

[8] *La Gazeta de Santa Fe de Bogotá,* January 30, 1820; *El registro judiciario de la República de Colombia* (Bogotá), February 1, 1826; *Codif. Nac.* II, 25, 362.

blamed for so many other evils of the body politic.⁹ It was undoubtedly heightened by the failure to make any provision for the families of conscripted soldiers. But the chief reason was almost certainly the harsh conditions of the service itself, which required danger and drudgery and offered very little in return. A common soldier's pay was fixed at $10 a month by the Congress of Cúcuta, and even when reduced to $6 by a later decree it compared favorably with normal wages in most parts of Colombia. However, a soldier never received his full pay. During most of the war there was not even an attempt to provide it all, for part was theoretically withheld to be satisfied later. Often nothing was paid: if a soldier obtained half-pay he was fortunate, and as late as 1823 wages might well go nine months in arrears.¹⁰

The inadequate pay was of course a direct result of the general financial circumstances of the Colombian government. It is no reflection on Colombia to point out that one reason for her readiness to aid Peru in the struggle for independence was the chance of arranging for Peruvian taxpayers to share the cost of supporting the Colombian army: as Santander bluntly stated to Congress, the troops "would ruin the country with their expenses" if they stayed home.¹¹ Moreover, when funds ran short hard-pressed Colombian administrators were frequently inclined to economize even more severely on military than on civil salaries. By and large, soldiers could well afford to wait longer for their pay than civilian bureaucrats, since they were less likely to have families to support, and since their rations were supposedly furnished either in food or in the form of a daily pittance with which to purchase their own meals. But sometimes the rations were given only in part, and if for the moment neither funds nor provisions were available, they were not given at all. In such cases the soldiers had to go hungry or else shift for themselves.

Still another hazard was disease, especially in the tropical lowlands where health conditions were always poorest, and where great numbers of troops were gathered either for coastal defense or en route to new battlefields in Ecuador and Peru. Some illness was caused simply by the difficulty of acclimatizing troops from the Andes to service on the *llanos* and the coastal plains, or lowlanders to the cool mountain air. General Páez did his best for *granadino* recruits in the *llanos,* even manufacturing *chicha* for their special benefit, but they still perished despite his care.¹² All in all, a relatively small proportion of Colombian casualties were actually caused by military action. It was not impossible for a third or

⁹ Cf. *La Gazeta de Santa Fe de Bogotá,* January 16, 1820.
¹⁰ *Codif. Nac.* I, 114; *The Present State of Colombia,* 207; *Acuerdos* I, 146.
¹¹ Message of May 12, 1823, A.C., Senado-22, 12.
¹² *Archivo del General Páez,* 268; Santander to Bolívar, September 26, 1820, Lecuna, *C.S.,* I, 121-122.

more of an army corps to be out of action due to sickness; half of the forces that retook Maracaibo in August, 1823, allegedly died of disease within four months of their victory.[13]

The lack of both money and doctors would have made it impossible in any event to provide real medical care for the Colombian army, but there is reason to believe that the best use was not always made even of resources that did exist. John P. Hamilton reported that in Bogotá it was impossible to obtain medicine for a sick soldier without written authorization from the *comisario;* if the latter happened to be away, the soldier would have to die.[14] The charge is perhaps exaggerated, but there are others like it. In fact the records of the period abound with examples of all kinds of inefficiency and downright negligence in caring for the material welfare of the troops. However, there are also examples of officers who cared for their men beyond the call of duty, and in the last analysis all the attenuating circumstances that were listed previously to excuse the inadequacies of the civil government can be repeated in this connection for the benefit of army leaders. They can in fact be multiplied, for the obstacles faced by the Colombian army in the liberation of northern South America were sufficient to strain even the best-run military system. The lack of material resources was bad enough, even without considering the physical tests of endurance that had to be survived from one end of the country to another. The Boyacá campaign was only the most striking of these tests, and it was nearly equalled by the legendary march of the *Alto Magdalena* Battalion from Guayaquil to Cuenca over Andean back trails and in tropical clothing prior to the liberation of Quito. Out of roughly 500 men, a fifth died on the way; 200 more were admitted directly to the sick-list on reaching Cuenca; and still others had been abandoned as unable to continue at various points along the march.[15]

The hardships resulting from sheer geography were thus a final deterrent to enlistment in the Colombian army; and when all deterrents were taken together they produced intermittent draft-riots, guerrilla bands, and the emigration of whole villages away from the main roads in order to escape recruiting officers. Santander complained of such disorders "even" in the mild-mannered Department of Boyacá; Bolívar at one point felt it necessary to make recruiting officers responsible with their lives for the

[13] Cf. Arcesio Aragón, *Fastos payaneses* (2 vols., Bogotá 1931-1941), I, 209; A.C., Actas del Senado (secret sessions), May 24, 1823; Francis Hall, *Colombia: Its Present State* (2nd ed., London 1827), 125.

[14] J. P. Hamilton, *Travels Through the Interior Provinces of Colombia* (2 vols., London 1827) I, 142.

[15] Alfonso María Borrero, *Cuenca en Pichincha* (Cuenca, 1922), 410-418, 481; R. Botero Saldarriaga, *El General José María Córdova* (Bogotá, 1827), 260-261.

success of their mission, as well as to threaten punitive action against the families of draft-dodgers.[16] When recruits were finally taken they were likely to be marched off with their hands tied lest they seek to escape, and sometimes infantrymen were given their arms and cavalrymen their horses only on reaching the fighting zone. If troops were headed for Peru, their destination would be kept secret not simply to deceive the enemy but to diminish incentives for desertion.[17] All the precautions, however, were unavailing. Armies dwindled in half by desertion en route from Cali to Popayán or a full third from Bogotá to Cúcuta. From time to time Bolívar fulminated threats of death as punishment for deserters, and occasionally the extreme penalty was actually enforced, but this did not work either.[18] Santander pointed out that a rigorous application of the death penalty, though prescribed by law for most cases of desertion, would do nothing but "destroy a great part of the population." By way of explanation he added that

". . . our soldiers are not like those of Europe. In the latter there is enlightenment, they know the cause which they defend, and know the laws to which they are subject. With the former it is just the opposite; their ignorance is well-known: it is regularly hidden from them for whom they fight; and however much they are instructed in the General Dispositions, very few succeed in understanding them." [19]

The Vice-President therefore made no attempt to impose the death penalty himself, recommending instead that deserters be compelled to perform such degrading chores as cleaning out the barracks in front of their fellows.

When desertion was carried out en masse it was barely distinguishable from mutiny, which was also much too common. An entire battalion mutinied at Santa Marta in November, 1823, demanding either pay or clothing; over thirty veterans returning from Peru were killed in a mutiny over pay at Quito some three years later; and similar outbreaks could be cited *ad infinitum*. The foreign legionnaires were not backward in following the Colombians' example. Indeed the classic example of an army mutiny is that of the Irish volunteers at Río Hacha in 1819, which

[16] A.C., Cámara-1, 408; O'Leary XIX, 113-114.

[17] A.H.N., Miscelánea de la República XI, 749-750, 761; Hamilton, *op. cit.*, I, 279; O'Leary II, 423-424, XVIII, 235.

[18] O'Leary XIX, 61-64; Karl Richard, *Briefe aus Columbien* (Leipzig, 1822), 211; *Archivo epistolar del General Domingo Caicedo* (Bogotá, 1943) I, 107.

[19] Santander to Congress of Cúcuta, September 7, 1821, A.C. (exact citation lost).

was set off by all the usual troop grievances plus an ill-defined dissatisfaction with the leadership of Mariano Montilla. Whatever the precise reasons for the mutiny, the result was total destruction of the city by fire.[20] Organized mutiny was naturally a trial for civilian bystanders as well as for commanding officers; but at least it was not an everyday occurrence. Far more serious, because of its monotonous regularity, was the inevitable tendency of the army to make up for its lack of material resources by living off the land. This was especially common in the early years when the lack of funds was greatest. As Páez wrote to one of his subordinates in January, 1820, "for the daily needs of the troops there is nothing whatever forbidden. . . . You are fully authorized to punish even with death any individual who shamefully refuses to hand over whatever is needed or to perform the service that is indicated to him."[21] Similar threats were issued by Bolívar, who prided himself on his dexterity in the violent extraction of both men and money.[22] Theoretically, everything would be paid for in the long run, but there was little guarantee that this would happen, despite all the decrees instructing military commanders to leave written receipts for what they took.

Probably the most important single variety of military extortion was the seizure of animals for the use of the army. If they were not eaten they were used as beasts of burden, and in many sections this led to a dangerous reduction in herds of beef cattle and an equally serious shortage of draft animals for private use. Most of the Colombian cavalry, it is interesting to note, was originally mounted on horses seized from private owners.[23] Such exactions as these, however, could at least be justified by reasons of military necessity. They were unpopular, but they were mainly unavoidable. There were always some exactions, on the other hand, that can be classed as simple robbery for the benefit of individual officers and men. Such conduct can be partially condoned in view of the privations which the military suffered, but angry soldiers did more than just help themselves to a solid meal: in August of 1826 the governor of Pamplona was authorized to raise a forced loan to support the soldiery frankly on the grounds that the only alternative was to see the troops "commit excesses, rob, or kill the citizens."[24] In a similar vein the *junta provincial* of Apure asked for the removal of a special bandit-hunting detachment

[20] A.C., Senado-XIII, 54; O'Leary IV, 8-9; A.H.N., Corresp.-Cámara (Hacienda), April 6, 1824; Hasbrouck, *op. cit.,* 130-134, 179-183.
[21] Páez to Ignacio Melean, January 28, 1820, *Archivo del General Páez,* 152.
[22] Bolívar to Santander, April 15, 1823, Lecuna, *C.L.* III, 168. Cf. Eloy G. González, *Al margen de la epopeya* (3rd ed., Caracas 1935), 105-108; O'Leary XIX, 509.
[23] Briceño Méndez, *Memoria . . . de Guerra* (1823), 5-6.
[24] A.H.N., Miscelánea de la República XXI, 291.

ostensibly because the troops themselves were as much to be feared as the bandits.[25] Indeed a very high proportion of the crimes of violence committed during the decade of Gran Colombia were cases involving the military, and they did not always have hunger or some other hardship as an excuse.

Nor were civilians the only ones who suffered by the misbehaviour of the armed forces. There was no lack of incidents among the military themselves, such as the drunken brawls of Generals Mires and Valdez that scandalized the Cauca valley before the arrival of Bolívar. Conduct of this sort was often associated with heavy gambling, and gambling with personal raids on the treasury. In any case, the shortage of funds for legitimate military purposes was aggravated by widespread corruption in military administration. One foreign visitor found that officers even boasted of their thefts of both government and private property, and the offenders regularly kept their positions. Colonel Guillermo Iribarren stole 600 head of government cattle in Apure, reselling them to the same *comisaría* from which he stole them; he built himself a solid reputation for being "careless of the property of others;" and he turned up again in 1825, ostensibly reformed, with an appointment as Governor of Margarita. In defending this selection Senator Soto argued forcefully that if everyone who had stolen anything in the first years of the republic were declared ineligible there would be nobody left to appoint. The President of the Senate added the wise observation that there was nothing to steal in Margarita anyway, and Iribarren was confirmed.[26]

The appointment of Colonel Iribarren is another illustration of the general shortage of qualified personnel that plagued Gran Colombia. However, this is only one of the reasons why the misbehaviour of the military so often went unpunished. Foreign officers were said to be unduly tolerant of abuses in their effort to gain the confidence of Colombian soldiers under their command. Likewise there were numerous cases in which members of a court-martial showed remarkable leniency toward one of their fellow officers. Military courts all too often declared that a few months' reclusion pending trial had been enough to purge an officer's guilt, despite the regularity with which the *Alta Corte* revoked such decisions; and imprisonment was often turned into something of a farce by allowing the "prisoner" to walk the streets at will. *El Correo del Magdalena* claimed that one officer was running a store while supposedly serving

---

[25] *La Gaceta de Colombia*, February 5, 1826.

[26] O'Leary IX, 445-448; Richard L. Vowell, *Campaigns and Cruises in Venezuela and New Granada and in the Pacific Ocean* (3 vols., London 1831) I, 213-214; Richard Bache, *Notes on Colombia* (Philadelphia, 1827), 170; A.C., Actas del Senado (Secret sessions), January 20 and 24, 1825; González, *Al margen de la epopeya*, 83.

out his four-year sentence.²⁷ Such examples of laxity, needless to say, destroyed any good effects that might otherwise have resulted from the occasional use of harsh exemplary punishments. The latter, moreover, were generally reserved for members of the lower ranks, including the sergeant who was sentenced to death for stealing a few cartridges and was flatly denied commutation by Santander. It was all too easy for officers who had done much worse to obtain a light punishment or none at all; but very few of them shared the civic zeal of José María Córdova, who hounded Bolívar for permission to return home from Bolivia so that he might publicly stand trial for having killed some *malvado* in Popayán without all the due formalities.²⁸

## Army Reduction and Alternative Means of Defense

In view of all that was wrong with the glorious *Ejército Libertador* it is not surprising that it was looked upon with mixed feelings by the mass of the population. Civilians were not ungrateful for the work of liberation, as military men so often imagined, but they showed a definite lack of confidence in the army's behavior, and they were not always ready to forgive and forget military abuses, which were loudly decried in Congress and the press. Nor was it only doctrinaire liberals who rushed to the attack, as historians of all parties have occasionally implied. The *Montaña* was as vociferous as the *Valle*, especially if the guilty officer was a friend of Santander or the victims were among its own adherents.²⁹ It was the oppositionist Caracas priest José Antonio Pérez who presented the fantastic bill to remove all troops eight leagues from Bogotá and condemn any officer to a traitor's death for even entering the place where Congress was meeting.³⁰ Indeed when Congress sought to pass a law which referred to the province of Río Hacha as "reduced to its ultimate annihilation" by the presence of the Colombian army, it was Santander who eliminated the offending words by the use of his veto, reminding Congress that the army had speeded the recovery of the very same province by its service in bringing in supplies and money.³¹ Santander was really a better friend of the army than either his admirers or his detractors

²⁷ Gaspar Theodore Mollien, *Viaje por la República de Colombia en 1823* (Bogotá, 1944), 210; *El Constitucional* (Bogotá), December 22, 1825, October 19, 1826; *La Gaceta de Colombia,* November 27, 1825 (citing *El Correo del Magdalena*), and January 15, 1826.

²⁸ *Acuerdos* II, 68, 141, 239; González, *Al margen de la epopeya,* 113-124; Córdova to Bolívar, April 26 and May 10, 1826, O'Leary VII, 363, 364.

²⁹ Cf. *Actas:* Cámara-1824, 34, and *El Correo de Bogotá,* April 23, 1824.

³⁰ A.C., Senado-33, 19-20. The most obvious implication of this proposal was of course that Santander might try to use the armed forces to coerce the Legislative Power; but this did not make it any less insulting to the military.

³¹ A.H.N., Corresp.-Cámara (Hacienda), August 1, 1823.

usually admit, even though he was civilian-minded enough to be highly critical of many fellow officers. For in the last analysis distrust of the army was not a simple matter of party loyalties but a general, popular phenomenon. The French visitor Mollien complained that more than once on his travels he was inhospitably received simply because he was believed to be conducting troops.[32]

No matter what form they might take, the greatest single cause of military abuses was the Colombian treasury's inability to supply the armed services adequately from its ordinary resources. The difficulties of the treasury, to complete the vicious circle, were due above all to the demands of an army larger than Colombia could afford. Hence the only real solution was to break the chain of events and abuses that led from a bankrupt treasury to a troublesome army and back again by drastically reducing the army's size. This principle was well understood, and the reduction was widely demanded by such public opinion as existed. To be sure, fairly little could be done until Peru was also freed; even then a state of war still existed, with Cuba and Puerto Rico in Spanish hands to threaten coastal raids if not a full-scale invasion of the Spanish Main. There were the normal demands of national defense and internal security to be considered, and ticklish questions of whom to retire and on what terms. There was little dispute, however, as to the basic objective. The Bogotá administration readily agreed that army reduction was necessary in order to save money, to revive agriculture, and to further "the stability and progress of public opinion," whatever that meant.[33]

The first significant attempt at demobilization occurred after the battle of Carabobo, when much of the *llanero* cavalry was disbanded, but this was a partial measure, and it was offset by the continued expansion of the armed forces in other parts of the republic. Only after the crowning victory of Ayacucho did a permanent reduction begin. General Bartolomé Salom, who then ruled Ecuador as *Jefe Superior* under the regime of "extraordinary faculties," carried out substantial dismissals in the southern departments, and Santander added his own orders for the reduction of various army corps in the center of the country.[34] In 1826 Congress itself stepped in with an "Organic Law of the Army" that provided for the number of troops to be fixed annually by legislative decree and limited the number of generals and colonels in active military service to 20 and 50 respectively. The former provision was not actually used until the following year, and there were various loopholes in the clauses relating

[32] Mollien, *op. cit.*, 241.

[33] Santander to Congress, April 7, 1825, Senado-35, 49.

[34] *La Gaceta de Colombia*, April 10 and July 10, 1825; *El Constitucional*, January 19, 1826; *Acuerdos* II, 29, 33. On the case of the *llaneros*, see below, pp. 279-280.

to generals and colonels, but at least Congress was pointing in the right direction. The surplus generals and colonels—who were probably about half the total number—were not to be fired outright; however, Congress decided that they should go into semi-retirement, and unless they were given some other job on the government payroll they should draw only half salary. Less severe measures were to be taken in cutting down the number of officers at the lower levels, but any who were then out on indefinite leave were to be considered as retired.[35]

The failure of Congress to attack the officers' corps still more energetically was presumably due not to the lack of a will but to the realization that many needless officers would not take kindly to forcible retirement, especially as the treasury was in no position to supply an adequate pension. However, demobilization was gradually moving forward. At first Santander actually gave full or "effective" tenure to fewer generals and colonels than the Organic Law indicated so as to have places left over for some who were then occupied in civil posts or were otherwise unavailable for the moment. Toward the middle of 1827, Bolívar asserted that there were only 8000 troops in all Venezuela and New Granada. This figure is almost certainly too low, being designed to prove a point politically, and it does not include a heavy troop concentration in Ecuador, where the last expeditionary forces had just arrived from Peru in a state of mutiny. At about the same time the Secretary of War, General Soublette, spoke of some 12,000 troops as existing in the various coastal departments, which in this case presumably should include Guayaquil. But either figure suggests a genuine reduction in army strength from the totals given a few years earlier.[36]

Unfortunately, the fact that 1826 and 1827 were both years of internal crisis and revolt tended to offset whatever advantage might have been derived from the process of demobilization, as well as to place definite limits on its continued progress. Moreover, the net reduction in the number of troops *within Colombia* was obviously much less than the overall decline, because so many had been serving in Peru and had returned home only lately.[37] This was an important point, since "bringing

[35] *Codif. Nac.* II, 293, 296-298. Only full colonels are referred to in the text, as the position of lieutenant colonel was abolished by the Organic Law.

[36] A.H.N., Congresos XXVI, 726; Blanco XI, 523; *Acuerdos* II, 240.

[37] In effect, whether there had been any appreciable reduction inside the country depends on the period selected for comparison. As compared to October, 1825, when official figures gave a total of nearly 25,000 men, over a third of whom were in Peru, there was little if any reduction; as compared to the years when fighting still raged in Colombia and the main expeditionary forces had not yet left for Peru, there was a very great reduction, possibly in the neighborhood of 50%. (Cf. footnote 1.)
Even at the time of the last figures given in the text, there remained a small Colombian force in Bolivia, at the disposition of Sucre.

the boys home" after the fighting meant that Colombia would have to assume the full cost of supporting them; unless they were disbanded the moment they reached Colombian soil, it also increased the number of potential participants in military disorders. Hence the reduction which had been carried out was still insufficient either to end the financial crisis or to meet the full theoretical requirements of Colombian liberals, whose true objective was to replace the regular army as far as possible by a national militia. Not only was a militia organization cheaper to maintain but also, although this was seldom explicitly stated, it was hoped that it might even protect the government against the standing army in case of need. Ever since the days of Lexington-Concord a militia had been the one truly republican way for a people to defend itself.[38] It was thus a great disappointment, to Santander among others, that the Colombian militia never really came close to fulfilling its prescribed functions; and this is one of the reasons why the army could not be disbanded more completely.

There had naturally been a militia of sorts under the viceroyalty, and it had been adapted as far as possible to serve the national cause. The militia of Bogotá helped to keep order between the flight of the Spaniards and the arrival of the patriots, and militia units provided a reserve defense for central New Granada when Bolívar's army swept back toward the Venezuelan border in the north.[39] But in the following years the Colombian militia organization still remained a rather haphazard affair. The Secretary of War announced in 1823 that in most cases it involved nothing but a meaningless general enlistment, limited essentially to the interior provinces. He added that there were only thirteen effective militia battalions in the whole country, and Santander made no concerted effort to improve the situation until August, 1824, when he decreed the organization of a uniform militia corps throughout the republic, based on a general obligation to serve and subject in each department to the broad supervision of the *comandante general*. However, this decree became the target of much irresponsible criticism, especially by the oppositionist liberal faction of Caracas, which absurdly claimed that it entailed the establishment of martial law or something of the sort. The new system went fairly well in Bogotá, but it caused a near revolution in Caracas, and General Soublette reported that in the nation as a whole enlistment was extensively thwarted both by citizen inertia and by the uncooperative spirit of many lesser authorities. One of the incidental problems that

[38] For arguments favoring the militia at the expense of the army—not all from pro-administration liberals—see *El Colombiano* (Caracas), March 1, 1826; *La Miscélanea* (Bogotá), January 1, 1826; Francisco de Paula Santander, *El Vicepresidente de Colombia da cuenta a la república de su conducta* (Bogotá, 1828), 65; A.H.N., Congresos XXVIII, 150.

[39] *La Gazeta de Santa Fe de Bogotá,* January 23 and 30, 1820.

arose was a bitter argument over the expediency of permitting militiamen to choose their own officers, which was a reform ardently desired by democratic theorists and strongly frowned on by the administration. Santander allowed the names of the lower officers to be suggested originally by their own corpsmen, but the *Gaceta* repeatedly attacked the general principle of elective officers as part of an unwise "mania" for democratization.[40]

There was obvious need for some definitive arrangement of militia problems by Congress, and the legislators rose to the occasion in 1826 with another of their various "organic laws." That devoted to the militia was a logical and systematic piece of legislation; it provided for both a semi-disciplined *milicia cívica* and a somewhat more effective *milicia auxiliar*, which would be ready to supplement the regular army on short notice in any of its functions, and it allowed Santander to have his way on the appointment of officers. The *milicia cívica* was to be generally under the civil authorities, the *auxiliar* under the military. But, alas, the new law was really no easier to carry out than previous measures, and to make matters worse the authority of the administration was soon undermined by civil war. The Venezuelan crisis of 1826 spurred *bogotanos* to cooperate all the more loyally, but it was the cooperation of other regions that had always presented the basic difficulty, and this still was not obtained.[41]

On a par with efforts to replace the regular army with a militia—and equally unsuccessful in the end—was the notion that Colombia should emphasize naval power at the expense of land forces. This thesis was put forward not only by Colombia's relatively few naval officers, but also by official and unofficial spokesmen for the Santander administration, and superficially it was a very sensible idea. It was pointed out that Colombia had a long and exposed coastline, whereas the only inhabited land frontier was the rather short Peruvian border. To ward off a Spanish reconquest or other foreign invasion a navy was thus more necessary than an army. By preying on enemy shipping and even carrying private freight shipments it might come close to paying its own way, whereas the very word "army" appeared synonymous with bankruptcy. Finally, navies were more compatible with free institutions, for it was a practical impossibility to overthrow a government in Bogotá by means of warships, and seamen

---

[40] Briceño Méndez, *Memoria . . . de Guerra* (1823), 11-12; A.C., Cámara-1, 408; *Codif. Nac.* VII, 222-224; *El Constitucional,* September 23 and 30, 1824, January 20, 1825, January 19, 1826; *La Gaceta de Colombia,* December 19, 1824, January 23, 1825.

[41] *Codif. Nac.* II, 251-268; A.C., Actas del Senado, January 6 and 21, February 10 (extra session), 1826; *El Constitucional,* October 26, 1826, February 8 and August 23, 1827.

were believed to be naturally less prone than soldiers to support military dictatorship. As Vicente Azuero's *Indicación* expressed it, "England has taught us that naval force is never dangerous or harmful to the freedom of the country." [42]

The main trouble with these arguments was that Colombia could not really afford the initial expense in acquiring a full-sized navy, had no adequate facilities for maintaining one, and lacked the sailors to sail one. Efforts at naval expansion were thus destined to become in a sense the great boondoggle of the Santander administration. On the other hand, it would be unfair to deny the services actually performed by naval forces in the War of Independence, both in the form of privateering and in conventional naval combat. Of these two, privateering was the more persistent activity, and for a while it greatly curtailed Spain's trade by Spanish vessels with the Spanish Antilles. The work of privateering was carried out in large part by foreign seamen sailing under Colombian colors, and neutral as well as Spanish commerce provided its victims, but Colombia was not the worst offender among Latin American nations in this respect. A certain amount of diplomatic wrangling over the seizure of neutral goods by Colombian corsairs seemed a small price to pay for the concrete advantages to be gained, and at first privateering was distinctly encouraged by Colombian military leaders.[43]

There were always exceptions, however, for some privateers caused more trouble than they were worth, while the lure of privateering in general unfortunately led the few bona fide Colombian seamen to neglect the equally important task of combatting the Spanish Caribbean fleet. As a result, privateering gradually lost favor in official circles, and more energy was devoted instead to building up a regular navy. At least something along this line was genuinely needed, since the Spaniards could retain their foothold along the Venezuelan coast west of La Guaira almost indefinitely so long as their ships controlled the coastal waters. Yet it was only in 1822, when Francisco Antonio Zea raised the first appreciable foreign loan, that three or four really adequate warships could be acquired. Two of them were soon lost in an attack upon the Spaniards, but the loss was partially repaired by the capture of a Spanish corvette off the shores of Cuba, and the final recapture of Maracaibo in August of 1823 was made possible when Admiral José Padilla boldly forced his way with a

[42] *La Indicación,* November 2, 1822. For additional discussion of the topic see *La Gaceta de Colombia,* March 4 and 25, 1827; Santander to Bolívar, June 21, 1823, Lecuna, *C.S.* I, 217; report of Admiral Padilla, December 30, 1823, A.C., Senado-4, 432.

[43] *The Present State of Colombia,* 215-216; E. Taylor Parks, *Colombia and the United States* (Durham, 1935), 81-85; Watts to Secretary of State, September 4 and October 20, 1824, N.A., Colombia Dispatches III; O'Leary XVIII, 215-217, 321.

Colombian fleet into Lake Maracaibo and won a sweeping victory over the Spanish warships stationed inside it. It is hard to find a completely objective estimate of Padilla's exploits, for he was a mulatto by race, had little technical knowledge of seamanship despite his brief service as boatswain in the British navy, and had attached himself at an early date to the fortunes of Santanderean liberalism. Santander himself was accused almost at once of unfairly giving Padilla all the credit for the fall of the city, to the neglect of an army cooperating on land. But even if Padilla does not deserve all credit, there can be little doubt that his victory altered the balance of naval forces in Venezuelan waters, and thus served indirectly both to forestall any future Spanish incursions and to hasten the surrender of Puerto Cabello to Páez a few months later.[44]

While an improvised navy of warships and privateers was fighting Spain in the Caribbean, Santander in Bogotá was issuing a number of comprehensive decrees designed to lay the basis for future naval greatness. The first in the series, on June 28, 1822, ordered the establishment of a naval academy at Cartagena endowed with half the income from suppressed convents in the Department of Magdalena. The school was actually set up, and its work was supplemented by that of a similar school founded by Bolívar in Guayaquil.[45] A second decree, coming on July 22, sought to organize a seamen's militia. It was supposed to replace the colonial *milicia marinera,* which was deemed incompatible with the principles of the Colombian constitution not only because it had made the business of sailing and fishing a monopoly in the hands of registered *milicianos* but also because it extended the military *fuero* to militiamen who were not on active duty. The basic provision of the Vice-President's system was simply to make all seafarers available for compulsory service when needed on Colombian warships, offering them in return little more than exemption from service in the army. On the same date Santander formally established a marine infantry, and later in the year he issued lengthy decrees regulating the administrative corps of the Colombian navy and setting up a network of naval arsenals. In due course he put the final touch on his naval establishment by separating naval affairs from the *Secretaría de Guerra,* to which they had originally been entrusted by Bolívar, and creating a new *Secretaría* for the navy alone. Nor did he neglect the interests of the navy in dealing with general problems of trade and navigation: he was a strong supporter of the principle of preferential

[44] *Present State of Colombia,* 209-210, 213-214; Carl August Gosselman, *Reise in Columbien* (2 vols., Straslund 1829), I, 99; Blanco IX, 164-167; Hasbrouck, *op. cit.,* 291.

[45] *Codif. Nac.* I, 176-178; A.C., Cámara-1, 484. Santander decreed the establishment of similar schools at Puerto Cabello and Maracaibo (A.C., Senado-38, 64), but apparently this was never done.

port duties and the like for native-built and native-manned ships as a means of building up a class of Colombian seafarers.[46]

The administration also continued the acquisition of warships, especially when it obtained the new and greater loan of 1824. Santander and his cabinet resolved that Colombia needed a total of three or four frigates, "a few" brigantines, from fifty to sixty small coast guard vessels, and an undetermined number of river craft. In fulfillment of these objectives the government began by acquiring a dozen *pailebotes* for coast guard duty and two excellent frigates, the *Colombia* and the *Cundinamarca*. All were purchased in the United States, the coast-guard vessels for a mere $174,774, and the frigates for some $1,068,845, which was around one-sixth of a normal year's revenue. These purchases definitely marked a turning point in Colombian naval history, and the turn was not favorable. The *pailebotes*, to begin with, were a complete fiasco—poorly designed, and constructed abroad despite the express terms of a Congressional decree authorizing the construction of up to fifty such craft "in the ports of the republic." It was no doubt true that North American shipyards were better equipped to handle the job, and Santander probably enjoyed enough discretionary power on the general subject of military procurement to cover the order for *pailebotes* even without specific instructions from Congress. But the administration cannot escape all responsibility for the bad designing, which clearly reveals the inexperience of the new republic in naval matters; and the entire transaction brought down upon Santander a storm of well-deserved criticism.[47]

There was fortunately nothing wrong with "those beautiful frigates," [48] which were admittedly worthy of any navy in the world, except that Colombia had scarcely enough capable sailors to man even one of them adequately. Colombia had few native seamen simply because her fishermen were not used to going much beyond their own harbors and because unfavorable winds and the absence of complementary regional economies had prevented the creation of a prosperous coasting trade: these were obstacles that Santander's militia organization could not possibly hope to overcome. Indeed the new naval militia was met with conspicuous lack of enthusiasm among the sailors themselves, many of whom appear to have missed the special privileges they had enjoyed under the colonial system. The civil authorities in the coastal provinces did not offer much cooperation either; they were constantly exposed to the more immediate

[46] *Codif. Nac.* VII, 97-103, 122-133; Santander to Congress, February 14, 1825, A.C., Senado-53, 471.
[47] Baralt and Díaz, *op. cit.*, 157; *Acuerdos* I, 189; *Codif. Nac.* I, 393-394; Felipe Esteves, *Observaciones que se ponen al conocimiento de los SS. de la Comisión de Marina* (Caracas, 1826), 6; *La Gaceta de Cartagena*, No. 189.
[48] Watts to Clay, October 21, 1826, N.A., Colombia Dispatches IV.

demands of the land forces, and many were actually pressing sailors into the army and the land militia.[49] The Cartagena naval school, finally, was faced with exactly the same sort of problems. Its opening had been delayed when the sudden loss of Maracaibo in September, 1822, compelled the intendant to use its operating revenue for other purposes, and even when it did open it could never be sure that its funds would not be diverted to swell the general revenues of the department.[50]

The navy was thus compelled to rely in large part on criminals, victims of the press-gang, and, above all, foreigners. The latter were sometimes shanghaied, sometimes lured onto Colombian ships by extravagant promises of enlistment bounties, extra pay, and Colombian citizenship and free land on completion of their service; but in either case their performance was often far from satisfactory. They were generally unfamiliar with the language and customs of the country; their morale naturally suffered from the inability of the Colombian government to keep all the promises it made; and in the end Colombia had to contend not only with the grievances of the foreign naval officers and seamen but with the foreign consuls who occasionally came to their defense.[51] All in all, this was not a very efficient system for manning warships, and it broke down altogether when it came to staffing the frigates *Colombia* and *Cundinamarca*. Not only this, but there was hardly money enough for their daily upkeep in Cartagena harbor, much less for putting them in shape to sail the sea.[52]

It is thus fortunate that the final surrender of the Spanish fortress of San Juan de Ulúa off Vera Cruz harbor in November, 1825, relieved Colombia of the need to fulfill her ambitious agreement with Mexico for a joint naval expedition against it; for even though an excellent fleet had been assembled, it was badly undermanned. For similar reasons, it is just as well that the next joint project of Mexico and Colombia to sweep the seas of the Spanish fleet guarding the Antilles and thus prepare the way for liberation of Cuba and Puerto Rico did not come off either. In this case there was no Spanish surrender to make the expedition unnecessary,

---

[49] *Present State of Colombia*, 211-212; Padilla to Chamber of Representatives, December 30, 1823, A.C., Senado-53, 433-437; Esteves, *Observaciones*, 23-24; A.C., Senado-4, 437, Senado-53, 408-411.

[50] Santander to Congress, March 3, 1825, A.C., Cámara-1, 483-489. One other difficulty was that the revenues assigned to the naval academy turned out to be considerably less productive than was originally thought.

[51] *Codif. Nac.* II, 111-112, 313-314, VII, 205-206; William R. Manning, ed., *Diplomatic Correspondence of the United States Concerning the Independence of the Latin American Nations* (3 vols., New York, 1925), II, 1219, 1220, 1222; A.C., Senado-2, 88. Further unhappy details can be found scattered through the U. S. consular dispatches in the National Archives.

[52] Gosselman, *op. cit.*, I, 97; Watts to Clay, October 21, 1826, N.A., Colombia Dispatches IV.

but the United States had made clear that for the present it would rather have Cuba and Puerto Rico remain in Spanish hands, and in the last analysis the practicability of the whole scheme was decidedly open to question. One of the difficulties that had arisen was the prospect that many officers, no doubt including a good number of race-conscious Anglo-Saxons, would resign in protest if the command of the Colombian contingent should perchance devolve upon Admiral Padilla, who was second in line for the post.[53]

This left the Colombian navy with very little to do except stand in readiness for use in some future emergency, for the war in home waters had virtually come to an end since the close of 1823, or even before the two frigates were purchased. In fact even while the San Juan de Ulúa expedition was still on the agenda the Colombian government had begun preparations to sell off some of its smaller ships at a fraction of their purchase price. One of them finally brought less than 4% of what Colombia had paid. Even so, it cannot be said that Santander ever truly learned his lesson. As late as February, 1826, his cabinet was busily negotiating with Juan B. Elbers for the repair of two large vessels that he had earlier contracted to supply but had not delivered in satisfactory condition. Bolívar later used this as a welcome excuse to cancel the contract altogether, but Santander merely arranged for Elbers to have the proper repairs made in the United States, after which the ships would be duly purchased for their intrinsic value. The official naval budget drawn up for 1826 was set at the fantastic sum of $4,809,078. No one seriously expected, of course, that more than a fraction of this amount would ever be found and spent, but it was still put down as a considered estimate of Colombia's theoretical requirements.[54]

## *Reforming the Military System*

In addition to desiring a reduction in the army's size—and its partial replacement by navy and militia—Colombian liberals fought to carry through assorted political and military reforms that would limit the general influence of the army and give it, supposedly, a more republican spirit. These reforms were not necessarily opposed by conservative-minded Colombians, and they were not invariably supported by Santander, who

[53] Pedro A. Zubieta, *Apuntaciones sobre las primeras misiones diplomáticas de Colombia* (Bogotá, 1824), 228-241; Anderson to Secretary of State, November 10, 1825, N.A., Colombia Dispatches III; Soublette to Bolívar, February 21, 1826, O'Leary VIII, 41.

[54] *Acuerdos* II, 27, 124; Baralt and Díaz, *op. cit.,* 158; Juan B. Elbers, *Representación dirigida a la honorable Cámara de Representantes* (Bogotá, 1833), 33; *El Colombiano,* April 5, 1826.

tended to urge caution even when he agreed with the ultimate objectives. In most cases, however, the driving force in the movement for reform came from the ranks of the liberals, including those who did not happen to be supporters of the administration.

Probably the most important of the concrete reforms affecting the position of the armed forces in the life of the nation was the legislation of 1825 that clearly separated civil from military administration and forbade the union of civil and military positions in the same hands. It has been pointed out in an earlier chapter that the Vice-President generally sympathized with the objective in this case, but that he had certain practical reservations on the matter of office-holding, and as a partial concession to his stand the separation was not made quite unconditional. Civil and military commands could still be united in cases of special emergency, and as late as January, 1826, there were no less than three provinces in which a sufficient emergency was deemed to exist. Moreover, Santander retained full power to name individual army officers to purely civil positions, and he did so often enough to arouse widespread criticism even among his own supporters. Senator Soto was one of those who felt he showed an undue favoritism to military men in making appointments. In reality, of course, there was usually good reason for what the Vice-President did, especially as the officers in question would automatically forego either the civil salary or their regular military pay. But the issue continued to be debated, and in 1827 at least one nominee for a position as governor was rejected by the Senate solely on the grounds that he was an army officer.[55]

Closely related to the technical separation of civil and military commands was the enthronement of clear civil superiority over the army as a whole. Here Santander was in much closer agreement with his liberal supporters, since for obvious reasons he was as anxious as anyone else that the military understand their sacred obligation to respect and obey the civil authorities. This theme was endlessly dinned into the army's ear by the liberal press, and it kept cropping up in official pronouncements as well. It was further emphasized by the definition of treason placed at the start of the Organic Law of the Army, which cited four different varieties of interference with constitutional legality as technically treasonable but did not bother to mention the specific act of giving aid to the nation's foreign enemies. Santander himself was sincerely horrified on one occasion when military authorities in Venezuela dared to question whether the civil power had requested the use of troops for a constitutional objective;

[55] *El Constitucional,* January 19, 1826; A.C., Actas del Senado (secret sessions), June 15 and 28, July 28, 1827; Francisco de Paula Santander, *El Vicepresidente da cuenta a la república de su conducta* (Bogotá, 1828), 65; *El Cometa* (Caracas), March 25, 1826. See also above, pp. 26-28.

the army, he explained, must do its duty without asking why.⁵⁶ The administration likewise showed a tendency to prefer the civil to the military authority in borderline cases where a particular function could logically be entrusted to either one: in regulating the expulsion of royalist suspects, for instance, the last word was given not to the departmental *comandantes* but to the intendants.⁵⁷ Santander was convinced, on the other hand, that there was a limit beyond which the subordination of the military to the civil authorities could not safely be carried. He thus objected very strongly to a legislative provision that would have expressly subordinated all "functionaries of any class" to the various intendants, arguing that if taken literally this would destroy the direct dependence of army units in military affairs on their *comandante general,* who was himself merely the agent of the Executive Power. When Congress passed the article over his veto he continued his protests in the official press, and Secretary of Interior José Manuel Restrepo reported in his next *Memoria* that the army itself had taken offense.⁵⁸ This, of course, was to be expected; and it is also quite possible that all the talk about sacred obligations to obey the civil authority may have so annoyed the army as to produce just the opposite effect from the one intended.

The same basic desire to maintain the army in a subordinate position could be seen in agitation to deny soldiers the right to vote. This proposal drew perhaps its greatest support from systematic oppositionists, including Father José Antonio Pérez of Caracas and various conservative members of the lower house, but some good liberals—not including Santander—were also in favor of it. Much was made of the fact that soldiers, like members of the religious orders, were trained to offer a blind obedience to their superiors; from this it followed that they were not really free agents, and therefore that they should be refused a chance to vote even if they could fulfill all the other requirements. At least this was the extreme form taken by the proposal, which some would have extended to both troops and officers.⁵⁹ A more immediate problem concerned application of the general suffrage requirements set up by the Constitution of Cúcuta. One difficulty seems to have been the rather indefinite residence status of the armed forces; then, too, there was the crucial paragraph that limited voting to adult citizens who possessed $100 in real property or else were "engaged in some business, trade, profession, or useful industry, having a house or place of business and not being dependent upon another

⁵⁶ *Codif. Nac.* II, 291-292; A.H.N., Corresp.-Cámara (Interior), January, 1825 (first message).

⁵⁷ This rule was not always observed on the spot. See A.H.N., Interior y Relaciones CXXI, 20, 100.

⁵⁸ A.C., Actas del Senado, April 5 and 7, 1826; *Acuerdos* II, 136; *La Gaceta de Colombia,* November 26, 1826; *El Constitucional,* June 28, 1827.

⁵⁹ Cf. A.C., Senado-50, 71, Senado-53, 125; A.H.N., Congresos XXV, 861.

as a day laborer or as a servant." [60] Obviously few common soldiers and by no means all officers possessed the necessary amount of property; on the other hand, the army was certainly one kind of "profession or useful industry," and for this reason all soldiers had been expressly granted the right to vote in elections for the Congress of Cúcuta itself. But, under the new constitution, were they now to be excluded as belonging in the same category with servants and day laborers?

If the soldiers' vote became an issue in the first Congressional elections of 1822, it did not arouse enough interest to win mention either in the press or in any major official documents. In the elections of 1825, however, when both Congress and the presidency were at stake, Santander specifically endorsed the principle that soldiers should vote, and he instructed their commanders accordingly. It was charged that in Bogotá soldiers were marched off to the polls with slips of paper in their hands,[61] although it does not necessarily follow that they all voted for electors who backed Santander in his race for a second term as Vice-President: he came in a poor second in Bogotá province. The principal disputes took place at Maracaibo and certain other points in Venezuela, where many soldiers presented themselves at the polls only to be turned away. It is not clear in each case whether the original objective was to declare the military automatically disqualified from voting, or to exclude only some classes, or merely to limit the suffrage to those members of the armed forces who possessed $100 in real property. Certainly the last alternative is the one that finally prevailed in Maracaibo, after a host of minor irregularities and altercations in which the intendant gave municipal officers a free hand to exclude whomever they wished. The highest military authority on the spot, General Rafael Urdaneta, very creditably refused to back up his soldiers' arguments by force, despite his personal conviction that they should be allowed to vote more or less *ex officio*.[62]

When news of this controversy reached Bogotá, the administration formally sided with Urdaneta and the military, but the arguments of the municipality carried more weight with a good many Congressmen. Indeed the Maracaibo affair appears to have paved the way for consideration of a bill expressly requiring all members of the armed forces to possess the legal property qualifications before they could be allowed to vote. This

[60] William Marion Gibson, *The Constitutions of Colombia* (Durham, 1948), 43.
[61] A.C., Senado-43, 204-206.
[62] A.H.N., Congresos XXIV, 760, Congresos XXVII, 533-535, 561, 607, 655; *El Constitucional,* January 19, 1826. For reference to incidents at Puerto Cabello and Caracas see Páez to Bolívar, October 1, 1825, O'Leary II, 57-60. In the case of Maracaibo and nearby Sinamaica it must be added that there were charges that Urdaneta's Chief of Staff and also Col. Nicolás Joly were seeking to influence the troops to vote in favor of certain military candidates, including Urdaneta (A.H.N. Congresos XVII, 657-658).

would have eliminated the vast majority from voting, and the additional requirement that they establish legal residence in the parish where they voted would have excluded even more. Apparently no final action was taken on this measure, but the whole subject came up once more in 1827 when Congress was called upon to decide who might vote for deputies to the extraordinary national convention scheduled to open at Ocaña in March, 1828. This time the demand was heard to exclude even generals automatically from voting, whether or not they possessed the other qualifications. In the end Congress did not go that far, but it did disfranchise the military from sergeant downwards, and it implicitly subjected the rest to both residence and property requirements. Since he was then having his own troubles with the armed forces, Santander does not appear to have raised any serious objections.[63]

The army was quite naturally offended at the campaign against its right to vote. It was also offended, by and large, at the attacks made upon the military *fuero*, which was argued over in much the same way as that of the clergy, and with about the same indecisive results. The *fuero* was regarded by almost all good liberals as a class privilege basically incompatible with republican institutions, and even some of the more enlightened army officers joined in the attack. The Senator-Colonel Judas Tadeo Piñango firmly proclaimed that the army had fought for national independence, not to preserve such outmoded privileges as the *fuero*.[64] The Santander administration itself moved by rather cautious stages towards the same point of view. In 1823 the Vice-President's personal organ of opinion, *El Patriota*, held the *fuero* to be a just reward for military service and dismissed its critics as a band of vain perfectionists. *La Gaceta de Colombia* defended it simultaneously in terms of the natural inequality of mankind. Three years later, the *Gaceta* was taking a rather apologetic attitude toward the *fuero* in view of the continuing press attacks against it, while the Secretary of War came right out in his *Memoria* for 1826 with the recommendation that all non-military offenses by members of the armed forces should be tried by civil judges. This would effectively have ended the *fuero* as a class privilege, even though he suggested that a special military jury might still be used to determine points of fact.[65]

The *fuero* had more reliable defenders outside the Santander administration. The army as a whole was strongly in favor of it, for the

[63] A.H.N., Congresos XXVII, 533-535, 607; A.C., Senado-43, 204-206, Senado-50, 71, Senado-53, 125; *Codif. Nac.* III, 307-308.

[64] A.C., Actas del Senado, March 21, 1826. Cf. *La Miscelánea*, January 8 and March 12, 1826; and Rafael del Castillo y Rada, *Discurso con que presentó a la Comisión de Guerra y Marina el proyecto de ley orgánica de esta arma* (Bogotá, 1824), 37-39.

[65] *El Patriota* (Bogotá), July 30, 1823; *La Gaceta de Colombia*, August 3, 1823 and February 5, 1826; *El Constitucional*, January 19, 1826.

*fuero* was one of the things that helped to offset the undesirable features of military life. Thus to attack the *fuero* was regarded by the military and their sympathizers as an affront to the glorious *Ejército Libertador*, a sign of base ingratitude, and so on and so forth. One commentator spoke of the total absurdity of dragging an army officer away in full uniform to the common jail.[66] Moreover, the close analogy between the military and ecclesiastical *fueros* served to protect the former against attack by many conservative civilians who otherwise took a dim view of military rights and privileges. Certainly the community of interests between the Latin American Church and the military class is less obvious than liberal historians have often assumed; but on the question of *fueros*, if nothing else, the army, the clergy, and all their respective defenders, quite naturally tended to stand together.

The work of gradually undermining the military *fuero* nevertheless began as far back as the Congress of Cúcuta. The Constitution of 1821 ruled that only members of the armed forces engaged in active duty were subject to military law, and it is this provision that made it impossible to give any real judicial privileges to militiamen except while they were actually in service. The same article presumably put an end to the *fuero* enjoyed by retired officers, although in this case it would seem that the constitution was not always logically applied; in particular, there was much confusion over the precise status of officers who were on extended leave or were in a state of semi-retirement.[67] Aside from this, much of what has been said already concerning the ecclesiastical *fuero* can be repeated with regard to the military. Thus the projected penal code which would have drastically curtailed all *fueros* whatsoever was never finally issued, but the *fueros* were still annulled completely in certain specific cases, including press offenses and all *negocios contenciosos de hacienda*. It is worth noting that in the latter case the loss of the *fuero* was more important for the armed forces than for the clergy, since the *negocios* in question covered such matters as theft of property from a government arsenal.[68] During the Congress of 1826, furthermore, a separate attack was made that concerned exclusively the military *fuero*. In the course of the debate on the Organic Law of the Army in that year, the liberal majority of the Senate wrote in a provision restricting military jurisdiction to purely military offenses, and the move was finally defeated only by an unexpected but wholly typical change of mind on the part of the lower house. The Chamber of Representatives had suggested the same reform

---

[66] Mollien, *op. cit.*, 210; *El Chasqui Bogotano*, No. 3 (1826); *El Indicador del Orinoco* (Cumaná), October 15, 1825.

[67] A.C., Senado-36, 76-78, 122-128; *La Gaceta del Istmo de Panamá*, May 12, 1826; *El Constitucional*, August 23, 1827.

[68] *Codif. Nac.* II, 164, 324; *La Gaceta de Colombia*, February 5, 1826; A.C., Senado-34, 292. Cf. above, pp. 220-221.

itself three years earlier, and it still felt the move to be justified; but it now refused to go along simply for fear of antagonizing the military.[69] This fear was amply justified, since even the minor alterations already made in the system of *fueros* had aroused considerable discontent. Indeed some army leaders appear to have done their very best to avoid full compliance with those changes. General Páez, to mention only the most prominent malcontent, was ready to concede that only the civil press jury was entitled to judge the legality of a publication under the law of press offenses, but he insisted that if the offender was an army officer the imposition of a penalty must be left to military jurisdiction. There is no reason to assume offhand that Páez was consciously defying the letter of the law, but he was certainly subjecting it to an arbitrary interpretation all his own. Perhaps the significance of his stand can best be seen from the letter of explanation which he submitted to the Secretary of War, attacking the municipal officers who opposed him, and speaking darkly about mere lawyers who "flatter the military when they are possessed with fear, and insult them in the prosperity of peace." [70]

Even though enough had been done to antagonize General Páez, only a few small dents had really been put in the army's *fuero*. This left the main edifice of military jurisdiction still standing, and it was widely felt that much needed to be done in order to bring it more closely into line with enlightened civil jurisprudence. Such a reform would supposedly be of benefit to the army itself, for one of the various arguments made against the *fuero* was the claim that it entailed the imposition of excessive penalties, and by a highly arbitrary procedure, upon the hapless defenders of the fatherland. This reasoning is sometimes difficult to reconcile either with the concept of the *fuero* as a special privilege or with the numerous instances of undue leniency shown in the treatment of military offenders, but the conflict is more apparent than real: a system of justice that could go to such unpredictable extremes obviously was not very satisfactory.[71]

The first step was to disentangle the conflicting orders that governed the military court system during the very first years of Gran Colombia. On the one hand there was a decree of Bolívar, dating from 1817, which established highly abbreviated rules of procedure and gave wide authority in making decisions to the military commander in the field; on the other, there was a law of the Congress of Angostura, passed in January, 1820, which was designed to offer more protection to the accused and gave the last word in military justice to a new *Alta Corte Marcial* composed of both civil jurists and army officers. Bolívar protested vigorously against

[69] A.C., Senado-35, 281, Actas del Senado, February 1, March 22, 27 and 31, 1826.
[70] *La Miscelánea*, April 2, 1826; A.C., Cámara-6, 206-207.
[71] Cf. *La Gaceta de Colombia*, November 21, 1824. Cf. *La Miscelánea*, January 8, 1826.

this law as a threat to sound discipline, and he formally instructed Santander to suspend its operation in New Granada. Santander complied, all the more readily no doubt because the new court was to function in far-off Angostura, but the law seems to have been enforced for the most part in Venezuela. When the Congress of Cúcuta met one more complication was added: Bolívar's decree of 1817 was in several important details against the letter and spirit of the new constitution, but at the same time nothing whatever was done to confirm the law of Angostura or make it extensive to all of Colombia. This left all court-martial procedure in doubt, with nobody clearly entitled to hand down a final decision, and for want of anything better to do Santander now ordered all cases suspended just short of the last instance. He left the matter for definitive treatment by the next Congress, and numerous officers under trial meanwhile languished in prison.[72]

The immediate bottleneck was relieved when Congress met in 1823 and established a special military high court at Bogotá, but this was only a temporary measure. The final solution came a year later and was roughly similar to that adopted by the Guayana Congress: it made several changes in court-martial procedure, but its basic feature was that the final authority in military law should henceforth be vested in the regular *Cortes Superiores* and the *Alta Corte* itself, sitting in each case *en calidad de marcial* with two army officers added to the number of civil jurists. Contrary to the advice of Santander, Congress left the civil judges in a majority even when purely military offenses were under consideration.[73] However, the new system served its purpose reasonably well, and there can be little doubt that the intervention of civil judges on so large a scale had a generally beneficial effect upon army justice. The judges of the *Alta Corte Marcial,* in particular, were always willing to increase the penalty imposed by an ordinary court-martial when it seemed that an officer had been let off too easily, but they were also eager to protect military prisoners against the persistent violations of fair play that were to be found at the lower levels of military jurisdiction.

The Santander administration would have been glad to see still further improvements made. It favored some reduction in the number of capital offenses in military law so as to bring it into closer accord with regular criminal jurisdiction, and on the advice of the *Alta Corte* Santander ordered the enforcement of one obscure Spanish decree that mercifully abrogated the death penalty for abandoning guard in wartime provided the act was not committed at a point of danger. The administration likewise favored a more extensive use of the technical services of trained

[72] Blanco VII, 93-98, 179; A.C., Cámara-4, 48, Cámara-6, 15, 22-29; *Actas:* Congreso-1823, 357; *Codif. Nac.* VII, 112-113.

[73] *Codif. Nac.* I, 278-280, 434-437; *Acuerdos* I, 240-241; *Actas:* Senado-1824, 658.

lawyers throughout the court-martial system, and a good bit else along the same lines.[74] But the only really basic reform that was carried out was the new system of military high courts, and in the last analysis most army spokesmen remained far more interested in defending the *fuero* as such than in any suggested improvement in military law or procedure. Certainly they displayed no very deep sense of gratitude for the benefits conferred on them so far.

[74] *El Constitucional*, March 23, 1826; *Codif. Nac.* VII, 324-325; *La Gaceta de Colombia*, September 5 and November 21, 1824.

Chapter XVII

## Military Claims and Veterans' Unrest

A COMPLICATING factor in all relations between the military class and the civil authorities was the annoyance caused by the government's failure to make good its full promises of material rewards to soldiers and officers. One aspect of this problem has already been considered in dealing with the general inadequacy of army pay, but there was more to it than just the inability to meet monthly payrolls. Wages that were not paid on time became an obligation that theoretically had to be paid at some future date, and this debt was closely bound up with an additional sum that was owed under the heading of military bonuses. Hence the accumulated salary and bonus claims of the military class formed a major part of the Colombian national debt. They remained a source of dangerous contention for as long as they were not settled, and they involved not only current members of the armed forces but also men who had already been retired without receiving payment of what was owed them.

Such claims were especially important to the veterans because on the whole Gran Colombia had little else to offer them. Some were actually receiving retirement and disability pensions, but in view of the state of Colombian finances no comprehensive pension system could be set up, and efforts in this direction were admittedly inadequate. Some officers were taken care of by the system of assigning limited military duties at part salary, and a number of both officers and men were given jobs in civil service on completion of their military duty. Indeed Bolívar once sought to put all bureaucrats on provisional tenure so as to save permanent appointments for returning veterans after the war. This scheme, however, was not very practical, especially at a time when capable public officials were so hard to find and retain. Certainly it was not generally adopted, and neither did anyone even think of devising the elaborate fringe benefits which veterans have learned to demand in more recent times. At one point Santander added insult to injury by specifying that veterans should take with them only their oldest uniforms on leaving the service.[1]

### The Handling of the Claims Backlog

In most cases, all that soldiers and veterans could look forward to

[1] *El Constitucional* (Bogotá), January 19, 1826, September 20, 1827; O'Leary XVIII, 396; *La Gaceta de Colombia*, April 10, 1825.

was to obtain some kind of settlement of their unpaid back salaries and in addition, if personally entitled to it, a bonus in national property. On these two points the government had assumed a firm moral and legal commitment, so at least something had to be done. With regard to the back salaries, military men were in roughly the same position as civil servants, who had not received their full salary either. The bonus, on the other hand, concerned almost entirely the military. As far back as 1816, when Páez occupied Apure for the patriot cause, he had found it expedient both to indulge the *llaneros'* propensity for looting and to promise his men the distribution of all government property in the area, meaning principally the confiscated holdings of former royalists. Páez later recognized Bolívar's supreme authority precisely on condition that he confirm these promises, and Bolívar had the Congress of Angostura extend the offer to his entire army. The law that did this started out by declaring military rank to be a sure indication of merit and then went on to pledge bonuses in national property ranging from $500 for a common soldier to $25,000 for a *general en jefe*. Privates and generals alike had to have at least two years' service in order to qualify for the regular amount, and certain classes of civil servants were also included in the legislation, to the frank displeasure of Bolívar. In due course the entire scale of rewards was confirmed by the Congress of Cúcuta. It is worth noting, however, that no bonus was ever declared to officers and men who had joined the patriot army after February 15, 1819, except in the case of a limited number of foreign volunteers. The bonus, in other words, was mainly a largesse for the hardy band that had fought for independence through the dark years of the withdrawal to the *llanos*. It was chiefly for the benefit of Venezuelans, and in the Colombian army as a whole a much higher proportion of officers than of men was eligible to receive it.[2]

Although bonuses and accumulated back wages were technically two different things, they were treated in much the same manner by the Guayana Congress. Both debts were given a special claim upon national resources, and both were paid in *vales* which the recipients were supposed to use in bidding for state property at public auction. This system did not prove very satisfactory, especially since it was hard for military men in active service to attend the auctions in person. Hence the latter were abolished by the Congress of Cúcuta, which provided for national property to be given directly to the claimants at an assessed value.[3] How-

[2] O'Leary XVIII, 393-395, 399-401; Blanco VII, 162; *Codif. Nac.* I, 74-78.

The bonus was not quite the same as a free gift, since it represented, among other things, a recognition that the military during the years in question had virtually received no pay—and that they never would be paid for those years in any other way.

[3] *Archivo del General José Antonio Páez* (Bogotá, 1939), 342; O'Leary XVIII, 393-395; Bolívar to Páez, January 18, 1821, Lecuna, *C.L.* II, 301. Both methods were also applicable to the claims of civil officials.

ever, neither method was very swift or effective. The certification of claims, formal condemnation of enemy property, and similar technical details all took time; furthermore, there was not enough desirable property to go around. Estates seized from royalist *émigrés* were obviously limited, and much of the confiscated property actually consisted of herds of cattle, which tended to be frittered away by mismanagement, if not just plain stolen, while awaiting distribution. There were substitutes available, including the properties that had once belonged to the Jesuits expelled by Charles III, many of which now ended up in the hands of patriot veterans; but these were also insufficient to fill the demand. The further alternative of obtaining payment from the general funds of the Colombian treasury, which was always held out as a last resort, was not of much help save during the brief heyday of the 1824 loan. And the one virtually limitless alternative—the unoccupied public domain—is one that aroused very little interest.[4]

Those who fared best in the face of all obstacles were of course the higher-ranking officers. Páez, for instance, obtained one estate worth $200,000 which not only covered all his past claims but represented in part an advance payment on salaries he had yet to earn. General Bermúdez also received property worth more than his total claims, and Congress graciously made him a special gift of the surplus. Another satisfied general was naturally Santander, with the estate outside Chiquinquirá which he had obtained through a rather questionable transaction with Bolívar.[5] Even among the officers by no means all received their full bonus and in addition had their salaries paid completely up to date; but the officer class as a whole admittedly fared better than either the common soldiers or, for that matter, the great majority of civil servants.

The relative good fortune of the officer class resulted not only from outright favoritism—which might occur whether payment was being made in land or otherwise—but also from the general failure to break up estates into small lots which any soldier could claim with the credits he had accumulated. An unfair advantage was likewise had by those who knew exactly what properties were available, for it was possible to receive preference in the distribution of a given estate by entering a request for it in advance. Needless to say, officers and speculators were most likely to have the necessary information to profit by this system.[6] If all went well a favored claimant could not only have an estate reserved for him but even have the estate and everything on it delivered to him "on deposit" pending final adjudication. This procedure had the advantage of

[4] *La Gaceta de Colombia,* November 17, 1822, August 3, 1823, February 26, 1826; *El Constitucional,* March 2, 1826.

[5] *Acuerdos* I, 8-9; *Codif. Nac.* II, 36. On the case of Santander see above, p. 40.

[6] Cf. *El Indicador del Orinoco* (Cumaná), December 9, 1825.

minimizing deterioration of the property while it was awaiting final distribution, but it really amounted to waiving the technicalities of adjudication in favor of the creditor involved. Many of the officers who obtained the most handsome rewards first had their lands on deposit; and only rarely if at all was a property first given in this fashion ultimately assigned to someone else.[7]

All these inequalities were aggravated by the widespread speculation in government obligations. The bulk of unsatisfied claims for bonuses and back salaries remained outstanding in the form of *vales,* and these were readily sold for a fraction of their value by anyone who doubted his chances of receiving payment or was momentarily in need of ready cash. There is no lack of complaints about soldiers who sold their right to national lands for 5% or less of the amount legally due them; very often they received even this token payment not in cash but in goods.[8] Numerous attempts were made to discourage speculation, as when the Congress of Cúcuta flatly prohibited circulation of all the military *vales* issued at Angostura, but such measures were hard to enforce, and they had to be qualified so as not to conflict with the rights which speculators had already acquired by legal means. Santander himself intervened to dissuade the Congress of 1826 from annulling the prior claims which second-hand purchasers of *vales* had staked out to individual properties.[9] Nor is there any reason to assume that this concern for the rights of speculators was solely a matter of personal favoritism. Speculation was not invariably evil, for it was a natural result of the time lag in paying off debt certificates; and in view of the financial instability of the new republic there was always a certain risk in holding government obligations. Santander's good friend Juan Manuel Arrubla accordingly implied that he had performed a very great public service in buying up *vales* at a time when final payment appeared extremely doubtful; and if he really paid the

[7] About the only case in which lands were actually taken back—and whether they had been given outright or on deposit in this case is not clear to the writer—seems to have occurred in Pasto, where the lands of royalist rebels were seized wholesale by order of Bolívar, and assigned to well-deserving members of the patriot army only to be given back to the original owners in considerable part by José María Obando when he became governor of the province. Obando claimed that many of the confiscations had been irregularly carried out, but in any event this action helps to explain the loyalty of the ultra-reactionary *pastusos* to the liberal Obando; and also the enmity between Obando and Juan José Flores, since Flores had been the chief instrument for carrying out the confiscations and himself lost an estate by the measure of Obando. See José María Obando, *Apuntamientos para la historia* (Lima, 1842), 28-29, 45; Blanco VIII, 594.

[8] Cf. O'Leary XVIII, 393-395; *El Argos Republicano de Cumaná,* August 21, 1825.

[9] *La Gaceta de Colombia,* September 8, 1822; *Codif. Nac.* I, 77, VII, 107-109; Santander to Congress, April 28, 1826, A.C., Senado-43, 467-468; A.C., Actas del Senado, May 9 and 12, 1826.

50% of face value which he claimed to have offered, it may well be that his boast was justified.[10] Moreover, despite all the complaints of soldiers and veterans against rapacious civilian speculators, it is impossible to place the blame solely on any one group. All kinds of Colombians took a hand in the game of speculation, and among the worst offenders were military leaders such as Páez, whose private fortune was due in considerable part to an *"agiotaje escandaloso"* with the *vales* of his own soldiers and officers.[11]

## The Veterans' Problem on the Llanos

Yet, no matter who was to blame for the speculation in *vales* and for the irregular payment of salary and bonus claims, these two problems could not help but create very serious unrest among both active and retired members of the armed forces. This unrest existed in some form almost everywhere. It was most acute, however, among the *llaneros* of interior Venezuela, who were an unruly group to begin with, and possessed the largest single share of outstanding military claims as a result of their uninterrupted service during the very years that served as a base for the calculation of bonus payments. Moreover, since many if not most of them had been sent home soon after the battle of Carabobo, they also provided the first substantial bloc of unemployed veterans.

As early as December, 1820—when most of the *llaneros* were still in active service—Páez reported that they were beginning to doubt the sincerity of the government's lavish promises of material reward, and he predicted the direst consequences if those promises were not speedily honored.[12] Bolívar fully shared in Páez' apprehension; he felt that the uncultured *llaneros* suffered from a kind of inferiority complex that made it impossible to inspire their confidence, and it was their sullen discontent that brought forth his much-quoted exclamation, "I fear peace more than war." [13] The state of mind of the *llaneros* certainly was not improved by placing a great part of them on indefinite, unpaid leave after the middle of 1821. This step made some sense militarily, for with the bulk of Venezuela already freed the main theatre of war was now in southern Colombia and then Peru, in both of which the terrain offered less room for cavalry, the *llaneros*' specialty; but it left them as dissatisfied as ever, and with nothing interesting to do. At times they suffered real privation, but they showed little desire to go to work, and instead a strong tendency

[10] *El Constitucional,* June 1 and July 20, 1826.

[11] A.C., Actas del Senado, March 30, 1825 (secret sessions). The term quoted is from Senator A. M. Briceño, himself a Venezuelan.

[12] Páez to Bolívar and to Secretary of War, December 23, 1820, *Archivo del General Páez,* 334, 341-343.

[13] Bolívar to Dr. Pedro Gual, May 24, 1821, Lecuna, *C.L.,* II, 348-349.

to continue living off the land. Colonel Francisco Conde, who knew them well, asserted that robbery was "their favorite inclination." He added that "in spite of their ignorance" they felt their military valor entitled them to all the places of importance in Colombia, and when they were left to shift for themselves they felt quite naturally offended.[14]

The situation was sufficiently ugly for Santander to grant the Intendant of Venezuela special powers in 1822 to distribute national property on the *llanos* almost as he saw fit, without reference to the central *Comisión de repartición* established in Bogotá. It was hoped that this move would quiet discontent, but in practice it was far from sufficient; merely cutting administrative red-tape would not remedy the concrete shortage of government estates that were available for paying bonus and salary claims. In 1823, therefore, Santander asked Congress to take other exceptional measures in favor of all men who had served in the armies of Apure and Casanare between 1816 and 1819, which meant chiefly the unruly veterans of the *llanos*. Congress responded by setting up an extraordinary commission in the province of Apure with full power to distribute national property to military claimants on the spot, much as the Intendant of Venezuela had been authorized to do the year before. The difference was that veterans were now required to take a quarter of their claims in vacant public lands, and that any part of their claims which could not be satisfied in land of one sort or another would be paid in cattle to be borrowed from private citizens at 5% interest. The latter provision seemed reasonable enough, since the land was not much good without animals to pasture on it.[15]

It is hard to be sure how this law worked in practice, although presumably it helped matters somewhat. The loan of cattle, however, was less successful than had been hoped, no doubt because no one wanted to lend anything to the Colombian government if he possibly could avoid it. For that matter, many cattle owners of Apure were themselves holders of military claims, and in such cases there would be little point in paying a man with cattle borrowed from his own estate. Santander therefore permitted anyone to exchange the old military claims directly for new treasury obligations bearing 5% interest, just as if he had lent cattle instead.[16] Even if interest was not regularly paid, it was a step in the right direction merely to have some promised, which had not been the case before; and with the coming of the English loan of 1824 the new obligations may

[14] Report of September 22, 1823, A.C., Cámara-5, 122-123. See also Cámara-13, 151; Restrepo VI, 287.

[15] *Codif. Nac.* I, 231-232, VII, 82-84. The background of the 1823 law can be found in A.C., Actas del Senado (secret sessions), July 2, 1823; *Actas:* Congreso-1823, 277, 305-306; *La Gaceta de Colombia,* August 24, 1823.

[16] A.C., Cámara-1, 252-254.

well have benefited from the general improvement in Colombian domestic credit.

On the other hand, there was little chance that any juggling with debt certificates could really solve the veterans' problem on the *llanos,* even when it was supplemented by active police measures and by calling the worst trouble-makers back to arms for military service in Peru. Santander optimistically pronounced in March, 1825, that unrest in Apure had finally been brought under control, but at the same time he reminded Congress that the only permanent solution was to turn the *llaneros* from "idlers and beggars" into "farmers or herdsmen," [17] and this had so far been accomplished only in part. Accordingly, the Vice-President recommended to Congress that it accept the "generous offer" of José Antonio Páez to sell the government his own valuable estates in Apure, together with his cattle at $8 a head and his horses at $10 and $20, all for distribution to veterans in payment of their claims. This was indeed a curious project to suggest, unless Páez was counting on quick cash payment from the funds of the English loan; undoubtedly he also hoped to cement his own prestige among the *llaneros,* for he observed that he should naturally have something to say in the distribution. However, Congress would have none of the scheme. Senator Soto expressed fear that Páez would exploit any rebuff he received as a means to curry favor with the *llaneros* at the expense of the Legislative Power, but Congress as a whole felt that Páez was asking infinitely more than either his land or his cattle had originally cost, and it was willing to run the risk of his displeasure.[18]

The payment of military claims on the *llanos* thus remained in the hands of the commission established in Apure by the law of 1823, and by the start of 1826 the commission had virtually completed its task, mainly by the technique of turning one kind of debt into another. This was enough for Castillo y Rada to pronounce the law a success, but whether the *llaneros* had actually settled down for good as peaceful farmers and herdsmen is highly doubtful. Nor was it possible to prevent much of the benefit of the law from going to speculators and outright falsifiers of military claims: Bolívar's secretary general declared some years later that the loan provisions had been applied with more generosity than justice.[19] All in all, one cannot escape the conclusion that the Colombian government's efforts to deal with the *llaneros*—and with all other veterans —were distinctly inadequate; the most one can say is that Colombia lacked the resources to handle the problem correctly, and that other American nations generally did no better.

[17] Message of March 29, 1825, A.C., Senado-35, 19.
[18] A.C., Senado-35, 19, 21, Actas del Senado, March 30, 1825 (secret session).
[19] A.C., Senado-43, 578, Cámara-13, 62; Blanco XI, 545.

## The Infante Affair

It is well to close this consideration of the veterans' problem and of military affairs in general with an examination of one of the most famous episodes in the entire history of Gran Colombia, a highly controversial murder case that had repercussions involving at least half the prominent figures of the period, served to underscore the distrust of civilians toward both past and present members of the armed forces, and demonstrated how the similar distrust of the military toward civilians might be exploited by interested politicians. It brought to light also, almost incidentally, a definite cleavage of opinion between Venezuelans and *granadinos*. The chief personage in the affair was Colonel Leonardo Infante, a veteran from the *llanos* who was noted for his bravery and not much more. In 1823 Infante left the army and settled down in Bogotá in the *barrio* of San Victorino, living on some kind of military pension. According to his principal defender he was feared in San Victorino for his valor, and hated both for his airs of a sultan and for his generally unruly behaviour.[20] Despite the fact that he lived in Bogotá, Infante was the perfect example of a turbulent *llanero* veteran. He was also the very symbol of oppressive militarism, and in particular of Venezuelan militarism, which to the *granadino* was much the worst variety. It is true that when the deputies of the *Montaña* raised a hue and cry over a minor scuffle between Infante and two of their own number, Drs. Baños and Chiriboga, the *llanero* officer was actually defended by the zealots of the *Valle,* and especially by *El Correo de Bogotá,* which reflected the views of Francisco Soto and Vicente Azuero. But this was simply out of dislike for his victims, not admiration for Infante, and when the final crisis arrived shortly thereafter his antagonists were headed by the same Soto and Azuero.[21]

The real trouble began on July 24, 1824, when Lieutenant Francisco Perdomo, a Venezuelan officer from Caracas, was found dead in the *barrio* of San Victorino. Various signs pointed to Infante as the probable assassin, for he had been reported in an altercation with Perdomo shortly before, and there was no doubt at all that he was capable of the deed. There were some confused stories of shouts heard in the night that seemed to bear out the charge, and also the rumor that some had even seen Infante commit the murder but were too frightened by his threats to say what they knew. The belief that Infante had murdered Perdomo was based more on the inherent likelihood of his guilt than on concrete evidence,

[20] Peña to Bolívar, January 25, 1825, O'Leary II, 256; see also Col. J. P. Hamilton, *Travels through the Interior Provinces of Colombia* (2 vols., London, 1827) II, 246; Enrique de Narváez, *Juan Salvador de Narváez* (Bogotá, 1927), 209.

[21] *El Correo de Bogotá,* April 23, 1824.

and the chief witnesses against him were two ladies of doubtful reputation who apparently had personal reasons to desire his undoing. Nevertheless, it was obvious almost from the start that a strong movement was on foot to make the charges stick, and thus to make an example of Infante that would show for once and for all that the civil government was supreme and that the military, regardless of their combat records, must behave themselves. Infante was accordingly brought before a court-martial in Bogotá, tried with record speed, and on August 13 unanimously condemned to death. Technical defects in the proceedings made a retrial necessary, but the death sentence was easily produced again with only one dissenting vote.[22]

On the very same day as the second verdict was handed down—again the speed is remarkable—Francisco Soto, acting as *fiscal* of the *Alta Corte Marcial,* recommended that the sentence be confirmed. However, the judges of the highest-ranking court of all were not quite so unanimous in their condemnation. The President of the court, the Venezuelan lawyer Dr. Miguel Peña, and one of the two military judges as well, voted for absolution; three other judges voted to condemn Infante to death; and Dr. Félix Restrepo, the judge whose verdict was least likely to be swayed by personal prejudice, voted for an "extraordinary penalty" of ten years' imprisonment. Restrepo did not doubt Infante's guilt, but he quite properly decided that there was insufficient evidence to warrant his execution; and not quite so properly, he chose to inflict a compromise sentence rather than follow the logical course of voting for acquittal. Thus a clear majority held Infante to be guilty of the crime, but a mere plurality of three out of six judges had voted for the legal penalty, which was death. Dr. Peña therefore insisted that no valid sentence had been given, and that Colonel Infante could not legally be executed. His view was opposed principally by Francisco Soto and the three judges who had voted for the death sentence, one of whom was Dr. Vicente Azuero. This was despite the fact that Soto and Azuero had declared in a previous case that a decision split along similar lines was flagrantly illegal; but the earlier decision had been one favoring the "Apostle of Facatativá," Father Fernández Saavedra, who was no friend of the liberals, so that both men now felt quite free to change their minds. Nevertheless, there was something to be said on either side of the procedural question; and it is sig-

[22] A good objective summary of the murder case can be found in Groot, 327-337; Miguel Peña, *Defensa del Doctor Miguel Peña* (Caracas, 1826), gives the best statement of the case from a pro-Infante viewpoint, and is quite as effective as the chief statements of the opposite viewpoint, which are Alta Corte Marcial, *Exposición a la Honorable Cámara de Representantes* (Bogotá, 1825) and *Conducta de la Alta Corte de Justicia reunida en calidad de corte marcial* (Bogotá, 1824).

nificant that in the end everyone concerned but Dr. Peña was willing to agree that Infante had been legally condemned to die.[23] For a time Peña's resistance was enough to prevent the execution, since the verdict could not be carried out until all members of the court had formally placed their signatures on it, and Peña, still claiming that no legal verdict existed, flatly refused to do so. In order to remove this obstacle it was necessary first of all to get Peña out of the way; accordingly, impeachment proceedings were begun against him as soon as Congress reopened in January, 1825, and in due course the Senate suspended him from the bench for a period of one year. As Peña himself pointed out, this was a rather strange outcome for an impeachment trial: if an offense were really serious enough to require use of the impeachment procedure, the latter should normally have led to either absolution or outright dismissal and worse. A one-year suspension bore an interesting resemblance to the "extraordinary penalty" suggested by Dr. Restrepo in his vote on Infante. Not only this, but the Senate acted against the spirit if not the letter of its own rules in refusing to disqualify from the final vote either Francisco Soto or two other Senators who had voted against Infante in court-martial.[24] However, Peña had temporarily left the court, which was the main thing. Infante's sentence now became valid without his signature; the *Consejo de Gobierno*,[25] with Félix Restrepo sitting as representative of the *Alta Corte*, voted unanimously against commuting the penalty; and four days later Infante was shot. He was unrepentant to the end, hurling insults at his foes as he was led to his death. But this was no ordinary execution: a body of troops was brought to witness it, and while Infante's corpse still lay in the public plaza Santander in person issued forth to harangue them on the duties of a soldier. There is some dispute as to the details of his speech, for the version printed in the *Gaceta* has been challenged. Its substance, on the other hand, was clear enough; for it was designed to stress the Majesty of the Law and the sacred obligations of the military to obey its commands. An example had thus been made—two examples, if we include Peña—and one English observer reports that the speech was quite well received by the troops.[26]

The latter detail is rather interesting, although under the circumstances it was obviously expedient for the troops to react favorably. It may also be that in Bogotá, at least, the average soldier had his heart in the right place provided he was not misled by unscrupulous schemers. It is some-

[23] See especially Peña, *Defensa*, 2-3, 44, 129-130.

[24] Peña, *Defensa*, 4-5; Peña to Bolívar, April 6, 1825, O'Leary II, 260-261; *La Gaceta de Colombia*, March 27, 1825.

[25] This was, in effect, a full cabinet session attended by the Chief Executive, all secretaries of state, and a voting representative of the *Alta Corte*.

[26] *Acuerdos* II, 35; Hamilton, *op. cit.*, II, 245; *La Gaceta de Colombia*, April 3, 1825; Groot, 335.

what more important to observe the reaction of the country at large to the whole series of events that began with the death of Perdomo and ended with that of Infante. In this connection it has long been customary to stress the subsequent activity of Dr. Peña, who left Bogotá in high dudgeon and immediately launched a campaign to convince the Liberator and anyone else who would lend an ear that the Santander administration was out to destroy both the military class and Venezuelans in general. Peña finally attached himself to General Páez, and he certainly deserved part of the credit when the Venezuelan chieftain finally rebelled against the central government in April of 1826.[27] On the other hand, it might be argued that Peña was a liability as well as an asset to his cause. Passing through Cartagena on his way home to Venezuela he was entrusted by General Mariano Montilla with the delicate assignment of carrying $300,000 in specie to the Caracas treasury; he received the sum in sound currency and, in effect, he then delivered most of it in the depreciated silver coin then current in Caracas, keeping for himself a profit of not less than $25,000. Peña sought to justify his action on the grounds that others had done the same thing and that as long as he had been unjustly treated by the national authorities he was merely repaying them in kind. However, his excuses were not very good; and the transaction not only caused Peña to undergo a second impeachment trial, which brought about his formal deposition from the *Alta Corte,* but also made his very name a symbol of financial corruption to *granadinos.*[28]

But even without the personal intrigues of the unscrupulous Dr. Peña, the summary treatment of Infante and his defender could not help but cause a disagreeable impression in much of Venezuela. Infante's fellow *llaneros* did not react as favorably as the troops in Bogotá plaza. Venezuelan politicians, whether sincerely convinced of Infante's innocence or merely guided by expediency, were for the most part publicly arrayed in his favor, and they tended to adopt at least some part of Peña's thesis that the entire episode was proof of Santander's undying hatred toward both the army and Venezuela. It is significant that in the three court decisions against Infante, Venezuelan judges, whether military or civilian, voted with only one exception for absolution, while the *granadinos,* with the exception of Félix Restrepo, uniformly voted for death. When the

[27] For two examples of this interpretation, see Restrepo VI, 344, and Gerhard Masur, *Simón Bolívar* (Albuquerque, 1948), 600. Cf. Peña to Bolívar, April 6, 1825, O'Leary II, 260-262.

[28] Montilla to Escalona, July 9, 1825, Blanco X, 13; *La Gaceta de Colombia,* October 30, 1825; *El Constitucional,* August 18, 1825; Peña to Bolívar, December 2, 1827, O'Leary II, 265-266.

What Peña did was receive good money and deliver only enough to make up the same face value in bad. As different sorts of currency are involved, there are slightly differing versions of the exact profit he made.

lower house of Congress instituted impeachment proceedings against Peña for refusing to sign the verdict, only one Venezuelan voted in favor of the motion, and he was a deputy from near the border of New Granada. In the Senate, three Venezuelans voted to condemn Peña, and one of them, the Senate President Luis Andrés Baralt, was among his bitterest accusers; but two of the three (including Baralt) were from the westernmost Department of Zulia. The vote of *granadino* Congressmen against Peña was not so overwhelming as that of the Venezuelans for him, but at least the "persecution" of Infante and his protector was not exclusively the work of the Santanderean liberals, for the *Montaña* also had a hand in it. Outside of Congress even the rabidly oppositionist *Gaceta de Cartagena* joined in the chorus of abuse against Dr. Peña.[29] This was no doubt highly gratifying to the administration. However, it was also true that the attempt to make an example of Infante had served to underscore all the dangers inherent in the Military Question. The loyalty of *granadino* officers was not apparently weakened; but that of the Venezuelan military class certainly had been.

---

[29] Peña, *op. cit.*, 104; *Actas:* Cámara-1825, 99 and Senado-1825, 558-559; *La Gaceta de Cartagena*, February 12, 1825.

Chapter XVIII

*The Venezuelan Problem*

VENEZUELAN opposition to the central administration is so constant a factor in the history of Gran Colombia that it is sometimes difficult to understand why Venezuelans ever accepted the idea of a unitary Colombian state in the first place. No doubt the will and magic name of Simón Bolívar had something to do with it, and so did the obvious expediency of combining Venezuela and New Granada as closely as possible in a single war effort against Spain. Then, too, the fact that the main work of the Constituent Congress was half completed before Caracas was finally liberated—and liberated by a Colombian army serving Bolívar—naturally presented the foes of central union with an inescapable *fait accompli*. However, the union could never be really stable unless it rested on a broad basis of popular support, and this is something that did not exist in Venezuela. Indeed a great many Venezuelans, notably including Dr. Miguel Peña, appear to have assumed almost from the start that once peace was attained Venezuela would ask complete independence from Colombia.[1]

It is easy enough to seek reasons for Venezuelan separatism in the basic social and economic diversity of Venezuela and New Granada. Yet diversity does not necessarily produce disunion; and if it takes the form of mutually complementary economies it can give rise to a profitable cooperation. To be sure, this was hardly the case with Venezuela and New Granada, both of which were essentially self-sufficient in agriculture and dependent on foreign supplies for manufactured goods. There were some products, such as the wheat of Tunja and Bogotá, that were produced in quantity in only one of the two, but here transportation difficulties ruled out any real interchange. On the other hand, neither was there any real conflict of interests. Venezuelans often tried to make out that they had been injured economically by their political union with New Granada, but for the most part their complaints can be dismissed as merely irrelevant. The disorganization of the tobacco monopoly was in truth more grievous to Venezuela than to New Granada, for the industry was centered in Venezuela, but the reasons for its decline had nothing to do with political organization. Nor did it make much sense for Venezuelans to complain on the one hand that the reduction of export duties hurt their revenues and on the other that the retention of export duties worked a

[1] C.J. Burckle to Todd, September 30, 1823 (enclosed with Todd dispatch), N.A., Colombia Dispatches II.

hardship on regional producers of coffee and cacao.[2] As a matter of fact, Venezuela is the region that always profited most directly from Colombia's foreign trade policy: the general tendency toward more liberal conditions of trade benefited Venezuela as a highly commercialized and exporting community, while at the same time the most glaring exceptions to that tendency—such as the prohibition of sugar and indigo imports—were specifically designed to favor Venezuelan interests.

There is certainly no basis either for charges that the Santander administration devoted all its attention and funds to New Granada, to the utter exclusion of Venezuela. The bulk of the funds appropriated from the English loan of 1824 for making agricultural loans was earmarked by Santander for Venezuela; Venezuelans likewise obtained a substantial share of the loan funds that were used in paying off government debts. It is true that Venezuela lagged behind New Granada in the expansion of educational facilities, but this was mainly because the war had lasted longer in Venezuela and because the revenues specifically assigned for educational purposes had a lower yield there. It was not for any lack of government decrees, which ordered the establishment of secondary schools even in such dreary spots as Guanare and Angostura.[3]

Systematic discrimination against Venezuela was likewise alleged in the matter of government appointments. Francisco Ribas complained that the *caraqueños,* "reduced to the state of semi-colonists, must not aspire except to cultivate the soil and to those subordinate jobs of doormen or *alguaciles.*"[4] There are even a few isolated statistics that would seem to bear out such charges: the three-man *Dirección de Estudios,* for instance, was made up exclusively of *granadinos,* and of Colombia's diplomatic employees abroad in October, 1825, fourteen were *granadinos* and only five Venezuelans.[5] But Santander can easily be forgiven for showing a certain preference for his fellow *granadinos,* with whose merits and capacities he was naturally best acquainted. This was no greater than the preference enjoyed by Venezuelans in the distribution of military commands, and it did not amount to an unvarying rule. In the Colombian cabinet the two portfolios of War and Foreign Affairs were always reserved for Venezuelans; Santander was also careful by and large to include a due number of Venezuelans in the nominations he submitted to Congress *en terna* for posts on the *Alta Corte,* and if Congress tended to make its final decision in favor of *granadinos* it was no fault of his. Actually

[2] *El Anglo-Colombiano* (Caracas), August 3, 1822; *El Venezolano* (Caracas), November 29, 1823; *El Observador Caraqueño,* February 12, 1824.
[3] *La Gaceta de Colombia,* February 8, 1824, September 10, 1826; *Codif. Nac.* VII, 226, 282. On the use of the loan see above, pp. 119-122.
[4] Letter to Pedro Gual, August 14, 1822, A.H.N., Interior y Relaciones CXXI, 180. For similar charges cf. *El Cometa* (Caracas), February 7, 1826.
[5] *Acuerdos* II, 159; *La Gaceta de Colombia,* October 16, 1825.

Congress cannot be blamed either, because experience had shown that Venezuelans were likely to reject even the most attractive appointments if they entailed making the long trip to Bogotá. This brings us to what was really the most valid of all Venezuelan objections to the scheme of central union: the geographical factor of excessive distances compounded by wretched transportation. This one factor was enough to cause Venezuela to be underrepresented in all three branches of government,[6] and lack of representation lent a tone of plausibility to each and every complaint that Venezuelan interests were being neglected at Bogotá. Geography also caused unreasonable delays whenever an official decision on government affairs in Venezuela had to be sought from the highest authorities of the nation. It was to prevent such difficulties as these that some of the Venezuelan deputies at the Congress of Cúcuta had strongly opposed making Bogotá the capital; similar motives were behind the proposal laid before Congress in 1824 to transfer the seat of government to Ocaña, although some liberal *granadinos* backed the move simply out of annoyance over the strength of clerical elements in Bogotá.[7] In the last analysis, however, the concrete grievances of the Venezuelans, whether real or imaginary, are only a partial explanation of their latent hostility toward everything that smacked of Bogotá. Venezuelans had looked upon their neighbors to the west as a band of backward mountaineers even during the colonial regime, and their feelings of superiority increased as a result of the War of Independence. *Caraqueños* insisted that their fair city was the one and only "cradle of liberty;" the *llaneros* insisted just as firmly that they had done the actual fighting almost single-handed. Neither claim, of course, was really justified, but Venezuelans still felt that they were entitled at the very least to an equal voice with New Granada in the management of the nation's affairs; and they were well aware that under a truly centralist regime the *granadinos* by sheer weight of numbers would always have the greater influence.

## Liberalism and Federalism in Caracas

Resentment against the Bogotá administration was always most pronounced at Caracas, which had exchanged its exalted status as head of a Spanish Captaincy-General for that of a mere Colombian departmental capital, subordinated to Bogotá on exactly the same terms as its own former satellites, Maracaibo and Cumaná. Hence as far back as December, 1821, the municipal government of Caracas swore allegiance to the Colombian Constitution only with the reservation that their representatives in Congress must feel free to propose whatever amendments they saw fit.

[6] On the case of Congress, see above, pp. 51-52.
[7] On this general topic cf. *Consideraciones sobre las leyes de repartimiento de bienes nacionales* (Caracas, 1823); *Actas*: Senado-1824, 256, 442-443.

This reservation was deemed frankly seditious by Santander, since it did not carefully specify that any reforms should be carried out under the terms of the constitution itself, which virtually excluded all important changes for a period of at least ten years.[8] However, the *caraqueños* were less inclined to respect the letter of the constitution since Caracas had been under Spanish occupation when deputies for Cúcuta were chosen and thus had not been formally represented in the Constituent Congress. In exactly the same manner the electoral assembly of Caracas province frankly instructed the men it chose for Congress in 1822 to seek some kind of constitutional reform. What it desired was a measure of administrative decentralization; and it was apparently felt that this could be obtained best of all by establishing a federation of three semi-autonomous departments, Venezuela, New Granada, and Quito.[9]

To some extent the federalist leanings of the Caracas area were inspired by doctrinaire political thinking, for Caracas was the most liberal of the larger Colombian cities, and it was a self-evident truth in the 1820's that federalism was the most liberal form of government. The liberals of New Granada had momentarily abandoned their support of federalism, but those of Venezuela, who did not have the same vested interest in the Colombian central administration, could afford to be more consistent. Thus federalism, which had become a strangely conservative force with the followers of Nariño in Bogotá, remained typically liberal in Caracas. On the other hand, Caracas federalists were just like Bogotá federalists in their bitter opposition to the whole Santander regime; and this was especially true of the group of radical zealots who were commonly lumped together by administration spokesmen under the heading of the "Caracas club," the "Caracas cabal," or some other term of mild contempt and abuse.

The most prominent member of this faction was no doubt Colonel Francisco Carabaño, a friend of Bolívar who had spent nearly ten years as an exile in Spain in punishment for his patriot activities; Carabaño seems to have united a very considerable personal popularity with the hallowed status of a patriot martyr, and both assets were fully exploited for the benefit of his party.[10] Then there was Colonel Francis Hall, an English disciple of Jeremy Bentham who was supposed to be making a scientific survey for the Colombian government but instead devoted himself to indoctrinating the *caraqueños* with all the most advanced liberal

[8] Blanco VIII, 235-236, 317-318. Later the municipality insisted it meant the reform should come by legal channels (Blanco VIII, 475-477), but this disclaimer is mildly suspect.

[9] Todd to Secretary of State, October 15, 1822, N.A., Colombia Dispatches I; *El Venezolano*, September 23, 1823; *El Anglo-Colombiano*, July 13 and August 24, 1822.

[10] Eloy G. González, *Dentro de la cosiata* (Caracas, 1907), 205.

theories.¹¹ A rather different element was represented by Tomás Lander and Pedro Pablo Díaz, both of them leading members of the business community. Díaz, Lander and several other chieftains of the "Caracas club" had been conspicuous for the fact that they stayed home and prospered during the Spanish "Pacification." This no doubt argued some lack of patriot fervor, although they certainly cannot be claimed as supporters of Bourbon absolutism: the one form of Spanish rule they had actively favored was the "liberal" and constitutional regime set up following the revolt of Riego in 1820.¹² Finally, one cannot overlook the part played in the same faction by Antonio Leocadio Guzmán, who was destined to become the real father of Venezuelan Liberalism. Guzmán had been brought up in Spain by his royalist family, but he returned to Venezuela a good patriot in 1822; he was promptly befriended by Colonel Carabaño and his associates, and in return he placed his unique gift for irresponsible propaganda fully at their disposal.¹³

The "Caracas club" did not by any means include all leaders of opinion in the Venezuelan capital, but it possessed a very wide appeal nevertheless. Nor is this at all surprising, since its special formula of liberal federalism—or federalist liberalism—was well suited to please both the enlightened minds and the irrational prejudices of central Venezuela. Even when it abandoned liberal orthodoxy, as in its indifference and even hostility toward the abolition of slavery,¹⁴ it was simply reflecting the sentiment of the local creole population. By and large, however, the leaders of the "club" sacrificed their liberal principles less frequently than did Vice-President Santander, who had practical problems to deal with. They naturally made the most of this fact in their various publicity organs, beginning with Col. Hall's *Anglo-Colombiano* in 1822 and finally culminating in *El Argos* of Antonio L. Guzmán. Not only did they paint the centralist form of government as illiberal in itself, but they went on to complain that the system of indirect elections was "aristocratic," that the Constitution of Cúcuta should properly have been submitted to the public for ratification, and that it was a crime against the separation of powers to appoint congressmen to executive and judicial office. The liberal agitators of Caracas were also much more frankly anti-clerical than Santander, whom they repeatedly accused of making a political alliance with the forces of "fanaticism;" thus his decree of 1822 banning certain items of obscene literature was promptly construed as a revival of the hated

---

[11] David Bushnell, "The Development of the Press in Great Colombia," *Hispanic American Historical Review* XXX, 441-442 (November, 1950).

[12] A.C., Actas del Senado (secret sessions), February 3, 1825; *La Gaceta de Caracas*, October 18 and 25, November 8 and 15, 1820.

[13] Pedro Briceño Méndez to Bolívar, December 23, 1825, O'Leary VIII, 185-186.

[14] Cf. *El Cometa*, September 22, 1824.

Inquisition." This charge, to be sure, was almost too extravagant to be believed; but it was fairly typical of a whole line of reasoning that presented Santander as an arbitrary tyrant sitting in viceregal splendor in Bogotá, ruining the nation for the sake of himself and a selfish clique of fellow *granadinos,* and all the while pleasantly inhaling "the aromas of adulation." [15]

It must be noted that Carabaño and several of his colleagues were among the Venezuelan deputies who resolutely refused to take the seats in Congress to which they had been elected, thereby forfeiting an opportunity to resist oppression by deed as well as by word. But in Caracas little if any stigma was attached to such truancy; and in the last analysis the Carabaño faction was just giving unusually vehement expression to sentiments which were shared by a great number of their fellow Venezuelans. Even the difference between *El Argos* and the eminently respectable *Colombiano,* which was published by English commercial interests in Caracas, was one merely of degree. The city council frequently served as an additional sounding-board for the liberal extremists; hence they in turn never ceased to sing the praises of municipal autonomy and to support municipal officers in their quarrels with the intendancy, which legally represented the central authorities. Good relations with the city government were especially valuable to the "club" since it was the municipality that chose juries for the trial of press offenses.[16]

In any case, the anti-government agitation in Caracas caused serious alarm at Bogotá from the very start. Not only did Santander finally remove Col. Hall from Caracas on official business, but he tried to remove Carabaño as well by offering him the job of *Comandante de Armas* in Guayana, an honor which Carabaño quite naturally refused to accept.[17] All attacks on Colombian institutions were promptly and specifically answered by *La Gaceta de Colombia* and also by Vicente Azuero's *Indicación,* whose essays on the Colombian Constitution were publicly endorsed by the *Gaceta.* The arguments of both newspapers were then reprinted throughout New Granada, and in Caracas itself by the semi-official *Iris de Venezuela.* Actual name-calling and mutual recrimination reached its height in 1823, when it was solemnly announced in administration circles that the Caracas liberal faction was dominated by *godos* who were trying to conceal their treasonable intentions behind a smokescreen of exaggerated liberalism. It was not claimed that all Caracas liberals were consciously

---

[15] See especially *El Venezolano,* November 12, 1822, November 29, 1823, and March 20, 1824; *El Anglo-Colombiano,* August 10, 1822; *El Argos,* June 20 and August 14, 1825; *El Cometa,* September 9, 1825.

[16] *El Anglo-Colombiano,* July 13, and August 17, 1822; *El Venezolano,* September 17, 1822, November 1 and 29, 1823; *El Cometa,* September 15, 1824; A.C., Actas del Senado (secret sessions), February 3, 1825.

[17] Santander to Bolívar, July 6, 1823, Lecuna, *C.S.* I, 224.

aiding the cause of the king, but much was made of the fact that their opinions were favorably and prominently featured, in the Puerto Rican press. *La Gaceta de Colombia* likewise took great pains to remind its readers of the activities of Lander, Díaz, *et al.* in royalist-occupied Caracas.[18]

Administration spokesmen rested their case principally, however, upon the vigorous opposition of *El Venezolano*, which was the successor to Hall's *Anglo-Colombiano*, to the expulsion of suspected royalists and *desafectos*. This was a serious issue chiefly because the Department of Venezuela is one of the few places where the expulsion law passed by the Congress of 1823 was taken very seriously. Royalist guerrillas were operating in the mountains east of Caracas, while regular Spanish forces were still stationed within the boundaries of the department at Puerto Cabello; similarly, the reoccupation of Maracaibo by the Spaniards the year before was evidence that they were still capable of offensive action. Hence General Carlos Soublette, who was serving as intendant at the time, attempted to exile all Spaniards who had not actively supported the patriot cause. The measure was perhaps extreme, but it was fully in line with the interpretation placed by Santander on the law that Congress had passed. And as at least one full-fledged member of the "Caracas club" was affected, not to mention numerous friends and relatives, it was only natural that *El Venezolano* should take huge offense. Many others took offense for similar reasons, since the Caracas area contained the largest concentration of European-born Spaniards anywhere in Colombia. The municipality joined wholeheartedly in the campaign, while businessmen pointed out that the sudden deportation of Spanish merchants would create utter confusion in the regional economy. Certainly there was ample reason to proceed with caution, and it is perhaps odd that Soublette did not diminish the severity of his measure even after the recapture of Maracaibo by the patriots in September, 1823. Even so, the Caracas liberals cannot escape blame for the generally irresponsible tone of their criticisms. They may well have been sincerely interested in obtaining justice for oppressed Spaniards, but they were equally interested in embarrassing the Santander administration, and in this they definitely succeeded. The expulsion was only partially carried out; the national government had been forced to take the defensive; and the tirades of *La Gaceta de Colombia* did little to increase Santander's prestige in central Venezuela.[19]

One year later a rather similar issue provided Carabaño and his friends

[18] David Bushnell, "Development of the Press in Great Colombia," *loc. cit.*, 434, 437, 442, and sources cited therein; cf. also *El Iris de Venezuela* (Caracas), October 7, 1822.

[19] *El Anglo-Colombiano*, August 3 and 10, 1822; *El Venezolano*, June 21, October 25, November 1, 8, and 29, December 6, 1823; Soublette report, October 8, 1823, A.C., Senado-26, 330; A.C., Cámara-4, 257-258, 268-279.

with one more fine opportunity to annoy the administration and obstruct the enforcement of its edicts. The immediate point at issue was Santander's provisional decree of August, 1824, for the creation of a national militia organization under the general supervision of the regular army. *El Venezolano* had at length expired, but its spirit survived in *El Cometa,* which attacked the militia decree as one more act of tyranny. The most absurd charges were voiced: it was stated that the decree entailed the creation of a state of martial law—"a military chain" to enslave Caracas— whereas in fact the militiamen would be subject to military authority only when on active duty. The city government gladly joined in, predicting the utter ruin of municipal independence in case its own members should be forced to join the national militia. So much opposition was aroused that the decree simply could not be enforced in Caracas. The new Intendant of Venezuela, General Juan Escalona, tried to effect a compromise by giving the *caraqueños* permission to organize a militia system of their own that was considerably more "liberal" than that of Santander, having popularly-elected officers and other democratic trappings. Unfortunately, Escalona was promptly overruled by the Vice-President, and he received no thanks from the Caracas liberals since he was still nothing but a tool of Bogotá. Instead he was accused of incompetence and worse for having broken the very laws that his critics were urging everyone else to break too, and Santander was sternly rebuked for not dismissing him forthwith. For the present, however, the "Caracas club" had won a sufficient victory. The militia organization in the Caracas vicinity remained in a state of suspension, and when the issue was finally revived in January, 1826, it served as a prelude to armed revolution.[20]

## *The Official Hierarchy*

The political turmoil in the Caracas area was aggravated by the state of disunity existing among the higher authorities of the Department of Venezuela. To begin with, almost the only permanent fixture in the regional government was General José Antonio Páez, whose personal idiosyncrasies were not the best calculated to ensure permanent cooperation with other officials. Páez was the rough *llanero* chieftain who had probably even more to do with the ultimate liberation of Venezuela than Bolívar, but he was also a would-be capitalist who originally made his fortune in large part by speculating in government lands and was trying to increase it, despite heavy gambling expenses, by engaging in both commerce and agriculture. As Fernando Peñalver aptly expressed it, he

[20] *El Cometa,* February 1, 1825; *El Colombiano* (Caracas), November 10, 1824; *El Argos,* June 11, 1825; Briceño Méndez to Páez, December 22, 1824, Blanco IX, 172-174; Santiago Mariño, *Observaciones sobre el reglamento provisional para la guardia cívica* (Caracas, n.d.).

was gradually shifting his love of command from troops of soldiers to herds of cattle and indigo plantations. He was also convincing himself more and more each year that he was a polished gentleman and statesman; and up to a point his vanity was justified, for wealth, authority, and the company of native and foreign men of distinction had necessarily exerted a civilizing influence on him.[21]

Needless to say, all of this heightened Páez' conviction that he had not been granted the power and prestige that he deserved. His sense of hurt developed at least as early as 1821, when Santander was made Vice-President of Colombia, Sucre was sent off to win glory for himself in Ecuador, and Páez was stranded in northern Venezuela with the local command of the forces besieging Puerto Cabello. He was given the additional honor of an appointment as *Comandante General* of the Department of Venezuela, but political command of the same department was entrusted to the intendant, General Carlos Soublette, and the latter was also given a broad provisional authority over all the provinces of colonial Venezuela with the special rank of *Jefe Superior*. In the words of Vicente Lecuna, this arrangement was made because Bolívar wished to leave his homeland in the hands of *un hombre culto,* a definition which admirably fitted the aristocratic Soublette but could not as yet be applied to Páez.[22] No doubt also the Liberator recalled that Páez had not always been amenable to his commands in the past, acting as his equal if not actually his superior in the conduct of war on the *llanos;* but whatever the reasons for the decision, it was hardly agreeable to Páez. The latter was thus ill-prepared psychologically to work with Soublette, and the vagueness of the latter's position as intendant and *Jefe Superior* served inevitably to increase the area of potential disagreement. Concrete wrangling occurred both over questions of military strategy and over affairs of state in which political and military considerations were closely interwoven. A case in point was Páez' open opposition to the expulsion of Spaniards and *desafectos*. Páez may have been influenced in this matter by the propaganda of *El Venezolano,* and he definitely felt that Soublette's zeal in enforcing the expulsion measure would prejudice his own efforts to gain the peaceful surrender of Puerto Cabello. But clearly Páez' attitude is one reason why the expulsion was only partially carried out, and in the process he succeeded in creating a rather sorry display of divided counsels.[23]

[21] Peñalver to Bolívar, May 12, 1826, O'Leary VIII, 396; Richard Bache, *Notes on Colombia* (Philadelphia, 1827), 146.

[22] Vicente Lecuna, ed., Baralt and Díaz, *Resumen de la Historia de Venezuela desde el año de 1797 hasta el de 1830* (2 vols., Bruges, 1939), II, 95, note.

[23] A.C., Senado-26, 331-332; *La Gaceta de Colombia,* July 9, 1826. Cf. Blanco VIII, 510-511.

In due course Soublette handed over the departmental intendancy to the *Marqués* Francisco Rodríguez de Toro, an old-line aristocrat who believed mainly in Bolívar and the status quo. The appointment of Toro was probably intended by Santander as a gesture of appeasement toward Soublette's enemies, who certainly welcomed the change. The new intendant also got along somewhat better with Páez, among other reasons because he was even more anxious to suspend the expulsion of Spaniards. This could not be done at once because Soublette remained on the scene as *Jefe Superior,* or *Director de Guerra* as the position was now called, and vigorously resisted Toro's efforts to take full charge of the expulsion process.[24] However, Soublette soon departed from Venezuela altogether, and his special command was not continued. The final surrender of Puerto Cabello, meanwhile, had made the expulsion of Spaniards almost a dead issue, and Toro was able to devote his energies instead to expelling Rafael Diego Mérida, a good patriot who was nevertheless violently *desafecto* toward the persons of both Bolívar and the *Marqués.* The *affaire* Mérida was enough to occupy Toro during the rest of his administration, for the *Corte Superior del Norte,* not to mention the military commandants of Caracas city and province, did their best to overrule the intendant's orders. It is perhaps significant that Páez himself in this matter did nothing to back up his military subordinates.[25].

In the end the Mérida episode was closed by the intervention of Vice-President Santander, who ordered first one thing and then another, and finally hit upon the happy expedient of naming Mérida as Colombian secret agent in Curaçao.[26] By that time the *Marqués* had also retired to private life, being succeeded by General Juan Escalona. The latter, like Soublette, was essentially a loyal servant of the central administration, so that the intendancy was once more involved in serious friction with the "Caracas club." Escalona was equally unsuccessful in his relations with Páez; but their differences did not actually reach a climax until early in 1826.

In some respects the most responsible of all elements in the official hierarchy of the Department of Venezuela consisted of the jurists of the *Corte Superior del Norte* and the second rank of civil administrators. In this group must be included such men as Cristóbal Mendoza and Francisco Xavier Yanes of the *Corte Superior;* Andrés Narvarte, who served as

[24] Francisco Rodríguez de Toro, *Manifiesto de sus hechos administrativos* (Caracas, 1825), 4-6; Santander to Congress, May 5, 1825, A.C., Senado-26, 336.

[25] *Correspondencia oficial que tuvo lugar entre las autoridades civil y militar sobre los auxilios que pidió la primera . . . contra el Sr. Rafael Diego Mérida* (Caracas, 1824).

[26] Blanco IX, 302, 304; Toro, *op. cit.,* 39-40; Rafael Diego Mérida, *A los colombianos del Norte* (Curaçao, 1825), 4. See also the biographical essay of Jorge Luciani, *El máximo turbulento* (Caracas, 1943).

deputy intendant during the Soublette regime and subsequently was named *fiscal* of the *Corte Superior;* and Fernando Peñalver, the venerable friend and adviser of Bolívar who became governor of the new province of Carabobo in 1824 when Congress separated the whole Valencia area from the province of Caracas. These men were all too independent to form a clearly-defined party, but in general they may be classed as experienced civilian patriots who had joined the emigration to the *llanos* and the Antilles and returned in 1821 to preempt the most distinguished places in both the judiciary and the departmental administration. What is more, they consistently exercised a wholesome influence for moderation against the Guzmán-Carabaño circle. Most of them were willing to say a good word now and then even for the much-maligned Santander.[27]

All this naturally won the moderates or independents—no one term is entirely satisfactory—a considerable amount of ill-will from the liberal extremists. With the intendancy, on the other hand, they were most of the time on reasonably good terms. The chief exception was the brief reign of the Marqués del Toro, who carried on a rather sensational feud with the *Corte Superior.* The latter strongly opposed his effort to deport Rafael Diego Mérida and on another occasion actually fined the intendant $500 for disobeying its orders; but Toro must take his full share of the blame for such wrangling, which was apparently due in part to his own laxity in paying the judges' salaries.[28] With regard to Páez, the court sided against him on the expulsion of *desafectos,* and also when he arbitrarily sought to invoke the military *fuero* on behalf of an army officer accused of violating the law of press offenses. In both instances, however, its stand was a reasonable one; and the court came to his defense when he himself was rather extravagantly accused in 1824 of callous trampling upon the civil prerogatives of the Puerto Cabello city council.[29] There is good evidence, moreover, that a policy of moderation made some appeal even to the Caracas electorate, which did not wholly trust Páez and was apparently losing its patience with the excesses of *El Venezolano* and the like. In October, 1825, the electoral college of Caracas province chose to support Cristóbal Mendoza for Vice-President of Colombia—in opposition, of course, to the reelection of Santander—while Dr. Yanes easily led the field in the vote for Senator.[30]

Yet when all was said and done, the destinies of Venezuela depended

[27] Cf. Peñalver to Bolívar, October 14, 1823 and November 9, 1825, O'Leary VIII, 379, 391; Yanes to Santander, September 7, 1825, O'Leary XI, 419; *El Venezolano,* November 29, 1823.

[28] *El Observador Caraqueño,* January 15 and 29, March 4 and 25, 1824; *El Venezolano,* March 6, 1824; A.C., Cámara-8, 41-45.

[29] Blanco IX, 373-399.

[30] A.H.N., Congresos XXV, 15, 94.

above all upon José Antonio Páez, who with all his faults was still behaving better than many persons had expected. It is true that his actions were a little high-handed at times, and it was seriously alleged in Congress that Venezuelans were simply afraid to speak out in public against the abuses he inflicted upon them;[31] but if this were so, it would have been easy enough to submit an anonymous letter of protest to *El Correo de Bogotá*. Not even in the secret sessions of Congress where these dark hints were made was anything at all presented in the way of concrete evidence. General Páez' conduct is all the more admirable, relatively speaking, when one considers that the disorderly state of Venezuela might have afforded ample pretexts for arbitrary military action. Until November of 1823 there was a Spanish army in Puerto Cabello; there was a persistent state of unrest on the *llanos* to the south; and even after the fall of Puerto Cabello royalist guerrillas remained active in the thinly-settled mountain area east of Caracas. For the latter problem Páez himself was in part to blame if one accepts the thesis later expounded in Bogotá that obstruction of Soublette's drive to rid Venezuela of *desafectos* was a significant contributing factor behind the guerrilla activity. But this view is far from proven, despite minor indications that the guerrillas continued to receive secret aid from royalists in the city of Caracas. Actually there was little need for such aid, since it was not difficult to establish contact with the Spanish Antilles; and even though the guerrilla bands fought in the name of Ferdinand VII, it is probable that their strength was due more to general social unrest than to orthodox royalism.[32] In any case, there was never a really serious threat to the security of the department from local guerrillas, Spanish invaders, Antonio L. Guzmán, or anyone else; and the well-earned military reputation of General Páez is one reason why no such threat developed. This does not mean that everything was peaceful in central Venezuela, but superficially, at least, conditions were gradually improving up to the day when Páez himself threw in his lot with the forces of disorder.

### *Páez, Peña, Guzmán: the Birth of an Unholy Alliance*

For some time the last group that might have been expected to rally behind General Páez was the ultra-liberal "Caracas club." Páez and his associates were at first distinctly hostile to its activities, while such organs as *El Anglo-Colombiano* and *El Venezolano* yielded to no one in their defense of civilian rights against military authority, their hatred of the military *fuero,* and their distrust of everything that smacked even remotely of military oppression. Guzmán himself became a martyr in the eyes of all civilians when he was attacked on the street by a colonel whom he had

---

[31] A.C., Senado-22, 102.
[32] Restrepo VI, 289; A.C., Actas del Senado (secret sessions), February 3, 1825.

offended in one of his articles.³³ It is no doubt significant, however, that the liberal extremists never indulged in personal attacks on Páez, even though he once had one of them prosecuted unsuccessfully under the press law of 1821. This remarkable moderation may have been due in part to a wholesome fear of the *llanero* chieftain; but it is probable that the little band of liberal agitators had always harbored some hope that Páez might be won over as an ally in their private war with Bogotá. They themselves professed to believe that his support was sorely needed as protection against the tyranny of Santander.³⁴ On his own part, Páez had very little directly in common with the liberal faction, but he did have an ambition that could not be fully satisfied under the existing central regime, and a concrete rivalry with its agents Soublette and Escalona.

The first step toward a rapprochement was actually taken by Páez himself as early as 1824 when he named Francisco Carabaño as secretary of the *Comandancia General*.³⁵ It is not clear what, if anything, Páez really meant by the appointment, but still it was an opening wedge. Then, at the end of the year, two minor crises arose that served at least indirectly to hasten his alignment on the side of the extremist faction. The first and less important of the two was set off by a decree of Páez, issued in late November, that declared the Departments of Venezuela and Apure in a state of siege. The principal though not the only reason for this declaration was a rumor about the hostile intent of a French squadron in the Caribbean; hence the state of siege was to have full effect only on receipt of clear evidence of hostility on the part of the French, and with this reservation it obtained the approval of Bogotá. However, it was soon obvious that France intended no harm to Colombia. The administration accordingly gave Páez specific instructions to lift the state of siege if he had not already done so, which he had not. There is no evidence that Páez was seeking to abuse the powers that it gave him, but he had personally felt it advisable to continue the state of siege for a short time longer in view of new outbreaks of disorder within the Department of Venezuela; and even though Santander later reversed himself on the issue, the whole affair obviously gave Páez some offense.³⁶ Not only this, but Páez had more to complain of than just the attitude of Santander, who at most had been slightly tactless in his order to end the state of siege. In Congress the eccentric *caraqueño* oppositionist Father José Antonio Pérez, who disliked the military class in general just as much as

³³ *El Cometa,* October 14, 1825.
³⁴ A.C., Actas del Senado (secret sessions), February 3, 1825; A.C., Senado-22, 104.
³⁵ A.C., Senado-22, 104.
³⁶ *El Constitucional,* February 3, 1825; *El Correo del Magdalena* (Cartagena), June 30, 1825; A.C., Actas del Senado (secret sessions), February 3, 1825; José Antonio Páez, *A sus conciudadanos* (Caracas, 1825), 19.

he disliked Vice-President Santander, had introduced a motion to impeach Páez for declaring martial law without due cause. The motion was supported by one other Venezuelan Congressman and by a handful of *granadinos,* none of whom, be it noted, belonged to the pro-administration bloc. It was then rejected by an overwhelming margin; but the accusation had succeeded in enfuriating Páez, who demanded that Pérez be compelled to prove his charges, and presumably to answer for them if he was unable to. There can be no doubt at all that the incident had much to do with Páez' growing disillusionment with legislative procedures and with civilian politicians in general, especially those in Bogotá.[37]

One reason why continuation of the state of siege had not been entirely unwarranted was the second of the two petty crises that closed out the year 1824. On December 9 the town of Petare on the very outskirts of Caracas was raided by a band of men who went armed with machetes and inspired by the shout of *¡ Viva el Rey y mueran los blancos!* The raiders appear to have been mainly slaves from nearby plantations, who may or may not have been associated with some pre-existing guerrilla band; and certainly the immediate practical effect of the raid was very slight. Far more important was the nation-wide wrangling that the Petare incident indirectly caused. In Caracas, to begin with, it was promptly alleged that the attackers had been in contact with local royalist elements, including certain members of the clergy. At this late date it is impossible to say how much truth there was in the charges, although anti-clericals everywhere seized upon all references to the clergy with unfeigned delight and at least a few arrests were made. General Páez, on the other hand, soon convinced himself that the whole affair had been nothing but a "small commotion," and he went out of his way to advertise this fact for the sake of Caracas' good name. He issued a proclamation just before Christmas in which he praised the city for its loyalty and announced that not one *caraqueño* was suspected of complicity; after the holiday he went on to offer a partial amnesty to the raiders themselves. And despite the fact that he minimized the importance of the incident, he became involved in a bitter dispute with the intendant, General Escalona, over the respective roles of civil and military jurisdiction in carrying on the needed investigations.[38]

This controversy was bad enough, but the agitation in Bogotá was worse. There the Petare incident was magnified far beyond its intrinsic importance, especially as it coincided with minor outbreaks of lawlessness elsewhere in Venezuela. Vice-President Santander asked Congress to grant

[37] A.C., Actas de la Cámara de Representantes, (secret sessions), January 21 and February 3, 1825; *El Constitucional,* June 30, 1825.

[38] *La Cátedra del Espíritu Santo convertida en ataque al Gobierno* (Caracas, 1825) ; *Acuerdos* II, 18; A.C., Actas del Senado (secret sessions), February 3, 1825; Restrepo VI, 292; Blanco IX, 470-471, 482.

him "extraordinary faculties" for dealing with similar incidents in the future, and one of the powers he specifically requested was the right to recruit a Foreign Legion for the maintenance of order in Venezuela. He also requested a special fund for the purpose of assisting right-minded journalists to counteract the propaganda of the "Caracas club." To be sure, there was not a shred of evidence that would show the Caracas liberals had aided the attack on Petare, but they had certainly helped to keep Venezuela in a state of latent political unrest, and administration spokesmen hammered away at the theme that they were at least indirectly responsible for the crime that had been committed. In a secret report to Congress the Secretary of the Interior, José Manuel Restrepo, carefully rehashed all the old charges about *godos* in liberal clothing, and when he came to the crisis of 1823 over expulsion of *desafectos* he even found room to cast some aspersions on the loyalty of Páez. The Secretary of War, General Pedro Briceño Méndez, was slightly more discreet in his own confidential report to the legislators; after all, he was himself a Venezuelan. However, he expounded at length on the possibility that the Petare raid had been engineered not by any known guerrilla band but rather by some "hidden hand" in the city of Caracas, and he lent his full support to the request for "extraordinary faculties." [39]

In the Senate there was from the start a general willingness to give the administration what it wanted. Francisco Soto was actually more inclined to proceed with caution than was the usually level-headed Jerónimo Torres of Popayán; among the Senators who were most anxious for vigorous action were Luis Andrés Baralt and Antonio M. Briceño, both from the Department of Zulia, and Father Ramón Ignacio Méndez, who represented the Department of Venezuela. The Chamber of Representatives, as might have been expected, was harder to convince. At first it insisted that the main cause of unrest in Venezuela was simply the abuse of power by subordinate officials, no doubt including José Antonio Páez. At long last, however, on March 10, 1825, Santander was duly voted his summary powers for the handling of armed rebels and conspirators. The clause about a Foreign Legion was omitted, since the administration had withdrawn its request on that point. The scheme for press subsidies (to cost $50 a month) apparently was not yet mentioned in public, but it definitely was approved.[40]

After so much excitement in Congress it is slightly ironical to note

[39] *Acuerdos* II, 17; Santander to Congress, January 28, 1826, *La Gaceta de Colombia*, July 9, 1826; A.C., Actas del Senado (secret sessions), February 3, 1825.

[40] A.C., Actas del Senado (secret sessions), February 4 and 14, and March 1, 1825; Actas de la Cámara de Representantes (secret sessions), January 31, February 19, 23, and 25, and March 7, 1825; Senado-22, 95, 100-105; Cámara-5, 141-146; *Codif. Nac.* VII, 256-258.

that Santander never seems to have used a single one of the powers he was granted.⁴¹ The long-range importance of the Petare debate, in fact, must be found in the impression which it caused in Caracas. And that impression was distinctly unfavorable. The "Caracas club," needless to say, was particularly offended, for it had enough friends in Bogotá to keep informed of everything that went on; it even obtained a copy of one of the many confidential reports that had been handed about in the course of the debate, and it published the document in *El Cometa* to the extreme annoyance of Santander.⁴² It would also appear that *caraqueños* in general were somewhat angry at the fuss made over the Petare incident, for it did not reflect very favorably upon their province, and they also disliked "extraordinary faculties" on general principle. Their representatives in the lower house had solidly opposed the grant despite the fact that they did not normally vote as a unit. The city council issued a formal protest of its own in which it expressed perhaps its greatest indignation over the provisions exempting clergymen from the death penalty for conspiracy and offering a reward to any slaves who would report on the subversive activities of their masters.⁴³

Moreover, it is unlikely that Páez enjoyed the spectacle of Santander and Congress feverishly taking measures for the preservation of law and order in his own bailiwick, even though he would presumably have been called upon to carry them out had the need arisen. The resurrection of the old expulsion issue can hardly have pleased him either, although it is possible that the more pointed remarks of Secretary Restrepo, which were addressed to the Senate only, were never brought to his attention. At the very least it was obvious that Páez' efforts to play down the Petare incident had been politely ignored, and he naturally blamed his rival Escalona for creating the state of alarm in Bogotá. His annoyance over the handling of the whole affair was naturally increased when he received a message from the Secretary of War supporting the intendant in the jurisdictional dispute that had arisen during the original investigation of the December 9 attack.⁴⁴

The Petare affair together with its aftermath was thus one more reason for the growing rift between Páez and the Santander regime that marked the year ·1825. There was not yet an open break or anything of

⁴¹ For a statement to this effect on the press clause, see *La Gaceta de Colombia*, November 27, 1825.

⁴² *El Cometa*, February 17, 1826; *La Gaceta de Colombia*, October 30, 1825.

⁴³ Municipalidad de Caracas, *Firme defensa de la ley fundamental* (Cartagena, 1825); *Revista Semanal* (Caracas), February 25, 1826. About the only defender of the Petare decree in Caracas was the English-managed *Colombiano* (cited in Blanco X, 13).

⁴⁴ Páez, *A sus conciudadanos*, 3-4, 18; *El Correo del Magdalena*, June 30, 1825; Briceño Méndez to Bolívar, April 26, 1826, O'Leary VIII, 197.

the sort, but there is every reason to believe that he was losing whatever respect he had felt for the constitutional order as represented by the Executive and Congress in Bogotá. If anything, it is surprising that this had not happened even sooner. Páez was still at heart a Venezuelan army officer from the *llanos,* and he could not entirely escape the prejudices that colored the thinking of his class when he saw the Vice-President and his associates whittling away at the *fuero,* making a martyr of Colonel Infante, and relentlessly upholding the supremacy of the civil authorities even in the concrete case of Escalona *vs.* Páez. Actually some of the severest critics of Páez in Bogotá were not friends of Santander at all, but it is unlikely that the general grasped these fine distinctions. They were civilian politicians, and that was bad enough. Páez was no doubt also subject to feelings of personal jealousy toward Santander; and in case he needed further arguments to show him that Santanderean liberalism was the enemy, Dr. Miguel Peña returned to Venezuela toward the middle of 1825 to supply them, attaching himself almost at once to the fortunes of General Páez. At the same time the Guzmán-Carabaño faction increased its own efforts to win Páez' favor: *El Cometa* suggested that he would make an excellent candidate for Vice-President in the next national elections, while Guzmán's *Argos* proclaimed that Páez himself was the "true liberator" of Venezuela. For good measure Guzmán also prepared a warm journalistic welcome for Dr. Peña, although apparently for some reason Carabaño was less enthusiastic about his arrival.[45]

Before the year was out Páez had made his first great misstep by writing to Bolívar, urging him to join a holy crusade against the "lawyers and merchants" who were out to ruin the *"pobres militares"* and against the wicked congressmen who "seek to reduce us to the condition of slaves." This tirade culminated in the frank suggestion that Bolívar could do much worse than imitate the example of Napoleon, which could only be a thinly veiled proposal to overthrow the existing regime in favor of some kind of monarchy.[46] Exactly who thought up the idea for this letter probably will never be known,[47] although Páez' authorship is fully established despite his later attempt to deny it. It is perfectly possible that the original inspiration came not from Páez or any other military leader but from Peña and/or the leaders of the "Caracas club," who were lawyers, merchants, and intriguing civilian politicians almost to a man;

[45] *El Argos,* August 4 and 14, 1825; *El Cometa,* June 22, 1825.
[46] Páez to Bolívar, October 1, 1825, O'Leary II, 57-60.
[47] The difficulty of establishing the origin of the scheme can be seen by contrasting such views as that expressed by *El Cometa,* February 17, 1826, which would trace it to the moderates who dominated the electoral college of 1825, and that of Pedro Briceño Méndez, who in a letter to Bolívar, December 20, 1826 (O'Leary VIII, 221), gives a highly romantic explanation involving a Polish Baron and the Holy Alliance.

as a group they were definitely in favor of the project, and it was the 22-year-old Guzmán who was chosen to present one of the two copies of the message personally to Bolívar in Lima.[48] The *pobre militar* Páez was apparently unable to see anything illogical in the company he was keeping.

It was no less odd, at first glance, for Guzmán and his allies suddenly to drop their vociferous liberalism in favor of a try at monarchy. Their about-face is particularly interesting in view of the fact that they had just been waging a press campaign in opposition to the expected reelection of Bolívar as president for the term beginning in January, 1827. Ostensibly they felt that as long as Bolívar was away in Peru the presidency ought to be given instead to someone who was on the spot to exercise it; otherwise the government might fall again into the hands of Vice-President Santander.[49] The obvious retort to such reasoning was that by the start of 1827 Bolívar could easily have come back—as actually turned out to be the case. In fact there is some reason to doubt the professions of respect for the Liberator that invariably accompanied all attacks on his reelection. The innate provincialism of the Caracas liberal leaders, which had led *El Cometa* to insinuate that Colombia should not waste her men and money on freeing Peru under Bolívar's leadership, was a factor making against any sincere *bolivianismo,* and the liberal faction may have been aware of the strong dislike Bolívar had recently expressed toward their own activities.[50] The precise reasons for the anti-reelectionist movement, however, can only be guessed at; it was probably as much a mere propaganda gesture as anything else. It did not hinder the liberal zealots from devoting their more serious attention to the coming struggle for the vice-presidency, in which they backed now Páez and now Carabaño, whose candidacy was recommended by *El Argos* on the basis of "his intense love for liberty, his popularity, his absolute disinterestedness, his superior talents, his valour. . . ."[51] When disinterestedness led *"El Justo Carabaño"* to suggest Pedro Briceño Méndez instead, the latter was also placed on the list of candidates.[52]

It is no doubt vaguely possible that the "Caracas club" had been opposing Bolívar for President simply because it now wanted him for Emperor instead, but an even likelier explanation for the apparent inconsistencies in the Caracas liberals' attitude toward Bolívar is that a

---

[48] Páez to Bolívar, October 21, 1825, O'Leary II, 60-61; González, *Cosiata,* 13; cf. Francisco Ribas to Bolívar, November 7, 1825, O'Leary II, 336.

[49] *El Cometa,* September 9 and October 14, 1825; *El Argos,* January 20 (citing *El Vigía de Puerto Cabello)* and August 1, 1825.

[50] Cf. Bolívar to Santander, May 8, 1825, Lecuna *C.L.* IV, 322.

[51] *El Argos,* August 1, 1825; *El Argos Republicano de Cumaná,* August 7, 1825 (citing *El Vigía de Puerto Cabello).*

[52] *El Argos (extraordinario),* October 4, 1825.

basic insincerity always underlay it. Their one unvarying objective was to embarrass and potentially to disrupt the Bogotá administration, and all their activities, including endorsement of the Páez letter, admirably served this end. In any case, they helped to get the monarchist scheme off to an excellent start. It was also supported, however, by numerous Venezuelan military leaders, including General Santiago Mariño, who ranked second in local importance only to Páez.[53] Another valuable conquest was General Briceño Méndez, who was neither a crony of Páez nor a sworn foe of Santander. Briceño had strongly criticized the Caracas liberals as Secretary of War at the time of the Petare incident. His principal loyalty was simply to Bolívar; and when he stopped off in Venezuela before journeying to Panama as delegate to the Inter-American Congress of 1826 he convinced himself that Páez' proposal was the only way to escape "the pretensions of some classes of our society . . . our legislative anarchy," and so forth. He rejoiced that the scheme offered at last a bridge of union between respectable elements and the Caracas "Jacobins," who by their acceptance of the monarchist formula had apparently shown a disposition to mend their ways.[54] For a time Páez may even have nourished the delusion that he could win the personal support of Santander, for whom he still had kind words on occasion,[55] but if he had any serious hopes on this score he had certainly lost all sense of Colombian political realities. For that matter, Bolívar firmly rejected the proposal too.

## The Other Venezuelan Departments

By and large it was always the Caracas area that gave most worry to the Santander administration, but the final outcome of General Páez' political evolution must be considered in a later chapter. In the meantime it is necessary to look briefly at the assorted difficulties that plagued other sections of Venezuela. These difficulties, it is true, have many points of resemblance with the turmoil existing in and about Caracas, and most of them have been touched on elsewhere in this study as part of the military, the racial, or some other general "problems." Even so, it is well to bring all the symptoms of unrest together in a short recapitulation in order to emphasize the fact that the "Venezuelan problem," applying the term now to the whole area of the former Captaincy-General, was in many respects the gravest of them all. It is well to keep in mind, moreover, that outside Caracas there was less of the tendency to blame everything that was wrong on Santander simply as a matter of general principle.

[53] Mariño to Bolívar, October 21, 1825, O'Leary II, 460.
[54] Briceño to Bolívar, December 23, 1825, O'Leary VIII, 184-185.
[55] Restrepo VI, 392; *El Constitucional*, June 8, 1826, citing Páez letter of November 19, 1825.

The other Venezuelans were more likely to have a concrete reason for their grievances, and some of them disliked Caracas quite as much as Bogotá.

The most tranquil area of Venezuela was undoubtedly the Department of Zulia, at least after the recapture of Maracaibo in 1823. It is significant that this area had been subject to Bogotá in the colonial period even while Caracas was a dependency of Santo Domingo, and that the Andean sections, such as Mérida, were socially very similar to the adjoining parts of New Granada. Families on one side of the border usually had close connections on the other; that of Santander is no exception.[56]

Conditions were not as peaceful on the Venezuelan side as they were over in the Department of Boyacá, but there was nothing to become really alarmed about. At most there were occasional vague reports of royalist guerrilla activity, which the administration blamed as usual on the laxity of local officials in expelling Spaniards and *desafectos*.[57] Actually the royalists may have been common bandits, although it is probable that the reports were partially justified: both Maracaibo and Coro had been royalist strongholds during the War of Independence. However, whatever royalist feeling still existed certainly did not pose a major threat to Colombian security. There was nothing like the ultra-liberal "Caracas club" to assist local royalists in the creation of unrest, and the long-standing jealousy of western Venezuela towards the turbulent city of Caracas was in itself a force operating in favor of law and order.

The state of affairs was more serious on the *llanos* that stretched south and east from Zulia all the way to Guayana, cutting across departmental boundaries. The *llanos* were the main center of the veterans' unrest that has been discussed in detail in the preceding chapter; they were also one focus of the antagonism between whites and non-whites that had been creating tension in Venezuela since before 1810. As the *llanero* veterans were usually of mixed blood, the two forms of unrest naturally tended to merge. On the other hand, despite persistent rumors that a major war between the races was about to break out, the immediate problem on the *llanos* was simply a wave of banditry, and by the early part of 1825 the worst was definitely over.[58] General Páez had done his part by revisiting the area to urge better conduct upon his former comrades-at-arms.[59] It is sufficient to repeat here that the basic causes of unrest, eco-

[56] Luis Eduardo Pacheco, *La familia de Santander* (3rd ed., Cúcuta, 1940).
[57] A.H.N., Interior y Relaciones CXXI, 20, 23.
[58] See above, pp. 279-281.
[59] Restrepo VI, 288. It should be noted that in the greater part of the *llanos* Páez had no direct legal authority. Both Apure and Barinas had originally been part of the Department of Venezuela, of which he was *Comandante General*, but the fall of Puerto Cabello had no sooner left Páez free to devote some attention to them than they were formed into the separate Department of Apure by the Congress of 1824.

nomic and otherwise, had by no means been eradicated, and they were easily sufficient to disturb the peace once again whenever the occasion should arise.

For the present, the most serious disturbances of all were in the easternmost Department of Orinoco, the major part of which lay outside the *llanos* proper. However, the same problems of racial tension and unemployed veterans contrived to create a condition of latent unrest. They were supplemented by at least a few authenticated intrigues on the part of Spanish agents, and also by serious regional and personal rivalries. Guayana was unhappy to be subjected to the departmental authorities at Cumaná, and kept up a vigorous stream of protests until the Congress of 1826 finally transferred the province to the Department of Apure. There was a similar separatist movement in the island-province of Margarita, which wanted to be dependent directly on Caracas; Cumaná, in turn, resented the fact that the Spanish government had made Guayana the seat of the ecclesiastical diocese to which they both belonged. In addition to all of this, the dominant figure at Cumaná was the *Comandante General*, José Francisco Bermúdez, who was not without his good points but had unfortunately inherited numerous personal antipathies from his service in the critical years of 1816-21. He apparently possessed a knack for creating new antagonisms also, especially in Guayana and Margarita.[60]

With so many elements of unrest at hand, it is hardly surprising that Orinoco was the scene of intermittent bandit activities, racial disorders, and minor conspiracies, all reaching a climax in the year 1824 thanks to the unpopularity of military conscription for the last stages of the war in Peru. In Guayana there arose a plot apparently designed to set off a mutiny among recruits gathered at Angostura and then carry out a general massacre of whites. There is no conclusive proof that bona fide Spanish agents were involved, but there is no reason to doubt the word of the local commander, Colonel José Manuel Olivares, to the effect that the ringleaders were trying to play upon the conscripts' ingrained fear of service in foreign parts. Fortunately the plot was discovered just in time, and the two main culprits were summarily put to death on the very day they were found out.[61]

The conscription issue also caused ill-defined disorders and guerrilla activities in the province of Barcelona, but the worst trouble of all occurred in Margarita, taking the form of an island-wide strike against military

[60] A.C., Senado-17, 396-397; Cámara-13, 206-207; A.H.N., Congresos IX, 817-819, 907-908. Soublette described Bermúdez as possessing a "genio desorganizador." (Letter to Bolívar, January 20, 1826, O'Leary VIII, 38).

[61] Restrepo VI, 289; A.C., Cámara-1, 468-472.

service outside the province. The *margariteños* had already acquired a reputation for insubordination of this sort, and their attitude was not entirely unjustified. The island was sparsely settled, it had lost many of its inhabitants since the war began, and its able-bodied men might always be needed at home to guard against a possible Spanish attack by sea. Both in 1819 and 1821 the islanders flatly refused to aid Bolívar's schemes for the conquest of Caracas, and both times they got away with it. Then, to make matters worse, after 1821 the island entered upon a period of difficult economic readjustment. It had prospered in colonial times by smuggling and during the war by privateering; but now the island's prize court was transferred to La Guaira and the regional *Comandancia de Marina* was set up at Cumaná, so that the importance of Margarita as a maritime center sharply declined. Thus when General Bermúdez in 1824 asked for a mere 100 troops to swell Bolívar's armies in Peru, all the local discontent broke out again worse than ever. Supported by the local garrison, which was itself composed of *margariteños*, the inhabitants simply refused to obey his orders.[62]

Since it was impossible to punish an entire province for rebellion, Santander had to authorize a policy of leniency. He did insist on the punishment of ringleaders, but they were far too prominent on the island, and this was never done. The islanders ultimately returned to at least outward allegiance to Bermúdez. Yet at the same time they thought it best to forestall any later retribution by sending Congress an elaborate petition in which they detailed their assorted complaints against Bermúdez and specifically asked for the transfer of their province to the Department of Venezuela, the establishment of a local prize court, the right to keep all their recruits for service on the island, and, finally, special economic relief in the form of tariff concessions. Congress listened attentively, and agreed to grant the last two measures. Santander, however, regarded the petition itself as a new sign of insubordination. He thus vetoed the concessions, suggesting merely that the islanders might be drafted for service in the navy, and adding that they should never be allowed to form their own military garrison under any circumstances lest they be able to revolt as easily again. As the Senate would not override Santander's veto, and as Congress did not act on his own suggestions either, nothing at all was done. The matter was taken up once more a year later when the *margariteños* repeated all their demands to Congress, claiming that they were now more terrified than ever at the prospect of Bermúdez' vengeance. A new bill for economic aid was taken under consideration, but it was never

[62] Mariano de Briceño, *Historia de la Isla de Margarita* (Caracas, 1885), 181-184; Restrepo VI, 289-291; A.C., Cámara-5, 105; A.C., Senado-30, 255-257.

passed. The islanders thus bided their time until they might have another opportunity for direct action, and meanwhile they gave vent to their feelings by supporting Páez for president and Carabaño for vice-president in the national elections of 1825-6.[63]

---

[63] A.C., Actas del Senado (secret sessions), March 10 and April 11, 1825; Actas de la Cámara (secret sessions), January 25, February 17, March 9, and April 20, 1825; Senado-30, 255-259; A.H.N., Corresp.-Cámara, February 3, 1825 (Interior) and April 29, 1825 (Hacienda).

Chapter XIX

*The Plight of Ecuador*

OUTSIDE of Venezuela there was just one other region with acute local problems that deserve separate consideration. This was the other extreme of the republic, Ecuador, where for the present discontent took the form mainly of simple frustration rather than the violence of word and deed that was so typical of Venezuela. The contrast no doubt reflects a difference between the passive Indian majority of Ecuador, which sought to live off to itself as much as possible, and the *pardos, mestizos,* and the like of Venezuela, who were perfectly willing to assert themselves when they took a mind to it; it also reflects a difference that is somewhat harder to define between the upper creole minorities of the two regions. A superficial resignation, however, could not conceal the fact that Ecuadoran grievances were actually far more real than those of Venezuela, and Ecuador was not lacking in elements of potential unrest that could become serious indeed once outside events brought matters to a head.

Ecuador is the part of Gran Colombia where regional unrest admits most easily of an economic interpretation. It has already been pointed out that the opening of Pacific ports to direct trade with Spain during the late colonial period dealt a serious blow to the primitive textile manufacturing of highland Ecuador, and the War of Independence dealt another with its frequent disruption of the normal routes of trade. This was particularly serious for the commerce between Quito and the minefields of western New Granada, which were cut off even after Pichincha by the royalist uprisings of Pasto. A third and final blow was the tariff policy of Gran Colombia, which was far more consistently liberal when Ecuadoran industry stood to suffer than it was when the interests of Venezuelan agriculture were at stake.[1] In any case, the troubles of Ecuadoran manufacturing naturally affected other interests as well. They were cited by the municipality of Quito as the root cause of all the region's economic problems. Landowners argued convincingly, with the support of the town fathers of both Quito and Latacunga, that they could not support the load of clerical *censos* on their estates because lack of specie had depressed the prices of agricultural and pastoral productions; and the lack of specie they ascribed to the decline of manufacturing and commerce. Whatever shortage of specie existed, needless to say, was merely an outward symptom of the more basic problem. Nor was the disruption

[1] See above, pp. 152-155.

of trade routes the only burden imposed on the Ecuadoran economy by the War of Independence. There was less actual fighting and destruction than there had been in Venezuela, but military conscription and forced loans still took their toll. The Liberators from the North liked to remind Ecuador how much longer Venezuela and New Granada had been making the same sacrifices, but Ecuador soon made up for lost time, footing roughly three-fourths of the bill for Colombia's share in the final liberation of Peru. About the only really bright spot in the economic picture was the cacao industry of Guayaquil, which was still in reasonably good shape and was able to benefit from a trend of increasing export prices.[2]

The situation might have been eased somewhat if the central authorities had taken a direct interest in Ecuadoran affairs, but usually they did not. In fact as long as Ecuador remained under the direct rule of Bolívar with his "extraordinary faculties" there was very little that Santander could do about Ecuador even if he desired. When Bolívar moved on to Peru he left the Ecuadoran departments under the special command of his own deputy, General Bartolomé Salom, who was to enjoy exactly the same broad powers. Only after the middle of 1825, when the Peruvian war was ended, was constitutional normalcy completely established. To be sure, the setting up of a separate administration for Ecuador under the regime of "extraordinary faculties" had certain obvious advantages, for it permitted a delay in enforcing the more objectionable features of the new customs legislation and also delayed various minor evils of union with Gran Colombia such as the *contribución directa*. It postponed the reestablishment of the tobacco monopoly in Guayaquil, where it had been abolished by the independent junta and was never restored by Bolívar. From the viewpoint of the creole minority, at least, the continuation of the Indian tribute by an emergency decree of Bolívar was still another benefit.[3]

However, the special status enjoyed by Ecuador was not an unmixed blessing. Bolívar's decision to charge higher duties on both imports and exports than those decreed at Cúcuta helped the treasury and helped those producers who were in need of protection, but it hurt exporters and it hurt all consumers. The treasury alone could benefit from the Liberator's refusal to carry out the abolition of the *alcabala*.[4] Finally, Bolívar inflicted on Ecuador his own unique version of the salt monopoly, which was far worse than that existing elsewhere in Colombia. Heretofore the saltworks at Guayaquil had been operated privately, and only a moderate

[2] A.C., Senado-4, 288-289; O'Leary XIX, 466 and XX, 225-226; *El Patriota de Guayaquil*, September 25, 1824; Carlos Cortés Vargas, *Participación de Colombia en la libertad del Perú* (3 vols., Bogotá, 1924) III, 368 and *passim*.
[3] O'Leary XX, 245-247; *Codif. Nac.* VII, 293; A.H.N., Corresp.-Cámara (Hacienda) March 17, 1825; *El Patriota de Guayaquil*, February 25, 1826.
[4] Bolívar to Santander, September 23, 1822, Lecuna, *C.L.* III, 95-96.

tax was paid to the state; but now Bolívar increased the tax and granted the exclusive right of distributing salt for four years to a group of Guayaquil merchants who agreed to pay $51,000 a year in return. The scheme was simple, it offered an assured cash return to the government, and the Liberator needed funds right away to pursue the war in Peru. Unfortunately, he was no economist to unravel in advance all the consequences of the measure. He simply earmarked the first two years' revenue for military expenses, and assigned the rest to the worthy end of road construction. And he did increase the salt revenues very considerably. But he allowed the contractors to make an exorbitant profit for themselves, amounting possibly to over 100%, and the result was a huge increase in the price of salt. The price was more than doubled at the salt-works, and at Quito it rose more sharply still. The "scandalous" salt monopoly thus worked a serious hardship on both pastoral interests and general consumers, and it was regularly lamented as one of the main burdens afflicting oppressed Ecuador.[5]

In recognition of Ecuadoran sacrifices in the later stages of the war Santander did finally obtain from Congress a decree providing that the sum owed by Peru to Colombia for war debts should be used in large part to pay government creditors in Ecuador.[6] However, Peru did not pay her debts, so the Ecuadorans had to take their chances for payment out of the inadequate resources already on hand in Colombia. Neither did they receive their due share of the one financial bonanza actually received by Colombia, the English loan of 1824. The agricultural development program, for instance, included only $20,000 specifically appropriated for Ecuador, and it is not clear whether even that much really got there.[7] Indeed it must be said that Ecuador had far more reason than Venezuela to complain of neglect on the part of Santander's administration, which offered sympathy but not much else even after the Ecuadoran departments were finally brought under its direct control. José Manuel Restrepo advised the Ecuadorans to overcome their manufacturing crisis by the adoption of European machinery, but he left them to obtain it all by themselves. Proposals for the introduction of vicuña-raising, the development of mineral deposits, and all varieties of economic assistance were met with the stock laissez faire argument that these were very laudable projects but that they should be undertaken by private initiative without official

[5] There is an unfortunate lack of reliable statistical data on this transaction, and there is no reason to take seriously reports that would imply an increase in salt prices at Quito of over ten times. The most informative *expediente* on the subject can be found in A.H.N., Congresos XXV, 775-788; see also *La Gaceta de Colombia*, April 1, 1827.

[6] *La Gaceta de Colombia*, January 8 and March 12, 1826; *Codif. Nac.* II, 203-204.

[7] A.C., Senado-43, 315.

action.⁸ Santander joined in the chorus of protest against Bolívar's salt monopoly; but as it had been set up by legal contract he merely referred the matter to Congress. The lower house then adopted a bill rescinding the contract, but the Senate refused to go along, feeling that the move violated sacred rights of private property.⁹

The Ecuadorans presented certain other demands that did not evoke even the vague sympathy of the administration but aroused instead its strongest opposition. The demand for outright tariff protection of industry was of course one of these, but even less agreeable was the campaign of the Quito aristocracy against all the liberal economic reforms that had been enacted since 1821 and were finally applied in Ecuador by the end of 1825 at the latest. The chief spokesman for this campaign was the frankly reactionary *Colombiano del Ecuador,* which assailed the *contribución directa* as worse than the *alcabala,* complaining that even with a personal exemption of only $50 the masses would give nothing at all. The same organ feared that abolition of the Indian tribute could only mean the imposition of unreasonable burdens on the white population, and dismissed the manumission of Negro slaves as "arms taken away from agriculture and applied to idleness and vice." ¹⁰ For such arguments as these, needless to say, the leaders of Santanderean liberalism had only contempt.¹¹

Although economic grievances always made up the greater part of the "Ecuadoran problem," they were not the only concrete grounds for complaint. To begin with, Ecuador to an even greater extent than Venezuela was underrepresented in all the branches of government at Bogotá. Because of such obstacles as Andean geography and unfriendly *pastusos,* there was virtually no one to speak for Ecuador when the first regular Congress began work in 1823, and there were always many more absentees in the Congressional delegation of Ecuador than in that of New Granada. No Ecuadoran ever was chosen for the cabinet or the *Alta Corte;* and of the Colombian diplomats abroad in October, 1825, not one was from Ecuador.¹² This neglect was no doubt due in part to the fact that Ecuador was originally separated from the direct control of the Santander administration, but from 1825 on there was little excuse for it, and it was tactless to say the least. Nor did Ecuador, like Venezuela, make up for its reduced voice in civil affairs by engrossing an extra share of high positions

⁸ *La Gaceta de Colombia,* October 1, 1826, and April 15, 1827.
⁹ A.H.N., Congresos XXV, 775; A.C., Actas del Senado, April 1 and 20, 1826.
¹⁰ *El Colombiano del Ecuador,* November 2, 1825; *La Bandera Tricolor* (Bogotá), November 12, 1826, citing the former.
¹¹ Cf. *La Bandera Tricolor,* October 1, November 12 and 19, 1826.
¹² *La Gaceta de Colombia,* October 16, 1825.

in the army: there was not one Ecuadoran general in active service, and Ecuadoran colonels were few and far between.[13] Ecuadoran officers had had little chance to accumulate military seniority until the Colombian Army of Liberation appeared on the scene in 1821-22, and by that time the commanding positions were already taken.

Quito in particular, like Caracas in Venezuela, had reason to "feel herself reduced from her ancient dignity" [14] by the mere fact of joining the centralized state of Gran Colombia. Cuenca and Guayaquil, which had been subordinate provinces of the colonial Presidency of Quito, were now erected into separate and equal departments: the "Department" of Ecuador comprised only the part that was left over. The *quiteños* were even more annoyed, it would seem, over the fact that their *Corte Superior* was deprived of the jurisdiction that the *Audiencia* of Quito had previously exercised over the greater part of what was now the Department of Cauca. The original intention of the Congress of Cúcuta had been to retain the traditional judicial connection, but no sooner had an appeal court been established at Quito than the Pasto rebellions came along to disrupt regular communications with Popayán. As a result Congress had to decree that appeals from the Cauca should be taken on a provisional basis to the *Corte Superior del Centro* in Bogotá; and this system was continued even after the reasons for it had largely disappeared. It was continued, in fact, until still another *Corte Superior* was established in Popayán itself.[15]

As long as the *quiteños* were unable to retain their old judicial district in its entirety they hoped for a time that they might recoup at least part of their loss by the outright annexation of the province of Pasto and the adjoining coastal strip of Barbacoas to the Department of Ecuador. By this measure the extreme South of New Granada would have been subjected to Quito in political as well as judicial administration. The demand was not unprecedented by any means, for Bolívar had briefly done just what the *quiteños* were asking by virtue of his emergency war powers; furthermore, the territory in dispute still belonged to the ecclesiastical diocese of Quito, and many of the principal landowners there were Ecuadorans. The *pastusos* themselves were not entirely averse to taking their legal business to Quito, and a few of them openly supported full political annexation. But those who opposed either full or partial amalgamation were just as numerous, and as usual the Ecuadorans pleaded in vain. Santander disapproved, and a bill in Congress to add just one canton

[13] *El Conductor* (Bogotá), February 6 and 20, 1827.
[14] A.C., Senado-42, 35; the quotation is from Intendant José F. Valdivieso.
[15] *Codif. Nac.* I, 143, 341-342; VII, 75, 105.

of the province of Pasto to the Department of Ecuador apparently got no farther than second reading.[16] What all the assorted grievances of Ecuador added up to was a vague sense of being just a subject people, disposed of at the whim of Venezuelans and *granadinos*. For some time, as a matter of fact, the description of Ecuador as a conquered territory was almost literally true. It would be unfair to minimize the part played by Ecuadoran troops in the liberation of their homeland, but certainly their commanders were almost all of them drawn from other sections of Colombia. These foreign liberators then proceeded to monopolize both civil and military commands in Ecuador and to treat the Ecuadoran inhabitants more or less as they saw fit. There was obvious need for a strong military authority at first both to consolidate the new regime and to mobilize Ecuadoran resources for the speedy completion of the war in Peru; but Colombian rule still appeared rather high-handed to the Ecuadorans. Bolívar himself remarked that in Ecuador

". . . everything has been violence upon violence. The fields, the cities have been left bare to take 3000 men and to take out 200 thousand pesos. I know better than anyone how far violence can go, and all of it has been used." [17]

Such conditions quite naturally created a state of tension between the local authorities and Colombian commanders, of which the best illustration is the open conflict that occurred in January, 1823, between the municipality of Quito and the departmental intendant, Col. Vicente Aguirre. The latter was one of the few Ecuadoran patriots to attain prominence in the new government, but his success was due to the fact that he had attached himself vigorously to the cause of Bolívar, and his attitude was essentially that of a Colombian military leader. His troubles began when the Quito city council asked for a reduction in the daily contribution of $50 that had been levied for the support of militia units in the local garrison. The plea was justified on the basis that the garrison itself had been curtailed in size, and it was accompanied by a request for general information on the use of the public revenues. Aguirre simply replied that the town fathers were being unpatriotic and should henceforth mind their own business. The city replied in turn that the Spaniards had published fiscal accounts every two weeks, but this argument was no doubt considered even more unpatriotic. This dispute was complicated by the fact that Aguirre simultaneously backed up a demand of the *Corte Superior* that the municipal authorities stop spending so much money on

[16] A.C., Senado-42, 33-42; Senado-49, 22-26, 29-31; Cámara-6, 192-193; A.H.N., Congresos XXV, 311-313.
[17] Bolívar to Santander, April 15, 1823, Lecuna *C.L.* III, 168.

candles for religious ceremonies; presumably the money should be used instead for maintenance of the army. Aguirre's official secretary, who was a colonel from New Granada, finally came forth with a note that accused the municipality of harboring seditious notions of Ecuadoran separatism, sprinkling his message for good measure with assorted insults. Two days later, on January 20, 1823, Aguirre ordered the military to arrest three members of the city government, who were promptly hustled off to Bolívar's headquarters.[18]

In due course the *Corte Superior* handed down its own ruling to the effect that Aguirre had committed no punishable act in his treatment of the municipality. On the other hand, the court included in its decision some severe criticism of the intendant, whom it squarely blamed for initiating the row,[19] and in this the court undoubtedly reflected the sentiments of most other *quiteños*. It need hardly be added that the ill-will engendered by the conflict was a long time in dying down. It produced, among other things, an unsuccessful campaign on the part of the municipality to have Aguirre impeached by the Congress at Bogotá. Bolívar himself now lost all patience whatsoever with Quito. In his private correspondence he hurled all sorts of epithets at the *quiteños,* and he threatened to abandon them to the Spaniards if they did not mend their behaviour. The recent crisis he blamed flatly on the machinations of an evil band of *bochincheros* and disappointed job-seekers. In reality, however, the *bochincheros* were old-line patriots who genuinely respected the Liberator but had opposed the annexation of Ecuador to Gran Colombia and personally belonged to a different local political faction from that of Aguirre. Their record as supporters of Ecuadoran autonomy lent some weight to the charges of sedition made against them, but there is no evidence that would show they had any immediate subversive action in mind at the time of their dispute with the intendant.[20] Santander probably gave a more accurate description of the Quito oppositionists when he lumped them with the "Caracas club" under the general heading of federalist agitators. He thus toyed with the idea of establishing a subsidized press in Quito as well as in Caracas for the purpose of upholding centralized institutions.[21]

It would nevertheless be misleading to equate the opposition movement in Ecuador too closely with that in Venezuela. Ecuadoran oppositionists had less need to fill out their remarks with purely irresponsible

[18] A.H.N., Congresos XXVI, 782-822.
[19] A.H.N., Congresos XXVI, 813-815.
[20] Lecuna, *C.L.* III, 141, 147 and IV, 8; Oscar Efrén Reyes, *Breve historia general del Ecuador* (2 vols., Quito, 1943-1945) II, 153-154.
[21] Santander to Bolívar, December 6, 1823, and March 21, 1824, Lecuna, *C.S.* I, 267, 288; A.H.N., Corresp.-Senado, May 10, 1824.

criticism, while at the same time the political atmosphere in which they operated was not quite so combustible. The only real outbreaks of disorder seem to have been of the purely military variety—draft riots, mutinies, and the like—that was common elsewhere too. Even Guayaquil, which had once enjoyed real independence and also knew something of the racial tensions that plagued Venezuela, was surprisingly peaceful under Colombian rule. About all that happened there was some minor royalist plotting, which was firmly repressed, and the arrest of a *jefe político* for allegedly espousing local independence in public.[22] No doubt part of the credit for this situation must be given to the firm military rule of the years 1822-24, but conditions quieted down even more after the establishment of constitutional normalcy. The partisans of separation or federation apparently came to accept the inevitable, and one of the latter, Mariano Miño of Quito, turned into a fairly consistent congressional supporter of the Santander regime. Miño actually rose to the position of Secretary of the Chamber of Representatives, which is about as high an honor as any Ecuadoran ever attained in Bogotá.

While at least some Ecuadoran liberals were making their peace with Santander, Ecuadoran conservatives were coming to the shrewd conclusion that Bolívar, despite the salt monopoly, was just the man to safeguard their long-term vested interests.[23] The military "oppressors" from Venezuela and New Granada, on their part, either moved elsewhere or began to accept Ecuador as an adopted homeland. Ecuadoran womanhood probably helped out in this respect, to judge from the number of Venezuelan officers who took Ecuadoran wives and settled down to stay: Sucre, Flores, Paz del Castillo head the list, but even Bolívar picked up an Ecuadoran mistress in passing through Quito. And yet, to repeat the observation so often made with regard to Venezuela, no really basic problem had yet been solved. The outward appearance of stability that had been reached by the start of 1826 was in many ways deceptive, and it would seem to reflect in part the mere fact that expression of public opinion was never so fully developed in Ecuador as it was in Venezuela or New Granada.

[22] Bolívar to Salom, April 9, 1824, Blanco IX, 467; *El Chispero* (Guayaquil), February 9 and 16, 1826.
[23] See below, pp. 332-334.

Chapter XX

## The Year of Crisis: 1826

AS THE year 1826 began Congress opened for the second time in a row on the very day when it was scheduled to meet, which was regarded in Bogotá as a sure sign of political maturity. The English loan was not yet entirely spent, and Venezuela was about as tranquil as might be expected. The war with Spain was finished except for minor naval encounters in the Caribbean. Business was good; the administration was making observable progress in the organization of a republican bureaucracy, in the expansion of educational facilities, and in all the related tasks that had been absorbing its attention over the past five years. Not everyone was pleased with all the administration was doing, but superficially, at least, there was every reason to expect that Colombia would continue to advance at an ever-accelerating pace.

### The Reelection of Bolívar and Santander

Among the various signs that all was well was the peaceful conclusion of Gran Colombia's first and only presidential election campaign. The next term of office did not begin until January, 1827, but the electoral colleges had cast their votes late in 1825, and the Congress of 1826 was assigned the task of certifying the returns and making a final decision in case there was no candidate with an absolute majority. For the presidency, of course, nothing of the sort was needed, as Bolívar's reelection was all but unanimous. Time, distance, and glories won in Peru had served to efface most of whatever open opposition to Bolívar had existed in the past; he was now the sacrosanct hero, Father of his Country. The few scattered votes for other candidates, chiefly Páez and Santander, (See Table, p. 320) were not necessarily votes against Bolívar. At least some and probably most were cast by electors who feared Bolívar would be unwilling or unable to assume the presidency in person and felt that there was no point in going through with the formality of his election if someone else was again to be the true Chief Executive.

As in the Congress of Cúcuta, the real struggle thus centered upon the race for vice-president. The reelection of Santander was strongly championed by Bolívar,[1] who had apparently recovered from his own past disagreements with the Vice-President, and also, save in Venezuela,

[1] Cf. Bolívar to Santander, February 23, 1825, Lecuna *C.L.* IV, 269.

318

by a clear majority of Colombian liberals. Santander further enjoyed the advantage of heading the party in power, to which all thanks were due for individual jobs and favors received and from which more of the same might be expected as a reward for political regularity in the future. His candidacy was vigorously opposed, on the other hand, by Venezuelan federalists, by the hardy band of Cartagena publicists who had been creating such a furor over the English loan,[2] and presumably by all those who had *not* received the jobs and favors they desired. In Caracas even the moderates who did not openly campaign against Santander did not actively support him either. There was also a marked lack of enthusiasm for his candidacy in most provinces of central and western New Granada. This must presumably be ascribed to dislike of the Vice-President's sporadic anti-clericalism, to the loan agitation, and to any number of purely local and personal factors, including a certain amount of lingering *nariñismo* in Bogotá.

Perhaps it is hardest of all to fathom why Ecuador voted almost solidly, though one may suspect unenthusiastically, for the Vice-President's reelection. One reason was undoubtedly the stated preference of Bolívar, whose opinion carried some weight with the higher authorities of the region. For the rest, the Ecuadorans may have decided that their grievances would be remedied more effectively if they stayed on outwardly good terms with what looked like the winning side, or they may have come to the reasoned conviction that Santander was the best qualified of all major candidates. But whatever the precise explanation may be, 112 of the 286 electoral votes cast in his favor came from the three departments of Ecuador, Azuay, and Guayaquil. Another 69 came from the Department of Boyacá, which was the home of Santander himself as well as that of Soto, the Azueros, and many other leaders of Santanderean liberalism. And since so much has been said about the irreconcilable hostility between Santander and Venezuela, it is well to take note that 38 of Santander's electors were Venezuelan, although all but six of them came from the eastern and western extremes of Venezuela rather than from the more important central provinces of Caracas and Carabobo. Thanks at least in part to Admiral José Padilla, he carried the city if not the province of Cartagena.[3] When all these votes were added to scattered ballots from the rest of New Granada, Santander rolled up a grand total of 286, which was 46% of the electoral votes cast.

Santander's runner-up, with a mere 76 votes, was General Pedro Briceño Méndez, a Venezuelan officer and firm friend of Bolívar. As

[2] Cf. *La Gaceta de Cartagena,* June 25 and August 6, 1825.

[3] *El Constitucional* (Bogotá), September 22, 1825; *La Gaceta de Cartagena,* October 8, 1825.

## ELECTION OF 1826

| Department and Province | Total Electoral Votes | Vice-President | | | | | | President | |
|---|---|---|---|---|---|---|---|---|---|
| | | Santander | Briceño Méndez | Castillo y Rada | Baralt | Sucre | Others | Bolívar | Others |
| Orinoco | | | | | | | | | |
| 1. Guayana | 10 | 10 | | | | | | 10 | |
| 2. Cumaná | 10 | 6 | | | | 4 | | 10 | |
| 3. Barcelona | 9 | 3 | 1 | | | 5 | | 9 | |
| 4. Margarita | 10 | | | | | | 10 | | 10 |
| Venezuela | | | | | | | | | |
| 5. Caracas | 35 | | 11 | 3 | | 1 | 20 | 35 | |
| 6. Carabobo | 35 | 6 | 7 | | | | 22 | 31 | 4 |
| Apure | | | | | | | | | |
| 7. Barinas | 19 | 13 | | | | | 6 | 18 | 1 |
| 8. Apure | 9 | | 1 | | | | 8 | 9 | |
| Zulia | | | | | | | | | |
| 9. Maracaibo | 11 | | | 1 | 9 | | 1 | 10 | 1 |
| 10. Coro | 10 | | 8 | | | | 2 | 10 | |
| 11. Mérida | 10 | | 6 | | | | 4 | 10 | |
| 12. Trujillo | 8 | 3 | 5 | | | | | 8 | |
| Magdalena | | | | | | | | | |
| 13. Cartagena | 32 | 9 | 19 | | | | 4 | 32 | |
| 14. Santa Marta | 10 | 1 | 9 | | | | | 10 | |
| 15. Río Hacha | 10 | | 10 | | | | | 10 | |
| Boyacá | | | | | | | | | |
| 16. Tunja | 46 | 38 | | | | 8 | | 46 | |
| 17. Casanare | 7 | 7 | | | | | | 7 | |
| 18. Socorro | 32 | 11 | | 3 | 12 | 6 | | 32 | |
| 19. Pamplona | 15 | 13 | 1 | | | | 1 | 15 | |
| Cundinamarca | | | | | | | | | |
| 20. Bogotá | 38 | 11 | 2 | 1 | 24 | | | 38 | |
| 21. Neiva | 11 | 7 | 1 | | | | 3 | 11 | |
| 22. Mariquita | 16 | 5 | 8 | | 3 | | | 16 | |
| 23. Antioquia | 23 | 4 | 17 | | 2 | | | 23 | |
| Cauca | | | | | | | | | |
| 24. Popayán | 14 | 3 | 1 | | | 10 | | 14 | |
| 25. Chocó | 10 | | | 10 | | | | 10 | |
| 26. Pasto | 10 | 10 | | | | | | 10 | |
| 27. Buenaventura | 10 | 10 | | | | | | 10 | |
| Istmo | | | | | | | | | |
| 28. Panamá | 11 | 7 | | | | 4 | | 11 | |
| 29. Veraguas | 10 | | | | | | 10 | | 10 |
| Ecuador | | | | | | | | | |
| 30. Pichincha | 45 | 45 | | | | | | 45 | |
| 31. Imbabura | 12 | 8 | | | | 4 | | 12 | |
| 32. Chimborazo | 28 | 21 | | | | 7 | | 28 | |
| Azuay | | | | | | | | | |
| 33. Cuenca | 18 | 18 | | | | | | 18 | |
| 34. Loja | 7 | 7 | | | | | | 7 | |
| Guayaquil | | | | | | | | | |
| 35. Guayaquil | 13 | 3 | 10 | | | | | 13 | |
| 36. Manabí | 10 | 10 | | | | | | 10 | |
| TOTAL | 609 | 286 | 76 | 56 | 50 | 39 | 102 | 583 | 26 |

Sources: The vote of individual provinces is taken from unofficial figures appearing in *La Gaceta de Colombia*, save in the case of Apure (figures from A.H.N., Congresos XXV, 19). The nation-wide totals are from the official count in A.C., Actas del Senado, March 15, 1826, and do not always agree with the sum of unofficial provincial figures.

Secretary of War in the Santander cabinet until early in 1825 he had been a non-controversial, almost a non-political figure; there is no evidence that he actively sought the election. Nevertheless, he carried most of the Department of Zulia, where he and his family were personally well known, and he also won Antioquia, Mariquita, and Guayaquil for reasons that are not quite so obvious. The third-ranking candidate was Finance Secretary Castillo y Rada, with 56 votes garnered almost exclusively from his home Department of Magdalena. There had been an active campaign waged in his behalf, with one full-page advertisement in *El Constitucional*,[4] but it is hard to detect who was behind it, or even whether Castillo himself favored the movement. He very possibly did, although he later denied it and could scarcely campaign openly in any case while remaining in Santander's cabinet. The President of the Senate, Luis Andrés Baralt, came in fourth with some 50 votes. There is no evidence that Baralt had seriously sought the election either, and his support came chiefly from just three provinces: Maracaibo, which was his home, Socorro, where he split the vote with Santander, and Bogotá, where he apparently had made friends during his service in Congress. The last major candidate was General Sucre, who had been outside the country for roughly three years and no doubt earned his 39 electoral votes purely on his status as a military hero; he won an actual majority only in Barcelona and Popayán. After the five leaders, finally, there was a scattering of votes for twelve others, including Colonel Francisco Carabaño, who obtained exactly seven votes, and José Antonio Páez, who had four.

Except perhaps in the case of provinces with a favored native son it is difficult to state the exact significance of the vote for Santander's competitors. Some Venezuelans lumped all of them together and affirmed that their total vote constituted a national repudiation of the Vice-President.[5] However, about all one can say with assurance is that there was not quite an outright majority in his favor. There was no figure of national importance who openly campaigned on an opposition platform, or even expressed himself publicly and formally as hostile to Santander's reelection; the only avowed, out-and-out oppositionist in the running was Carabaño. This does not mean, of course, that there was not a sizeable protest vote, especially as the vote for Congress which was taken at the same time showed a perceptible, though hardly precipitous, shift toward the right. Numerous administration stalwarts were not returned, including notably Juan Manuel Arrubla and Francisco Montoya, both of

[4] *El Constitucional*, August 25, 1825.

[5] Cf. *Revista Semanal* (Caracas), February 25, 1826; this was not one of the more rabidly oppositionist organs.

whom were too closely associated with the English loan.[6] On the other hand, there could be no effective nation-wide opposition to Santander until Bolívar himself decided to head it. At the very most the vote for Briceño Méndez and Sucre, both of them military figures firmly attached to Bolívar, might be regarded as a vague anticipation of the later conservative *bolivianismo*. The same certainly cannot be said in the case of Castillo y Rada, who shared direct responsibility for all the controversial economic policies of the Santander regime. As for Baralt, he had been a consistent supporter of administration policy in the Senate and was himself, rightly or wrongly, one of the main targets of the loan agitators. Hence a part of the "opposition" vote probably must be ascribed not to any fundamental dislike of Santander but to the belief that for one reason or another—perhaps just to appease Caracas—it was time for a change.

In any case, Santander was so far in the lead that Congress had little choice but to vote for him when it came time to make a final choice from among the top three contestants. This decision was warmly praised by Briceño Méndez, in particular, and also by numerous others who had not originally supported Santander's reelection.[7] When Santander went through the motion of offering his resignation to Congress, only five members voted to accept it, of whom one was Dr. Juan Nepomuceno Azuero, an eccentric government supporter who presumably made the gesture for reasons of his own.[8] No doubt a certain amount of dissatisfaction with Santander's administration can be detected in the eagerness shown simultaneously by the lower house to summon Bolívar home from Peru so that he might rule in fact as well as in name; but the Senate refused to go along, insisting that Bolívar must be allowed to do whatever he thought best for the welfare of America.[9]

[6] Juan Manuel was the brother of Manuel Antonio Arrubla, who was loan negotiator alongside Montoya. For detailed congressional returns see *Actas de las sesiones de la Cámara de Representantes* (Bogotá, 1826), 34-65 *passim*. It is easy to exaggerate the importance of the turnover, which was high among oppositionists also; in many cases, moreover, failure to reelect a man was really a favor to him. The main fact is simply that the new Congress was distinctly more conservative than the last.

[7] Briceño to Bolívar, April 13, 1826, O'Leary VIII, 194. Among the organs of opinion that did not campaign for Santander but praised his reelection when it happened were *El Constitucional* and *El Chasqui Bogotano* (No. 4). The latter was edited by José Félix Merizalde, a former backer of Nariño who himself had voted for Baralt in the provincial electoral college (A.H.N., Congresos XXV, 40).

[8] *La Gaceta de Colombia*, May 7, 1826.

[9] The Senate made it clear that Santander was wholly capable of taking Bolívar's place. *Actas de . . . la Cámara de Representantes* (1826), 68; A.H.N., Congresos XII, 549; A.C., Actas del Senado, January 18 and 27, 1826.

## The Revolt of Páez

The Congress of 1826 accomplished much more than just the re-election of Santander. Its legislative activity marked a high point in political, economic, and religious liberalism that was not regained until the middle of the century. Another of its achievements, however, was to begin impeachment proceedings against the *Comandante General* of the Department of Venezuela, José Antonio Páez, and this one step led through a long and devious chain of events to the final dissolution of Gran Colombia. The projected impeachment of Páez, needless to say, was no exclusive cause of the final outcome, which was due essentially to all the underlying weaknesses and disunity that have already been surveyed in detail. It merely happened to be the event that brought the first of those weaknesses fully into the open.

The attack made against General Páez was not based on his ill-defined monarchist activities, although they were no secret at Bogotá, but rather was a direct result of the latest developments in the great militia controversy that had been raging in Caracas since 1824. The *caraqueños* had generally continued to resist Santander's enlistment decree, and in the face of their opposition the Vice-President had authorized Páez to proceed cautiously in its enforcement. Under the circumstances this meant very slowly. Then, in December, 1825, rumors were circulated hinting at new disorders reminiscent of the Petare incident of a year before. As a result of this alarm Páez redoubled his efforts to organize the local militia, and on January 6, 1826, when his summons to enlist had not produced the desired effect, he sent out troops to scour the city for able-bodied men, authorizing them to raid private homes and even to open fire if need be.[10]

At least this is what the Caracas city council and General Escalona, the intendant, subsequently asserted. Páez himself claimed that he recalled the patrols soon after they went out, and that his own orders had said nothing about raiding homes or shooting down civilians. The Caracas municipality had never been noted for responsible criticism of anyone, while General Escalona was no friend of Páez, whom he accused simultaneously of improper gambling activities. It is clear that no very horrible abuses took place on January 6.[11] On the other hand, it is unlikely that the charges were fabricated entirely; and, what was more important, the military class had acquired such a bad reputation that many Colombians of all shades of political opinion were prepared to believe the worst of a *llanero* soldier like Páez. In Bogotá the Chamber of Representatives promptly voted by 38 to 16 that Páez should be tried before the Senate for his arbitrary conduct, and the Senate readily voted by a similar margin

[10] *El Constitucional,* July 20, 1826; A.C., Senado-35, 81-82; Blanco X, 154-155, 163-165.

[11] Blanco X, 594-609; A.C., Cámara-15, 53; *El Constitucional,* November 30, 1826.

to accept the indictment and proceed to formal trial. In both houses there were liberals and conservatives, *granadinos* and Venezuelans, arrayed in opposition to Páez; this is one issue on which Francisco Soto and Bishop Lasso were in agreement. Indeed the chief criticism of the move came simply from moderate-minded independents such as Senator Joaquín Mosquera, who felt that it would be wise to avoid acting hastily when dealing with a man like Páez.[12]

The foregoing should be enough to refute the claim first made by the associates of Páez in 1826 and still being repeated today that the accusation was all a base intrigue of Santander. It is true that Soto and others of the Vice-President's political friends warmly supported the move against Páez, but they were far from alone in their stand. Nor is there the slightest indication that Santander himself did anything to promote the agitation. All he did was to give Congress what information he had on the militia incident when requested to do so, point out that the evidence of Páez' personal responsibility for whatever abuses might have occurred was far from sufficient, and reprove the Chamber of Representatives for listening to an "abundance of frivolous complaints."[13] Santander's personal sentiments, to be sure, were much more sympathetic to Congress; to Bolívar he wrote that the action of Congress was in effect an attempt to find out "whether it had the moral force . . . to make the first chiefs of the Republic understand that their services and heroic deeds are not a safe-conduct to abuse the citizens."[14] Yet the Vice-President's public conduct was correct throughout. All one can say against him, in the light of subsequent events, is that he might have exerted some pressure on his supporters in Congress either to moderate their tone or else to drop the accusation altogether. Of course it is conceivable that Santander did make such an effort and that it had no effect, since men like Soto were not mere puppets of the Vice-President.

Santander can be criticized on much better grounds for his choice of General Escalona to replace Páez temporarily as *Comandante* while the latter came to Bogotá to stand trial. Since Escalona had been serving as intendant he was already on the spot, was well acquainted with affairs in Venezuela, and was able to take over on a moment's notice; but he was also one of Páez' accusers, and he had numerous enemies of his own among Venezuelan military leaders. Páez nevertheless determined at first to obey the Congress. He made preparations to leave for Bogotá, and he ordered his troops to recognize the authority of Escalona. He also requested Santander, rather pathetically, to use his full influence in Bogotá to win an acquittal. Almost certainly Santander could ultimately have done just that, because he did have great influence in the Senate, and the

[12] A.C., Actas del Senado, March 27, 1826; Cámara-15, 60.
[13] Blanco X, 206-209.
[14] Santander to Bolívar, May 6, 1826, Lecuna, *C.S.* II, 203-204.

Senators would probably have come to their senses soon enough to avoid condemning Páez at the risk of civil war unless much more decisive evidence were presented against him. And since the Senate was sure to vote acquittal, as Santander saw it, it would be a very noble thing for Páez to make the gesture of submitting to trial. Citing numerous precedents from classical antiquity, the Vice-President told Páez that this would powerfully impress upon public opinion the Majesty of Law, and would assure Páez himself of lasting glory far greater than the fame he had won on the battlefield. The argument was good—but it arrived too late.[15]

It was on April 28 at Valencia that Páez had acknowledged Escalona as his successor. On the 29th he wrote his humble letter to Santander; on the 30th he reassumed his former command and announced defiance of the government at Bogotá. Ostensibly this change in plan was in response to the urging of the Valencia city council, which announced wide indignation over Páez' separation from office and declared that he must return to his job in order to preserve the tranquillity of the state. There can be no doubt that tranquillity was really threatened: Páez' withdrawal had been followed immediately by an outbreak of minor disorders in the Valencia neighborhood. The fact is, however, that these were disorders of a rather suspicious character. There is good authority even for the statement that a group of army officers went out and killed two men, and dragged their bodies into the public plaza precisely in order to show the necessity for Páez' return to power. Thus one need not assume hypocrisy on the part of the city council or even General Páez, although in either case it is wholly possible; but there were certainly some shady dealings somewhere behind the scenes.[16] It is hard to resist the conviction that Dr. Miguel Peña must have had a hand in them. He was present in Valencia throughout the proceedings of the last week in April and his violent ill-will toward the Bogotá regime was notorious; if anything, it had recently been augmented by the knowledge that he was now being impeached by Congress all over again, this time for improper manipulation of the government funds that he had taken as courier from Cartagena to Caracas the year before. Peña could not, of course, prepare a revolution all by himself; but there was no lack of unscrupulous military leaders surrounding Páez who were equally capable of provoking one.[17]

Once Valencia had taken the first step the movement rapidly spread throughout central Venezuela. One town after another pledged its allegiance to Páez, including Caracas, where the same councillors who had led

---

[15] Páez to Santander, April 29, 1826, *Arch. Sant.* XIV, 294-295; Santander to Páez, May 10, June 12, July 14, 1826, Lecuna, *C.S.* II, 208-209, 220-230, 242-246, and August 27, 1826, *Arch. Sant.* XV, 112-117.

[16] Blanco X, 288-289, 292-294; O'Leary VIII, 425 and XXIV, 130-133.

[17] Restrepo VI, 385-386; Eloy G. González, *Dentro de la cosiata* (Caracas, 1907), 192.

the accusation against him in January now proclaimed him saviour of Venezuela. This about-face in Caracas was obviously brought about, or at least hastened, by the news that a band of Páez' troops was fast approaching from Valencia, and undoubtedly the fear of military coercion had much to do with the almost unanimous support that was offered to Páez in all sections of the department.[18] On the other hand, one cannot deny that the Valencia rebellion was honestly backed in its early stages by a large segment of Venezuelan opinion. The Guzmán-Carabaño faction, for obvious reasons, was delighted with the new development. Even the eminently respectable Fernando Peñalver, although he condemned the rebellion in his capacity as Governor of Carabobo, expressed definite sympathy with Páez in a personal letter to Bolívar. Perhaps more significant still, he agreed to continue serving as governor under Páez' command. A similar decision was made by Dr. Cristóbal Mendoza, who had succeeded Escalona as departmental intendant only a few days before.[19]

The Valencia rebellion was able at first to enjoy such wide support in large part because so little was said about its precise objectives: it was against Santander, it was in favor of "reforms," and so was most everyone else. As early as May 11 it was proposed that a special national convention should be called for the purpose of amending the constitution, which was quite illegal since the Constitution of Cúcuta had directed that no such assembly might be held for at least ten years, or until 1831. But Venezuelans had little reverence for the constitution, and in any case Páez had solemnly promised that no major reforms would be undertaken until Bolívar should return to Venezuela and act in the role of arbiter.[20] Only gradually did it become evident what sort of "reforms" the Venezuelan leaders really had in mind. Páez' letter to Bolívar of the previous October and an ambiguous Caracas manifesto on May 16 both afforded some justification for the view that the movement was monarchist in nature, and this interpretation was duly exploited in the Bogotá press.[21] From the month of May onward, however, more and more municipal councils and organs of opinion in Venezuela began to declare themselves in favor of the federalist system of government. Páez did nothing at all to discourage these declarations, which apparently were not wholly spontaneous. On the contrary, it was increasingly clear that he had fallen under the influence of Peña, Carabaño, and their associates, and that they were firmly committed to the federalist cause. The question then was simply

[18] On this point cf. *La Gaceta de Colombia*, July 2, 1826. For a full collection of municipal *actas*, see A.C., Senado-41, and Blanco X, 295-325.

[19] Peñalver to Bolívar, May 12, 1826, O'Leary VIII, 397; Blanco X, 294, 301-302.

[20] Blanco X, 321, 331-335.

[21] Cf. *La Bandera Tricolor*, July 16 and August 6, 1826; Carlos A. Villanueva, *El Imperio de los Andes* (Paris, 1913), 65-66.

what kind of federation Venezuela should have. There could be a loose confederation of Venezuela, New Granada, and Ecuador, each of them managing its regional affairs under a unitary government of its own; or there could be first and foremost a "federation of Venezuela," consisting of numerous small provinces raised suddenly as in the *Patria Boba* to the status of sovereign states, and deciding freely whether it would choose to remain within the framework of Gran Colombia. Both solutions were publicly proposed, although it is extremely hard to disentangle who was behind either plan.[22]

Even so, the more clearly the nature of the movement was defined, the more its support began to dwindle. Moderates especially disliked the prominence assumed by such irresponsible figures as Dr. Peña, fearing that Páez would be rushed into the adoption of radical reforms even before the return of Bolívar. Their fears were justified, moreover, for the extremists were already trying to overcome Páez' deference toward the Liberator's opinions.[23] At the same time Páez was antagonizing the merchant class by suspending the payment of customhouse *vales* and refusing to execute the tariff legislation of 1826, which had provided, among other things, for the assessment of duties *ad valorem*. Both moves were essentially fiscal expedients, as was Páez' demand for a semi-voluntary loan of $240,000. Finally, Páez was strongly criticized by many different elements for a series of political acts that ranged from merely unwise to distinctly arbitrary; a typical example was a decree ordering the interception of all *granadino* newspapers, a measure which drew the formal protest of a British consul.[24]

By the end of August, therefore, Páez' strength was definitely on the wane. Fernando Peñalver finally refused to serve longer under Páez and fled for his own safety to territory that was loyal to Santander. He then gave the administration detailed advice on how to overcome the Páez revolt. Even Carabaño briefly toyed with the idea of seeking a compromise settlement with Bogotá. The most disturbing sign of all was the appearance of counter-revolutionary action within the armed forces. Under the leadership of the *comandante de armas* of Caracas province, and with the secret sympathy of the intendant, Dr. Mendoza, the *Batallón Apure* formally repudiated the rule of Páez on August 28 and marched off to

[22] *El Colombiano* (Caracas), May 17 and 24, June 28, July 12, August 2, September 6, 1826; *Memorial de Venezuela* (Caracas), July 20, 1826; *El Cometa* (Caracas), October 19, 1826; O'Leary VIII, 419.

[23] González, *Cosiata*, 192-195; O'Leary VIII, 400, 420, 424-425. For some interesting comments by members of the "Caracas club" see also O'Leary II, 326, 330-331.

[24] *El Colombiano*, July 12 and August 16, 1826; Foster to Clay, La Guaira, August 2, 1826, in William R. Manning, ed., *Diplomatic Correspondence of the United States Concerning the Independence of the Latin American Nations* (3 vols., New York, 1925) II, 1301; Blanco X, 522, 615-617.

join the loyalist troops of José Francisco Bermúdez in the Department of Orinoco.[25] For the fact is that Páez had so far won control only of his own Department of Venezuela and the single province of Apure that lay outside it. The other sections of colonial Venezuela, to his vast disappointment had continued to accept the rule of Bogotá. This was probably due in large part to the personal loyalty of Bermúdez at Cumaná and General Rafael Urdaneta at Maracaibo; both rejected Páez' advances and implored him to return to his senses. Urdaneta regarded Páez' course as a betrayal of the Liberator, and ascribed it frankly to the evil machinations of Peña and Carabaño.[26] But it is unlikely that the other Venezuelan provinces were swayed solely by the personal leanings of their commanders. They also had their traditional rivalries with Caracas, while their relations with Bogotá had been in most cases at least superficially cordial. After all, no less than three of the lesser provinces had given a majority to Santander in the last elections.

To be sure, the idea of "reforms" appealed to many who rejected the rule of Páez.[27] Furthermore, Páez did have at least some partisans almost everywhere in Venezuela, and in the East, where Bermúdez' personal enemies inevitably looked to Páez for support, they were numerous enough to be a real menace. In fact the *Batallón Apure* reached the Department of Orinoco only to find that since the end of August one town after another in the territory under Bermúdez' command had issued a call for constitutional changes, aligned itself with Páez, and repudiated both Bermúdez and Bogotá. The island of Margarita eagerly embraced this opportunity to carry out its earlier ambition of joining the Department of Venezuela. Fortunately, however, the movement was never complete. Bermúdez kept himself a foothold, and the province of Guayana remained virtually undisturbed under the leadership of its governor, Colonel José Manuel Olivares, one of the few prominent Venezuelans who had consistently supported Santander. At one point troops at Angostura organized a mutiny in favor of Páez and "federalism," but Olivares bought them off and the mutineers left peacefully for Cumaná.[28]

[25] Peñalver to Bolívar, September 15, 1826, O'Leary VIII, 398; González, *Cosiata*, 201-203; Sagarzazu, "Ligeros apuntes en las diferentes épocas de disensiones políticas," *Boletín de la Academia Nacional de Historia de Venezuela*, XIII (1930), 353-356. Cf. also O'Leary VIII, 415-422.

[26] *La Gaceta de Colombia*, July 9, 1826; Urdaneta to Páez, June 27, 1826, in Carlos Arbeláez Urdaneta, *Biografía del General Rafael Urdaneta* (Maracaibo, 1945), 185-189.

[27] Petitions for a convention were tolerated if not actually encouraged by Urdaneta himself, and also by General Miguel Guerrero, the loyalist intendant of the Department of Apure. See *La Gaceta de Colombia*, August 27, 1826.

[28] A.C., Senado-41, 45-153, 228-230; Blanco X, 560-562, 574-575, 593.

## The Reaction of Santander and Bolívar

In Bogotá and in New Granada as a whole public opinion was generally hostile to Páez' rebellion from the start, although the bitterest comments, naturally enough, came always from the administration camp. Santander himself obviously had no choice but to condemn the movement as wholly illegal, and he accordingly declared all its acts to be null and void. He quite properly assumed "extraordinary faculties" in order to deal with the situation in Venezuela, and he warned Colombian writers that they could be punished for sedition if they advocated illegal reforms on the Venezuelan model. On the other hand, he did not take any immediate action against the revolutionists. He discreetly prepared to fight Páez if necessary, and unleashed a bitter propaganda campaign against him; he urged loyal officials in Venezuela to do all they could by peaceful methods, including censorship of the press and correspondence, in order to undermine the insurgent cause; but the government carefully instructed its agents to avoid firing the first shot.[29]

The Vice-President's caution reflected his original realization that the Venezuelan problem could not be solved without either civil war or a willingness to forgive the insurgents, and he obviously hoped to avoid the former. He believed that the authority of the law should be vindicated at least to the extent of compelling Páez to answer the Senate's charges against him, but he now wrote that he was willing to name Páez' own ally, General Santiago Mariño, as provisional *Comandante General* of Venezuela while Páez came to Bogotá. As a last resort he was even prepared to countenance a sufficiently strained interpretation of the constitution to allow Congress to summon a constituent convention before 1831.[30] However, Santander's mood gradually changed when reports of Páez' declining strength began to reach Bogotá. He then spoke frankly of "punishing" Páez for his rebellion and warned Bolívar that if he compromised with the Venezuelan leaders all respect for law and order would be destroyed.[31] Yet Santander was still cautious enough not to specify the punishment to be meted out, and when he insisted that there be no compromise he probably meant chiefly that any settlement must be generally based on a restoration of the legal *status quo* as of April 29.

Santander and his ministers, like Cristóbal Mendoza and Peñalver in Venezuela, believed that the revolt could very possibly be overcome by

---

[29] *Arch. Sant.* XIV, 368-370; A.C., Senado-44, 268; *Acuerdos* II, 165. The propaganda campaign included publication of Páez' personal correspondence to Bolívar, which had been intercepted and opened at Bogotá (*La Gaceta de Colombia,* July 9, 1826).

[30] Santander to Páez, June 12 and July 14, 1826, *Arch. Sant.* XIV, 385-386, XV, 64-68.

[31] Santander to Bolívar, July 31 and September 21, 1826, Lecuna, *C.S.* II, 265, 284-285.

the mere presence of Bolívar in the city of Caracas. Accordingly, the Vice-President wrote repeatedly to Bolívar in Lima urging him to speed his return home. He continued to bank on the intervention of the Liberator even when such administration zealots as Vicente Azuero, no doubt heartened by the signs of growing opposition to Páez, had come to the conclusion that it was time to seek a settlement by force of arms.[32] As it turned out, however, Bolívar's reaction to the Venezuelan revolt was not quite what Santander had hoped. When he first heard of the Congressional agitation against Páez, Bolívar expressed strong sympathy with the accused, and on one occasion he suggested that Páez might feign illness so as to avoid appearing before the Senate until he himself could arrive on the scene and devise a solution.[33] Over the following weeks the Liberator naturally received conflicting reports of the origin, aims, and strength of Páez' rebellion, including Páez' own version that it was all a result of Santander's machinations in Bogotá, and he appears to have agreed with the latter interpretation at least to the extent that he regarded Santander's appointment of Escalona as a major cause of the revolt. Certainly he expressed only a rather perfunctory disapproval of Páez' course of action. Bolívar was most favorably impressed by Páez' pledge not to introduce any reforms before his own return to Venezuela; and to Sucre he wrote that the Venezuelan problem ought to be solved by some kind of "amicable transaction." [34]

Bolívar's idea of an "amicable transaction" was unlikely to be the same as Santander's; in particular, the prospect of constitutional reform was by no means unwelcome to him. The Liberator was a convinced republican, so that he had already rejected Páez' earlier suggestion that he imitate Napoleon Bonaparte.[35] He ascribed at least in principle to most of the liberal theories that were fashionable in his day. But Bolívar was also convinced that the people of Colombia were unprepared for the enjoyment of genuinely liberal institutions. He had therefore urged the Guayana Congress to create a Senate whose members would serve for life, and he felt from the start that the Constitution of Cúcuta was actually too liberal. The unrest that prevailed in Spanish America, especially in his beloved Venezuela, simply confirmed him more and more each year in his opinions.[36] It was thus natural for Bolívar to regard Páez as a victim

[32] Santander to Bolívar, July 31, August 21, September 21, October 8, 1826, Lecuna, C.S. II, 265, 270, 284-285, 289; *Acuerdos* II, 200-204.

[33] Bolívar to Páez, May 6, 1826, Lecuna, C.L. V, 285.

[34] Bolívar to Sucre, July 3, 1826, Lecuna, C.L. VI, 6-7; Bolívar to T. C. Mosquera, August 1, 1826, Lecuna, C.L. VI, 22-23.

[35] Bolívar to Páez, March 6, 1826, Lecuna, C.L. V, 239-240.

[36] For an excellent brief study of Bolívar's political thinking, see Caracciolo Parra-Pérez, *Bolívar: contribución al estudio de sus ideas políticas* (2nd ed., Caracas, 1942).

of the excesses of Spanish American liberalism; the very letter in which he gently chided Páez for his revolt contains the interesting statement that the military had suffered less from the Spaniards than from ungrateful civilians who sought to "destroy their liberators." In a similar vein he attacked the press as a "deceitful tribune" that had guided the executive —presumably meaning Santander—to seek a "premature perfection" in a maze of well-intentioned but impracticable legislation.[37] Probably the main reason, in fact, for Bolívar's failure to rebuke Páez more strongly was that the Valencia revolt appeared to offer a golden chance to wipe out all previous efforts and start Colombia afresh under the semi-authoritarian constitution which he had just finished preparing for Bolivia, and which he termed "the ark that is to save us from the shipwreck that threatens from all directions." [38]

The Bolivian Constitution was designed as a panacea that would cure Latin America's political ills and at the same time reconcile monarchical, democratic, and federalist opinions. Bolívar thought that he had found the true principle of stability in a president serving for life and automatically succeeded by a vice-president whom he himself had a part in selecting. The president's powers were restricted to war, foreign affairs, and certain other carefully defined activities, but the government would still be more like a constitutional monarchy than anything else. Indeed it was perfectly possible for the president to choose as successor a member of his own family. To please liberal elements, however, these provisions were supplemented by an almost fantastic system of checks and balances guarding against the abuse of authority—a system that made the constitution totally unworkable in the opinion of Sucre, who, as first President of Bolivia, was the only man ever to govern under it. As for the federalists, they were to be conciliated by certain aspects of the Bolivian "Electoral Power," which consisted of local electoral colleges with fairly wide powers of nomination and appointment as well as the function of presenting popular petitions to higher governmental bodies. Federalists would again be pleased, Bolívar hoped, by his accompanying project which would have abolished Colombia in its present form and joined its three great sections together with Peru and Bolivia in a vast Confederation of the Andes. In this scheme both the confederation itself and the five component states would have charters modelled on that of Bolivia. But even if the Confederation of the Andes did not work out, Bolívar felt

[37] Bolívar to Páez, August 8, 1826, Lecuna, C.L. VI, 49.
[38] Bolívar to Antonio Gutiérrez de la Fuente, May 12, 1826, Lecuna, C.L. V, 295. This was written before Bolívar received notice of Páez' rebellion.

that it would be desirable at the very least to adapt the major provisions of the Bolivian Constitution to the government of Gran Colombia.[39]

In order to prepare the way for acceptance of his plans in Colombia, Bolívar resolved to employ the services of none other than Antonio Leocadio Guzmán, who had come to Lima bearing the Napoleonic scheme of Páez. Guzmán was given copies of the proposed constitution to distribute as widely as possible, as well as form letters in which Bolívar urged his friends throughout Colombia to start campaigning for its adoption at the national convention which was ostensibly to take place in 1831. At least Bolívar gave no hint as yet of desiring an earlier date. At the same time, Bolívar asked his correspondents to pay close attention to all that his emissary had to say about the immediate political crisis, for Guzmán would describe the practical measures that Bolívar himself suggested for solving it. It is impossible to state exactly what these measures were, since Bolívar did not write them down; and he subsequently declared that Guzmán apparently exceeded his instructions in some instances. Nevertheless, from the results of Guzmán's mission and from the later statements of Bolívar it is clear that he was instructed to mobilize public opinion in favor of granting some kind of extraordinary powers to the Liberator. The immediate purpose of such a grant would be to enable Bolívar to settle the Venezuelan revolt in his own way; apart from this, it is probable that Bolívar himself did not yet know what he really intended.[40]

## The Subversion of Ecuador and the Pilgrimage of Guzmán

The Bolivian Constitution had awakened friendly interest among military leaders and disgruntled aristocrats in Ecuador even before Guzmán returned to Colombia, and no doubt in many cases even before they had given much thought to what it really said.[41] It vaguely offered hope of a conservative reaction, and that was enough. There were many others, of course, who wanted not a genuine conservative reaction but simply a measure of local autonomy along federalist lines; this group was particularly strong in Guayaquil. However, the mere fact that Bolívar was known to be sponsoring some new system of government, when added to the rebellious example of Venezuela, was enough to bring all the assorted unrest of the Ecuadoran departments fully to a head. Not all factions were agreed on the precise objectives to be sought, least of all on the Bolivian Constitution, but they did want a change.

[39] Vicente Lecuna, ed., *Documentos referentes a la creación de Bolivia* (2 vols., Caracas, 1924) II, 312, 314-317, 326, 335-339; Parra-Pérez, *op. cit.*, 101-102, 114; Bolívar to Sucre, May 12, 1826, Lecuna, *C.L.* V, 292-293. There would be six component states if Peru were split in two, a possibility that Bolívar seriously considered.

[40] Lecuna, *C.L.* VI, 28-45, 118-119.

[41] Cf. O'Leary IV, 6-8, 364, 458, 461-462; IX, 75-76, 439-440.

The first step had been taken at Guayaquil early in July, when the municipal government, in response to pressure from both local federalists and partisans of the Bolivian Constitution, held a public meeting and decided that in view of the apparent separation of Venezuela from the rest of Colombia it was high time for Bolívar to summon a convention for constitutional reform. Soon afterwards an open meeting was held at Quito to consider the advisability of making a similar pronouncement. It would almost seem that the *quiteños* had as much or more to say about the need for immediate restoration of the colonial tax system, but the departmental intendant, Col. Pedro Murgueitio, saw to it that the final resolutions merely gave a general endorsement to the motion of Guayaquil. With Quito and Guayaquil thus presenting a united front, it was only natural for numerous smaller centers to follow suit with declarations of their own. The only important opposition came from the province of Manabí, which was no doubt influenced by its local rivalries with Guayaquil, and from the Intendant of Azuay, Col. Ignacio Torres, who simply frowned on the mention of federalism. As a matter of fact, Murgueitio, Juan José Flores, and all the other military leaders who ultimately gave their support to the campaign for reforms were just as much opposed to bona fide federalism as was Col. Torres; their first loyalty was to Bolívar, and they were all actual or potential supporters of the Bolivian Constitution. They went along with the movement that began in Guayaquil in the belief that it might be diverted to some more suitable ends. General Manuel Valdés, who had helped to inspire the original manifesto, was quite frankly dismayed when municipal leaders insisted on injecting the issue of federalism but still preferred not to start a public controversy over it. In any case, the higher authorities of all three Ecuadoran departments proclaimed that nothing would be changed without the presence of Bolívar, and unlike Páez they really meant what they said.[42]

Bolívar's attitude toward developments in Ecuador seems to have been much the same as that of the military commanders on the spot. When he was sent a copy of the Guayaquil manifesto his official secretary dispatched an ambiguous reply vaguely suggesting that Bolívar approved of its contents and at the same time recommending the Bolivian Constitution as his "profession of political faith." [43] When Antonio L. Guzmán finally reached Guayaquil at the end of August his principal task was thus to forge some more tangible link between the local separatist movement and the Liberator's profession of faith. In this he was admirably assisted by the newly-arrived intendant, Col. Tomás Cipriano de Mosquera, who personally considered the Bolivian Constitution to be a "gift from heaven"

[42] Blanco X, 475-477, 496, 516-517; Torres to Bolívar, August 29, 1826, O'Leary IV, 451-454; Manuel Valdés to Bolívar, July 8, 1826, O'Leary IX, 440-441; A.C., Senado-41, 265.
[43] Blanco X, 523-524.

and felt that "the sun in the center of the universe, Chimborazo there in its heavenly elevation, and the firmament encompassing the works of nature, are less, physically, than Simón Bolívar in the society of mortals."[44] The result of the combined efforts of Guzmán and Mosquera was certainly one of the most remarkable of the hundreds of manifestos that were issued all over Colombia in the memorable year 1826. Not only did the people of Guayaquil now formally endorse the Bolivian Constitution but they went on to declare that in view of the evident dissolution of Colombia they gladly transferred their fundamental sovereignty to the person of Simón Bolívar, who should act with full dictatorial powers. This declaration was distinctly less spontaneous than that of the previous July. However, all its provisions were promptly endorsed at Quito, where it probably found more general support than at Guayaquil, especially among the local aristocracy. A good number of lesser towns again followed suit, under the urging of their respective governors, but still no immediate changes were made in the political system. Dictatorship would have to await Bolívar's arrival.[45]

From Guayaquil Guzmán had continued on to Panama and Cartagena. As in Ecuador, he found that army officers—especially those of Venezuelan origin—were generally in favor of the Bolivian Constitution and anything else that Bolívar might have to offer. But he also encountered unexpected opposition, especially in Panama; and as a result was not as successful as he had hoped. The Panamanians signed a fairly innocuous statement about the need for Bolívar to come home and the prospect of holding a national convention, but they included a compliment to themselves for having remained steadfastly loyal to the constitutional regime. Cartagena went farther and offered the Liberator whatever extraordinary powers he might need to "save the republic;" some pointed attacks on the Bogotá government were thrown in for good measure. Yet the Cartagena manifesto still contained nothing expressly to indicate that its recommendations could not be carried out under the terms of the existing constitution.[46]

At Cartagena Guzmán was ordered to suspend his journey by Santander, who rightly feared that if he continued on to Venezuela he would try to undermine the administration's policy of firm and watchful waiting in dealing with Páez' revolt. As an added justification for his action Santander suggested that Guzmán had been spreading false reports about the Liberator.[47] Nevertheless, Guzmán could not be stopped, and reentered

[44] O'Leary IX, 76; Blanco, X, 558-559.

[45] Blanco X, 556-557, 570-572; O'Leary IV, 364; A.C., Senado-41, 270-274.

[46] Ernesto J. Castillero, "Los panameños y la dictadura de Bolívar," *Boletín de Historia y Antigüedades* (Bogotá), XL, 141-144 (January-March, 1953); Blanco X, 610-614.

[47] Santander to Bolívar, October 15, 1826, Lecuna, *C.S.* II, 298.

Venezuela by the port of Maracaibo. There General Urdaneta was still resisting Páez' advances, having used his own power and influence to thwart all attempts anywhere in the Department of Zulia to join forces with the Venezuelan rebellion. But Urdaneta was by no means averse to the idea of constitutional reform. He was simply awaiting Bolívar's orders; and with the arrival of Guzmán he encouraged the city of Maracaibo to transfer its sovereignty into the hands of the Liberator in order that he might call the much-needed convention.[48]

Only in Caracas, his final destination, did Guzmán meet with obvious and complete failure. There the movement of Páez had not developed in quite the way Bolívar hoped, for in recent weeks the cause of federalism —and especially the more radical demand for a "Federation of Venezuela"—had made rapid progress. It had won the formal endorsement of a number of municipal juntas, and an assembly of delegates was summoned to meet at Caracas on November 1 in order to decide what should be done next. Antonio L. Guzmán arrived on the scene just in time to inform the assembly of Bolívar's sympathy for Venezuelan aspirations, and to explain the nature both of the Bolivian Constitution and of his own mission. He was kept on the defensive, however, by the extremists in Páez' faction, who were the chief movers of the whole federalist agitation. The *síndico procurador* of Caracas, José de Iribarren, boldly assailed the Bolivian Constitution as contrary to republican ideals and attacked the Liberator himself for daring to propose it. It was thus increasingly apparent that central Venezuela had not thrown off the rule of Santander simply to follow wherever Bolívar might choose to lead. But in the assembly itself there was no clear decision. If there was a winner at all it was really Santander, for the delegates resolved that a special committee should draw up a list of Venezuelan demands, and that as long as it had not truly been demonstrated that Colombia was in a "state of dissolution" the list should be presented to the next session of the regular Colombian Congress.[49]

This outcome reflected mainly the influence of such moderates as Cristóbal Mendoza, and it was wholly unwelcome to Páez. He therefore summoned a new assembly more to his own liking. He himself appeared, claimed Bolívar's backing for his rebellion by virtue of the personal letter he had received from the hands of Guzmán, and obtained from the meeting a virtual declaration of Venezuelan independence. The assembly did not rule out the eventual inclusion of Venezuela in a broader Colombian confederation, but it demanded first a separate constitutional convention for Venezuela which should organize all the provinces of the former Captaincy-General into a federal union of their own, and it at least en-

[48] *Acuerdos* II, 194; Blanco X, 548, 644-645.
[49] O'Leary XXIV, 425, 463-470; José Joaquín Guerra, *La Convención de Ocaña* (Bogotá, 1908), 101, 103.

visaged the possibility of complete separation by asserting that under any form of government Venezuela would naturally assume her just share of the Colombian foreign debt. Similar proposals were endorsed at Valencia by such notables as Peña and Carabaño, and the summons for a constituent convention actually went out, in flagrant violation of Páez' pledge to make no innovation until the Liberator returned.[50]

In the meantime Santander had remained in Bogotá, condemning each and every proposal to solve the nation's problems by unconstitutional methods. The territory under his immediate influence, which meant chiefly the central provinces of New Granada, turned out its own batch of manifestos urging firm support of the constitution and denouncing especially the revolt of Páez. Some of these were apparently no more spontaneous than many of the opposition manifestos from Venezuela and Ecuador, and when Santander presented Congress in 1827 with a definitive collection of the proclamations put out by either side, those favorable to his government filled only 73 folios and those unfavorable filled 217.[51] But no matter what the *granadinos* may have thought about the shortcomings of the Santander administration or the need for "reforms," they definitely preferred Santander to Páez. Nor were they at all enthusiastic about the Bolivian Constitution, despite the original hope of Bolívar that even Santander might support it. Presumably he hoped that its more liberal features would win the Vice-President's fancy, and in truth Santander's first letters to Bolívar concerning the project were somewhat favorable. The speech with which Bolívar had introduced the constitution was described by Santander as a "masterpiece of eloquence, ingenuity, liberalism, and learning." [52] And yet by mid-October the Bolivian Constitution was drawing mild but open criticism in the official *Gaceta*. A month later Santander was the first signer of a manifesto which started out with a conventional eulogy of Bolívar, declared it an insult to the Liberator to believe him capable of dictatorship, and then proceeded to assail the Bolivian Constitution with particular reference to the life presidency. The document had been written by Vicente Azuero, but Santander supplied the printing costs from his own pocket. Nor was it a mere outburst of the liberal extremists, for it was also signed by the far from liberal Dr. Ignacio Herrera, the universally respected Félix Restrepo, and virtually all the notables of Cundinamarca.[53]

[50] O'Leary XXIV, 473-484.

[51] A.C., Senado-41. See also Blanco X, 615, 631, 634-640, 643-647, 658-659, and *La Gaceta de Colombia,* May 27, 1827.

[52] Santander to Bolívar, July 19, 1826, Lecuna, *C.S.* II, 260; see also *C.S.* II, 197-198.

[53] *La Gaceta de Colombia,* October 22, 1826; Guillermo Hernández de Alba and Fabio Lozano y Lozano, *Documentos sobre el Doctor Vicente Azuero* (Bogotá, 1944), vi, 183; Jorge Hernández Carrillo, *Santander y la Gran Colombia* (Bogotá, 1940), 104-135.

Santander's final stand on the Bolivian Constitution is a little hard to reconcile with his earlier letters to Bolívar, but it is definitely more in keeping with his record as a political liberal. Even more than this, it reflects a growing rift between the two men. Bolívar never fully informed Santander of his intentions with regard to the immediate crisis, if indeed he knew them himself; he had merely lamented the state of Colombia and suggested his new constitution as a permanent cure for the nation's ills. Santander, in turn, originally hoped that Bolívar could be induced to take a strong stand in favor of constitutional legality, and it was probably a long time before he gave up this hope entirely. However, the hope had already begun to dwindle. Bolívar's response to the first pronouncement of Guayaquil was somewhat disturbing; the actions of Guzmán were sufficient to cause a rapidly growing distrust of the Liberator's intentions. It was obvious that Bolívar had not heeded the express warning of Santander to the effect that Guzmán was a scheming, malicious character and that he had probably been sent to Lima originally as some sort of spy.[54] On the contrary, Bolívar's trust in his chosen emissary was apparently so complete that Santander could not help but suspect that Guzmán's various activities reflected the true policy of the Liberator. If this was the case, it seemed to follow that Bolívar was seeking dictatorial authority so as to impose an extra-legal settlement in Venezuela and then prepare the way for adoption of the Bolivian Constitution—with or without the Confederation of the Andes—at a National Convention that would probably be meeting well before 1831.

[54] Santander to Bolívar, January 6, 1826, Lecuna, *C.S.* II, 139-140.

## Chapter XXI

## *The Return of Simón Bolívar and the Fall of Santander*

ON SEPTEMBER 3 Bolívar finally set out from Peru, leaving the Peruvian government already organized in general accord with the Bolivian Constitution, and soon afterwards he arrived in Guayaquil. It was widely and fervently hoped that his mere presence in Colombia would put an end to internal dissensions. However, his task would not be easy. The country was fundamentally divided among Venezuelan separatists, the partisans of Santander, and proponents of a Bolivarian dictatorship, not to mention the various shadings in between. Each of the major factions had at least some ideals and aspirations all its own; it would be hard enough to reconcile any two with one another, and to find a solution that would be reasonably satisfactory to everyone was totally out of the question. In the last analysis, Bolívar had to choose either Páez or Santander, and the drama of the next six months centers upon his gradual realization of this fact and the process by which he finally made his choice.

### *From Guayaquil to New Granada*

When Bolívar reached Guayaquil, publicly expressed displeasure at the talk of dictatorship, and affirmed his intention to uphold the legal order, Santander was at least temporarily reassured as to his intentions. Unfortunately, the Vice-President's suspicions were promptly revived by the events that followed. Bolívar embarked on a triumphal tour through Ecuador in which he was feted on every hand as an almost supernatural being, and he gave very little indication of displeasure at such treatment. For the present he rejected the title of Dictator, but he calmly ignored the fact that his previous delegation of executive authority within Colombia into the hands of Santander was still in force, and that his personal "extraordinary faculties," which he had enjoyed simply as a commanding general, had been annulled by the controversial law of July, 1824. He proceeded to act as though still invested with those faculties, and he used them to grant military promotions to the chief backers of the movement for dictatorship.[1] He paid close attention both to the laments of the military against ungrateful civilians and to the observations of the

---

[1] Blanco X, 592; José Joaquín Guerra, *La Convención de Ocaña* (Bogotá, 1908), 80-81, 88; Santander to Bolívar, October 29, 1826, Lecuna, *C.S.* II, 320.

338

Ecuadoran conservatives who felt all would be well if only the major part of the social, fiscal, and economic reforms enacted since 1821 were cancelled outright. Bolívar wrote frankly to Santander that he had informed the Ecuadorans of his desire not to be blamed for the "absurd laws" which had been issued at Bogotá "against the will of the people." [2]

In his private correspondence Bolívar admitted that his public statements against dictatorship should not be taken too seriously:

> "In this confusion dictatorship will compose everything, because we shall take time to prepare opinion for the great reform of the Convention of '31; and in the meantime we calm the parties of the extremes. With laws . . . we can do no more in the Páez business than to punish the rebellion; but if I am authorized by the Nation I can do everything." [3]

He thus showed obvious annoyance when he reached Popayán in New Granada and found not only that there was wide popular opposition to his latest political ideas but also that the intendant, José Hilario López, was a firm supporter of Santander who refused to countenance any municipal proclamations of the type sponsored by Guzmán. Bolívar's officers made matters worse by their mocking of the Colombian Constitution and their rather high-handed treatment of the local population; and the Liberator on his part was sufficiently free with hostile remarks about the Santander administration for the Vice-President to become fully aware of them.[4]

When Bolívar arrived in Bogotá in mid-November he was greeted with speeches and slogans extolling the sacredness of the Constitution and Laws of Colombia. Everything was obviously—and rather tactlessly—designed to compromise him in favor of the policies advocated by Santander, and he made no secret of his displeasure. The day after his arrival he wrote to General Páez—whose latest disloyalty was not yet known in Bogotá—that his one motive in coming had been to save Páez, and with him Venezuela; that Páez "had a right to resist injustice with justice;" and that he himself was "surrounded by calumny and enemies" in Bogotá.[5] In the course of the following week, however, relations between Bolívar and Santander began to take a turn for the better. Bolívar felt that he was winning the Vice-President and his party over little by little to his own way of thinking, and he wrote to Lima that Santander was strongly in favor of the scheme for a Great Confederation of Peru, Bolivia, and Colombia. The latter statement finds some support, as a matter of fact,

[2] Bolívar to Santander, October 8, 1826, Lecuna, *C.L.* VI, 81-84.
[3] Bolívar to Santander, September 19, 1826, Lecuna, *C.L.* VI, 74-75.
[4] Angel and Rufino J. Cuervo, *Vida de Rufino Cuervo* (2 vols., Paris, 1892) I, 80; Joaquín Mosquera, *Carta al Sr. Felipe Larrázabal* (Bogotá, 1869), 8; José María Obando, *Apuntamientos para la historia* (Lima, 1842), 48.
[5] Bolívar to Páez, November 15, 1826, Lecuna, *C.L.* VI, 99. Cf. Groot, 430.

in a letter which Santander wrote soon afterward to Marshal Santa Cruz. At the same time Bolívar consented to regularize his position by formally reassuming his place as constitutional Chief Executive. He also assumed the "extraordinary faculties" which the Executive was entitled to use in national emergencies under the terms of the constitution itself. This was not quite the same as being dictator, and it certainly did not mean that Bolívar had become reconciled to the constitution in its present form; but the powers he received were broad enough for most purposes, and the legality of the procedure could not be seriously questioned. Santander had assumed exactly the same faculties a few months earlier.[6]

The next step was for Bolívar to issue a series of emergency decrees that met at least some of the complaints about the "excessive liberality" of Colombian institutions but wholly annulled only a few of the great reforms of the last five years. The decrees were principally justified, moreover, on the grounds that they would revive the Colombian treasury, and there could be no doubt that this was urgently needed; Colombia had defaulted on her foreign debt since the previous July, and the disorders now afflicting the country had further disrupted the always harassed fiscal administration. Thus one group of decrees carefully instructed Colombian officials to do their duty in the collection and distribution of revenues, in case they were not doing it already; increased the normal penalties against smugglers and tobacco bootleggers; and gave revenue-collectors direct coercive jurisdiction in arresting and seizing the property of tax-payers. But only two real changes were made in the tax structure itself. The *derecho de consumo* on imported merchandise—which in practice had amounted to a surtax of 3% over and above the regular customs duties— was reimposed despite protests from Santander and Castillo y Rada; and the *contribución directa* was diminished, with the loss in revenue to be made up by a head-tax of $3 a year on "all free men, without exception of class, condition, or estate." The head-tax clearly indicated the reactionary trend of Bolívar's economic thought, but at least the *contribución directa* was not yet abolished outright.[7]

Other decrees had the purpose of saving money by reducing the government payroll. The Departments of Guayaquil and Ecuador were each reduced to a single province, wiping out at the stroke of a pen three provincial divisions set up by the Congress of 1824. The *jueces letrados de primera instancia* were eliminated, their functions passing to the municipal *alcaldes;* similarly, the superior courts of Guayaquil and Zulia

---

[6] Bolívar to Páez, November 18, 1826, Lecuna, *C.L.* VI, 107; Bolívar to Santa Cruz, November 21, 1826, *C.L.* VI, 110; Bolívar to Heres, November 30, 1826, *C.L.* VI, 115; Santander to Santa Cruz, December 3, 1826, Lecuna, *C.S.* III, 11; *Codif. Nac.* II, 409-410.

[7] *Codif. Nac.* II, 408-409, 413-416; *Acuerdos* II, 211; *La Gaceta de Colombia,* April 8, 1827.

were abolished. The post of Secretary of the Navy was abolished also, and the portfolios of Foreign Affairs and Interior were provisionally united in the same hands. The diplomatic corps was slashed, in a decree originally classified as confidential; Colombian representatives were completely withdrawn from all Latin American nations save Mexico and in Europe from the Holy See. The armed forces, finally, were called upon to accept their full share of the economy drive. Retirement pensions were suspended, again over the protest of Santander, and all payments to officers not holding *destinos efectivos* were halted until further notice; both army and navy were to undergo a further reduction in size; numerous departmental and provincial *comandancias* were dismantled, and those that remained were entrusted as far as possible to officers who held political command in the same regions.[8] Of these measures the abolition of the *jueces letrados* and the union of civil and military commands were the most repugnant to liberal theorists, but neither move was irrevocable, and the immediate financial situation afforded a good excuse for both. The further reduction of the army, moreover, was a favorite demand of all civilian liberals.

At the same time Bolívar issued a number of miscellaneous decrees laying down some rather obvious rules of good conduct for government employees, setting up regulations for the exclusion of subversive foreigners from Colombia, and prescribing ways to improve the administration of justice. Only two measures dealt directly with the political crisis of the moment. One was a decree setting up the office of *Jefe Superior del Sur,* with broad powers over all three Ecuadoran departments; General Pedro Briceño Méndez was named to fill the position, but until he could get there it was entrusted to Bolívar's former Secretary General, José Gabriel Pérez. The other strictly prohibited all unauthorized popular assemblies or juntas such as those from which Guzmán had extracted his various proclamations, and singled out the military for particularly severe penalties if they became involved in anything of the sort.[9]

The last decree was obviously framed to please Santander, giving the impression that Bolívar had assumed "extraordinary faculties" and made his economies precisely to strengthen the constitutional regime. Taken as a whole, Bolívar's recent burst of activity in Bogotá is an excellent indication of the energy and capacity for rapid decision which were normally among his most distinctive traits; though a few of his measures were perhaps adopted too hastily, others were long overdue. Yet the concrete improvement in relations between Bolívar and Santander was not destined to last. The Liberator continued on his way to settle affairs with Páez, leaving Santander with "extraordinary faculties" over all territory where

[8] *Acuerdos* II, 210-212; *Codif. Nac.* II, 416-427, VII, 461-462; O'Leary VII, 427-428. The suspension of retirement pensions did not apply to *inválidos.*

[9] *Codif. Nac.* II, 411-412, 419-422, 424-425.

he could not exercise them in person. However, Bolívar had no sooner resumed his journey than he reverted to the same bad habits he had shown on his march up from Guayaquil. He listened attentively to anyone who had a grievance against the Santander administration, and though many of the charges he heard were true enough he appears to have made little effort to distinguish the true from the false, or the concrete mistakes of the regime in power from conditions which no government could remedy with the human and material resources at hand. All the complaints he carefully relayed back to Bogotá. Bolívar later denied that he meant to ascribe everything that was wrong to the personal failings of Santander and his associates, but this obviously was not the impression gained by the Vice-President in reading the Liberator's reports. Nor can Bolívar's word be entirely reconciled with the unfriendly comments about Santander that he and his party were continually making, with particular reference to the English loan.[10]

Bolívar's official correspondence was also proof that he regarded his Bogotá decrees as only a start in the right direction. He frankly indicated his entire disapproval of the *contribución directa,* and his strong preference for the Spanish financial system; the *alcabala* did not agree with the "doctrines of economists," but it had the great advantage of being "habitual." He compared the republican bureaucracy most unfavorably with that of the colonial regime, and his complaints were promptly echoed by the *junta provincial* and various municipalities of the province of Socorro through which he passed.[11] Needless to say, the Santander administration could not be expected to agree with many of these opinions. With regard to the *alcabala* Castillo y Rada was prompt to reply that it might have been habitual in 1821, but that this was no longer the case in 1826; instead, the people were gradually becoming accustomed to the *contribución directa,* whether they actually paid it or not.[12] Nevertheless, Santander now ordered the immediate suspension of the *contribución directa* and the restoration of the *alcabala* in its place. He even took the first preliminary steps toward restoration of the *aguardiente* monopoly as well. At least outwardly, all this was done as a gesture of submission to the will of Bolívar, who received full credit for the revival of the *alcabala* in an extended prologue to the decree that ordered its collection.[13] On the other hand, it is entirely possible that Santander's extreme haste in complying with the Liberator's wishes arose from a desire to discredit Bolívar and all his critics for once and for all by showing without further

[10] *La Gaceta de Colombia,* April 15, 1827; O'Leary XXV, 193-197; Blanco XI, 70-71, 190; Cuervo and Cuervo, *op. cit.,* I, 103.
[11] *La Gaceta de Colombia,* December 17, 1826, February 11, 1827; A.H.N., Congresos XXV, 861-865, 870-873.
[12] Castillo to Revenga, December 9, 1826, O'Leary VII, 110-112.
[13] *Codif. Nac.* II, 433-435; *Acuerdos* II, 213.

ado what a return to the colonial tax system would really be like. As he well knew, it was one thing to talk nostalgically about the famous Spanish sales-tax, and something else to pay it. It was also alleged that Santander's method of enforcement made Bolívar's head-tax even more burdensome than the Liberator had intended, presumably again with the purpose of discrediting the measure itself. Whether this charge was literally true or not, the head-tax probably aroused more popular criticism and actual disorder in a matter of weeks than the *contribución directa* in all its five years of existence.[14]

## *The Settlement of Venezuela and the Final Breach with Santander*

While Bolívar and the government at Bogotá were engaged in long-distance debate over fiscal policy, the Venezuelan situation was deteriorating faster than ever. Páez' recent decision to go ahead with his reorganization of Venezuela without waiting for the Liberator's arrival, together with more instances of arbitrary action on the part of Páez and his followers, had brought the popularity of the revolutionary regime to a new low. Cristóbal Mendoza, after being finally deposed from the Intendancy of Venezuela, thought it best to take flight to the Antilles. Toward the end of November Puerto Cabello formally withdrew its allegiance from Páez and announced that it would obey only Bolívar.[15] To make matters worse, the first actual bloodshed of the rebellion had already taken place. It began in the East, between the partisans of Páez and those of General Bermúdez; the latter thereupon placed himself under the exclusive protection of Bolívar's name, issuing a manifesto roughly similar to those of Guzmán. This step, in turn, provoked a countermovement in favor of the Colombian Constitution and Santander on the part of Colonel Olivares in Guayana, which left eastern Venezuela in a three-way conflict. A second outbreak of violence occurred between Páez and Puerto Cabello, the command of whose forces was provisionally accepted by General Briceño Méndez, who conveniently happened to be on hand. And a third was almost provoked by the Páez faction in the latter part of December when it staged an invasion of the province of Barinas, which had so far remained loyal to Bogotá under the rule of General Miguel Guerrero. Fortunately the invasion was a bloodless one, since the

[14] On this point see report of the Comisión de Hacienda of the lower house, May 25, 1827, A.C., Senado-48, 396; J. G. Pérez to Bolívar, January 21, 1827, O'Leary V, 449. For general protests against the head-tax: A.C., Senado-49, 49-51, 53-56, 135-137; Cámara-13, 396-397.

[15] Eloy G. González, *Dentro de la cosiata* (Caracas, 1907), 222-229; Mendoza to Bolívar, December 15, 1826, O'Leary II, 290-293; O'Leary XXIV, 501-502.

defenders retreated without a fight and then, when their attackers found no local support, compelled them to accept a bribe and withdraw.[16]

The basic trend of developments in Venezuela was already known to Bolívar as he embarked upon the semi-final lap of his journey, from Cúcuta to Maracaibo. His immediate reaction was to dispatch urgent messages to both Bogotá and Cartagena, asking for men, money, and supplies so that he might restore order in Venezuela by force if necessary. Meanwhile he emptied provincial coffers of all available funds, including those specifically earmarked for service on the national debt. This procedure, however, merely served to increase the Vice-President's growing distrust of Bolívar's intentions, with the result that he deliberately put off sending the men and supplies.[17] Indeed the more radical liberals of Bogotá, including even Castillo y Rada, insisted that Bolívar was more likely to use troops to subvert the constitution than to restore it, and that therefore New Granada should copy Venezuela and turn federalist herself in order to escape from his threatened tyranny. Even Santander appears to have toyed with the idea of staging a separatist movement in New Granada, although he did nothing about it and saw to it that the others did nothing either.[18]

Santander finally realized that Bolívar's warlike preparations were directed against Páez and not himself, and he then agreed to give the aid that was requested.[19] By that time, however, his assistance was no longer needed. Seeing his forces waver at the mere approach of Bolívar, Páez had made one last determined show of force with a view of extracting more favorable terms from Bolívar; he commissioned Dr. Peña to inform the Liberator that he must either accept the demands of Venezuela or halt his march, and he talked quite openly of armed resistance. Peña had the misfortune to be arrested before he reached Bolívar's headquarters, but otherwise Páez' tactics were brilliantly successful. In return for a general amnesty, a guarantee that Páez and all his followers would retain their property, rank, and public offices, and the promise of a Great Convention for constitutional reform, the *llanero* chieftain on January 2, 1827, deigned to recognize the Liberator's supreme authority. Bolívar was then

[16] A.C., Senado-41, 212-214, 216 ff.; *La Gaceta de Colombia,* January 7 to February 11, 1827.

[17] See the surprisingly frank admission about "doubts" and delays in *La Gaceta de Colombia,* January 28, 1827; also Watts to Clay December 27, 1826, N.A., Colombia Dispatches IV.

[18] *La Bandera Tricolor* (Bogotá), January 7, 1827; Joaquín Mosquera to Santander, December 29, 1826, *Arch. Sant.* XVI, 101; Restrepo VI, 479, 499-500; *Apelación al público de Colombia* (Bogotá, 1827), 32-33.

[19] *Acuerdos* II, 220-223; *La Gaceta de Colombia,* February 18, 1827.

welcomed into Caracas by a populace that was heartily glad to be rid of Páez.[20]

Thus far all that Bolívar had done could be justified on the grounds that it was necessary in order to avoid further bloodshed. Páez' submission might well have been bought more cheaply, but Bolívar could not be sure, especially as he still did not realize the full extent of Páez' weakness. Yet not content with Páez' submission, Bolívar now adopted a set of policies that made his open breach with Santander inevitable. He not only declared that his recent amnesty had cleared Páez of any obligation to answer the charges originally made against him in Congress but went on to affirm that the Venezuelan *caudillo* had "saved the republic." Páez' leading supporters, similarly, were lavishly rewarded with jobs and favors; Carabaño, for instance, became deputy chief of the Liberator's general staff. Press criticism of Páez and his adherents was forbidden lest it disturb public tranquillity.[21] At the same time former loyalists such as Bermúdez and the *Batallón Apure* received little or nothing from Bolívar's hands; he himself admitted that they had "lost everything." [22] Mendoza and Peñalver received the Liberator's thanks for their constant friendship, and got back their old positions, but they obtained nothing else. This situation was not entirely to the liking of Bolívar, who was distinctly critical of Páez in private conversation; but he frankly confessed that he was afraid to antagonize Páez unduly. If the loyalist faction received any material rewards at all it generally had to be from Santander, who sought to match the promotions that had been handed out by Páez during his rebellion and later by Bolívar so as to keep up what remained of constitutionalist sentiment in Venezuela. The three leaders together thus managed to create a new surplus of generals and colonels over and above the normal quota set by the Organic Law of the Army.[23]

Bolívar also found time in Caracas to carry out additional reforms of the type decreed in Bogotá the previous November. The main difference was that the measures he took in Caracas were of purely local effect, applicable to Venezuela but not to the rest of the republic, which he had assigned to Santander. Bolívar suspended his own head-tax, but definitely restored the *alcabala*. He abolished numerous offices for the sake of economy, but he wisely increased the meager salaries of those public servants who were not dismissed. He fired corrupt fiscal employees, replacing them with inactive army officers who had been cut off from

[20] Daniel F. O'Leary, *Ultimos años de la vida pública de Bolívar* (Madrid, 1916), 109-114; Blanco XI, 74-77; O'Leary II, 318-319, VI, 20-21.

[21] O'Leary XXV, 19-22, 27, 32.

[22] Bolívar to Santander, February 6, 1827, Lecuna, *C.L.* VI, 180-182.

[23] *La Gaceta de Colombia,* March 4 and May 13, 1827; A.C., Senado-22, 219; Sagarzazu, "Ligeros apuntes en las diferentes épocas de disensiones políticas," *Boletín de la Academia Nacional de Historia de Venezuela* XIII, 356-357 (1930).

payment of salaries or pensions by his own Bogotá decrees. Bolívar also suspended the acceptance of government *vales* in payment of customs duties, while at the same time issuing lurid threats against all who did not at once pay what debts they owed to the state. This particular combination of measures was well fitted to help out the government treasury, but it showed little regard for the merchants, several of whom had to undergo arrest as a result. One United States businessman held *vales* expressly countersigned for the payment of debts at the Maracaibo customs house; Bolívar's order came out, and the *vales* were no longer acceptable; whereupon he was arrested for non-payment of the debts in question and his property was temporarily confiscated.[24]

Some of the most significant of Bolívar's reforms were contained in a number of detailed *reglamentos* whose purpose was to reorganize with military dispatch the entire Venezuelan administration, especially in its financial aspects. Their spirit was consistently reactionary. The separation of powers was violated in order to give the intendants back their legal jurisdiction in treasury cases (*negocios contenciosos de hacienda*), which they had received on a provisional basis from the Congress of Cúcuta but had lost in the legislative reforms of 1825; the death penalty was established for any theft of government funds, "by force or clandestinely, however small their amount;" and an entire new tariff system was introduced, with substantial increases in both import and export duties over those being charged in New Granada. Another decree reorganized the University of Caracas, generally following Santander's Plan of Studies but making no mention of the required texts. Many detailed provisions of these measures were undoubtedly beneficial, but still their total effect was to give Venezuela a system of government distinct from that prevailing in the rest of Colombia. It is quite possible that Bolívar was frankly preparing Venezuela to take her separate place in his projected Confederation of the Andes.[25]

In fact it was widely assumed in Venezuela at the time that Bolívar was still hoping to impose at least some form of the Bolivian Constitution, despite the rather dubious reception it had received in most of Colombia. The latest journalistic forays of Antonio L. Guzmán were seemingly designed to further this objective,[26] although there is little real evidence of Bolívar's long-range intentions. For that matter, neither the Confederation of the Andes nor the Bolivian Constitution as such was very

[24] *Codif. Nac.* III, 13-14, 52, 57; Blanco XI, 546, 551; *El Reconciliador* (Caracas) April 10, 1827; Watts to Clay, May 14, 1827, N.A., Colombia Dispatches IV; consular report March 17, 1827, N.A., Maracaibo I.

[25] *Codif. Nac.* III, 23-24, 53, 78-81, 225-272. See summary of measures by José R. Revenga in Blanco XI, 538-552.

[26] Williamson to Clay, May 9, 1827, N.A., La Guaira I; Heres to O'Leary, July 2, 1827, O'Leary V, 252.

popular in Venezuela, and the agitation for and against them helped to keep the region in a state of latent unrest. This unrest was further augmented by minor troop mutinies and by various social and racial disorders of the usual Venezuelan type.[27]

In any event, Bolívar's conduct in Venezuela had naturally aroused the bitterness of Santander to a new height. The Vice-President frankly complained to the Liberator that "Páez being the saviour of his country, I, as ruler, and Congress, are guilty and delinquent; we have to defend ourselves against this charge." [28] Moreover, Santander could not defend his own policies without publicly attacking those of Bolívar. In *La Gaceta de Colombia*, at least, criticism of the Liberator was still rather mild, and often indirect, but it was expressed with much more frankness by Santander's political supporters in their private conversation and in the liberal press. Nor was it only the out-and-out *santanderistas* who took a dim view of Bolívar's policies in Venezuela. *El Constitutional*, which more closely reflected the opinion of moderates and independent liberals, was perfectly willing to accept Bolívar's judgment in regard to the amnesty he granted Páez, but it had harsh words indeed for his press curbs and for his new fiscal arrangements.[29]

The hostility of Santander and his circle had in turn evoked the deepest indignation in Bolívar, who did not believe the Vice-President should allow even private newspapers to attack him. The ideal solution, he felt, would have been to allow no criticism of Santander in Venezuela and no criticism of himself or Páez in Bogotá. For a time Bolívar actually tried to enforce this system at the Venezuelan end, but it was not for long.[30] At heart, in fact, Bolívar was now far more bitterly opposed to Santander than Santander yet was to Bolívar. The Vice-President still professed to hope that Bolívar would mend his ways, provided that the *granadino* liberals would refrain from "irritating" him too much; he went out of his way to compliment Bolívar on his apparent resolve to leave the formal convocation of the Great Convention to Congress, and he vigorously proclaimed his belief that Bolívar must remain at the head of the government for the maintenance of law and order.[31] However, it is probable that the kind words of Santander were irritating in themselves, since they were

[27] Blanco XI, 170, 204, 220-221, 243, 539-540; O'Leary II, 87, 98. Rumors were circulated even to the effect that Bolívar was selling people to the English as slaves in payment of the foreign debt.

[28] Santander to Bolívar, March 9, 1827, Lecuna, *C.S.* III, 88.

[29] Cf. *El Constitucional*, February 1, April 5, and July 19, 1827.

[30] Bolívar to Soublette, March 16, 1827, Lecuna, *C.L.* VI, 230-232.

[31] Santander to Rufino Cuervo, March 1 and 30, 1827, Luis Augusto Cuervo, ed., *Epistolario de Rufino Cuervo* (3 vols., Bogotá, 1918-1922) I, 31, 37; Santander to Bolívar, March 2, April 16, 1827, Lecuna, *C.S.* III, 82, 119; Santander to Urdaneta, April 10, 1827, *Arch. Sant.* XVI, 328.

invariably phrased in such a way as to put across some rather obvious pleading for the constitutionalist cause. To Bolívar this was rank hypocrisy; he wrote to Soublette on March 16 that Santander's "perfidious ingratitude" had at last become insupportable, and on the same day he wrote to the Vice-President requesting him to consider their friendship at an end.[32]

## The End of the Santander Regime

Even before he received Bolívar's letter of March 16, Santander's growing antagonism had led him into a course of action which immeasurably deepened their estrangement, and has permanently marred the Vice-President's reputation as the Man of Laws. The origins of the trouble really go back to January 26, 1827, when First Commandant (i.e., Lt. Col.) José Bustamante led a mutiny of the Colombian Third Division still stationed at Lima. In justifying his action Bustamente announced the existence of "very grave and well-founded suspicions" that the head of all Colombian forces in Peru, General Jacinto Lara, was engaged in treasonable activities against the Colombian Constitution. But actually, the main treason Lara had committed was his foolish indifference to the reports of plotting within the Third Division itself that he had been receiving since the previous December. Exactly what was behind this unrest has never been fully established, and probably never can be. Part of it was certainly the natural demoralization of troops on occupation duty in a foreign country increasingly hostile to them. Then there was some rivalry between *granadino* junior officers such as Bustamante, whose home province was Socorro, and the Venezuelans surrounding Lara who monopolized the higher posts. José María Córdova believed that the men, though not necessarily their leaders, were quite sincere in believing that their objective was to protect the constitution against monarchist intrigues by the Bolivarian party; according to this argument, careless statements by a number of Colombian officers had aroused genuine suspicions in the soldiers' minds. Finally, there are "grave and well-founded suspicions" that Peruvians hostile to the government Bolívar had left established in their country took a hand in the affair, since a Peruvian coup d'état followed suspiciously close on the heels of the Colombian troop mutiny.[33]

Whatever the precise origins of the mutiny may have been, for Colombia its immediate importance lay in Bustamante's attempt to rationalize his conduct as part of a struggle for the defense of constitutional legality, decking out his manifesto accordingly with attacks on both Páez and the Bolivian Constitution. The strategem was eminently successful

[32] Lecuna, *C.L.*, VI, 230-232.
[33] Blanco XI, 104-107, 511; O'Leary V, 175-182, VII, 370-371, XXV, 260; *El Constitucional*, April 5, 1827.

from the start, for when news of the mutiny reached Bogotá it occasioned an impromptu celebration in which Santander himself took part. Obviously Santander was swept off his feet by the enthusiasm of his friends, for we also know that he had to search the archives even to discover who Bustamante was. But when an official reply was finally dispatched to Bustamante at Lima it was sufficiently favorable to give rise to a false yet widespread belief that Santander had personally inspired the mutiny. The administration informed Bustamente that mutiny, as such, could never be approved, but that if his charges against Lara proved correct his action was to be highly commended, and that the patriotic sentiments expressed by the mutineers were duly appreciated. To this communication Santander added a personal note in which he stated that the motives cited in justification of the mutiny did in fact appear extremely serious, but that Bustamante should still have warned the government soon enough for it to deal with Lara in legal fashion. At the same time Santander authorized Colonel Antonio Obando, an old associate from the Vice-President's days in Casanare, to go and take command of the Third Division, giving him blanket authority to reward it with any promotions he felt advisable.[34]

As Santander later pointed out to Congress, there was no apparent reason to doubt Bustamante's word on the basis of the first reports reaching Bogotá, and it would have been unwise to alienate the Third Division at once by condemning it sight unseen; in any event, he added, it would have been unfair to inflict a severe punishment upon Bustamante after pardoning Páez who had done exactly the same thing.[35] Even so, the Vice-President could have been more guarded in his answer to Bustamante, and his attempt to equate the Bustamante revolt with that of Páez was a virtual admission that his original confidence had proved unfounded. Indeed the Third Division had departed secretly from Lima soon after its mutiny, and in April proceeded to launch an armed invasion of Ecuador. Once again, the motives behind its actions remain somewhat obscure. The new Peruvian government admittedly helped the Division on its way, and it was widely believed that its leaders had been bribed to bring about the annexation of southern Colombia to Peru. That such a bribe was offered is entirely possible, although the Peruvians' desire to speed the departure of their Colombian guests could easily be explained on other grounds. That the offer was ever seriously accepted is perhaps less likely, although the possibility cannot be excluded. The leaders of the Division themselves merely announced that they came to defend the constitutional order that had been disrupted by the dictatorial proclamations of the year before. They further declared that they could offer no obedi-

[34] *Arch. Sant.* XVI, 285-289, 303, 281-282; Joaquín Posada Gutiérrez, *Memorias histórico-políticas* (4 vols., Bogotá, 1929), I, 66-72.
[35] O'Leary XXV, 358-363.

ence to Bolívar until he appeared before Congress to give account of his actions in Peru; nor would they accept any constituent convention not expressly decreed by Congress.[36]

At Guayaquil the Division found prompt support in the form of a local fifth column that deposed the departmental authorities and laid open the province to its invaders. The fear of Peruvian intrigue was heightened when the sovereign people of Guayaquil then installed as their new intendant General José La Mar, who, though a Colombian by birth, was now a Marshal of Peru following in the train of the Third Division. On the other hand, no really important party in Guayaquil seriously favored annexation to Peru. Even the victims of the local insurrection had to admit that it had fairly wide popular support, certainly more than the movement hatched by Guzmán and Tomás C. Mosquera the year before in favor of dictatorship. This support resulted in part from purely local issues; it reflected dissatisfaction caused by several of the Liberator's Bogotá decrees, including the ones that abolished the departmental *Corte Superior* and suspended all salary payments to army officers in full or partial retirement; and it reflected a certain distrust of the national policies for which Bolívar and his chief advocates now stood. The true political objective of Guayaquil now as before was simply to obtain a greater measure of regional autonomy.[37]

The invasion of Ecuador was nevertheless too much even for Santander. Even before the mutinous division reached its destination the government at Bogotá had come to admit that Peru probably had a hand in the January uprising. When it heard of the proceedings at Guayaquil the government sent an immediate message of protest and instructed its special agent, Col. Antonio Obando, to reestablish the state of affairs that had existed before the recent disturbances. However, Santander was disinclined to take strong measures. He had not given up all hope that the Third Division might ultimately be proven innocent, and he expressed full confidence in Obando even when the latter delayed taking command of the Division as instructed and actually chose to recognize the provisional authority of La Mar. Santander likewise issued a curious order, which was not carried out, for the Venezuelan troops of the Third Division to remain isolated in the South while the *granadinos* continued on to Bogotá. The conduct of both Obando and Santander was in fact somewhat erratic throughout. The same can be said of the Governor of Pasto, José María

---

[36] Blanco XI, 191-192; Guerra, *op. cit.* 155-157; O'Leary XXV, 232-233, 252, 253-254, 381-382. Bustamente himself, when captured later on, said that the Peruvian offer had really been made but that he never intended to carry out what the Peruvians proposed; after regaining his freedom he then repudiated the entire statement (Restrepo VII, 31-32).

[37] *La Gaceta de Colombia*, June 10, 1827; Pedro Fermín Ceballos, *Resumen de la historia del Ecuador* (5 vols., Guayaquil, 1886) IV, 199; *El Constitucional*, August 23, 1827; O'Leary IV, 312-319, V, 172, 451-452, IX, 78-81, 86.

Obando—a firm *santanderista* but no relative to Antonio—who flatly refused to cooperate with the authorities at Quito when the latter prepared to take action against units of the Third Division that had marched inland through Cuenca. Yet there is no reason to doubt that all three sincerely desired to avoid bloodshed; they were merely dealing with Bustamante as Bolívar had dealt with Páez. Moreover, the actual danger inherent in the movements of the Third Division was sharply diminished when Juan José Flores as *Comandante General* of the Department of Ecuador succeeded in provoking a counter-insurrection among the Division's troops at Cuenca. For a time Bustamante himself was held under arrest. Flores' efforts to follow up this success with the military conquest of Guayaquil were thwarted by the hesitations if not the outright hostility of Santander and Antonio Obando; but their attitude was at least partially vindicated when Flores finally obtained the surrender of the city by peaceful intrigue on September 29.[38]

All of Ecuador thus fell again under the rule of Flores and the other military partisans of Bolívar, while Venezuela continued subject to the quasi-independent regime set up by the Liberator since his compromise with Páez. In the meantime, Santander at Bogotá had been attempting to reestablish at least a semblance of constitutional normalcy. His first objective was to obtain the opening of Congress, which had been delayed far beyond the legal date of January 2 since the prevailing state of unrest afforded a new excuse for unwilling members to stay home, and also because the present authorities in Venezuela and Ecuador were not always very helpful in speeding Congressmen on their way. Hence the first meeting was delayed until May, and it took place in Tunja rather than in Bogotá so that the Senate could muster a quorum by the inclusion of a member too sick to finish his journey.[39]

Once regular sessions were resumed in the national capital, Santander delivered a formal message that was an odd mixture of conciliatory gestures and frank hostility toward Bolívar. He was sharply critical of the entire Páez affair and of Bolívar's subsequent actions in Venezuela; yet he reiterated his earlier suggestion that as a last resort Congress might legalize a National Convention at some time in the near future by taking a rather broad interpretation of the Constitution of Cúcuta. He requested a legal amnesty that would confirm the one granted by Bolívar to Páez and at the same time excuse the January mutiny of the Third Division; he opposed extending it to cover the invasion of Ecuador, on which he re-

[38] O'Leary XXV, 302-303, 319, 460-461, 477-514, 518, 584-585; *La Gaceta de Colombia*, May 23, 1827 (extraordinario), July 1, and September 9, 1827; Ceballos, *op. cit.*, IV, 213-217.

[39] A.C., Cámara-12, 312, Senado-49, 218; *El Colibrí* (Caracas), June 23, 1827; *Codif. Nac.* III, 155-158. Bolívar while at Bogotá had stated that he hoped Congress would not meet (Soublette to Montilla, December 7, 1826, O'Leary VIII, 122).

served judgment, even though Congress subsequently did this just the same. Finally, the Vice-President reaffirmed what had been his own stated opinion throughout the recent months: "The well-being of the Republic . . . is obtained if only the Liberator is the one who directs the administration . . . under the regime of laws."[40] Should Bolívar act according to this principle, Santander was convinced that no convention would really be necessary until the year 1831, since everyone would gladly abide by the present constitution if the Liberator would set the example.

Exactly the same course was urged upon Bolívar by General Carlos Soublette,[41] one of the few Colombian statesmen still actively working for a reconciliation of the President and Vice-President. But it is doubtful that Santander really thought the Liberator would agree to such a compromise, and certainly his leading supporters did not even regard it is a remote possibility. They consequently launched a campaign to have Congress accept the latest of the formal resignations from the presidency that Bolívar submitted from time to time almost as a matter of routine, principally to obtain renewed expressions of confidence. They supported their demand by citing all possible instances of the Liberator's disregard for the laws of Colombia, and they argued further that acceptance of the resignation was necessary in order to appease the Third Division. Santander himself opposed the resignation, not so much on general principle as for fear of Bolívar's armed supporters. In the end the Congress as a whole also voted to reject it, but only after a long debate that left both houses bitterly divided between the partisans of Bolívar and those of Santander. The division became so deep that it took twenty-five hard-fought ballots to select a Vice-President of the Senate.[42]

The fact that such serious squabbling had now taken root even in the Senate is a clear sign of the declining fortunes of Santanderean liberalism, and it is only partly due to the turnover in Senate membership at the last elections. Another sign of the same shift in party strength is the fact that the sessions of 1827 witnessed the most vigorous attack yet on the anti-clerical and fiscal legislation of the previous years. But the Bolivarian party of 1827 was not merely a stronger edition of the old *Montaña*. It had absorbed a good part of the *Montaña*, but it incorporated other disgruntled elements as well, especially from Ecuador and Venezuela, and also a number of *granadino* independents who were not always happy

[40] *Arch. Sant.* XVII, 42-57; cf. Santander to Urdaneta, April 1, 1827, Lecuna, *C.S.* III, 113. On the question of amnesty for the Third Division, see *Acuerdos* II, 237; and *Codif. Nac.* III, 177.

[41] Soublette to Bolívar, April 27, 1827, O'Leary VIII, 47-49.

[42] Santander to Rufino Cuervo, May 22, 1827, *Epistolario de Rufino Cuervo,* I, 47; A.C., Actas del Senado, May 19 and June 11, 1827; Manuel José Forero, ed., *Santander en sus escritos* (Bogotá, 1944), 107-108.

about having to choose between Bolívar and Santander but still in the last analysis preferred Bolívar. Typical of the latter group was the Popayán oligarchy of Mosqueras, Arroyos, and Arboledas, whose principal spokesman in Bogotá was Senator Jerónimo Torres.[43] The latter, if anyone, was the real leader of the Bolivarian faction in Congress. He was definitely a moderate compared with many of his fellow partisans, and his arguments usually made sense while theirs all too frequently did not. The moderate wing of the Bolivarian party must receive much of the credit for the fact that Congress in 1827 showed remarkably little interest in either a Bolivarian dictatorship or the Bolivian Constitution. Indeed a law restoring the legal status quo as of April 27, 1826, and cancelling all "extraordinary faculties" anywhere in the republic was put through with remarkably little difficulty, and with the general support of Jerónimo Torres.[44] In this way Congress essentially gave its approval to the policy suggested by Santander in his recent message: Bolívar should rule, but he should come to Bogotá and rule by the constitution until it was actually changed.

If it had not been for the Vice-President's use of his veto the same law for the restoration of constitutional normalcy would likewise have annulled all the emergency decrees lately issued by either Bolívar or Santander by virtue of the faculties in question. As it was, the law in its final form gave Santander wide discretion in modifying those decrees as he saw fit, and he used this authorization primarily to reestablish the three suppressed provinces in Ecuador and also, with certain reservations, the *jueces letrados de primera instancia*. The restoration of the former had been requested by many of the Ecuadorans themselves, and the restoration of the latter chiefly by the higher judiciary, which complained that the return of original jurisdiction to the municipal *alcaldes* under the terms of Bolívar's decree had caused new delays and confusion in the administration of justice.[45]

Santander was quite powerless, however, to dissuade Congress from summoning at last the Great Convention for constitutional reform, which it called to meet at Ocaña in March, 1828. Even his cabinet secretaries openly supported the proposal. The Vice-President's congressional supporters tried out their best delaying tactics, all to no avail; the most they could do was dictate a clause forbidding the Convention to tamper with any of the basic principles of popular sovereignty and republicanism. As a matter of fact, it is likely that many adherents of Santander were

[43] Cf. *El Bobo Entrometido* (Bogotá) July 1, 1827; for the views of Jerónimo Torres, see *El Ciudadano* (Bogotá), *passim*.
[44] *Codif. Nac.* III, 219-220; A.C., Actas del Senado, May 17, 1827; *La Gaceta de Colombia,* June 24, 1827.
[45] *Codif. Nac.* III, 280-281, 290-291; *El Registro Judicial de la República de Colombia* (Bogotá), June 22, 1827.

distinctly half-hearted in their opposition to the Convention. At the very least the Santanderean party promptly realized that the next step was to make the best of a bad bargain by joining the reform movement and trying to direct it into liberal channels. When Congress got around to deciding who might be elected to attend the Convention, Santander saw to it that the Liberator would be excluded and he himself would not.[46] Still more significant, perhaps, is the fact that the Vice-President's supporters were becoming more and more frankly the party of federalism, a scheme of government they had strongly condemned while the Chief Executive was Santander, but one which would have obvious advantages whenever Bolívar should finish his work in Venezuela and come back to take full command of the presidential office to which he had legally been reelected. As a last resort, outright independence for New Granada was advocated, all as a means of escaping the Bolivian Constitution and related evils.[47]

This evolution was hastened by news that Bolívar had at long last decided to leave Caracas. Bolívar's resolve, on the other hand, had been hastened if not actually determined by Santander's handling of the Third Division. In the eyes of the Liberator, the failure of "the iniquitous administration of robbery and rapine which has reigned in Bogotá" to take firm action against the invasion of Ecuador showed outright complicity in the hostile designs of Peru, and further revealed the scheme of Santander to destroy Colombia for the sole purpose of destroying Venezuela and Bolívar.[48] He therefore commissioned Páez to rule Venezuela as *Jefe Superior* in his absence and set out from Caracas early in July. Even before his departure he had begun to organize a great force to combat the rebels in the South. He did not desist from these plans even when he learned of the arrest of Bustamante and the desertion of much of the Third Division to Flores, although he frankly recognized that these events "exterminated the anarchists forever." [49] On the contrary, he continued to order troop movements from Maracaibo and Cartagena southward into the interior of New Granada just as if Bustamante still represented an immediate threat to Colombia. He expressly decreed that the cost of these preparations should be paid from whatever government

---

[46] A.C., Senado-6, 132, 142-146; A.C., *Actas del Senado*, June 18-20, July 17, 1827; *Codif. Nac.* III, 311; *Acuerdos* II, 254.

[47] *El Bobo Entrometido*, July 1, 1827; *El Fiscal* (Panamá), March 11, 1827; *El Granadino* (Bogotá), May 19, 1827; *El Conductor* (Bogotá), July 18, 1827.

[48] Bolívar to Cristóbal Mendoza, July 18, 1827, Lecuna, *C.L.* VI, 340-341.

Bolívar's decision was taken before he learned of the law that restored the legal and constitutional status quo and thereby ended the powers he was using in Venezuela; but undoubtedly he sensed what was likely to happen, and this was another reason for him to hasten his march.

[49] Bolívar to Peñalver, June 28, 1827, Lecuna, *C.L.* VI, 323.

funds his lieutenants could lay hands on, regardless of any orders that Santander might issue to the contrary.[50]

In his official statements Bolívar appears to have cited only the disturbances in Ecuador and the rumored designs of both Spain and Peru as reasons for his military preparations. To the government at Bogotá he also remarked that it would be easier and cheaper to support his troops in the interior than on the coast. Bolívar's correspondence, however, reveals that the political situation in the capital was also a major reason for his present course of action. Until Congress finally got around to calling the Great Convention he was frankly distressed at its apparent indifference toward the expressed will of the people, and he vaguely promised that this state of affairs could not be tolerated. Especially after reaching Cartagena, moreover, he showed great consternation over the alleged conspiracies of the Santanderean faction in Bogotá; and though he may have been misinformed on specific facts, his fears were not altogether imaginary.[51]

Yet Bolívar's own activities were the principal cause of the latest "conspiracies" in Bogotá. Santander rightly believed that the immediate danger in Ecuador had passed, he was unaware of any new peril from Spain, and he was not seriously alarmed over the current hostility of Peru, which he conceived to be directed primarily against the Liberator in person. These views were mainly shared by Congress, which chose the present occasion to decree the reduction of the army to exactly 9,980 men.[52] The Vice-President and his party thus concluded that Bolívar's preparations must be aimed specifically against themselves with a view to setting up some sort of dictatorship. These suspicions seemed to be confirmed when Bolívar's advance was preceded by a number of bloodcurdling manifestos against the Santander regime which were issued by military corps in Venezuela and Cartagena. Equally serious in the eyes of the constitutionalists was the fact that Bolívar was now acting as Chief Executive endowed with "extraordinary faculties" over both Venezuela and New Granada, in open violation of the recent law cancelling all such powers, and despite the fact that he had not yet even taken the oath of office before Congress for his new term as President. As his previous term had expired in January, his position had been slightly obscure for some time, but as long as he remained in Venezuela he had not really attempted to be any more than an extraordinary regional official. Santander's position had also been obscure until Congress finally managed

[50] A.C., Senado-54, 275-276.
[51] O'Leary XXV, 392-395, 463-464, 516-517, 538-540; *Acuerdos* II, 251.
[52] *Codif. Nac.* III, 296-297. For evidence of the wide support for this measure, cf. A.C., Senado-53, 36-38.

to receive his oath as Vice-President in May; but certainly now he had a far better legal claim to rule than did Bolívar.[53]

In any case, the *granadino* liberals now talked openly of offering armed resistance and if necessary setting up an independent state under Santander. The Vice-President himself was presumably more discreet in public, but he, too, seriously considered the possibility of fighting back. According to José Manuel Restrepo, who was present in his cabinet at the time, Santander was dissuaded from this course only by the refusal of his Secretary of War, General Soublette, to lend support. Santander also informed his cabinet that he "hated Bolívar to the death" and would still welcome a chance to fight if Bolívar struck the first blow.[54] Many other liberal leaders, including Senator Soto, were so afraid of Bolívar's vengeance that they left Bogotá for reasons of "health," but Santander remained in the capital, assailing Bolívar's recent actions in messages to Congress and in the official *Gaceta*. He had Soublette write to Bolívar's camp suggesting that the new law reducing the size of the armed forces—which had proved highly offensive to the Liberator—be implemented precisely at the expense of the units now moving on Bogotá. Then, as Bolívar finally drew near, Santander instructed Congress to prorogue its sessions expressly to receive his oath of office. By this means Bolívar was given a last chance to assume command of the government legally, and to rule by the Constitution.[55]

\* \* \* \* \* \*

The Liberator's return to power was not immediately followed by either disaster or dictatorship as so many liberals had expected. He continued his policy of conservative reform, obtaining the consent of Congress to increase customs duties throughout the republic and removing Bentham from the official school curriculum, but there was no complete subversion of liberal institutions, and Santander's cabinet was retained intact. Vicente Azuero was assaulted on the street with impunity by a *llanero* officer, and other liberals in both New Granada and Venezuela suffered violations of their civil rights from time to time, but there was certainly no general reign of terror. Santander was personally harassed over his alleged misuse of the English loan; but nothing was proved against him and no punishment imposed. Most striking of all, Santander and his followers were allowed to win the largest single bloc of seats, though not an outright majority, in the Great Convention which finally opened at Ocaña in March of 1828.[56]

[53] *La Gaceta de Cartagena*, August 5, 1827; A.C., Senado-22, 227-231; *La Gaceta de Colombia*, August 26, 1827; Guerra, *op. cit.*, 179-180.
[54] Restrepo VII, 63, 67.
[55] A.C., Senado-11, 60, 62; *Acuerdos* II, 251, 257; O'Leary XXV, 538-539, 544.
[56] *Codif. Nac.* III, 325, 331-332, 354; Forero, *Santander en sus escritos*, 117-125.

By this time the change in Santander's political thinking was complete. He refused to be deceived by any outward show of moderation on the part of Bolívar, insisting that the government was being run solely in the interests of a militarist clique. Civil rights, the Laws, the Constitution were being trampled; the Liberator himself had become "the supreme Perturber of the Republic." Santander thus concluded that it was necessary

> "to bind that colossal power which Bolívar exercises, to secure the rights . . . of citizens, and to divide executive authority in order to contain it. . . . I am for federalism as the only recourse left to us to save the national liberties." [57]

In the Convention itself Santander found some strange allies among the more radical Venezuelan separatists who had not been won over to Bolívar along with Páez, and on occasion he was able to enlist the cooperation also of a group of moderate deputies headed by Joaquín Mosquera. In the end federalism as such was voted down, for the moderates did not approve of it, but the federalist faction was able to command a majority for the draft of a new constitution which had definite federal characteristics despite its ostensibly centralist outline.[58]

This was a major defeat for the Bolivarian party, which aimed to increase rather than to diminish the power of the national executive, but the easy victory of Santander was snatched away by the decision of Bolívar's more vehement supporters to withdraw from the Convention entirely and thus make it impossible to procure a quorum for a final vote on the new code. Next came the open proclamation of a dictatorship in the hands of Bolívar by an improvised junta at Bogotá on June 13, 1828. The Bogotá declaration was rapidly copied, in almost identical terms, throughout the republic. Such uniformity is of course suspicious, and concrete instances of military coercion can be detected behind some of the proclamations that followed. General Montilla demanded that the military governor of Mompós produce a "popular" demand for dictatorship on 24 hours' notice, *"aunque cueste sangre."* [59] However, in all probability the Bolivarian dictatorship enjoyed wide popular support at the outset. The elections for Ocaña and the decisions of the Great Convention had shown that the following of Santander was far from negligible, and that not everyone who opposed Santander as Vice-President was automatically a last-ditch supporter of Bolívar. Many of the Liberator's professed supporters had been too indifferent to campaign actively on his behalf. But with the failure of the Convention to produce any

[57] Santander to Alejandro Vélez, May 17, 1827, Lecuna, *C.S.*, III, 139-141.
[58] Guerra, *op. cit.*, 315-358 and *passim*.
[59] Montilla to Adlercreutz, June 25, 1828, Caracciolo Parra-Pérez, ed., *La cartera del Coronel Conde de Adlercreutz* (Paris, 1928), 56-57.

concrete result there was an obvious feeling that no ordinary or parliamentary expedient was enough to "save the Republic," to use the stock phrase of the period. Out of despair and resignation, many were willing to accept the dictatorship who normally would not have countenanced anything of the sort.

It took the dictatorship less than two years to end in even more spectacular failure than the administration of Santander, and any detailed recital of its fortunes would lie beyond the scope of this volume. As dictator Bolívar issued a never-ending stream of decrees altering in one way or another the political, military, and financial organization of the country, always seeking to find by military directness and efficiency a perfection that had not been attained by the joint efforts of Congress and Santander. However, it is enough to say here that perfection was never found. Instead, for every problem that was solved a new one was created, while internal disorders continued from month to month and year to year. Santander himself was sent into exile for alleged complicity in the attempt on Bolívar's life of September 25, 1828, but the charges against him were unproved, and certainly his absence did not make things much easier. By the middle of 1830 Gran Colombia had dissolved completely.

In the opinion of most historians this outcome was really inevitable from the very foundation of the republic, and probably it was. Indeed the reasons for the creation of a united Colombia must be found essentially in a combination of transitory factors: above all, the requirements of the war with Spain and the personal will and prestige of Simón Bolívar. For the rest, Gran Colombia was accepted as a noble ideal but answered few fundamental needs of its peoples that could not be answered equally well or better by smaller and more convenient national units. Colombia might still have survived if the war had lasted long enough to endow the people permanently with a sense of common patriotic effort; if there had been a reasonably unified climate of opinion on such issues as religion and taxes that in themselves had nothing to do with the territorial size of the country; or if there had been money constantly in the treasury. Some official compromise with federalist sentiment might have helped, although it is doubtful that this could ever have offered a real solution: if not consciously, at least unconsciously, the ultimate tendency of all federalist movements was the outright destruction of Gran Colombia. In any case, not one of the immediate conditions for survival was met, and any major civil conflict could lead straight to national dissolution.

Whether this outcome was truly "inevitable" in a strict sense depends on one's definition of the term, and no final answer need be given in a general discussion of the Santander regime, which sought principally to carry out the moral and material improvements that would allow Latin Americans to catch up with the progress of the Western World in as short a space of time as possible. Gran Colombia—even the conquest of independence from Spain—was never an end in itself with Santander: Colombia was only the geographic framework in which he happened to be carrying out his policies. Needless to say, those policies were not always successful, and his concrete objectives have not found favor with all his compatriots. The fact remains, however, that his work was not necessarily undone by his own deposition from office or by the dissolution of Gran Colombia. Despite the temporary reverses of the Bolivarian dictatorship, Santander laid the foundations for the subsequent development of liberalism in New Granada, which he himself returned to lead. His influence also persisted, in more attenuated form, in Venezuela and Ecuador. Or to put it differently, both Santander and Bolívar went down to defeat in their efforts to govern Gran Colombia, but in laws and institutions if not in military victories and popular renown Santander had even more to show for his efforts by the time he failed.

APPENDIX

## A Note on Colombian Financial Statistics

COLOMBIAN statistics for the period under consideration are by and large so incomplete and so inaccurate that they can be taken only as extremely rough approximations of the actual totals. The table of government receipts which is inserted in the text on page 93 is no exception; it is included only in the belief that to offer no figures at all would be worse.

The colonial figures that are given for purposes of comparison are derived from a table in Restrepo I, xxxi. There can be no particular reason save perhaps convenience for preferring Restrepo's table over other alternative estimates; however, differences between the various estimates are seldom so substantial as to alter the general picture. The second column of figures is taken from *El Constitucional* of Bogotá for February 16, 1826, and the third is based on figures in the Archivo del Congreso;[1] but all the republican figures are ultimately derived from statistics of the Secretaría de Hacienda in Bogotá, which all too frequently did not have records of the exact yield of a tax in a given department. In such cases there were various methods of arriving at the figures for the country at large, and these methods do not always inspire confidence.

The customs figures are the ones that require most extended comment. In the first place, the overall Colombian customs totals include tonnage duties, some port charges, etc., in addition to the taxes specified by name in the table; some similar items are presumably included by Restrepo in the colonial figure. Even including these minor revenues, it is hard to understand the phenomenal increase in customs receipts for 1825-6. In part it merely reflects the sharp increase in Colombia's foreign trade during that year, due in large part to purchases made with the funds of the English loan of 1824, but this is not the whole answer. The principal source of error seems to be the fact that in Venezuela the customhouses not only submitted incomplete reports on the basis of which figures for the whole year were calculated at Bogotá but also administered certain other revenues that should normally have been handled separately. It should also be noted that the total customhouse receipts include payments made in government obligations as well as in cash.[2]

With regard to the *alcabala*, the colonial figure of Restrepo is in this case probably too high. The listing of fairly substantial receipts from

[1] A.C., Senado-38, 104-105. Virtually the same figures can be found in Restrepo VII, 298-299. There are a few discrepancies, which seem to result at least in part from differences in the handling of certain minor revenue classifications.

[2] A.H.N., Aduanas de la República I, 420-431, 466.

this source even as late as 1825-6—long after the *alcabala* was abolished for most purposes by the Congress of Cúcuta—is due to the fact that it was retained as a special sales tax on real estate, and also to the fact that overdue payments were still being made from earlier years. Much the same can be said in the case of the Indian tribute; overdue payments were still being made in Venezuela and New Granada, where it had been abolished in 1821, while in Ecuador its abolition became effective only in 1825.

The receipts listed under the heading of "foreign loans" represent funds changed into pesos and transferred to Colombia, as distinct from sterling credits spent directly abroad. Hence they do not include all the republic's income from foreign loans, but they do help to swell the grand total of revenues for the year 1825-6 to $12,156,375, which is the most remarkable figure of all. This total reflects all the defects previously noted and others to match. It includes, for instance, nearly $1,000,000 of unspecified origin reported from the Department of Magdalena, which may mean almost anything. Several entries in the detailed statement of receipts prepared for the republic as a whole represent either bookkeeping maneuvres or at least something other than normal revenues—e.g., $233,000 balance on hand July 1. Such items help to swell the grand total; whereas the government's regular income from taxes and monopolies combined was probably less than $7,000,000. The 1824-5 total has some of the same defects, but not enough to give so patently false an impression as the figure for 1825-6.

# BIBLIOGRAPHY

## Manuscript Sources

1. *Archivo del Congreso, Bogotá.*

This was the most important single source of data used in preparation of the present volume, containing not only minutes, committee reports, and other by-products of the legislative process but a great number of valuable *expedientes* on particular topics especially assembled for the benefit of Colombian Congressmen. The collections used by the author are:
> Cámara de Representantes
> Senado
> Miscelánea
> Actas

2. *Archivo Histórico Nacional, Bogotá.*

This is a much larger archive than the Archivo del Congreso, but it is harder to use for that very reason. There is a much greater amount of inconsequential material to be sorted out from the documents of lasting importance, and the arrangement of material by series and volume is often haphazard. Many of the more important documents may be found in duplicate in the other archive. The author confesses that he has barely scratched the surface; the collections he has consulted, whether exhaustively or not, are:
> Aduanas de la República
> Congresos
> Correspondencia del Libertador Presidente
> Correspondencia del Poder Ejecutivo con la Cámara de Representantes (Secretarías of Hacienda and Interior)
> Correspondencia del Poder Ejecutivo con el Senado (Secretaría del Interior only)
> Departamento de Boyacá
> Departamento de Venezuela
> Historia de la Colonia
> Indios
> Libro Primero de Contratos
> Miscelánea de la República
> Secretaría de lo Interior y Relaciones Extranjeras

3. *Biblioteca Nacional, Bogotá.*

Miscellaneous manuscripts scattered through collections of printed pamphlets, broadsides, etc.

4. *National Archives, Washington.*
> Colombia Dispatches
> Consular correspondence from: Cartagena, Guayaquil, La Guaira, Maracaibo, Puerto Cabello, Santa Marta

BIBLIOGRAPHY 363

PRINTED SOURCES

1. *Published Documents and Correspondence.*
The items under this heading are few but on the whole invaluable. The *Acuerdos del Consejo de Gobierno* and the printed *Actas* of the Colombian Congress contain more solid information per inch of type on the internal affairs of Gran Colombia than any other published source known to the author, while the *Codificación nacional* presents a definitive collection of liberal aspirations even if it does not always mirror hard realities. Such old and exasperating standbys as Blanco and Azpurúa, the *Memorias* of O'Leary, and the *Archivo Santander,* not to mention Vicente Lecuna's fine edition of the *Cartas del Libertador,* are of course heavily weighted on the side of military events, but they are so extensive that they cannot help but contain some information on all phases of national life. The other titles listed were of unequal value for this study—e.g., the *Epistolario* of Rufino Cuervo, which is an outstanding collection in its own right but chiefly contains material from a later period. However, certain others were used extensively indeed, and all those which are cited anywhere in the footnotes are given again below.

A great amount of documentary material can also be found scattered through the journals published by national and local historical societies. The *Boletín de la Academia Nacional de Historia de Venezuela* deserves particular credit in this respect. On the other hand, many items first published in this manner have appeared again in volumes of collected documents and correspondence, and it should be sufficient simply to call attention to this source without specifying the available items in the present bibliography.

*Actas de las sesiones de la Cámara de Representantes.* Bogotá, 1826. (Contains *actas* through January 28 only.)
*Acuerdos del Consejo de Gobierno.* 2 vols., Bogotá, 1940-1942.
*Archivo del General José Antonio Páez.* Bogotá, 1939. ("Vol. I," referring to the years 1818-1820, but none other has been published.)
*Archivo epistolar del General Domingo Caicedo.* 3 vols., Bogotá, 1942-1947.
*Archivo Santander.* 24 vols., Bogotá, 1913-1932.
Blanco, José Félix, and Ramón Azpurúa, eds., *Documentos para la historia de la vida pública del Libertador.* 14 vols., Caracas, 1875-1878.
*Bolívar y Santander. Correspondencia 1819-1820.* Bogotá, 1940.
*Codificación nacional de todas las leyes de Colombia desde el año de 1821.* Bogotá, 1924—.
Cortázar, Roberto, and Luis Augusto Cuervo, eds., *Congreso de Angostura: Libro de Actas.* Bogotá, 1921.
_____ *Congreso de Cúcuta: Libro de Actas.* Bogotá, 1923.
_____ *Congreso de 1823: Actas.* Bogotá, 1926.

_____ *Congreso de 1824, Cámara de Representantes: Actas.* Bogotá, 1942.
_____ *Congreso de 1824, Senado: Actas.* Bogotá, 1931.
_____ *Congreso de 1825, Cámara de Representantes: Actas.* Bogotá, 1947.
_____ *Congreso de 1825, Senado: Actas.* Bogotá, 1952.
Cuervo, Luis Augusto, ed., *Epistolario de Rufino Cuervo.* 3 vols., Bogotá, 1918-1922.
Gibson, William Marion, trans., *The Constitutions of Colombia.* Durham, 1948.
Hernández de Alba, Guillermo, and Fabio Lozano y Lozano, eds., *Documentos sobre el Doctor Vicente Azuero.* Bogotá, 1944.
Humphreys, Robert A., ed., *British Consular Reports on the Trade and Politics of Latin America, 1824-1826.* London, 1940.
Lecuna, Vicente, ed., *Cartas del Libertador.* 10 vols., Caracas, 1929-1930. Vol. 11, New York, 1948.
_____ *Cartas de Santander.* 3 vols., Caracas, 1942.
_____ *Documentos referentes a la creación de Bolivia.* 2 vols., Caracas, 1924.
Leturia, Pedro, ed., *La emancipación hispanoamericana en los informes episcopales a Pío VII.* Buenos Aires, 1935.
Manning, William R., ed., *Diplomatic Correspondence of the United States Concerning the Independence of the Latin American Nations.* 3 vols., New York, 1925.
O'Leary, Simón B., ed., *Memorias del General O'Leary.* 32 vols., Caracas, 1879-1888.
Parra-Pérez, Caracciolo, ed., *La cartera del Coronel Conde de Adlercreutz.* Paris, 1928.
Rodríguez Piñeres, Eduardo, ed., *La vida de Castillo y Rada.* Bogotá, 1949.
Webster, C. K., ed., *Britain and the Independence of Latin America.* 2 vols., London, 1938.

2. *Periodical and Pamphlet Literature.*

A source of equal importance with the published documents is the periodical and pamphlet literature of the period. Virtually every newspaper or propaganda tract published during the years of Gran Colombia has at least been looked at, and a glance at the footnotes will show how helpful they have been. But there is little to be gained by listing all the titles consulted or even the most significant. Unfortunately, few are readily available in this country either in the original or on microfilm, while the investigator who wishes a complete listing can find all of them, with unimportant exceptions, in the convenient printed catalogues of the Colombian Biblioteca Nacional. Hence those catalogues are listed below instead of the separate titles. It is sufficient here to single out *La Gaceta de Colombia*—the official gazette—and *El Constitucional,* which was for Bogotá in the 1820's what *El Tiempo* is for Colombia today. For the rest, the chief items bearing on any one topic will be found in the footnotes to the relevant chapters in the text.

Biblioteca Nacional, *Catálogo de todos los periódicos que existen desde su fundación hasta el año de 1935.* 2 vols., Bogotá, 1936.

────────── *Catálogo del "Fondo Anselmo Pineda."* 2 vols., Bogotá, 1935.

────────── *Catálogo del "Fondo José María Quijano Otero."* Bogotá, 1935.

3. *Secondary sources.*

By and large, the secondary sources are distinctly the least valuable. Even if every book or article bearing on the internal history of Gran Colombia were included the list would not be long, but neither would it be of much help, since relatively few historians have yet studied domestic affairs with the same extensive documentary research that has been lavished on the military and diplomatic history of the independence period. The most useful items are probably the accounts of contemporary travelers who visited Gran Colombia, although they must naturally be used with care. As for biographies, those of Bolívar are legion but are mostly substandard panegyrics. The other figures of the period are for the most part even worse off, and few had the forethought to remedy this neglect by writing acceptable memoirs of their own careers. Economic and social history has barely been touched: only religious matters form an honorable exception, and even under this subheading there is no adequate treatment covering Gran Colombia as a whole but only serviceable monographs on a regional or some other limited basis. Indeed the general inadequacy of the available secondary works serves only to underscore the merits of the two classic nineteenth century histories of Restrepo and Groot.

However, it is difficult to generalize further. Presumably it will be more useful to list below merely those books and articles which seemed of greatest interest for the topics covered in this volume, together with a few descriptive comments. This is admittedly a very personal selection, but the scholar who wishes further titles will have no difficulty unearthing them by the usual procedures, and the general reader (if one should happen to consult this bibliography) is referred to the card catalogue of the nearest major library.

POLITICAL HISTORY AND GENERAL.

Baralt, Rafael María, and Ramón Díaz, *Resumen de la historia de Venezuela desde el año de 1797 hasta el de 1830.* 2 vols., Bruges, 1939. A fairly competent survey, with valuable editorial notes by Vicente Lecuna.

Borrero, Alfonso María, *Cuenca en Pichincha.* Cuenca, 1922. More general than the title indicates; one of the best sources on local conditions in Ecuador during the late stages of the war.

González, Eloy G., *Dentro de la cosiata.* Caracas, 1907. A highly suggestive treatment of the Páez revolt and its origins, by one of Venezuela's most original historians.

Groot, José Manuel, *Historia de la Gran Colombia*. Caracas, 1941 (Vol. III of his *Historia eclesiástica y civil de la Nueva Granada*). Biased but extremely well informed; draws on both personal recollections and exhaustive acquaintance with the periodical and pamphlet literature of the 1820's.

Guerra, José Joaquín, *La Convención de Ocaña*. Bogotá, 1908. A detailed survey not only of the Convention itself but of the crisis that led up to it, with numerous documents; old, somewhat disorganized, but still useful.

Rivas, Raimundo, *Escritos de Don Pedro Fernández Madrid*. Bogotá, 1932. Part biography, part documents, part general history; especially helpful on religious and diplomatic problems. "Vol. I," but never continued.

Restrepo, José Manuel, *Historia de la Revolución de la República de Colombia*. 3rd ed., 8 vols., Bogotá, 1942-1950. Dry, factual, almost wholly military and political; authoritative on all matters it takes up.

Zubieta, Pedro A., *Apuntaciones sobre las primeras misiones diplomáticas de Colombia*. Bogotá, 1924. Detailed, with much information on foreign loan negotiations.

DESCRIPTIONS OF COLOMBIA BY FOREIGN WRITERS.

Cochrane, Charles Stuart, *Journal of a Residence and Travels in Colombia*. 2 vols., London, 1825. Detailed observations, by an author personally engaged in countless projects for economic development.

Duane, William, *A Visit to Colombia*. Philadelphia, 1826. By a militant Philadelphia democrat, but more objective than one would expect.

Gosselman, Carl August, *Reise in Columbien*. 2 vols., Straslund, 1829-1831. Sound though unexciting, especially useful on mining developments and the like.

Hall, Francis, *Colombia: Its Present State*. 2nd ed., London, 1827. Rather opinionated, by a disciple of Jeremy Bentham who himself became a controversial figure in Colombian politics.

Hamilton, John P., *Travels Through the Interior Provinces of Colombia*. 2 vols., London, 1827. Detailed and often penetrating, an account of very broad interest.

Mollien, Gaspar Theodore, *Viaje por la República de Colombia en 1823*. Bogotá, 1944. A lively narrative, always to the point; also available in the original French and in English version (London, 1824).

*The Present State of Colombia*. London, 1827. "By an officer late in the Colombian service;" especially informative on problems of trade and production.

BIOGRAPHIES AND MEMOIRS.

Acevedo Latorre, Eduardo, *Colaboradores de Santander en la organización de la república.* Bogotá, 1944. Biographical data combined with selected documents; an extremely useful reference tool.

Arbeláez Urdaneta, Carlos, *Biografía del General Rafael Urdaneta.* Maracaibo, 1945. Not always scientific, but contains solid information as well as some interesting correspondence.

Bierck, Harold A., *Vida pública de Don Pedro Gual.* Caracas, 1947. A scholarly account, concentrating on foreign relations.

Cuervo, Angel and Rufino J., *Vida de Rufino Cuervo.* 2nd ed., 2 vols., Bogotá, 1946. A classic by any standard; deals mainly with a later period, but treats the administration of Vice-President Santander with a rare combination of sympathy and objectivity.

Forero, Manuel José, ed., *Santander en sus escritos.* Bogotá, 1944. Contains various writings by Santander in defense of his conduct, though not his *Apuntamientos,* which are listed below.

Hernández de Alba, Guillermo, *Vida y escritos del Doctor José Félix de Restrepo.* Bogotá, 1935. Sketchy, but a worthwhile account of the noblest Colombian of them all.

García Ortiz, Laureano, *Algunos estudios sobre el General Santander.* Bogotá, 1944. Interpretative essays and miscellaneous *santandereana.*

Masur, Gerhard, *Simón Bolívar.* Albuquerque, 1948. Massive though not quite definitive, sometimes inadequate on domestic background; definitely the most useful work on its subject.

Obando, José María, *Apuntamientos para la historia.* Lima, 1842. Obviously unreliable, but at least suggestive.

Ortiz, Juan Francisco, *Reminiscencias.* 2nd ed., Bogotá, 1944. Of marginal interest for the period of Gran Colombia, but useful as giving the views of a civilian conservative.

Otero Muñoz, Gustavo, *Semblanzas colombianas.* 2 vols., Bogotá, 1938. A valuable collection of short biographies, especially on cultural figures.

Romero, Mario Germán, "Apuntes para una biografía del doctor Francisco Margallo y Duquesne." *Boletín de Historia y Antigüedades* (Bogotá), XXXVIII, 1-116 (January, 1951). A rambling biography of a key figure in religious controversy.

Sagarzazu, Miguel, "Ligeros apuntes en las diferentes épocas de disensiones políticas." *Boletín de la Academia Nacional de Historia de Venezuela* XIII (1930), 353-365, XIV (1931), 58-72, 235-251. Páez' revolt seen from the loyalist side.

Santander, Francisco de Paula, *Apuntamientos para las memorias sobre Colombia y la Nueva Granada.* Bogotá, 1837. Patronizing and self-laudatory.

Vejarano, Jorge Ricardo, *Nariño.* 2nd ed., Bogotá, 1945. An outstanding biography; justly fond of its subject, but meticuously fair to Santander.

ECCLESIASTICAL AFFAIRS.

Leturia, Pedro, *La acción diplomática de Bolívar ante Pío VII.* Madrid, 1925. Like the next item, a definitive treatment of its special subject, with much of interest on general religious topics as well.

―――――― *Bolívar y León XII.* Caracas, 1931.

Navarro, Nicolás E., *Anales eclesiásticos venezolanos.* Caracas, 1929. A competent summary, by a life-long specialist in ecclesiastical history.

―――――― *La política religiosa del Libertador.* Caracas, 1933.

Tobar Donoso, Julio, *La iglesia ecuatoriana en el siglo XIX.* Quito, 1934. A neglected mine of useful information. Another "Vol. I" without sequel.

Watters, Mary, *A History of the Church in Venezuela.* Chapel Hill, 1933. Exceptionally detailed on the period of Gran Colombia.

GENERAL SOCIAL AND ECONOMIC HISTORY.

Arcila Farías, Eduardo, *Economía colonial de Venezuela.* Mexico City, 1946. Of only indirect bearing on the period of Gran Colombia, but a model treatment of the colonial economic background.

Bierck, Harold A., "The Movement for Abolition in Gran Colombia." *Hispanic American Historical Review* XXXIII, 365-386 (August, 1953). A definitive treatment of the manumission program in both conception and operation.

Friede, Juan, *El indio en lucha por la tierra.* Bogotá, 1944. Based on original research, an excellent treatment of the Indian problem throughout Colombian history, mainly in its social and economic aspects.

―――――― "La legislación indígena en la Gran Colombia." *Boletín de Historia y Antigüedades.* (Bogotá), XXXVI, 286-298 (April, 1949).

Galindo, Aníbal, *Historia económica y estadística de la hacienda nacional.* Bogotá, 1874. Brief, with tables; useful for want of anything better.

Gilmore, Robert Louis, and John Parker Harrison, "Juan Bernardo Elbers and the Introduction of Steam Navigation on the Magdalena River." *Hispanic American Historical Review* XXVIII, 335-359 (August, 1948). A definitive treatment of its topic.

Nieto Arteta, Luis Eduardo, *Economía y cultura en la historia de Colombia*. Bogotá, 1941. The only general economic history; stimulating but scarcely exhaustive.

Tovar Ariza, Rafael, "Causas económicas, políticas, sociales, y culturales de la disolución de la Gran Colombia." *Revista de las Indias* (Bogotá), January, 1938, pp. 73-107. A brief but ambitious synthesis, summing up and extending the conventional interpretation of modern Colombian liberals.

# INDEX

*Academia Literaria Nacional*, 188 f.
Administrative problems and policies, 26-44 and *passim*
  *See also* Bureaucracy, Departmental organization, Finance, Municipalities
Agriculture, 1-4, 87 f., 128, 143, 146, 152-154, 159-161, 310 f.
  loan program, 119 f., 129, 288, 312
  *See also* Land policy
*Aguardientes*, taxation of, 77 f., 92 f., 108, 153 f., 342
Aguirre, Vicente, Intendant of Ecuador, 315 f.
*Alcabala*
  abolished for most purposes, 77, 79, 81, 92, 130, 311
  restoration proposed, 108 f., 123, 313
  restored, 342 f., 345
  yield, 93, 360 f.
*Alcaldes*, 17, 20, 28, 47, 340, 353
*Alta Corte*, Colombian, 47 f., 68, 170, 173, 189, 221, 227, 251, 285, 288, 313
  functions defined, 18, 45 f.
*Alta Corte*, Venezuelan, at Angostura, 13, 272 f.
*Alta Corte Marcial*, 35, 48, 256, 273, 283 f.
Ambato, 36
*Anglo-Colombiano, El*, 42, 291, 293, 298
Angostura, 12, 211, 288, 307, 328
  Congress of, 10, 13, 100, 168, 170 n., 231, 272, 276, 330
Antilles, *see* specific islands and West Indies
Antioquia
  city, 187
  province, 98, 150, 168, 321
Apure
  department and province, 28, 133, 255, 299, 306 n., 307, 328
  veterans' problem in, 276, 280 f.
*Argos, El*, 291 f., 303 f.

Arias, Buenaventura, 204, 237 n.
Army, 249-274
  abuses in and by, 101, 128 f., 253-257, 317
  bonus and salaries, 100, 105 f., 252, 275-281, 350
  and civil authority, 26-28, 267 f., 341
  civilian distrust of, 257 f., 282 f., 298, 323 f.
  clergymen in, 199
  cost, 95, 120
  disaffection towards Santander regime, 74 f., 107, 249, 286
  and Freemasonry, 212
  officer class, 106, 122, 174, 205, 250, 277, 314, 334
  seizure of property by, 99
  size and reduction of, 249, 258-260, 341, 345, 355 f.
  suffrage of, 14, 268-270
  *See also* Conscription, Courts-martial, *Fuero*, War
Aroa, mines of, 136, 142
Arrubla, Juan Manuel, 132, 145, 278, 321, 322 n.
Arrubla, Manuel Antonio, loan negotiator, 115-117, 119 f., 124
Arrubla and Montoya, firm, 97, 121
Arvelo, Cayetano, 74
Atrato River, 139, 157
*Audiencias*, 11, 45 f.
Augustinians (Discalced), 201, 217 f.
*Auxilio patriótico*, 82 f., 125
Ayacucho, battle, 72, 258
Azuay, department, 319, 333
Azuero, Juan Nepomuceno, 60, 103 n., 206, 209, 229, 245, 322
Azuero, Vicente, 11, 60, 88, 122, 145, 330, 356
  in *Alta Corte*, 48, 133, 283
  at Cúcuta, 16, 80
  and education, 192-194, 241
  liberal publicist, 29 n., 62, 64, 130, 211, 229, 262, 282, 292, 336

371

Bache, Richard, 205
Baños, Manuel, 14, 56, 282
Baralt, Luis Andrés
   Senate President, 121, 256, 286, 301
   vice-presidential candidate, 321 f.
Barbacoas, 170 f., 314
Barcelona, province, 133, 307, 321
Barinas
   city, 132
   province, 1, 306 n., 343
Baring Brothers, 114
Bello, Andrés, 188
Beltrán de los Ríos, Andrés, 239
Bentham, Jeremy, 55, 192 f., 207, 241, 244, 290, 356
Bermúdez, José Francisco, *Comandante* of Orinoco, 297, 307 f., 328, 343, 345
Bible Society, British, 207 f., 216
Bible Society, Colombian, 208 f., 238, 245
Bierck, Harold A., 114
Blanco, José Félix, Col., 199
Bogotá, 2-4, 60 f., 287, and *passim*
   archdiocese, 88, 197, 200, 203, 208, 215, 220-223, 231, 233, 236 f., 239-241, 244
   city, 6 f., 13, 30, 35, 46-49, 63, 84, 97 f., 132, 138, 141, 148, 154 f., 206, 211 f., 260 f., 282, 357
   education in, 183, 185-190, 193 f., 209 f.
   (*see also* San Bartolomé)
   province, 199, 269, 319-321
   status as capital, 21, 289, 306
Bolívar, Simón, 83, 101, 136, 138, 178 n., 296
   and Church, 197 f., 212, 218, 223, 227, 230 n., 237
   in constitutional crisis of 1826-7, 330-348, 350-356
   dictator (1828-30), 124 n., 224, 227, 239, 357-359
   and Ecuador, 24, 32, 103, 131, 140, 311-317, 333, 341
   and education, 183, 185, 188, 190
   election as president for first term, 20, for second, 304, 318, 322
   and establishment of Gran Colombia, 10-13, 16 f., 22
   and financial policy, 77, 79, 81 n., 98, 100 n., 103, 107, 110, 112, 114, 156, 159 f., 176, 311 f., 340, 342, 346
   and military administration, 175, 250, 253-255, 259, 275 f., 278 n., 279
   and navy, 263, 266
   relations with Páez, 295, 303-305, 326 f., 330, 335, 339, 344 f., 354
   relations with Santander, 11, 40, 64, 69-75, 318, 336-339, 341 f., 344, 347 f., 351 f., 354-357
   and slavery, 167 f., 173
   in war, 7-9, 69 f., 74, 308
Bolivia, 237, 259 n.
Bolivian Constitution, 331-338, 346, 348, 353 f.
Bollman, Justus Erich, 114 f.
Boyacá
   battle, 9
   department, 89, 95, 154 f., 187, 243, 253, 306, 319
Briceño, Antonio María, Senator, 279 n., 301
Briceño, Domingo, 217
Briceño Méndez, Pedro, Gen., 303 n., 341, 343
   vice-presidential candidate, 304, 319-322
   War Secretary, 22, 63, 101 n., 301 f.
Brión, Luis, Admiral, 79
British
   admiration for, 148, 210, 262
   in Colombia, 207 n., 215, 250, 327
   (*see also* Bible Society, Hall, Hamilton, Investment, Lancaster)
   Minister, 118
   *See also* Great Britain
Buenaventura
   port, 140
   province, 139
Bureaucracy, 28, 34-39, 83 f., 275, 340, 345
   abuses and corruption in, 43 f., 85 f., 101, 121 f.
   criticism of, 109 f., 342
   salaries and pensions, 37, 94, 100, 105 n., 107, 119, 121 n., 276
   *See also* Diplomatic service
Bustamante, José, *Primer Comandante,* see Third Division

*Cabildos, see* Municipalities
Caicedo, Domingo, Gen., 88
Caicedo, Fernando, 191, 208, 232, 239, 241, 244 f.
Calcaño, Juan Bautista, 117

## Index

Caldas, Francisco José, 4, 189
Cali, 189
Canning, George, 124 n.
Capital, foreign, *see* Investment
Carabaño, Francisco, Col., 52, 290-292, 297, 299, 303 f., 309, 321
  in Páez revolt, 326-328, 336, 345
Carabobo
  battle, 279
  province, 297, 319
Caracas, 1, 4, 121, 167, 169, 285, 296, 306 f.
  archdiocese, 197, 201, 236 f., 240
  city, 98, 141, 185, 187, 190, 209, 212, 242, 246
  in independence movement, 6-8
  as opposition center, 42, 61 f., 260, 289-294, 298, 300-305
  and Páez revolt, 323, 325-327, 335, 345
  province, 13, 23, 90, 102, 146, 297, 319
Cartagena, 6, 66, 102, 153, 319, 334
  Bishop of, 196
  city and port, 46, 91, 97, 138, 156 f., 164
  diocese, 200, 234
  naval academy, 263, 265
  province, 11, 77
Casanare
  province, 37, 95, 128
  Indians of, 179-181
  in war, 8, 10
Castillo y Rada, José María
  Finance Secretary, 22, 35, 83-85, 87 f., 92, 94, 104, 110, 119 f., 123, 157, 281, 344
  and tax policy, 76 f., 80, 85, 90, 109, 153, 159, 161, 340, 342
  and religious problems, 208, 216, 220-222, 224, 232, 234
  vice-presidential candidate, 321 f.
Castro, Vicente, Governor of Loja, 44
Cattle-raising, *see* Grazing
Cauca
  department, 94, 97, 187, 314
  valley and vicinity, 140, 157, 167, 172, 195, 205, 256
*Censos*, 4, 102 f., 105 n., 169, 223-228, 310
Central America, 158
Chamber of Representatives, 95, 317
  *See also* Congress
Chile, 158

Chimborazo, province, 36
Chiquinquirá, 203, 205
Chocó, province, 91, 139, 157, 189
Church, Roman Catholic
  and anti-clericalism, 202, 205-228, 238, 244, 291, 319
  attacks on property and income of, 132, 178, 211, 215, 217, 220-228, 242
  clergy, 195-207, 300, 302
  defended by Nariño faction, 61, 67
  disaffection towards liberal regime, 240-242, 244-248
  and economic and social policy, 133, 148, 169, 171
  and education, 183, 187, 190-195, 238, 241
  and Indians, 178, 222 f.
  (*see also* Missions)
  religious orders, 183 f., 197, 199-203, 205 f., 209, 212, 216-219, 224, 226-228, 240
  (*see also* Dominicans, Franciscans, Jesuits)
  and state, *see* Patronato, Santander
  and toleration issue, 145, 206, 210 f., 214-216, 232
  *See also* Censos, Fuero, Mortmain, Papacy, Tithes
Civil servants, *see* Bureaucracy
Cochrane, Charles Stuart, 136, 142
Coinage, 90 f., 162, 285, 310
  *See also* Mints
*Colegios, see* Education, Rosario, San Bartolomé
*Colombiano, El,* 150, 207 n., 292, 302 n.
*Colombiano del Ecuador, El,* 313
*Cometa, El,* 169, 202, 213, 294, 302-304
Comettant, Pierre, 154, 185
Commerce, 130 f., 133
  foreign (colonial), 2-4
  foreign (republican), 89, 147 f., 151-165, 181 f., 310 f., 360
  *See also* Customs duties, Smuggling
Conde, Francisco, Col., 280
Confederation of the Andes, 331, 332 n., 337, 339, 346
Congress, 18, 50-57, 94, 288, 318, 351, and *passim*
  (*see also* Chamber of Representatives)
  and Executive Power, 31, 38 f., 42, 51, 54-57, 110 f., 239 f., 242 f., 257, 291

geographic and social composition, 51 f., 174, 199, 220, 239 f., 292, 313
impeachment proceedings in, 44, 65-68, 89, 284-286, 300, 316, 323-325
political factions in, 52-54, 63, 214, 246 f., 321 f., 352 f.
See also Elections, *Montaña*, *Valle*
Congress of Angostura, *see* Angostura
Congress, Constituent, *see* Cúcuta
Congress of Panama, *see* Panama
Conscription, military, 71 f., 167 f., 251-254, 265, 307 f., 311, 315
exemptions from, 89, 138, 142, 179, 263
*Constitucional, El,* 33, 118, 322 n., 347
Constitution of 1821, 16-19, 31, 46, 48, 114, 130, 231, 232 n., 247, 263, 268 f., 271
criticism of, 59, 61 f., 289-291, 330
reform of, as political issue 1826-7, 326, 328-330, 333-336, 339, 343 f., 348, 351-354 (*see also* Ocaña)
*Consulados,* 130
Contraband, *see* Smuggling
*Contribución directa,* 81-84, 92 f., 108 f., 311, 313, 340, 342 f.
*Contribución extraordinaria, see* "Extraordinary contributions"
Convention of Ocaña, *see* Ocaña
Córdova, José María, Gen., 257, 348
Coro, province, 7, 306
*Correo de Bogotá, El,* 53 f., 64, 211, 282
*Correo de la Ciudad de Bogotá, El,* 62, 135
Corte Superior del Centro (Bogotá), 35 f., 38, 46 f., 49, 66-68, 221, 314
Corte Superior del Norte (Caracas), 296 f.
Corte Superior del Sur (Quito), 44, 132, 314-316
Cortés Madariaga, José, 239
Courts, 18, 45-49, 340, 353
commercial tribunals, 130 f.
relations with other branches of government, 19 f., 26-28, 36, 38 f., 346
See also *Alta Corte, Corte Superior, Juez Letrado*
Courts-martial, 45, 48, 256, 272-274, 283
See also *Alta Corte Marcial*
Cuba, 1, 258, 262, 265 f.

Cúcuta, 37, 186
Congress of, 12-22, 26, 58 n., 133, 290, and *passim*
Cuenca
city and province, 131, 185, 239, 246, 314, 351
diocese, 200, 239
Cuervo, Nicolás, 232
Cuervo, Rufino, 194
Cumaná, city and province, 146, 169, 307 f., 328
Cundinamarca
department, 7, 13, 15, 35, 41, 59-61, 63, 94, 118, 130, 154, 336
vice-presidency of, 12 (*see also* New Granada, provisional regime)
Curaçao, 296
Customs duties, 76, 93, 106, 125, 129, 140, 181 f., 263, 288, 311, 327, 346, 356, 360
*derecho de consumo,* 79 f., 130, 340
export, 79, 85, 90, 159-162, 164, 287
import, 79 f., 85, 151-158, 163-165
internal, 77, 130

Debt, foreign, 96, 112-126, 340, 361
English loan of 1824, 99, 115-118, 124, 319, 342, 356
proposed new loan, 104, 123 f.
use of 1824 loan, 89, 91, 97, 118-122, 129, 163, 264, 288, 312, 360
Debt, internal, 96-106, 112 n.
loans, 93, 96-99, 147, 198, 255, 280, 311, 327
payment of debts, 104-106, 119-123, 125, 312 (*see also Vales*)
salary and bonus debts, *see* Army, Bureaucracy
De Francisco Martín, Juan, 43, 109, 117 n., 118, 121, 123, 145, 157 n., 170
Denmark, 94 n.
Departmental organization, 18-20, 26-30, 36 f., 84, 94, 267 f., 346
*Derecho de consumo, see* Customs duties
*Desafectos, see* Royalists
Díaz, Pedro Pablo, 291, 293
Diplomatic service, Colombian, 94, 288, 313, 341
*Dirección de Estudios,* 192 f., 288
Dominicans, 188, 202-206, 208
Durán, Higinio, Bishop of Panama, 196, 198, 239

INDEX

Economic policy and affairs, 127-150 and *passim*
See also Agriculture, Commerce, Finance, Grazing, Immigration, Indians, Land, Manufacturing, Mining, Slavery
Ecuador, 34, 310-317
  Church in, 200, 204-206, 208, 218 f.
  in crisis of 1826-7, 332-334, 338 f., 341, 349-355
  Department of, 314 f., 340
  economic and social conditions, 4, 103, 107, 129 n., 140, 152 f., 155 f., 159 f., 162, 176, 225, 250 n., 310-313
  in 1826 elections, 319
  incorporation in Colombia, 12, 14, 17, 22-24
  under regime of "extraordinary faculties" (1822-5), 32, 72-74, 156, 159, 176, 258, 311-317
  relative voice in national affairs, 51 f., 313 f.
  in war, 5 f., 8, 311, 314
Education, 173 f., 183-195, 211, 238, 356
  of clergy, 190, 203 f.
  of Indians, 176-178
  secondary, 184, 187-194, 217, 224, 226, 288
  See also San Bartolomé, Universities
Elbers, Juan B., 123, 137 f., 266
Elections
  for Congress, 21 f., 321 f., 352
  for Congress of Cúcuta, 13 f.
  for Convention of Ocaña, 356
  municipal, 20, 30
  for president and vice-president in 1821, 20 f., in 1825-6, 269, 297, 303 f., 309, 318-322
  See also Suffrage
Encinoso, Mauricio, Col., 149 n.
England, English, *see* Great Britain, British
Entailed estates, 81, 131, 150
Escalona, Juan de, Intendant of Venezuela, 141, 294, 296, 299 f., 302, 323 f., 326, 330
Esmeraldas, 140
Executive Power, in Constitution, 18
  See also Administrative problems
"Extraordinary contributions," 82 f., 93
  See also *Auxilio patriótico*, *Subsidio*

"Extraordinary faculties"
  granted and defined, 20, 31-33, 72-75, 301 f.
  use of, 32, 42 f., 72 f., 86, 131, 156, 161, 176, 311, 329, 338, 340 f.
  withdrawn by Congress of 1827, 353
Federalism, 6 f., 29, 331, 358
  at Cúcuta, 15-17
  in Ecuador, 61, 316 f., 332 f.
  Nariño and, 58-64
  Santander faction turns to, 344, 354, 357
  in Venezuela, 61 f., 289-291, 326-328, 335
Ferdinand VII, 5 f.
Fernández Saavedra, Manuel, 221 n., 283
Fernández de Sotomayor, Juan, 217, 239
Finance
  administration of, 83-91, 110 f.
  revenue and expenditures, 92-96, 107, 258 (*see also* Army, Bureaucracy)
  Secretary of, *see* Castillo y Rada
  tax policy, 76-83, 107-109, 221, 340, 342 f.
  See also Debt and specific revenues
Fishing industry, 264
Flores, Juan José, *Comandante* of Ecuador, 109, 278 n., 317, 333, 351
Foreign Relations, *Secretaría*, 94 n., 288, 341
  See also Diplomatic service, Gual, Revenga; for actual relations with other countries, see the latter
Foreign trade and investment, *see* Commerce, Investment
France, 159, 165, 299
  See also French
Franciscans, 198
Freemasonry, 185, 206, 210-213, 221 n.
  hostility to, 239-241, 244-247
French, in Colombia, 190
  See also Comettant, Mollien
*Fuero*
  ecclesiastical, 220 f.
  military, 47, 263, 270-272, 274, 297 f., 303

*Gaceta de Cartagena, La,* 117, 239, 286
*Gaceta de la Ciudad de Bogotá, La,* 210, 238, 244
*Gaceta de Colombia, La,* 57, 64, 110, 120, 169, 191 f., 261, 270
  and Church affairs, 196, 219, 235, 238 f., 243

criticizes Bolívar, 336, 347, 356
and political opposition, 62, 117 f., 292 f.
Germany, 165
Great Britain, 24, 181
trade with, 158, 163 n., 164 f.
*See also* British
Goajira, Indians of, 149 n., 181 f.
Goldschmidt and Co., 115 f., 124 f., 126 n., 136, 146
Gómez, Diego Fernando, 63, 67, 145, 246
Grazing, 1, 128, 161 f., 255, 312
Gual, Pedro
at Cúcuta, 18
Governor of Cartagena, 77, 79
Foreign Secretary, 22, 208
Guanare, 288
Guayana
Congress of, *see* Angostura
diocese, 236 n., 307
missions, 81 n., 179-181
province, 10, 86, 197, 200, 306 f., 328, 343
Guayaquil, 159, 164, 174, 311, 317, 321
city and port, 72, 84, 103, 160, 165 f., 208, 263
in crisis of 1826-7, 332-334, 338, 350 f.
department, 94, 314, 319, 340
independent junta, 22-24, 156
Guilds, 130
Gunpowder monopoly, 80, 152, 154
Gutiérrez, Antonio María, 206, 208
Groot, José Manuel, 40, 193, 210, 212, 241 n., 243, 247
Guerra y Mier, Francisco Xavier, 64, 232
Guerrero, Miguel, Intendant of Apure, 328 n., 343
Guzmán, Antonio Leocadio, 291, 297 f., 303 f., 332-335, 337, 346, 350

Haiti, 144, 172
Hall, Francis, Col., 42, 290-293
Hamilton, James, 81 n., 138 f., 144, 211
Hamilton, John P., 206, 253
Herrera, José Ignacio, 53, 60-63, 66-68, 230, 247, 336
Herring, Graham, and Powles, 113, 115
Hurtado, Manuel José, Minister to Great Britain, 136, 146
and 1824 loan, 115, 117, 119, 124 f.

Ibagué, 187
Ibarra, 217
Immigration, 143-148, 181, 245
Indians, 149 n., 166, 172, 174-182
and Church, 222 (*see also* Missions)
land tenure of, 131, 176 f.
*See also* Tribute
*Indicación, La,* 29 n., 62, 130, 262, 292
Infante, Leonardo, Col., 282-286, 303
Inquisition, 210, 214 f., 292
*Insurgente, El,* 59 n., 60, 63, 80, 108
Intendant, office of, *see* Departmental organization
Interest rates, 132 f., 226
Interior, *Secretaría,* 341
*See also* Restrepo, José Manuel
Investment, foreign, 81, 87, 134-142, 145-148
*See also* Debt, foreign
Iribarren, Guillermo, Col., 256
Iribarren, José de, 335
*Iris de Venezuela, El,* 292
Irish, in Colombian army, 254 f.
Istmo, department, *see* Panama

Jamaica, 137, 140, 153, 157, 165, 181
*Jefe político,* office of, 28, 30, 37, 39
Jesuits, property of, 277
Jiménez de Enciso, Salvador, Bishop of Popayán, 191, 196-198, 200, 204, 208, 232, 236, 245
Joly, Nicolás, Col., 269 n.
Judiciary, *see* Courts
*Juez letrado de hacienda,* office of, 27 f., 37, 109
*Juez letrado de primera instancia,* office of, 28, 36 f., 54, 109, 340 f., 353
*Juez político,* office of, 18, 20, 28
*Juntas provinciales,* creation of, 29

Labor legislation, 166
*See also* Slavery
La Guaira, 141, 147, 165 n., 308
La Mar, José, Gen., 350
Lancaster, Joseph, 185 f.
Land policy, 144-146, 149 f.
and corporate tenure, 131 f., 176 f.
(*see also* Church)
use of national domain, 81, 105 f., 179, 276-280
*See also* Agriculture
Lander, Tomás, 291, 293
Lara, Jacinto, Gen., 348 f.

INDEX  377

Lasso de la Vega, Rafael
  Bishop of Mérida, 180, 190, 192, 196-198, 200-204, 209, 211 f., 222, 231, 234 n., 236 f., 245
  as Senator, 22, 133, 203, 221, 235, 246, 324
Lecuna, Vicente, 295
Leo XII, 236 f.
Leturia, Pedro, 231, 237
*Llaneros, Llanos,* 1 f., 28, 128, 149, 161, 174, 180, 205, 282
  unrest, 46, 144, 279-281, 285, 306
  in war, 7-10, 70, 252, 276, 289, 295, 297
  *See also* Apure
Loans, *see* Debt
Loja, city and province, 44, 185, 202
López, José Hilario, Intendant of Cauca, 339
López Méndez, Luis, 113 f.
López Ruiz, Sebastián, 67 f., 69 n.
Lowry, Robert, 136

Magdalena, department, 153, 321
Magdalena River, 46, 137-139, 166
Mannhardt, Christian Louis, 139
Manabí, province, 333
Manrique, Manuel, Gen., 212
Manufacturing, 4, 135, 142 f., 154 f., 310, 312 f.
Maracaibo
  city and province, 98, 121, 186, 196, 199, 212, 263 n., 269, 321, 328, 335
  in war, 7, 24, 262 f., 293, 306
Maracaibo, Lake, 139, 263
Marcos, José Antonio, 56, 122
Margallo, Francisco, 241 f., 244-246
Margarita, province, 256, 307-309, 328
Mariño, Ignacio, 202, 212
Mariño, Santiago, Gen., 101, 305, 329
Mariquita, province, 7, 321
Márquez, José Ignacio de, Intendant of Boyacá, 39, 194
Márquez, Remigio, Col., 65 f., 85
Masons, *see* Freemasonry
Maturín, department, 28 n.
Medellín, 189
*Medias anatas,* 221
Méndez, Ramón Ignacio, Senator, 246, 301
Mendoza, Cristóbal, 296 f.
  Intendant of Venezuela, 326 f., 329, 335, 343, 345

Mérida
  Bishop of, *see* Lasso
  city and province, 98, 196, 306
Mérida, Rafael Diego, 296 f.
Merizalde, José Félix, 48, 61, 118 n., 190 n., 322 n.
Mexico, 125, 265, 341
Military affairs, *see* Army, Militia, Navy, Veterans, War
Militia, 260 f., 265, 271
  in Caracas, 294, 323
  naval, 263 f.
Mining, 3, 90, 135-137, 162, 164
  school of, 189
  and slave emancipation, 167 f., 171
  *See also* Mints
Miño, Mariano, 317
Mints, 90-93, 119, 162
  *See also* Coinage
Mires, José, Gen., 256
*Miscelánea, La,* 213
Missions, Indian, 81 n., 179 f., 202 f., 222, 240
Mollien, Gaspar Theodore, 204, 258
Mompós, city and province, 65 f., 217, 357
Monarchism, 303-305, 326, 331, 348
  For support of Spanish monarchy specifically, *see* Royalism
Monasteries, *see* Church
Moniquirá, 36
Monopolies, fiscal, *see* Aguardientes, Gunpowder, Platinum, Playing-card, Salt, Tobacco
*Montaña,* faction in Congress, 52 f., 56 f., 65, 109, 133, 247, 257, 282, 286, 352
Monteagudo, Bernardo, 70
Montilla, Mariano, Gen., 145, 255
  *Comandante* of Magdalena, 117, 285, 357
Montoya, Francisco, 97 n.
  congressman, 154 n., 321
  loan negotiator, 115-117, 119 f., 124
  *See also* Arrubla and Montoya
Mora, Sebastián, 184 f.
Morillo, Pablo, 8, 196, 201
Mortmain, 81, 150, 223-227
  *See also* Church
Mosquera, Joaquín
  Senator, 73, 104, 123, 170 n., 194, 324
  at Convention of Ocaña, 357
Mosquera, José Rafael, 170 n.

Mosquera, Manuel José, 204
Mosquera, Tomás Cipriano, Intendant of Guayaquil, 333 f., 350
Mosquito Coast, 181 f.
Municipalities, 17 f., 20, 39, 105, 133
  common lands, 131 f.
  reform of, 28-31, 36, 134
  See also Alcaldes, Jefe político, Juez letrado de primera instancia
Murgueitio, Pedro José, Intendant of Ecuador, 333
Museo Nacional, 189
Mutis, Facundo, 89
Mutis, José Celestino, 4, 188 f.

Nariño, Antonio, 39, 57, 80, 107
  and Congress of Cúcuta, 20 f.
  early career, 5, 7
  feud with Santander, 53, 58-64, 290
  struggle continued by his followers, 65-69
Nariño y Ortega, Antonio, 65
Narvarte, Andrés, 296
Navy, Colombian, 70, 85, 166, 261-266, 308, 341
Negroes, unrest and discrimination, 65, 144, 172-174, 306 f.
  See also Slavery
New Granada
  economic and social conditions, 2-4, 152-155, 159, 161, 166, 205 f. and passim (see also Mining)
  earlier patriot regime, 112
    (see also Patria Boba)
  independence movement in, 6-10, 22-25
  political alignments in, 11, 15 f., 319, and passim (see also Nariño)
  provisional regime (1819-21), 10-13, 77, 79, 98, 273
  reaction to Páez revolt, 329, 336
  relative voice in national affairs, 22, 52, 250 n., 288 f.
  rivalry with Venezuelans, 13, 15 f., 60, 282, 285 f., 287-289, 348
  separatism in, 344, 354
  Viceroyalty of, 1 f.
Noticiosote, El, 118 n., 154

Obando, Antonio, Col., 349-351
Obando, José María, Governor of Pasto, 25, 278 n., 350 f.
Ocaña, 289
  Convention of, 270, 353-357

Oficios vendibles, 78
Olivares, José Manuel, Governor of Guayana, 307, 328, 343
Olmedo, José Joaquín, 188
Orinoco, department, 17, 28, 129 n., 307 f., 328
Orinoco River, 138 f.
  basin, see Llanos
Ortiz, José Joaquín, 67-69
Osío, Juan José, 74
Osorio, Alejandro, 11, 17, 61, 217

Padilla, José, Admiral, 262 f., 266, 319
Páez, José Antonio
  Comandante of Venezuela, 14 n., 52, 245 n., 250, 272, 277, 279, 281, 294-306, 309, 318, 321
  Jefe Superior, 354
  proposed impeachment and revolt, 323-331, 334-336, 338 f., 343-345, 347-349, 351
  in war, 8, 98, 252, 255, 263, 276, 294 f.
Palacio, Miguel, 138 f.
Pamplona
  colegio, 191, 211
  province, 11, 186, 255
Panama, 91, 97, 153, 162 n., 165, 225, 334
  Bishop of, see Durán
  canal projects, 139 f.
  city, 218
  Congress of, 237, 305
  terms of incorporation in Colombia, 23, 103, 105 n.
Papacy, 197, 201, 203, 209 f., 212 f., 220, 230 f., 234-237, 341
Pardos, see Negroes
París, José Ignacio, 136
Pasto
  province, 199, 218, 314 f.
  royalists in, 22-25, 61, 172, 197 f., 278 n., 310
Patía, 172
Patria Boba, 6 f., 20, 29, 58, 60, 64, 101 f., 168, 172, 230, 236
Patriota, El, 62 f., 213, 242, 244, 270
Patronato, 190, 201, 229-240
Paz del Castillo, Juan, Gen., 317
Peña, Miguel, 48, 158 n., 283-286, 303, 325-328, 336, 344
Peñalver, Fernando, Governor of Carabobo, 294, 297, 326 f., 329, 345
Pensions, 107, 275, 341

INDEX    379

Perdomo, Francisco, Lieut., 282
Pérez, José Antonio, 38 f., 118, 240, 257, 268, 299 f.
Pérez, José Gabriel, 341
Peru, 23, 158
    Colombian military aid to, 69-74, 251 f., 259, 281, 304, 307 f., 311
    debt to Colombia, 125, 312
    and mutiny of Third Division, 348-350, 354 f.
Petare, 300-302
Pichincha, battle, 24
Piñango, Judas Tadeo, 270
Pius VII, 236
Plan of Studies, 184, 190, 192 f., 246, 346
Platinum monopoly, 137
Playing-card monopoly, 78
Popayán
    Bishop of, see Jiménez
    city and province, 37, 46, 64, 90 f., 102, 170 n., 187, 205, 314, 321, 339, 353
    diocese, 204, 232
Popes, see Papacy
Powder monopoly, see Gunpowder
Pradt, Abbé de, 237
Presidency, in Constitution, 18
    See also Administrative problems, Elections
Press, in Colombia, 61, 211, 327
    Bolívar and, 331, 345, 347
    law of press offenses, 19, 216, 242, 246, 271 f., 292, 297, 299
    official, see Gaceta de Colombia
    treatment by Santander, 42, 63, 301, 302 n., 316, 329
    See also individual newspapers
Privateering, 261 f., 308
Protestantism, 207 f., 210 f., 216, 238, 245 f.
Provincial government, see Departmental organization
Puerto Cabello, 297, 343
    in war, 22-24, 263, 295 f.
Puerto Rico, 258, 265 f., 293

Quinto, 81, 85, 90, 93, 142
Quito, 24, 36, 101, 140, 185, 187, 200, 212, 254, 310, 312-317, 333 f., 351
    Bishop of, 196, 200 f.
    diocese, 204, 314
    Presidency, 4-6, 8, 12, 14, 17, 23 f.

Rebollo, Manuel Benito, 103 n., 203 n.
Religious affairs, see Church
Revenga, José Rafael, 57, 85, 185
    Foreign Secretary, 22, 116 f., 202
Restrepo, José Félix, 104, 121, 181, 192, 194, 336
    in Alta Corte, 48, 283 f.
    at Cúcuta, 14, 168, 217
Restrepo, José Manuel, Interior Secretary, 22, 26, 41, 48 f., 122, 226, 268, 301 f.
    cited on Santander, 11, 75, 356
    at Cúcuta, 168
    and economic affairs, 96, 104, 134, 150 n., 155, 312
    and education, 183, 194
Ribas, Francisco, 288
Río Hacha, city and province, 128 f., 182 n., 186, 254 f., 257
Rivero, Mariano, 136, 189
Rocafuerte, Vicente, 125, 209
Rodríguez de Toro, Francisco, Intendant of Venezuela, 296 f.
Roman Catholic Church, see Church
Rosario, Colegio, 188, 208, 239
Royalists, 12, 24 f., 98, 172, 175, 180, 251, 268, 310, 317
    in clergy, 196-198, 240, 241 n.
    lands of, 105, 276-278
    in Venezuela, 292 f., 296-298, 300 f., 306 f.

Sabanilla, 156 f.
Salom, Bartolomé, Jefe Superior of Ecuador, 72, 74, 258, 311
Salt monopoly, 80, 87, 90, 93, 152, 154, 311-313
San Bartolomé, Colegio, 188, 190-192, 208, 241
Sánchez de Tejada, Ignacio, 236
San Gil, 187
San Juan de Dios, order of, 219
San Miguel, José Ignacio de, 60-64
Santamaría, Miguel de, 216
Santa Marta
    Bishop of, 196, 200
    city and province, 24, 66, 138, 156, 199, 254
Santander, Francisco de Paula
    administrative duties and achievements, 22, 26-35, 38-44, 358 f.
    and aid to Peru, 69-72, 252
    and Church affairs, 103, 195, 197, 208, 212-215, 218 f., 222 f., 225 f., 229, 232-234, 236-244, 248

conflict with Nariño faction, 58-69
and Congress, 38 f., 42 f., 50 f., 54-57, 110 f., 242
and economic development, 127-135, 139-150, 157
and Ecuador, 311-314, 316 f.
and education, 183-188, 190-193
elected vice-president for first term, 20 f., for second, 318-322
and federalism, 16, 58, 62, 354, 357
and fiscal policy, 77, 79, 81-83, 86 f., 94 n., 97 f., 102-104, 106 n., 109 f., 152, 154, 159, 176, 340, 342 f.
and foreign loans, 114-122, 124 f.
and Indian policy, 175-179, 181, 182 n.
and military and veterans' affairs, 253 f., 257-261, 266-270, 273, 275, 277 f., 280 f., 284 f.
and naval expansion, 261-264, 266
and Páez revolt, 323-330, 334 f.
relations with Bolívar to 1826, 11, 64, 69-75, in final conflict (1826-8), 336-345, 347 f., 351-358
and revolt of Third Division, 348-351
and royalist problem, 12, 24, 197, 293
salary, 100, 107
and slave emancipation, 167, 169, 173
and Venezuela, 285, 288, 290-297, 299-306, 308
Vice-President of Cundinamarca (New Granada), 10-13, 83
in war, 8
Say, Jean Baptiste, 191
Senate, *see* Congress
*Sisa*, 77
Slavery, Slaves, 140, 153, 164, 166-173, 291, 300, 302, 313
Smuggling, 65 f., 85, 90, 153 f., 156, 162, 181, 182 n., 308, 340
Socorro, city and province, 60, 90, 187, 321, 342
Soto, Francisco
Senator, 11, 38, 60, 63, 122, 149, 201, 211, 256, 267, 281-284, 301, 324, 356
at Cúcuta, 16, 18, 21
and education, 127, 191, 193
Soublette, Carlos
Intendant and *Jefe Superior* of Venezuela, 114, 293, 295-297, 299

War Secretary, 22, 129, 259 f., 270, 352, 356
Spain, 113, 164, and *passim*
debts left by, 102-104
revolt of 1820 in, 25, 197, 291
*See also* Royalists, War
Stamped paper (stamp-tax), 76, 80, 93, 105, 221
*Subsidio*, 221
*See also* "Extraordinary contributions"
Sucre, Antonio José, 24, 74, 176, 259 n., 295, 317, 321 f., 331
Suffrage regulations, 13 f., 18 f., 30, 214, 268-270, 291
Sweden, 158

Talavera, Mariano, 220
Tariffs, *see* Customs duties
Taxation, *see* Finance and specific revenues
Third Division, 348-352, 354
Thomson, James, *see* Bible Society, British
Tithes, 80, 87 f., 93, 98 f., 143, 204, 209, 221 f., 231, 243
Tobacco monopoly, 77 f., 80, 88-90, 92 f., 119 f., 125, 152, 154, 287, 311
Torres, Ignacio, Intendant of Azuay, 333
Torres, Jerónimo, Senator, 64, 73, 140, 145, 171, 173, 301, 353
Tovar, Martín, 52
Transportation, improvements in, 137-141
*See also* Magdalena River
Tribute, 77 f., 93, 107 f., 175 f., 182, 311, 313, 361
Tunja, city and province, 100, 187, 190, 194, 218, 287, 351

Ucrós, José, Intendant of Magdalena, 99
United States, 24, 115, 266
businessmen in Colombia, 141, 147, 346 (*see also* Lowry, Mannhardt)
trade with, 89, 152, 158, 163 n., 165, 264
Universities, 184, 187 f., 190-192, 206, 346
*See also* Education
Urdaneta, Rafael, *Comandante* of Zulia, 122, 269, 328, 335
Urquinaona, Francisco, 211, 212 n.

*Vacantes*, 93, 222
Valdés, Manuel, Gen., 256, 333

Valdivieso, José F., Intendant of Ecuador, 227
Valencia, 297, 325, 336
*Vales* (debt certificates), 106, 123, 145, 149, 226 f., 276-279, 327, 346
*Valle*, faction in Congress, 53 f., 65, 214, 247, 257, 282
*Venezolano, El*, 224, 293-295, 297 f.
Venezuela, 15, 32, 287-309, and *passim*
 completion of war in, *see* Maracaibo, Puerto Cabello
 Department of, 17, 28, 84, 94, 294-297, 306 n.
 earlier patriot regime, 6-8, 112
 disaffection in, 34, 61 f., 70, 130, 171, 285-294, 298-309, 318 f.
 economic and social conditions, 1 f., 89, 128, 152 f., 161 f., 164, 172, 205, 225, 287 f. (*see also Llanos*)
 and loan of 1824, 118, 120 f., 129
 provisional regime (1819-21), 10, 12 f.
 rebellion of 1826, 124, 325-332, 335 f., 343 f.
 relative voice in national affairs, 22, 51 f., 250, 288 f.
 reorganized by Bolívar, 345-347, 354
 rivalry with *granadinos*, *see* New Granada
Vergara, Estanislao, 11, 192

Veterans, 254, 275-282, 306 f.
Voltaire, 210, 244

War, *Secretaría*, 263, 288
 *See also* Briceño Méndez, Soublette
War of Independence
 in Colombia, 5-9, 22-24, 253, and *passim*
 economic and social effects, 87 f., 90, 95, 127 f., 167 f., 179 f., 202, 225, 310 f.
 naval aspects, 262 f., 265 f.
 *See also* Army, Peru
West Indies
 patriot emigration to, 8, 297
 Spanish, 71, 298 (*see also* Cuba, Puerto Rico)
 trade with, 90, 157 f., 161, 165
 *See also* Haiti, Jamaica

Yanes, Francisco Xavier, 296 f.

Zea, Francisco Antonio
 Colombian agent in Europe, 112-115, 137, 159 n., 189, 262
 Vice-President of Colombia, 12, 81 n.
 Vice-President of Venezuela, 10
Zipaquirá, 87
Zulia, department, 17, 251, 286, 306, 321, 335, 340
Zulia River, 139